England's Dreaming
Sex Pistols and Punk Rock

Jon Savage

'The best book about punk rock and pop culture ever.' *New Musical Express*

England's Dreaming

Jon Savage was born and brought up in West and Central London. His books include *The Kinks: The Official Biography*, *Up They Rise – The Incomplete Works of Jamie Reid*, and *The Faber Book of Pop* (edited with Hanif Kureishi). *Time Travel*, a collection of his articles, was published in 1996. *England's Dreaming* won the 1993 Ralph J Gleason Music Book Award.

by the same author

THE KINKS: THE OFFICIAL BIOGRAPHY
UP THEY RISE: THE INCOMPLETE WORKS OF JAMIE REID (with Jamie Reid)
THE FABER BOOK OF POP (with Hanif Kureishi)
TIME TRAVEL

faber and faber

ENGLAND'S DREAMING

Sex Pistols and Punk Rock

Jon Savage

To my grandfather: Malcolm James Grant 1/1/1904–12/2/1977

First published in 1991
by Faber and Faber Limited
3 Queen Square London WC1N 3AU
This paperback edition first published in 1992
Reissued and updated, 2001

Photoset by Wilmaset Ltd, Birkenhead, Wirral
Printed in England by Clays Ltd, St Ives plc

A CIP record for this book
is available from the British Library

ISBN 0–571–20744–8

10 9 8 7 6 5 4 3 2

Contents

Parliament Square, London, 1 May 2000 (photo: Russell Boyce/Reuters)

Introduction

The juxtaposition is simple yet complex enough to be iconic: the monolithic swagger of war-winner Winston Churchill – as bulky as the cliffs of Dover in his army greatcoat – topped by a brow-to-nape mohican made out of Parliament Square's finest lawn. This is not a tasteful cut, but a full-blown cider punk affair: a lurid green splash against the grey gun-metal sculpture. Conceived by anonymous artists during the May Day anti-capitalism protest in central London in 2000, it became the chief press image of that day, for some a symbol of violence and desecration, for others an example of creative protest – a national icon detourned.

The mohican has had a long journey from its native American beginnings. Indian stories by authors like Karl May, Buffalo Bill and Edward Sylvester Ellis were already a staple of boys' literature by the last quarter of the nineteenth century, around the time that the last homelands were disappearing in the US. In these action tales, Indians were the underdog: vicious, exotic and savage – the perfect role model for teenage malcontents and all those who felt put upon. Indian trappings became popular among delinquents in 1890s London,

1900s Paris and 1930s Berlin, and of these, the mohican was the ultimate. It still is.

As Travis Bickle boils over with rage in Martin Scorsese's 1976 *Taxi Driver*, his transition into a killing machine is symbolised by a brutal mohican: an idea that was not lost on the emerging punk movement – which shared much of the film's incandescent disgust. The shape of a strip of freshly shorn scalp, the mohican means war, pure and simple. There is a famous Robert Capa photograph of US paratroopers in Northern France, March 1945, with their hair cut 'mohawk style for luck and esprit de corps' for their next day's jump over the Rhine into Germany. Clearly, like any potent symbol, this can work several ways.

Attended by 4000 protestors and 5500 police, the May Day 2000 riots provoked a furious national debate, with the punked-up Churchill providing a convenient rallying ground for all parties. One letter writer to the *Guardian* dared to suggest that, indeed, if Churchill had had such a mohican, he'd have kicked Hitler's ass in two rather than six years. In an emotional article, Emma Soames wrote about the 'photographs of my grandfather so defaced and dishonoured I could hardly believe my eyes'. There was even a prolonged discussion of the man's life and crimes in the letter pages of the music press. And the *Mirror* pitched in with the simple question: 'Where would these yobs have been if the Nazis had won?'

For the children of the 50s and the 60s, Churchill was the ultimate grand/father – his funeral in January 1965 was a national event on the scale of Princess Diana's funeral. For the last sixty years, he has been held up as a national hero, perhaps even more sacrosanct than the Royal Family (until the Sex Pistols got involved, but you'll notice even they did not question Churchill's human-being status). He has thousands, perhaps millions of unquestioning admirers, and rightly so: for, as Michael Korda observed in the May 2000 *Harpers*, 'it can truly be said of him, as of perhaps no other figure of the twentieth century, that he saved the Western world . . . without him we would very likely be living in a world dominated by Hitler's heirs and Hitler's ideas. Because of him we are not.'

And yet, like all heroes, he has feet of clay. An unreported but significant feature of the May Day painting, apart from the blood coming out of Churchill's bulldog jaw, was a simple acronymic graffiti – TIKB – placed by the Turkish Communist Party, protesting the botched invasion of Turkey at Gallipoli in 1915 for which Churchill, as First Lord of the Admiralty, was responsible. Then there were his actions during the 1926 Miners' Strike when, as Chancellor of the Exchequer, he orchestrated what Robert Graves called 'the news service of the Law-and-Order party'. For others, the sight of Churchill with Punk/anarchist insignia was delicious payback for the siege of Sidney Street in January 1911, when Churchill – as Home Minister – sent in the guns against armed police killers who, in the intervening press hysteria, had grown into an army of anarchists led by the Russian Peter the Painter.

For many protestors, Churchill served as a prime avatar of the ruling class. The sacking of his statue might well have served to obscure the global nature of the urgent demonstration at hand, but it also served to reintroduce the spectre of Punk as the bourgeois demon, the harbinger of the anarchist apocalypse – just like that 1911 bogeyman, Peter the Painter, who was never clearly identified and never found. And it plugs straight into a debate about national identity, between the haves and the have-nots, the included and the excluded, between those who accept or reject the dominant perception. As the Sex Pistols sang: 'now is the time to realise, to have real eyes'.

A quarter century after Punk, England is still dreaming, its New Labour consensus brittle, fearful, beset by demons both imaginary and real. It is fair to relate the government to the country partly because of the sheer weight of the May 1997 election victory, but also because national identity has been an explicit project of New Labour – the 'reclaiming of the flag' for modern Britishness, the wresting of it away from malign, Thatcherite nationalism. You only need to look at the incidence of the Union Jack in political and pop iconography to see that national identity was a hot issue throughout the 90s: whether it be Neil Kinnock's 1992 party platform, Noel Gallagher's guitar, or Liam and Patsy's pillows and duvet on the March 1997 *Vanity Fair* 'London Swings Again' cover.

The Union Jack is the symbol of the political union between England, Scotland, Wales and Northern Ireland. It is far from being an equal partnership. England, and the South East in particular, dominates the economy, class system and perception of these islands. The Union Jack-strewn Britpop – a case in point – did not reflect Britain's multicultural reality but highlighted, almost exclusively, white rock groups from the South East. So it wasn't Britpop – because dance music is mainstream pop – but Engrock, and this is a small example of the problem. Yet this kind of unquestioning English superiority is under constitutional attack as never before, with the successful institution of assemblies in Scotland and Wales and with the increasing centralisation of Europe.

The reality of the situation is that England is going to have to re-examine some of its dearest shibboleths. Hugo Young is right to say (in the *Guardian*, March 2000), that 'Britain can't survive if England remains the centralised and dominant substate'. The mutual resentments will pull it apart. That little-island mentality that loathes Europe and will do anything to sabotage closer European links ignores both the wishes of a substantial part of Britain's young and the fact that Britain's 'special relationship' with an increasingly isolationist US cannot be taken for granted. History is on the side of devolution and monetary union, yet there are many, from Conservative leader William Hague down – with his xenophobia and anti-Europeanism – who stand like King Canute before the waves.

That old England erupted across the world's media in June 2000, when a strongly nationalistic contingent ran amok in Brussels and Charleroi during Euro 2000. Despite the fact that they comprised a tiny proportion of England football followers, there was even talk about expelling the country from the championship. Football had been part of the new Britain ever since the ecstatic summer of 1990 – marked by New Order's halfway decent official England theme, 'World In Motion' – but now the middle-class/media worship of the great game and its worst attitudes had run up against the reality of the hooligan rump. Within lad culture's heavily marketed worship of sexism, alcohol and machismo, it was possible to see this splenetic bout as one logical conclusion to the whole rotten idea.

The most revealing moments of the whole fracas came during a BBC *Panorama* special report: for the 'fans' profiled, the fact that Britain had won the war was justification enough for their behaviour. 'If it wasn't for England you'd be Krauts,' they shouted in Amsterdam. As Billy Bragg noted shortly afterwards: 'The mythology of 1940, fed by heroic war films and the soft stereotypes of *'Allo, 'Allo* and *Dad's Army*, is rooted deeply within our national consciousness.' Yet it was this very Churchillian myth that, thirty years after VE Day, Punk set out to challenge across a broad front: England had not won the war but lost. There was no longer the cushion of empire, just dreams of historic glories, of Douglas Bader and Jack Warner, of the Silver Jubilee and all that red, white and blue bunting.

And so Winston Churchill looms up like a Kings Road punk from the early 80s. You know, one of those who'd charge you several quid to take their picture so you could make your very own punk postcard. Punks didn't look like that in 1976, but nobody cares any more: it's twenty-five years on – at least five pop generations – and the direct experiential link has gone. Today's teens weren't even born when Mrs Thatcher was elected: they are now as far away from the Sex Pistols as Punks were from Johnnie Ray. Punk is there as a past pop style to be sourced, just as it remains in the media as a casual cruelty which feeds the viciousness of the English élite, but its long period of dominance over British pop has passed, wiped out by the late 80s dance explosion. Punk insisted on living in a hyper-intensive present, but now it's history – just another English dream.

This process was inevitable as soon as Punk occurred – as Wire sang in 1977: 'don't just watch, hours happen, get in there kid and snap them' – and was confirmed by Fred and Judy Vermorel's brilliant Polaroid of the Sex Pistols in early 1978. For a long time, the subject was off-limits – too close, everyone knew everything – but in the early 90s a cluster of books appeared, including Greil Marcus's *Lipstick Traces* and this one, which helped to make Punk a publishing issue. The subsequent decade has seen many group biographies, revisionist histories (check out David Dalton's hilarious *El Sid: Saint Vicious*), picture books (Nils and Ray Stevenson's *Vacant* has the best words and photos) and autobiographies – of which John Lydon's 1994 *Rotten: No Irish, No Blacks, No Dogs* is mandatory reading.

Many of the principal Britpunk players – all now in their forties – have got to grips with the new technology and their past during the last decade. The Buzzcocks continue to perform new material and have the best official website. The Clash put aside their differences in 1999 to work on a double-headed history: the *From Here To Eternity* live CD and the *From the Westway to the World* documentary, directed by Don Letts. Premiered with a big media party, the film broke little formal or historical ground: the contradictions in the group's position (which gave them much of their original power) were glossed over, the contributions of women like Caroline Coon ignored, that whole explosive moment tidied up within current laddish rock modes.

With their keen sense of rivalry intact, the Sex Pistols waited for the Clash package to pass through the culture before launching their own documentary in May 2000. Titled *The Filth and the Fury* after the famous *Daily Mirror* headline in December 1976 which made the group national scapegoats, the film reunited director Julien Temple and the group to retell the McLaren-inspired 'The Great Rock 'n' Roll

Swindle' from John Lydon's point of view. The fact that Temple was rewriting his own contribution to The Swindle didn't seem to bother him at all, although it should have done: Lydon's insistence on telling the story his way – which means ignoring McLaren except to insult him – is psychologically understandable (that terrible fight that pop performers have to get control of their work) but ultimately belittling.

Like the 'Filthy Lucre' tour, *The Filth and the Fury* continues to encode tabloid cynicism and criticism in its title. It's as though the whole scandal that the Sex Pistols went through during 1976 and 1977 have so marked the participants, Lydon in particular, that they have never got over it. Well, could you? But it also marks the moment when the Sex Pistols became a national obsession, and *The Filth and the Fury* quite rightly tells the Sex Pistols story from a national perspective, relating them to that chaotic late 70s moment that became a pivotal point in late twentieth-century political and social history. Despite the film's faults – an overlong prologue, several irritating directorial tics – *The Filth and the Fury* sees the Sex Pistols tell their own story, and what a great story it is.

'No feelings' was one of the Sex Pistols' three great negations – the other two being 'no fun' and 'no future' – and, with the personal authenticity routinely required by rock, many people took this to apply to the group members themselves. The most memorable parts of the film – apart from the unseen archive footage – is the quiet way in which Paul Cook, Steve Jones, John Lydon and Glen Matlock unfreeze emotions long blocked. They talk about childhood traumas (Jones's lack of father and family, Lydon's severe meningitis); the difficulties they had in getting on with one another (JL: 'a monkey's tea party'); the national scandal (PC: 'we were public enemy number one'); the problem of Vicious (SJ: 'Sid was dark, man'); his awful death (Lydon cries on camera); and the legacy (GM: 'it's a big albatross, you know').

Two quotes from Steve Jones cut to the quick. His pride in the group strips away the cynicism that the packaging implies: 'We gave it fucking 200 per cent for two years and that was it. We ran out of steam. I loved being a Sex Pistol. I'll always be a Sex Pistol. At least when I die I can say I've *done something*.' And he reveals the human cost of chaos: 'I didn't have a life. I had nothing to lose. And I was a miserable sod deep inside. So the more havoc I created, the more I felt better at doing it because I was a tortured soul. I think the fighting came through lack of musical ability. It was like, "Oh, this is what gets you headlines".'

Place 'no feelings' next to the Sex Pistols' famous broadside in 'Pretty Vacant': 'we know what we feel!' From today's standpoint – after a quarter century of therapy – the late 70s now seem like, to use Ian Curtis's and Margaret Drabble's phrase, the Ice Age. It wasn't just the Sex Pistols who couldn't cope: it was almost all of the people involved in Punk, as the pop culture that they loved expressed raging emotions from behind a blank sarcastic, hostile facade. In Ridley Scott's Punk-saturated *Blade Runner* (just look at Pris's costume and gesture) the Lexus 6 humanoids turn, Frankenstein-like, on their creators. What they want is directly Punk-relevant: a longer shelf life ('the light that burns twice as bright burns half as long'), and, most urgently, past and present emotions. They don't have feelings but recognise their necessity.

There was a great deal of unrecognised hurt and damage in Punk which, because unacknowledged, has taken several decades to work out – whether it be in *The Filth and the Fury*, Deborah Curtis's memoir of her husband Ian and his group Joy Division (*Touching from a Distance*), or Paul Morley's relentless *Nothing*, an unflinching examina-

Insane in the City: February 1977 (© Jon Savage)

tion of his father's suicide in June 1977, the moment of high Punk. Much of this hurt and damage was standard teenage stuff: the usual problems that young people have in getting their voice and perception heard. But there were specific problems in the late 70s: the start of family break-up; the collapse of the 60s hippie dream; hard drug usage following patterns of supply; a new, harsh political and social environment.

The Clash located this in one of their most famous early songs, 'London's Burning': 'The wind howls through the empty blocks looking for a home/ I run through the empty stone because I'm all alone.' Punk was an international outsider aesthetic: dark, tribal, alienated, alien, full of black humour. It spread from the US through the UK and France and through Europe, Japan, and Australia during the years following 1975. For anyone in the UK at that point who felt cast out because of class, sexuality, perception, gender, even choice, who felt useless, unworthy, ashamed, the Sex Pistols were an attraction/repulsion machine of, as Paul Morley notes, 'infernal' power that offered the chance of action, even surrender – to something larger than you – and thus possible transcendence. In becoming a nightmare, you could find your dreams.

Like the Adverts exulted in summer 1977: 'I found some friends with a little faith/ Less money and no taste.' During 1976 and 1977, Punk brought together suburban stylists, Bowie victims, teenage runaways, hardened sixties radicals, gay men and women, artists, disco dollies, criminals, drug addicts, prostitutes of all persuasions, football hooligans, intellectuals, big beat obsessives, outcasts from every class. It wasn't just the groups: the power that they had came from their audience. (In taking this broad view, Paul Tickell's 1995 *Arena*, 'Punk and the Pistols', remains the most ambitious filmed punk history). This broad church – repeated, with regional variations, throughout the US – makes a mockery of today's thirtysomething nostalgia, the type you can see in witless travesties like BBC2's *Never Mind The Buzzcocks*. Punk did not reproduce dominant lad modes: heretical sex and gender politics were key to its original impact.

Suddenly, you didn't have to be alone. You *submerged*. You had a good time by having a bad time. You were full of the poison. You acted out Iggy's edict in 'Death Trip': 'sick boy, sick boy, learning to be cruel'. You attacked the generation of World War Two: all that they could not express you'd flaunt in their faces, stiff upper lip morphing into blank stare and violent gesture. 'Gimme World War Three we can live again.' This was tough stuff, telling England what it did not want to hear. Punk demanded a commitment that many pop fans and obsessives were not prepared to undertake, and indeed the dangers of such a dark aesthetic quickly began to play out in deaths, drug addiction, cynicism – a black cloud that has haunted many ever since. There was that awful, self-aware, headlong flight to destruction: 'you can always tell,' sang San Francisco's Sleepers, 'if you are going to hell.'

This emotional perplex is culturally specific to Punk – and remains an issue for those involved – but falls within pop's general remit to explore the private. But Punk was also in the world: determinedly so as soon as John Lydon put those acronyms into 'Anarchy in the UK'. The Sex Pistols had the most power when they remained undefined – 'God Save the Queen' was a grandstanding 'fuck you' to England that seemed to come out of nowhere – but what they set up was so explosive that, in the polarising political climate of the time, it soon required definition. Punk thrust itself into politics and politics came back to claim it, whether resolving into the far right, the left (Rock against Racism), anarchy (Crass), or a wider form of autonomy which stressed cultural and social independence.

It's easy to forget, now that pop music is diffused throughout all media, that Punk was actively discouraged if not banned during 1976 and 1977, first by the music industry, then the newspapers and the politicians, then the public at large. This resulted in an underground distribution and production network which turned necessity into a virtue: it was easy and cheap, go and do it. These ideals of access – which have since been expanded by the internet – have become one of Punk's enduring legacies. The Sex Pistols had sung 'no future' with such force that it seemed like a curse: doing it all yourself – making, producing and releasing your own record/fanzine/book/film (like Crass) – and federating with other like minds became the hidden positive to Punk's much-flaunted negative, a practical decentralisation with infinite possibilities.

Another forgotten aspect of Punk is its anti-consumerism. 'Don't be told what you want/ don't be told what you need', warned John Lydon, while the Buzzcocks noted: 'I used to only want, but now I need.' On X-Ray Spex's 'Germfree Adolescents' – a virtual reality concept album before its time, with songs about 'Identity' and 'Genetic Engineering' – Poly Styrene projected into a nightmare future. Although Punk turned into music industry business after early 1978, at its heart was a furious disgust with consumption, and the place of pop culture and Punk itself within it. As John Lydon said on the day of his last concert as a Sex Pistol, 'I just wanna ruin everything. I don't like rock music. I don't even know why I'm in it.'

In Nic Roeg's *The Man Who Fell to Earth*, a spring 1976 release that had a great impact on Punk, David Bowie as Newton begins to lose his precepts. He forgets why he is on earth and begins to succumb to the seduction of pleasure. In one of the film's most memorable scenes, Newton lolls back in his chair, booze-blitzed, and becomes immersed in a vast ocean of white noise emanating from dozens of television sets with a myriad moving pictures. In 1976 England, this was definitely futuristic – simultaneously exciting and terrifying – and this duality of response corresponded to Punk's simultaneous fascination with, and condemnation of, the media: a contradiction that would play out with predictable results as Punk became assimilated into the media industries. And now that we're all Newtons, isn't it a bore?

But, just as the hippie movement highlighted concerns about ecology and its own version of autonomy, so these Punk ideals remain vigorous because they remain unresolved. The contradiction on which Punk foundered was its attempt to critique and change consumption and media from within – an attempt doomed to failure. In the 90s, the nearest US equivalent to the Sex Pistols, Nirvana, foundered on exactly that contradiction, this time from within a global pop/media economy of unprecedented relentlessness, and with correspondingly more serious results. The central problems thus remain for those who want to question the basis of society: how do you avoid becoming part of what you're protesting against? If everything exists in the media and you reject it, how do you exist?

This perhaps is the real message of the May Day riots which, like the 30 November 1999 anti-World Trade Organisation action, sprang from a thoroughgoing critique of global capitalism that has its roots in the Punk strands of anarchy, anti-consumption, federalised access and participation. While no organisation assumed full leadership, the ideals expressed by the participants had a common core: 'A variety of protest groups are building on a growing unease about environmental degradation, the growth of big corporations, and what is seen as a widening global gap between the haves and the have-nots. There's definitely something going on. People know that the world is threatened by an ecological crisis. Unlike in the 1960s, they despair of conventional political parties to do anything about it. So it is up to us. That's what direct action is all about.' (*Observer*, 30 April 2000).

Despite the usual conspiracy theories bandied about in the tabloids, the May Day action lacked any overt leaders. The demonstration encompassed violence and vandalism, thoughtfulness and subversive play, if you can include Winston Churchill's makeover and the planting of cannabis seeds in Parliament Square in the latter. The lack of an overall, defined ideology was heavily criticised but, just like Punk was at its most powerful when impossible to define, this is not a weakness but a source of strength. In sharp sentences like 'capitalism at its core rewards the darker side of human nature – greed and egotism', you hear the start of something big, something that echoes John Lydon's climactic snap at the end of *The Filth and the Fury*: 'All I want is for future generations to go, "Fuck it. Had enough. Here's the truth."' Well, here you are.

The simple, temporary reclaiming of Winston Churchill's statue for Punk radicalism is one of those freeze-frame moments that reveals a profound gap of perception: between 1940 and 2000, between those who think it a desecration and those who think it the perfect metaphor for a country, England, that refuses to squarely face the present, indeed, even to admit that the present exists. It also asserts the continued vigour – twenty-five or so years after its heyday – of the Punk DNA, not as music or culture or one group, but as a global symbol for youth disaffection, rebellion, sheer trouble. After all, if nothing gets challenged, nothing gets changed.

430 King's Road, London, October 1976 (© Bob Gruen)

1

> In the city we can change our identities at will, as Dickens triumphantly proved over and over again in his fiction; its discontinuity favours both instant heroes and instant villains impartially. The gaudy, theatrical nature of city life tends constantly to melodrama.
>
> **Jonathan Raban: *Soft City* (1974)**

> We wander through London; who knows what we may find?
>
> **Lionel Bart: 'It's a Fine Life', from *Oliver!* (1960)**

It is the early seventies. All the participants of what will be called Punk are alive, but few of them know each other. They will come together during 1976 and 1977 in a network of relationships as complicated as the rabbit-warren London slums of Dickens's novels. The other beginnings of Punk – the musical texts, vanguard manifestos, pulp fictions – already exist, but first we need the location, the vacant space where, like the buddleia on the still plentiful bombsites, these flowers can bloom.

That space is a small, oddly shaped shop at 430 King's Road, at World's End; the extended ground floor of a four-storey, late Victorian house, it was cheaply converted in the early years of the century. An iron pillar in the middle of the floor supports the roof. The only natural light comes from the front window. There is no inside toilet. It stands at a commanding position at the end of a row of similar, slightly larger shops; directly to the east is the local Conservative Association.

The building's changes of function illustrate the social shifts within this marginal area, a microcosm of what Malcolm McLaren has called 'the human architecture of the city'. The corner on which it stands is the first major deviation in the King's Road. World's End itself is named after a large pub that stands nearby. This name in turn derives not from the apocalypse but from the fact that, at the time when it was built, in the eighteenth century, it was the last house on the outskirts of the city, a boundary moving inexorably westwards from the World's End of Congreve, near Markham Square.

During the second half of the nineteenth century, this area of dead roads became associated with Cremorne Gardens, a stretch of land bounded by Lots Road in the south west and the World's End in the north east. Initially fashionable, the gardens degenerated, as public urban spaces will, into harbours of prostitution and low life of all types, and were closed in 1877. During the last two Victorian decades, World's End became a poor area, creating an atmosphere which, despite gentrification, lingers in the World's End estate of seventies tower blocks.

After the First World War, 430 King's Road was occupied by Joseph Thorn, who carried on a pawnbroking business there for over thirty years. By the early 1950s, it had become a café, run by Mrs Ida Docker. The World's End was still a down-at-heel area belonging to the poor, the Bohemians, the transients of Pamela Hansford Johnson's 1937 novel *World's End*, whom Evelyn Waugh described (reviewing in Graham Greene's *Night and Day* magazine) as people 'economically, politically, socially, theologically, in a mess'.

As the upper reaches of the King's Road became fashionable in the mid-1950s, boutiques, coffee bars and other meeting places slowly spread down the street's eastern stretches. As a part of this process, number 430 ceased to be a shop that served only its immediate locality. For a time, it was a yacht agents, then the premises of a motor scooter dealer called Stanley G. Raper. In the winter of 1967, when Michael Rainey moved Hung On You from its previous site on Chelsea Green, it became chic.

Hung On You is a good example of the social mix that fuelled the synthesis of fashion, music and politics which has become London's principal export to the world. Along with David Mlinaric, Tara Browne (immortalized in the Beatles' 'A Day in the Life'), and Christopher Gibbs, Michael Rainey had been one of the original, aristocratic Chelsea stylists: an elite based, not on breeding or manners, but on pop values like style and glamour.

By the mid-1960s, the English music and culture industries were increasing exponentially – a process officially marked by the Beatles' investiture as MBEs in October 1965. Pop groups like the Beatles, the Animals and the Rolling Stones – with roots ranging from the suburban to the truly poor – were not only becoming rich and famous, but the new aristocracy: in John Lennon's phrase, 'the kings of the jungle'. They had few better role models than the Chelsea Dandies, whose taste for exotica was already well developed.

One can see the clothes on the Beatles or the Rolling Stones in early 1966: narrowly cut, high double-breasted suits in velvet or stripes, worn with garish, hand-painted forties ties, or thirties crêpe-de-Chine scarves. This was the pop modernism of the mid-1960s on the cusp of hippie collage. As this style spread, it was principally sold in Carnaby Street or on the Portobello Road. Too remote, the World's End didn't directly profit from the bonanza. Although other shops like Granny Takes A Trip had opened in 1966, the corner was not a mass-market thoroughfare but a place for drugs, eccentricity or special pilgrimages.

Michael Rainey closed Hung On You early in 1969. He had helped to originate the idea of multiple identity in fashion – of clothes worn not in a uniformity of caste or taste, but in a riotous confusion of colours, eras and nationalities – but the next occupants of 430 took the idea of 'Fun Clothes' to a sickly conclusion. Trevor Miles had supplied Hung On You with kaftans; more recently, he had made waistcoats for Tommy Roberts' Kleptomania. They decided to set up a shop together, with a new name taken from an underground movie title.

Mr Freedom was like a gigantic playpen. Once inside the ice-cream-sundae, Deco frontage, customers were greeted by a giant stuffed gorilla dyed fun-fur blue. While a revolving silver globe in the ceiling gave an authentic Palais feel, they could buy jars of sweets from the counters with inset televisions twinkling away. Influenced by the 1950s, the clothes were trivial, garish and fantastic, pastiching the past thirty years of 'comic-strip, Hollywood vulgar'.

'I did appliqué lightning bolts, long T-shirt dresses with rockets coming up them, Mickey Mouse T-shirts and all that,' says Miles. Other items included Lucie Mabel Atwell-style print dresses, appliqués with catchphrases like 'Slip It To Me' and 'Pow' worn by deliberately ugly models, Superman jackets and fake leopard skin everywhere. From the outset, the shop was a success. 'I've never seen so much publicity on anything,' muses Miles: 'there was nothing else for them to grab onto. It was all very, very groovy.'

This was one source of a pervasive mood in early seventies pop culture: a mixture of camp and infantilism triggered by the hippies' celebration of childhood as the ideal state. Evocations of the thirties environment characteristic of the babyboomer childhood – a process which would peak with that palace of fun, Biba's superstore – went hand in hand with the fine-art codification in 1968 of thirties styles under the term Art Deco. As the sheer drive of pop modernism faltered, the era of decade style-revivals began. Style replaced content; clothing became costume.

Popcult phenomena like Mr Freedom shook loose individual items from time referents like 'the 30s' or 'the 50s' and ran wild with the past, like a child in an antique shop. To aesthetes like Nik Cohn, this cheerful plunder was total anathema: 'for the moment, Fun reigns supreme. At middle-aged joint-smoking parties, balding fatties come on as Johnny Weismuller and their wives play Rita Hayworth. It is not a pretty sight.'

For Miles, this total visibility brought rather more pressing problems: the rip-off. It happened with his most celebrated design, the 'Star' T-shirt, instantly copied by the established rag trade, which then flooded the market with cheap imitations. This is a perennial problem for the successful yet small entrepreneur: Tommy Roberts went for broke, opening a bigger, better shop at the bottom of Kensington Church Street, while Miles, less of a businessman, remained in 430: 'We fell out and I took the Mustang and the shop.'

It was time for a new concept: Pacific exotic. Miles went off to New York with £5,000 and bought piles of used jeans, Oshkosh dungarees and Hawaiian shirts. To suit 430's new incarnation, the shop front was done in green corrugated iron, with Hawaiian-style bamboo lettering, and featured an antique petrol pump. Inside, the Electric Colour Company put bamboo everywhere, rush matting on the floor and covered Miles's Mustang with flocked tiger-skin fabric.

Paradise Garage was one of the first shops to do pop retro and assemble a collection of old clothes with some overriding taste. Miles

Trevor Miles outside number 430, 1970 (courtesy of Trevor Miles)

was ahead of his time again, but the familiar problems reappeared. Not only was the shop undercut by more businesslike dealers, but he was getting bored. 'I thought, "Right: used clothing, done that, next idea." So I sprayed the floor black, put a jukebox and a mobile floor in so that people had the option of going in there to dance. Then I just left for a few months. It seems extraordinary now, but that's the way you did business in those days.'

By 1971, the gloss had gone off the King's Road and the shop faced strong competition from immediate neighbours like Alkasura and Granny Takes A Trip which hit the spot, selling crushed velvet finery to the English musicians touring the lucrative American market. As hippie bottomed out, the World's End became awash with drugs, a market centred on the 'Golden Triangle' of pubs that followed the chicane: the Roebuck, the Man In The Moon on the corner with Beaufort Street, and the Water Rat, right opposite the shop.

It was into this jaded environment that Malcolm McLaren drifted one summer day in 1971. McLaren had just left Goldsmiths' College without completing his degree; his final-year project – also uncompleted – was a psychogeographical film about Oxford Street, which had led him into a fascination with fifties Rock'n'Roll in general and Billy Fury in particular. In his account: 'I'd used my grants over 1969, 1970 to collect various records from the fifties and sixties from all the markets like Portobello Road and Club Row. By the time I left I had this enormous collection. I didn't know quite what to do, and I had this idea of selling these records and hooking up with an art student friend of mine called Patrick Casey, who had this great taste and flair for finding used clothing of a unique kind – particularly old leather jackets and strange zoot jackets that related to the period of those records. No one in those days – 1970, 1971 – knew that was a style to do.'

On his way to an open market near the corner of Edith Grove, McLaren was accosted by a man who was struck by his lurex trousers: these had been made for McLaren by his friend Vivienne Westwood. The man was 430's manager, an American hustler called Bradley Mendelson. Once inside the shop, McLaren was impressed: 'They were obviously down in the dumps; the guy inside was looking for money. But they had a jukebox blazing away and it was all black, they had no sign, no front at all. I was thrilled because it was so fifties.'

In October 1971, McLaren moved into the back of number 430 with Vivienne Westwood and Patrick Casey. When Trevor Miles returned from his honeymoon, he was not pleased: 'Bradley Mendelson rented out half the shop without me knowing. When we came back, I found myself in a shocking state. I declared myself bankrupt and literally walked away from it. Malcolm took over the shop; he took the jukebox and the whole thing and did Let It Rock.'

For Miles, it was the end of an era: 'Malcolm and Vivienne were probably very down to earth, but they felt like aliens to me. I've always been fascinated by Malcolm's attitude and approach – the way he gets away with things. I find Vivienne's way of getting her message across almost embarrassing sometimes, very intense. But then it was early days: they had very strong convictions and the sort of clothes they were doing there were really out on a limb.'

> Apart from the twitching rock'n'rollers, who often resemble Charlie Chaplin in *Modern Times*, we are becoming a nation of spectators.
>
> **Nina Epton: *Love and the English* (1960)**

> Frustration is one of the great things in art; satisfaction is nothing.
>
> **Malcolm McLaren: college notes (winter 1967/8)**

Despite the fact that they were of a similar age and had dipped into a similar pop culture, McLaren and Westwood had very little in common with the beautiful people of the King's Road. In 1971, they both hated hippies with a vengeance: 'hippos', McLaren called them. Their interest in fifties clothes had nothing to do with fun or camp. 'It goes without saying', writes Susan Sontag, 'that the Camp sensibility is disengaged, depoliticized – or at least apolitical.' In their different ways, Westwood and McLaren were politicized: this gave them a *moral* purpose in their approach to clothes.

Both deeply mistrusted the apparent social progress of the free and easy hippie culture that was all around them. McLaren *liked* the guilt that flaked off the busty magazines, like *Photoplay* and *Fiesta*, which he sold at the back of the shop. With their peroxide coiffures, large breasts and leopardskin costumes, these Evas and Audreys were anachronisms, yet their sheer exaggeration highlighted the real dynamics of desire, exchange and sexual repression which were being fudged in an area where a shop could be called Liberated Lady.

England wasn't free and easy: it was repressed and horrible. Both felt that the claims of hippie culture to have changed the world were false: it was just window dressing, like the façades so quickly erected and demolished in consumer enclaves like Oxford Street. Consider the music of the time – then called 'Rock' in a bid for respectability. What a pompous, middle-class facsimile of the anarchy that was fifties Rock'n'Roll! The music industry was now in control and conning everyone: how could that industry's 'Rock' retain any trace of Rock'n'Roll's original teenage revolt?

Their solution was to turn, not just to the music, fashion and accoutrements of the 1950s, but to the people who lived out the style: the Teddy Boys who, in the early 1970s, were experiencing a resurgence. They were the descendants of those youths from Tottenham, Clapham and the Elephant and Castle who had created the very first English youth style. Although organized along traditional class, criminal and territorial lines, their dress had marked them out as being something different: harbingers of a new age.

The original Teddy Boys had grafted the shape of an American gangster's suit or zoot suit – with its exaggerated annexation of space – onto details stolen deliberately from a specialized Savile Row fashion of 1948: the Edwardian look. Originally floated as a nostalgic evocation of the pre-First World War Edwardian era, this precise, rather mannered style failed to catch on amongst its target market but, in one of those ill-documented shifts that happens in urban culture, had passed into London's criminal vernacular by the early 1950s.

In the hands of 'petty criminals' like Colin Donellan, profiled in the *Picture Post* in 1953, the effect was simultaneously brutal and foppish. The 'Edwardian' quickly caught on: in assuming an upper-class style, it had the added spice of subtly cocking a snook at its betters. The Edwardian was smart, flash and advertised his profession – petty criminal – by his clothes. In an era when everyone knew their place, vulgarizing what the nobs wore was a definite act of class warfare.

In the early 1950s, the Edwardians were clothes obsessed, as maniacal as the Mods who would follow them: they would think nothing of spending all their money on an embroidered waistcoat, a dark suit with finger-tip length sleeves and fourteen-inch trouser bottoms. As the name was edited into Teddy Boys, and then Teds, the style became degraded and brutish – a process captured by Colin MacInnes's description, in *Absolute Beginners*, of racist Teds at the Notting Hill Gate riots of September 1958. With the onset of new, cooler styles – 'The Italian Look' of 1958 – Ted dropped from sight.

But Teddy Boys never stopped reproducing. Their original composition had been working class and many hung onto the style as an act of cultural faith and class solidarity, bringing up their children in the same dress. Occasionally, they came up into the glare of the media spotlight – as in 1968, when Bill Haley's 'Rock Around The Clock' made the Top Twenty. Or when, as Richard Neville describes in *Play Power*, with a sharp eye for class detail, Teddy Boys rioted at the Albert Hall in July 1969: fired up by Chuck Berry, they revolted when the Who came on stage.

This was the sort of culture gap that McLaren and Westwood wanted to explore. By the early 1970s, the second Teddy Boy revival had already gathered some steam. Its focus was the Black Raven pub in Bishopsgate where, ever since 1967, the original Ted landlord, Bob Ackland, had been keeping the faith. The jukebox stocked Richie Valens, Billy Riley, Carl Perkins, Elvis; the bar soon stocked a regular,

Malcolm McLaren outside number 430, December 1971 (© David Parkinson, courtesy of Valerie Olins)

large following which, by the autumn of 1970, was getting mass-media attention.

McLaren and Westwood were greatly impressed by the Teds' foppish brutality and their *hard* style, which seemed like a subversion of the status quo. But both of them were from a different class: educated, Bohemian, even thinkers. It was Vivienne (as would often happen) who put theory into practice and went down to the Black Raven. She quickly found that these Teds had to get all their clothes hand made – a costly and time-consuming process. There was a gap in the market. And what better place was there to exploit this gap than the World's End, right in the heart of enemy territory?

How had this combustible pair come to this point? Obtaining coherent biographical data from McLaren and Westwood is not easy: both tend to rewrite their history according to the demands of their current project. The question of authorship that bedevils the whole story of Punk doesn't help either. Westwood will only draw out biographical data if they fit the point she wants to make at that particular time. Her accounts of the life she and McLaren had together are now coloured by their bitter break-up in 1983.

McLaren's accounts of his life and feelings, in the abstracted world of the mediated personality, are a shifting, constant parade of mythologizing, selective perception and acute self-analysis. He is quite capable of delivering devastating self-criticism, yet at such breakneck speed that it could be taken as just a spasm of his celebrated hyperactivity. Myths and dreams play a large part in McLaren's life, as he adheres to the First Pop Law of Andrew Loog Oldham: 'I believe that if you lie enough it becomes a reality.'

McLaren's fantasies, or even his half-lies, are as revealing as the truth. As he has managed to turn many of his fantasies into reality, it is worth giving them credence. This is, after all, pop, the modern Hollywood: the one place in English society where you can reinvent yourself, where the donning of a new jacket can appear a political act. 'Never forget that clothes are the things in England that make your heart beat!' he says. 'There's a constant attempt to step out of that class structure of the two-piece suit.'

For all the propaganda of classlessness – whether the sixties popcult model or the eighties entrepreneurial model – England is a highly static society, with a strongly defined ruling class and a narrow definition of the acceptable. If you fall outside it for any reason, you're marginal. As with any cluster of minorities, if you put them together, you make a majority: pop – a marginal industry in itself – is a place where many of them meet, as dreamers and misfits from all classes, to transform, if not *the* world, then their world.

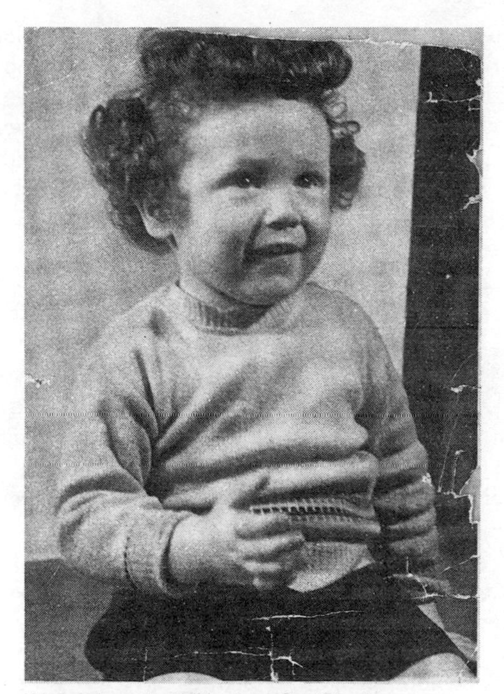
Malcolm McLaren, circa 1950 (courtesy of Stuart Edwards)

Modern society puts every child in a straitjacket.

R. D. Laing and A. Esterson: *Sanity, Madness and the Family* (1969)

30 September: To use a kid's eyelevel to describe ordinary situations and to get the utmost out of these situations. Showing the structure of Oxford Street thru the eyes of a child and the effect it has on him and his elders. The child is unknowing of the media and thus the basis for being there is to see it without commenting on it. Cut into this an older person's viewpoint, equally subservient to it but serving it. That one has no control over one's life. Showing how an adult is still a child still no control. Important then to relate how he combats that predicament.

Malcolm McLaren, notes for *Oxford Street* (1970)

A constant echo through McLaren's rhetoric is the ideal of childhood: whether in the voice-over for his projected *Oxford Street* film, in his 1984 *Fans* album, or in the figure onto whom his fantasies were projected, Sid Vicious, that he placed in the heart of pop myth. These were not original ideas: they were current during the underground that existed in the time of McLaren's studenthood, whether in the radical psychology or the pop songs of the age.

What marks out McLaren is the particular intensity with which he has pursued these ideas; this has much to do with his own life story. Celebrity suits him, being 'the one adult mode that inhabitants of the adolescent mode can imagine living in – because it is not really an adult state but is rather the ultimate adolescent fantasy of adulthood'. Born marginal, of a marriage between religions and cultures, and further subjected to a bizarre childhood, he has enacted the best revenge of all: that of an outsider on society.

McLaren was born on 22 January 1946, the younger son of Peter McLaren, a Scottish engineer, and Emily Isaacs, who came from a proud Jewish family. The pair were ill-suited in age, race and intellect and they separated just over eighteen months later. After one further meeting with his two sons in 1948, Peter McLaren was 'wiped out of history' by Emily and her powerful family.

It was as though he had never existed. It took McLaren another forty years, some psychotherapy and a private detective before he found his father again, in 1989. 'It happened by letter,' McLaren says. 'He lives in Romney Marsh, right by Old Romney Church. He's had six wives, and now looks like those pictures of W. H. Auden near the end of his life. I've got another family that I never knew existed: when I was in England last, I met my half-sister and half-brother, who's a fellow of King's College, Cambridge.'

The separation was a shattering event for Malcolm and his brother. 'I was very angry and resentful,' says Stuart Edwards, who retains the surname of his stepfather, 'I carry those things today.' Although only two and a half years older than McLaren, there could be a whole generation between the brothers. Whereas McLaren can, on occasion, be as quicksilver as a spoilt adolescent, Stuart is solid: a balding family man with two daughters and a steady job as a night-time taxi-driver. Yet if one scratches the surface, one can see the similarities between the brothers: the voice, the imaginative intensity, and the thirst for knowledge.

Both brothers retain considerable hostility for their mother. 'She hurt us,' says Stuart: 'Sir Charles Clore had a big relationship with my mother; why I don't know. They had liaisons in the Hotel du Paris in Monte Carlo, then she married my stepfather Martin Levi, who later changed his name to Edwards, and she changed her christian name to

Eve. He was Jewish, of course, which made him acceptable, but my grandmother didn't really like him. He was very limited, but he was clever enough to open a clothing factory, Eve Edwards Limited, which became quite a big concern . . . It happens to a lot of people, but my mother never spent any time with her children. She went off and furthered her career, and left us in the clutches of our grandmother who I now realize was imposing on us her values and her outlook. Which was weird anyway. We missed a generation. We were being brought up by a woman whose childhood was in the Victorian era.'

'When I was first manager of the Sex Pistols it was like returning to my childhood with my grandmother,' Malcolm says of the dominant influence in his life. 'She was a woman who created her own world and everybody else had to live in it or live without it. Her world was far better than the world we live in, because it had a lot more soul and a lot more passion. It was a world that was fairly inventive but that had brilliance. It shone and I felt for it, because it was the world that I was protected by.'

Rose Isaacs was born Rose Corré in 1887; her father, Abram Corré, was a diamond merchant who had emigrated to England from Holland sometime in the middle of the nineteenth century. 'His ancestors had come from the landowning Sephardic community in Spain,' says Stuart, 'but they had to leave the country after the Inquisition.' Born into some wealth, Rose married Michael Isaacs just before the First World War: the family house in Carysfort Road was a wedding present. There's no doubt who was the stronger character: 'I remember that my grandad never used to sleep in my grandmother's house,' says Malcolm, 'he hardly lived there. He had to come and visit.'

'I thought my grandmother was a total idiot,' says Stuart. 'She adored Malcolm, she didn't like me very much. She saw in me the reflection of my father, who had upset her life. I was very like my father, while Malcolm was the image of his grandmother. Mannerisms, everything. She was a very strange woman, an eccentric for her time. She wanted to be an actress and took elocution lessons, so she had an affected way of speaking. During the First World War she and her other sister, who was quite pretty, cavorted with officers; she was a Bohemian and had strange friends.'

Rose spoilt the young Malcolm. 'She made me challenge every notion of the established viewpoint because that's what *she* wanted to do,' he says. 'I think Stuart must have felt pretty bad because I was lavished upon and he was starved. But I was never allowed to play or

Rose Isaacs (centre) and Emily Edwards (right) during the 1950s (courtesy of Stuart Edwards)

to have friends. I had to stay inside. He was allowed to run amok, because she didn't care about him. We had no idea what family unity was. But my grandmother had such a strong alternative world that I could exist by creating my own in the same fashion.'

The brothers entered William Patton school in Stoke Newington in 1954. Malcolm lasted one day: 'I was an obstreperous little bastard. I couldn't understand why the school was so full of rules and laws.' He was then taught by a private tutor, who, by his own account, force-fed him *Jane Eyre* and *A Christmas Carol*. When the Edwards began to make money, they moved out to Cheyne Walk in Hendon and sent Stuart and Malcolm to a private Jewish school, Avigdor, in Lordship Lane, which both hated. Stuart was asked to leave at fifteen, while Malcolm went on to a grammar school at Burnt Oak called Orange Hill.

Neither boy was a good student. 'I could have been academic at school,' says Stuart, 'but I rejected that life totally. My rebellion was a total withdrawal.' Malcolm, however, found that his bad behaviour got him attention and, perhaps more importantly, his grandmother's approval: 'She used to write these wonderful letters to the headmaster which always ended with the phrase "Boys will be boys". I got away with murder. I was such a snob, really fucked up in those schools. Refusing to listen to any kind of authority and refusing to learn anything.'

One refuge was the pop culture now flooding in from America. 'The first pop we had in the house was Bill Haley and the Comets,' says Stuart. 'You'd had Frank Sinatra and Bing Crosby, then suddenly we had this wild music. I wasn't really interested in the velvet collars and the long jackets that the Teddy Boys wore; I liked the creepers and the drainpipes and the Italian box jackets with the little collars and the three buttons.'

'Stoke Newington, Clissold Park and Stamford Hill – that was a very potent place to be,' adds Malcolm, 'because it sported some of the first Teddy Boys, and Tottenham, which was close by, had this enormous ballroom, the Royal, where Rock'n'Roll gathered a lot of momentum. I often remember crossing the road going to school, because I went to a Jewish school and had a cap on. These Teddy Boys would come up and they'd put their hands in their jackets as if to motion that they might be carrying something dangerous. I was always terrified.'

These were neighbourhoods fierce in territorial loyalties, inner-urban enough to be city-wise, yet not poor enough to be a ghetto: English pop was a product of comparative affluence. Marginal zones, such as these areas of London, promised the illusion of transformation. 'Dressing up was always a big part of going out,' McLaren remembers. 'My parents were always involved in fashion, and I was always inspired by my brother. Every Saturday night he would take over the bathroom, and you couldn't get in. No matter how desperate you were: it was his domain.'

These were the London suburbs that produced the very first Mods. If anything, their parents' move to the more genteel Hendon increased both the brothers' restlessness and the range of movement open to them. 'We used to go all round North London and Soho,' says Stuart, 'all these suburbs had to do with Jewish society, and no matter how he tried to break away, Malcolm was always linked with that. There was a night club in Swiss Cottage called the El Toro and one in St John's Wood called the Coronet, where I met my wife. In Soho, I used to go to a club called the Poubelle and to St Anne's, a disco in a church.'

Soho was multi-racial, and had traditionally harboured outcasts and oddities. Its caste system was not the standard elitism of class. It didn't matter who you were – you could be criminal, existential, homosexual, vicious or teenage – as long as you had an interesting angle, or a good story. The hustler, immortalized in Wolf Mankowitz's *Expresso Bongo*, was king. In the early 1960s, there was a brief period when French, existential-style coffee bars coexisted with all-night raves.

'I'd get the Bakerloo Line to Charing Cross and just hang around the coffee bars,' says Bernard Rhodes, whose thirty-year, on-off friendship with McLaren began with a meeting at Stamford Hill Bowling Alley. 'I saw Paul Simon for half-a-crown: it was a working class, Bohemian thing and there was no media, you just locked into it. You met people who were on your wavelength, and you could actually go out Friday night and come back Monday morning. There was no stopping you: there was everywhere to go.'

After leaving school in 1961 with three GCEs, Malcolm was confronted with the problem of what to do with his life. His mother made him take a job with Sandeman's, the wine merchants, in Piccadilly. 'I was with all these boys from public school,' he says. 'They thought I had much better clothes than they did. When Sandeman's asked me to go to Spain and work in the vineyards, I decided that I really did have to spend my life in Wardour Street.' Various temping jobs followed, from which he was fired almost as a matter of policy.

In autumn 1963, Malcolm started evening classes in life-drawing at St Martin's School of Art on Charing Cross Road but his mother objected to the nudes on display, so, still under the thumb of his family, he transferred to three-D design and graphics. To be accepted by the new system of art education, Malcolm needed two extra O levels, and enrolled in an Edgware school for a booster course. He passed, but was in the wrong educational area for St Martin's: instead, he was accepted by Harrow Art School to begin a Dip.AD in autumn 1964.

Before that, however, there was a break with his parents. 'The anti-establishment side of him started to come out,' says Stuart. 'He spent his time at a club called the Witches Cauldron at Hampstead which was a place for beatniks, Bohemians, subversives. Then he decided to bum around the world, sleep on beaches. What was emerging was something we didn't understand: I supposed it was a throwback to my grandmother.

'My parents thought this was all too much. Like all Jewish parents, they thought in terms of doctors and lawyers. Their customers were the foremost thing in their lives. They were all Jewish men with stores up north, and they'd say "My son's been called to the bar, what does your son do?" My parents would say: "One of them's rejected everything and has gone to work in a men's clothing store." That was me.

'But Malcolm had BLACK FRIENDS! He mixed with all kinds of

low life. He got arrested in the south of France for being a vagrant. How could my mother tolerate that when she was cavorting with Charles Clore in Monte Carlo? So she completely disowned him. The only link with the family was with the grandmother, and there were secret meetings. Always these meetings meant that he was in dire straits and needed money and she would give him money. This went on until he found a niche with Vivienne Westwood.'

'I have an in-built perversity,' Vivienne says, 'a kind of in-built clock which always reacts against anything orthodox.' In person, Vivienne Westwood can be single-minded to the point of obsession. She has a similar verbal pattern to both McLaren and Bernard Rhodes, often changing mid-sentence in a logic that is hard to follow but which, after a while, begins to make sense. Often, the patterns revolve around her project of the moment: beneath an apparent diffidence, Westwood has a very definite view of the world and is confused when people do not share it.

This is born from her own moral authority – a mixture of radical and class certainty that has paralleled Mrs Thatcher's thrifty, polarizing certitude. In April 1989, Westwood posed as Mrs Thatcher for the cover of the *Tatler* in an 'eerie resemblance'. Westwood and Thatcher are mirror images of the same national archetype, an impression further reinforced by Vivienne's obsession with the Queen as national symbol – either negatively (1977) or positively (1987). As a fashion designer, Westwood has been insistent that her clothes connect with the English psyche.

In Gillian Greenwood's 1990 *South Bank Show* profile of Vivienne Westwood, a child wanders through her many outfits, trying them on, as in a dressing-up box. Like Malcolm, Vivienne is fascinated by the child, but with a deeper-rooted innocence: 'A good idea is a perfect surprise,' she has said, and she retains a childlike wonder about the world that reflects the isolation of her early life.

Born on 16 April 1941, Vivienne was the first child of Gordon and Dora Swire, and was raised in Hollingworth, a small village near the Snake Pass in Derbyshire. Her grandfather had died very young and her grandmother turned the family shop into a greengrocery, which she ran all her life. Dora (née Ball) was a cotton-mill weaver who married Gordon Swire during the war, while he was working in aircraft munitions. After the war, they ran the Tintwistle Post Office, eventually moving to Harrow in the late 1950s.

Vivienne had a sheltered adolescence, imbued with a Calvinist insistence on hard work. 'My parents were not uncultured,' she said in 1990, 'both were very bright, clever people with lots of initiative.' All three of the Swires' children – Vivienne, Olga (born in 1943) and Gordon (born 1946) – went on to higher education in art colleges and universities, although Vivienne's course was less straightforward than those of her siblings.

After leaving school, Vivienne held temporary jobs, such as a stint in the local Pickering's pea factory. She was already wearing clothes in an individual way and had developed a taste for nightlife which led to her marriage in July 1962 to Derek Westwood. 'My dad Derek used to run a night club and that's where they met,' says their son Ben Westwood, who, unlike many of those closely involved with McLaren and Westwood, seems free of bitterness. 'He did clubs in different places with his brother and some friends. My mum used to do the cloakroom, my uncle would be on the door. They married, had me, and divorced in 1966.'

Before Ben was born, Vivienne had entered Harrow Art School, near her parents, to study silversmithing. Her first love was painting but to do a foundation course would have been too simple. She left after a term: the other students were 'still at the titillation stage'. Her independent streak reasserted itself: after working in a factory to put herself through secretarial school, she then decided to become a teacher. After a spell at St Gabriel's Teacher Training College in Camberwell, she left Derek Westwood and returned to Harrow with Ben in 1965.

At this point, she met Malcolm McLaren (or Edwards as he was still known) and so began, according to Fred Vermorel and Malcolm himself, a period of pursuit. Westwood claims otherwise. McLaren was more interested in himself, and romantic notions of art as lifestyle: bound to his grandmother, he was a virgin at twenty. By 1966, he had enrolled in drama school: 'My grandmother always had visions of being an actress and she was going to support me if I took drama seriously,' he says, 'so I went to drama school and there I also took piano lessons, studying Bartók.'

Malcolm had already met Vivienne at one of Derek's club nights – at the Railway Hotel, Harrow and Wealdstone. 'I was sharing a house with a friend of mine from Harrow,' he says, 'and with Vivienne's brother Gordon Swire, and a bunch of American draft-dodgers who were all going to film school. Vivienne was running away from her husband, and she came to live there, to my shock and horror, because I hated the idea that girls should come and inhabit this house. It was boys only, as far as I was concerned, and girls coming in made it all look dreadfully slimy. I brought her to tears and she had this little kid who I hated and loathed, and I brought him to tears as well. This turned out to be Benjamin Westwood.

'I almost persuaded her to leave, but because of her northern stubbornness, it defeated that end, and instead, three or four weeks later I decided to feign sick. Curiosity at the thought of being inside a woman's bed – even though I was twenty-one, God knows why I didn't think of this before – I decided I would try this out on Vivienne. It was very slow and uncertain. She was a schoolteacher, and I felt I was in bed with one. There was something harmlessly perverse about the whole notion of this spoilt brat being in bed with a schoolteacher.'

Westwood was by no means committed to any relationship and was mildly appalled by McLaren's juvenile behaviour: although only five years younger than her, sometimes he seemed like a child, particularly when jealousy reared its head: McLaren couldn't control his emotions at all. Vivienne quickly became pregnant. Risking the end of relations with Rose Isaacs, who disapproved of the whole affair, McLaren and Westwood failed to go through with a planned abortion, and their son Joseph was born in 1967.

After the birth, Vivienne made a more definite emotional commitment to Malcolm. 'She appeared warm and in a sense more practical and maternal and stable and I think those were the attributes that attracted Malcolm,' says Robin Scott, who lived with them both in 1969. 'I always think the only stable relationship he seemed to have, the only person he seemed to trust was his grandmother. Vivienne helped to wean him off that strange relationship with his grandmother. I always saw Vivienne as the woman behind the man.' Before he committed himself to Vivienne, Malcolm was experimenting with a variety of costumes, situations and artistic styles. Within an art school context, his eccentricities were acceptable, even approved of, but none of this activity was focussed. Vivienne provided a backbone built out of her insistence on hard work, and her extreme commitment to a variety of beliefs, not the least of which, initially, was in Malcolm himself. She entered his fantasy world: her strength enabled them both to turn fantasy into reality.

But their partnership always had the qualification of McLaren's self-obsessed restlessness. 'Stuart had to get married to create a real world for himself,' says McLaren, 'because that's what his friends had. He got married to the first girl he met: he was sacrificial and I think it's only now that he resents it, but he's accepted it. It was the same with me: I fucked the first girl, got her pregnant and ended up by living with her for fifteen years. I settled down as well, but I wouldn't allow the normality to grow around me completely. I did at least in my own fucked-up way create an environment I could run wild in. I did try.'

Drawing by Malcolm McLaren, October 1969 (courtesy of Malcolm McLaren)

3

'Black is the most exciting colour' (Goya). Black when used in different ways appears the most infinite and mysterious, the most spatial and loose.

Malcolm McLaren: essay, Croydon Art School (winter 1967/8)

In the autumn of 1964, Malcolm went to Harrow Art School, which, in his account of McLaren's early life, Fred Vermorel describes as 'the centre for miles around for Bohemian frenzy, mixing the local gay community with beatniks, drug pedlars, sexual delinquents and Mods'. In those days, art schools were less result-orientated than they are now. 'It was the place where everybody went who didn't fit in anywhere else,' says Malcolm; 'it was a brilliant hangout.'

His first teacher was a dapper, aristocratic Royal Academician called Theodore Ramos. 'I didn't enjoy teaching very much,' he says, 'but I enjoyed meeting that curious suburban generation. In a lot of cases, their achievement was to liberate themselves from their background. Malcolm was one of the odd ones: one couldn't tell then that he was going to go far, or in any direction. He had this white skin and red hair and was far more angry and intense than most of the students, an entirely different calibre.

'I liked him because he talked to me; I don't think he talked to many people. He detached himself from his contemporaries. He would be excited by the inexplicable. I didn't think he was a good artist at all. If one were to compare him with my contemporaries, we all drew much better, but art schools are such interesting places. All sorts of things happen outside of art. So I didn't think Malcolm was ever going to be a painter; he was playing with art in a sense. He was enjoying what the art school gave, which was not necessarily an ability to paint, but discovering oneself.

'He saw himself as the creator, the thinker. This is what he learnt at art school, to draw quickly, to think on paper and having thought something out, to discard it and pick up something else. But because of his incomplete training, Malcolm learned ideas about art but not the motives. He happened during a time when students were frightened and ignorant, trying to find motivation for themselves. They over-declared themselves. The student was his own creator, his own critic, his own destroyer.'

This was the start of Malcolm McLaren's independence, and the start of a seven-year drift through further education. From 1965 on, when Malcolm resumed his place at art school, he began trying out ideas. 'I learnt all my politics and understanding of the world through the history of art,' he says. Malcolm was interested in knowledge and in its practical application: 'Plagiarism is what the world's about. If you didn't start seeing things and stealing because you were so inspired by them, you'd be stupid.'

By degrees, Malcolm began to see himself as an avant-gardist, searching for a key with which to unlock his deep anger and resentment. Between 1965 and 1968, he passed through a number of art schools and polytechnics (Reigate, Walthamstow, Chelsea, Chiswick) under a series of names falsified for the purpose of getting grants. Throughout this period, he took up and discarded ideas from ideas then in currency: Fluxus, Pop Art, Andy Warhol. Common to these was the idea of art being indivisible from everyday life, indivisible particularly from commerce and the environment.

Space had been the idea behind Malcolm's first installation, in spring 1966, when he took over the now defunct Kingly Street Gallery, just off Carnaby Street. 'It was a forty-eight hour environment,' he says, 'I was very influenced by those Yoko Ono-style happenings. I took a lot of six-foot-high corrugated cardboard which I completely stuffed into the gallery.' Inside this maze, films blared and spotlights shone: a series of photographs show a mod Malcolm orchestrating what looks like total chaos.

By the time he was in his first year of vocational painting at Croydon, Malcolm was experimenting with shapes and colours in Pop-Art packaging. From his research and discussions, he had learnt the knack of verbalizing practice in a written manifesto. 'Stimulated by my environmental experiences,' he wrote at the time, 'shop windows, museums, the kitchen, I find myself working with these associations. Shoe shops as opposed to grocery shops as opposed to meat shops as opposed to jewellers' shops.'

In a series of photos taken on Clapham Common in early 1968, the results of these ideas, fragmented black on black, geometric shapes or hardboard box constructions which look like display trays, are shown *in situ* – outside a bakery where they blend in with the Hovis and the Sunblest. Another painting sets two repeated pink, yellow and orange shapes – very similar to Warhol's famous 1967 'Flower' series – against a matt black background.

Guided through whatever disciplines the school was attempting to impose, Malcolm's early statements carried a heavy burden of negation. His Croydon portfolio contains a drawing of two chairs where the black is so furiously applied that there is almost no white space left. Other sketches and primitive lithographs depict a black and white world dominated by the monolithic, abstract shape of the tower block that would become an art director's cliché a decade later.

Urban space – then the hyper-modernistic celebration of the mediated commercial world – is an idea that runs not only through the history of postwar utopian art but also through the specific currents of postwar English society. Malcolm's art-school period coincided with the heyday of postwar development – office blocks, motorways, huge council housing schemes. During this period, he made several sculptures inspired by Frank Stella: disturbing, angular shapes from the subconscious which were hung in concrete environments.

The sculptures were in part inspired by the particular spatial quality of Croydon itself. As Croydon native Jamie Reid says in *Up They Rise*: 'In the early 1950s, Croydon was about to boom. The plans for new skyscrapers, a new shopping centre and governmental Croydon already existed. It was to be a whole new citadel of commerce for postwar Britain. London's mini-Manhattan was born.' Malcolm took photographs of office blocks like Luna House, turning them into threatening charcoal shapes, or totally abstract designs. Reid's 1968 gouache, *Up They Rise: A Playground For The Juggler*, depicts Malcolm as an alchemist – a manipulator of the new urban space.

Malcolm had entered Croydon in the autumn of 1967: the course provided him with more freedom than hitherto and, as importantly, a community of peers. Robin Scott, the future pop singer 'M', remembers Vocational Painting as 'full of people who'd broken some ground in some way or were mature students. It was pretty broad in its possibilities, but rather vague.' This is confirmed by Jamie Reid: 'Because you didn't need any qualifications, there was a very odd combination of people at that college. The other thing was that there was no qualification at the end of the course.'

Both Reid and Scott were Croydon natives. Born in 1947, the son of John MacGregor-Reid, City editor of the *Daily Sketch*, Jamie Reid had been brought up in Shirley, the thirties 'dream suburb' east of Croydon. It is a neat, highly ordered environment which at the time it was built accorded with the spatial fantasy of the age: *sub*-urbanism. 'In principle it's a very good system,' Reid says, 'why shouldn't everybody have their own garden? But I've always had a love/hate relationship with suburbia: I hate what it's become.'

The family was politically active: Jamie's grandfather, George Watson MacGregor Reid, had been head of the Druid Order and stood for Parliament just before the First World War, at the time when socialist politics and utopian occultism were mixed. Jamie's brother Bruce was a press officer for the Committee of 100 in the early 1960s, and was a fund of information about London: not only about the 'secret' underworld of bunkers and nuclear command posts, but about the teeming metropolis of Boswell and Hogarth.

Jamie had gone straight to Wimbledon Art School from John Ruskin Grammar School, where he was an unwilling student. It had been a toss-up between art and football, but painting won: Reid was obsessed by Jackson Pollock, whose canvases he saw as landscapes. At Wimbledon, the teaching methods were very traditional and Reid rebelled: 'I was a typically obnoxious young art student.' He was in the right area for Croydon Art School, and the course offered more freedom: full of the romance of painting, he started there in autumn 1964.

As a teenager, Robin Scott found Croydon exciting: 'It was like nowhere else,' he says. 'The Saturday morning market in Surrey Street was a fantastic place: it was like somewhere in the Caribbean – full of intrigue and corruption, very lurid.' After leaving Croydon Technical College, Scott had kicked around as a beatnik hustler. A self-confessed opportunist, he went to Croydon Art School 'to grasp what was happening in London'.

'It was very quiet in our studio,' he remembers: 'Malcolm and I used to wander round and look in the other studios: we'd managed to break down the partitions in our studio, but down the other end it still was a serious business, suitable for what Jamie was doing. He was very preoccupied with being a painter; he was thought of as a serious student. Then came the sit-in and that's when he became closer to Malcolm.'

> To describe the essential theory of anarchism is rather like trying to grapple with Proteus, for the very nature of the libertarian attitude – its rejection of dogma, its deliberate avoidance of systematic theory, and, above all, its stress on extreme freedom of choice and on the primacy of the individual judgement – creates immediately the possibility of a variety of viewpoints inconceivable in a closely dogmatic system.
>
> **George Woodcock: *Anarchism*, reprint (1975)**

> MUSICIANS – SMASH YOUR INSTRUMENTS
>
> **King Mob flyer**

The near-revolution that occurred in Paris and the rest of France during May 1968 had an immediate, galvanizing impact on youth throughout the world: partly because it was the first properly televised urban insurrection, partly because it marked a generation claiming its political rights. The American destruction of Vietnam may have been a trigger, but 1968 turned aesthetic style into political gesture. The violent intensity of the pop that had flooded the world from 1964 was translated into a public demonstration of the utopian promise: that the world could be transformed.

The virus of anarchy had returned with symptoms suited to the age. The term most commonly used for the 1968 rioters, *'les Enragés'*, made reference to the precise moment in French history, the late stages of the Revolution, when the words 'anarchy' and 'anarchist' were first used freely – and pejoratively – in the sense of social chaos. During the next century, through the writings of libertarians like Proudhon and Bakunin, anarchy became anarchism: in George Woodcock's words, 'a system of social thought, aiming at fundamental changes in the structure of society and particularly at the replacement of the authoritarian state by some form of non-governmental cooperation between free individuals'.

Lacking dogma, anarchism could be defined – and attacked – in many ways: despite the seriousness and cogency of its arguments, it was easily misunderstood and coopted by more dogmatic political systems. 'I destroy and I build up,' Proudhon wrote in his *Economic Contradictions*; and in the popular eye, anarchism became more associated with the first, and to many, more exciting part of Proudhon's programme. But, as Woodcock notes, in this lack of definition lay anarchism's strength: 'It can flourish when circumstances are favourable and then, like a desert plant, lie dormant for seasons and even for years, waiting for the rains that will make it burgeon.' Although the events of 1968 were not directly inspired by French anarchists – by then 'ageing intellectuals' – the rhetoric of the groups and, in particular, the spontaneity of communications, updated anarchist ideas and methods.

The most identifiable signals in Paris of 1968 were posters and graffiti. Their cryptic phrases were the perfect medium for this mediated revolt – novel, easily packageable and paradoxical. Phrases like 'Demand The Impossible' or 'Imagination Is Seizing Power' inverted conventional logic: they made complex ideas suddenly seem very simple. They were art works but not in the traditional sense of being attributable to one person: anonymous, spray-canned slogans like 'Never Work' or 'Sous les Pavés, la Plage' acted as polaroids of an instant.

The instant passed quickly – on 30 May, de Gaulle reaffirmed his power through a televised ultimatum – but it became a powerful symbol to those who had participated, either in person or by proxy. Many of that generation were profoundly moved by that incandescent moment (as 1988's media coverage of the twentieth anniversary gave witness). For the bored students in the concrete cage of Croydon, it acted as a starting pistol. Why not go one further than just putting on visiting lectures: why not *dispense* with lecturers?

Malcolm McLaren had already put his toe in the radical currents of the time, picking up ideas from a South African called Henry Adler while still at Chelsea. Jamie Reid had grown up with utopian politics; Robin Scott was just up for the crack. Whatever their motivations, all were involved in a sit-in that developed in Croydon a week after the famous Hornsey Art School action. On 5 June, the art students barricaded themselves in the annexe at South Norwood and issued a series of impossible demands.

'We put up a sort of sixth-form manifesto about tearing down the partitions. Most of the demands were directed at the staff; it didn't go beyond that,' says Robin Scott. 'We felt their role was pointless and that the existing walls between authority and the students should be torn down. Hornsey had more grievances than we did, but we were in a very apathetic situation and boredom was the main complaint. It was time to test the system: see what the limitations were.'

'The idea was in the air,' says Jamie Reid; 'at the time it was imperative just to contribute to what was going on and take your own action. There was genuine contact between the Sorbonne, Croydon and Hornsey.' The action was as much a media event as anything else: inside the annexe, the students pumped out press releases and manned the telephones. On 12 June the sit-in made the press. Robin Scott fielded the *Times* press call: 'We have been tricked,' he said. 'The authorities have created a situation which could have become ugly and violent.'

'Our solution to all the talk about network structures and changing years and departments was just to tear the dividing walls down. So we did,' says Jamie Reid. But after the initial enthusiasm had passed, the question remained of where to take it now. 'I was singled out to represent the student interest,' says Robin Scott, 'and to confront the staff. I wasn't interested, but time was running out; people weren't sleeping and we had to get out.'

By the time the summer holidays arrived, the sit-in had dissipated: 'It was a weekend picnic,' says Scott, 'the fun was over. I don't think Malcolm's intentions were any more serious either, because when it came to the crunch, having anything constructive to say or do, he had nothing to say. Indeed when the opportunity arose to actually change the system, or do anything about the Croydon School of Art, he was gone, he fucked off. All the time he was creating a position for himself elsewhere at Goldsmiths'.'

Jamie Reid remembers it differently: 'Both McLaren and I, as instigators of the sit-in, were pressurized, busted, stopped by the police. At one point, the Board of Governors tried to get McLaren committed to an insane asylum.' For Reid, the sit-in was an eye-opener: 'I went from being a student worrying about my little niche into being someone who was very aware of what was happening in other parts of the world – what was taking place in Paris, the riots in Watts. I really felt that I had control over my own life and over my environment.'

This was the mythology of May 1968 in a nutshell. Although none of the Croydon students was in Paris during the actual disturbances, it suited both Malcolm and Jamie Reid – who visited Paris later in the year – to say that they had been there: it was perfect for the Sex Pistols' own radical mythos. In as much as dealing with myth, their actual presence or absence is irrelevant: both felt themselves challenged and altered by the moment. Once they had drunk of that elixir, the challenge was not only to retain the feeling, but to make it happen again.

The riots of 1968 coincided with a revolt in perception, as the first postwar 'media' generation reached adulthood, saw the way the world worked and saw that it did not accord with their experience. The playful techniques of the Situationist International (SI) not only helped to instigate the riots themselves – the Situationist-inspired *'De la Misère en Milieu Etudiant'* had fired the student protest in Nanterre that sparked *les événements* – but also set the paradoxical style of the graffiti and posters which, photographed *in situ*, were collected in their magazines.

'I'd heard about the Situationists from the radical milieu of the time,' says McLaren. 'You had to go up to Compendium Books. When you asked for the literature, you had to pass an eyeball test. Then you got these beautiful magazines with reflecting covers in various colours: gold, green, mauve. The text was in French: you tried to read it, but it was so difficult. Just when you were getting bored, there were always these wonderful pictures and they broke the whole thing up. They were what I bought them for: not the theory.'

As much as the psychedelic graphics contained in the English and American underground press, these slogans and posters, which both parodied and trashed media practices, showed how a vertiginous sense of possibility could be transferred into the imagination of people who had not witnessed the events themselves. If the aggressive rhetoric blended with the Maoism of the time, the occluded perceptual tricks developed by the SI would lie dormant, like anarchism, until reactivated by the right conditions.

As Michèle Bernstein wrote in 1964,'The Situationist International was founded in 1957 at a conference held in Italy and attended by a number of artists from several European countries. Some of them came from the avant-garde movements that had emerged around 1950 but were still almost completely unknown at the time: COBRA in Northern Europe and Lettrism in Paris. As a start they aimed to go beyond artistic specialisation – art as a separate activity.'

'In its first phase,' wrote Peter Wollen in 'Bitter Victory', 'the SI developed a number of ideas which had originated in the Lettrist International, of which the most significant were those of *urbanisme unitaire* (integrated city-creation), psychogeography, play as free and creative activity, *derive* (drift) and *detournement* (diversion, semantic shift). Artists were to break down the divisions between individual art forms, to create *situations*, constructed encounters and creatively lived moments in urban settings, instances of a transformed everyday life.'

This was an ambitious but fluid project. Pinot Gallizio's *pittura industriale* – rolls of canvas produced at random with painting machines and spray guns – could cover a whole city, as well as being a sharp comment on the industrialization of fine art. In 1959, Asger Jorn showed his *Modifications*, over-paintings of kitsch art bought at flea-markets. Subconsciously unsettling, paintings such as *The Disturbing Duck* or *The Avant-Garde Will Not Give In* both mocked and celebrated notions of 'bad art'.

By the early sixties, the SI became dominated by the more theoretical, dogmatic Guy Debord. In 1962, he published *Society of the Spectacle*, a book which plundered philosophers like Sartre, Lefebvre and Lukács, and urbanists like Lewis Mumford. From his brilliant collage of avant-garde art, Marxist theory and existential obnoxiousness, Debord fashioned a language that battered on the subconscious like a negative mantra. *The Society of the Spectacle* is a series of numbered aphorisms, like the *Poésies* of Lautréamont which Debord, in homage, plagiarizes.

The book updates the critique of everyday life to describe postwar conditions, where people are held in thrall by a unified media system which includes TV, newspapers, pop music and culture itself. 'Culture turned completely into commodity,' wrote Debord in aphorism number 193, 'must also turn into the star commodity of the spectacular society. In the second half of this century culture will hold the key role in the development of the economy, a role played by the automobile in the first half, and by railroads in the second half of the previous century.'

Debord's personality came to dominate the SI during the 1960s, both within the dynamic of the movement itself – expressed in a series of scissions and expulsions – and in the way that the products and ideas of the SI began to filter through into the UK. As early as 1960, there had been an SI conference in Britain, held in the suitably Dickensian surroundings of Whitechapel: there were also British members, such as the painter Ralph Rumney and the Scottish poet and beat novelist Alex Trocchi. Apart from Trocchi's utopian 'Sigma' movement, Britain largely bypassed the first, more conventionally artistic phase of the SI and consumed it in rhetorical pamphlets.

SI material came into the country in dribs and drabs. Within its own context, there was much that was pop about the Situationists, and this was how it was understood in Britain: as a philosophical update on Pop Art. For, because of Britain's connection with America, the future was seen, not in terms of philosophy, but in the terms outlined by Richard Hamilton in his 1956 manifesto: 'Popular; transient; expendable; mass-produced; young; witty; sexy; gimmicky; glamorous; big business.' By 1966, this future was being transmitted around the world by aggressive pop groups like the Beatles, the Kinks and the Rolling Stones.

One early English reponse to the SI was a magazine called *Heatwave*, the first, July 1966, issue of which collaged material from the Provos in Amsterdam and American anarchist publications like the *Rebel Worker*. The keynote pieces are about British pop culture: John O'Connor wrote a critique of the first 'teen takeover' novel, Dave Wallis's *Only Lovers Left Alive*, which describes a near future where 'the adults have committed suicide with "Easyway pills" and the teenagers have taken over'.

In 'The Seeds of Destruction', Charles Radcliffe laid the foundations for the next twenty years of subcultural theory. Radcliffe isolated six 'unofficial youth movements' – 'The Teddy Boys', 'The Ton-up Kids', 'The Ravers', etc. – which simultaneously represent a symptom and a critique of postwar capitalism. 'The facts proclaim,' he concluded, 'that youth revolt has left a permanent mark on this society, has challenged assumptions and status, and has been prepared to vomit its disgust in the streets. It has made its first stumbling political gestures with an immediacy that revolutionaries should not deny, but envy.'

The second issue of *Heatwave* reproduced material from the SI, which Radcliffe, co-editor Christopher Gray, Timothy Clark and Donald Nicholson-Smith had joined in late 1966. SI texts were percolating through: '*Ten Days That Shook The University* was widely distributed among students interested in contemporary radical activity,' says Paul Sieveking, a Cambridge student who completed the first English translation of Raoul Vaneigem's *The Revolution of Everyday Life*; 'it was a discovery: you felt it gave you a certain edge over people who didn't know about it. That was followed by Vaneigem's *Totality For Kids*, in a dark blue cover, which was hawked by this strange character who travelled the country called Martin Housden. *Heatwave* had a fairly small distribution, only in London I'd guess. You'd have got this stuff at the Wooden Shoe Bookshop in Old Compton Street, anarchist bases like Freedom. Better Books' basement was packed with samizdats, rants and manifestos. The initial impact of the SI was less in the Urbanist side: I think the term was "hermetic terrorism".'

In December 1967 Gray, Radcliffe, Clark and Nicholson-Smith had fallen victim to the SI's favourite motion: exclusion 'for maniacal excesses'. 'It was thought their support for this rather nebulous street gang, the Motherfuckers, was somewhat uncritical,' says Sieveking. 'Vaneigem went over to the US and met this guy called Hoffman, who was into Tarot cards. When Gray and Smith refused to recant and say they were mistaken, they were excluded.'

Some of the excluded formed their own group, an SI/Motherfucker mutation, King Mob, and declared themselves and their politics through their tabloid magazine, *King Mob Echo*. On the cover of the first issue, published in April 1968, was a masked *blouson noir* with a Molotov cocktail and a quote from Marx: 'I am nothing but must be everything', while inside were aphorisms that fused Marx, Hegel and Emerson in a 'poetic' style: 'My utopia,' it declaimed, 'is an environment that works so well that we can run wild in it.'

King Mob took their name from Christopher Hibbert's 1958 book, then the only one available, on the Gordon Riots of June 1780, which John Nicholson calls the 'Great Liberty Riot' – the anarchic week that was akin to the French Revolution a few years later. In applauding this hidden moment of British history, the group were attempting to reemphasize a disordered, anarchic Britain that had previously been swept under the carpet. It was an attempt to give a specifically British context to the rumblings of discontent that, even before the events of the following month, were growing louder.

King Mob weren't unique – another pro-Situ group was formed in October 1968 at Cambridge, the Kim Philby Dining Club – they were part of a continuing process. As such, specific details of membership, still heavily disputed, are not vital: as King Mob linchpin Christopher Gray says, 'The spirit is more important than the facts.' The extent of McLaren's involvement with King Mob has been disputed in subsequent pro-Situ pamphlets: although Gray wishes to say little, he remembers McLaren as 'just a wide-eyed art student – he wasn't very involved'.

The only active involvement that can be attributed to McLaren was during King Mob's plagiarism of Black Mask's 'Mill-in at Macy's', when in December 1968, twenty-five members or affiliates, one dressed up as Santa Claus, crammed into Selfridges' toy department and started thrusting toys into the hands of passing children and their startled parents. This action was accompanied by an anonymous, one-page, broadsheet manifesto: 'Christmas: it was meant to be great but it's horrible,' ran the headline. 'Let's smash the great deception. Light up Oxford Street, dance around the fire.'

McLaren was one of the twenty-five: 'We were all handing out the toys and the kids were running off. The store detectives and the police started to pounce: I ran off into the lift. There's just me and this old lady: the doors start to open and I can just *see* all these police. I grab the old lady really tight and walk through like I'm helping her. As soon as I got out of the store, I belted out of there.'

Malcolm was watching hard. King Mob were as much involved with Anglo-American pop revolt as they were with French theory, attempting to make contact with 'delinquents' between 'fifteen and twenty-five or those who were mental'. They considered football hooligans 'the avant-garde of the British working-class'. There were graffiti campaigns in and around Notting Hill Gate, where anonymous slogans like 'The Road of Excess leads to the Palace of Willesden' conducted an opaque, fleeting dialogue.

Seeking utopian metaphors, King Mob fetishized both revolutionary violence and pop culture. They held up Valerie Solanas as an exemplar: author of the pre-feminist tract 'SCUM Manifesto', Solanas had put theory into practice when she shot Andy Warhol in 1968. The cover of *King Mob Echo* has a Motherfucker-inspired drawing: bursting out of frame is a bearded figure with a bubble: 'Reich, Geronimo, Dada: Revolutionaries with a message for England'. In between scattered pistols ran the legend: 'We're looking for people who like to draw.'

Another *King Mob* tabloid reprinted a 1968 Motherfuckers' handbill with slogans such as 'We are the forces of CHAOS AND

King Mob Echo flyer, late sixties (from *BAMN*, Penguin Books, 1970)

ANARCHY'. At the bottom were the sentences – 'We are everything they say we are and we are proud of it. We are obscene lawless hideous dangerous dirty violent and young' – which found their way onto the hit album, *Volunteers*, by the Jefferson Airplane, for whom, it was claimed, Radcliffe was the 'official political adviser'; Chris Gray also had an idea for a totally unpleasant pop group for whom graffiti was sprayed near Victoria Coach Station.

The twinning of revolutionary rhetoric with pop culture came to little. This was partly due to revolutionary priorities – terrorist groups like the Weathermen in the USA, Baader/Meinhof in Germany, and the Angry Brigade in the UK were moving towards real armed struggle – and partly due to the marginality of groups like King Mob. By the late sixties, pop culture was a monolith: the Bohemian, if not revolutionary attitudes of the Beatles and the Rolling Stones, both of whom wrote about the events of 1968 from an equivocal standpoint, were bankrolled by multi-national corporations.

No pop radicals, then, confronted this central contradiction: that their radical styles were uttered from within a powerful, Anglo-American music industry, which, by the late 1960s, could afford to stifle trouble with large advances. Nobody had the language to formulate this critique, outside obscure publications like Raoul Vaneigem's *Revolution of Everyday Life*. 'Already the idea of "teenager",' he wrote in 1963, 'tends to define the buyer in conformity with the product he buys.' This was not fully translated until 1972.

King Mob's attempt to bridge the gap between pop culture and revolutionary theory failed. As group members the Wise brothers stated in the (anonymous) *End of Music* pamphlet: it 'gave an extra fillip to the marketing of disintegration and ironically became more noticeable in the late 70s than in the late 60s because of the scale of the mass market of artistic anti-art'. In the late 1960s, the dream of 'Youth Culture' was still too powerful.

The libertarian currents of the late 1960s shaped the lives of many of those that they touched: for Malcolm McLaren and his associates like Fred Vermorel and Jamie Reid, life would never be the same. In those currents they could swim, and select a language for their multiple angers, resentments and ideals. It was largely through the SI's influence that they developed a taste for a new media practice – manifestos, broadsheets, montages, pranks, disinformation – which would give form to their gut feeling that things could be moved, if not irreversibly changed.

Location photograph from *Oxford Street* film, 1970 (courtesy of Malcolm McLaren)

4

The middle classes invented the commodity. It defines our ambitions, our aspirations, our quality of life. Its effects are repression – loneliness – boredom.

Malcolm McLaren: 'Intentions for film' (May 1971)

Life is so boring there is nothing to do except spend all our wages on the latest skirt or shirt. Brothers and Sisters, what are your real desires?

The Angry Brigade: *Communiqué* 8 (1971)

After the Croydon sit-in, Malcolm Edwards entered Goldsmiths' in autumn 1968 to study film and photography. The first person he met there was Helen Mininberg (later Wallington-Lloyd). The child of rich South African parents, Helen had arrived in London for education and excitement. As a dwarf, she was also a very visible misfit. Fascinated by the extravagant behaviour and language of the (then) subterranean gay world (and its coded language, *Polari*) she made a vivid, magical companion, lover, and once, LSD partner, for Malcolm, who was essaying a flamboyant marginality.

'It was just before the summer term at Goldsmiths',' she says, 'and the last people to be interviewed were Malcolm and me. These were the days of flower power, and Malcolm had this peaked cap, a long Army and Navy coat, miles too big for him, newspaper rolled under his arm, smoking Woodbines. He asked me what I'd do if I didn't get in. I said, "I'll go to San Francisco and join the hippies. What would you do?" He said: "I'd go and cause a revolution." I was so sheltered in South Africa: although the Mandela thing had started, you just didn't hear about revolution.

'When I started at Goldsmiths', I saw Malcolm and he goes, "Oh hello, you got in!" We stuck together. He'd say, "What are you being so precious about? Don't tickle the canvas, you're more important than the canvas." He was an agitator. There were debates at the students' union, and Malcolm used to put things in terms they could relate to because he's not an intellect: he had a more ducking and diving kind of life. He loved art, but he didn't want to make pictures for people to buy. He wanted to instigate something and be an imp. An itch in somebody's knickers.'

Six years into his art-school wanderings, Malcolm was still floundering. He and Vivienne were constantly separating for various reasons: lack of money, parental pressure or simple waywardness. In 1968, Vivienne had briefly returned to her mother's in Harrow: Ben Westwood was packed off to live with his father. 'Before I went we were incredibly poor,' he says, 'we used to go down to the market after it had closed and pick up all the vegetables, and down to the building sites and get dandelions and blackberries and stuff. I went to my dad because it got to the stage where we couldn't afford to survive.' Both children were sent to boarding school as soon as possible.

By 1969, 'Malcolm and Vivienne had a relationship where they were educating each other,' says Robin Scott, who lived with them briefly. At this point, Vivienne was supplementing Malcolm's grant with money made from selling her jewellery on Portobello Road: 'She had to be confident,' says Scott, 'because she was doing all the bloody work back at the flat. She knew she was holding it together and if she were to pull out the whole thing would fall apart. Plus she was looking after the kids: she had everything on her plate.

'Vivienne was crucial. I admired her: I thought she was and still is a great person, much more prepared to commit at an emotional level and admit one's vulnerability. She's more down to earth. She was very supportive and she was happy for Malcolm to be the centrepiece in a conversation, when she had just as much to say. Malcolm was happy to have a line and repeat it endlessly. If you were with him all the time it could get a bit exasperating. He would pick up something he'd heard and decide that he liked it; he would then use it all the time. He was very tenacious and wouldn't tire; he'd carry on in the face of adversity.'

If Vivienne's tenacity rubbed off, so did her moral certitude, which matched the absolutist political rhetoric of the time: 'One time when we were living together,' says Scott, 'she said, "I want you to go, Robin." I said: "Why?" "I don't think you're part of the revolution." God! She was bound up in the rhetoric of that time.'

Just like Malcolm, Vivienne retains many of the ideals which they both lived out in the late 1960s and propagated, at the same time as they were denying them, from the mid-1970s on. 'The artists who created Punk,' says script-writer Johnny Gems, 'were Malcolm and Vivienne, and they created it in this very sixties art-school, hippie kind of way. All that Revolution, anti-materialism, Yippie, pro-minority.' Yet their commitment was not the same: 'Little did Vivienne know that Malcolm wasn't committed to the revolution,' says Robin Scott, 'he was committed to himself and it took her a long time to realize that.'

In the summer of 1969, Malcolm manoeuvred himself into a position where he could cause trouble. The week before the huge Rolling Stones' concert in Hyde Park, Malcolm talked into existence a free festival in the Goldsmiths' buildings. He roped in Robin Scott, by this time working with a group called Mighty Baby, and Fred Vermorel, billed to give a lecture called 'All in a day's work'. On the final day, there was to be a discussion with 'R. D. Laing, William Burroughs, Alex Trocchi, Michael X, Jim Dine, squatters, radical students and workers'. Others 'awaiting confirmation' were 'Pink Floyd, the Living Theatre, Rolling Stones and John Lennon'.

None of these turned up; neither did many of the lesser-known, billed acts. Vermorel remembers the festival as a fabulous disaster: 'Hardly any of the bands advertised turned up and in the resulting chaos the police were called and a mini-riot developed.' But Malcolm remembers it as a success, his first taste of showbiz. If nothing else, he was learning the value of old-fashioned, carnival hype: what did the reality matter as long as you made an impression? The ensuing events made it clear that a disaster was just as interesting as a success.

Malcolm's inability to see anything through became apparent with his major Goldsmiths' project, the *Oxford Street* film, which he worked on with Helen Mininberg and Patrick Casey. The bulk of this occurred during another spell away from Vivienne, who had been packed off with Joe to a Welsh caravan site the previous autumn. In 1969, McLaren married a Turkish French Jew called Jocelyn Hakim: 'She needed to stay in the country,' he says. 'We married in the registrar's office at Lewisham. We didn't have a ring so I had to rush out and get one from a bubblegum packet.' It was with the £50 from this wedding that the *Oxford Street* film was begun.

Due to lack of money and lack of conceptual focus, *Oxford Street* drifted along for eighteen months before being left unfinished. Very little remains of the film except a few tiny reels of negative, yet it is clear from the shot lists and scripts that if one piece of work in Malcolm's vagrant art-school career can be called a precursor to the Sex Pistols, this was it. As an old man comments in one of the many synopses for the film: 'I wouldn't want to be born today, everything is so expensive and everything is so dull. There's no future for the kids.'

The film on Oxford Street began as a piece of pro-Situ psychogeography in this prime consumer thoroughfare, which, on a bad day, can still seem like a living example of everything that is wrong with civilization. Consumption, and its new temples, department stores, had for some time been an object of fascination to the millenarian left, whether in the leaflets published by the German Kommune 1 after the fire in the Brussels store 'À l'Innovation' on 22 May 1967, the 'mill-ins' practised by Black Mask and King Mob, or the bombs planted in Frankfurt by Baader/Meinhof in 1968.

The photos that Malcolm and Helen took as a guide for the 16mm footage act as a manifesto: they depict an inhuman landscape, peopled by ciphers. Here the shop assistants persuade customers to look like mannequins; the empty public space is dominated by obliterating traffic; passers-by are threatened by a blown-up gun from a cinema poster; rows of stockinged mannequin legs freeze a sterile sexuality; everywhere are monolithic office blocks.

When it came to shooting, Malcolm involved a variety of his friends: at various points, Jamie Reid was used as cameraman and Helen as assistant director. They worked around Oxford Street: the shot list includes many shop façades and exteriors, as well as close-ups of advertisements and human gestures of frustration and incorporate hostility. They were hampered by the fact that hardly any of the stores would allow them access: only Selfridges let them in.

As well as the dehumanizing effect on shoppers and staff alike, the film-makers became interested in Oxford Street's transience: the sleights of hand used to keep the customer bedazzled. Many of the shots concentrate on the zoning of the street, itself offering 'no relaxation, geared totally to work and consumption': the quick erection over the weekend of 'new' façades; the quick-turnover nature of the design itself, displayed in the Wimpy Bars where the seats and the lighting are ergonomically shaped to make the customer leave quickly.

The film slowly took shape: a May 1970 treatment, worked on by Malcolm and Jamie Reid, concentrates on fashion's alienation: the film begins in Mr Freedom's interior, with a TV screen blaring the importance of female fashion in society and its function as business. Pop has its place here too: the Rolling Stones' hymn to dis-'Satisfaction' cuts in and out, while a pop star says 'how he loves his work. Thinks everybody is happy with their work. Hates football vandals.'

The frustration and claustrophobia build, in the stores and on the tube. In front of a window with the word H-O-L-I-D-A-Y-S running across it a young man is kicked into unconsciousness. The film ends with a grand parade of London stores. In the middle of this spectacle is a scene straight from Situationist demonology: 'Smoke seen coming from a building, a restaurant is on fire. Procession stops.'

In the first quarter of 1970, Jamie Reid worked with Malcolm on the history of Oxford Street 'as a set of attractions; respectability is invented for people to better themselves as they pay highly for it'. Their version traced the history of Oxford Street from Tyburn at Marble Arch on the western end: the hangings on Monday, execution day, were 'London's largest free spectacle'. The street was slowly taken over by the middle class: in 1760, the Pantheon opened, a fashionable amusement palace where one lady dressed 'one half of herself smart and other half in rags'.

Their account of the Gordon Riots then begins: 'the middle class started it against the Catholics. Then hundreds of shopkeepers, carpenters, servants, soldiers and sailors rushed into the streets. There were only a few Catholic houses to smash. So they started to smash all the rich houses. The middle classes did not want anything to do with this.' The rioters then 'burned down all five London prisons. They wanted to knock down everything that stopped them having fun and made them unhappy. They wanted to set all the mad people free and free the lions from the Tower.' The film was still not finished.

A final script from May 1971 takes another course. This time there is a star – a real attraction who skews the film away from revolt into homage. On top of the old structure, pop is everywhere: the head of the Billy Fury fan club talks about her idol, while a kiosk on Oxford Street displays 'all the glitter of the signs'. The commentary is spoken by a nine-year-old with a jarring voice. Inside the Oxford Street dolphinarium, dolphins 'perform stupid tricks'. Press cuttings juxtapose commercial boosterism with random violence.

A last shooting schedule shows the 'glitter of the signs' slowly enveloping Malcolm. Rock'n'Roll crowds the soundtrack: we see 'a living room full of photos of Billy Fury'; 'his fans outside theatres and their style of dress'; 'Billy in performance, portraits on record covers.' Malcolm was getting bored and discouraged: one last, despairing letter to his tutor has him hoping for finance from Larry Parnes, Billy Fury's manager. Sometime in June 1971, he walked away. 'It was very hard to film,' says Helen. 'It had to do with life, in the end.'

It was time for life outside the cloister. Within six months, Malcolm had a new identity and a new outlet: using his disappeared father's name for a passport application, he was now Malcolm McLaren, Rock'n'Roll couturier and hustler. Ignoring the admonitions of the Angry Brigade, who stated in their communiqué for the 1971 'Biba' bombing that 'in fashion as everything else, capitalism can only go backwards', McLaren began to sell 'authentic' fifties fashions to a small but fussy crowd. Why this change?

By summer 1971, active pro-Situ politics were becoming positively dangerous: Angry Brigade suspects were being rounded up by Detective Inspector Roy Habershon, who used a well-worn copy of *The Society of the Spectacle* as his guide. The process of the law took a long time; it was over eighteen months from arrest to final sentencing in December 1972. During this time, constant reports provided the popular press with potent images of an enemy within that had to be extirpated.

In many ways, this trial marked the farthest reach of late sixties utopianism in Britain. The postwar economic boom that had provided the foundation for this fantasy had ground to a halt as early as July 1966, when a six-month wages freeze was instituted and the pound devalued. The economy began its long decline: by 1972, inflation was running at thirteen per cent, and in January of that year unemployment went over the 1 million mark for the first time since the 1930s.

The new political mood reflected this. In June 1970, a Conservative government was elected for the first time in six years, under Ted Heath: a new, tough 'realism' was its signature prefigured by the Tories' January 1970 conference in the Selsdon Park Hotel. As Hugo Young notes in his biography of Margaret Thatcher: 'Selsdon Man was born in Labour rhetoric: a hairy, primeval beast threatening to gobble alive all the benefits which socialism spread around postwar British society.'

The first cracks were showing in the postwar consensus that had been so heavily promoted by both Labour and Conservative. The pendulum was swinging away from the social liberalization that had been going on since the early 1960s: nowhere was this clearer than in the coining, by Mrs Whitehouse and the proto-New-Right Festival of Light in the early 1970s, of the term 'permissive society' to describe the 1960s.

The process of absolutism which had led the Angry Brigade to the only logical conclusion, armed violence or terrorism, had not only split the utopian underground down the middle but was part of a wider process that was affecting British society as a whole. The alternative society split between, in Richard Neville's phrase, 'the sober, violent puritan left extremists versus the laughing, loving, lazy, fun-powder radicals'. Neither could find a way into conventional politics: by the end of its six-year tenure, the Labour Party was seen as having been just as another branch of Multinational Inc., with its failure to condemn the Vietnam war and its collusion with local and international capitalism.

At the same time, instead of the consensus epitomized by Harold Wilson, there were the first signs of a polarization typified by Enoch Powell's famous 'rivers of blood' immigration speech in April 1968. As Stuart Hall writes: 'The resolution of the state to resist, and the panic and fear of the "silent majority" at having their routine way of life threatened and shattered, made a fateful *rendezvous*. Out of this convergence the drift into reaction and authoritarianism was born. In Britain the greatest casualty was the disintegration of liberalism.'

From 1970 on, there was a diaspora of the underground community, however illusory that community might have been. The many new roles and ideas that had been thrown up were becoming institutionalized. Squatters became home-owners; local activists become adventure playground leaders; utopians joined the Labour Party. Many went into the various authoritarian, Eastern religious movements that oddly paralleled the rise in Christian fundamentalism.

And now the most mysterious and glamorous radicals of them all, the ones that had struck moral fear into those who hadn't gone all the way, had their reward: ten-year gaol sentences.

The hedonists disappeared into normality or spiralling drug use, itself more risky after Labour's 1970 Misuse of Drugs Act. Some of them became the entrepreneurs that they had always had the potential to be. Within McLaren's circle, his contemporaries were following their own paths: Fred Vermorel continued in higher education, while Robin Scott composed ditties for the day on BBC 2. Helen Mininberg married a gay man and spent her life as a 'fag hag'. Jamie Reid, perhaps the most affected by the events of 1968, returned to Thornton Heath. Together with Nigel Edwards and Jeremy Brook, he founded a local printing company called the Suburban Press in 1970.

There was another reason for Malcolm's new identity. After Billy Fury, the glamour of the signs took hold of McLaren: at the same time as he took his father's surname, he slowly built up his Jewishness in imitation of Larry Parnes, the most outrageous, flamboyant Rock'n' Roll impresario of them all. And, although he did not know it, McLaren had the blueprint for his ideal product in all the research for his failed film. It was on Oxford Street that he would have the Sex Pistols' first offices, in a forgotten, now demolished, rabbit warren. It was here that he had shot the exterior of EMI records in the spring of 1970. It was for this film that he had written the manifesto: 'Be childish. Be irresponsible. Be disrespectful. Be everything this society hates.'

alcolm McLaren outside number 430, arch 1972 (© *Daily Mirror*)

5

The Spui, at midnight each Saturday, suddenly became the popular centre for everyone who was bored. And everyone is bored. The real importance of the Spui scenes was that they broke the system of isolation, based on permanent movement, characteristic of modern urban control – to rule, divide – and succeeded to a large extent in turning a public space in the middle of the city into a small uncontrolled enclave of freedom. This vortex rapidly drew in together all the city's dissident, bored and aggressive elements. (Beatniks, pleiners, nozems, teddy boys, blousons noirs, gammler, raggare, stiljagi, mangupi, mods, students, artists, rockers, delinquents, anarchists, ban-the-bombers, misfits . . . those who don't want a career, who lead irregular lives.)

***Heatwave*, 2 (1967)**

During November 1971, McLaren, Westwood and Patrick Casey took control of number 430. In photos taken at the time, McLaren appears in orthodox Ted wear: a powder-blue drape with black velvet trim, a gold waistcoat and slim-jim tie, black shirt, black drainies, black crêpes and black-and-blue striped nylon socks. Vivienne's bleached, razor-cut hair is matched by a wild, canary-coloured mohair sweater, black stretch pants and shorty boots with high heels.

Ever the chameleon, McLaren is trying on a variety of poses suitable to his new situation. In some photos, he plays the proud Jewish salesman – showing off the pink lining of a blue drape jacket, a particularly extravagant cowboy boot. In others, he is the cultist, clutching the *Buddy Holly Story* LP or standing in front of a shrine to Rock'n'Roll heroes past and present. He has already developed an air of glaring, proletarian menace which embodies his infamous future protégé. 'He looks exactly like me!' blurts John Lydon, when he finally sees the pictures in 1988.

There wasn't much construction work to be done. The corrugated iron façade of Paradise Garage was sprayed black, and the words Let It Rock were picked out in pink fluorescent paper and shaped into musical notes. Prominently displayed was a flyer for Screaming Lord Sutch, an early patron. One of the first British Rock'n'Roll singers, Sutch had been, before his better known electioneering activities, an outrageous, stunting showman, blissfully careless about his lack of any conventional musical talent.

Inside the shop, the back sales area was painted black. The clothes were hung on an antique stand: they were a mixture of vintage items and reconstructions – the trousers made by Vivienne, the jackets by an East-End tailor named Sid Green. Other items included blue and silver pegged pants, several scarlet shirts, and a beautiful fifties flecked jacket, in black with white strands woven in like TV static. Dotted around were dayglo socks, records, and original handbills for films like *Rock Around The Clock*, *Vive Le Rock*, and Joseph Losey's apocalyptic *The Damned*.

The front half of the shop was the hangout area. This was dominated by Odeon wallpaper and a peculiar trompe-l'oeil window under which stood an original fifties cabinet, picked out in pink taffeta and containing plastic earrings, Brylcreem, and pendants. On top of this sat a picture of Sutch, his hair flying wildly as though from an electric shock. On the wall, Billy Fury leered from within a garish glass frame.

Dotted in between the utility furniture – 'just like a fifties Brixton living room' – were stacks of magazines which you could sit and read: *Mad* take-offs like *Sick*, cinema sheets like *Photoplay*, or the more blatant *Spick*, *Span* and *Carnival*. McLaren's idea (not totally shared by

Vivienne) was to make the shop more than just a sales machine. 'On good days,' ran the first piece on Let It Rock, 'Malcolm says that he sometimes buys cakes and Coke to give to his customers. Thinking that "Capitalism stinks", he has doubts about running the shop.'

McLaren and Westwood quickly found themselves in a contradictory but agreeable situation: still searching for a revolutionary metaphor, if not subculture, while finding themselves in fashion. Something that was provisional, at least on McLaren's part (though everything was provisional to him), was not only boosted but also fixed by media attention, as Let It Rock got immediate press. Within two months, the shop had spreads in the *Evening Standard*, the *Daily Mirror*, and *Rolling Stone*. 'There was no doubt,' as Bevis Hiller wrote in the contemporary *Austerity Binge*, 'that 1972 was to be the year of the Fifties' Revival.'

The Ted revival had moved from its inner urban fastnesses to London's outer limits. 'The slice of Greater London that goes between the A1 in the North and across the A40 to Ealing in the West has always thrown up a lot of Rock'n'Roll kids,' says Ted Carroll, a balding, bulky Dubliner who pioneered the selling of pop's past in England. 'It's Greenford and all those areas like Northolt. It's a bit boring and neat, a fairly safe existence. If you wanted to shoot a movie about the 1950s or early 1960s, you would find loads of locations even today.'

Rock'n'Roll landed in the British Isles like a Martian spaceship. There was scarcely the Afro-American music or subculture here that could prepare anyone for the brutality and sheer sexual explosiveness of the records that, between 1954 and 1959, seemed to drop from heaven like the offerings of a cargo cult. These records were so transforming that nobody who heard them could find a language to explain them except in the phrases of the songs themselves, which talked in tongues: 'A Wop Bop A Loo Bop', 'Be Bop A Lula'. From these alien incantations was born the quasi-religious fervour with which the British still celebrate pop.

This intensity heralded the religion of the teenager. In 1948, 60 per cent of English people under thirty wanted to emigrate. To teens in the mid-1950s, Rock'n'Roll carried, encoded within its arcane language, the promise of a new world: a world where they did not have to do National Service, where they didn't have to keep on hearing stories about the war, where they could reject sacrifice, where they could have sex and consume freely, where they could drift, cruise, run wild. Most of all, they wanted to do as much as they could as soon as they could and this first-time intensity – epitomized by Rock'n'Roll – is the hallmark of the teenage dream.

'The Americans had Rock'n'Roll under their nose and they took it for granted,' says Ted Carroll, 'whereas over here it was very difficult to hear that music – in 1957, 1958, the BBC didn't play Rock'n'Roll at all. You had to listen to Luxembourg or the American Forces Network to hear Rock'n'Roll. It was almost as though there was a plot to keep it from you and that added a mysticism to it.'

Because the first-time impact of hearing Rock'n'Roll was so strong, many Britons became obsessed with trying to recapture, or at least simulate, that enveloping rush. Having no indigenous tradition (and very little media), the celebrants had to build their religion in blocks, out of cult objects like the 'brothel creeper' crêpe-soled shoe or those visiting stars who, like Little Richard or Buddy Holly, seemed totally immersed in the big, bad noise. As the Scandinavians did with Charlie Parker, the British not only supported, but also idolized, rockers like Gene Vincent way after their peak of success in the USA. In this vicariously self-destructive ritual, commitment to the brutal beat was everything.

'It never died here,' says Ted Carroll. 'When the British beat boom went soft it turned a lot of people off and they just stayed with Rock'n'Roll throughout the sixties.' As the main tide of youth culture floated downstream, the Teds were left with rituals that had become fixed by routine. Specific objects – a particular forty-five on the black and silver London label, or a velvet-trimmed, finger-tip length drape jacket – became all-important. One principal way in which the British had absorbed a youth culture that was, initially, outside their experience was to consume, and in this apotheosis of *the thing*, the shop was the temple.

Like McLaren and Westwood, Carroll had noticed a gap in the commercial infrastructure serving the Ted revival. 'When I went to America in 1970,' he says, 'I discovered that they had oldies shops there which specialized in selling fifties and sixties records, and many of those records were still in print. Most of the majors had actually kept a lot of their hits in the catalogue. This was also the time of junk shops where you could get albums for about ten shillings and singles for a shilling. By 1972 I'd amassed this stock and started importing records from America. I was looking for a retail base: I couldn't afford the overhead of a shop and I found the ideal solution in the weekend market place.'

Rock On, at 93 Golborne Road, quickly attracted a hardcore

following. Going there was in itself an act of faith. Golborne Road was at the wrong end of Portobello Road, ten years before urban regeneration; Rock On was right at the back of a long, deep store space heavily guarded by several impenetrable junk stalls and a smelly café. Inside you could not only buy, but also obtain an education, listening to records that were almost impossible to find anywhere else: forty-fives of Doo Wop, Deep Southern Rockabilly, New Orleans.

Like Charlie Gillett, whose *Honky Tonk* radio programme began in March 1972, Carroll was offering, not only a service, but also a taste. 'Instead of having to go to a second-hand shop and churn through thousands of singles to find maybe two or three, a lot of people liked the idea of everything being gathered together and put into sections.' Carroll's stall was not the first oldies shop but it was accessible and, along with *Honky Tonk* and a new monthly magazine, also called *Let It Rock*, it supplied an infrastructure for the exhaustive interest in pop history that was an undercurrent of the early 1970s.

Inevitably, Carroll crossed paths with McLaren, supplying records for number 430: 'Malcolm was an opportunist and always keen to make a buck. In his research for his Billy Fury movie, he'd found that there were old shoe companies in Leicester that still had old stock. When he produced some of these, people freaked out and wanted more, so he was just reacting to the demand. People wanted winkle-picker shoes and drape jackets and cheesecutter hats and pictures of Rock'n'Roll stars, and he was digging these things out and then charging quite a lot of money.'

With its commanding position, Let It Rock attracted a mixture of genuine, working-class Teds, fanatical about their lifestyle, and a few Chelsea sophisticates and disaffected teenagers, who were swamped by the shop's principal clientele. There were a few disasters but the shop was making money. Encouraged, McLaren and Westwood decided to expand: a large Rock'n'Roll festival was scheduled for Wembley Stadium in August 1972 and they printed up hundreds of T-shirts in their own design – Little Richard with the overprinted slogan 'Vive Le Rock'.

This festival marked the commercial high watermark of the grass-roots Ted revival: up to 50,000 people attended to hear Chuck Berry, Bill Haley, Screaming Lord Sutch, and Billy Fury. Dressed in a leopard-skin cap and a drape suit, McLaren took a stall there, but the produce didn't go as expected. 'The only things that sell at those events are the hot-dogs,' says Ted Carroll, who was paid twenty pounds by McLaren to mind the stall. 'He just about covered his costs and was left with 500 or so T-shirts.'

Quite apart from any personal disappointment for McLaren, the festival's events reinforced the contradictions behind the Rock'n'Roll revival as a trend. While many of those freshly attracted to Rock'n' Roll's primal energy had participated in the libertarian culture of the late 1960s, most of the fans retained the stolid conservatism implicit in the recreation of a sixteen-year-old style. When a very heavily made-up Little Richard made some comments about Black Power and then began disrobing in an extremely camp manner, the Teds booed viciously. The only new acts on the bill, Gary Glitter and the MC5, were hardly allowed the luxury of exhibiting any attitude at all.

For all his posturing, McLaren was much closer to the post-hippie MC5 than he was to the dogged traditionalism of the Teds. At Wembley, the reality behind the revolutionary metaphor intruded with a jolt: far from being the proletarian vanguard, his customers were revealed to him in conversation as boring, repetitive and narrow-minded. The Rock'n'Roll revival had been a useful polemic with which to crash through the detritus of hippie culture, but both Malcolm and Vivienne began to realize that it was itself even more ossified than the decadent King's Road culture they were trying to upset.

In the religion that is pop, the Teds were fundamentalists. The simple fact was that many of 430's customers were upholders of that very society which McLaren and Westwood abhorred: they were not true marginals but mildly extravagant examples of a deep strain of English conservatism. Aside from their costume, the Teds were as straight-ahead, rigidly working-class as one could get: bound by tribe to violent dislike of anyone who was different. In contrast, McLaren and Westwood were committed to the idea of minorities. The Teds were as English as meat pies and racism: McLaren and Westwood ate vegetarian food and wouldn't buy South African oranges.

'Malcolm was very disappointed,' says Ted Carroll, 'but he got a lot of his ideas from dealing with them. Because there was a lot of press about the shop at that stage coupled with the Teddy Boy thing, it helped him to form his ideas about how the press and society looked at something like that. He was a bright boy: he picked up things fast. It was at that time that I happened to mention casually that I was managing Thin Lizzy and he got very excited. It wasn't a big thing to me because the band hadn't had a hit at that stage, but he wanted to know everything.'

> There was something satisfying about the way in which a traffic stream on a hot Saturday, stalled, crammed with sweaty pink families trapped with one another as the Mini-Minor was trapped in the queue, could be utterly *negated*, cancelled, by a group of gleaming rockers hurtling past.
>
> **Jeff Nuttall: *Bomb Culture* (1968)**

Any change at 430 was a gradual, unplanned process, despite the air of certainty which hindsight gives the whole enterprise. Just as the Teddy Boys were beginning to obstruct custom, the Rock'n'Roll revival was percolating through into the mass market. Late in the summer of 1972, Let It Rock was commissioned to provide outfits for Ray Connolly's *That'll Be The Day*, the first major British film to look back at the 1950s. David Essex and Ringo Starr modelled Let It Rock drapes and leopard-skin jackets. By the time the film was released, it was competing with other Rock'n'Roll nostalgia items such as *Let The Good Times Roll*, the stage version of *Grease* and the influential film *American Graffiti*.

Slowly, the clothing began to deviate from the Ted tablets of stone: McLaren and Westwood could not hope to compete with the serious rag trade once it got hold of a style. A strong biker element started to creep in from the autumn on, reflecting another of the origins of the Rock'n'Roll style, in outlaw movies like *The Wild One* (the principal influence on future teen movies such as *Rebel Without A Cause*). By the late 1950s, the biker's black leather jacket had become a visual shorthand for the generic juvenile delinquent: frightening but fascinating.

Bikers – or 'ton-up boys' – had become a British cult in the late 1950s: the first to celebrate, not only a new mobility, but the impulse to pure, destructive speed that had been impacted into youth culture with the death of James Dean. In races around the North Circular Road, you were not only fighting the other rider, but also yourself. As befitted existential gladiators, their clothes were dramatic to the point of being fetishistic: as the plot of the 1964 film *The Leather Boys* made explicit, they were also a mask for sexual ambiguity.

By 1972, the sleek look of the early bikers had been cross-bred with the shaggier Hell's Angels style. Bikers, now called Rockers, had been the epitome of bad style ever since the Mods had fought pitched battles with 'the grease' at sundry seaside resorts from 1964 onwards. This element of a forbidden style was immediately attractive to McLaren and Westwood, with their sharp awareness of subcultural shifts. More than with the Teds, there was a dramatic potential in the clothes themselves that could be heightened: laden with associations, biker gear links sexuality, violence and death, in a twentieth-century archetype.

McLaren and Westwood began by studding the backs of leather

Clothing by Too Fast To Live, Too Young To Die, *Mahler*, 1974 (courtesy of the Cinema Bookshop)

jackets. They then started to explore clothing technology, finding a method of glitter-printing onto cloth. Using a particular form of glue, you could bake slogans onto a T-shirt: they took the logo that Gene Vincent had on the Blue Caps' drum kit and transferred it onto tight, sleeveless T-shirts. T-shirts began to sparkle with blue glitter, picking out names like Elvis, Eddie and Chuck Berry. 'Then we came up with the idea of studding the T-shirts,' says McLaren. 'We became more inventive and started to stud the T-shirts with the names of certain brands of fifties motorbikes that also had sexual connotations like Triumph and the Norton "Dominator".'

Another idea was to pick out keywords – like 'Rock'n'Roll' – by making letters out of boiled chicken bones and attaching them to the cloth by tiny chains, like the raw material for a magician's curse. 'Then we thought "What would make it more sexy?" So we cut two lines down the breastplate of the T-shirt which went across the breast and Vivienne put in two little ball-and-chain zips rather than just a flat end so they'd be hanging. Then we went further: really mad and bikish. The nearest thing I could think of was getting an actual tyre: I had this image of a tyre round your armpit. So we got hold of old two-wheel bicycle tyres and started to cut them in half: you'd place them round your armpit and stud them. They were called bike-tyre T-shirts; they were very special.

'We started to get involved with a lot of rockers: some of them were so good at customizing things themselves. One boy we employed was brilliant: he painted one slogan that said "Too Fast To Live, Too Young To Die". I thought it was such an extraordinary phrase. He said it was a slogan that American gangs took up as an anthem after James Dean's death. Then, as we decided to get into making more things of our own, we decided to change the name of the shop in the spring of 1973. For the façade, we had a black hoarding made and painted with a white skull and the words above "Too Fast To Live" and below "Too Young To Die".'

McLaren had learnt well from Oxford Street's hyperactive motion: this was the first of many attempts by him and Vivienne Westwood to get rid of an unwanted clientele by changing their shop's name, design and attitude. The Teds had proved themselves to be ideologically unsound and had to be excluded. Their cash wasn't entirely unwelcome however: the Let It Rock range remained on sale and the phrase was retained as the brand label for McLaren and Westwood designs.

As the shop began to move away from the cult of proletarianism, McLaren set about surrounding himself with other marginals, many of whom would reappear later in his story. New recruits for the shop included Gerry Goldstein, whom Malcolm had met in Stamford Hill; by 1973, Goldstein was an intellectual Jewish *flâneur* straight out of Alexander Baron's London novel, *Low Life*. Another was Roberta Bayley, a Californian Anglophile who had fled the West Coast: 'It already felt like you'd lived here, listening to all those Kinks' records. When I first arrived, I worked as a waitress in this vegetarian restaurant in Langton Street called the Chelsea Nuthouse. Malcolm and Vivienne used to come and eat there and they really liked Americans. They'd hired a friend of mine called Gerry Goldstein to work in the shop and he couldn't start straight away so I filled in for him. Maybe it's because he's Jewish, but Gerry seemed more American. He knew about people like Lenny Bruce, and he was the one that turned me on to writers like Joe Orton and Mervyn Peake – he was dating Mervyn Peake's daughter at the time.

'I didn't work there more than a few weekends and days. The shop was just between Too Fast To Live and Let It Rock. Malcolm was at the point when he was really hating the customers: they all came down on Saturdays and he really disliked selling to them. Vivienne didn't spend much time in the shop: she'd just drop by. She was strong. Malcolm seemed really spacey and a gentle person: he still has that side to him. He was in a formative stage, still trying to make money. He was interested in all these political ideas, and had other weird obsessions: he really liked Roger Vadim, he really liked this black girl who used to come in.

'One day Gene Krell from Granny's came by and said "Picasso died" and Malcolm just said "Oh good". I never heard anybody say anything like that. I'd never been exposed to that type of attitude. I was from San Francisco, a girl, never hurt anyone's feelings, peace and love, all this stuff, so it was a shock. That was my first exposure to anybody saying something really outrageous; it was just what he felt at that moment.'

Fuss ripped off Cruz's floppy tie and tore open his pink-and-black polkadot shirt, the buttons popping off like overripe cherries. He pulled the shirt open, exposing deep razor-blade cuts crisscrossing Cruz's thin, hairless chest, some cuts old and scabbed over, others open and festering. Cruz's face-blurred before Fuss as his own eyes filled with

tears. 'You punk, Cruz! You dumb little punk! You've gone and bitched up on me! You've gone on the Horse! You're jacking right into your bloodstream!'

Thomas Sanchez: *Zoot Suit Murders* (1978)

McLaren and Westwood kept on reversing into tomorrow. As far as they could see from the musicians who came into the shop – Jimmy Page, Marianne Faithfull, the Kinks – there was little that was genuinely new in a pop culture that was, after all, mining the same vein of nostalgia. If there were harbingers of a new age, or even musicians who harked back to pop's first intensity, then neither McLaren nor the culture at large noticed them. When Iggy Pop and James Williamson, in the middle of recording *Raw Power*, visited 430, McLaren disdained them as untidy hippies.

The clothes gradually went back further into the 1940s, with the zoot suit fashion that the pair thought was the root of Rock'n'Roll style. According to Vivienne, 'The surface of the Teddy Boy was full of racism, that's why we went through to the black roots that lay behind. We started to tailor really generously cut trousers, padded shoulders and double-breasted jackets, but we did it with feel. It was almost more than authentic.'

In the early 1940s, the zoot suit had come to prominence as a minority badge: the wonderfully exaggerated insignia of negroes and in particular the rapidly increasing number of Mexican immigrants – brought by an expanding wartime economy into Southern California. As Stuart Cosgrove suggests in *Zoot Suits and Style Warfare*, the zoot suit signified the contradictory experience of the immigrant for the young *pachucos*: it was an underclass style taken to the point of absurdity.

Zooters expanded Rhett Butler's Western suit every which way: out at the shoulders, in at the waist, but especially down at the hem. The same went for the trousers, which were 'pegged' into a high-waisted shape that billowed out like a sail at the knee, before tapering almost to nothing at the turn-up. These suits would be tailored in wild, ice-cream colours like yellow and lime-green, and would be accessorized with long chains, pointy shoes and long, 'conked' (i.e. heavily sculpted) hair.

The whole effect was deliberately alien. Like the English Edwardian later, the *pachucos* signalled their revolt with their clothes: dressing up like a demented ice-cream sundae was not the way that ethnics were expected to behave in war-time America. Their revolt was instinctive and existential: 'Their attitude reveals an obstinate, almost fanatical will-to-be,' wrote Octavio Paz in *The Labyrinth Of Solitude*, 'but this will affirms nothing specific except their determination not to be like those around them.'

This sartorial aggressiveness provoked violent hostility: from June 1943 on, thousands of people were involved in race riots that began in Los Angeles and spread throughout the country. These were named after the garb that was their hair-trigger: the Zoot Suit Riots. Tailoring itself became the object of a moral panic: steps were taken in California to impose regulations on 'the manufacture of suits'. But by the mid-1940s, the style had blended back into the black, American jazz look from which it had come and in this guise, came over with the GIs and Hollywood films into Britain.

A variation on the zoot was quickly taken up by spivs and petty criminals as an advertisement for their trade: what better way to display your command of America's allure and your contempt for rationing? This alien, American shape moved through spivs and cosh boys to be taken up by the first Edwardians, who liked its annoying flash and who were also attracted by its similarity to the Western suits Alan Ladd was wearing in their favourite films.

McLaren and Westwood found that these clothes were attracting a new clientele. Apart from the pop glamour market, they were catching on with Chelsea-ites like Michael and Gerlinde Kostiff, cruising trendies on the way to Granny Takes A Trip or Alkasura, and younger teenagers like the brothers Johnny and Ollie O'Donnell, Chris Sullivan and the milliner Steven Jones, who, under a decade later, would fuel the club and clothing industry of Swinging London Mark II.

Let It Rock's successful costumes for *That'll Be The Day* had also led to another commission, this time for Ken Russell's flamboyant *Mahler*. Asked to work out something for the climactic dream sequence where the Jewish composer confronts his Aryan anima, McLaren and Westwood worked on 'this huge German Catholic creature with a Nazi helmet', as McLaren remembers. 'We used a "Dominator" bike-tyre T-shirt and the skirt was very short, in leather, and had a zip right down the front of it. Either side of that we had this huge Jesus cross in brass studs. This was right down the centre of the crotch and then on the back was this huge swastika in brass studs.'

Despite this small *succès d'estime*, McLaren was restless. The demon boredom had him in its grip. The shop wasn't going anywhere exciting. His relationship with Vivienne was marked by the usual arguments and walkouts. If there was an 'ejector seat' available in any situation, McLaren would press the button – if for nothing else, just to see what happened – and in August 1973, his chance came. With several other King's Road shops, Let It Rock was asked to exhibit designs at the National Boutique show at New York's MacAlpin Hotel. As Let It Rock, Vivienne Westwood, Gerry Goldstein and McLaren went to try their luck in the America of their dreams.

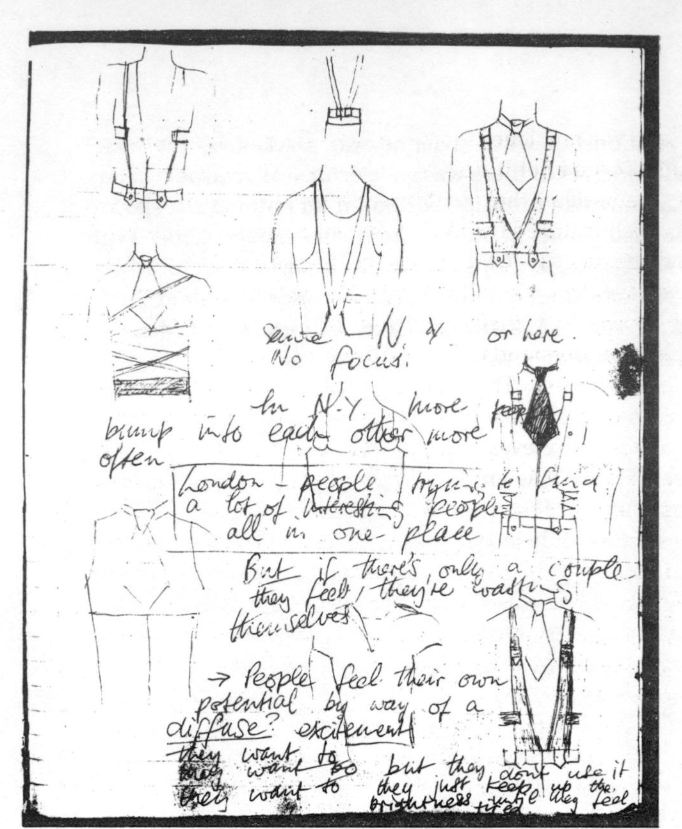

Ledger page from number 430, March 1974 (courtesy of Malcolm McLaren)

6

Actually I can't believe it's 1973. It ought to be 1935. I thought it would all blow up by now. I think when I was 16, I thought everything would blow up by the time I'd be 20.

Syl Sylvain: 'Talking with the New York Dolls', *Mercury Records Press Release* (June 1973)

Rimbaud would write about the monstrous city and the effects it would have on the species. And here it is 1973 and everything is very fast moving and I try to understand how people feel about it, how they relate to the environment. That's what a lot of my songs are about.

David JoHansen: 'Talking with the New York Dolls'

'It was the first time we'd ever been in New York,' says McLaren, 'we didn't know anyone. It was ridiculous because it was all so square. We pinned all these *Spick* and *Span* photos on the wall of our little bedroom – everyone had a bedroom in this hotel where you were supposed to show your clothes – and we tried very hard.' The trio took a few zoots, a few drapes, and for ambience, some of the fifties records and fan photos that had adorned Let It Rock.

To promote themselves they had cheaply printed some single-colour leaflets which featured the skull and crossbones from the front of the shop and the legend, 'Clothes by Let It Rock 430 King's Road England'. They then sat back and waited. 'We had all these blouses with cigarette burns on them,' remembers McLaren, 'all the Americans couldn't understand it because there were all these holes in the T-shirt or in the blouse. The T-shirt had contrived holes turned back and sewn, wild things like that. We never took a single order.'

This was almost irrelevant. Both McLaren and Goldstein encountered sensations that are familiar to everyone visiting New York for the first time. At first, the city is just like the image you have seen in countless films, only jerking out of synch; then you mesh into Manhattan's adrenalin rush. These sensations were heightened by the situation they found themselves in: the McAlpin was a chaotic rout of hippies selling incense, stall-holders playing drums in the street, finger-snapping hustlers weaving in and out of the Dolly Wog Bar.

'That's when I met Malcolm McLaren,' says Sylvain Sylvain, 'because I used to make clothes also, so you'd get all these invitations: in those days, if you were weird, you had a boutique show. He had this little room where he sold his clothes: we knew about them because we'd gone into Let It Rock on our first visit but Malcolm wasn't there. I've still got one of their forties satin ties with snow scenes; Johnny got a drape in blue with a black velvet collar. We loved to dress up. Here in America, nobody gives a shit about clothing, but in Europe, somebody will go "What the fuck are you doing with those crazy pants". That might get you to be cool.'

Sylvain was a founder member of the group that, by summer 1973, was the toast of New York. 'Johnny Thunders, Billy Murcia and I formed the New York Dolls out of New Town High School, Queens,' he says. Clothes obsessives and Anglophiles, the trio scuffled around Manhattan's music and fashion worlds, teenage hedonists trying to find a way into Max's Kansas City. An embryo group was formed at the beginning of 1972, with college drop-out Arthur Kane on bass and singer David JoHansen, whose intelligence, Jagger-like appearance and highly developed sense of the ludicrous gave the group of bombed-out suburbanites just the right edge of irony.

As their name implied, the New York Dolls intended to play high-energy, sluttish Manhattan Rock'n'Roll. The Dolls, said JoHansen, were 'a reflection of their audience', who congregated in the tiny Oscar Wilde Room at the Mercer Arts Center right in the middle of SoHo. The Dolls were sharing space with the tail end of the sixties Warhol scene, which had been the venue for drag queens, speed freaks, every possible outcast. 'We played Max's Kansas City: that was the scene,' says Sylvain, 'Candy Darling, Jackie Curtis, Warhol stars would hang out there in the back rooms.' At Mercer Arts, the Dolls played with the Magic Tramps, fronted by former Warhol superstar Eric Emerson, performance artists like Alan Suicide, or serious drag queens like Wayne County.

The Dolls instinctively swam with the tide of excess. Their costume regularly included make-up, high heels and women's clothes picked up in thrift stores. Arthur Kane was the most heavily into drag, sometimes dressing up in a tutu, while Sylvain pioneered the fashion for spandex, a cheap, shiny material which, when worn as trousers, revealed all. 'The fact that the Dolls wore lipstick connotated homosexual,' says Bob Gruen, 'but they weren't. Somebody asked JoHansen if he was bisexual, and he said, "No man, I'm trisexual. I'll try anything." This was their attitude but behind the soft pose, they were putting on make-up because these young, beautiful girls liked it.'

The Dolls shuffled the musical deck with which they had all grown up: Rock'n'Roll, the early-sixties Girl-Group sound, the Rolling Stones and the Beatles. They learned in public and flaunted the fact. This made them unpredictable, but their insouciance about lack of musical expertise was inclusive and meant that their audience could grow with them. Although there was a distancing irony, this wasn't Camp: the Dolls transcended ghastly bad taste through their enthusiasm and the way in which their music perfectly mirrored what they had to say.

Alongside JoHansen's burlesque, Jagger-like leers, Johnny Thunders' guitar slid in a series of drones that, like John Cale's viola in the Velvet Underground, gave an edge of harmonic instability – you never knew when they would explode. Beneath this near-chaos was Arthur Kane's bass, which thudded along on the beat in a minimum of notes. The tension between the two was terrific. The Dolls sang about subway trains and that's what they sounded like: the screech of the IRT.

More than Alice Cooper, they brought Hard Rock up to date for a new, nihilist generation who, in Dave Marsh's words, 'were growing up when the economy was contracting rather than expanding, when the innocence of the sixties was curdling into seventies cynicism'. 'We like to look 16 and bored shitless,' David JoHansen declared to *Rolling Stone* in the autumn of 1972. The New York Dolls' early song titles and lyrics read like a manifesto for this generation of Frankenstein's monsters, gorged on sixties excess but lacking the idealism with which that excess had been inaugurated.

Initially, things had moved fast for the Dolls: within six months of their first performance, they had a professional management team: booking agents Steve Leber and David Krebs and veteran 'plugger' Marty Thau, who had broken bubblegum hits like 'Yummy Yummy Yummy' by the Ohio Express. But the New York Dolls were the products of a very specific milieu and as a consequence they found it hard to make headway in a conservative music industry that was just beginning to formulate the concept of 'adult-oriented Rock'.

Their image didn't help: 'I remember when Clive Davis, CBS Records president, told Lisa Robinson,' says Bob Gruen, 'that if you wanted to work in the music business, you didn't go round admitting that you saw the New York Dolls. That was like admitting that you had friends that were homosexual. It was not popular in the mainstream.' Then there were the drugs: on their first visit to the UK the previous autumn, drummer Billy Murcia had died in the bath in unexplained circumstances. 'They were stoned,' says Gruen, 'but at the time it didn't seem to be so bad: everybody was. To be cool in a band, you were supposed to be drunk or on drugs.'

'After Billy's death, we were a big smash,' says Sylvain, 'it got us a lot of publicity. We were living this movie: everybody wants to see it, and we were giving it to them.' By the time they came across the Let It Rock leaflet, the Dolls were on a high: after months of negotiations, Marty Thau had finally signed them to Mercury Records, where they had quickly recorded an album. The record contained a slightly watered-down version of their music and, perhaps because of this, had the potential for nationwide sales. The Dolls were the toast of New York: their imprimatur gave McLaren, Westwood and Goldstein the keys to the city.

Under the Dolls' aegis, the trio were moved into the Chelsea Hotel, where celebrities like Alice Cooper and Michael J. Pollard came to see these odd clothes. Let It Rock were admitted into Andy Warhol's *Interview* offices at 33 Union Square West: Bob Colacello interviewed while Warhol filmed. There were endless parties: in the McAlpin; in the Dolls' loft, where Goldstein encountered a young poet called Patti Smith; or in the Chelsea, which was filmed by Eric Emerson – the Dolls wore zoots while the soundtrack of the film *The Harder They Come* played endlessly.

One night McLaren and Goldstein found themselves, amid the usual maelstrom, at David JoHansen's flat. The first album was on the point of release. Their accounts differ: Goldstein remembers the singer being 'very full of himself' and surrounded by yes-men, but in McLaren's description, the mythologizing process has gone into overdrive. As he tells it, the Dolls were diffident about their music, thinking he was a fifties man. When JoHansen eventually put the album on, McLaren shrieked for him to take it off after a few minutes. It was awful, he thought, but so awful that it crashed through into the other side, into magnificence. Upon this inverted aesthetic his interest in pop was fully rekindled.

For McLaren, New York was like a jump-cut into the present. The city seemed boundless, unfolding a series of freedoms – from class, from stasis, from puritanism – that had seemed a distant dream in England. With the New York Dolls, McLaren at last found himself in the world of celebrity – and he wanted more. The group themselves were impressive. Beginning from a similar point in fashion and fifties music, they had managed to update the original wildness of teenage Rock'n'Roll to suit the 1970s. They had attitude, they had style, they had media attention, they lived out what they sang, and most of all, they made him feel that he belonged.

On his return to England in September, McLaren felt grounded. In the depression that usually follows the New York adrenalin rush (and jet-lag), he found London static and provincial, a crushing reverse from the future he had anticipated in New York. Anything or anybody American was almost like a talisman to him. He began yet again to tinker with the content of 430 King's Road, but this time he had the germ of a new idea: something that was current rather than nostalgic.

The New York Dolls seemed to hold the key to this. When they returned to Europe in November 1973, McLaren stuck to them like glue and this time, they had a considerable impact. On 26 and 27 November, they played two dates in Biba's Rainbow Room; a day later, they gave a memorable performance on BBC2's 'serious' Rock show, the *Old Grey Whistle Test*, where their deliberate taunting of the programme's adult ambience had a galvanizing effect. 'Mock Rock' whispered compère Bob Harris, instantly adding thousands of teens to their fan club.

'The first time I saw Malcolm was when the New York Dolls played

Biba's,' says Nick Kent, then the doyen of English music journalists: 'There was some fuck-up because he wasn't on the list. Later he got in. I had seen Vivienne a few times before, obviously she stood out. Malcolm was in Paris just after that: I'd gone off to do a piece about the Dolls playing Olympia. Malcolm had got completely obsessed with the band and he'd gone on the whole tour – he was sitting around with JoHansen most of the time. He was like this guy that had seen the light.'

Kent laid out the group's allure in the *New Musical Express* on 26 January 1974: 'Five minutes off the plane in Paris, walking up towards the airport entrance, and Johnny Thunders throws up. Bl-a-a-a-a-g-g-h-h! God knows how many photographers there are: *Paris Match*, *Stern* magazine – all the European rock press and the nationals. The record company folks have arranged a special little welcome. Bl-a-a-a-a-g-g-h-h! David JoHansen, who's always one to inject a little humour into any situation, pulls out his best German officer impersonation: 'Vee did not co-operate viv de Nazees'. The massed media minions look just a little more nervous. Bl-a-a-a-a-g-g-h-h!'

The Dolls had begun with a script and now – in the confusion between person and *persona* that always occurs in pop – they were living the movie for real. Simple good times had been replaced by obnoxiousness as drugs and fatigue took hold. In Paris, Johnny Thunders smashed a guitar over the head of a spitting fan, and in Germany, had participated in the following exchange:

> *Press*: How do you enjoy being in Germany?
> *Johnny*: We . . . we wanna play a benefit gig at Belsen or someplace like that, y'know?
> *Press*: For all the Jews who died in the camp on the site?
> *Johnny*: Narrwww . . . for all the Nazis who gotta hang out in trees in fuckin' South America.

For those trying to locate pop's id, the basic punk attitude wasn't enough: it had been done countless times. A sharp shock was needed to get a reaction from dulled reflexes. As well as exhibiting their exciting incompetence, the Dolls occasionally used the swastika. 'In grammar school you get a looseleaf book and the first thing you draw in it is a swastika and a skull and crossbones,' JoHansen said in 1973. 'You carve a swastika in a desk. You don't know what fascism is, it's not anti-Jewish at all. Kids don't care anything about that shit. When you want to make a statement about how BAD you are, that's how you do it.'

This was raising the stakes. At the time, it went unremarked: the film *Cabaret* had been very popular and the swastika was just something to add spice to divine decadence. The New York Dolls were far too wayward ever to be considered coherent about anything, so that an occasional swastika band on Thunders' arm was just a good metaphor for obnoxious intent. But the ideas went into the heads of those close to them: 'Viva Rock'n'Roll Fascism', wrote Nick Kent at the end of that year, while McLaren just added it to his checklist of the components that made the Dolls so great.

Travelling with the Dolls made McLaren realize that he was not as alone as he had thought. Good ideas occur to many different people at the same time, and what he had been fumbling for in London had already been set in motion in Paris. 'In 1973,' Marc Zermati told Chris Salewicz in *The Pretenders*, 'we were calling ourselves Punks. We were very fond of those pre-psychedelic groups like the Shadows of Night. McLaren came to my shop when he had come to see the New York Dolls. The scene in Paris was really moving at the time. There was a lot of action.'

An intense man, Zermati ran a shop called The Open Market in Les Halles district of Paris, where he sold the sixties Punk codified by *Nuggets*. This compilation by Lenny Kaye had a diffuse reception in England, but in Paris, it initiated a full-blown cult, whose high priest was Yves Adrian, a journalist for the monthly French magazine *Rock and Folk*. Zermati was also forming a label, Skydog Records, whose first release was a live EP by the Flamin' Groovies, one of the few concise Rock'n'Roll groups around at that time. It was on this trip also that McLaren met Charles Castebaljac, a young designer who was struck by the similarity between their ideas.

Early in 1974, McLaren returned to London with some catching up to do. He cultivated Nick Kent: 'I had my first conversation with him at the shop,' Kent says. 'We talked about the Ronettes. I used to pass by there a lot: Granny Takes A Trip, where Keith Richard used to get his heroin at the time, was just down the road. I'd hang out there with a couple of Americans, Gene Krell and Marty Breslau. Spanish Tony Sanchez, who later wrote *Up and Down with the Rolling Stones*, was always around. One day, we were sitting around talking and Malcolm came in: I thought, "God this guy is really in a bad state." He was wearing this tweed jacket, a pair of mock leather trousers and those little shoes and the curly hair and the tie, and he was very nervous indeed.

'About that time, I did a piece on the Dolls called "Farewell Androgyny" where I said that Glam Rock had backfired because any idiot with a beard was putting make-up on and it just had to be dumped. People should get back to singing about premature ejaculations, something that meant something to teenage audiences instead of people pretending to be gay when they weren't. Bowie was watering down, Bryan Ferry was off on a Gatsby trip and I thought: "That's it, it's over." It could have provided some interesting insights, but of the groups the Dolls were the only saviours left. Malcolm loved the piece and we got close.

'He wanted to know about everything that had happened between 1963 and 1974. For him, Billy Fury was the archetype. Malcolm was obsessed with Larry Parnes; he adored him. He claims he saw the Rolling Stones at Eel Pie and then stopped, was not interested. So I told him about the Doors and Jimi Hendrix. He started going out to gigs and clubs all the time, and he really researched.'

Malcolm McLaren at the World's End, March 1974 (© Pennie Smith)

The central problem, boredom, still remained. McLaren scanned the cityscape for portents. 'Same NY or here,' he scribbled in a shop ledger in the early spring of 1974: 'In NY more people bump into each other more often. London – people trying to find a lot of people all in one place. But if there's only a couple they feel they're wasting themselves. People feel their own potential by way of a *diffuse excitement*. They want to but they don't use it. They just keep up the brightness until they feel tired.' How to unlock Pandora's box?

Modernity killed every night.

Name for 430 King's Road: after Jacques Vaché (May 1974)

Fired by what he had seen in Paris and New York, McLaren wanted to fast-forward number 430 into the present. The shop had already hit the *impasse* which happens to most sellers of second-hand goods: what happens when the good stock begins to dry up? According to McLaren, 'I just wanted something new, I didn't know what but I couldn't stand the idea of anything retro. Black seemed to be the best colour: it seemed to be where all our ideas were most exciting.

'I decided to open a shop that was more strictly black and design oriented, which would bring out all the sexual clothes that people normally sold as a fetish but which we would sell as street clothing, on the boutique strip.'

McLaren and Westwood began their research. They started to contact the specialist suppliers of rubber and leather wear: John Sutcliffe at Atomage, and the hardcore London Leatherman in Battersea.

To fit the new concept, 430 had to be totally revamped. McLaren and Westwood closed Too Fast To Live, Too Young To Die in April 1974. The rebuilding process took several months. A builder was hired, but he couldn't do the job and left the shop in a mess of debris. 'All those Teddy Boys were going mad banging on the shop and we had to sell shoes out of boxes,' McLaren says, 'there was dust and shit everywhere, the shop was smashed to smithereens.' McLaren and Westwood had to do the redecoration themselves.

The dance floor was dismantled. The wood was stripped down, varnished and bevelled, and placed on the wall in the shape of gym bars. For the wall coverings, McLaren and Westwood were obsessed by the idea of something soft: rubber was too expensive to cover the whole place, but a thin, sponge-like material was found on a trip to the

Pentonville Rubber Company. McLaren chose a grey, and rolled it like wallpaper: it was interspersed with bunches of the same material fashioned into seams. This design was carried onto the ceiling so that the shop's interior was like a womb.

'After that was done, I realized it needed something else,' McLaren remembers. 'It needed something mad and street again. I just got some spray guns and I chose all these phrases out of fetish books – like Alex Trocchi's *School for Wives* – that finally became printed onto T-shirts by making wooden little blocks that we could dip into printing ink and then just press onto your breast.' There were graffiti on the walls: phrases like 'Does passion end in fashion?', as well as quotes from King-Mob heroine Valerie Solanas. This riot of references was topped off by a pro-Situ epigram: 'What counts now is to get out of the suburbs as fast as you possibly can.'

The shop's public face came next. The lintel was sprayed with a slogan from Rousseau: 'Craft must have clothes but Truth loves to go naked.' The window displays each side of the door were lined by more sponge material, this time in a flesh-like, pale apricot colour. In one window, McLaren put an old, paint-spattered wooden chair, with the Let it Rock leather jacket slung over the back. The name remained uncertain. In May, McLaren was still toying with a pornzine quote: 'The dirty stripper who left her UNDIES on the railings to go hitch-hiking said you don't THINK I have stripped off all these years just for MONEY do you?'

In the other window was a series of extraordinary drawings that harked back to the existential roots of postwar utopianism: signed Tabou (after the club), they depicted Left-Bank life in picaresque vignettes whose subjects ranged from beatnik drunkenness to chic slumming. McLaren claims he bought them from a man who simply came in off the street: 'That's the way the King's Road was then.' The Tabou drawings show most of the existentialists as Lettrists, with writing on their clothes. The slogans that adorned the walls were soon to turn up on McLaren and Westwood's new clothes.

The tactile surfaces of the shop framed new clothes that accentuated the body. After two years of intermittent tailoring, Vivienne found her own style, suddenly turning her inexperience to her advantage. One day, she was tinkering with two simple squares of cloth, attempting to make a sleeved T-shirt. Then she thought, 'Why bother with the sleeves?', and made the simplest possible T-shirt instead, sewing the two squares roughly together, the seams highlighted as much as possible, with holes for the head and the arms. Beautifully androgynous, they fitted the torso like a glove. The heavy, pinkish, felt-like cloth made a suitable backdrop for printing slogans.

These T-shirts became the fashion staple of the new shop, whose commercial base was the strict fetish clothing in rubber, leather and vinyl. Most sexual byways were explored: it was a less sexually specific era and McLaren behaved as a classic small entrepreneur, seeking to satisfy every demand. Ranged on the walls and the wall bars were inflatable rubber masks, 'tit clamps', whips, chains, lacy rubber petticoats and boots with fantastic, foot-high heels filed down to pinpoints.

'The great thing about their clothes,' says Chrissie Hynde of the Pretenders, 'was they were doing everything that was the antithesis of fashion. It really appealed to me because it was saturated with all these Virgo qualities, all this attention to detail. I began walking round wearing all this stuff, like a rubber skirt, fish-net stockings, and these high-heeled shoes: it was the first shop I'd ever seen where I thought "I can wear this gear exclusively, and never go to another store." It was so hip and well thought-out.'

After her arrival in England during 1973, Hynde's intensity and her commitment to the hard-living Rock myth quickly led her to Nick Kent and, through him, to Malcolm and Vivienne. 'I started writing for the *NME*,' she says. 'Then I became "Chrissie Hynde of the *NME*", which I didn't like. The scene was so bad in 1974 that there was nothing to write about. The turning point for me at the *NME* was that one day they said: "Look, we want you to write an article looking back at the Velvet Underground", and I thought about it, why always looking back? Working in this shop seems so much more happening than looking back at the past, so I left.

'The job didn't last long. One day, we were just closing up – Malcolm was there – and Nick Kent came in the shop. He thought I had been seeing someone else, so he took off this belt he was wearing, which had big coins on, real cheap and nasty, and started whipping me with it. I hit the floor then ran into the dressing room and Malcolm hid underneath the counter. I still have a tiny scar. The next day, Malcolm said: "It's too confusing you working here." So I went to three record companies a few days later, got about forty albums, sold them and got a ticket to Paris.'

Violence stalked the shop. With their radical redesign, McLaren and Westwood intended to make their break with the Teds final. A few Let

It Rock items remained, such as the shoes, satin ties and the Jerry Lee Lewis T-shirts. But the intention was clear, and this rebuff earned them the undying enmity of some hardcore Teds, whose anger had already spilled over into violence. One day, just before the change-over, fifty-two Teds stormed the shop: McLaren noted the number by counting the cups of tea they ordered after their looting.

In just over two years, McLaren and Westwood had learned through their trading and their travelling how subcultures work, both culturally and commercially: how membership was not casual but involved a frantic, committed lifestyle that ignored orthodox convention at the same time as it observed strict rules of behaviour. In 1973, they'd seen how those subcultures interacted with the media, music and fashion industries. Though they didn't analyse it, both felt that it was time to begin marrying this experience with their fundamental politics.

It was at this crossover point that McLaren gave his first extended interview. In April 1974, Nick Kent wrote a piece in the *New Musical Express* about the interface between pop and fashion. It was called 'The Politics of Flash', and covered the couturiers of the day. Wearing high heels, pegged pants and a mohair, McLaren is captioned as 'togs for NEW YORK DOLLS and others'. Kent speaks a very different, very new language: 'McLaren sees it all as an artistic statement. Clothes are getting more transexual and . . . Malcolm is trying to get reknowned [sic] philosopher R. D. Laing interested in designing suits for him.'

But McLaren was bored again. In May 1974 he wrote to Roberta Bayley, who had returned to New York. In the same breath as he talks about the new designs for the shop, he mentions that he is 'still fucking trying to sell it. No luck so far. Hopefully soon I will. Because I will be heading for New York when I do. I want to come this time for a long time.' The letter ends with his latest brainwave: 'I've written lyrics for a couple of songs, one called "Too Fast To Live Too Young To Die". I have the idea of the singer looking like Hitler, those gestures, arm shapes etc. and talking about his mum in incestuous phrases.'

Steve Jones at the Furniture Cave, early 1974 (courtesy of Warwick Nightingale)

7

The phenomenon exploded in some four million viewers' eyes. Suddenly, as if catapulted from top-secret rocket installations, Johnny and his men charged. Broke through the security veneer. Gained the stage. Johnny sensed the magic of being in front of an audience. On stage. He charged forward, sent Bobby Sharp flying as he grabbed the mike. He swung, saw his 'Jolly Green Men' take care of their instrumental opposites. He glowed. This was it . . .

Richard Allen: *Teenybopper Idol* (1973)

'If it wasn't for Steve Jones, there wouldn't be any group,' says McLaren. 'Because Steve is a street kid. He was the one that was constantly thieving, the one I had to grab, and ultimately, through that grabbing, there was some fateful eye contact. I was seduced by him. It was like Larry Parnes with Billy Fury. You had this marvellous, secret eye contact. You didn't have to talk about T. S. Eliot or Gene Vincent, there was just a sense of understanding.'

The accepted view of the Sex Pistols is that McLaren, Svengali-like, hoisted a group of no-hopers to international prominence, that he is the group's alpha and omega. In fact, it was Steve Jones who first had the idea of putting the group, or any group, together with McLaren. He chose McLaren, not vice versa. It was Jones's persistence, and ultimately, his presence, which convinced this restless yet ambitious shop owner to commit himself to the group that would become the Sex Pistols.

'You need the mix of working-class roughage with middle-class kids to make a group work,' says Bernard Rhodes, who was as much responsible for the Sex Pistols' initial guidance as was McLaren. Pop is one of the very few areas in English society where members of different classes can mix on anything resembling equal terms. Its history is full of interactions between middle class, often Jewish, often homosexual entrepreneurs and working-class, male performers. If sex is not involved, another kind of fantasy is: the performer, Trilby-like, can often act out what the manager himself is unable to do, because of either age or inhibition.

McLaren was obsessed by Larry Parnes, the doyen of English Rock'n'Roll and the creator of what we today understand as the English music industry. In the late 1950s, Parnes packaged and dominated a squad of English Rock'n'Roll singers with marvellous, technicolour pop names: Billy Fury, Vince Eager, Duffy Power, Dickie Pride. This was McLaren's role model. 'Malcolm baldly stated to me that Johnny Kidd was more of an influence on his generation than Bob Dylan,' says Nick Kent, 'he really was in love with the myth of the working-class, barely articulate Rock star.'

Steve Jones was a perfect Artful Dodger to McLaren's Fagin. Born on 3 September 1955, he was the only child of a professional boxer and a hairdresser. 'I was brought up near Goldhawk Road, down Benbow Road,' he says, 'little streets. West Indian and Irish people. Wild.' His childhood was scarred by the breakdown of his parents' marriage and his mother's subsequent remarriage. Jones didn't get on with his step-father and the first signs of trouble emerged in his schooldays, which were interrupted by truancy from an early age. In 1972, he was the subject of a council care-order.

Despite his considerable quick-wittedness, Jones was left with poorly developed verbal skills, and by the end of his teens he could read and write only with difficulty. His real schooling came from outside, where he quickly learnt street smarts, the ability, often denied to those with a more extensive education, to size up situations at a glance. 'I was a skinhead,' he says, 'used to go to football matches and cause trouble. QPR, Chelsea, Fulham. Never watched the game. Go on the rampage afterwards, down Shepherd's Bush market.'

Jones was irrepressible but, behind his bullish attitude, he was sensitive and surprisingly vulnerable. His frustrations found their vent in hyperactivity. From his early teens he was, as he now admits, a kleptomaniac. 'One of my earliest memories is down in his basement,' says Paul Cook, 'he was fiddling around with these bikes he'd stolen, changing all the bits and pieces around on them.' Another facet was an obsession with sex: from his mid-teens, Jones had a compulsion to have sex as often as possible.

Paul Cook grew up in the same area of London as Jones, on the south-west side of Shepherd's Bush – a large, predominantly working-class area just to the west of rich inner London. It was composed mainly of Victorian terraces. During the mid-1960s, Shepherd's Bush was a principal Mod site and the stamping ground of the Who. Towards Hammersmith, the housing was artisan rather than council-brutal: 'Steve lived around the corner from where I lived in Carthew Road,' says Cook, 'which is now a very desirable area. We went to different primary schools, but his mum knew my mum.'

Jones was headstrong and fearless, but Paul Cook represented bedrock. Today, he retains a spry stability: of all the principal players in the Sex Pistols drama, he remains the most unaffected. He was born on 20 July 1956, the second of three children and the only boy. His father was a carpenter and joiner, and his mother did casual work. The family was stable and he grew up into a hard-working, 'quiet and conscientious' adolescent, until he started hanging round with Steve Jones: his report cards show a marked downturn from the age of fourteen.

From the age of eleven, both boys went to the Christopher Wren School, on the Wormholt estate to the north west of Shepherd's Bush. 'It was where all the kids went from the estates around White City,' Cook says, 'it was quite tough.' Although only a mile away from Hammersmith, Wormholt, just over the road from White City, was quite different. It was a sprawling council estate that, despite the benefits of thirties town planning, was as much of a rabbit warren as the slums of Dickens's London had been a century before.

'It was a lot rougher,' says Cook. 'We used to hang around there a lot though: all our school friends lived there. A certain crowd of us was always into music and fashions, and that's how we got to be friends.

Tonics, skinhead stuff. If there was a club going we'd go down there: it was all Reggae, Motown. I was never into Rock music at the time. I liked growing up there, up to all sorts of mischief. There was so much to do: you had the whole of London to explore.'

By the age of fifteen, Jones had left his parents and had lived with his friend Stephen Hayes, before moving in with the Cooks. The three were usually up to something: Jones was the active instigator and Cook the sometimes unwilling sidekick. 'He was never a bounder for villainy,' Jones says. They began to play truant systematically and, as Cook remembers, they soon found a base. 'There was a guy called Wally who lived around the corner of the school, in Hemlock Road, and at fifteen, we were always round his house. He was into playing guitar and we slowly got into the idea of playing together that way.'

'It could have been anybody,' says Warwick Nightingale, the embryo group's first guitarist. 'Paul was in my class at school; Steve was in the lower class. There were twelve hundred kids there: it was a hard school. I got through the first and second years and by the third year I'd got it sussed out and I'd stopped attending. I started to try to get a group together. I had a guitar and an amplifier, a Les Paul copy. After I left school I started to hang around with them, 'cos I liked Steve. He was funny and things happened around him: he would make them happen.'

The ritual of pop stardom requires bloodletting, and it was Warwick Nightingale's lot to be the Sex Pistols' Pete Best, sacked before success. Wally, the diminutive of his Christian name, has a colloquial meaning of idiot, and this is how the Sex Pistols myth has labelled him. Today he is withdrawn, troubled, prone to occultism, with a blighted family background. His father, a film technician, was sacked for embezzlement and died, years later, in suspicious circumstances; Warwick himself went to prison in the early 1980s, for drug-related offences.

It is hardly surprising that his account of those years is spiked with bitterness. 'None of the others would have formed a group,' he says, 'Paul was heavily into an apprenticeship as an electrician. Steve was going to be a petty criminal, as simple as that. Stephen Hayes just ended up being a Punk, a weak personality. I was the only one that could play.'

The Sex Pistols began here, as a way to spend days bunking off school. Steve Jones and his satellites had accepted the pop fantasy of transformation hook, line and sinker, but they were ordinary youths, with their noses pressed against the window, and no way in. The

(left to right) Steve Jones, Warwick Nightingale and Paul Cook in the garden at Hemlock Road, early 1974 (courtesy of Warwick Nightingale)

mainstream pop of the day was Rock, which was fantastic, expensive and still populated by the Mod generation of the mid-1960s by now ten years older than the 'Sixteens' for whom they composed self-conscious anthems. Steve Jones wanted to be Rod Stewart, but what chance was there for a bunch of scruffy herberts from the Wormholt?

Jones decided to move in closer in the only way he knew. 'We could always find a way to get in for nothing if Steve was there,' says Warwick, 'It didn't matter if we had to tear a door down. We went to Wembley to see the Faces and the Dolls. To get in, we had to rip a panel out of a door. We got right down to the front, then went backstage, drinking all their drink in the dressing room. Rod Stewart was just standing there. We were just doing all their champagne, having a great time. They didn't know who the fuck we were, they just let us get on with it.

'At that time we were hanging out down the King's Road, and we got our clothes from the same place that they got theirs – Alkasuras, Granny Takes A Trip. Steve would nick stuff because he wanted to wear the same clothes as Rod Stewart was wearing in the Faces. There was a guy called Tommy Roberts: we turned him over, took every single bit of clothing that he had in that shop City Lights. This is where David Bowie and Bryan Ferry had their suits made. We used to dress in all the clothes, and go down the King's Road in a stolen Jag, to the Drug Store or the Roebuck.'

Once the idea of the group started, in the winter of 1972–3, Jones became much more methodical. For the next three years, he performed a tour of the houses of the pop stars of the day: from those he liked, he stole. 'It was the thrill of doing it, the excitement, the adventure,' he says: only then did he feel alive. From The Wick, Ronnie Wood's mansion on Richmond Hill, came a fur coat: from Keith Richard's house, on Cheyne Walk, some clothes and a colour TV. Much more pressing was the need to accumulate instruments and a PA for the fledgling group. 'It gave us somewhere to channel our energies,' says Paul Cook, 'we knew we wanted a band and there was no way we could afford to buy the gear so we stole it.'

Anything was fair game, although the riskier it was, the better. Some of a Premier drum kit was removed from the BBC studios at Shepherd's Bush: Paul Cook saved up to buy the rest, being the only one working at the time. Most of the PA came out of a van parked near the river at Hammersmith: it belonged to a cabaret group. Two columns and an amp came from a Reggae group in Watford. A Fender bass was 'walked' from a van in Acton, and a strobe tuner was the prize from a Roxy Music concert. Two guitars, including a genuine Les Paul, came from Rod Stewart's mansion in Windsor.

The gang's greatest coup came in July 1973. David Bowie, then at the height of his first flush of fame, was playing a big concert at the Hammersmith Odeon. The event was to be filmed by D. A. Pennebaker for future circuit release. Entrance to the venue was no problem as it was their local: once in, they hid until nightfall. 'There was a security guard, asleep,' says Warwick. 'We walked on stage with a pair of pliers, snipping the wires. We took the whole PA, every single one of their microphones. RCA were recording it, so they were Neumann microphones, about five hundred pounds apiece. Prior to that, Steve had gone out and nicked a minivan to cart the stuff away in. It was me and Steve: Paul didn't want to go.'

They'd got the gear, now what were they going to play? In a bizarre homage, they had stolen from the groups that they wanted to be like: their criminal catalogue illustrates the sort of pop that was attractive to working-class males in 1973. It constituted a polarity between the lads' Rock of Rod Stewart, with or without the Faces, Gary Glitter's terrace chants and the sexually ambiguous hard Rock of David Bowie and Roxy Music. The Faces showed that Rock could include good-humoured camaraderie, while, beneath their lurex sheen, David Bowie and Roxy Music gave pride of place to ideas.

An autodidact, Bowie instinctively understood that media and pop culture were – in England at least – where the bulk of disaffected teens got their information about the world. In the early 1970s, Bowie paid explicit homage to the Velvet Underground, Andy Warhol, William Burroughs and Iggy Stooge. His breakthrough album, *Ziggy Stardust and the Spiders From Mars*, was the first Postmodern record: a sequence of songs about a mythical pop star. With a dazzling sleight of hand, it in turn made him a star.

In a fragmented market, Bowie made an ambitious attempt to codify a new pop generation: the artificial, trebly shriek of the Spiders From Mars deliberately alienated the older hippie audience. Apart from the wish-fulfilling power of *Ziggy Stardust*, his most resonant record was as producer of Mott the Hoople's 'All The Young Dudes'. In the gap left by the failure of hippie idealism, so its script went, a new kind of vicious, teenage nihilism was breeding: 'Is it concrete all around or is it in my head?'

Roxy Music also came to prominence in the middle of 1972, but they were more cerebral. Bryan Ferry had been taught by Richard Hamilton at Newcastle, and introduced a highly referential Pop Art sensibility into big hits like 'Virginia Plain'. If anything, Roxy were more outrageously constructed than Bowie: their record sleeves displayed extravagantly dressed models, named stylists and showed the band frozen in the amber of pan-stik. Musically, too, Roxy were more radical. Their greatest innovation was the use of Brian Eno as an untutored synthesizer player. Like the New York Dolls, they were making a point welcome to teenagers alienated by technoflash: that *style*, not musicianship, was important.

Lyrically, Bryan Ferry summed up the era in a series of brilliant epigrams that caught the dying curve, or so it seemed, of a civilization: 'Well I've been up all night again,' he quavered on 'Mother of Pearl'; 'Party-time wasting is *too* much fun.' On his three peak albums, David Bowie also laid out this minatory pop mood: *Aladdin Sane* hinted at imminent world war while *Diamond Dogs*, a concept album loosely based on Orwell's *1984*, dealt with the aftermath. In *Ziggy*'s 'Five

Years' he counted the apocalypse down: if that's all the time we had, then world's end was due in 1977.

Like the best pop, this connected with what people were feeling. In 1974, the lights were going out: the OPEC oil-price rise of the previous year was pushing an already unstable economy into recession. Reeling from the three-day week of the previous December, the Heath Government had finally fallen in February to a successful miners' strike and the collapse of its credit boom, which had been devised to buy the way out of trouble. The long postwar party was over, and with it the democratic consumer ideal. Advertisements which had celebrated, indeed taken you *into* the teenage experience now looked nervously at youth as a problem. Vandals and dead-end kids were not consumers.

This feeling had been dramatized by Stanley Kubrick's film *A Clockwork Orange*. Ostensibly a science-fiction vision of a hypothetical, nightmare future, it seemed to many people uncomfortably close to a documentary about England, as bizarrely dressed, drugged youths ran amok through a post-industrial cityscape. *A Clockwork Orange* was translated into the playground by Richard Allen's *Skinhead* series, which charted the various early seventies working-class subcultures. New English Library (NEL) paperbacks like *Suedehead*, *Boot Boys* and *Glam* depicted a brutal, randomly violent world closing in.

This was the pop with which the future Punk generation grew up. Cook and Jones were naturally appreciative of the Faces, but Glam's foppish violence broadened their outlook on what was possible. If they had any preference, it was towards groups that mixed Glam with lads' Rock, such as Mott the Hoople and the New York Dolls. 'They were so funny on the *Old Grey Whistle Test*,' says Paul Cook, 'they were so anti-everything, lurching about, falling into each other on their platform boots.' Despite the fact that the Sex Pistols were later presented as a radical break with all of pop's past, Glam's cadences are always lurking in the rhythm section of guitar and drums, whether in Jones's stolen Mud riffs or Cook walloping his kit like his hero, Paul Thompson of Roxy Music.

The group that formed in 1973 around the stolen equipment were called the Strand after the Roxy Music song. Steve Jones was the singer, with Paul Cook on drums, Warwick Nightingale on guitar, Jimmy Mackin on organ and Steve Hayes on bass. 'We rehearsed at the Furniture Cave, right down the very end of the King's Road,' says Warwick: 'we played Rod Stewart covers like "It's All Over Now",

"Twisting The Night Away", and Small Faces stuff like "All Or Nothing" or "Sha-La-La-La-Lee". We pumped it out, but Steve wasn't a good singer. He really wanted to be like Rod Stewart, but there was something holding him back.'

Within a few months, Jones's friends began to fall away: 'They weren't exactly in it at the death,' comments Paul Cook. That left the nucleus of Cook, Jones and Nightingale. Like Johnny Holland and his Jolly Green Men in Allen's *Teenybop Idol*, the Strand needed a focus for their delinquent energy. As far as Steve Jones was concerned, there was some urgency if he was to avoid a gaol-bird's life: by the spring of 1974, he had already been convicted of burglary, breaking and entering, stealing ignition keys, theft of a motor vehicle and driving without a licence while uninsured and under-age.

The answer surely lay in the King's Road, which Jones had by now been haunting for a good two years. 'When I started going down to Malcolm's shop it was called Let It Rock,' says Steve Jones. 'There was the other shops where the Rock'n'Rollers all used to go, Granny's and Alkasura, but Malcolm's was cool because you could hang out there: no one would rush up and say "Can I help you". We just used to sit there and watch people come in. I thought Malcolm was a bit of a weirdo, a bit of a pervert kind of guy. But he was different. I used to try to nick stuff, though.'

McLaren was the obvious candidate: he knew a bit about music and he had the contacts through the shop's clientele. Jones had already tried in vain to get McLaren interested: 'He was in such a dream he didn't know who he was,' Jones remembers, 'we thought him a right cunt.' After the appearance of Nick Kent's 'The Politics of Flash' piece, Jones redoubled his efforts. Eventually, he came straight out with it: 'Do you know where I can get a rehearsal place? I'm trying to get a group together.' Busy with rebuilding the shop, McLaren didn't bite for another couple of months, until, worn down by Jones's persistence, he paid for a room in the Covent Garden Community Centre.

When McLaren came to hear them a few days later, he was presented with a group that had no permanent bass player and no stage presence. As they launched into the number they had rehearsed endlessly, 'Can't Get Enough of Your Love', Jones forgot the lyrics and broke down in the middle of the song. Nightingale had the riff down but little else. Cook was in and out of time on the drums, and his cousin Del Noones made it quite clear that he was just filling in. The group then lurched through 'Wild Thing' several times. It was a shambles but McLaren was held: 'I had some sympathy with these guys, because they seemed a bit roguish and a bit mad.'

The first thing was to find a more committed bass player. To cover during the previous summer's trip to New York, Vivienne Westwood had used a young art student, Glen Matlock, who used to help out in the shop on Saturdays. Although McLaren found him quiet and reserved he detected a certain Bohemian liveliness. Matlock had already met Cook, Jones and Nightingale but nobody had thought of connecting them until McLaren discovered that Matlock had played the guitar at school. One night at the Marquee Club, McLaren pushed the four of them together.

Although he came from the same side of London as Cook and Jones, Glen Matlock might have come from a different world. He was born (by Caesarian) on 27 August 1956, and was the only child of white-collar parents: his father was a coach builder and his mother an accounts clerk with the Gas Board. Like many only children, he grew up to be a solitary person: 'Even now I consider myself a bit shy,' he says, 'I just like to go out on my own.' He spent his early adolescence in Kensal Rise, a traditionally working-class suburb to the north west of the city. 'It's like a village within London,' Matlock says, 'but it's quite central.'

By his own account, Matlock got on well with his parents. In 1968, he passed his 'eleven plus' and entered St Clement Danes Grammar School, right next to Wormwood Scrubs. Here he first met Paul Cook, playing impromptu games of football on the Scrubs itself. While still in his last year at school, Matlock started working on Saturdays at 430 King's Road. 'I went down to this Teddy Boy shop to get some creepers. I liked it and asked whether they needed any casual help: I got seven pounds for a seven-hour day. When I started the shop had just changed: Michael Collins was working there and a girl called Elaine Wood. They'd just begun the zoots, but a lot of younger kids were coming in.'

Matlock and Warwick Nightingale provided McLaren and Westwood with unpaid labour for the shop's refurbishment in spring 1974. Matlock was good-looking and eager, and had some musical expertise.

'My first audition with them I went round to Wally's house and they said: "Well, what can you play?" I said that I liked the Faces and so did they. I'd learned this Faces song called "Three Button Hand Me Down" that had this quite intricate bass part and I could play it, much better than I can now. So I said I knew this one and before I'd finished they said: "He'll do".'

After his parents moved to Greenford, a dull outer suburb, Glen rarely lived at home, but to McLaren and the others in the group, the suburbs never quite left Glen, who, through no fault of his own, remained the group's perpetual outsider. Quiet, affable, often bemused, he was not well cast for McLaren's gallimaufry of deviants and delinquents. 'When I first met McLaren he was a bit offhand to me because I was pretty straight,' Matlock says. 'I never really got on with Glen,' says Steve Jones, 'I found him a bit poncified, he weren't one of the lads.'

Jones quickly exploited this class gap by playing on Matlock's innocence of his criminal activities. Just after they had begun playing together, Jones had run off with a bass guitar out of a Shaftesbury Avenue shop to impress his current girlfriend. He later gave the bass to Matlock to sell: Glen took it down to Charing Cross Road, and, as he was wondering why they were taking so long to get to the point, he was collared and bundled into a police-car. All his fellow students at St Martin's lined up in the windows opposite, watching.

In the summer of 1974, the group found an ideal situation. 'The biggest thing that got the ball rolling,' says Matlock, 'was that Wally's dad was an electrician and he got this contract to work on what is now Riverside Studios in Hammersmith: it was an old BBC studio and he had to strip out what wasn't needed. He got a set of keys cut and it's got this acoustic room in it which was one of the best in Europe, so we started rehearsing there. Paul worked in Watney's in Mortlake, so we had this bar set up. It was like Aladdin's Cave. There was all this equipment, which had been stolen, lying around.'

The Strand made the first steps towards a basic competence. 'Glen could play well,' says Warwick Nightingale, 'about as well as I could play on the guitar. Steve could hardly play a note, and Paul was way behind on the drums.' The four started rehearsing in earnest, using a repertoire influenced by Matlock's obsession with concise, yet raucous, Mod pop: sharp explosive songs by the Kinks and the Rolling Stones, or football-style chants like 'Build Me Up Buttercup' by the Foundations and the 'The Baker' by the Small Faces. This brought them into line with the times.

It was the year that people started cutting their hair. There was a steadily growing idea that pop should be made accessible again. By mid-1974, one of the hottest things in London was Pub Rock. *Let It*

Rock magazine began to chart the rise of groups that disdained any flash and played simple R&B on a rapidly growing circuit of pubs – most notably Islington's Hope & Anchor. The music was almost like honky-tonk come to life: it was funky, accessible, performance-led, a deliberate return to the basics, 'back to mono'.

Most of the early Pub Rock groups were content to play rehashed R&B and Country. The only sign of anything new was a group called Kilburn and the High Roads, which featured the menacing, twisted performances of polio victim Ian Dury, with razor blades in his ear and venom in his heart. However, the breakthrough of Dr Feelgood, who electrified the metropolis with razor-sharp performances, tightened up R&B into a menacing mesh. They weren't just something to drink your beer by, but were downright threatening: Lee Brilleaux and Wilko Johnson, the group's front pair, looked like villains you might see on *The Sweeney*.

The pop 1960s were coming back, with fans' attempts to recall British pop's first rapture. 'After opening the stall at Golborne Road,' says Ted Carroll, 'I very quickly realized that there was a market for sixties stuff, particularly obscure British beat groups. The Northern Soul boys were beginning to come in as well. All sorts of interesting people used to come through the shop: Andrew Lauder started buying records for himself and Greg Shaw, who was sending over records. In 1973, Andrew brought one of the early copies of 'Who Put the Bomp' and I started stocking that; Lenny Kaye came in, around the time of the *Nuggets* album.'

Released in America at the end of 1972, *Nuggets* codified a critical idea that had been current in America since the turn of the decade. In the midst of hippie excess, writers like Lester Bangs and Dave Marsh began to celebrate the unconscious, noisy pop of the mid-1960s. In America, the unprecedented success of the Beatles had triggered an overproduction much like that which had characterized the Doo-Wop craze in the mid-1950s, when the national and local charts were crammed with groups that, because of intense competition or industry ineptitude, only had the luxury of one hit.

In ignorance of the music that was on their doorstep, most of these groups were copying white British pop groups – like the Rolling Stones or the Yardbirds – that were themselves attempting to capture the spirit of black American R&B. This double refraction resulted in a purely white, blue-collar style, in which any black rhythmic influence was bleached out in favour of pure noise and texture: fuzz guitar, feedback, drones and whiny vocals. The flatly rhythmic repetition of a song like ? and the Mysterians' '96 Tears' seemed to be the perfect form through which to express a numb nihilism.

The whole idea of Punk, as coined by Marsh and Bangs, marked a process of deliberate *un*learning: a new pop aesthetic that delighted 'in Rock's essential barbarism (and the *worth* of its vulgarism)'. Implicit in this definition of Punk was an underclass menace. In searching for the key, these Punk cultists – just like McLaren and Westwood – went back into history: just as the subconscious was to be tapped through self-consciousness, the future was to be brought about through the past. The process of recycling waste, that today is a pop commonplace, had begun.

In summer 1974, Ted Carroll found another retail outlet, a small stall in Soho Market, a temporary site awaiting redevelopment in Soho's Newport Court. An old friend from Belfast, Roger Armstrong, started to run it, first for three days, then all week. 'We instantly sold stuff, right across the board,' says Armstrong, a music enthusiast whose energy makes him larger than life. 'A lot of Rockabilly, the Blues of course, as well as a bit of sixties Soul, there were still a lot of Mods around. One of the biggest things was the New York Dolls, the Flamin' Groovies, Iggy and the Stooges. We found they were available, and sold them by the bucketload. Also sixties garage and Small Faces records. One of the big things that kept us going as a stall was that no one else had thought of phoning up Decca and finding out what was in catalogue. They still had Small Faces and Them albums, and hundreds of singles. It was the old system where if a record dropped below a certain level of sales it was automatically deleted: if it didn't, it stayed in catalogue.

'We used to get a wide cross-section at both stalls. There was this guy, Jesse Hector, who had a band called the Hammersmith Gorillas; they did a version of "You Really Got Me" in 1974. There were the Blues bores, the Rockabillies, and for the Dolls and the Stooges and the sixties garage stuff, what was to become the Punk bands. People like Shane MacGowan, when he worked in a bank somewhere, Joe Strummer, Paul Weller. I'm sure there were a lot more. The ones you remember are the ones who once they join bands, still come in. To this day kids go to hang about in the West End on a Saturday.'

Carroll's stall now supplied McLaren with the Yardbirds rather than Jerry Lee Lewis. Taking Cook and Jones, Helen Wallington-Lloyd and Gerry Goldstein, McLaren also started to tour London's pubs and clubs like the Speakeasy. In a more innocent pop era, Parnes had instilled 'showbiz values' into his protégés; McLaren would inculcate ideas. 'Malcolm started to open up a little more,' says Matlock, 'but what I really enjoyed was the discussions I had with Bernie Rhodes. He fancied himself as a statesman of the world: he was into minimalism and dadaism. I found that a good way of opening up because they'd been through the sixties and knew about the King's Road scene.'

As McLaren and Westwood's ideas for the new shop became more ambitious – and there was nothing contradictory for McLaren in being enthusiastic about the shop at the same time as he wanted to leave it – they started to gather round them friends with specific skills. Vivienne wanted to expand the sleeveless T-shirt line to take on more complicated ideas, mixing sexual taboos with Situationist slogans.

Bernard Rhodes was an ideal colleague: not only did he have the practical skill of printing, but his complex, meandering discourse threw up many new ideas. 'The idea of the Sex Pistols wasn't important then,' says Rhodes. 'The relationship between Malcolm and I and other characters around was; all of a sudden half a dozen people were around, getting on with it. We still weren't that interested in being involved with Steve and his band: we were more interested in the T-shirts and the whole idea of the shop.'

By the autumn, however, McLaren had had enough. His relationship with Vivienne was going through another bad patch: domesticity didn't suit, excitement did. He was still bedazzled by his dreams of Gotham: the New York Dolls, fashion, sex, pop, freedom. 'He wanted to sell some clothes and get away from Vivienne,' says Sylvain Sylvain. Some time in November 1974, McLaren left for New York: 'He said to me, "Look after Steve",' says Rhodes, 'meaning, "He's got this sort of group, maybe we can do something".'

Before McLaren left, however, the three collaborated on a new T-shirt, their first manifesto. Entitled 'You're gonna wake up one morning and *know* what side of the bed you've been lying on!', the design had a list of 'hates' on the left, a list of 'loves' on the right. The shirt was the blueprint for a new, polarizing style that echoed the heated rhetoric of 1968 in which fathers are killed, contemporaries dispatched, lone heroes rewarded in an incantation that, transcending nostalgia, brought the new age into being through an act of will.

This 'visual rap', to use Rhodes's phrase, is an accidental sequence so meticulous and complete that it holds in one small patch of cloth strands that would unravel over the next few years. The 'hates' mainly comprise the dead culture of the time: pompous rockers, faded rebels, repressive institutions, 'a passive audience'. The 'loves' include sex professionals, renegade artists, hard Rockers, IRA terrorists, working-class heroes and, well hidden, the first printed mention of 'Kutie Jones and his SEX PISTOLS'.

> You're gonna wake up one morning and *know* what side of the bed you've been lying on!
>
> **(Hates:)** Television (not the group)/Mick Jagger/
> The Liberal Party/John Betjeman/George Melly Kenny & Cash/Michael Caine/Charles Forte/Sat nights in Oxford Street/SECURICOR impotence or complacency (slogan & Robert Carr)/Parking tickets/19, Honey, Harpers, Vogue in fact all magazines that treat their readers as idiots/ Bryan Ferry/Salvador Dali/A Touch of Class/BRUT for – who cares?/The Presidents Men/Lord Carrington/The Playboy Club/Alan Brien, Anthony Haden-Guest, Vic Lownes, to be avoided first thing in the morning/ ANTIQUARIUS and all it stands for/Michael Roberts/POP STARS who are thick and useless/YES/Leo Sayer/David Essex/Top Of The Pops/Rod Stewart oh for money and an audience/Elton John – quote in NME 25 Sept re birthday spending/West End shopping/Stirling Cooper, Jean Junction, BROWNS, Take Six, C&A/Mars bars/Good Fun Entertainment when it's really not good or not funny Bernard Delfont/a passive audience/arse lickers/John Osborne Harry Pinter Max Bygraves Melvyn Bragg Philip Jenkinson the ICA and its symposiums John Schelsinger André Previn David Frost Peter Bogdanovich/Capital Radio/The Village Trousershop (sorry bookshop)/The narrow monopoly of media causing harmless creativity to appear subversive/THE ARTS COUNCIL/Head of the Metropolitan Police/Synthetic foods/Tate & Lyle/Corrupt councillors/ G.K.N./Grey skies/Dirty books that aren't all that dirty/Andy Warhol/Nigel Waymouth David Hockney & Victorianism/The Stock Exchange/Ossie Clark/The Rag Trade/E.L.P./Antiques of any sort/Housing Trusts who profit by bad housing/Bianca Jagger/Fellini/John Dunbar/J. Artur's/ Tramps/Dingwalls without H/Busby Berkeley MOVIES/Sir Keith Joseph and his sensational speeches/National Front/W.H. Smith/Censorship/ Chris Welsh and his lost Melody Makers/Clockwork soul routines/Bob Harris (or the Sniffing Whistler as we know him)/The job you hate but are too scared to pack in/Interview magazine – Peter Lester/rich boys dressed as poor boys/Chelita Secunda, Nicky Weymouth, June Bolan, Pauline Fordham halitosis/Rose & Anne Lambton Chinless people/ Antonia Frazer/Derek Marlow/Anne Scott-James/Sydney Edwards/ Christopher Logue/Osbert Lancaster/Shaw Taylor – whispering grass/ The Archers/BIBAS/Old clothes old ideas and all this resting in the country business/The suburbs/The Divine Light Mission/All those fucking saints.

(Loves:) Eddie Cochran/Christine Keeler/Susan 602 2509/My monster in black lights/Raw Power/Society For Cutting Up Men/RUBBER Robin Hood Ronnie Biggs BRAZIL/Jamaican Rude Boys/Bamboo Records/ Coffee bars that sell whisky under the counter/THE SCENE – Ham Yard/ Point Blank/Monica the girl who stole those paintings/Legal Aid – when you can get it/Pat Arrowsmith/Valerie Solanis/The Price Sisters/Mervin Jones article The Challenge To Capitalism in New Statesman 4th Oct. 74/ Buenoventura Durutti The Black Hand Gang/Archie Shepp Muhammed Ali Bob Marley Jimi Hendrix Sam Cooke/Kutie Jones and his SEX PISTOLS/This country is run by a group of fascists so said Gene Vincent in a 1955 US radio interview/Seven Days with Alexander Cockburn/ Olympia Press/Strange Death of Liberal England – Dangerfield/Mrs Scully love goddess from Shepherds Bush her house slaves and Search magazine/Labour Exchanges as your local/FREE RADIO stations/A chance to do it for more than a month without being ripped off/The Anarchist Spray Ballet/Lenny Bruce/Joe Orton/Ed Albee/Pauslovsky/ Iggy Pop/John Coltrane/Spunky James Brown/Dewey Redman/KING TUBBY'S sound system/Zoot suits and dreadlocks/Kilburn & the High Roads/Four Aces Dalston/Limbo 90 – Wolfe/Tiger Tiger – Bester/Bizarre Humphries/Woolf – Waves/Walt Whitman poet/Exupery, Simone de Beauvoir, Dashiell Hammett, Dave Cooper, Nick Kent, Carl Gayle writers/ Mel Ramos painter/David Holmes the newsman/Mal Dean cartoonist/ Guy Stevens records/Mal Huff funny stories/D.H./Valve amps/Art Prince/ Marianne Faithfull/Jim Morrison/Alex Trocchi – Young Adam/Patrick Heron v. The Tate Gallery and all those American businesslike painters/ Lady Sinthia 908 5569/Experiment with Time – Dunne/John Lacey and his boiled book v. St Martin's Art School experiment to be seen in New York. Imagination . . .

(left to right) Arthur Kane, Sylvain Sylvain, David JoHansen, Jerry Nolan, Johnny Thunders: the New York Dolls, 1974 (© Bob Gruen)

Strange, well-built young men
Some of them have exploited *your* worlds
Equipped with frightening voices and several dangerous talents,
They are sent into town to take it from behind,
Tricked out in *disgusting* luxury.
A paradise of violence, of grimace and madness.

Arthur Rimbaud: 'Parade' (1872)

By the autumn of 1974, the New York Dolls were in trouble. Their script was running to a conclusion as predictable as those in the trash movies that the Dolls loved. *Too Much Too Soon* was the title of their second album, taken from the biography of Diana Barrymore: as everybody pointed out at the time, the title was more than applicable to the Dolls themselves. 'Johnny had got into junk,' says Sylvain, 'and Jerry had hepatitis. It was heavy, heavy drinking.'

The Dolls had made it into the teenage press but neither press nor cult esteem sells records in America: without sales or record company back-up, the business problems started. Leber and Krebs were more traditional types who believed the industry word on the Dolls and began to get cold feet: Marty Thau operated on flair and belief, and actively promoted those very 'bad boy' aspects of the Dolls that were so worrying to his partners.

Like any partnership that turns sour, factions formed. Johnny Thunders and Jerry Nolan were shooting-buddies, which excluded everyone else. Arthur Kane was so alcoholic that he was replaced late in 1974. That left the uneasy relationship between Sylvain and JoHansen: neither could decide on the group's direction. Leber and Krebs then dangled a tour of Japan and a renegotiation of the Mercury contract, which was up in August 1975. Unable to make a choice between the two sides, the Dolls were in a state of suspension.

'Suddenly Malcolm was there in New York,' says Sylvain. 'He was making the Sex clothing. We had a meeting with Marty Thau, myself, David and Malcolm about what to do with the band. Marty was devastated, but Malcolm was enthusiastic: I always said the guy has a lot of power. Arthur was the one we convinced: we took him uptown to the detox centre. Malcolm's investment was maybe eight hundred dollars. He called up the guy who ran the Hippodrome, he hated us, but Malcolm convinced him. He's like a preacher: if he gets you to believe, you will see the light. That was his magic.'

McLaren's relationship with the group was never formalized. His principal action was to change the group's tired façade. Out went Glam, in came Communism. 'It started with one pair of red trousers,' says Sylvain, 'we were so into clothes that it was natural for us. This is the only thing that Malcolm and David agreed on: to make the hammer and sickle flag. Cyrinda Fox and David made the flag in their apartment with Malcolm, and that's when America gave up on the Dolls.'

The Dolls now had a complete new package: a uniform made by Vivienne Westwood back in England, consisting of red vinyl trousers, red ciré T-shirts, high heeled Sex boots, a hammer and sickle backdrop, and a manifesto. 'To me it meant "Let's eat the rich",' says Sylvain, but McLaren had his own concept and language, taken from the Chinese revolutionary posters that adorned the flat at Thurleigh Court: 'WHAT ARE THE POLITICS OF BOREDOM? BETTER RED THAN DEAD!'

The first 'patent leather' Dolls' concert was held on 28 February. The material had been thoroughly overhauled, but the New York Rock media was against the Dolls and McLaren in particular. 'Everything was built around this *Rock Scene* magazine,' says Nick Kent, 'and Lisa Robinson. Because there was no weekly London press there, groups would measure themselves by it. It was the first time I realized just how much groups need the media as a mirror. After the show Lisa Robinson came backstage. She thought Malcolm was mad. She rounds on JoHansen, "What is this Communist shit?" who, being the old trouper that he is, says "It ain't nuthin' serious, y'know". Malcolm was looking at him and thinking, "You bastard", because Malcolm *was* serious. Lenny Kaye went over to Thunders and asked him the same question. Much to Malcolm's delight, Thunders said: "What's it to ya?" Malcolm would tell this story over and over again, to him that was attitude.'

'They went to Florida a week after that show,' says Bob Gruen. 'Jerry's mother owned a motel and they played there. They broke up because Jerry and Johnny got on a plane back to New York to cop dope, and David left. Syl and Malcolm ended up with the rented car. So they headed for New Orleans to pick up musicians there for a new band. To get across the country they bought uniforms to look like guys off an army base, so they wouldn't get arrested for being weirdos.'

Three years is a long time in New York, and the Dolls had been superseded by a new, more austere generation of groups centred on a downtown bar, CBGBs. First to unearth this unlikely spot was a group called Television, formed by Richard Meyers and Tom Miller, two dropouts from a boarding school in Virginia. 'Tom and I kind of hated each other from the beginning but there was some mutual ground which we didn't share with anyone else,' wrote Meyers later. 'All the people whose work I was interested in, the self-conscious, twisted aestheticism of the French 19th century, were not the popular ground for the writing of the time.

'When you're a kid you think you know everything. I felt I was seeing the reality of human existence that everybody else was deluded about. The best way to reach these people, I thought, was with a Rock'n'Roll band. When I was a teenager, there was a feeling of radio as a secret network. Songs were the secret teenage news and you'd get the news by listening to the radio. I thought we should start a band. We saw ourselves as slum kids with big visions. I was trying to penetrate the conventions and the lies of mass culture and undermine this idea of 'rock star as idol' and have it be sharp-eyed kids talking to each other about what they saw.'

PATTI SMITH

with Lenny Kaye, guitar, and Richard Sohl, piano

TELEVISION

Richard Lloyd   Tom Verlaine   Richard Hell   Billy Ficca

At Max's Kansas City

213 Park Ave. South at 17th St. 777-7870 shows at 9:30 and 11:30

Wed. Aug. 28th-Mon. Sept. 2nd

The new generation, August 1974 (courtesy of Roberta Bayley)

Meyers and Miller had made themselves over by way of homage: Richard became Hell and Tom became Verlaine. With drummer Billy Ficca, they recorded two tracks: 'That's All I Know Right Now' and 'Love Comes in Spurts' – trebly songs of teenage rejection with guitars clanging like a fire engine. Hell had also worked out a visual package to go with the chopped musical style: large fifties shades, leather jackets, torn T-shirts and short, ragamuffin hair.

This was a severe aesthetic, that carried a series of messages: the existential freedom of the fifties beat, the blazing, beautiful self-destruction of the *poète maudit*, and the razor-sharpness of the sixties Mod. It spelt danger and refusal, just as the torn T-shirt spoke of sexuality and violence. If such a thing is possible to identify, it was the origin of what would become the Punk style.

Certainly, Richard Hell thinks so. Today, he is sick of the whole thing. Or, rather, the day I went to see him, he was sick of the whole thing. His look has gone around the world, yet he has been left with little. His *poète maudit* script has overtaken him. After a fruitless decade, he is trying to live in the here and now, but all everyone is interested in is a past which reminds him of how much he has lost. 'Look,' he says, fixing me with his bug-eyed glare, 'I shouldn't have told you to come at all to waste your time.'

After a routine sparring match, he gives me a copy of his latest poems, *Cuz*, for which I give him $2.95. There is no communality here which makes me want to accept a gift. Hell's bitterness – caused, as he admits later, by the fact that the Sex Pistols achieved what he desired – is an index of the antagonism that begins to colour the relationship between London and New York from this point. By March 1975, England was nowhere: in New York, there was already a thriving culture in CBGBs.

Hilly Kristal's bar on the Bowery was in the centre of the 'bum zone' – on the upper floors of the club was a flophouse hotel called the Palace – and the clientele was rough. Throughout 1974, Television played every Sunday night. The hardest thing for any musician is to find a place to learn in public: after Kristal inaugurated a 'Rock only' policy in December, CBGBs became a testing ground for other new groups like the Ramones.

Early in 1975, Hell wrote a protean song of escape. The idea was borrowed from an early sixties beat cash-in, Rod McKuen's 'Beat Generation', but Hell was ambitious, attempting to turn fake culture – for what, in the saturated 1970s, was not mediated, and therefore suspect? – into real culture. 'Blank Generation' laid out the attractions of vacancy: not just being or looking bored, but the deeper vacancy of the subconscious. In one chorus, Hell removed the word 'blank', leaving a pause before the following 'generation': nothing was defined, everything was up for grabs.

The Ramones twisted this into a repertoire of refusal. 'I don't care!' they sang: 'Don't it make you feel sick?' Formed by four suburbanites from Forest Hill, who all took the surname 'Ramone' in homage to Paul McCartney's first pseudonym, the Ramones knew their pop history, but they played dumb. '1–2–3–4!' bass-player Dee Dee Ramone shouted at the start of every song, as if the group could barely master the rudiments of rhythm. Eventually, it became a ritual.

The Ramones learned on stage, fighting, slowly refining all the time. What had emerged by early 1975 was a *reductio ad absurdum* of the story of pop music so far: the Beatles, the Girl Groups, the Beach Boys, the Stooges, Herman's Hermits, pulped down into songs so brief that they reflected the fragmented attention timespan of the first TV generation. There was no melody, only distortion and sheer, brutal speed. 'The first time they got a gig at the Bottom Line,' says Leee Black Childers, 'you could see the audience holding onto things, like they were on a rollercoaster.'

The new affiliation without a name proclaimed its difference, as all pop movements must: downtown rigour instead of midtown glitter. There was a new musical lineage that was the authorized version: sixties Punk coupled with despised bubblegum groups, but this was a deliberate simplicity, a sophisticated naivety. Although new CBGBs groups such as Blondie and Talking Heads were playing what they thought was pop, it was a long way from the industry expectations. As a result they had time to develop.

One CBGBs group was already on the point of crossing over. As a New Jersey teenager, Patti Smith had been entranced by a picture of Edie Sedgwick in the August 1965 *Vogue*: 'She was such a strong image that I thought, "That's it". It represented everything to me, radiating intelligence, speed, being connected with the moment.' In 1968, Smith moved into the Chelsea Hotel with a young photographer called Robert Mapplethorpe: together, they'd hang around the entrance of Max's: outsiders looking in.

By 1974, Smith had published two books of poetry, written for *Rolling Stone*, and had worked in the theatre with Sam Shephard and Tony Ingrassia's Theatre of the Ridiculous. Her first single was recorded in June. One side is a version of the Folk-Rock commonplace, 'Hey Joe' with Tom Verlaine on added guitar: Smith's improvisation feminizes the old 'Stagger Lee' Blues myth that is the song's root. The new renegade is not a murderer but a woman terrorist: Patti Hearst, whose exploits with the Symbionese Liberation Army during 1974 provided an instant myth.

On the other side, 'Piss Factory' both celebrated her escape from New Jersey and laid down the script for the autobiography in which she was now starring. Despite the addition of musicians, Smith was the focus. Each performance would see her launch into the unknown, through her improvisations on songs like the Punk classic 'Gloria'. Androgynous, she would invoke Rimbaud, Reich, even the CBGBs dog, in her attempt to achieve unconsciousness, to dissolve, as she sang on her centrepiece, 'Land', into 'the sea of possibility'.

When McLaren returned to New York, the Patti Smith Group were in the middle of a seven-week engagement at CBGBs, four nights a week. At the end of this season, the group signed a deal with Arista, the first sign of industry interest in the CBGBs groups whose development McLaren had been observing. 'He copied the New York groups,' says Sylvain: 'he loved Richard Hell.'

McLaren had a new hero. Before he returned to England, he tried to persuade Hell to front the group he had back home, but Hell was already having fights with Tom Verlaine about who was the star of Television, and was too old and too proud to allow himself to be manipulated. Yet McLaren had learned his lesson well: during his six months in New York he had seen a musical subculture develop that was self-generated, mutually supportive, yet potentially commercial, that radiated 'intelligence, speed, being connected to the moment'.

Yes. Sex is the only way to infuriate them. Much more fucking and they'll be screaming hysterics in no time.

Joe Orton: Diary (26 March 1967)

By the time that McLaren left for New York, the identity of the new shop had been established. There was no long quotation, but one short, sharp declaration of intent. 'That sign said Sex, in those big pink

Sex business card, 1975 (courtesy of Marco Pirroni)

sponge letters,' says McLaren, 'making you think that this is not just another shop on the King's Road, this was a shop selling things you would normally send for by mail order. You didn't have to think in such a voyeuristic fashion, you could come in and get it first hand.'

In its downtown baldness, the new name described what was inside and acted as a provocation, but McLaren and Westwood intuitively understood that new front people were needed to flesh out this polemic. It wasn't enough just to have the name and the ideas: they needed to be translated into physical form – sexy and threatening. To *be pop*, the shop had to take one into the experience and the feelings that McLaren and Westwood were attempting to invoke, but neither of them, at that stage, had the confidence or commitment to carry it off themselves.

With the arrival of Jordan, the story moves into a different gear. She is the first Sex Pistol. By apparent accident, the new shop gained a front woman who was living out the tenets that Sex consciously promoted. She was a living advertisement for the new shop, having turned her own body into an art object. From her teens, she had cultivated an appearance so startling that, every time she stepped out of the door, she put herself on the line. Her life was a *pas de deux* with outrage.

Born Pamela Rooke in 1955, Jordan was brought up in a council estate on the hills just outside Seaford in Sussex, a genteel, fading seaside resort. 'I started ballet when I was about four,' she says, 'and carried on until I was about eighteen. It gives you a sense of physical confidence when you've done a tight discipline like that. I liked to treat myself like a painting. I didn't consider that people would be offended by it. It's got to do with the way you carry yourself and the way you walk. If you hold yourself right, then you can carry it off.'

From her early schooldays, Jordan experimented with her appearance: first was a hairstyle cropped and dyed after the example of Mia Farrow. 'At school I didn't want to make too many friends. I was very strict about my lifestyle. It was about that time that I changed my name. I always liked the sound of just one name, and Jordan stuck. Then I started going to discos in Brighton: I cut my teeth there. It's quite an outrageous place: if you could hold your ground in Brighton, you were somebody.

'When I came up to London, I went to the Masquerade Club in Earl's Court, a gay club, which was outrageous even by today's standards. It was very difficult for a woman to get into those clubs, the male gay scene was very insular. They were very worried about women coming into their clubs and the only way you got in was by how you looked. If you looked crazy and outrageous you were alright. It so happened that I liked good dance music and the only places you could get that was those gay clubs. They played things like "Rock Your Baby", "Rock The Boat", lots of Bowie.

'When I started at the shop, not many people were wearing the stuff out. That was the great thing, you could go out and not see anyone with the same outfit. There were still a lot of drapes, a few lamé things, creepers, penny loafers. There was also the vinyl wear, the rubberwear and some leather trousers. There was an old metal hospital bed there that just had a rubber sheet on. The rubber men were a mixed bunch. We had regular customers who would have things made to order for them, whole rubber suits, which were terribly expensive. The first thing you learned was that they didn't mind being told what you thought. That's why they came back; if something looked terrible on someone, you said so.'

Jordan's own appearance began to reflect the shop's wares. 'I used to take real pride in the way I looked when I went to work. I kept the job because of the way I looked and because I could do the job. When I started, the beehive was already there: I used to go to work in that vinyl leotard and fishnets, and once in just fishnets and those big mohairs with satin padding at the front. And a Teddy Tinling tennis skirt with rackets up the side: very, very short.

Jordan opening up, late 1975 (© Joe Stevens)

'After I got the job, I lost my flat in Drayton Place so I had to come back to Seaford to commute. And whatever I wore at work, I wore on the train and I didn't wear a coat. I had a lot of trouble but what did I expect? Sometimes I'd get on a train and all I had on was a stocking and suspenders and a rubber top, that was it. Some of the commuters used to go absolutely wild, and they loved it. Some of the men got rather hot under the collar, paper on the lap.'

With Jordan as a scandalous sandwich board and with Michael Collins' contacts on the gay scene, the shop developed a new ambience which reflected the shop's stock. 'Michael's friends used to hang about,' says Jordan. 'Like Amadeo, who used to be the host down the Sombrero, which was another of our hangouts. This was after the Masquerade, which just outraged itself eventually. It was closed down because it was a public nuisance.'

Another Masquerade habitué and new Sex employee was Alan Jones. 'I used to wear the tight jeans from Let It Rock on the gay circuit,' he says. 'It worked. Don't forget this was the era of Glam Rock and on the gay scene, it was all long hair and sweaters tied around the necks. I had four major things from Sex: a T-shirt that just said "Sex", the porno story, the very first nude little boy T-shirt, and the T-shirt which said "P-E-R-V" in chicken bones. I worked there for nine months. We'd have all the sleazy old men coming in, pretending they wanted to have a look at the stuff, and they were desperate for Jordan to try it on. She used to complain about having to clean down the changing room curtains. I didn't drink and I never took drugs then, so I posed. That was the way I had fun. People used to stop at the zebra crossing and we'd walk out and they'd go mad. That was the first time I realized how people must be noticing it. Jordan was amazing, she pushed it to the limit, and got away with it.'

By early 1975, there was a slow, imperceptible shift on Chelsea's strip. By this time, the popularity of Bowie and Roxy Music had had a deep stylistic impact: as they changed their image with each major concert or album release, the more dedicated fans followed them. By early 1975, Bryan Ferry had his famous 'GI' look and David Bowie had his updated zoot image for *Young Americans*: the henna'd wedge, the forties-style checked shirt.

This popularized the fashion underground of the time. 'The first person I saw who looked totally brilliant,' says Simon Withers, who worked with Vivienne Westwood in the early 1980s, 'was in late '74 at a bus stop in Kentish Town. He was called Matt Scottley and he had blue two-pleat pegs, plastic sandals and a blue mohair jumper, with a blonde wedge.' This was what would be later called the 'Soul boy' look: at the time the term denoted not only a musical preference but also some sartorial extravagance.

In another ripple spreading out from London's centre, the outer suburbs were now playing host to their own cruising culture. From 1974, teenagers from Ealing, London Colney, or Bromley would dress up and drift, going to pubs like the Royal Oak in Tooley Street, or discos like the Global Village. The most stylish of these groups came from Canvey Island: the year before, they'd been into Glenn Miller but now assumed the shiny, retro-futurism of the 'Soul boy' with the added innovation of *period cars*.

'The first big change was in 1975 where you had people going to the Lacy Lady in Ilford,' says Withers, 'and the Room At The Top. Then there was the Water Splash at London Colney. They were crucial: they were the town versions of the Goldmine in Canvey Island, and they began to cross over really quickly. Everybody was improvising. Gradually you started noticing the six or seven people with ciré T-shirts, mohair jumpers and flashes in their hair, and after a while cut-up clothes started and oddities started to creep in.'

King's Road is nothing if not market-led and several boutiques, including Malcolm and Vivienne's, began to cater to this new demand. In 1974, everything was like *The Rocky Horror Show*, but soon after Sex opened, Lloyd Johnson started selling old Mod outfits. Other stalls opened: Shades at the Antique Market and Acme Attractions, run by John Krivine, whose retro stock changed with the faster-pulsing cycles of nostalgia.

Like every good shop, Acme began to create its own atmosphere. With the front pair of Don Letts and the small, extremely pretty Jeanette Lee, Acme was excitingly subterranean, but more accessible than the chilly Sex. Pork pie hats, Wemblex pin-collar shirts from the sixties, and a variety of sunglasses were brought in by freelance clothes obsessives like Jack English, a first-time Mod, who scoured warehouses in the north for unsold sixties lines.

Letts, the only black to attend Archbishop Tennyson's Grammar School in Brixton, began to play dub Reggae at the stall: 'The dub stuff had started, Keith Hudson, Skin Flesh and Bones, and the DJs, Big Youth. I played it very loud and that's what attracted everybody, apart from the third who came for Jeanette. I had it done up like a third-world living room, with a Lambretta scooter in the middle, and I'd sit around posing in my dark glasses. Sex was happening, and there was competition: Vivienne didn't like me because I was working for the enemy.'

While Malcolm was in New York, Vivienne was running the business, making clothes and bringing up Ben Westwood and Joe Corré at the same time. She was gaining confidence, even though the shop was barely breaking even. 'A lot of money would be going through the shop,' says Andy Czezowski, another ex-Mod who worked as Vivienne's accountant, 'but there wasn't any structure there at all. Because Vivienne's whole viewpoint was non-business – she wanted to *do* things, create things, instigate things – there was no sense of profit margin or growth. That wasn't the point.'

'The customers were half and half,' says McLaren, 'half were MPs and fetish buyers from out in the country, but half were kids. Because the shop was so extraordinary, it swept them up and made them feel very dangerous and unique. And they suddenly found themselves experimenting with a kind of clothing that took them into dark places in their heart. They found themselves excited by whatever it was that they were discovering.'

McLaren returned to London in May 1975 with Sylvain's guitar as a lucky charm. The King's Road was different from the one he had left. He was impressed by Jordan's appearance and the way in which a few teenagers were incorporating the shop's clothes into their look. There was competition from Acme Attractions as a spur, and most of all, there was his desire, fired by what he had seen in New York, to mould a pop group that captured the here and now. He had six months' grace before everyone else caught up.

The Strand had rehearsed steadily under Bernard Rhodes's guidance, making it to the point where they had played for the first time in public. 'I'd hang out with Steve and his mates,' says Rhodes, 'it was a very banal type laugh, but I was drawing him into getting something done.' Some time in the new year, the group lurched through three numbers – 'Scarface', a new song written by Warwick Nightingale and his father, 'Can't Get Enough of Your Love' and 'Twisting the Night Away' – at a party above Salter's Café on the King's Road. 'It was a nightmare,' says Steve Jones.

McLaren went down to Riverside Studios: 'I was quite impressed that they had something together,' McLaren has said, but as he watched them over the next few weeks, he felt that they'd gone as far as they could go. The rhythm section was tight, and Warwick could play with some virtuosity, but there was something lacking. 'They weren't being themselves. They were singing songs that didn't really relate to their own feelings.' The problems were Jones and Nightingale.

As the lead singer, Jones was something of a sore thumb, but there was an emotional bond between him and McLaren. Nightingale was a more proficient player, but the CBGBs groups had wiped out the previous generation's belief in musical skill. Warwick was obstinate, withdrawn, not up for a bit like Jones. 'He wasn't right,' says Paul Cook. 'We were all having fun and he was one of these "don't touch my guitar" merchants. We wanted to get rid of him. Malcolm did instigate it, but we didn't need much persuading.'

Discreetly, McLaren gave Sylvain's white Les Paul guitar to Steve Jones. Some time in June, Warwick went to rehearse as normal. 'Steve was playing guitar behind my back. I was too naive to think he wanted my position in the group. Malcolm was there, and they just said: "You're not in the group any more." It was very hard. I was virtually in tears. Didn't cry, but I was so gutted that I didn't say anything. I even went for a drink with them that evening. As far as they were concerned, it was no reaction.'

McLaren was making fruitless attempts to bring over a New York musician. 'The Sex Pistols were supposed to be my band,' says Sylvain. 'He said he had these kids hanging outside his store; they'd love to play with me, not like JoHansen. I believed him. But then I got stuck in New York: Bob Gruen brought up a Dolls' tour of Japan. We were going to make thirty thousand dollars, more money than I ever heard of. Malcolm got mad at me: I went with David, and he wrote me, saying "I don't trust David, he's a bastard." So I made a mistake.'

The next thing to do was to find someone who could speed up the learning process. 'I'd had a very bad experience with the *NME*,' says Nick Kent, 'I felt I'd done my three years and hit a plateau. So I got interested in playing: I wasn't anywhere near as good as I thought I was, but that was good enough for the group at the time. I liked them: we were worlds apart, but then being older and being able to get into the Speakeasy, they hung onto me like limpets, frankly. I never felt I was in the group.

'Jones's voice was very much like Steve Marriott's, but he didn't know what to do with his hands, so the guitar was a prop. That was the original idea, but within six months Steve was playing. After a few weeks I felt that no one had direction so I gave them an ultimatum. I went to Malcolm on a Friday and said that I proposed to take the group over and change the name. Malcolm thought about this and on Saturday Matlock called me and told me it was out of the question. It was an amicable parting: it wasn't wasted time.

'Malcolm was probably one of those people who were never in a gang, and he wanted to be in a gang like they were. You have this gang and after six months you're bored stupid by it, particularly if it involves music. That's why there's hardly such a thing as groups any more, like the New York Dolls, where there is a sense of comradeship. Malcolm wanted this: he was constantly phoning Sylvain and getting him to talk to Steve Jones. There was this constant thing: they are the New York group, we are the London group.'

By the summer, McLaren's advantage was slipping away. The idea of a rough, teenage, Rock group was current in the capital's claustrophobic streets. Rock On had their own group, with a name taken from a New York street gang: the Count Bishops. The group played the usual R&B, but with an edge given by their wild front man, Mike Spencer. 'Malcolm was looking for a singer to form this ultimate garage band,' says Roger Armstrong. 'He was seeing all these street bands and Spencer was a candidate at one point.'

McLaren's idea for his group wasn't fully formed: he still had a fixation about Larry Parnes. Early in that summer came the zenith of the Scottish group, the Bay City Rollers. The group was an update of a late fifties pop mode: five working-class teens, a manipulative, gay manager, cute sartorial gimmicks and music that was tepid but effective. Older Rock fans sneered at the Rollers' reheated fifties pop, but young audiences went mad.

McLaren and Rhodes drove up to Scotland to attract some sympathetic magic. They didn't get a Roller, but they found a young Glaswegian, Midge Ure (later of Ultravox), who had a group called Slik. Ure wasn't interested. Slik had just been signed to Bell, the Rollers' label, and were being groomed as the next off the production line. The group also continued their own search: 'We did try a singer out,' says Paul Cook , 'a rocker called Dave. He was a really good-looking guy with fair hair, but he was more of a model, know what I mean?'

With the singer problem still unsolved, McLaren began working more closely with Westwood on the clothes and the ideas for Sex. Up went the handbills and posters for the New York Dolls, Television and their 'Blank Generation', and in came a more extreme sartorial correctness. Jordan was an inspiration, as she slipped into the role of dominatrix. 'People became terrified of coming in,' she says, 'it was just my attitude. I felt powerful, and I looked powerful.'

Another important influence was a new customer, Linda Ashby, a *maitresse* working from her flat in St James's. Ashby was excited by the fact that she could find her specialist clothing in a retail outlet, and that she didn't have to change to go to work. This was the kind of existential danger that McLaren and Westwood had always wanted to capture: they watched the ripples caused by these strong women and began to formulate theories around them.

'It was a good team,' says Ben Westwood, 'a very fortuitous meeting between the two of them. They had more of an intellectual relationship than a love affair. Malcolm would come up with an idea and mum would come up with a way to make it work: she would decide which cloth to use and how to make the clothes. Malcolm used to come up with styling ideas at the last minute. What mum got out of him was someone to back her up and someone through whom she could express her ideas. And so did Malcolm: they backed each other up.'

The first line to be expanded was the sleeveless slogan T-shirt, by now the shop's best-selling item: not cheap at two pounds each. Ciré and leather were used as fabrics while zips, tears and studded leather or plastic pockets were added. In addition to the earlier manifestos came a number of new designs from pornography's shadows. There was a naked black footballer with pendulous cock, Alex Trocchi's fervid lesbian fantasies, or the troubling image of a twelve-year-old boy, suggestively exhaling a cigarette, which came from *Boys Express*, a small paedophile magazine sold openly with a contact address in Essex.

One blatant design acted as an implicit graphic manifesto for the Sex Pistols. The image was drawn in the style of Tom of Finland, who exaggerated the parts of the anatomy that were desired by his target audience: two cowboys pose outside a dancehall, on Saturday night. Both wear cowboy hats, long boots and no trousers. One, in a leather vest, grips the lapel of the other's faded Levi jacket: at the exact height of the latter's gun in its holster, two large, flaccid penises are a whisker away from contact.

Printed in brown on pink, or red on green, these images were simple but complex: as McLaren and Westwood knew, there was a world of difference between an image in a brown-bag pornzine and a silk-screen blow-up worn in public display. The effect could be

"Ello Joe, Been anywhere lately
Nah, its all played aht Bill,
Gettin to straight."

curiously asexual. Both McLaren and Westwood had strong elements of puritanism in their own sexual make-up, and their blow-ups of fetish imagery were polemical, a comment on the images' primary use. The overt sexuality became an abstraction of sex.

This reflected the deadening of the sexual impulse in the newly industrialized sex districts like Soho, where, by the mid-1970s, the great promises of liberation had been honed down into a series of stock postures. One of McLaren and Westwood's most brilliant early designs captured this: a cut-out of a photograph of a pair of female breasts was placed at breast height on T-shirts worn by either sex. The effect was both androgynous and, in the double-take it forced upon you, distinctly unsettling.

These designs were pushed through by McLaren against the will of his helpers. Glen Matlock objected to the young boy T-shirt on moral grounds. He was backed up by Bernard Rhodes: 'Malcolm likes to titillate, but I like to get down to substance.' On this score, McLaren was amoral: like Nietzsche, he believed that 'without cruelty there is no feast'.

Even the blasé Michael Collins had had twinges of conscience, this time about the T-shirt which showed a picture of the hood worn by the Cambridge rapist, then terrorizing the university town with a series of brutal rapes. Collins was sure that one of their customers was the rapist and informed the police while McLaren was away in New York. The design was withdrawn; incensed, McLaren added more to the rapist's hood on his return: overlaid in red were some musical notes bearing the legend 'A Hard Day's Night'. Underneath was a tabloid-style legend which made public some unsavoury music-industry gossip: 'Brian Epstein – found dead Aug 27th 1967 after taking part in sado-masochistic practices/S&M made him feel at home.' This was the darker side of the managerial stereotype so dear to McLaren's heart: clearly, there were few fathers McLaren would not kill in his bid to get some reaction.

In late July, McLaren's fantasy world collided with exterior reality. 'It was the day they'd just brought out the Cowboys T-shirts,' says Alan Jones. 'I bought that and the Cambridge rapist T-shirt. I wore the Cowboys shirt and blue jeans, and walked along King's Road, got to Piccadilly Circus, and these two plain-clothes policemen came up behind us and said, "Ah, what are you wearing here. Will you accompany us to Vine Street police station?" I hadn't noticed but the friend I was with said that everybody was looking at us as we went. I was had up under a nineteenth-century law. I told Malcolm what happened and he said: "We're going to do everything we can. We'll get you a really good lawyer, you're going to get off." What happened? Fuck all. I went to court on my own, not knowing what to do, and in the end I pleaded guilty. If Malcolm had given me the back-up he promised it would have been fine.'

Alan Jones's arrest made the national newspapers in a front-page *Guardian* story on 2 August, which connected the incident with the season's great moral panic: the scandal about teenage-boy prostitution in Piccadilly which had been uncovered by the book and ITV documentary *Johnny Go Home*. This form of prostitution became an issue at exactly the time as the beginning of the real backlash against the 1960s and 'permissiveness'.

Politicians such as Labour MP Colin Phipps complained that Jones's arrest was 'merely one aspect of what seems to be a concerted attack on the more open and liberal view of nakedness and sex which is becoming widely adopted,' but McLaren thought their views a fraud. He wanted to provoke the state, in the way that the Yippies or the Baader/Meinhof gang had done, in order to reveal the real repression that lay beneath the permissive veneer.

That week, the police paid a visit to Sex and removed a selection of items, including all copies of the Cowboys T-shirt. On 7 August, McLaren and Westwood were charged with 'exposing to public view an indecent exhibition'. By the time their case came up at the end of November, action had been taken against the social problem with which they had become associated. In typical fashion, the law followed the media in the clean-up of Piccadilly including the arcade called 'Playland'.

McLaren and Westwood got off with a fine. Theodore Ramos was brought in as a character witness in the case: 'Malcolm was continuing his experimentation, but with live subjects, so that they were graphic experiments. Having overreached himself, he was too frightened to do it himself and required somebody else to follow it through. A lot of those things were mad ideas that he picked up in art school. A lot of them are literary: he had the ability to assimilate and pursue an idea. In that case, he became a true impresario. A catalyst, precipitating an action.'

'The writing on the wall', The Chippenham, W.9., 1975 (© Roger Perry)

9

Behind the repressed darkness and the personal shadow – that which has been and is rotting and that which is not yet and germinating – is the archetypal darkness, the principle of not-being, which has been named and described as the Devil, as Evil, as Original Sin, as Death, as existential Nothingness, as *prima materia.*

James Hillman: *Insearch – Psychology and Religion* (1967)

Poor luvs. Trained to rule the empire; trained to rule the world. Englishmen could be proud then. They could, George. All gone. Taken away. Bye bye world.

Beryl Reid as Connie Sachs in John Le Carré: *Tinker, Tailor, Soldier, Spy*, as dramatized by Arthur Hopcraft for BBC TV (1979)

Author's Diary 2.12.75: . . . London suburbia: sterility – cynicism – boredom ready to spill into violence; incipient right-wing backlash. Fuck London for its dullness, the English people for their pusillanimity and the weather for its coldness and darkness.

Sixteen years later, it's hard to recollect what England felt like in 1975. The media were full of an apocalyptic rhetoric. 'Already the vultures are darkening the skies,' ran a *Sun* leader in October 1974. 'The high summer sunshine of 1975, historians of 2000 AD may decide, induced in the British people a fatal indolence,' thundered the *Sunday Times*: 'through the summer haze dim shapes could be perceived, but they were quaint, unreal, abstract. Those who listened could hear a distant thunder.'

By July 1975, England was in recession. The unemployment figures for that month were the worst since the Second World War: school-leavers were among the most vulnerable. Not only had output shrunk, but public spending had risen to 45 per cent of the national income, and was threatening to unbalance the whole economy. In November 1975, Chancellor Denis Healey presented a package of public expenditure cuts totalling three billion pounds.

This didn't seem like a temporary crisis but the acutest angle of a long, slow decline. 'Winning the war' had left Britain with a fearful cost. This first fully global war had twisted the balance of power from its previous axis so that Britain was no longer a world power. It was merely a small island held in thrall by the USA, both strategically and economically. When America called in its Lend Lease agreement five days after VJ day, Britain owed three billion pounds.

There had been a collective refusal to look the facts in the face. 'Britain's postwar decline began in wartime British dreams,' writes Correlli Barnett in *Audit of War*. 'As a consequence, the British people never had to face the reality about themselves and their future place in the world.' The 'year-zero' conditions undergone by Germany and Japan encouraged a complete overhaul of their manufacturing economy, then capitalism's motor. In contrast, Britain's manufacturing base had been poorly run and chronically under-invested ever since the 1880s, when the appeal of manufacture first paled before the lure of paper profit on the foreign markets.

The country carried all the psychic baggage of a Pyrrhic victory. Despite the postwar burst of Socialism, the war had seemed to vindicate the status quo. The incidence of films celebrating England's endurance and victory was in a direct ratio to the refusal of its people to see the need for change. England was smug and static, full of imperial pretensions, even in areas such as the celebration of the Beatles' worldwide fame after 1964 – one of the country's few successes. Pop was a hitherto unrecognized and rapidly expanding source of capital.

The whole idea of 'consensus' that had dominated postwar politics and social life was disintegrating: it was as though the whole postwar ideal of mass consumer enfranchisement fostered by Prime Ministers of both parties was being proved a sham. The bright colours, the 'classlessness', and especially the optimism of the sixties, now seemed like a mirage. Just as the pop culture of its mid-decade had fragmented into small segments, so the country's social life seemed to be degenerating into warring factions.

'Fool your friends and fool yourself, the choice is crystal clear,' sang Richard Thompson in his terrifying 'Roll Over Vaughn [sic] Williams': 'Live in fear, live in fear.' There were enemies within. The targets were many for a tabloid press discovering its own power. The *Sun* had remained left-ish in the few years after Rupert Murdoch had taken over, but from 1972 it developed a new language of fear and anxiety which began saying the previously unsayable.

After the tabloid 'mugging scares' of 1972–3, which targeted West Indians, there were scares about pornography, education, vandalism and sexuality in general. All of these, collected under the label of 'permissiveness', served notice on sixties libertarianism. These scares amplified deeply felt and understandable fears into an apocalyptic shriek. It seemed to many as though the country's fabric was being attacked, from within and without: in 1974, the IRA took the war to the mainland in a bombing campaign worse than any since the war.

4.10.75: Graffiti – TORIES WANT WAR. Worrying thing about Thatcher is that she has that blind belief/certainty about her own rectitude that may attract plenty of followers. Certainty in age of impossibility of (real) certainty. Back to the golf club image – in effect the 50s.

Confronted by the proliferation of morbid symptoms, a considerable section of the middle classes felt that their backs were against the wall: they began to lash out in fear and revenge. In November 1975, the hardline National Association for Freedom was formed: a week earlier one of its founders, Ross McWhirter – the man who had brought a civil action against ATV's 1972 Warhol documentary – had been assassinated by the IMLA.

Just as Tony Benn had shifted the Parliamentary Labour Party leftwards, so there was an equivalent shift on the right, as Mrs Thatcher became the middle classes' secret weapon: by 1977 she was speaking at the National Association for Freedom's inaugural subscription dinner. A party outsider, the MP for Finchley became Conservative Party leader in February 1975 after Edward Heath's two 1974 poll defeats.

Although at the time of her election Mrs Thatcher had an image problem, being 'plastered with suburbia', by the summer she was observed to be having a favourable impact on the population at large. As a minister, Thatcher had been less overtly critical of the Heath line than might now be expected but, from 1974 on, influenced by Keith Joseph and Alfred Sherman, she began to develop her own ideology. At the time when State control, through nationalized industries and a vast bureaucracy, seemed to be on the way to Orwell's dystopia, Mrs Thatcher asserted the primacy of the individual. Her style was important in this: not only was she combative, but she played on tabloid fears of internal decay. In her first conference speech as leader, she launched a major attack on those 'who gnaw away at our self-respect, rewriting British history as centuries of gloom, oppression and failure'.

23.11.76: . . . fascism here won't be like in Germany. It'll be English: ratty, mean, pinched, hand in glove with Thatcher as mother sadist over all her whimpering public schoolboys.

In *The Ice Age*, Margaret Drabble embodies the period's miasma in the person of Mike Morgan, a comedian with a 'rat-clown face': 'The English are guilty, they are self-denigrating, they are masochists, they love to be kicked, he said, because of their deeply ingrained inalienable disgusting *certainty* of superiority. They are island xenophobes, and they love to be kicked because they know it does not hurt. They are rich bitches who like to be degraded.'

There was another factor which made Thatcher a national symbol. The long decline of the 1970s had created, not only a mood of fear, but also a sense of guilt. In her speeches, Mrs Thatcher began to resolve this guilt by confidence building, but it was her presence that supplied the back-up that these ambitious, ringing phrases demanded. With her hectoring rhetoric, privet-hedge propriety, and thick hair piled into a steel wave, she had the air of a professional dominatrix.

Thirteen years later, John Lydon is talking quietly about his first vision of the Sex Pistols: 'Glen Matlock wanted us to be a camp version of the Bay City Rollers. I'm sorry, I was completely the other way. I saw the Sex Pistols as something completely guilt-ridden.' In 1975, an Adam Ant besotted by Jordan painted a picture of Mrs Thatcher as dominatrix: with her upswept hair, suburban sadism and milky-white skin, the Sex front woman was the mirror image of the Conservative leader.

> Do you remember what the squatters in Piccadilly wrote on the great derelict house they'd taken over before the police moved in? 'We are the writing on your wall.'
>
> **George Melly: *The Writing On The Wall* (April 1975)**

There still exists a visual record of the capital in 1975. Roger Perry's book of 110 photos concentrated on those run-down areas of London that, perversely, harboured a type of free speech. The graffiti that Perry highlights are a generation away from the three-dimensional designs that we have now become accustomed to. Slogans were sometimes sprayed, sometimes awkwardly painted or scrawled in a hand that tails off, as if the effort of communication was too much.

The messages themselves are not so much the territorial markers or the frantic assertion of self that we have become used to, but are anonymous, allusive and cryptic, a window into the world of the culturally or socially dispossessed: 'Dada is everywhere', 'Words do not mean *anything* today'. Pride of place is given to the graffiti that snaked between Ladbroke Grove and Westbourne Park tube stations: 'SAME THING DAY AFTER DAY – TUBE – WORK – DINER [sic] – WORK – TUBE – ARMCHAIR – TUBE – WORK – HOW MUCH MORE CAN YOU TAKE – ONE IN FIVE CRACKS UP'.

Notting Hill Gate is the location of most of Perry's photographs. Its position as a large, marginal, inner city area with an unusual class and multi-ethnic mix was captured in novels like Colin MacInnes's *Absolute Beginners*, and Wyndham Lewis's *Rotting Hill*, as well as post-Profumo 'exposés' like *Jungle West 11*. Films that made use of the area's faded ambience included *Performance* (1969) and *The Blue Lamp* (1949), a seminal UK gangster movie, in which Dirk Bogarde flees through a cityscape of crumbling columns that has now totally disappeared.

'Notting Hill has been looked upon as something of an unusual area in London and the UK,' state the Wise Brothers in their history of the area. 'It was a place to escape from the insufferable constraints of the family background, away from entrenched working-class prejudices and a too strait-laced world altogether. Far more than elsewhere the lower slopes of Notting Hill sponsored the entrance of post-war "anarchism" – more precisely an anarchic sentiment – into the political arena and the party system.'

This was the return of the repressed. Notting Hill's radical pretensions and realities both highlighted and masked the real hardship that existed at its outer fringes. In 1975, the areas around Chippenham Road and Elgin Avenue, Freston Road and Lancaster Road were a scrapyard vista. Where there wasn't rubble, there were remnants of Victorian housing stock. Just like parts of Camden Town, most of Docklands, and pre-media Soho, these empty spaces seemed then to embody an emotional truth: this is what England is *really* like.

Freston Road and Elgin Avenue/Chippenham Road were the site of mass squats. 'There were streets and streets; a real community,' says Joe Strummer, the son of a diplomat who had dropped out of art school for a Bohemian life of busking and casual labour. 'In Elgin Avenue the GLC had decided to knock down about a hundred Victorian terraced houses: it was between deciding and actually knocking them down that the squat culture flourished there. We even had a Squatters' Union. You'd go in there, bang, change the locks. Possession is nine-tenths of the law. We were very organized.'

In July 1975, it was estimated that of the country's 50,000 squatters, at least 60 per cent were in London. Squatting was then an ideological choice – 'based on a recognition of the futility and stupidity of work' – as well as a practical solution to the most basic need for housing. This was a harsher version of the hippie dream, with a soundtrack by the group Hawkwind, but it was none the less potent. With the dole, squatting made living in central London accessible and affordable. This access allowed the rapid city-transits of the Punk period.

24.9.75: Young men wait at street corners, with hungry eyes; like hyenas, they wait for the kill.

Nowhere was England's 'poverty of desire' more obvious than in youth culture. Any trip outside London's elite havens revealed shoddy styles which were the bottom level of hippie and Glam. Lank, bedraggled hair topped baggies (cheap, maroon or deep brown trousers that began with pleats and a high waist and spread out from there). The whole effect was of adults crammed into children's clothes or adolescents forced, through poverty or habit, to wear clothes which they had long outgrown.

'The image and the empire may be falling apart,' sang Murray Head that autumn; 'The money is getting scarce/One man's word'd hold the country together/But the truth is getting fierce.' The only thing stirring within the nation's youth appeared to be a desire for order and power. In October 1975, the magazine *Let It Rock* profiled some Roxy and Bowie fans: 'We should rule the world like we used to,' they said, 'I believe in anything to purify the race.'

Thirty years after a lost victory, the overdraft had to be paid, with accumulated interest. The English stage was finally set for a protracted drama of conflict, guilt and punishment, as stress revealed the dark shadows that populated the English psyche. As Mrs Thatcher began to wield the lash of ideology, so the figureheads of Sex instinctively began to act out the chaos to which she appeared to offer a solution.

John Lydon at eighteen months (© Joe Stevens)

Impressive ideas which are hailed as truths have something peculiar about them. Although they come into being at a definite time, they are and always have been timeless; they arise from that realm of creative psychic life out of which the ephemeral mind of the single human being grows like a plant that blossoms, bears fruit and seed, and then withers and dies.

C. G. Jung: *Freud and Jung: Contrasts* (1929)

While Malcolm was in New York, a group of youths, all called John, had begun to come into number 430. Although they kept to themselves, they were different from the other teenagers, like Adam Ant or Marco Pirroni, who fled suburbia to lurk in the shop's corners. Coming from working-class north and east London, they were combative, articulate and carried themselves with a certain arrogance.

The most immediately charismatic John was tall and goofy, and he always had the most money. He sometimes answered to the name of Sid. The quietest John of the four, with his green hair, hunched stance and ragged look, looked like a cross between Richard Hell and Uriah Heep. He was first approached by Bernard Rhodes, who was struck by the youth's customized 'Pink Floyd' T-shirt: the eyes had been torn out and over the group's logo were the words, scrawled in biro, 'I hate . . .'

'Sex were doing something different from everybody else,' says John Lydon, 'and they weren't liked, which was absolutely brilliant. They were totally horrible people. Vivienne was the most awful old bag and that really fascinated me. Vivienne's a killer, a vicious lady. To buy anything in that shop was a real fight. I loved the rubber T-shirt, lock, stock and barrel. I thought it was the most repulsive thing I had ever seen. To wear it as a piece of clothing rather than part of some sexual fetish was hilarious.

'Jordan was always friendly. Genuinely interested. She'd obviously seen us for what we were, which was silly little kids who didn't have a clue. We'd go to the King's Road just to annoy people: it was necessary then. Long hair was everywhere. What was there to do then? There was Soul boys and Roxy Music kind of clothes: all that was naff, very weedy and not going anywhere. People were very stiff and boring. I was bored with everything.'

'Anger is an energy,' sang John Lydon years later. At nineteen, his shyness masked a volcano of sarcasm and verbal hostility. The four Johns were all in the same predicament: 'We were all extremely ugly people. We were outcasts, the unwanted.' The group were caught in an impossible double-bind: intelligent in a working-class culture which did not value intelligence, yet unable to leave that culture because of lack of opportunity. The result? An appalling frustration.

'My father was a crane driver,' John Lydon begins, and then interrupts himself with a characteristic disclaimer, 'but I don't see that any of my background has any effect on me whatsoever. I think you are what you are from the day you are born: using things as a cultural disguise doesn't hide what you are deep down.' His experiences in his twenty-first year have scorched mistrust into his brain.

Lydon's subsequent success has given him some distance from his anger. There are two subjects, however, on which he is insistent to the point of pomposity. The first is Malcolm McLaren. The second is his decision to be a 'completely honest human being'. Yet he contradicts what seems to be the truth. But even if his statements are not true, Lydon at that moment believes them to be true. This is a moral certainty easily to match that of Westwood or McLaren.

John was born on 31 January 1956, the first child of Eileen and Jim Lydon. Three brothers followed – Jimmy, Bobby and Martin. 'My old man was from Galway; Cork's my mother,' he continues: 'first generation in England. I don't even know where I was born. We moved around a lot, for all kinds of reasons. We lived on the ground floor of a place right on the sea in Hastings until I was about six. I suppose it was really squalor, but my memories of it aren't bad. Kids don't see the dirt and the peeling wallpaper.'

Like others who later become shamanistic performers, Lydon had a severe illness in his childhood, contracting meningitis when he was eight. In the Vermorels' book *Sex Pistols*, Eileen Lydon (who died in 1979) described its effect: 'It frightened me, naturally. I had it when I was eleven and I knew what it was. It left him with bad eyesight and I don't know if you ever notice John, he stares. Sort of stare in his eyes.' 'I didn't go to school for a year,' John says, 'still have problems with my ABC.'

If anything, the illness deepened the young Lydon's sense of being different. 'I can remember my parents having parties and my brother Jimmy doing his soldier dance to some dismal Irish folk song, and I'd be sitting in a corner going: "This is awful." I never talked to any of them. I used to hate my mother's clothes, she used to wear that Crimplene stuff that was fashionable then, a huge beehive hairdo, and the smell of the hairspray used to repulse me. I remember the smell of sweaty corsets, and all the men had stinking armpits.'

When Lydon resumed his education, he was 'quiet, reserved' and artistic. When the Lydons returned to London after some years living around the country, they got a council flat in Pooles Park, by Finsbury Park station. At the age of eleven, John went to William of York, the Catholic comprehensive school prescribed by the local educational authority. It was in Gifford Street, a particularly grim Victorian backwater near Pentonville. 'A shit hole,' says Lydon, 'Catholic schools should be pulled down: they separate you from everybody else. I learnt hate and resentment there. And I learned to despise tradition and this sham we call culture. The religious classes were just excruciating: in the end I said I wanted to be a Muslim, just to get out of that class. It was rubbish. You're not allowed to question. You have to accept as a fact: "You'll die and go to hell if you don't believe in the lightning rod of Jesus Christ almighty and the sanctity of his virgin mother." What nonsense.

'I used to have hair way down my shoulders. At fourteen that was quite rebellious. I was the freak of the neighbourhood: a jean shirt, no jackets and hob-nail boots painted bright green. My long hair was part of the reason I got thrown out of school. They called me a Hell's Angel because my parents were poor, they couldn't afford the uniform. Because I was just inside the three-mile limit I had to cycle to school and I'd have to wear a leather jacket in the rain. So: Hell's Angel.'

Lydon pursued the required lifestyle of the time with John Grey. 'The Roundhouse was particularly good. I saw Iggy and the Stooges at the Scala in 1972: James Williamson was playing the most out of tune guitar. Iggy wasn't liked: in fact he was ignored. He'd run around and bash himself with the microphone. I liked it. Later I used to go to a Reggae stall underneath Finsbury Park station. I had to go in for a year with my long hair and denim shirt before I knew what to order: the black customers were so hostile and surprised that I had to wait until the shop was empty.'

After leaving school in 1972, Lydon desultorily pursued a higher education interspersed with various dead-end jobs. In 1973, he went to Hackney Technical College to study for some more O levels. 'That's where I met Sid. He was a Bowie fan. He'd do silly things to get his hair to stick up, because it never occurred to him to use hairspray. He'd lie upside down with his head in an oven. Sid was such a poser, a clothes hound of the worst kind. Anything *19* told you to wear, he'd have to have it. I called Sid Sid after my pet hamster. It's true! It's the most useless, stupid answer in the world! Vicious came later, after the Lou Reed song. He was a Soul boy when I first met him. You know the uniform: it could be mid-winter and snowing, but he wouldn't wear a jacket. He had naivety, which is a good quality, a kind of innocence, but he lost that. He couldn't see dishonesty in people. He was funny: he would laugh at everything all the time. Everything would be the ultimate amusement to him.'

Born John Simon Ritchie, Sid Vicious already had so many names that one more didn't matter. Like discarded clothes, they fell away from him. He was Simon or 'Sime' to his mother Anne; John or Sid to his friends. Until he got his nickname, he had the surname Beverley from his mother's second husband. This fragmented identity reflected what had already been a chaotic life: 'He was never in a stable situation,' says Anne Beverley, who brought him up single-handed, 'it was like a mirror of my early life.'

Simon seemed fated to repeat the childhood of his mother, abandoned by her own single-parent mother when she was twelve. Fleeing from a loveless family, Anne Randall joined the Air Force at eighteen, married hastily, then 'jumped into the arms of John Ritchie'. Their only son, Simon, was born on 10 May 1957: his parents, who never married, separated two years later, when Ritchie left Anne penniless in Ibiza. To survive, she lived on credit, typed scripts, and 'earned money rolling joints for people. When I returned to London in 1961, there was I with a little kid. I had hair an inch long when everybody else had a great big beehive, and everybody else's dress was two inches below the knee, and mine was two inches above. I got every remark you could think of, and Simon heard all this. I tried to inculcate into his psyche: "You are you, you can do anything you like providing you don't hurt anybody else while doing it. You should be able to do what the fuck you like." At four, five, six, that's gone in.'

Simon moved schools as fast as his mother moved house. 'He hated school,' says Anne Beverley, 'but then so did I. The longest period we ever stayed in one place was in Tunbridge Wells from 1965 to 1971. His last school was off Stoke Newington Church Street. He left at fifteen, against my wishes, but I knew that school wasn't really for him. He then went and worked at Simpson's, the factory that makes the DAKS slacks, before going to Hackney to do a course in photography.

'He loved the art classes, they showed him how to paint and then let them do what they wanted to do, but he quit after the second term because they tried to make him do particular subjects. Simon was always the person who could not be told what to do. That was where he met John Lydon: the first time he came round he had hair down to here, a beautiful head. He was shy. If I just looked at him, he went beetroot red. Couldn't say a word. I'd never met someone that shy before.'

Simon was very close to his mother – sometimes they seemed more like conspirators than parent and child – but the family spectre of abandonment was ever present. 'He left home when he was fifteen, he lived in some squat, but after a couple of months he came back home. Then when he was seventeen, we had a row. "Simon, it's either you or me and it's not going to be me, so you can just fuck off." "But I've got nowhere to sleep," he said, and I said: "I don't care if you have to sleep on a fucking park bench: just go."' As a squatter and Bowie Boy, Simon flirted with prostitution.

By 1974, John Lydon was just hanging on at home. After Hackney, he attended Kingsway College: 'What a dump that was,' he says, 'that's where I met Wobble. The other students thought we were sick.'

'John and Sid were exactly what I was looking for when I was sixteen,' says John Wardle, more usually known as Jah Wobble. 'All I knew then was that I desperately didn't want to work. I was already an angry young man. I had images of being enclosed by council flats, feeling very claustrophobic.'

Only John Wardle's icy blue stare now betrays his past. During Punk, Wobble, like Sid, resembled a random-destruction machine, wound up and placed in the middle of an event to see what would occur. Today, he speaks of his past as if of another life: 'I loved to drink. I had rather a bad problem years later. There's a lot of suppressed anger in everyone, and drink opens up that grille just a little bit too much. I cultivated that "Wobble the Thug" image: it's that process of re-inventing yourself.'

An East Ender, Wardle was expelled from the London Nautical School, and ended up at Kingsway. 'John looked in the Roxy Music sort of line then,' he says, 'and me rather a thug. That Great Gatsby thing: grey pinstripe suits. Sid was into the trendy scene then: we used to go out to the stores out Ilford way. John had long hair, a black tux and baggies but one day he came along with dyed, shaved hair and saying that he'd found his new way of life. It all seemed to happen on one day: he was excited about something.'

In 1975, John Lydon was thrown out of the family home as a result of the severe hair cut. 'You see, at the time, long hair was accepted, and I thought "Sod that", so I hacked it off and dyed it green. I looked like a cabbage. "Out! Out! You dirty bastard and don't come back!" My old man never spoke to me until the day I left home: then he suddenly started showing signs of respect. It's like birds, they've got to kick them out of the nest at a certain age.

'So I went squatting with Sid. Hampstead, not the posh end, but those awful Victorian dwellings round the back of the station. Really desperate people lived up there. It was awful. I liked it: it was better

'I'm Hymie: try me', Sid Vicious, August 1975 (courtesy of Viv Albertine)

than home. I don't remember a great deal from that period because I loved getting wildly drunk. It was good fun: it was freedom, but then responsibility rears its ugly head when you realize you're flat broke. When I was living at home I'd worked at a sewage farm, killing rats in Guildford, and laying concrete with my dad. Seventy quid a week: outrageous then. After I got thrown out, I got a job in a shoe factory. What a farce.'

Then there was a job with Sid in Cranks restaurant, at the top of Heals in Tottenham Court Road: 'If only those health food hippies knew who was cleaning out their kitchen. We cleaned it out in more ways than one. Night after night we stuffed our faces. We'd wait for the boss to go, then we'd run round Heals trying out beds. There was nobody else in the building: it was like an adventure playground. There was no time limit on when we had to finish, so we waltzed out of there at one in the morning. You couldn't actually steal anything, but you could use it all as much as you wanted. We'd move furniture, the way you'd like your house to be. You remember *Dawn of the Dead*, where the zombies are in that huge department store. That's what it was like. A dream come true.'

It was at this time that the forays down the King's Road began. 'John was very image conscious,' says Wardle: 'He's the kind of fellow who would want *c* effect and "to get to *c* I have to go from *a* to *b* to get to *c*".

He's got an assumed logic. Sid had found out where Bryan Ferry lived and he wanted to go round there with a bottle of Martini and demand to be let in. John would have had too much pride to want to be seen trying to get in, even though he desperately wanted to. Sid wouldn't worry about that, he'd just steam in. I think it was him who first went down and met McLaren: he introduced John to all of them.'

When the call came however that late August, Sid was off on a stall in the Portobello Road. John Lydon, on the other hand, was coming more and more into the shop: his inquisitiveness was tempered, even then, by antagonism. Responding to Bernard's enthusiasm, McLaren confronted him one night and asked him if he could sing. 'What? What do you mean? What for? No: only out of tune and anyway I play the violin,' Lydon replied, as if to an idiot. McLaren, naturally, was further intrigued and left him with an invitation to meet the group at the Roebuck at seven that evening. Despite Lydon's apparent indifference, McLaren was aware that this was an offer he couldn't refuse.

Lydon did turn up, with John Grey as moral support, and, sitting silently, just looked at the rest of the group. 'We'd had a few idiots,' says Steve Jones, 'and then Rotten came in. He looked really interesting, there was something about him that magnetized you to him. He had all the Punk stuff on, the safety-pins and everything: that was nothing to do with McLaren. He was wild looking: his brothers were boot boys. So he came down and I really didn't like him at all, because of his attitude: he seemed like a real prick.'

Jones got increasingly irritated with Lydon's superciliousness and, on the verge of violence, went up to McLaren, who was lurking at the end of the bar. The only solution was to hold an impromptu audition. Lydon was hesitant and nervous but persuaded by Jones's threats and John Grey's enthusiasm, he allowed himself to be steered back to the shop. There he was placed in front of the jukebox, with a shower attachment in his hand as a microphone, and told to sing along to Alice Cooper's 'Eighteen'. Everyone retreated, leaving Lydon alone in the centre of the shop.

'I was terrified,' says Lydon. 'It never occurred to me that the music biz could be a place for me to vent whatever talent I had.' He froze, but then, egged on by Grey, who realized that there was some real potential in this ridiculous situation, he begun to jump up and down in a spastic fashion, gabbling improvised lyrics: 'I'm eighteen, sex in the grass, I'm eighteen . . .' Jones growled further threats of violence and, under considerable stress, Lydon launched into a sequence of hunchbacked poses – screaming, mewling and puking, until his first audience dissolved into laughter.

The group wasn't sure, but McLaren was. 'I had an eye,' he says, 'and my eye saw Rotten's ability to create image around himself. It was a gut feeling. I knew he had something, just as I knew Jones had something.' He persuaded Cook, Jones and Matlock to rehearse with Lydon for a week above a pub called the Crunchie Frog in Rotherhithe: the first day nobody except Lydon turned up. 'I felt a fool walking round Bermondsey Wharf,' he says, 'it's dangerous down there, particularly the way I looked at the time.'

'I called him the next day to say I was sorry,' says Glen Matlock. 'He said, "I'll kill you, I will, I'll kill you, I'll come round with a hammer." I thought: "Here we go".'

'We had one rehearsal,' says Malcolm McLaren, 'and none of them showed up because they thought Rotten was a cunt. Right there, first day. They never liked him. I liked Jones; Jones didn't mind me. I quite liked Cook, but to me he was a bit boring. I brought Matlock into the group as an anchor of normality: he had a certain intelligence that I thought could be used to help Cook and Jones construct songs. Rotten was just an arrogant little shit who thought he knew everything. He hated their music. Cook and Jones were going for the tradition of mutated, irresponsible hardcore raw power: Iggy Pop, New York Dolls, MC5, the Faces. Rotten wanted it like the sixties – Captain Beefheart, all weird.'

Thus the Sex Pistols began in a miasma of antagonism, misunderstanding and mutual suspicion. With his nose for trouble, McLaren liked this volatile atmosphere: he thought it might set up sparks. Yet this instability also caused real damage, not least to the person who thought he was in control. McLaren liked to play with fire but, in entering the world of John Lydon and his friends, he would be dealing with psychic material far more combustible than the stuff he was used to with Cook, Jones and Matlock.

With Lydon's arrival, the other problem for McLaren was his claim to sole authorship. 'What brought us all together first was that we hated what was on TV,' McLaren says. 'Rotten liked *Eighteen* and *School's Out*, but he thought they were a bit mindless. He thought being mindless was a good pose. As soon as I got that sense, that he was terrified of being in a group, of having to announce himself, I knew there was a star there. I knew people would see that vulnerability and go for it, and they did.

'We knew he couldn't sing, that he had no sense of rhythm, but he had this charm of a boy in pain, trying to pretend he's cool. That was the most accessible thing. You knew all the girls were going to love him. I thought they could be the Bay City Rollers: that was in my head, I was so out of it. To think he would be the alternative to the Bay City Rollers: dour and tough and the real thing. A genuine teenage group. For me, that was anarchy in the record business: that was enough for me. That was the best selling point: they were like young assassins. The rest was the cream on the cake, and not something I necessarily promoted. It took on a life of its own.'

John Lydon provided that life: it would have been impossible for the Sex Pistols to have had the impact they did without him. Despite McLaren's scorn, it was Lydon's very interest in the quirks of post-hippie pop – the expressionist Peter Hammill, the disruptive Captain Beefheart, the spaces of Keith Hudson – that gave the Sex Pistols an exit from nostalgia or lads' Rock into new, uncharted territory. Lydon's interest in musical experimentation gave the Sex Pistols the edge to back up their increasingly extravagant demands. McLaren wanted to whip up a storm, and Lydon would hurl himself into its eye, attempting to offload his anger and guilt.

'The kids want misery and death,' snorts Lydon, 'they want threatening noises, because that shakes you out of your apathy.' Here John Lydon intersects with an archetype. McLaren was attracted by the character that Graham Greene has defined for all time in *Brighton Rock* (a book that Lydon had studied for his English O level): the vengeful, Catholic boy-gangster, Pinkie. 'There was poison in his veins, though he grinned and bore it. He had been insulted: they thought because he was seventeen . . .' Like Pinkie, John Lydon was ready to murder a world.

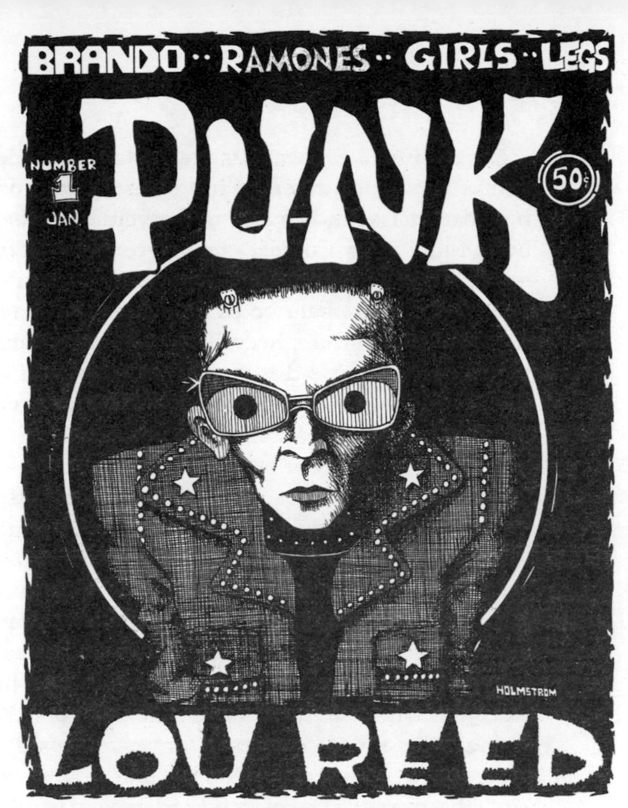

The new generation gets a name, December 1975 (© John Holmstrom)

10

The first work of the hero is to retreat from the world scene of secondary effects to those causal zones of the psyche where the difficulties really reside, and there to clarify the difficulties, eradicate them in his own case (i.e. give battle to the nursery demons of his local culture) and break through to the undistorted, direct experience and assimilation of what C. G. Jung has called 'the archetypal images'.

Joseph Campbell: *The Hero With A Thousand Faces* (1948)

In the autumn of 1975, the mainstream music industry was not sympathetic to new groups that wanted to make an abrasive socio-cultural noise. As Dave Laing notes in *One Chord Wonders*, the music industry had reacted to the huge market opened up in the 1960s by organizing itself globally: over 60 per cent of the English market was dominated by six multi-national companies. Their 'gigantism' dominated pop music, in the market approach of 'flinging mud against a wall' and in the favoured musical style, progressive Rock, which was expensive to record, package and promote.

New industry innovations were as much to do with marketing as music. Abba fully emerged in the last quarter of 1975 as 'the classic transnational sound of the mid-seventies'. After winning the 1974 Eurovision Song Contest, they recorded in Sweden, leased their records to an American based multi-national, and sang in an English which was the global pop esperanto, synthesized from fifty years of American pop culture. Recycling of a more blatant kind occurred with the music industry's discovery of the power of television: in 1972, a company called K-Tel had had immediate success with a series of TV-advertised compilation albums. By 1976 these compilations would account for 30 per cent of all sales.

Television adverts, streamlined retail outlets, tax dodges, institutionalized nostalgia, all filled up the space in the airless room that was pop culture. A *Melody Maker* piece on the 'State of Rock' in June 1975 summed up the situation: 'At the heart of the Rock Dream is a cash register.' In the same feature, independent producer Pete Jenner stated: 'I'm thinking of someone who's 16, who's going to start saying, "Look, all this stuff these bands do with these huge PAs and lights, that's not where it's at. It's down to the people."'

There was already one space for young musicians who spurned the current path of intense grooming and high investment. By autumn 1975, the impact of Dr Feelgood had opened up the pub circuit to a new generation of more intense groups: the Stranglers, Eddie and the Hot Rods, and Joe Strummer's 101'ers. 'We realized we had to move fast,' says Paul Cook, 'there was an undercurrent of all these people who were going to start bands. You could feel something was going to happen.'

Quick to compete, Bernard Rhodes was attempting to fashion his own teenage pop group from the pool of musicians around a group called London SS. Formed by art student Mick Jones and Brunel maths graduate Tony James, London SS was a highly style-conscious group: according to James, 'long-haired, like a London New York Dolls with girls' shoes'. Rhodes's first act was to try to shame the group out of their name; his second was to find the group a base, the Praed Street Café in Paddington, where the group auditioned scores of would-be guitarists, singers and drummers.

'Thousands of people now claim to have been in London SS,' says James. 'Chrissie Hynde came and went. We did make recordings at the time, covers of MC5 numbers and "Protex Blue". Bernie and Malcolm were most instrumental in turning the understanding. They introduced us to Glen and Steve and Paul: at that time they had very short hair and we had very long hair. We hated the idea of getting our hair cut: long hair was still a symbol of rebellion. There were the two factions. The Sex Pistols were King's Road, we were Paddington, but we fell apart because we couldn't find a singer.'

Even with a singer, the newly constituted 'Sex' group had a mountain of problems to overcome. A month after their first full rehearsal, things were still very temporary. Apart from their own musical shortcomings, the four had problems finding a place to rehearse: un-soundproofed pubs like the Crunchie Frog or the Rose & Crown in Wandsworth were not ideal. At this point, in September, McLaren finally made a committment to the group: when Glen found an advertisement for a rehearsal space in the *Melody Maker*, McLaren guaranteed the £1,000 deposit.

Owned by Bill Collins, the space comprised an attic over a small ground floor rehearsal room, reached by a crumbling passage between numbers 6 and 8 Denmark Street. John liked it because it was dank and depressing; Steve Jones liked it because he now had a W1 address; Malcolm McLaren liked it because it was a kind of Trojan horse right in the heart of Tin Pan Alley, which had been the nub of English pop in the 1940s, 1950s and 1960s. Never mind that the centre of the music industry was now elsewhere: with this tiny room, he could *be* Larry Parnes or Laurence Harvey in *Expresso Bongo*.

The next day, Paul Cook phoned McLaren to tell him he'd been up all night thinking, and wanted to quit the group. He thought the group was a shambles and that McLaren was wasting his money on the rehearsal space. 'I thought Malcolm was bullshitting all the time,' says Cook, 'he'd say these things would happen all the time and they never did.' McLaren bought time by setting up auditions for a competent guitarist. The advertisement – for 'WHIZZ KID GUITARIST Not older than 20 Not worse looking than Johnny Thunders' – went in the *Melody Maker* on 27 September: they got an immediate response.

According to McLaren, 'They got some incredibly funny, mad kids. One was called Fabian Quest and he turned his head to the wall as he tried to play guitar. When they came to do the audition, they suddenly realized that they were at least better than this guy. Jones was pissing himself laughing. Everybody was terrible. So suddenly they found themselves having an identity from that: they had all these kids coming in, so it wasn't like anyone could join. They had some common cause: they could all criticize these people with their various ideas that didn't seem to appeal to theirs, even though they didn't know what theirs were.'

Cook was persuaded to stay and full rehearsals were fitted in around his working hours: Lydon and Jones were on the dole, while Matlock had just gone back to St Martin's.

'I lived by myself in Denmark Street for a long time,' says Steve Jones: 'I used to take black bombers and play along to records for hours on end. "Raw Power" and the New York Dolls. My fingers would be down to the bone.' 'We'd rehearse almost every day,' says Glen, 'even if we just did half an hour. John would come down in the evening.'

The Sex Pistols did what any other group in their position does: they played their favourite oldies as a touchstone. During October they rehearsed a repertoire mainly derived from experimental, mediated Mod pop: 'Psychotic Reaction' by Count Five, 'Through My Eyes' by the Creation, five songs by the Small Faces, including 'All Or Nothing' and 'My Mind's Eye', the thuggish R&B of Dave Berry's 'Don't Gimme No Lip Child', and the incestuous phrases of the Who's 'Substitute'. Despite the violence lurking beneath these songs, Lydon wasn't satisfied: 'Everybody thought I was vile and loathsome because I wouldn't do covers or Small Faces' songs: we did a few good songs, we really mutilated them, but you have to start somewhere. "Don't you give me no lip, *child*, don't you talk back to me": God, from an eighteen-year-old that's pretty sarky stuff! As soon as I was given the opportunity, I came up with ideas: "Sod them," I thought, "they're going to go do Who rip-offs, I don't care. I'll write the songs I want to write." I hated rehearsing. I'd feel too insecure, so I'd write these little things and crawl into a corner and mumble, hoping that no one would hear.'

To avoid being just a superior Pub Rock band, the Sex Pistols needed their own material. McLaren pushed them into it. 'At the time, Malcolm was like another member of the band,' says Cook, 'he got off on hanging around younger people, feeding off their energy.' Lydon had already changed the lyrics to 'Scarface' – which became 'Did You No Wrong' – before Matlock came up with 'Pretty Vacant'.

'Malcolm had not long come back from the States with these posters,' Matlock says, 'one was for Television with Richard Hell in the band. It had all these great songs in it, "Blank Generation", "Venus De Milo" and that's where we got the idea for "Pretty Vacant".'

The song begins with a simple but dramatic repeated guitar figure, before sliding into one of Matlock's best melodies and most concise structures. The song's hook, 'We're so pretty', echoed a *Sunday Times* piece on the Bay City Rollers, where a picture of a pouting '17-year-old art student' was captioned with the phrase: 'They're so pretty.' Lydon's addition to Glen's chorus skews what could be just a pleasant Rock ditty into something different: his negative verses are a powerful refusal, though, at the same time, they act as a baffle against definition: 'There's no point in asking: you'll get no reply.'

'Pretty Vacant' captured the tension between Lydon and Matlock. 'Me and Glen have never seen eye to eye,' says Lydon. 'The things he likes, the nice clean-shaven side of pop, I find offensive and dull.' 'There was a thing between John and Glen from the first,' says Paul Cook, 'they both went to college, maybe there was a rivalry there.' 'John's a fucked-up Roman Catholic,' says Matlock, 'and that came out in the lyrics. One of the songs we never used was about waiting for the Archangel Gabriel.'

More to the point, a struggle for control was already developing. 'Glen was Malcolm's henchman,' says Bernard Rhodes, 'he would do everything, find the college gigs. It became a scene between John and Malcolm: they got on very well, because John was coming to the shop and was impressed, but then you promote the troublemaker in order to solve a problem, and in the end you're working for the troublemaker. Glen was Malcolm's strong card in this.'

Lydon had a strong streak of morbidity to work through. 'The one job I really wanted when I was on the dole was to work in a funeral parlour and they would not take me seriously,' he says. One early song, in an echo of Hell's 'Please Kill Me' T-shirt, was called 'Kill Me Today'. Yet there are many kinds of death: under pressure to come up with generation-gap anthems, Lydon began a systematic disordering of the senses, which led him to reject self-conscious attempts like 'Concrete Youth' and 'Mindless Generation' in favour of a more instinctive, unconscious approach.

'I would think about it for a week,' says Lydon, 'and then it came out in one go.' The result was allusive rather than specific. 'You're only twenty-nine, got a lot to learn, but when your business dies, you will not return,' he sang on 'Seventeen', perhaps the nearest thing that the Sex Pistols came to an initial manifesto: 'We make noise 'cos it's our choice, it's what we want to do. We don't care about long hair: we don't wear flares.' 'I don't work,' it concluded, 'I just speed – that's all I need.'

The various edicts of McLaren and Lydon, issued annually through the media, state quite clearly that neither had an influence on the other, and worse: 'We were never friends, ever' (Lydon); 'Never, never' (McLaren). Ignoring these squabbles, another story emerges. 'I saw McLaren a few weeks after he'd found John,' says Nick Kent, 'and he was just raving about him. The thing that finally made me think he'd done it was him saying: "He's the best thing about the group, he's got these great lyrics, he's got this song called 'You're only twenty-nine, but you got a lot to learn'".'

'John liked Malcolm basically, in the beginning,' says Helen Wallington-Lloyd, 'perhaps as a father figure, or as a mirror of himself. And, to Malcolm, John was this younger version. Malcolm's got this thing about youth: when you're young, you're fearless, you can do things.' In 1975, Malcolm left Vivienne to live with Helen, just returned from South Africa, in her Bell Street flat. 'He was wearing leather jeans and talking like an American; I met Johnny and his mates. Johnny looked amazing in a mohair jumper: like a young Albert Steptoe. Very queenified: always moaning.

'He had definite opinions about things and he would voice them: loud. I'd look at him and think: "What has Malcolm got himself into?" To me his friends seemed like those National Front types, louts: nudging each other about poofters and yids and blacks, anything. John was a bit like that: very suspicious of middle-class people. I spoke to his mother on the phone. She asked me, "What is this Malcolm McLaren really like? Do you think he's for real? Is he thinking about the boy?" I don't think they liked him being Jewish very much. There's an innate Catholic thing about Jews, especially someone like Malcolm who pulled the strings.

'I got quite close to John: he liked me. He always talked in opposites. His mother used to say: "He's a funny boy, talking in opposites." I think he's a closet case. I think with Malcolm, they had a sexual thing. It was narcissistic: they looked so much alike. Both aquarians, the same bone structure: they've got those eyes and they're absolutely fearless of other people's opinions. They're hard: obviously different things in their background made them different and also they had the gift of the gab. They'd come up with the most bizarre innovations.'

There is no doubt that a spark was lit between them, for however brief a time. The tension came out, however, in another of the Sex Pistols' early songs, 'Submission'. 'He was such a poseur, Malcolm,' says Paul Cook, 'with his fantasies about sex and violence.' To go with the shop, McLaren told the group to write a song about submission: S&M, bondage, domination, that sort of thing. With Glen, Lydon wrote something completely different: a slow, almost mystical song to the unattainable female.

McLaren's control was far from absolute. In November 1975, he was also having problems in getting the group to agree on a name. After a month's hard rehearsal, the Sex Pistols were just about ready to face the world, but, although they had been working under that name, no final agreement had been made. Glen had been deputized to find college concerts and had arranged two: one at Central School of Art and Design in Holborn, on 7 November, and, at the very last minute, one in a small upstairs room at St Martin's, the day before. The group's identity had to be finalized.

As part of this process of transformation and group bonding, individual names were changed first. Although they'd known Lydon for three months, he was so secretive and mistrustful that he hadn't told the group his surname. John was always spitting, blowing his nose and inspecting his rotting teeth. Steve Jones found this repulsive and used to say to John, 'Your teeth are rotten, you look Rotten.' The name was annoying enough to stick. It was a negative of Larry Parnes's Pop-Art pseudonyms: not Wilde, but Rotten; Sex Pistols but not sexy.

The others didn't have quite the same conviction: Paul nearly became 'Slave' Cook, while Glen added an extra 'n'. Jones stayed as he was. McLaren then insisted that they went out under the name that he had coined in the autumn of 1974: as far as he was concerned, the group were promoting the shop and Sex had to be in the name. Now that Jones wasn't the singer, Kutie Jones could go. What was wrong with Sex Pistols, with its associations of 'a pistol, a gun, assassins, young and vicious and sex'?

As ever, the accounts differ. 'I liked that name very much,' says Lydon, 'I thought it was hilarious. The word "Sex" had never been used in that blatant way before and to put it into a pop band was very funny. I thought it was perfect to offend old ladies.' 'Rotten wanted just to be called "Sex",' says McLaren, 'it was only Jones that loved it. Cook thought it was reasonable but wanted something more normal sounding. Matlock, being a genuine sixth-form character, sided with John. They still went out as Sex Pistols. I wasn't having it: I was in control and I wasn't going to waste my time with a bunch of herberts going out with a name like Sex. I was out to sell lots of trousers.'

I'm so young/I'm so young/I'm so goddam young/I'm so young/I'm so goddam young/I'm so young/I'm so goddam young . . . we created it: *let's take it over.*

Patti Smith (29): Improvisation at the end of 'My Generation', live in Cleveland (26 January 1976)

You know what I think?
I think the whole world stinks
& I don't need no shrink
I just hate it

The Electric Eels: 'Agitated' (1975)

The week that the Sex Pistols played their first performance, the six-year-old 'Space Oddity' by David Bowie took over the number one UK single slot from Art Garfunkel's version of a sixteen-year-old song, 'I Only Have Eyes for You'. The number one album was the TV-advertised *40 Golden Greats* by Jim Reeves, who had died in 1964. In returning, the 1960s showed up the poverty of the present: 'Remember Those Fabulous 60s?' ran the cover byline of that week's *New Musical Express*, catching the crest of a marketing wave which would result in Top Ten hits for old songs by the Beatles and the Small Faces.

Inside, however, was a feature that made this nostalgia seem irrelevant. Entitled 'Are you alive to the jive of . . . THE SOUND OF '75?', it revealed the New York scene that McLaren had been keeping as his secret. Charles Shaar Murray's two-page spread on CBGBs gave pride of place to the Ramones. 'They used to play 20-minute sets because they only had eight songs, but now they're up to 45 minutes. Joey spits out the title of the song, Dee Dee shouts "1–2–3–4" and they're off again, maybe with "53rd and 3rd".' *One and a half minute songs; 1–2–3–4 countdown intros; Byrds haircuts: perfect.*

The CBGBs scene had grown considerably. During the second half of July 1975, the club hosted a Rock Festival which showcased over thirty new groups: although the crowds were variable, the festival attracted the first concerted press attention. Within the small, incestuous world of the English weeklies and New York media the festival was a hit but it was still small-time: most of the groups wanted Top Forty success.

Nobody could agree on the name for the new movement: Hilly Kristal called it Street Rock, but a new magazine published that winter finally codified it. *Punk* was started by two high-school friends from

Cheshire, Connecticut, Legs McNeil and John Holmstrom. Holmstrom was studying cartoon under Will Eisner and Harvey Kurtzman at the School of Visual Arts in New York. McNeil, an Irish Catholic high-school dropout joined him there in September 1975: 'John had this definite attitude: he wanted to call it "Teenage News", which I thought was really stupid. I said to John: "Why don't we call it "Punk"? We were driving and John said, "I'll be the editor"; our friend Jed said, "I'll be the publisher"; and they both looked at me and said, "What are you going to be?" "I'll be the resident punk." It was all decided in two seconds. On TV, if you watched cop shows, *Kojak, Beretta*, when the cops finally catch the mass murderer, they'd say, "you dirty Punk". It was what your teachers would call you. It meant that you were the lowest. All of us drop-outs and fuck-ups got together and started a movement. We'd been told all our lives that we'd never amount to anything. We're the people who fell through the cracks of the educational system.'

'It was pretty obvious that the word was getting very popular,' says Holmstrom. *Creem* used it to describe this early seventies music; *Bomp* would use it to describe the garage bands of the sixties; a magazine like the *Aquarian* would use it to describe what was going on at CBGBs. The word was being used to describe Springsteen, Patti Smith, and the Bay City Rollers. So when Legs came up with it we figured we'd take the name before anyone else claimed it. We wanted to get rid of the bullshit, strip it down to Rock'n'Roll. We wanted the fun and liveliness back.'

'The war in Vietnam ended, which I think helped a lot,' says McNeil. 'If you were a kid, you grew up afraid that you were going to have to go, and that was a release, a party. The previous year you'd had Watergate, it was a time of change. Something was going to happen: it confirmed your feeling, this government sucks, Nixon's an asshole, and then we had Ford, who was a real klutz. No one in New York had any money: the city was nearly bankrupt and that's when Ford said to the city: "Drop dead" .'

Punk: How old are you?
Tommy: 23, 24.
Punk: Oh, that's us!
Tommy: Lovely generation.

***Punk* 1: 'Ramones – Rock'n'Roll – The Real Thing'**

Johnny, Joey and Dee Dee Ramone at CBGBs, early 1976 (© Roberta Bayley)

The first issue of *Punk*, in a folded broadsheet format, hit the news stands in December 1975. Almost straight away, it pulled together the disparate elements of the CBGBs scene into a powerful fantasy. Its cover story was an interview with Lou Reed about his current record, *Metal Machine Music*, but, instead of a photo, there was a wickedly accurate cartoon of Reed as metal man: the feature inside was not typeset but told in fumetti.

'I wanted to see something new in comics,' says Holmstrom, 'it fitted the music. Johnny Ramone would always wear cartoon logo T-shirts.' In issue number one of *Punk*, the surrounding artwork is as important as Reed's insults: the Ramones play on the interview tape and one can see them in photograph form. When the interviewers follow Reed down the block, there they are in the cartoons. The effect was both immediate and distanced, a formal innovation on a par with *Mad* magazine or the Ramones' own manipulations: 'Third verse, different from the first,' they shout on 'Judy is a Punk', and of course, it is.

Mary Harron, a Canadian who had edited *Isis* at Oxford, interviewed the Ramones for *Punk*'s first issue. 'When I first saw the

Ramones,' she says, 'I couldn't believe people were doing this. The dumb brattiness: "Beat on the brat with a baseball bat." There was this real cartoon element, and yet you're in a real place, you want to do something real, so you're in a situation where they could be real, they could be genuinely delinquent. It had an edge to it: they looked dumb-smart, smart-dumb.

'Hippy culture had gone very mainstream: for the first time Bohemia embraced fast-food. It was about saying yes to the modern world. Punk, like Warhol, embraced everything that cultured people, and hippies, detested: plastic, junk-food, B-movies, advertising, making money – although no one ever did. You got so sick of people being so nice, mouthing an enforced attitude of goodness and health. Punk was liberating and new: the idea of smoking sixty cigarettes a day and staying up all night on speed.'

'One of the Punk things was going to the past to pick the right influences out,' says Holmstrom, 'we weren't starting anything new, we were taking our favourite influences and playing with them.' This version of Punk contained as many contradictions as there were groups: there was the cartoon quality of the Ramones, the preppiness of Talking Heads, the confrontations of Suicide, the breathy sixties pop of Blondie, and the fin-de-siècle romanticism of Verlaine and Hell. In its early issues, *Punk* featured Patti Smith on Rimbaud, Television on Gérard de Nerval and Richard Hell on Nietzsche.

'There was something about it that was very rigorous,' says Harron. 'It had an art element in it, always. There's a great interview with Richard Hell that Legs did in *Punk*. It captured the attitude: people needed to say something that negative. I liked that time of decay. There was nihilism in the atmosphere, a longing to die. Part of the feeling of New York at that time was this longing for oblivion, that you were about to disintegrate, go the way of this bankrupt, crumbling city. Yet that was something almost mystically wonderful.'

> Jarry's writing expressed an almost unthinkable code of conduct, which he did not shrink from applying to his own life. Dream must invade every waking moment to become the element in which we exist. The conscious and the unconscious fuse into a continuum which coincides with the fusion of thought and action, art and life, childhood and maturity.
> **Roger Shattuck: *The Banquet Years – The Origins of the Avant-Garde in France – 1885 to World War I* (1955)**

Ahead the dim blur of an alien land/Time to give ourselves into strange gods' hands.

Pere Ubu: *30 Seconds Over Tokyo* (1975)

Urbanism, romantic nihilism, musical simplicity as a door to the unconscious, the 'teenage news' – these impulses were not exclusively the preserve of New York and London. 'In Cleveland from 1968 to 1975, a small group of people were evolving styles of music that would, much later, come to be called "New Wave",' writes Charlotte Pressler. 'Misleadingly so, because that term suggests the current situation, in which an already evolved style exists for new bands to aim at. The task of this group was different: to evolve the style itself, while struggling to find in themselves the authority and confidence to play it. And they had to do this in a total vacuum.'

'Cleveland is a working-class town with very unsophisticated tastes,' says historian Mike Weldon, 'but for some reason it's a major music media city. Records break there: maybe it's the way into the Midwest. In the early seventies, Cleveland was a major market for Bruce Springsteen, David Bowie. The New York Dolls, Television played there before they had a record out, and at the same time, because of the strength of the local radio stations, we got the best British bands of the time: T. Rex, Dr Feelgood, Roxy Music.

'You always had a small group of people who loved that kind of music: they formed bands and did original songs, but they never got support in Cleveland. The local media didn't write about them: there was no label interest at all, until 1978. In 1973 to 74, there was a small underground scene that included Rocket From The Tombs, who later became Pere Ubu, and who had members in the Dead Boys. There were the Electric Eels and the Mirrors. From Akron, there were the Bizarros, Devo. Most of them had fallen apart by 1977.'

'Most of these people were from middle or upper-middle class backgrounds,' writes Pressler. 'Most were very intelligent. There was no reason why they should not have effected an entry into the world of their parents. Yet all of them turned their backs on this world, and that meant a number of very painful choices. Yet they were not drop-outs in the sixties sense: they felt, if anything, a certain affection for consumerist society and a total contempt for the so-called counterculture. The sixties drop-outs dropped in to a whole world of people like themselves; these people were on their own.'

The Cleveland groups used the same building blocks as New York or London, but their development in isolation resulted in a Bohemianism that was proud to fail. 'The most nihilistic were the Electric Eels,' says Weldon. 'John Morton was the leader: he and Dave E., the singer, wrote the songs, which had funny, clever lyrics. There was a lot of violence attached to that group. John liked to call it Art Terrorism. Brian McMahon, the guitarist, and John would go out to working-class bars where people worked in steel mills, and dance with each other. That caused serious fights.

Electric Eels handbill, December 1974 (courtesy of Mike Weldon)

'In 1974, they were wearing safety pins and ripped-up shirts, T-shirts with insulting things on them, White Power logos and swastikas: it was offensive and they meant to be offensive. They meant to distract people, but I don't think they were exceptionally racist: they were being obnoxious and outrageous. Live they were often too out of control. I don't think they seriously thought anything was going to happen except they were going to go out there and get arrested.'

It was the problem that would be endlessly repeated during the next few years: in trying to blast through the culture's complacency, the Electric Eels succumbed to the very nihilism that was their tool. Their first forty-five, recorded just before they broke up in mid-1975, mixed impossibly distorted production with words that seemed to crawl up the wall. 'Cyclotron' spins flashing, surreal images taken from a vast wasteland of pop culture and suburban plenty, while 'Agitated' goes into the eye of the storm, a closed cycle of frustration and rejection: 'I'm so agitated/So agitated/So agitated/That I'm so agitated/I'm so agitated . . .'

'I would like to know the source of the deep rage that runs through this story like a razor-edged wire,' writes Charlotte Pressler. 'It wasn't precisely class hatred; it certainly wasn't political; it went too deep to be accepting of the possibility of change. The Eels perhaps came closest to embodying it fully; but it was there in everyone else. It was a desperate stubborn refusal of the world, a total rejection: the kind of thing that once drove men into the desert, but our desert was the Flats. It should be remembered that we had all grown up with Civil Defense drills and dreams of the bomb at night; we had been promised the end of the world as children, and we weren't getting it.'

For the isolated Clevelanders, there were two main ways of acting out this refusal. The first was to throw all your rage outwards. The second was to write your own script of self-destruction, a script that harked back to the founding teenage intensity of James Dean. 'Ain't it fun when you know you're gonna die young,' sang Peter Laughner early in 1975: within two and a half years, he had achieved his aim. At seventeen, Laughner had posed in a leather jacket and bound a heavy chain with a padlock around his neck: his ceaseless efforts to reproduce the negation of the Velvet Underground and the Stooges made him 'central to the Cleveland underground in those years'.

In 1973, Laughner formed Rocket From The Tombs with David Thomas, a large, Ubu-ish bear of a man who had planned to be an English professor: after Laughner's departure, the group became Pere Ubu. The group's first forty-five continued the romantic notion of the avant-garde that had begun in Jarry's Paris. One side, built around Scott Krauss's loping drum rhythm and Tim Wright's sinister bass pattern, journeyed straight into the 'Heart Of Darkness': 'Image Object & Illusion: go down to the corner/Where none of the faces fit a human form/Where nothing I see there isn't deformed.'

Pere Ubu were formed out of a loose group of people centred around an apartment block called the Plaza. 'It was a really nice old building in a terrible neighbourhood,' says David Thomas. 'We were into this Urban Pioneer thing, which was a bunch of kids born in the suburbs to middle-class families, moving back into the city, because they thought the city should live. The city I loved everybody else hated: it was totally deserted, people fled when the sun went down. It was run down, but we thought it was beautiful at the time of youth when you're prone to romanticism.

'I wondered at what point a civilization hits its peak and then begins to decline. All those deserted cities, the jungle overgrows them: at what point does the city die? At what point do the people who live there no longer understand the vision of the builders? We felt that we owned Cleveland at that point because nobody else wanted it. But that's all gone now. The city has become revitalised: they're tearing down all the really neat old deserted stuff and putting up condos.

'This Urban Pioneer movement was the context of what we were doing; a lot of us loved the city because we appreciated the almost naive vision of the people who had built it. Clearly we were dark at that point, but it was no more dark than Country and Western is dark. "Heart of Darkness" was describing a certain bend in the freeway: we saw all that in the city, but it wasn't that we embraced it. It was more journalistic, and when we saw that people were embracing it, we tried to make it clearer.'

Pere Ubu were the first new Cleveland group to make it out of the city: in the winter of 1975 they travelled to New York to play Max's and CBGBs. In March 1976, they released 'Final Solution', a stripping down of Blue Cheer's 'Summertime Blues' into a 'dumb teen angst song' so nihilistic that the group, concerned by the Nazi images in the new culture, refused to play it live. But it was their first A-side that defined the dreamscape that Pere Ubu would make their own. Punctuated by a synthesizer that gusted like a buffeting wind, '30 Seconds over Tokyo' took one on a 'suicide ride' so enveloping that you were dissolved in a future that was at once hopeful and dread.

'Lose his senses,' sang Television in 'Little Johnny Jewel'. This exploration of the subconscious began to disinter the strange gods of the time. Lurking under nihilism's cloak was a slight but persistent trace of the right-wing backlash that was brewing in the West from the mid-1970s on. 'We don't believe in love or any of that shit,' says one of the editors of *Punk* in its first issue, as they state in the Ramones interview: 'Dee Dee likes comic books, anything with swastikas in it, especially *Enemy Ace*.'

Final solutions of various types were invoked to hasten the death of the old culture, but Nazi images persisted. The Ramones were initially packaged by an artist called Arturo Vega, who lived in a loft next door to CBGBs: 'Everybody hung out there,' says Legs McNeil: 'Arturo was a gay Mexican and a minimalist artist who made dayglo swastikas.' The Ramones' early material was spattered with references to militarism and acronymic organisations like the CIA or the SLA, with more explicit references in 'Blitzkrieg Bop' and 'Today Your Love, Tomorrow The World'.

'What they want, I don't know,' sang the Ramones about *their* generation: the formal severity of their music lent such slogans an absorbing ambiguity. 'I would have arguments about this stuff,' says Mary Harron. 'Arturo had some really nasty ideas, but Joey Ramone was a nice guy, he was no savage right-winger. The Ramones were problematic. It was hard to work out what their politics were. It had this difficult edge, but the most important thing was needling the older generation. Hating hippies was a big thing.'

'The Dictators came from Co-op City in Detroit, the Ramones came from Forest Hills, we came from Cheshire,' says McNeil. 'We all had the same reference points: White Castle hamburgers, muzak, malls. And we were all white: there were no black people involved with this. In the sixties hippies always wanted to be black. We were going: "Fuck the Blues; fuck the black experience." We had nothing in common with black people at that time: we'd had ten years of being politically correct and we were going to have fun, like kids are supposed to do.

'It was funny: you'd see guys going out to a Punk club, passing black people going into a disco, and they'd be looking at each other, not with disgust, but "Isn't it weird that they want to go there." There were definite right-wing overtones, but we didn't feel like, "Let's go out and start a youth movement about fascism" or anything. I don't think anyone wanted to read too much depth into it: it was more emotional. When the imagery was used, it was more like "Look at these guys, isn't it stupid?"'

This element of polemic and put-on masked the real return of the repressed: a white, suburban, adolescent nihilism that had been forgotten since sixties Punk Rock. Just as much of the music bled out any black influence in favour of a monolithic, unsyncopated sound, some of the accompanying attitudes held both the excitement of the broken taboo and queasiness about the possible implications. Yet this examination of the forbidden was the source of Punk's power.

Nothing epitomized this more than the one garment that above all would become associated with Punk; which Punk brought out of taboo and into the high street. 'You had to buy the black leather jacket,' says Legs McNeil. 'You had to make that initial investment. We went to see the Ramones at CBGBs. We were wearing these nerdy T-shirts and denim jackets. It was embarrassing. The Ramones were wearing leather jackets: Joey has said they got it from *The Wild One*. I walked out the next day and bought my first.

'It was a return to the fifties. You know *The Lords of Flatbush*? The Fonz was on TV: in the first episodes of *Happy Days* he wore a windbreaker because it was too threatening for him to wear a leather jacket. Nobody in New York wore black leather: if you wore one the streets parted in front of you, it wasn't like now. It was the mood of the country: people wanted to get back to the aggression, prove we weren't wimps, put on the leather jacket.'

In *Punk*'s definition of the new aesthetic, there was one final problem: homosexuality. The word may have had all the Rock-specific meanings already mentioned but another source lay, as Peter Crowley pointed out in issue 3 of *Punk*, in 'a prison word meaning the boys who give up their ass to the "wolves"'. At the same time as the Ramones were baiting the liberals, they sang '53rd and 3rd', a song which recorded Dee Dee Ramone's experiences on the corner that was a hustler hangout. The ripped jeans and skimpy T-shirts, elements of their style that would soon pass around the world, were taken from the hustlers who worked that strip.

Punk had to disavow any taint of homosexuality, not only because of suburban prejudices, but, because, in Leee Black Childers' words, 'gay people made up most of the audience'. This became another way for *Punk* to say the unsayable in a pluralistic, liberal milieu. 'John and Legs wrote a few things about Wayne County and it created a huge war. But a lot of the bands they tried to champion, like Blondie, would have no part of this anti-homosexual number. That's fine: when you have a growing scene, for a little while it's fun to have a feud. It creates interest.'

These ambiguities were coded into American Punk as the CBGBs groups made their steps towards the American mainstream and, in the constant oscillation between London and New York, began to influence England. In the autumn of 1975, the Patti Smith Group released their first album. Television were attracting record company attention, as were the Ramones, Blondie and Talking Heads. This was a level of attention unusual for the ingrown New York Rock scene, and was partly due to *Punk*'s successful translation of CBGBs into a package that record executives like Seymour Stein could readily understand.

However, contained in this package were problems which would take several years to work out. How could you be tough and a loser at the same time? How could you play with right-wing imagery and not get trapped by it? How could you take a script from Rimbaud and avoid the mythological trajectory of that poet's life? Built into Punk from the beginning was not only a tendency to self-destruction, but a short shelf-life. Despite what many of the groups professed, the movement enshrined failure: to succeed in conventional terms meant that you had failed on your own terms; to fail meant that you had succeeded.

John Lydon at St Albans, Hertfordshire College of Art and Design, February 1976 (© Ray Stevenson)

11

Can't go on/Drag along/Can't go wrong/Sing along/Pied Piper will lead you to the water.

John Lydon for PiL: 'Pied Piper' (1980)

Trying to tart the rock business up is getting nearer to what the kids themselves are like. Because what I find, if you want to talk in the terms of rock, a lot depends on sensationalism, and the kids themselves are more sensational than the stars themselves.

David Bowie: *New Musical Express* (28 February 1974)

'For their first ever gig,' says Adam Ant, 'the Sex Pistols were support group to the band I was in, Bazooka Joe. I'll never forget it. They came in as a gang: they looked like they couldn't give a fuck about anybody. John had baggy pinstripe trousers with braces and a ripped-up T-shirt saying "Pink Floyd" with "I Hate" over it. Jonesy was tiny, he looked like a young Pete Townshend. Matlock had paint-spattered trousers and a woman's pink leather top. Paul Cook looked like Rod Stewart, like a little Mod really.

'I watched them play: Malcolm was at the front, orchestrating them, telling them where to stand. Viv was there. There weren't many there: maybe a dozen of their people – Jordan, Michael Collins, Andy Czezowski. They did "Substitute", and "Whatcha Gonna Do About It" with the lyrics changed: "I want you to know that I *hate* you baby." Then John lost interest. He'd eat sweets, pull them out and suck them and just spit them out: he just looked at the audience, glazed.

'There were no guitar solos, it was just simple songs. They did five and that was it: goodnight. The rest of my band hated them because they thought they couldn't play: in fact somebody said as much to Glen and he said: "So what?" But I thought they were very tight. It was only John who hadn't learned how to make the voice last, but over a fifteen minute burst, he was very clear. At the end Rotten slagged off Bazooka Joe as being a bunch of fucking cunts and our guitarist Danny Kleinman leapt from the front row and pinned John against the back wall: he made him apologize.'

'It was fucking wild,' says Steve Jones; 'I was so nervous I took a mandrax. When we started playing the mandrax was hitting me and I cranked the amp up. It was a 100w amp in a little room with no stage and it was great. Everyone was looking at us. It seemed like millions of people at the time. You could tell there was a buzz.' 'We had carried the equipment over from Denmark Street,' says Paul Cook, 'we were all highly charged and nervous. It must have been a terrible racket, because someone pulled the plug on us, there was a big fight.'

'The impression they left on me was total,' says Adam. 'They had a certain attitude I'd never seen: they had bollocks and they had very expensive equipment and it didn't look like it belonged to them. They had the look in their eyes that said: "We're going to be massive." I stood there transfixed. When Danny jumped John, I didn't jump in to help him. I left Bazooka Joe the next day: I came out of that gig thinking, "I'm tired of Teddy Boys" and it seemed to me that the Sex Pistols were playing simple songs that I could play. I just wanted to go away and form my own band.'

'Whether they were *good* or not was irrelevant,' says Andy Czezowski: 'I *wanted* to be excited and they filled a spot.' Performers are only as interesting as the emotions that they generate, or the situations that they catalyse: the audience gives them their power. The Sex Pistols began as a hype, a group of four disparate teenagers thrown together to sell trousers, but they quickly became a prism through which the present and a future could be clearly seen.

The power of sound is unpredictable and potentially dangerous. In the Anglo-German folk tale, the Pied Piper is hired to draw away a plague of rats from a large city: cheated by the elders of his fee, he spirits away the children of the city through the sound of his pipe. Lost in the spirit world, they are never seen again. From the very first, the Sex Pistols polarized and galvanized their tiny audiences. 'We started getting a reaction instantly,' says Paul Cook, 'so we thought we must be doing something right.'

That reaction was, at first, composed of 50 per cent indifference, 25 per cent hostility, 20 per cent hilarity and 5 per cent immediate empathy. Until their first TV broadcast in August 1976, the only way to see the group was live: for nine months they toured the country. To most of their small audiences, their music was just scraping and gnawing sounds, but at each concert, one or two people listened and, instantly converted, laid aside their previous lives to follow them.

'It must have been very satisfying for them to get such a violent response to everything they did,' says Al McDowell, who was approached by Glen Matlock to put on their second concert, at the Central School of Art, the day after St Martin's. 'They had a mirror standing in front of them all the time. I think the media side of it was very well controlled. It was presented as a package all the time. Graphically it was all together; everything had an atmosphere. It was threatening and there was that feeling of revolt, based on the Paris '68 approach. It was immediately attractive to anyone who was feeling hostile.'

On 5 December, McLaren organized a concert at the Chelsea School of Art. For this, their fifth, the group had no support except a disco. 'There was a little buzz about Malcolm's group,' says Ted Carroll, 'so he contacted a lot of people and invited them to Chelsea. Roger Armstrong and I went and we thought they were great, because there was so much energy. They were disorganized but powerful. People didn't know what to make of them: there was no definite reference point.'

Finding suitable venues for the Sex Pistols quickly became a problem, particularly as McLaren, with his ignorance of the music business, refused to take the easy route. He wanted to avoid the standard Pub-Rock circuit, with its pecking order and its stock responses, but in the pre-video age, live exposure was still the way to gain attention. After studying the music press, McLaren realized that there was still a lively college circuit, but after a few calls, he found that the name 'Sex Pistols' tended to trigger a reaction that, although satisfyingly negative, failed to result in bookings. The only thing to do was to lie and cheat.

The routine went something like this: McLaren would call the social secretary or some other minor college official. 'We're the support group. I phoned up Fred from the office and he said to come along. It only takes us ten minutes to set up and we'll play for half an hour. OK?' Or, 'we're friends of the group – they said we could come along and fill in for half an hour'. Between November and February, the Sex Pistols played about fifteen concerts in and around London: at St Albans, Ravensbourne, North East London and City of London Polytechnics and Westfield College.

'It wasn't very exciting,' says Paul Cook. 'There would be all these hippy bands on. We just laughed at them. We'd just turn up and there'd be a few people standing round watching. It was good practice for us, and it kept us out of the way. Everyone knew to stay together at that stage because we were all nervous. John was pretty stiff but he'd have the verbals if there was any barracking. We'd get that at some of the colleges, but John handled himself so well on stage that he had everyone in stitches. We improved really well.'

'Around Halloween a band just turned up and played at St Albans Art School,' says Shanne Hasler, a foundation student who become one of the group's first fans. 'We didn't know who they were. We hardly even bothered watching them, but we were dancing because they were terrible. We thought they were a piss-take of a sixties group: afterwards one of them was crying because they were so terrible. They were very slow, very amateurish. It was peculiar because they had the same hairstyle as I had. That was how we got talking.

'I hated the world. I had a terrible childhood. I came from a middle-class background, brought up in Ware, Hertfordshire. I was illegitimate and I hated that thing of everyone trying to be nice and well-mannered, and behind the scenes, people weren't really. I didn't want to be part of it, so I ripped my clothes, scalped myself, pierced my ears. I was dyeing my hair; I used to get old grannies' corsets and things from thrift shops. I just wanted to be noticed, but I was very shy at the same time. It was my hatreds coming out with a sense of humour.

'John Lydon came up to me because he couldn't believe I dressed like that. He asked if I'd ever been in a shop called Sex; there was a girl called Jordan there who dressed like me. I went down there with a friend: we got taken out to lunch by Malcolm McLaren. He took us all around the shop and explained how all the clothes were made. Later I met Johnny: he took me back to Finsbury Park and put me on the train home. He was really well-mannered; nothing like the image.'

As the group appeared unheralded and unannounced, they picked up supporters from London's dormitory towns. The dreamscape of suburbia has a powerful and unrecognized place in England's pop culture. 'Bromley is perfect,' says Simon Barker. 'It's a twenty-minute train ride to London, so even when I was thirteen it was quite easy to get a day return to London. You'd walk down the King's Road and see it, then come back to Bromley. Living in the suburbs gives you a bigger and better perspective on things. If you go to London and see people wearing flares, you'll come home and you'll want your mum to sew triangles in your trousers and stuff: then you're more fashionable than anyone else in Bromley.'

The Sex Pistols' performance on 9 December plugged them into a network of teenage stylists, who would, more than anyone else, create a subcultural ambience around the group. 'It was Saturday night and there was nothing to do,' says Barker. 'We went to Ravensbourne College: there was a band on called Fogg, but we didn't go to see them. I got there and saw Malcolm: I'd seen him in the shop and I thought, "Wow, what's he doing here?" Then the Sex Pistols came on and I was the only person clapping. All the students were going mad, shouting and crap. The group were awful but it was visually really brilliant. You could tell what they were trying to do with the sound.

'We had this group of people. Steve Bailey and I went to school together, the Bromley Technical High. Billy Broad went to another school in Bromley: I met him through college. Siouxsie, we met going to a Roxy Music concert. We liked to be noticed: we were influenced by Bowie, Roxy and *Clockwork Orange* but we were doing it in our own way. Bowie had dyed his hair red, but we went into a hairdressers and saw all these tubes of crazy colour and went mad.

'When Bowie and Roxy came along that was a focus for me, the way I wanted to look and the ideas on style, but parents hated them. It was really brilliant. You started to realize that it wasn't just you and your friends, that it was more than just music and clothes: it was what films you saw and everything. It became a lifestyle. Roxy perpetuated that: seeing Eno have tea with Salvador Dali. Bowie had paved the way but they took it a little further: he didn't understand what he was doing half the time.'

'I always gravitated to the city,' says Siouxsie, 'I hated suburbia.' Born Susan Janet Ballion, she was brought up strange in Chislehurst: 'I hated the street we lived in, bordering on middle class. More puritanical than proper middle class in a way, almost spiteful. My sister was a Go-Go dancer; that was one of my routes for getting out. I used to go with her on her dates, to the Gilded Cage, the Trafalgar: I loved it, bright lights, total unreality. Some of the pubs would be half gay, half straight. It was Disco Tex and the Sex-O-Lettes, Bowie and Roxy; Barry White was huge.

'After school, I went to a secretarial college for a few months. I'd go round to the model agencies, and already I was into heavy make-up, bright colours. They said I was too skinny and too made up. They wanted busty and natural models. So I worked in pubs and clubs in the West End: the Valbonne. At night it was disgusting, full of Arabs, but during the day it was businessmen, pretty much just the local punters. I'd bring my record collection and dance to it on the floor by myself: Bowie, Brass Construction, "Hard Work" by John Handy.

'I'd been to the shop before I knew about the group: I'd bought some fishnet tights with gold and black tassels on them. I remember Vivienne, she looked gorgeous: she had blonde hair with purple pink lips. I was really attracted. Simon told me about the Pistols: the first time I saw them, there was just a few students wandering about and everyone kept their distance. It wasn't aggressive. They just played their music. Rotten didn't glare at anyone the way he did later. Glen was the loudest. I thought he was trying too hard. He was the one who'd be decked out in the Sex gear and it would look squeaky clean on him.'

The appearance of these oddly dressed teenagers at every concert gave the Sex Pistols a boost. Internally, they oscillated between arrogance and bickering, but the tide was beginning to turn. The group had mastered the basic level of competence, they had fanatical supporters, and a hustling manager. At Christmas, McLaren and Rhodes made an abortive trip to Paris to stimulate interest about the Sex Pistols in the Punk centre of Europe, but London was acquiring an allure of its own. 'I left everything I had in France at the beginning of 1976,' says Chrissie Hynde: 'I could smell something was happening in London. When I saw the Sex Pistols, I remember thinking London was the thing.'

The Sex Pistols' first wider impact was as the harbingers of a new sensibility, within a very specific London milieu. On 4 February,

Malcolm and Vivienne gave a talk about their clothes as part of a season called 'Fashion Forum – New Designers' at the Institute of Contemporary Arts (ICA); the group sat in the audience. Others on the bill included Swanky Modes, Howie and Miss Mouse. 'The idea at the time,' says Max, one of the ICA staff, 'was the whole fashion, art, anthropology, popular culture crossover which has become quite common since.'

'There had definitely been a feeling in London for the previous six months,' she adds. 'I remember noting two boys wearing leather jackets and bleached blond hair. Now that sounds so ordinary, but at the time people were divided into being gay and tough Rocker fifties revivalists, so the combination of the two was a real development. You'd be walking down the street and there'd be a thread that was emerging: straight trousers, not wearing jeans at all, or if you did, 501s. The whole idea of men having short hair again, of women dyeing theirs: that mixture of gay, Soul boy and Rocker styles.'

On 14 February the Sex Pistols played a 'Valentine's Ball' at Andrew Logan's studio in Butler's Wharf, appearing on a set that had been constructed out of materials from the children's department of the dismantled Biba superstore – closed in late 1975 – and some scenery from Derek Jarman's film *Sebastiane*. This was an important test for the group. It was a good opportunity for wider exposure – many people were there with cameras of all types – but this exposure had to be specific: because all concerned with Sex were so close to the Logan's world, they had to find a way forcibly to disassociate themselves from it.

Logan's parties were a gathering of the clans for a particular generation, too young to benefit from the full sixties explosion but old enough, by 1976, to have established themselves as London's leading artistic/Bohemian circle. They were as concerned with style outrage as McLaren and Westwood: indeed, they formed a significant proportion of Sex's clientele. Later that year, Peter York codified the group as 'Them' (after the 1950s science fiction film) just at the point when their influence was beginning to wane: 'An awful warning was sounded in November 1975 with the closing of big Biba.'

This was the generation that had dominated the King's Road since the early 1970s. Their aesthetic was a mixture of Pop Art and retro: Duggie Fields' fifties living room had been photographed for Bevis Hillier's *Austerity Binge*, but his large paintings unblinkingly created their own modern world. Andrew Logan made sculptures and installations out of broken mirrors: they were decorative, but they also had a real wit and warmth. They 'pushed the boat out for the new sensibility,' York wrote: 'Self-conscious, equivocal, eclectic, Post-Modern.'

These qualities were exactly what McLaren and Westwood had built on and had already reacted against – in the cast list for the 'Which side of the bed' T-shirt – as they searched out the generation gap (and what better way was there of creating one than turning on your peers?). Never mind that there had been real kindness, manners and talent in that milieu, these were qualities that would be swept away in a new, committed age. The 'Them' striving for effect would be superseded by a new shock aesthetic.

'All that crowd loved Vivienne and Malcolm for what they were doing,' says Simon Barker, 'but Vivienne and Malcolm held them in contempt. They didn't like that set-up, everyone patting each other on the back. Malcolm used that, got them to play at Andrew Logan's party, and then invited everyone. Logan was freaking out because he had this nice space and there were all these people. John was shut outside and finally he persuaded them to open the door and he was so mad: by the time he got in all the drink had gone. He said to Vivienne: "Where's our fucking drink?" He gave Vivienne the biggest black eye she ever had in her life.'

'Malcolm was really excited,' says Jordan. 'He rushed up to me saying, "The *NME* are here!" It's funny to think of it now. "The *NME* are actually *here*. Do something Jords!" He wanted to get them a bit of outrageous publicity. He said: "Take your clothes off, girl." "Naw, I'm not going to." "Go on, we haven't got much time." "I'll do it if John knows and we can do some sort of act." I jumped onstage and John ripped my clothes off. The photos were used everywhere.'

'John Lydon was on three trips of acid and god knows how many grams of speed,' says Nick Kent. 'It was the first time anyone had confronted me like that. It was "Nothing's happening at the *NME*, is it?" I agreed with him, but he had this look on his face which said: "I'm going to really shove you down; your time has come." It reminded me of when I used to stay in All Saints Road and I'd always have to walk past these black guys who would never touch me, but it was running a gauntlet. That's where he got it, from listening to Reggae and hanging round with those guys.

'Lydon had got so out of it. They were doing this version of "No Fun", kept doing it over and over. Lydon got it in his head to start

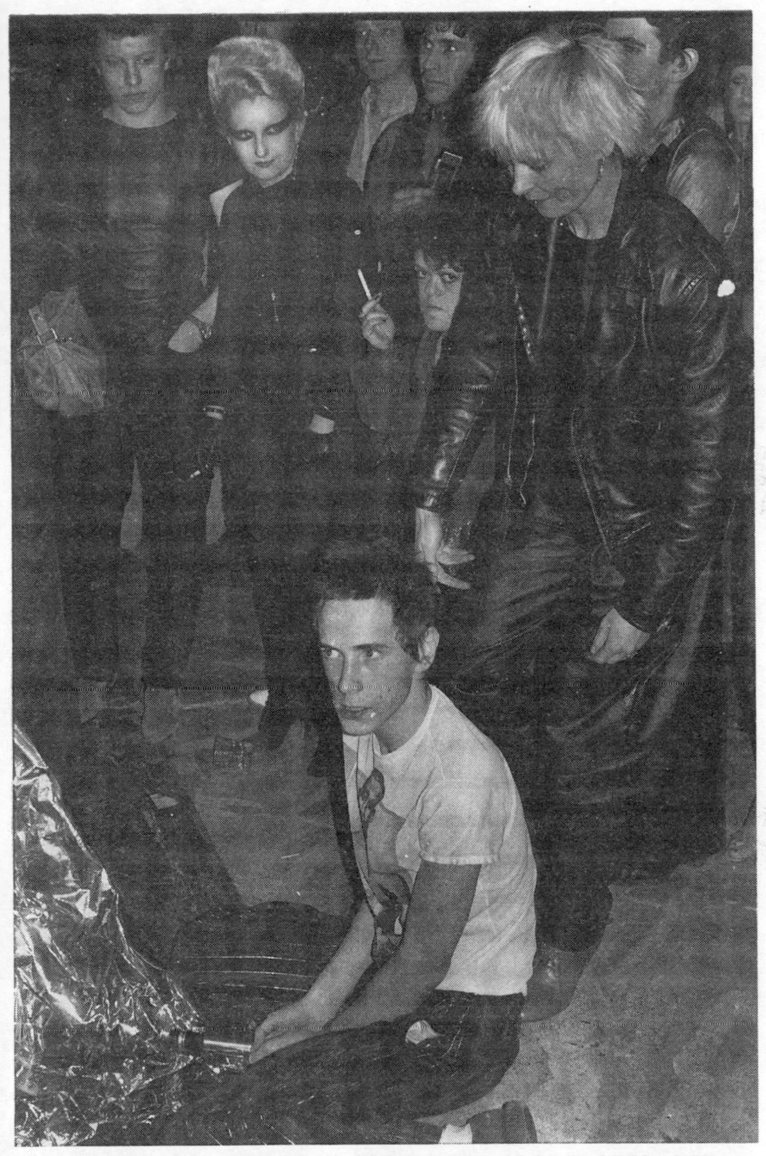

(left to right) Jordan, John Lydon, Helen Wallington-Lloyd and Vivienne Westwood, Butler's Wharf, 14 February 1976 (courtesy of Joseph Stevens) smashing the equipment: flying around with this mike stand, throwing things around. It wasn't aimed at the audience: they didn't matter. Lydon was in this state, it was obviously drug-induced but he clearly wanted to get completely out of himself. He wanted to go straight into the eye of the hurricane, and the group was backing him up.'

I'm interested in anything about revolt, disorder, chaos, especially activity that appears to have no meaning. It seems to me to be the road toward freedom.

Jim Morrison of the Doors: *Time* (24 January 1968)

To me, the most haunting, prophetic cry of the nineteenth century is Theophile Gautier's *'plutôt la barbarie que l'ennui!'* If we come to understand the sources of that perverse longing, of that itch for chaos, we will be nearer an understanding of our own state, and of the relations of our condition to the accusing ideal of the past.

George Steiner: *In Bluebeard's Castle* (1971)

It quickly became clear, as they moved out into the world, that the Sex Pistols were programmed for confrontation. McLaren was ambitious for this group: as his instrument, they would act out his fantasies of conflict and revenge on a decaying culture. From the very beginning, their attitude polarized their peers: soon the name of the game was for the group to stay on stage as long as they could, to ram their noise home. This taste for chaotically staged events would soon become an addiction.

No matter how antagonistic they were, the Sex Pistols still had to make some concessions to music-industry practice. Now that they had mastered the rudiment of performance, they would be tested in venues around the country. And as they gathered momentum, they would soon be encountering the press. McLaren began casting for the group's infrastructure.

First to be hired was Nils Stevenson, as the group's road manager, or, as he has claimed, the group's co-manager. A self-styled King's Road casanova, Nils was only a year or so older than the group, but wise beyond his years. Brought up in Dalston, he had lived on his wits and his appearance after quitting Barnet Art School in the early 1970s. 'I ended up working for Richard Buckle, ballet critic at the *Observer*. That was great fun: dress up in this mad purple Edwardian suit and high heels and open the door for Frederick Ashton, and pretend to be his boy.

'Alan Jones had taken me in the shop. I got to know Vivienne first: I used to hang around with her a lot because I used to really fancy her. Nothing ever came of it, because I got to know Malcolm as well: the two of them would come to my house in Barnes. They'd bring Chrissie Hynde along with them, and the four of us would go to Andrew Logan's parties. Eventually Malcolm asked me to come and work with him on the Sex Pistols.

'I'd met Steve and Paul in the pub already. They were being very nice to me and I just thought: "Why are they being so nice?" They were being nice because they were nice, and I wasn't used to it in the King's Road: people were all starfuckers in one way or another. These two cockney boys being pleasant made me feel odd. They didn't look anything, just a couple of football hooligans. So I thought I wanted to see the group first. I hadn't seen Rotten until I went to the Marquee: when I saw him I just knew I had to be involved.'

Two days before the Logan party, the Sex Pistols were booked in to support their Street Rock rivals Eddie and the Hot Rods in the Marquee, the heart of enemy territory. It was another test for the group, and they rose to the occasion magnificently. 'It was like Iggy when he played King's Cross,' Nils says. 'The band were all over the place. Rotten said: "I've always wanted to watch this group play." He just walked offstage with this long microphone lead and sat in the audience. He threw Jordan across the floor, threw chairs about: they smashed Eddie and the Hot Rods' equipment.'

Nils also brought in his older brother Ray, a photographer who had cut his teeth on the mid-sixties folk scene and emerging hippie superstars like Marc Bolan and David Bowie. Apart from a trickle of reportage shots, the group had already posed individually for Hipgnosis employee Peter Christopherson, but his concept of the group as psychotic rent-boys was unsuitable. With his rock experience, Ray Stevenson was perfect. 'There was also an element of me working for free, which obviously made me interesting.'

There was some urgency for photographs, as the Sex Pistols' kamikaze approach had immediate results. Six days after the group's first proper London date, they had a national publicity splash, when the *New Musical Express* printed a review of the Marquee concert. Staffer Neil Spencer had wandered in and, struck by the Sex Pistols' arrogance, talked to them backstage. The result was a review that, unusually, carried interview quotes. From a manager's point of view, it contained everything required: there was a picture, an arresting caption and best of all, it didn't mention the headliners, the Hot Rods.

Spencer caught the group's appeal in a series of slogans. Under the banner headline, 'Don't look over your shoulder but the Sex Pistols are coming,' coded references leapt out at the reader: 'Iggy and the Stooges'; 'moronic'; 'a musical experience with the emphasis on experience'. The picture of Johnny Rotten, all hair and staring eyes, said almost everything, but best of all was the quote at the end, supplied by Steve Jones: '"Actually we're not into music," one of the Pistols confided afterwards. Wot then? "We're into chaos".'

This was small beer: the main live reviews were of Emmylou Harris and Alice Cooper. Patti Smith might have been on the cover, but features inside concentrated on James Last, Gong, and Genesis. The Sex Pistols were a long way from a full page, but they had the first taste of publicity's power. 'I was sitting in a café in Kensington High Street,' says Glen Matlock: 'I had just bought the *NME* when I saw the review. It didn't mention the Hot Rods; it just said Sex Pistols. I thought "Whoooo – here we go!"'

The impact was immediate, and it was remarkable that the Sex Pistols got instant feedback, not only from the media, but from the next stage in the process: the media's consumers. The references in Spencer's review leapt out at those who, provoked by boredom, were attempting to tap the same archetype. 'I wished to annoy, to be exhibitionist, to be self-destructive,' says Howard Devoto. 'Listening to the Stooges' records, it sounded easy to do. Iggy's personality and the music attached to some unfortunate trait I had. In my mind it didn't get much beyond performing at college, but it had to be confrontational.'

Together with a fellow student at Bolton Institute of Technology, Peter McNeish, Howard Trafford (as he was then known) tried to carve some modern music out of the air. 'Howard was doing a video project and needed some electronic music,' says Peter. 'The next thing was, there was an advert on the college notice board which said "Wanted: people to form a group to do a version of 'Sister Ray'". I was well into Glam and I knew all the Velvet Underground albums back to front, so I gave him a ring.'

'We tried Eno's "The True Wheel",' says Howard, 'and "Your Pretty Face Has Gone To Hell". It came to nothing, but we stayed in touch, such that we were reading the *NME* in the bar together, when we read the first review of the Sex Pistols. It was the fact that they played a Stooges song, and said "We're not into music, we're into chaos".

Oooh, that's interesting, and off we went down to London.'

'I'd known Howard from Leeds Grammar School and Peter from Bolton,' says Richard Boon. 'Howard phoned up after the *NME* review, saying "Did you read this? I just called the *NME* and it seems that they're playing this weekend and I'm coming down with a friend, can you put us up?" I was very glad someone had organized something like that for me, so we all went down to Sex to get the details from this bemused character, Malcolm, who was very struck that these two people had turned up from Manchester wanting to see them. We went to see them in High Wycombe and Welwyn Garden City.'

'It was great,' says Shanne Hasler, 'High Wycombe was the first big fight.' According to McLaren, 'We were supporting Screaming Lord Sutch and the microphone which Rotten was using suddenly went dead and you couldn't hear what he was singing. He was aware of this and suddenly got incredibly embarrassed. He got hold of the microphone and smashed it to the ground, jumping on it. The PA guys and roadies swarmed on stage from every direction but Big Jim, Steve's mate, was there very pissed, and as they came on stage he was holding them back. The audience was wondering what was going on.'

'There were all these louts who really couldn't relate to the Sex Pistols at all,' says Boon. 'They were very disappointed: they were sitting along the front of the stage as Johnny crept along the front of the stage and tousled their hair. One of their mates from the back came running and picked Johnny up and threw him on the floor. The Sex Pistols' friends started piling in and – this was during "No Fun" – there was this throng of thrashing people.

'Johnny kept on singing and crawled out from this mêlée and crept back onstage and finished the number. It also ended the show: this terrible DJ came on and said, "Oh yer, in the *NME* they say we're not into music, we're into chaos and I think we know what they mean. Har har." We got chatting to them afterwards: Johnny was very twitchy and charismatic and off in a corner: not hostile, but totally wired. The lads were interested that two people had travelled two hundred miles to see them. It must have been the first time it had happened, so a link was established.'

'Rotten was certainly being very abusive and moody,' says Devoto, 'we thought they were fantastic: it was, we will go and do something like this in Manchester.' They returned with an increased sense of urgency: 'After we'd seen them, Howard and I were sleeping in the living room,' says Peter, 'as we were going off to sleep Howard was quizzing me, like if we got our band started, what was my commitment. Would I stick with it? Was it a hobby or was I into living the life? And I said: "Yeah, I'm into living the life".'

There was already an element of showbiz *schtick* in the Sex Pistols' performances but that confrontation was rooted in reality. While they might unite in the face of a common foe, relations within the group were very volatile. Cook and Jones were close to each other and with McLaren: Matlock tended to be left by himself and Lydon was barely tolerated by all the rest of them, including McLaren. 'Once everything was working,' says McLaren, 'John felt cool and one of the lads, but not before he told Jones he was a member of a Hell's Angels gang. It was in the Cambridge: everybody stopped themselves from laughing as they ordered another Pils.'

'What kept on winding me all the time in those early days was that I never felt part of the band,' says Lydon. 'I was very insecure. I got on OK with Steve and Paul, particularly Steve. He's hilarious; he'll never change. Although he's a tea leaf, Steve is one of the most honest people I ever met. If you ask him something outright, he cannot lie to you. Glen was a bit of a mummy's boy. I spent a lot of time with the friends I already had: John Grey, Sid, Wobble.

'But it would always be with Malcolm and Vivienne that, if they were going out after a gig, I wouldn't be invited. A lot of the fashionables, Little Nell and that lot, would always be around but I wasn't allowed to know them. I was never introduced and they always looked at me as scum. Until of course the Sex Pistols started to take off and then it was: "Oooooh Hiiii!" Jones and Cook knew all these people because Malcolm had taken them out all the time but not me. They wanted me to be this mystery figure that they could hide in the cupboard and spring out like a Jack-in-the-box. Close the lid when it's not needed anymore.'

A positive result of the High Wycombe fiasco was firm interest from Ron Watts, who booked them into his club at the end of March. Watts ran the 100 Club, a nondescript basement near the Centre-Point end of Oxford Street, which had a long and illustrious history as a jazz and folk venue. 'I don't know what we did right,' says Glen Matlock. 'Everyone was going apeshit after the Sutch gig and John totally denied that he had smashed anything: "Oh I didn't." But everybody had seen him do it. In the end both Sutch and Ron Watts just burst out laughing.

'At the first 100 Club, John was out of his box: he always used to have quite a bit to drink before we went on anyway, but this night I don't know what he was on, but it sounded abysmal. He was singing the right words but to the wrong songs so I just went up to him and said, "Look you're acting like a cunt now, you're doing it deliberately." This was in the middle of a song. He says, "Do you want to fight?" I said, "No, not particularly, I'm playing the bass you know, we're doing a gig." He said, "Come on." I said, "John just get on with it." So he just stormed off the stage.'

'John was just fed up with it and he started to leave,' says Nils Stevenson, 'he walked up the stairs and started waiting for a bus to go home. Malcolm saw, and shouted in front of everybody – mind you there wasn't many people there: that was part of the reason that John was fed up, because everybody there had seen them before. Malcolm shouted "You get back on that stage or you're over." John did: finished the set and even did a couple of encores.'

The group just avoided breaking up that night and their situation was still parlous that early spring. The Sex Pistols' earnings were purely from concerts (when they were paid at all). The shop had to underwrite any extra costs. The rehearsal rooms had already been paid for out of Sex and McLaren also had to pay for petrol and occasional hall hire. Equipment was no problem, as it was stolen. Likewise, living expenses for the group were no problem: there weren't any. All four members were either squatting or living at home: Paul Cook had a job, and the others were living off sporadic dole money.

'None of them had any money,' says Nils. 'Steve was really hustling about: I lived in Denmark Street on and off for nine months and Steve used to support us by stealing. We lived on baked beans: it was what you could nick easiest. Malcolm's priority was the shop. If the group happened, well fine, but it was all advertising for the shop. He wanted to quit the group many times, as did Rotten. In that period, Malcolm was all right because he could just get rid of the group and not lose money.'

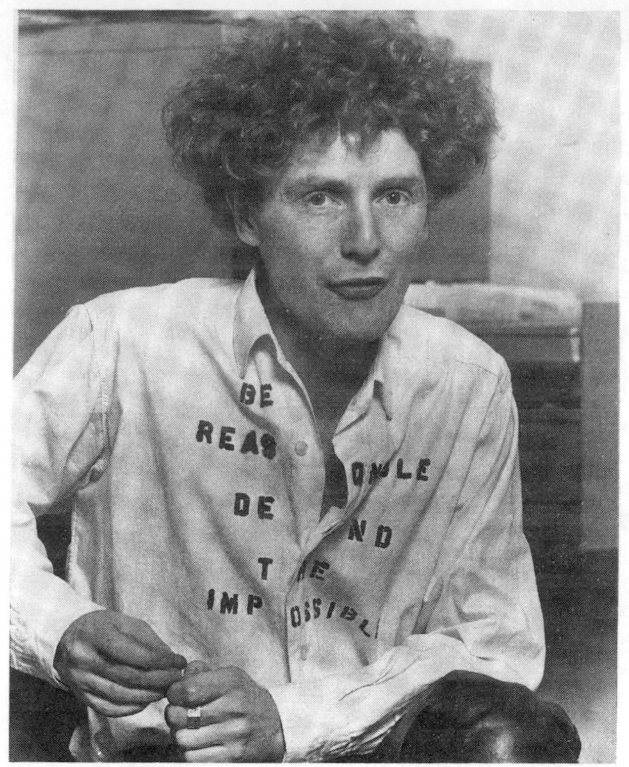

McLaren, couturier Situationniste, April 1976 (© Joe Stevens)

Right!
Here we go now
A sociology lecture
A bit of psychology
A bit of neurology
A bit of fuckology
No fun!

John Lydon, improvised intro to 'No Fun' (October 1976)

In April 1976, the Ramones' first album was released. Along with the Patti Smith Group, the Ramones were the vanguard of the CBGBs scene and their record delivered on the hype. 'It cost six thousand dollars to make,' says their manager Danny Fields. 'All the approaches had been thought out already, so the album was just making the statement. Like the picture on the cover, you put them in the alley behind CBGBs and make sure it's in focus. They had invented themselves, and they could have probably done the album for six hundred dollars.

The Ramones was a formalist's delight. The mix was simple but artful: a minimal drumbeat (both channels) provided a basic structure for clipped vocals (centre); a bass guitar carried both melody and minimal rhythmic variation (left) and the guitar sound (right) was merely a distorted, rhythmic texture. *The Ramones* now sounds laughably simple: at the time it was brutal and divisive. After hearing it, everything else sounded impossibly slow.

In the competition to lay claim to the seventies' 'teenage news', New York was the clear leader. 'London, the trend centre of last decade's mod rebellion, has been running a poor second this time around,' wrote Greg Shaw in April.

'In music and sheer pop energy, New York is far and away the new mecca, with at least half a dozen of the most important acts of the next few years emerging. The audience in Paris is the most advanced, and may provide a crucial breaking ground for the new wave of "street" bands that everyone seems to agree are the coming thing.'

In comparison, the Sex Pistols were nowhere: all they had by late April was one proper piece of press, about fifty hardcore fans, a couple of club bans, and an organized sequence of songs. After the 100 Club fiasco, the pressure was on. Once installed in Mininberg's flat in Bell Street, McLaren issued a stream of stamped Ray Stevenson pictures and a barrage of phone calls. He had no set plan, just a series of ideas and obsessions, one of which was to avoid an already hostile rock circuit. With Nils Stevenson, McLaren scouted the Soho of his youth to secure a suitable venue for a Sex Pistols happening. After a few false starts, Stevenson lighted on El Paradise.

It was a sleazy Brewer Street strip-club with, according to McLaren, 'a stage the size of a Punch-and-Judy show and a few fucking filthy seats. The whole place smelled like a shit-hole but we thought it looked good as it had this terrific entrance with these huge nude women in gilt frames. We argued with the Mafia and traced the owner which took us two weeks: when we found him he said we could take the place for a hundred pounds. So we did. We campaigned it by doing little leaflets and sticking them up and throwing them around at the 100 Club, Nashville and places.'

Early Sex Pistols events were never far removed from farce. 'It was typical,' says Jordan. 'Malcolm gets this club, doesn't let the people know what's really going on. There was no drinks licence at all. Michael Collins and I did this punch which looked like grapefruit juice but we'd laced it with tequila. It was really potent. People kept coming

Sex Pistols' first handbill, April 1976 (© Helen Wallington-Lloyd and Nils Stevenson, courtesy of Alan Jones)

back for more and then collapsing. Halfway throughout the evening these Maltese guys turn up to check that we're not selling alcohol because the licence would be lost, and they're not very well in the head people. Michael and I screamed out, "Drink the evidence" and about seven of us did.'

'You're in this room which is like the size of a good-sized living room,' says Jonh Ingham, 'and there's a stage which couldn't have been more than ten feet wide and four feet deep with a mirror behind it. All the early Pistols crowd were there: Jordan, Kate Crockford, Viv Albertine, and then others like the Arrows pop group. A strange assortment of people. Ray Stevenson walked in and started setting up umbrella strobes and I was getting really cynical at this point: "What is this shit? Who is this idiot with strobes?" And then they came on.

'John's got this red sweater on and it's ripped and his hair is up and he's wearing old Ben Franklin glasses. I liked him immediately. The group looked funny and I found myself laughing a lot: John was trying to be Johnny Rotten and it was like a comic book. It wasn't the madman you saw nine months later at all. He was going, "You'd better like what I'm doing otherwise I'm wasting my time." All the songs sounded similar but they were clearly different: some songs were clearly good and the others were over quickly.

'You couldn't intellectualize the band. You couldn't analyse it. I got the sense that something was going on here, that this was something to follow, a movement. It wasn't called Punk then: Malcolm was insisting we call it "New Wave", like the French cinema. Caroline Coon was there: it was the third time I'd met her and it was the first time we'd ever talked about it. She'd been following them: she knew all about it because she used to go to Sex all the time. She got very peeved that she was going to be scooped: unfortunately for her she had Ray Coleman to deal with.'

Coon and Ingham were working for rival rock weeklies: *Sounds* and *Melody Maker*, two of the trinity completed by the *New Musical Express*. Another weekly, *Record Mirror* had a stronger disco/dance base. The existence of these three weekly papers, which are principally dependent on music industry advertising, may be a publishing quirk but they have had an influence on English pop out of proportion to their sales. A survey of record buyers conducted by the British Market Research Bureau (BMRB) in 1975 revealed that only a tenth bought (as opposed to read) the *MM* or the *NME*.

The weeklies hold up a mirror to musicians, the music industry and the pop obsessives who comprise their readership. With over fifty broadsheet format pages to fill a week in 1976, the papers were copy-hungry, demanding an extremely high turnover both of subjects and of writers and thus opening a door to musicians and to young journalists in a hurry to make their names. Competition and deadline fever produced a media literacy among musicians unthinkable outside this hothouse atmosphere.

The music papers were and are overwhelmingly geared towards novelty. England is a small country with a centralized media and a strategic importance to the worldwide music industry that is disproportionate to its size. Not only is the English music industry a vigorous exporter, but it has also been an important springboard for the American music industry. England is very quick to respond to this novelty. The time between the first piece of press coverage – often in the weeklies – and an appearance on *Top Of The Pops*, seen by up to a fifth of the population, is sometimes only a matter of weeks.

From the perspective of the record companies that support it, the music press is most useful when writing about new performers: initiating or confirming 'artist development' decisions. There is a constant stream of weekly journalists who have become Artist and Repertoire (A&R) men or managers. This momentum works against analysis and investigation in favour of impressionism and enthusiasm. The weeklies excel in a time of fast movement, but if the music industry is static, the demanding weekly deadline becomes a crushing grind.

The first quarter of 1976 was not a good time for the music press. New groups like Moon, Cado Belle, Racing Cars were Pub-Rock journeymen all, a 'tasty' mixture of R&B, Rock and Soul, but hardly mythic. Of the three papers, only the *NME* showed a circulation gain, reflecting its alert coverage of the New York scene. Still stuck in the progressive era, the *MM* was only held afloat by its small-ads revenue. *Sounds* was desperate: a recent change in regime had lost it over a tenth of its circulation, which was down to about half that of its rivals: it was wide open.

'I felt like I had only two or three competitors,' says Ingham, then a *Sounds* staff writer. 'Nick Kent had had two or so years of being the best guy going and it was my turn next so I went out to grab it. That was my attitude. The only new group that I liked was the Doctors of Madness. They had a guitarist called Urban Blitz and Richard Strange had a good sense of what was going on. One day I opened up the *NME* and read Spencer's review of the Sex Pistols and the name alone was like, "My god, this is brilliant." Right away I wanted to see this band: I was loading so much imagery into this name.

'I didn't have a clue of how to go about finding them. A few weeks later there was a message for Vivienne Goldman from Malcolm McLaren: he wanted to talk to her about the Sex Pistols. He was calling all the papers trying to get people interested. I just leapt: "Vivienne, you are not going to like this band." So I called him back: it was about El Paradise. I saw them and wrote a quick review. Alan Lewis said, "What was this like?" I started talking. He said, "I want a feature." I said, "Wait a minute: I've only seen them once. I don't want to write it." He said, "Give it to me, I want a feature."

'So I called Malcolm and said that I wanted to do an interview. He named some coffee bar in the King's Road. I walk in and there's only

Malcolm there. I said, "Where's the band?" He said, "I just want to talk to you first." So we started talking, and he did the whole rap from top to bottom. I admired him immensely because he'd seen how to package that frustration I'd been feeling for a couple of years. What's popular now? Do the opposite. People were wearing flared trousers: wear straight legs. They got long hair: cut your hair short. People are taking drugs: the Sex Pistols don't take drugs.

'So I talked with Malcolm for an hour and a half. He's wearing this flesh nylon turtle-neck T-shirt and a leather jacket, and these drain-pipe Sex trousers. I was really impressed that someone would dress like that. I went back and Alan asked me about it; I said, "This is incredible." I'd made an arrangement to meet the Pistols: Malcolm said to come to Denmark Street at 12.30. I arrived there dead on 12.30 and he's standing there with Nils. "You're late. They've gone already." "What do you mean I'm late? You told me 12.30." "No, I told you 12 a.m. They hung around for twenty minutes and they split, they got tired waiting."

'So we made another appointment at 7.30. I show up at 7.20 and he's standing there with Paul, Steve and Glen. Malcolm says: "You're late again." "Come on," I said, "stop it. I'm wise to this one. You're winding me up," and he started laughing. I'd passed the first test. So we go to this awful pub, the Cambridge, and I'm talking to the three of them as we're walking along. We were talking about bands, and they were questioning me as much as I was questioning them.

'We get there and John's sitting in a corner with two girls, Tracey and Debbie. Steve and Paul are sat next to me: I'm getting on well with them. The interview starts and Malcolm is still talking, answering questions directed at them if it's relevant. John is still sitting there, very politely bored, and they are talking about him like he's not there. After a while I'm feeling a little intimidated but at the same time I think, "No 20-year-old kid is going to intimidate me," so finally I looked him right in the eye and said, "OK. I've heard it from everybody else: why are you doing it?"

'It was like one frame, moving imagery. He's very normal. Next frame, the kilowatts are on: there is no transition at all. He just ranted. I'm looking at Malcolm who has this nervous look on his face, "Don't look at me." Everyone is looking at me: what am I going to do? Half way into the second sentence I just cracked up laughing. Then, because he was going, "I hate hippies," and just glaring, I found myself saying: "I'm not a hippy: I just haven't shaved." That's when I got very impressed: the fact that I was defending myself to this kid and at the same time wondering, "Why am I defending myself?" I was sold.

'The feature was straightforward propaganda. A lot of this comes out of what Malcolm said the first time I met him, but, in a nutshell, when it is the first time you've got kids in five years saying "Move over" to groups like the Who, then what is the point of taking the musical analysis approach when clearly this group is going to appeal to fifteen-year-olds? No fifteen-year-old wants to read about that: they want to get excited about all the cool shit, like what clothes did they wear, what was the noise?'

Kev elucidates on Nottingham Forest graffiti: 'It used to be We Hate Pompey or We Hate Derby. Now it's just We Hate.'

Idris Walters: 'Is Northern Soul Dying on its Feet?'
***Street Life* (2 November 1975)**

Teenagers from London's Shepherd's Bush and Finsbury Park: 'We hate everything'.

Malcolm McLaren: Sex Pistols press handout (April 1976)

Today it is evident, to the point of tedium, that every new pop group or performer has a ready-made manifesto. In early 1976 however, the keywords were either a carefully constructed authenticity or a musician's humility. In direct contrast, the Sex Pistols were an explosion of meaning encoded into their clothes, their choice of songs, their action photos printed in stark black and white, their photocopied handbill and press release, and the inflammatory slogans that punctuated Ingham's feature.

McLaren's ambitions were extensive: according to Ingham, 'he wants a rumbling, anarchic, noisy anarchic rock scene, the likes of which haven't been seen since the mid-1960s'. The Sex Pistols existed 'for English rock to finally get to grips with the seventies'. In order to do so, that meant taking on the burden of pop theory and self-consciousness that had developed in England during the 1970s. They were 'so tuned into the present' that they had to take on the past.

In the mid-1960s, pop had been modernistic: revelling in an everlasting present, without reflection or theory. In the late 1960s, pop became 'progressive', an idea still implying some forward, unitary motion. Early seventies stars like Bowie and Roxy Music broke up this linear motion with a plethora of references taken from high art, literature and Hollywood kitsch. As the new generation, the Sex Pistols were a finely tuned mixture of the authentic and the constructed. The members of the group embodied an attitude into which McLaren fed a new set of references: late-sixties radical politics, sexual fetish material, pop history and the burgeoning discipline of youth sociology.

'I've always been involved with cults,' McLaren said in a May 1976 interview in *Street Life*. 'The subterranean influence on people and that's what fashion is predominantly about. The fashion market at the moment has separated the kids into all different factors. They can be fashionable either by going to the Portobello, or a chain like Take Six, because all commercialism feeds on diversification. I think now that kids have a hankering to part of a movement (like the Teddy Boys of the fifties and the Mods of the sixties). They want to associate with a movement that's hard and tough and in the open like the clothes we're selling here.'

This was very English. America had inaugurated both Rock journalism – with the work of Paul Williams in *Crawdaddy* and Robert Christgau in the *Village Voice* – and the 'new journalism' of Tom Wolfe and Hunter Thompson. If new journalism took you there, and 'there' was pop for a while, then Rock journalism took pop phenomena seriously, teasing out their meaning and importance in language that was no less high-flown. By the mid-1970s, these two approaches were reaching stasis in mainstream magazies like *Rolling Stone*, where pop music came to be seen as an entity on its own, disconnected from the rest of society.

From the start, English pop had to be interpreted: a commercial and social process to be mastered before the music itself could have its effect. Pop was alien, the spearhead of an American, commercial construct summarized by Mark Abrams' *The Teenage Consumer*, whose demographic argument is partly echoed by Colin MacInnes's February 1958 article about 'Pop Songs and Teenagers'. MacInnes's favourite subjects were outsiders, such as teens then were: a subterranean culture whose rituals were impenetrable to all adults.

As McLaren had so closely observed in his tour through the West End Boys, the Teds, the Rockers and now the lost seventies generation, America's pop products, planned for rapid obsolescence, underwent a transformation when they arrived in England. Grafted onto older methods of social organization like the multiple codes of the homosexual world and the territorial flash of working-class gangs, pop styles became badges of pride and tribe, not so much something to wear for a season but a way of life, a way to construct an identity out of an often unforgiving, static class system.

Early accounts of British pop culture concentrated on 'the pop process'. The ways in which the products of this process were used were rarely detailed, let alone woven into a coherent theory. George Melly's sharp mixture of journalism and analysis of the commercial cycles that turn potential *Revolt into Style* located the origin of the English pop sensibility in the ICA Group and its motor in the country's class resentment. With its extended sections on pop design, literature, film, TV and radio, *Revolt into Style* captured the beginning of pop's cross-media integration in England.

The next phase was to interpret Style as Revolt. From the 1960s on, English pop came loaded with meanings and uses that were political, aesthetic and social and which, once interpreted, were fed back into pop. In 1964, Charles Hamblett and Jane Deverson published a rare piece of teenager 'vox pop' material. *Generation X* was pegged to the recent riots between Mods and Rockers which had begun at Clacton on the Easter Bank Holiday and which, just like the 'Rock Around the Clock' disturbances in 1956, had been fanned by some hyped news reporting.

Teenagers had read accounts of the 'riot' and, stimulated by official disapproval, had initiated several 'copycat' events. In *Generation X* they replay the roles required of them in phrases taken from the media: 'Yes, I am a Mod and I was at Margate. It was great – the beach was like a battlefield. It was like we were taking over the country.' Clipped directly from the book, this paragraph found its way onto an early Clash handbill in October 1976.

In 1972, Stanley Cohen argued that youth subcultures like Teds and Mods are announced to the world through media-generated 'moral panics', usually about violence and drugs. Using the Mods and Rockers 'battles' as a test case, Cohen drew up, in *Folk Devils and Moral Panics*, an archetypal cycle for the emergence of youth cultures in Britain: the 'lost' origin of a cult in an individual action or costume, the formation of a group identity, the increasing visibility of this group, and its eventual revelation to the country, in pejorative and simplistic terms, through the media.

In these announcements, the media engages in a self-fulfilling prophecy: more people will be attracted to the cult, which they then join on the titillating terms outlined by the news reports. The cycle then intensifies. Under this overall definition, no youth culture was 'real'; all cults were heavily mediated by the time they came to the public's attention. Again, academics were only schematizing what was occurring in popular culture itself. (Again, this theory, clipped from the book, found its way onto a Clash artwork, this time for their first single, 'White Riot'.)

During 1973, Pete Townshend worked on what would be his second 'thematic' album, *Quadrophenia*: the plot line was based on the Who's own 1964 Mod past. The Who had always been the most self-conscious and media-aware of pop groups, as well as one of the most violent. This hit record mixed pop history with the contemporary urban experience of recession. At the same time, the brutal prose of Mick Norman's 'Guardian Angels' series and Richard Allen's 'Skinhead' books reflected deviant youth cults, real and imaginary, back at the very people who were likely to become their members.

Allen's books in particular were prime examples of the process described by *Folk Devils and Moral Panics*. 'Despite his outspoken condemnations of the news media,' writes Stuart Home, 'Allen's books serve as an encouragement for youth to enter the media's discourse on style.' Apart from their right-wing bias, the 'Skinhead' books simultaneously condemned and glorified violence, in what was becoming the true tabloid style. Most importantly, the climaxes of the books were always marked by sensational media reports. The media had colonized all areas of cultural and subcultural life by the early seventies.

'When we first met John Lydon in the Roebuck,' says Paul Cook, 'I remember saying to him how nothing was happening in music and how this whole youth movement needed something to get them going again. After the Skinheads, Teds and Mods, everything had been in a bit of a lull since 1970 and it was now 1975. Five years had passed.' None of the Sex Pistols was an intellectual (neither was McLaren for that matter), but they didn't have to be: they were already immersed in this media/youth-culture discourse and in the history of pop itself.

Guided by McLaren, the band were easily capable of parroting this discourse when it came to their turn to deal with the media. Just as they mirrored the media – in their songs, in their interviews and in their clothes – so the media were to mirror the Sex Pistols, in an intense symbiosis that very quickly led to distortion, but which set the style for the future decade. 'The media was our helper and our lover and that in

Vivienne Westwood and Sid Vicious at the Nashville, 23 April 1976 (© Kate Simon)

effect was the Sex Pistols' success,' wrote Malcolm McLaren and Jamie Reid in a final manifesto during the dying days of the group, 'as today to control our media is to have the power of government, God or both.'

McLaren had interviewed well for the job of creating the Sex Pistols' all-important first piece of press: Jonh Ingham and *Sounds* had nothing to lose, and all to gain, by constructing the Sex Pistols with a knowing innocence. Ingham was not fifteen, neither were many of his readers, but by projecting himself and the Sex Pistols for that age group he created a classic self-fulfilling prophecy. He cast himself as a fan and the group as the spearhead of a new generation, which they weren't necessarily at that point. But, given the intimate relationship between pop culture and the media, such an outcome was now more likely.

Two days after the *Sounds* interview came out, the Sex Pistols played their second date at the Nashville. 'That's when they started getting good,' says Nils. 'They weren't playing very sophisticated music, were they? It was just a matter of keeping in time with each other.' Though the group now had some sense of discipline, and better sound, thanks to the addition of the experienced Dave Goodman on the PA, they found that competence by itself does not excite.

This event was high profile and the pub was full of future members of Punk Rock groups such as Tony James, Mick Jones, Adam Ant, Vic Godard and Dave Vanian, as well as journalists and photographers

Malcolm McLaren at the Nashville, 23 April 1976 (© Kate Simon)

such as Kate Simon and Joe Stevens. Neither the group's performance nor the audience were particularly inspired; they were failing to live up to the expectations aroused by Ingham's hyperbole. 'I'm standing at the back and watching them,' he says. 'I knew some of the songs, like "No Feelings" and "I'm Not Your Stepping Stone". They're not being very good. It was in the middle of "Pretty Vacant". All of a sudden Vivienne is slapping this girl's face. She's right in the front row slapping this girl: her boyfriend has been standing six feet away and he just comes barrelling over and grabs Vivienne and starts to hit her. I don't know whether Malcolm had watched the whole thing, or whether he just saw some guy trying to bash up his girl, but the next thing you saw was a clear image of this guy ten feet across the front of the stage with Malcolm a foot behind him with his fist flying out – a classic photograph.

'John, with this look of glee, immediately dived off the front of the stage and started throwing punches. Steve came forward and started trying to pull them apart. It was complete chaos but they went on to finish. Vivienne said to Caroline afterwards that she was bored, the Sex Pistols were boring, she decided to liven things up. So she slapped this girl for no reason, just did it. It was extremely electrifying. Up until that point it was just another date.'

Joe Stevens and Kate Simon snapped furiously. Simon captured the sequence leading up to the group jumping off stage but Stevens got the group composition. Violence was sexy then, it was visible in the way that Sid Vicious, now a Sex Pistols follower, licked his lips as the fight began, or in Lydon's look of glee caught by Stevens' lens. It was also newsworthy: all three music papers ran coverage of the event, while the *NME* ran it as a mini-feature, together with an excited piece of writing by future Pet Shop Boy, Neil Tennant. 'So how do the Pistols create their atmosphere when their music has failed? By beating up a member of their audience. How else?'

'That fight at the Nashville: that's when all the publicity got hold of it and the violence started creeping in,' says Paul Cook. 'I don't know what caused that, except that I think everybody was ready to go and we were the catalyst. People just wanted to go mad, but we didn't instigate it.' The die was cast. 'Each successive pop explosion has come roaring out of the clubs in which it was born like an angry young bull,' wrote George Melly in his 1969 book *Revolt into Style*, and here were the Sex Pistols fulfilling the first criterion. For they were nothing if not ambitious, with a moral certainty that was so right for the times: 'I hate shit,' says Johnny Rotten in Ingham's feature, 'I hate pub bands. I want to change it so there are Rock bands like us.'

John Lydon in Soho, April 1976 (© Ray Stevenson)

13

I got you in my camera
I got you in my camera
A second of your life, ruined for life
You wanna ruin me in your magazine
You wanna cover us in margarine
Now is the time, you got the time
To realize, to have real eyes.

John Lydon for the Sex Pistols: 'I Wanna Be Me' (1976)

Punk was out of the starting blocks, and, just as the Ramones' first album accelerated a generation of English musicians, the competition to form Punk Rock groups intensified. During the spring of 1976, McLaren and Bernie Rhodes were actively trying to fashion groups out of the musicians that had ebbed in and out of London SS. Understanding that the Sex Pistols would be more impressive if they could appear as the spearhead of a new generation, McLaren embarked on a policy of nurturing an environment where people make things happen.

'The 101'ers were doing well,' says Joe Strummer about his first group, named after their squat at 101 Walterton Terrace. Nurtured by a resident spot at their local pub, the Chippenham, and the surrounding squat community, the 101'ers had just released their first single, a fast, intense Pub Rocker called 'Keys to your Heart'. 'We were working very hard: we did twelve gigs in fourteen days in places like Sheffield, and it was up and down every day, but we were invisible.

'In April the Sex Pistols played the Nashville for the first time, supporting us. I walked out onstage while they were doing their soundcheck and I heard Malcolm going to John, "Do you want those kind of shoes that Steve's got or the kind that Paul's got? What sort of sweater do you want?" And I thought, "Blimey they've got a manager, and he's offering them clothes!" The rest of my group didn't think much of all this, but I sat out in the audience. Lydon was really thin: he pulled out his snot rag and blew into it and he went, "If you hadn't guessed already, we're the Sex Pistols," and they blasted into "Substitute".

'They did "Steppin' Stone" which we did but they were light years ahead of us. The difference was, we played "Route 66" to the drunks at the bar, going "Please like us". But here was this quartet who were standing there going, "We don't give a toss what you think, you pricks, this is what we like to play and this is the way we're gonna play it." They were from another century, it took my head off. They honestly didn't give a shit. The audience were shocked.

'After that I started going down to Tuesday nights at the 100 Club. That's when Bernie Rhodes came up to me and said, "Give me your number, I want to call you about something." We had some dates supporting Kilburn and the High Roads but I split the group up. They thought I was mad. They were probably right, but it was a case of jump that side of the fence or you're on the other side. Remember the T-shirt that Bernie and Malcolm designed, "Which side of the bed"? It was so clear.'

'Strummer came rushing up to me in the Red Cow: "Have I done the right thing?",' says Roger Armstrong. ' "What?" "I've left the 101'ers." He was in tow with Mick Jones and Bernie, and he started on a whole rant about how this was the future. I knew Bernie from the great King's Road triumvirate. Malcolm, Bernie and Andy Czezowski: the tailor, the rabbi and the accountant. It was a funny alliance: they all got their band out of it.'

Solidarity, however, was not the main spur. Both the Ramones and the Sex Pistols had already shown the way: it was possible to make a loud noise, express hostility, learn in public and get attention. This temporary advantage had to be exploited quickly: the result was a frantic jockeying for position, like a game of musical chairs.

'I saw Bernie and Malcolm as competitors,' says Chrissie Hynde, 'when they could have been working together. Everything that Bernie did seemed like a pale version of what Malcolm was doing with the Sex Pistols. For instance, when I finally came back from France, I was going to do something with Mick Jones. Mick phoned me up one day and said, "I want you to talk to Bernie who's going to manage us." "I'm in a band with *you*, I don't want to talk to this other guy." He goes, "Alright, I'll try to explain. You won't sing at all, you'll just play the guitar and be in the background. The band's going to be called School Girls Underwear." I thought, "I'm going to be in a band called School Girls Underwear, I'm *sure*."

'I had a meeting with Malcolm over some won ton soup. The Sex Pistols were going and he wanted another band. What Malcolm did at this point was he would meet people at parties who were personalities and put them together. He said he'd met this great kid drummer called Chris Miller, who was Rat Scabies by now, and he had these other people. So we went to meet this guy coming off the train from Hemel Hempstead, and it was David Zero, who later changed his name to Dave Vanian: he looked like Alice Cooper.

'Later on we went to some retro clothing store in Covent Garden and there was another David who they'd tried out for the Sex Pistols. He didn't want to be in a band at all, but Malcolm dragged him into it because he thought he had the right personality. That was very Malcolm: he didn't care about the music at all, he was just interested in personalities. So we had the black David and the white one: they were the singers. I was supposed to play guitar, not sing at all. We were to be called the Masters of the Backside.'

London SS had finally split two ways: guitarist Bryan James teamed up with drummer Chris Miller, now named Rat Scabies after a bout of the disease. Miller's old Croydon friend Ray Burns was brought in on guitar. He was a working-class drop-out whose manic behaviour masked real sensitivity. 'Tony James was the bass player,' says Burns, 'they gave him the elbow because he was too interested in his clothes, so I got the job. Then they chopped my hair off. I didn't mind: I was like a hippy with teeth. That was London SS: when Chrissie Hynde joined it became Mike Hunt's Honourable Discharge.

'Malcolm came and put us in rehearsal for two days and then came down with Helen and Rotten and all those people, and they sat down watching us, laughing, and told us to fuck off. No commercial possibilities. Malcolm was good to us: he gave us money and talked sense. Chrissie left: we started playing ourselves. Brian and Rat had met Vanian at the Nashville – they thought he looked good. The name "The Damned" was Brian's idea. We were damned really: everything that could go wrong did.'

Within weeks of forming, the Damned were given rehearsal space by John Krivine and Andy Czezowski and were being groomed as Sex competitors. Meanwhile, Bernard Rhodes was working on the other half of London SS. 'One morning I was signing on,' says Joe Strummer, 'and there were these people staring at me on the bench. I was thinking there was going to be a ruck. It was Paul Simonon, Mick Jones and Viv Albertine: these were the weeks that Bernie had pulled Mick and Paul out of London SS and put them together. If they'd have come up to me, I'd probably have swung at one of them. Get it in first: Lisson Grove was the worst place on earth.

'By that time Bernie had fallen out with Malcolm over the swastika, because Bernie's mother was a refugee from Europe. Bernie called me and I agreed to meet him and Keith Levene. We drove over to Shepherd's Bush to the squat where Paul and Mick and Viv had been staying – that's why they'd been staring at me – and we put the group together there and then. For about a week we were the Psychotic Negatives, then we were the Weak Heartdrops, after a Big Youth lyric, then Paul thought of the name the Clash.'

The Sex Pistols had had great publicity but it worked both ways. After the reports of violence, doors were closing in their faces: they were banned now from the Marquee and the Nashville, and El Paradise had proved too unstable as a regular venue. The day that the *NME* piece about the Nashville fight came out, the group played a club called the Babalu halfway up the Finchley Road: 'That was the best concert we ever did,' says Glen Matlock: 'there were about thirteen people there, including us.'

McLaren and Helen Mininberg collected what press material the group had and wrapped it with an A3 poster, two photos printed at the Labour Party Press at Peckham Rye by McLaren's old friend Jamie Reid, who had been brought into the fold for his printing expertise. Armed with this pack, McLaren approached booking agencies, but without success. McLaren then decided to ask John Curd, a bearish man who promoted concerts at the Roundhouse, if the Sex Pistols could be added to the forthcoming Ramones bill. Malcolm and Nils went to Curd's home, where they were thrown bodily down the stairs.

'That was the incident that made McLaren want to go totally outside the music industry,' says Jonh Ingham. 'His idea was to create your own, total alternative to what was going on in the business at that time. Malcolm was trying to get his band into situations. One of his things was, "You have to pay to see them, because then you're making an active effort." That was the opposite to what the Pub Rockers were thinking, which was get your band in front of any audience: what he was doing was creating an audience that was specifically *for* the band.'

During May, the group were set a new challenge: a tour of the north of England. 'That was ridiculous,' says Nils Stevenson. 'Malcolm would give us just about enough money to get there, then you have to fend for yourself. Steve would steal chocolate bars to eat. You had to make sure you got your money as most people didn't want to pay after seeing the group. Frightening times playing these really straight places. I'm totally non-aggressive, but my adrenalin was so whacked up that I'd be up on stage kicking punters off.

'In Barnsley, we played this awful place out in the sticks, just this pub in the middle of nowhere. The place filled up and things got a bit hairy, so I made the landlord call the police, who escorted us out. In Hull things got very nasty, we had to high-tail it out of there. Rotten would get very lippy and put the crowd down, but it wasn't too bad. It was just that the look of the band and their lack of professionalism used to incense these people. They wanted a hippy group with long hair but these kids really pissed them off.

'We'd have the cheapest, cheapest vans: we had one to go to Scarborough that wouldn't go up hills, so we had to look at the Ordnance Survey map. Glen worked out this ridiculous route, all the way round everywhere, but it was flat so we could get to the venue. You'd tell Malcolm about all these problems when you got home and he'd be very apologetic, but the same thing would happen again the next week.

'There were ridiculous arguments going on in the van. You can imagine how petty John could be, depending on his mood. Rotten would always insist on going in the comfy seat: "I'm the star, fuck off." It could be quite uncomfortable with all four of them together, but it was all superficial: as soon as they were on their own everyone would be as sweet as a nut. Rotten would generally want the company of everybody but would be too insecure and would put on this weird front all the time and wander off by himself, watching people to see if they had noticed.'

'It was vile, horrible, a nightmare,' says John Lydon. 'No chance to relax, nothing, nylon sheets. What you can never get in your book is the utter, total boredom of being in a band.'

'It was like little boys,' says Glen Matlock. 'Imagine being in a van with Rotten. And the places! We were playing in Whitby and they kept telling us to turn it down. In the end we were just larking about pretending to mime. This bloke comes up and says: "It's no good lads. Look we'll pay you what you're due, but you can't hear the bingo in the other room." We'd played for about 15 minutes.'

The pattern was the same in or outside London: rejection by most people and instant identification on the part of a tiny but significant minority. 'My boyfriend then, Peter Lloyd and I lived in Ferryhill just outside Durham,' says Pauline Murray of Penetration, 'but we'd go to see everything in Newcastle. We'd seen pictures of the Sex Pistols looking great. We were real provincial fans. When we eventually got to London, and saw Johnny Rotten on a bus, we followed him into this shop: the jukebox had songs like "Little Johnny Jewel" and Jonathan Richman, which we hadn't heard.

'In Newcastle, you could watch things as they came along, track it all through – T. Rex and Roxy Music, Mott the Hoople, Hawkwind, Cockney Rebel and then nothing for a long time. We started to go and see Doctors of Madness, who were a real record-company type band: then we saw the Sex Pistols in Northallerton, in this tiny club. A short while later they played with the Doctors of Madness in Middlesbrough and they wiped them out. They wiped a lot of bands out. It sounds a cliché now but I saw it happen. All those bands lost their confidence when the Sex Pistols came along.'

'My life changed the moment that I saw the Sex Pistols,' says Howard Devoto. 'I immediately got caught up in trying to make things happen. Suddenly there was a direction, something I passionately wanted to be involved in. It was amazingly heady. I'd said to Malcolm, "Do you want to come and play at my college?" and he said, "If you can set it up, we'll do it." I tried to persuade the Students' Union to put them on, but they wouldn't go for it. Not because of their reputation, just that they had never heard of them. There was still very little in the press.'

Howard and Peter had already formed their own Sex-Pistols type group and had changed their identities to seal this pact of transformation. Instead of McNeish, there was Shelley, the name Peter would have had if he was a girl. Howard Trafford became Devoto. The group name, the Buzzcocks, came from a February *Time Out* review of *Rock Follies* which ends, 'get a buzz, cock'. The next thing was to play out, and promoting a Sex Pistols' concert was the easiest way: 'Someone told me about this little hall above the Free Trade Hall,' says Devoto, 'I got it for the fourth of June, and meanwhile we were planning to play ourselves.'

'The other two bottled out,' says Shelley, 'so we got this band, the Mandala Band, to play with the Pistols. We were organizing this thing and we put an ad in the *New Manchester Review* for a drummer and bass player. On the Friday afternoon we arrived at the Lesser Free Trade Hall and Howard said to me, within earshot of Malcolm, that a bass guitarist had called him, and they were calling back. As the doors were getting ready to open, I was in the box office taking the money: Malcolm was in the street saying to people, "Come on in, there's a great band from London, you know, they're going to be famous. Roll up! Roll up!"

'There was this guy standing on the steps, saying he was waiting for somebody, he probably said he was waiting for a guitarist. So Malcolm said: "Oh, you're a bass guitarist?" "Yeah." Malcolm said: "Oh, they're in here," and brought him inside to the box office and said to me, "Here's your bass guitarist." And there was the bemused Steve Diggle, with collar-length hair. It was a real Brian Rix farce. So I said, "Now you're here, come and see this group." And he liked it, and so we said, "We've got a band, we're not too dissimilar," and we made arrangements.'

Advertised by a four-side, folded A4 leaflet, the Manchester concert was a good opportunity to establish the Sex Pistols outside London, since Manchester is England's third largest city and the gateway to the North and North West. The concert was poorly attended but, again, the seventy or so people there included future performers and media names, – such as Peter Hook and Bernard Sumner of Joy Division/New Order, Morrissey, Factory's Tony Wilson – who would lay the foundations for Manchester's future musical preeminence.

'That first appearance was quite difficult,' says Morrissey; 'There weren't any instructions. Being northern, we didn't know how to react: people were very rigid. There was a support group from Blackburn, and their hair swept off the stage. People were unwilling to respond to the Sex Pistols; the audience was very slim. It was a front-parlour affair. The Sex Pistols still had slightly capped sleeves and flares were not entirely taboo at that point: their jeans were somewhere in the middle. I liked them, but they seemed like a clued-in singer and three patched musicians.'

'At that time, I'd never known what a good audience was,' says John Lydon, 'but when an audience behaves badly to you, it does tend to make your work better.' Bolstered by their rejections, the Sex Pistols were building up speed. 'There was a sudden point when I realized how good they were,' says Ray Stevenson. 'It was at the 100 Club: that telepathy and tension, where John would be slagging off the audience, Steve and Paul would be doing something, and they would just go into a number at the perfect moment. John's control. I was seeing them as amateurs, and to imagine this bozo kid from Finsbury Park with no schooling was phenomenal.'

'They were having such fun,' says Caroline Coon; 'Steve told me he wanted to play guitar like Jimi Hendrix. Chris Spedding gave them a confidence they hadn't had: after he produced their first demo tape he said they had the most expressive guitar lines he'd heard in two decades of working in Rock'n'Roll. Steve was a typically underprivileged child, but he was the musician in the Sex Pistols. Johnny was like a young Rimbaud: thoughtful, angry, beautiful. I don't think he ever realized how beautiful he was.'

Tapes exist of both the Manchester concert and a performance at the 100 Club on the 29th of the month. Manchester is a quantum leap from the Nashville in April, but the 100 Club tape is something else. Here the Sex Pistols are wound up to a pitch of impossible tautness: they swoop and drive through their set of fifteen songs (more than half of all they would ever play in their brief life). They begin with an improvisation, 'Flowers of Romance', loosely based on Mud's 'Dynamite', over which Lydon chants and rants. Phrases leap out of the aural streetfight: 'True love and peace', 'Jah Rastafari'.

The songs are a series of musical manifestos: each sets up a statement which is only partially resolved at the song's end. They pass in a strip of rough harmonies from Glen, sounds of aerial battle from Steve Jones's guitar, and a rhythm section that never lets up. Lydon is mesmerizing: taunting both McLaren – 'you always hide when I want money from you' – and his audience of peers. Just after 'Flowers of Romance', Jones breaks a string but Lydon keeps the crowd entertained with a non-stop stream of squeals, sarcasm and invective, delivered in a bewildering variety of voices.

In the intimate setting of the 100 Club, the group could relax enough to take risks with their material and their performances. There they began to master their environment, using the acoustics of the small club to experiment with overload, feedback and distortion. Electric amplification had provided much of the excitement of early Rock'n' Roll: pushing their equipment to the limit – even further than the early Who – the Sex Pistols twisted their limited repertoire into a noise as futuristic as their rhetoric.

'Electricity come from other planets,' quipped Lou Reed in a song released that summer. In return, the audience took the electricity of the group's performances to develop a sympathetic new style. Apart from the gelled, spiky, electric-shock hairstyle, there was 'gobbing', the habit of spitting which began as a response to Lydon's constant expulsion of phlegm over the audience, and pogoing, the frozen leap, as though on a pogo stick, to gain a view: an action born out of necessity in the club's packed space.

But, just as the Sex Pistols inspired loyalty, then they deliberately fostered division. There were still fathers to be killed, people to be forcibly alienated. New material like 'I Wanna Be Me' was a diatribe against a 'typewriter god' suspiciously like Nick Kent. The lyric was quickly accompanied by a physical attack. 'It was a week after seeing the Rolling Stones in Paris,' says Kent, 'where somebody pulled a gun on Mick Jagger backstage. There was a lot of violence in the air. I went over to Malcolm and for the first time ever he was quite cold. I just thought: "Well, he's in a bad mood", and sloped off to the very back of the 100 Club where I waited for the group to perform. I was sitting there, fairly drugged-out: my reactions to what did occur were very slow. I started noticing that this guy would, whenever he walked past, kick me in the shins. At first it seemed like a clumsy mistake: the second time, this was on purpose.

'I knew his name was Sid, because at the final night of the Stones at Earl's Court, all the future hierarchy were gathered in their Sunday best to get in and were unable to. He was obviously wearing his father's old clothes, he had the bog-brush hair and he looked really lairy. It was quite interesting to see that guy with the Richard Hell hair: Bryan James and Chrissie pointed Sid out to me. They'd tried him out as a singer. So he was starting to harass me and then he disappeared for a while. Then I noticed he was following Lydon around: everywhere Lydon went, he would go.

'Lydon by that point was the Don: he was top cat. In the classic star tradition, he didn't take the stage with the other three members: he would wait until they had turned up. I remember seeing Malcolm, Lydon and Sid, and Lydon was pointing my way. My mind was like a stranger: I remember this really malevolent look on all three. It all happens very quickly: Lydon goes on stage, and Sid decides to stand directly in front of me. I tapped him on the shoulder and I said, very careful: "Could you move over?"

'Sid immediately pulled this chain out. He made some remark which he thought was insulting like: "I don't like your trousers." The guy next to me immediately makes a motion towards Vicious and then pulls his knife out and he really wants to cut my face. Years later I find his name is Wobble. This was a real speed freak, and this is when it got very unhealthy. I remember putting my hands up and not moving a muscle, and then Vicious tapped him on the shoulder and he disappeared immediately. It was all set up: Vicious then had a clear aim and got me with the bike chain.'

'I used to get violent on a few occasions,' says Wobble. 'The one with Nick Kent was not one of those. Kent was with some geezer who demanded that we step aside, they couldn't see the band. I said "Fuck off", which was pretty standard. Sid wasn't a rucker, but he lashed him with a chain and then I had a go, but we were just mucking about. What I didn't know then was if you set yourself up as a hard man someone will come looking for you who's harder than you are.'

'It wasn't painful,' says Nick Kent: 'The main thing was that it drew a lot of blood, which was just pouring down my face and my chest. Ron Watts grabbed Sid off me. All those guys there like Mick Jones didn't do a fucking thing. I was just trying to get the hell out of there – it had been years since I had been involved in any violence – and Vivienne comes up and says: "Oh God, that guy's a psychopath. He'll never be at one of our concerts again, I promise that. It's not our fault, we're so sorry."

'I saw Vivienne a month after that; the Ramones were playing and guess who she was with? With Sid, pogoing around. She came up to me and started to give me this: "You can't handle violence; you're just a weed." I was completely dazed: what is this macho shit? Lydon then came up to me and said: "What's all this shit you're saying about us? You're trying to get us banned, aren't you?" "The people that were telling you this aren't telling you the truth," I replied; he just turned round to me and said: "I know the truth."

'I just thought, what have I done to bring this on? It was like a shower of abuse. It was really like that T-shirt, going from one side to the other side. I think for that gig Malcolm worked out a thing that a fight was going to occur, because it made the publicity. Having seen the three of them work it out, it was quite clear. Malcolm is one of those people who gets an idea and he is going to see that idea through hell and high water.'

Another new song was 'New York', a diatribe aimed this time at David JoHansen and Syl Sylvain. Lydon's lyrics are fluently vituperative, but they originate from McLaren. 'Malcolm was real disappointed in me when I went with David JoHansen to Japan,' says Syl Sylvain, 'he wrote me this letter where he got really mad. But if the song says anything bad about New York, it has to do with Malcolm as much as with us: he was so in love that he got bitter.'

But then it suited everybody to slag off New York: in the competition to patent Punk, London was coming up fast. On 4 July, there was the first chance to see 'New York' live, when the Ramones played the Roundhouse. 'They had never played a larger venue than a club,' says Nick Kent, 'and all of a sudden they are on a much larger stage. Culture shock. They plugged into this huge PA stack and started playing – and it just went off. Kaput. It was a damp squib. Then they came back on and just did it. It was good, but there was a lot of violence. It got very territorial.'

The same night, the Sex Pistols played at the Black Swan in Sheffield with the future Clash. 'It was a Sunday,' says Joe Strummer, 'but two hundred people turned up: they were very receptive.' Two days later, the Damned played their first concert supporting the Sex Pistols at the 100 Club. 'They were so bizarre,' says Jonh Ingham. 'They never rehearsed. They were all playing this white-light speed, and just by chance things would mesh and fall apart and mesh again. It was like this phasing up and down: very odd, but funny.'

On the 9th of the month, the Sex Pistols played their first concert on a large stage, at a Lyceum all-nighter. 'They were absolutely petrified backstage,' says Ingham. 'They were taking it as very important: it had never occurred to me that they really wanted to win people over. That was the night that John stubbed out cigarettes on the back of his hand when he was singing: that frightened me. He was the most maniacal thing alive: it was back to Iggy, that unpredictability. He already had cigarette burns on his wrists: it was one of the games Sid and he played in their Hampstead bedsit.

'At the Lyceum, there was suddenly this major step up in musical ability. Glen was phenomenal, Paul was right on the beat. It was in one night: they were all just there. Suddenly you knew this was a great band. By now everyone was being very serious about making this happen, it was quite clear that this was the only thing that was going to break through and create a new generation of music.'

Steve Jones and John Lydon at the Lyceum, 10 July 1976 (© Kate Simon)

(left to right) Nils Stevenson, Helen Wallington-Lloyd, Paul Cook, Steve Jones, Debbi Wilson, Steve Severin, Siouxsie, John Lydon, Glen Matlock, autumn 1976 (© Richard Young)

14

> The whole point of Sex is that we want to inspire other people with the confidence to live out their fantasies and to change. We really are making a political statement with this shop by attempting to attack the system. I'm also interested in getting people to wear some of our sex gear to the office. 'Out of the bedroom and into the streets!', now that would really be revolutionary!
>
> **Vivienne Westwood: 'Buy Sexual', *Forum* (June 1976)**

In the first half of 1976, two National Film School students, John Sansom and Mike Wallington, shot a documentary called *Dressing for Pleasure*. The film concentrates on rubber fetishism, then still a subterranean human activity. The novelty of the subject is expressed in the interviewees' postures: unused to the light of exposure, they are stiff and vulnerable. Suddenly, there is a shot of Sex and Jordan: she speaks a different language: 'we're trying to bring everything together and not to segregate things.'

Now pop culture is shot through with fetish material, it is hard to imagine how surprising Sex was. The shop had fetish credibility, boosted by the June feature in the sex magazine *Forum*. The pictures show regulars like Jordan, Chrissie Hynde and Steve Jones camping around, but it is Vivienne who speaks. 'I usually wear a T-shirt that reads: "Be Reasonable, Demand The Impossible". People are always coming up to me and asking: "Excuse me, but what's the impossible?" They want to find out what it is so they can be part of the inner circle.'

McLaren's concentration on the group increased both Vivienne's confidence and her mastery over the shop. You can see that confidence in a series of photos taken then by Will English: dressed in black leather leggings, skirt and a T-shirt with chains across the front and 'Venus' spelt out in studs, Vivienne grins gleefully from behind a black rubber bra. Left to her own devices, she had started designing: 'I couldn't put it down because I'd begun something, the culmination of that is communicating with a big audience. I can't think of a better way of putting yourself on the spot. Fashion is the strongest form of communication there is. I've always worked through a process of research. The Punk Rock thing came out of the fact that I got so intrigued, when I started to make clothes in rubberwear in Sex, by all those fetish people and the motives behind what they did, that I really went into it. I wasn't content with thinking: "Oh I'll just do something that looks a bit like what they want to wear." I wanted to make exactly what they wore, to understand all the things there.'

With confidence came an increased certitude and didacticism: 'You could never just buy something in the shop,' says Jordan. 'It was always, "*Why* are you buying it?" I'd just managed to get someone to buy a whole expensive outfit and she turned round and asked them what was the motivation behind it. I think they ended up not buying it in the end. They just wanted to buy the clothes. They didn't want a book written about them. Vivienne could always rationalize what she was doing; she could always make it into some political statement about the world today. Michael and I just sold the clothes: the customers didn't want to know about that.

'I think she was a pretty sheltered sort of person. She'd had a revelation late in life, much later: she didn't know much about life when she lived in Manchester. She's always amazed by things. But Vivienne worked as a teacher, and she has never lost that attitude, of teaching and wanting to teach. That's why Debbie and Tracey, who were so young, were the perfect vehicles for Vivienne to sculpt, to nurture.'

During the latter part of 1975 and the first half of 1976, Vivienne cultivated her own inner circle of performers, mainly women, who would act out the implications of the Sex clothes. This was vital because, by themselves, the Sex Pistols were not sexy enough. The sexiest, Steve Jones, was only so in a laddish way: Paul Cook and Glen Matlock were conventional, and John Lydon was unformed and unsure. In comparison, the women and men that Vivienne collected acted out their wildest fantasies. By doing so, they became part of the Sex Pistols and gave Punk its Warholian edge.

'People think that the early days of Punk were all banging along at Sex Pistols gigs,' says Debbie Wilson. 'But for me it was camping it up down Park Lane with a gang of trannies. All my friends, John, Blanche, Tracey, Berlin, were on the game. Linda of course was on the whipping sessions. It was all in Park Lane: it was the most outrageous place in the world. All these queens going around in Punk gear and black leather going, "Ooooooh!" They actually became quite famous down there: it got to the stage where prostitution wasn't that bad a thing to do. It became part of the new London.'

In the pictures of the time, Debbie is all surprised eyes and short, spiky blonde hair – an androgynous changeling. A refugee from boredom in Burnt Oak, she was, as she admits, a blank slate. 'I was about fifteen, so I was pretty naive. I started going out a lot, not going to school. I'd got to know Simon and Siouxsie: they'd all teamed up and we'd go to the Global Village or Crackers. That's how I met Tracey O'Keefe: she came from Bromley. Her father was a chartered accountant, middle class, but she was wild. I wasn't wild at school but I got wilder as we started going to more clubs.

'Suddenly I was involved with all these people. I saw the Sex Pistols at El Paradise. I met Linda Ashby then as well. That part of my life gets really confusing. Girls would really fancy me then and because I was young I thought it would be the craze to just go with girls. I didn't know whether I was supposed to be gay or not. I know we started going to Louise's, but it was the Bromley Contingent who introduced the Pistols to the gay scene.'

'Before it got a label it was a club for misfits,' says Siouxsie. 'Waifs, male gays, female gays, bisexuals, non-sexuals, everything. No one was criticized for their sexual preferences. The only thing that was looked down on was suburbia. I hated Bromley: I thought it was small and narrow-minded. There was this trendy wine bar called Pips, and I got Berlin to wear this dog-collar, and I walked in with Berlin following me, and people's jaws just hit the tables. I walked in and ordered a bowl of water for him, I got the bowl of water for my dog. People were scared!'

In the 1910s Bromley had provided the setting for Richmal Crompton's *William* books; by the 1970s, it epitomized suburban affluence. 'It was so oppressive,' says Berlin. 'There was no place to go. When I was fifteen I started this flirtation with a black girl called Simone, whose boyfriend was Simon Barker. I began a friendship with these two because he was a Bowie clone, and she was like Ava Cherry, with blonde hair. I was more like a Liza Minnelli clone: up Camp tree basically. The next person I met was Simon's best friend Steven Bailey: it was the four of us going about together.

'When you make a big change in your head about who are, you change all the way through. I started calling myself Berlin, because I was so enamoured by *Cabaret*. Steve started calling himself Steve Spunker and Sioux used to call herself Candy Sue. After that I started to go out with Steve, and we'd go round his house and listen to the Velvet Underground. In a way, Siouxsie mirrored herself on all those pop stars, Nico and Patti Smith, and Severin modelled himself on John Cale, Lou Reed, which is where he got the name Severin from: "Venus in Furs". I was their little plaything.

'*Cabaret* was such a big influence then: Joel Grey, a man with loads of make-up on. It was a very strong image, that Weimar thing. That was how my dress developed. I'd wear nothing but a white shirt, black tie, cropped black hair, black tights, imitation leather, a black jumper, and this fabulously high pair of black boots. It was naive. Remember I was fifteen, Siouxsie was eighteen. What do you know? It was to do with dare and finding your adolescent self.'

'We were carrying the Bowie and Roxy looks in our own way,' says Simon Barker. 'Siouxsie's jagged eye make-up was an extension of the *Clockwork Orange* look. Sioux was the first to dye her hair, with every shade of white. We'd all come up to Vidal Sassoon's to get our hair cut and coloured for free. We'd be used as models and they'd take a picture.'

'My hair went through so many changes,' says Siouxsie. 'It was very very short with coloured bits at the front, then I had longish bits round the sides and I'd just sweep them round and I'd have flame colours going round like a halo. Then black and red: pretty short then up at the side with a red streak. I got it bleached and I remember hating the bits at the side, getting home and just cutting them off – the very, very short hacked blonde hair. Blonde is something all brunettes think they want to be.'

'When I saw the Sex Pistols it was just noise, basically,' says Berlin. 'There was Paul Getty, Vivienne, Malcolm, Helen, Steve, Siouxsie, Debbie, Tracey, Sharon, all those people around the shop. Johnny was crouching on stage in a red jumper with a white collar, safety-pins, jeans, orange hair and screaming. I said to Steve: "Where is the energy coming from?" It was totally different: aggressive, violent, and at that point it didn't incite the audience much.

'Sulphate: that's what got them going. I had a party for them afterwards, and there was amphetamine sulphate everywhere. It was in May 1976, 8 Plaistow Grove, Bromley, two doors down from David Bowie's old address. It was on a Saturday and it was called "Berlin's Baby Bondage Party". You had to come as your kink. Simon had invited them after the 100 Club. Paul was the nicest one: he was lovely, like a puppy dog. Steve Jones was the macho bastard. Glen I didn't like at all. He was arrogant, naff. Johnny was totally aloof, out of his head.

'I can just remember walking into my bedroom: all the clothes were on the floor, all the books, all the records. The curtains were wide open, so all the neighbours were getting the benefit of Marilyn Monroe singing "I Wanna Be Loved By You", and Johnny lining up sulphate on the grooves of a record as it went around. He was wearing a black rubber T-shirt, those fifties trousers with the glitter, the glasses. He was young, open, and obviously the most intelligent of that lot.

'The party was a complete and utter riot. There was Siouxsie who was dressed in a plastic apron and tights, that was all. No knickers, nothing. And she had a leather whip. My parents had these awful polystyrene tiles, and there were whip marks all over the ceiling. Everybody was screwing everybody else. The stains on the sheets, honestly.

'I had to move to Chelsea, Oakley Street, to live with Tracey. There was also a transvestite, who's now a transexual, called Blanche. We'd go to Chaugeramas, a dingy dive where the worst transvestites went and all these businessmen. There was the Masquerade in Earls Court, there was Rob's, which was Bryan Ferry's hang-out, very chic. There was the Sombrero. I can't tell you the parallels between those days and *Goodbye to Berlin*. We were living it out, the whole bit.

'Siouxsie introduced everybody to Louise's. Six of us went out one night to this very exclusive lesbian club in Poland Street. We pressed on the doorbell looking like a cartoon probably. Madame Louise at the door: "Hello, darlinks, OK?" And her faggy American boyfriend going, "Hi! Three quid to get in." We went in, and it was very quiet. Red tableclothes, mirrors everywhere. They played soul, and Doris Day, and lush disco. Diana Ross's "Love Hangover" was a very pertinent song: we used to practise that dance at Siouxsie's place.'

(left to right) Sue Catwoman, unknown, McLaren, Nils Stevenson, Linda Ashby, Simon Barker, Siouxsie at Louise's, Poland Street, October 1976. Berlin is reflected in the mirror. (© Bob Gruen)

In 1976, London's gay scene was still in the 'wedge' era, just before the rigid separatism of the 'clone' look, which, as gay historian Peter Burton writes, 'started in New York from about 1976 and percolated to Britain at around the same time'. The 'clone' image: cropped hair, 'tache, Levi jeans and working-men's shirts, aimed to subvert traditional ideas of masculinity. It also appealed to a slightly older age group. Amongst the teenagers, the softer wedge hairstyles and outrageous camping proclaimed their difference and their liberation from the world of work.

'Purely because of the way we looked we were a distraction, a threat,' says Simon Barker. 'The straight clubs either didn't want you in there or they wanted to cause a fight. We used to go to Bang sometimes: there were two thousand people there, and none of them would hassle you. None of us were looking for sex in clubs so we went to this lesbian club where we would dance all night and not get hassled. Malcolm then asked us where we went and then he and the Pistols came down and it became trendy.'

'We used to take acid at Louise's,' says Lydon. 'It heightens the enjoyment. That's when I used to hang around with prostitutes, who I think are the most honest and open people on this earth. It was a very pure time then towards sex. People took it as it comes. One of Chrissie Hynde's jobs was to write letters for *Forum*, and I wrote a few with her. Used to sit there making up this utter gunk and then buy it the next month, thinking: "People are masturbating to this nonsense!" It didn't matter what your sex was then. It was very good, very open.'

'Neither John nor Sid was sexually mature,' says Jordan. 'Totally opposite to Steve. Because John was such an innocent, there were connotations. Sid had more of a physical presence than John, who I suppose didn't want the trappings of a normal person. He was John Rotten, and much the same as myself, I didn't go out with anyone either. The image was everything. When John used to stay at my flat, he used to take his trousers off in bed, he didn't like to show his body. When he performed, it was never masculine: it was postured.

'Punk wasn't necessarily a sexual thing: it was something that enticed people. People were scared out of their wits of me. Absolutely, I would have people write to me, adoring letters. I could do anything with them: I could kick them around the floor, they'd be my slave for life, but nobody would say it to my face. I never got anyone saying they'd like to take me out. I exuded a leave-me-aloneness.'

In the summer of 1976, this ambiguity was an important part of the group's shock tactics. Nobody knew where they were coming from. In this, Sex was vital: 'What came first, the chicken or the egg?' says Jordan. 'The shop did create such a great buzz about the band. The clothes were an important part of their make up, but also a lot of things were sold because of them. Initially the Sex Pistols were just a vehicle. The real T-shirt boom came after the group came along: that was the vehicle to sell the band.'

Fetish T-shirts weren't the only Sex clothes the group were wearing: pleated trousers, corduroy straight-legs, suede slingbacks and velvet-collared fifties jackets were all supplied to the group. Members also offered their own innovations: Matlock with his artfully paint-spattered black drainpipes, or Lydon with his hand-painted shirts and torn-up 'Steptoe' clothes – tiny sweaters, huge cardigans and fifties flannels. The effect was striking but indefinable, something like a skewed Mod with both Bohemian and hooligan touches.

As the group took off, the shop's range began to expand, not only with more specific sexual items but with new, designed clothing that blurred the lines between fetish wear and high fashion. There was a series of diaphanous shirts made out of parachute material, with legends from Alex Trocchi's novels on the breasts. There was a sequence of T-shirts and shirts with 'sexy' playing cards attached in plastic pockets, and Eton-collared shirts with a voyeuristic card design printed in red and orange on white, or in gold and blue on green.

There was a lot of discussion about anarchy that summer: Lydon was working up a set of lyrics to one of Glen's tunes. Vivienne set about making a parallel item of clothing. The resulting 'Anarchy' shirt was a masterpiece. Taking a second-hand sixties shirt, Westwood would dye it in stripes, black, red or brown, before stencilling on a slogan such as 'Only Anarchists Are Pretty'. The next stage was to stitch on more slogans: hand painted on rectangles of silk or muslin. These made explicit references to Anarchist heroes and to the events of 1968: 'Prenez vos désirs pour la réalité'; 'A Bas Le Coca Cola'. The final touches were the most controversial. Small rectangular portraits of Karl Marx (from Chinatown) were placed on the side of the chest, and on the other, above the pocket or on the collar, was placed an (often inverted) flying swastika from the Second World War. To ensure that the message was received, the whole shirt was finished off by an armband which simply read 'Chaos'. The intention was the group should not be politically explicit, but instead should be an explosion of contradictory, highly charged signs.

As in the 'Which side of the bed' T-shirt, in this one garment are contained the ambiguities and density of references that would take several years to unravel. The 'Anarchy' shirt created a chaos of meaning but managed nevertheless to make a coherent statement. The intention was clearly to deliver a political manifesto that avoided simplistic solutions. In this context, the use of Anarchist and Situationist slogans indicated the desire not to be easily labelled and a wish for change, of an intensity not usually associated with a pop group.

But the shirt didn't exist in isolation, even within the confines of Sex. Both Westwood and McLaren had already used the swastika on their clothes, and had a stock of Nazi memorabilia. 'Malcolm was in awe of the symbolism,' says Jordan. 'Not just the swastika, but a lot of artefacts from that era. The Nazi Youth badges. They were extremely rare. He had a lot of rings, including gold *SS* wedding rings, which weren't for sale because they were originals. There were a few things for sale: mock-ups from the regalia shops, the straight wing badges, swastika hankies.'

'I had a woollen thing with plastic gloves and zips,' says Alan Jones, 'it had Nazi emblems all over it and a swastika armband. I got a terrible reaction to it: this guy in Notting Hill Gate turned round and said, "It's disgusting: I can't believe you're wearing this." Our stock remark at that time was: "We're here to positively confront people with the past." It was something Vivienne and Malcolm told us to say. He followed me down the street and ended up by hitting me very hard. From that time on I turned my armband round.'

'The shop was about breaking taboos,' says Jordan. 'The Epstein T-shirt was another aspect of it. I suppose the swastika was the ultimate shocking symbol. We got banned from an all-night club, the Candy Box. John and Sid and I all got memberships for it; it was a place for people who worked in clubs to go to. I went there with an anarchy shirt on and somebody took offence, there was an argument and that was the end of our membership. I just liked the shirts, and I didn't really understand Vivienne's argument for the swastika: that it was demystifying the symbol.'

Just as McLaren and Westwood simultaneously used and despised sixties libertarianism, the Sex Pistols gained power at exactly the moment when the freedoms of the 1960s were reaching their high water mark. In summer 1976, they existed on the cusp of the New Right: nothing shows this more than their confused use of the swastika and their attitudes to sex. For, despite the free and easy milieu within which the Sex Pistols moved, the strongest element to come over from their songs is sexual disgust.

'By the time you're twenty you just think – yawn – just another squelch session,' Lydon said about sex that summer. When asked to write a song about submission, Lydon had produced a lyric with a punch-line which was a dissolution of the ego, submerged in the mythical female: 'I'm going down you're dragging me down/Submission I can't tell you what I found/Submission/Submission/Going down down/Under the sea/I wanna drown drown/Under the water/I'm going down down/Under the sea.'

This accords with the fear of the female described by Klaus Theweleit in *Male Fantasies*, his masterly study of the image of woman in the collective unconscious of the German Freikorps, the early fascist shocktroops. 'A river without end, enormous and wide, flows through the world's literatures: the women-in-the-water; woman as water; as a stormy, cavorting, cooling ocean.' In the company of the sexually unconventional, this fear could be briefly disguised.

'I loooove you,' John Lydon sang in one of the summer's new songs. But he doesn't. 'Satellite' is a scathing put-down of a girl modelled on Shanne Hasler: 'Looking like a big fat pink baked bean.' 'Glen said that I was Johnny Rotten's girlfriend and he wrote the song about me,' says Shanne. 'I was really insulted! The nearest thing we ever did to going out was walking around St Albans hand in hand. I used to speak to him on the phone and he mentions that. I could have written one back: but what's the point?'

This sexual fluidity, or denial, would quickly go sour. The group's link with the subterranean sexual world would be conveniently forgotten once the music they played became part of the music industry and once the people that actively supported them and contributed to the package became mere 'fans'. Once defined, the Sex Pistols became a Rock band and Rock bands are not usually tolerant of homosexuality, either in their music or in the way they are treated by the media. Just as in New York, ambiguity would turn to disavowal and then, under the wrong conditions, prejudice.

The sun does funny things
It's like some prankster's cheat
I could swear the city's like some magic beach
'Cause against the curb
I can see those street waves beat.

Pere Ubu: 'Heaven' (1976)

Do you think it's really the truth that you see?
I've got my doubts it's happened to me.

The Byrds: 'Artificial Energy' (1967)

'The great thing about the Sex Pistols was the people they attracted,' says Julien Temple. 'The scenes in Oxford Street that summer were wonderful. The sun sets at Marble Arch and so you get that incredible shaft of light, a very epic feeling. I remember Sue Catwoman walking in a see-thru raincoat, backlit in the sunlight down this Victorian Street. They were like a velcro ball that attracted all these other people: it was like a snowball rolling down a slope.'

'When the Ramones played at Dingwalls,' says Bruce Gilbert of

Wire, 'there was a kerfuffle at the door. It was obviously McLaren and he was trying to get his group in. They were so dangerous-looking, these boys. It wasn't contrived, but they looked like Dickensian urchins. They had shoes on but no socks, and they looked like they couldn't have got that way without being alcoholics, but they were young boys. They were perfect.'

There were two other factors which added to the Sex Pistols' perfervid momentum, as, for three months, the group and their supporters ran wild through the crumbling capital city like the historically dispossessed. Since June, the country had been undergoing a heatwave, the hottest since 1940. In England, heat changes everything. The English national emotion is depression and it is endemic, brought on by long, grey winters whose dampness never quite leaves the air, even during summer. Extra-hot summers boil out both the dampness and the national reserve, as life takes to the streets and English isolation melts. 'Caroline and I used to stay up until four in the morning,' says Jonh Ingham. 'The windows would be open all night, and then the sun's coming up: that was in the spring, and the weather just kept on going. You want to get out; you feel really great because it's sunny and warm and there's this great *joie de vivre*. The weather had a lot to do with everyone's positiveness.'

There is also pop's hidden motor to consider. If, as Ingham claims, 'drugs have influenced the entire course of twentieth-century popular music', then the Sex Pistols and the music that they generated were inextricably linked with amphetamine sulphate. 'I loved the stuff,' says John Lydon. 'I'm normally a very slow person and it made me more intense. I'm naturally paranoid and it made me feel better. But you get bored with these things, the thrill wears off.'

First synthesized in 1927, the amphetamine, then known as benzedrine, came into its own during the Second World War, where it was regularly given to pilots and other combat personnel on both sides. Until 1957, it was possible to obtain benzedrine inhalers over the counter without a prescription; their withdrawal was followed by an increase in pill consumption. 'Drynamils' and 'French Blues' were the fuel for the Mod movement: that era of smart, violent pop that was the Sex Pistols' first influence.

Changing fashions in drugs pushed amphetamine use underground during the late 1960s in the UK, but in America the use of powdered amphetamine became widespread. It was broadcast to the world when Ondine flamboyantly shot up on the screen in Warhol's

Chelsea Girls. In the early 1970s polydrug abuse began, the choice of drugs being amyl nitrate, cocaine and mandrax (the UK equivalent of the quaalude popular in the USA). Speed went underground into Northern Soul, where its use became statutory to keep feet dancing all night.

A government report to the United Nations shows the rapid spread of amphetamine sulphate; one gram sold for ten to fifteen pounds in 1975. Sulphate was a bathtub drug, easily concoctable at home using chemicals readily available in the UK. The 1977 government report shows the existence of twenty-five LSD and amphetamine factories spread around the country. Speed was the drug of the squatters, the hippie rump: it was effective, Bohemian and obliterating.

'Speed came in during the summer,' says Ingham. 'It had all the advantages of being very cheap, you don't take much, it lasts a long time, and it's great to have that energy feel. When Malcolm was doing that "No Drugs" thing the Sex Pistols weren't taking a lot of drugs: but they got into it because of older people around them who weren't going to give up their drug habits just for the sake of Malcolm's party line. Of course the drugs get broken out, and they're not going to say no: that wouldn't be Punk.'

'Development of amphetamine tolerance leads to larger and larger doses to maintain the effect,' writes Barbara Harwood in a homeopathic report on drug abuse. 'With an increased dose different effects are experienced: often irritability, suspicion, restlessness, overexcitement. Eventually a serious mental disorder resembling paranoid schizophrenia may ensue – the development of delusions and hallucinations of a persecutory nature, often linked with grandiosity, hostility and aggression.'

Just as the Ramones speeded up the pace of Punk, so amphetamine defined its mental state and its attitude. The movement that developed around the Sex Pistols was the first full working out of the legacy of Andy Warhol's Factory in this country. With the Sex Pistols and their many supporters, McLaren and Vivienne Westwood collected a similar carnival of the oppressed and the Bohemian, prostitutes and drug addicts, the brilliant and the publicity-seeking. These teenagers changed their lives in pop acts of transformation, using bizarre dress codes, cartoon pseudonyms and amphetamines.

The Warhol 'superstars' had taken on their pseudonyms, not to assimilate, but to advertise, their wish for celebrity, but the Punk use of the pseudonym was more complicated. Many originated as insults –

like Rat Scabies or John Rotten – which were then taken on board and flaunted as a badge of pride. This not only turned the insult on its head, but meant that the owners of these pseudonyms were often required to act out the pejorative definitions of others. Identity was thus created and reinforced by hostility.

'I was Girl of the Year and superstar and all that crap,' says doomed Warhol superstar Edie Sedgwick in the tapes for her 1971 biopic *Ciao Manhattan*. 'Everything I did was really underneath, I guess, motivated by psychological disturbances. I'd make a mask out of my face because I didn't realize I was quite beautiful, God blessed me so. I practically destroyed it. I had to wear heavy black eyelashes like bat wings, and dark lines under my eyes, and cut all my hair off, my long dark hair. I'd freak out in a very physical way. And it was all taken as a fashion trend.'

The Sex Pistols and their followers were playing with a gun loaded by McLaren and Westwood. Drugs also fragmented already frail teenage identities. If one person embodied these changes even more

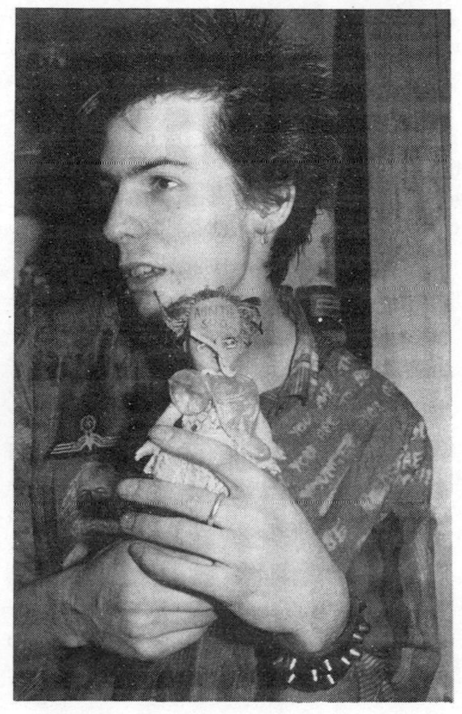

Sid Vicious, late 1976 (© Ray Stevenson)

than John Lydon, it was John Beverley, now settling into his role as Sid Vicious, Sex Pistols follower number one. 'Sid was a nice kid that was doing too much speed,' says Nils. 'We'd go to the shop and Vivienne would just put a pair of trousers on him,' says Viv Albertine, 'he was like a toy almost.'

'Sid began as quite conservative,' says Jordan. 'He was worried about getting exams. Being in or near the Sex Pistols changed all their lives dramatically. Sid worked with me for a little while as a stand-in while someone was on holiday. He was useless as a shop assistant. But he was very adaptable: he'd make a lot of things out of what he already had. John would need someone to tell him what to do half the time. Sid was very imaginative: wearing garters outside of his jeans, and a padlock over his crotch.'

'He didn't have much sexuality about him then,' says Viv Albertine. 'When I first met him, he was quite polite. I'd heard a lot about him, a friend of John's: they looked like bookends, the pair of them with their spiky hair. I was expecting spiky hair but when I got there he'd shaved his head, looked hideous. I can't remember how we got friendly, I think I just rang him up. I was very bold in those days. I always felt very uncomfortable with him: he was so strict, and so idealistic and so clever. This is what people don't realize: Sid was so sharp.

'We had a group called the Flowers of Romance: John thought up the name. It was perfect: you're the flowers and what's romance? Lies. These children are the flowers of romance. There was me, Palmolive, Sarah Hall: we spent all summer in this horrible squat, every day, we did have discipline. It was so hard because I could hardly play. Sid picked it up like that. One night I went to bed, and Sid stayed up with a Ramones album and a bass guitar, and when I got up in the morning, he could play. He'd taken a load of speed, and he'd taught himself. He was so quick: that's why he had to look thick, to slow himself down.

'He was strict about everything. You'd have to wear leather, black and pink, high heels, practically everything from Sex in fact. I remember Sid teaching me about the size and shape of collars. I'd never taken notice of men's collars before and they are such a revealing sign of the way things are going. It was down to the way you looked, the way you spoke, the things you were hung up about. If he could find something you didn't have worked out, he'd home in on it, and you'd be in pain from his verbal haranguing.

'Sid had this fantastic disguise of a loping, playful, get-wise, Jamaican expression, and if you ever did confront him with something that he was embarrassed about, he would just be barefaced and admit it, so you'd lost your power. The reason he went scooting downhill was that he really couldn't stand the world and its pettiness. He could be a pain in the arse, but he was the type of person, like a lot of junkies, who are so idealistic that they can't handle life as it is.

'Sid couldn't be bothered with principles. He taught me that in different situations you should always be ready to change your ideas. As quickly as the situation changed, you had to reconstruct your whole mind, and that's how Sid lived. I can't tell you how hard it was to be around somebody like that.'

One definition of nihilism is that it is not the negative or cynical rejection of belief but the positive courage to live without it: the Sex Pistols and their supporters were an explosion of negatives and between them encompassed the rejection of most values. They displayed all the trappings of mindlessness, and were quickly defined as being such, a definition which was instantly assumed and which inexorably took over their script. For a while though, they tried to make a way of life that borrowed from the Maoist and Situationist miasmas that hung around Sex.

'I used to leave Shepherd's Bush with not a penny in my pocket,' says Albertine, 'get in the tube and at the other end say I left my purse at home, go to the Speakeasy or Louise's, blag your way in through the door, get bought drinks all night, then share a taxi or get the night bus home. It wasn't ligging, but an adventure: you'd just rely on ingenuity, you knew you could do it. There was an absolute horror of boredom. Rather than spend a night in, you'd go out every day in that hottest summer and practise, just to fill up your time with worthwhile things.

'You would have your hair cut in the most hideous way, but it was an interesting thing for a woman to have done. Or Siouxsie wearing something with her tits hanging out. It was like wearing your thoughts and your attitudes to life, clothes reflected it in a very obvious way. It was that strictness: I couldn't talk to my mother for ages. It was too convoluted and complex, and too much needed to be explained to talk to someone about it.'

This wholesale existential leap into the everlasting present of the teenage overlapped with a normal adolescent obnoxiousness and lack of respect for limits. 'Give me World War Three we can live again,' sang Lydon in 'I Wanna Be Me'; 'Now is the time to realize, to have real eyes.' The Sex Pistols' gang were undergoing a rite of passage of particular intensity: what had begun as an excuse to annoy people quickly took on an almost messianic flavour as the inner circle surfed through the city on a diet of sun, sex, sulphate and swastikas.

Like Warhol, McLaren and Westwood created an arena where the burning youth – strong and vulnerable alike – could run wild, behaving as they liked, as children freed from the imposition of adult compromises and lies. Like Warhol, their very lack of conventional morality – a prankster's cheat – was both liberating and the source of their power. It meant that the emerging movement could not be easily defined, yet, through its childlike aspect, it was particularly vulnerable to perversion, once defined.

Punk began as hostile and became nihilistic in the deepest sense. Although it had had a moral intent, it became convoluted and clouded by the violence, the shock tactics, and cynicism. Yet there was also enough existential truth in it for it to interact with society beyond Soho and Louise's, and it did so with great impact.

'SNIFFIN' GLUE...
AND OTHER ROCK'N'ROLL HABITS,
FOR ~~PUNKS~~ GIRLS! (3) SEPTEMBER '76.

THE MAG THAT DOESN'T LIKE GIVING YOU 'UP TO DATE' NEWS ON THE MUSIC SCENE.

WITH
THE DAMNED ✱ SEX PISTOLS ✱ IGGY POP +

The first *Sniffin' Glue* picture cover, September 1976 (© Mark Perry)

15

It is certainly time we got a super new thing like the Beatles. The music business needs a shot in the arm.

Wayne Bickerton: 'Sheet' (August 1976)

Let us put our trust in the eternal spirit which destroys and annihilates only because it is the unsearchable and eternally creative source of all life. The passion for destruction is also a creative passion!

Michael Bakunin: *Reaction In Germany* (1842)

In the high summer of 1976 there was a sequence of larger-scale events, planned to increase the visibility of the Sex Pistols and their movement. The first was the return match at Manchester's Lesser Free Trade Hall, on 20 July. Within just a month and a half, things had changed considerably. 'It brought all kinds of people out of the woodwork,' says Richard Boon. 'People thought they were left alone in their rooms with their obsessions. They began to meet: they were saying to each other, "Didn't I see you last month?" A pocket-size community was forming as a result.'

'We'd heard about this band Slaughter and the Dogs,' says Howard Devoto. 'We'd never seen them play, but they sounded vaguely appropriate. We opened the show: Slaughter went on second. It sold out. I don't remember having time to be nervous, because I'd organized it, and there was all this other stuff going on: Malcolm bitching about the PA. Suddenly we were on in five minutes. I can't remember planning that much but certainly what we did was strongly based on what we'd seen with the Pistols.

'We were following some kind of brief. Looking back, certain things surprise me. There was an affected aggression, but you're bound to be like that when you start out. "I'll give you a subterranean profile." I think there were insults I'd written earlier. Not everything that went into those early songs was written in that period. Partly diary, partly for songs if they ever happened. Partly poems. I wrote a song called "Boredom", but I think that was of a moment.

'It's surprising how quickly you can pick things up and make them right. Quite obviously there was a feeling that certain things were right and certain things weren't right at all.'

'The day we wrote "Boredom",' says Pete Shelley, 'Howard was working a night shift at the tie factory, and during the night he'd written these words. I looked at these words and before he went to bed, I wrote the music.' The words were straight out of Ouspensky: 'I've taken this extravagant journey or so it seems to me. I just came from nowhere and I'm going straight back there.'

'I was in South Manchester cemetery sketching one day,' says Linder, a striking woman whose designs for Buzzcocks would help to create the Punk graphic style, 'I walked out and there was this van parked outside saying, "Malcolm McLaren presents the Sex Pistols". It was the names: McLaren sounded all tartan, and tartan with sex and guns. When we got there, I just knew that something strange was going to happen that night. These people looked so separate: not threatening at all, just fascinating. It was a shimmery night: all energy and light.'

'The Buzzcocks were very, very fast,' says Richard Boon. 'They did a Ramones song and they were two seconds faster. They were cheap and nasty, but they were uncomfortable. They just wanted to get off stage as quickly as possible.' The performance ended with Shelley entering a prolonged feedback solo which was cut abruptly short. 'It was stage-managed,' says Shelley cheerfully. 'I'd bought the Audition guitar especially. We ended up wrestling with the guitar and pulling the strings off, before smashing it up.'

'Malcolm was using that concert as a publicity exercise,' says Shelley. 'He put on a coach for journalists to come up from London to see what was happening elsewhere in the world. So we got reviewed on our first concert by Jonh Ingham, and I even got a name check. As soon as the magazine came out, I rushed out and bought three copies of it: instant stardom. I was thrilled because it was actually about doing things and entering the mystique of being written about. There was no turning back then.'

Some things were right, others weren't, in the new order as it was being defined. Slaughter and the Dogs *were* much more what the Punks of rhetoric were supposed to be: four working-class hooligans from a vast thirties estate, Wythenshawe, in south Manchester. 'They were a bit more football-terrace,' says Shelley. 'It was arrogant, so we kept our distance. I'm quoted as saying they weren't really Punk. They were into Mick Ronson and *Diamond Dogs*.'

(left to right) Pete Shelley, John Maher, Howard Devoto, Steve Diggle: the Buzzcocks, Manchester, summer 1976 (© Phil Mason)

In order to penetrate the mass market, a new form of music and fashion must be defined – and definition is as much about exclusion as inclusion. In this process, commentary is all-important, as the weekly tabloids interpret and shape often contradictory and surprising new phenomena. In this, the very minutiae of clothing and attitude are all-important: as Ingham noted, Slaughter and the Dogs were 'well outside the boundaries being drawn by the Pistols'.

'The atmosphere among the punky bands on the circuit at the moment is positively cut-throat,' wrote Caroline Coon in the *Melody Maker* two weeks later. 'It's the Before or After Sex Pistols debate: "We saw Johnny Rotten and he CHANGED our attitude to music" (the Clash, Buzzcocks), or "We played like this AGES before the Sex Pistols" (Slaughter and the Dogs), or "We are miles better than the Sex Pistols" (the Damned). They are very aware that they are part of a new movement and each one wants to feel that he played a part in starting it.'

Coon had finally resolved her arguments with the *Melody Maker*. If Ingham had concentrated on the minutiae of style with a Mod obsessiveness, Coon wrote for both a wider, unconvinced audience and for the music industry itself. This 'new cultural movement' is unequivocally defined as 'Punk' and if, in order to pump up a new movement, she put in a couple of groups – like Eddie and the Hot Rods and the Stranglers – that weren't part of the inner circle, its significance was outweighed by her description of the Sex Pistols as inspiring 'a fourth generation of rockers'.

Coon says, 'I reported that things were happening: what I personally felt about it was irrelevant. They were exciting and fun, there was so much good humour in it, and I was fascinated by the dilemma of an artist who has an idea and not yet quite the technique with which to express the idea. To see them struggling with their technique to get the songs across was superb: that got a white-hot fire going onstage.'

This was everything that McLaren could wish. There was a problem however: nobody was defining 'Punk' from within. The established writers were inevitably compromised both by age and the minimal demands of objectivity required by their papers: Coon had to share space with knocking copy. The established media could propagandize and comment, but they could not dramatize the new movement in a way that fired people's imagination. A new medium came from an unexpected source, boosted by developments in printing technology that made photocopying cheap and accessible for the first time.

'God, did we sell fanzines at Rock On,' says Roger Armstrong. 'Mark P.'s [Perry's] *Sniffin' Glue* was the first one. His girlfriend's dad had an office where they had a photocopying machine, and that was where he got his stuff photostatted. He used to work in a bank and he was so excited about Punk, it was the best thing that ever happened to him. The first one was on the Gorillas and the Flamin' Groovies; it was based around what was coming out of Rock On. I helped him to the extent that when he brought copies in I'd pay him straight away for the lot because I knew I'd sell them.

'*Sniffin' Glue* was being planned before I ever saw the Pistols,' says Perry. 'It was based on the Ramones album. All that stuff about *Glue* being the first fanzine is crap. Brian Hogg's *Bam Balam*, which was all about sixties music, was in its fourth issue by then: it showed that you could do a magazine and you didn't have to be glossy. Also Rock On used to carry Country and Rock'n'Roll fanzines. It was the first time I'd ever done anything like that: I approached it like a project in school.' With economy and honesty, Mark Perry wrote himself into the role of 'Punk Everykid', much as Legs McNeil had in New York. The first few issues of *Sniffin' Glue* chart Perry's own conversion: 'Even I've got cropped hair now,' he wrote in issue 3, 'you just can't help getting into it!' Produced on up to ten A4 sheets photocopied on one side, with hand-drawn graphics, *Sniffin' Glue* lacked the professionalism of *Punk*, but was nevertheless in the tradition of American fanzines, if filtered through the medium of Sex Pistols handbills.

From the El Paradise concert on, the Sex Pistols had been advertised by a series of one-sided, A4 collages. At first, crude, hand-painted logos were laid over pictures of the group. These were later replaced by a sequence of logos in 'ransom-note' lettering – individual letters cut out of existing media and then jumbled together. 'You know who invented that?' says McLaren; 'it was Helen: I remember her sitting on the floor of the Bell Street flat cutting up the *Evening Standard*.'

Ransom-note lettering is typically used by criminals or freedom fighters because printed letters avoid the 'fingerprint' of the typewriter or handwriting. Like communiqués, the Sex Pistols handbills spoke in codes to the initiated only, but there was also a strong wish to involve the mass media. Even at this early stage, pieces of the tabloids were built into the Sex Pistols package.

From April, McLaren had collected the group's press cuttings and handbills and like any aspiring manager, had them collated into a press pack to be handed out to journalists and record companies. These press packs were like no others: printed in a variety of colours by Jamie Reid at the Labour Party Press at Peckham, there was no written manifesto, but a montage of vitriol, praise and indifference, reflecting both the confused response to the group and the group's wish not to be defined. As more coverage came, it was added to this pack, which became more like a magazine.

This was the form taken up by *Sniffin' Glue*. Perry had no problems about definition: the cover of *Sniffin' Glue* announced itself to be 'FOR PUNKS'. Taking its name from a Ramones song and a Lenny Bruce sketch, Perry's magazine began by covering Eddie and the Hot Rods, but by issue 3 it had honed down its coverage to 'pure' Punk groups. It quickly distinguished itself from the weeklies even though it boosted the scene in a similar way. The difference was an enthusiasm which reflected the musical ideology put forward by the groups.

'Most of the things in the *Glue* were written straight down, no looking at it later,' says Perry, 'which is why you get all the crossing out. People never believed me at the time, but I didn't really care about the magazine. It was the ideas that were important.' The point was *access*: anybody with a certain command of English and a few pounds could make their statement. The economics were simple: the cost of photocopying – then about 3p a sheet – would just be met by the cover price of 20p or so. Free access to a photocopier meant instant profit. The fanzine was a living exemplar of this access aesthetic.

This inclusivity was at odds with a simultaneous exclusivity. Another early fanzine, Paul Morley's *Out There*, talks of 'priding ourselves on attractive elitism' – but that summer, Punk's breakthrough was to unite people who saw pop in terms of social realism and those who viewed it as artistic expression. Perry was smart enough to see the differences between the Sex Pistols' rhetoric and the reality: 'Punks are carefree and don't care a shit. The Pistols crowd are not Punks, they're too vain. But what's wrong with that so am I.'

Nevertheless Perry (renamed Mark P. to avoid dole snoopers), committed his magazine to a populist, accessible aesthetic, with unforeseen results. 'I did realize the importance of what it encompassed, and I also had that enormous ego that was necessary to get on in Punk,' he says. 'John Lydon had it, Strummer had it, Rat Scabies had it. I thought, "If I say this in the *Glue*, it's going to happen." I knew that, and that's what fueled me, knowing that it was being taken seriously.'

The Manchester concerts were a watershed for the group: they gave the impression that the Sex Pistols were the spearhead of a nationwide movement. They also led to their first appearance on nationwide television. 'Granada was preparing its third series of *So It Goes* to be a quick-moving, groovy TV show,' says Tony Wilson, a former editor of *Granta*, who was the show's presenter. 'We didn't want to have too much respect for the music because the music was pretty shitty then. People didn't like it because it was irreverent; it wasn't the *Old Grey Whistle Test*, which was dull and dead.

'In February it was announced that *So It Goes* was going to be a network show in the summer, and I got two letters within a couple of weeks. One was from a kid called Steven Morrissey, containing a battered copy of a New York Dolls album, saying, "Why can't we have more music like this, Mr Wilson?" I have to say that I hadn't heard of them. Then I got a cassette from a guy called Howard Trafford, with a letter talking about this really wonderful group coming up to Manchester on 4 June, and that of course was the Sex Pistols.

'I went to see them, and didn't know what the fuck was going on, until they played "Steppin' Stone". Then it was clear that they were deeply and fabulously exciting. I went back to Granada and said "We absolutely must put them on the show." We decided to make a virtue out of our last show of the series, with three unsigned bands: Gentlemen, the Bowles Brothers and the Sex Pistols.'

The Sex Pistols' first encounter with the mass media was not without moments of mutual incomprehension. 'Malcolm asked me to go to the recording to lend a bit of ambience,' says Jordan. 'Tony Wilson turns up to greet us with clogs on. There was another band on wearing blue satin suits; all the kids were drinking coke. You've got Clive James, who is a terrible Australian straightie, being huffy and shocked, so we just waded in. I called him a baldy old Sheila. John just called him "Bruce" for an hour.

'They got my back up because they wouldn't let me wear my swastika armband: they eventually put a piece of sticky tape over it. But that's why the performance was so good: because we were really pissed off. The band had already had an argument with this band Gentlemen. They said they liked Joni Mitchell, and you could imagine what John said: "You fucking arsehole". We realized we were like fish out of water, but there was a definite ability to make the show work for us.'

'They'd drunk quite a bit,' says Wilson. 'They were meant to do three and a half minutes – they agreed that and rehearsed it – and there was five minutes left. They just kept playing for seven minutes and kicked their equipment apart. Two days later the director edited it down to three and a half minutes. The audience was dumbfounded. As they came off stage there was complete silence except for the footsteps of the producer coming down from the box to try to hit somebody. Everybody was wound up. The next day I was in trouble at Granada: there was bad feeling.'

It was at the second Manchester date that the Sex Pistols unveiled 'Anarchy in the UK'. An index of their increasing ambition, their wish to get into the world beyond the confines of the music industry, it was a call to arms, delivered in language that was as explosive as the implications of the group's name. In the first two lines – 'I am an antichrist/I am an anarchist' – it is not only the half-rhyme that jars: within the space of ten seconds, two taboos have been broken.

Today, Lydon denies all intent, but he was deliberately using inflammatory imagery. The word 'antichrist' goes back directly to the pseudo-messiah of Revelation: in Norman Cohn's words, 'an all-destroying demon whose reign was to be lawless chaos, but was also to be the prelude to the Second Coming'. During the Middle Ages, the antichrist became Europe's monster from the id, a terrifying figure who could arise out of nowhere, the harbinger of the Last Days. Even in 1976, the word carried a clear threat of apocalypse.

In this social demonology, the anarchist was only a more recent, secular version of antichrist. To the general public, the word carried associations of riot and of anonymous, lethal disorder; such as seen in the Chártist Riots, the Sidney Street siege of 1911 or the more recent Angry Brigade bombings. These associations were deliberately evoked: although the authorship of 'Anarchy in the UK' is now a matter of dispute, there seems little doubt that Lydon was fed material by Vivienne Westwood and Jamie Reid, which he then converted into his own lyric.

McLaren and Westwood had woven slogans by Spanish anarchist Buenaventura Durruti into their clothes and Jamie Reid had, during his time at the Suburban Press, familiarized himself with libertarian thinkers like Charles Fourier and articulate British exponents of anarchist thought like William Morris and Digger Gerrard Winstanley. In 1974, he did the design for Christopher Gray's translation of SI texts, *Leaving the 20th Century*.

'We used to talk to John a lot,' he says, 'about the Situationists, about Suburban Press. The Sex Pistols seemed the perfect vehicle to communicate ideas directly to people who weren't getting the message from left-wing politics.' Whatever their precise provenance, the ringing phrases of 'Anarchy in the UK' were powerful enough to insert the idea of anarchy, like a homoeopathic remedy, into a society that was already becoming polarized.

'Anarchy in the UK' was one of seven songs recorded during July 1976 by Dave Goodman on a four-track machine in the rehearsal room at Denmark Street. The others were also originals – 'Pretty Vacant', 'Seventeen', 'Satellite', 'Problems', 'I Wanna Be Me' and 'Submission'. 'They needed some good tapes,' says Goodman. 'The Spedding tapes sounded like rough mixes, guitars not loud enough. I said I could do it better with my four-track, so they said, "Do it then." We recorded four or five takes of each song, then overdubs were added on an eight-track machine at Riverside studios.'

With these tapes, McLaren made his first assault on the music industry. Now that the stylistic changes that the Sex Pistols set in motion have become a cliché in pop's vocabulary (even today, barely a week passes without a group being described in the music press as 'influenced by' or 'sounding like' the Sex Pistols) the first batch of Goodman tapes sound very familar but they were very surprising to A&R ears of the time, however educated.

The music industry is, in general, not in the position of initiating trends, but reacting to them. Collectively, the ten or so major labels have, to some extent, the power to dictate the market because of their new monopoly of the means of production and promotion. They are however, vulnerable to the speed with which fashions can arrive and disappear, particularly in a centralized, fast-moving music economy like Britain's. In effect, they are in the position of attempting to catch the lightning. They can never predict exactly where it will strike, nor with what power.

The primary purpose of the music industry is to make money, a fact usually masked by the fervid rhetoric that always surrounds English pop. It is not surprising then, that A&R men will opt for what is understandable to them and to their superiors. These twenty-five to thirty-five-year-olds would often judge pop music by the criteria of their youth, rather than through the eyes of the (then) fifteen to twenty-four-year-old target market. In 1976, the prevailing fashion was for tasteful Country, Pub or progressive Rock styles, with a dash of Hard Rock, such as City Boy or Lone Star, rightly forgotten groups signed by major companies that year.

With their sound alone, the Sex Pistols drove a wedge into the musical standards of the time. When production values were complex and smooth, the Goodman tapes capture the group's live sound 'of broken glass and rusty razor blades'. When British vocalists sang with a mid-Atlantic accent, Lydon's voice skated in and out of tune in a tone of bored sarcasm mixed with the Cockney stylings of Lionel Blair and David Bowie. And at a time when songs generally dealt with the pop archetypes of escape or love, the Sex Pistols threw up a series of insults and rejections, couched in a new pop language that was tersely allusive yet recognizable as everyday speech. In 1976, they must have sounded to the uninitiated like a rougher, more inept version of the new wave of Pub Rock groups, none of whom had reached the attention of the industry.

'We can't play' was the rhetoric, but the Sex Pistols could. By the summer of 1976 everything was there: short declamatory openings, carried by guitar riffs, staccato drumming, basic song constructions of verse and chorus, simple solos (often of repeated chords), and very definite endings. They are manifestos in which the lyrics function as slogans. Unlike the Ramones, the Sex Pistols do not continue at one breakneck pace, but each song ebbs and flows in the winding up of tension and its resolution. Glen Matlock's bass is crucial to this. There are also gaps where all but one of the instruments drop out in an effective use of surprise.

On 'I Wanna Be Me', the group take things fast but they are in total control, and Lydon is in full command of his *persona*: righteous, bitter, accusatory yet mocking. His occasional hoarseness only adds to the song's urgency. In the song's bridge the tension winds up until everything goes dead with Lydon's ascending scream of 'Nooooooow!': there is the gratifying, distorted sound of amplifier hum, and then Paul Cook hits the snare drum and the whole group smashes in as one.

McLaren had very little experience in dealing with the music industry except in a 'hands off' manner, and he was attempting the difficult trick of attracting investment with as few strings attached as possible. He concerned himself initially with making the standard approaches: hassling A&R men to see the group live, playing demos, issuing press kits. It was an uphill struggle: 'You'd had all these front pages but they just didn't understand who you were,' he says. 'All they knew was, one, you couldn't play and, two, they just didn't want to understand it.'

The Sex Pistols' penchant for problems didn't help either: the *NME* had held back from covering the group after the Nick Kent attack, and Island Records A&R man Howard Thompson had happened to be in the club with Kent at the time. There were problems with Polydor: Chris Parry liked the group, but there was the matter of Steve Jones's activities at Middlesbrough in May when he had gone through the pockets of the headlining band, Doctors of Madness (who were contracted to Polydor) while they were on stage. McLaren also tried Simon Draper at Virgin, Mickie Most at RAK, and Dave Dee at Warner Brothers, all with negative reactions.

McLaren decided to hold another big event. Through an old art-school friend, Roger Austin, he set up a concert at Islington's Screen on the Green at the end of August. Advertised by the first handbill designed by Jamie Reid – a silhouette image of Lydon and Jones framed by contact sheets from the 100 Club – the 'Midnight Special' pulled together the Clash and the Buzzcocks in Punk's first metropolitan test of strength. Waiting for all three groups were not only the fans but journalists, photographers and A&R men.

The running order was: Buzzcocks, Clash, Sex Pistols, after Kenneth Anger's Kustom Kar Kommandos and Scorpio Rising. There was also a warm-up disco to which some of the Louise's regulars danced. 'It was a marvellous event,' says Nils Stevenson, 'but very hippy in a way. Malcolm and I had carte blanche to do what we wanted, and both being from that arty scene, we came up with a very 1967 type of event. All the artistic people who picked up on it and could be some help were old hippies who had cut their hair.'

The Screen on the Green was the nihilistic, mediated Warhol version of the mid-1960s, an odd mixture of innocence and decadence. The crowd was in full regalia: Siouxsie with her breasts out and a swastika, Alan Jones zonked on acid, Debbie in enormous dungarees with short, blue hair and a zippered T-shirt. 'I was still finding my way,' says Debbie. 'I don't think anybody really knows their way with clothes at fifteen. We created the style by not being educated about dress.'

'In Manchester and London, there was a sense that you had to make your own entertainment,' says Richard Boon, who had started managing the Buzzcocks. 'I used to answer that phone, book that rehearsal studio, but there was nowhere to play. There was a degree of mutual support, so as the people that became the Buzzcocks had arranged for the Pistols to play in Manchester, so we got to play with the Pistols in London as well.'

But, despite the front of solidarity shown to the outside world, Punk was already riven with competition. 'There was a feeling that we were outsiders,' says Howard Devoto, 'the Clash and the Sex Pistols were Londoners and we weren't.'

'There was a sense of people competing for copyright on presenting ideas,' says Richard Boon. 'At the Screen on the Green, the Clash went out into the alleyway to get dressed so that no one could see that they were wearing slogans and paint-spatter. There was that urge to secure their turf.'

Guided by a Bernard Rhodes in hot competition with McLaren, the Clash were being carefully groomed for stardom. Still a five-piece with Keith Levene, they had announced their presence to the world a couple of weeks before with an invitation-only 'first' concert for the press at their studio, Rehearsal Rehearsals, in Camden Town. There, playing in front of a car-dump mural painted by Paul Simonon, they unveiled a strong look to boost a three-chord blur that was already becoming familiar.

'All the stuff about Pollock was a veneer,' says Strummer. 'What actually happened was that Bernie rented that British Rail warehouse in Camden Town and we painted it. We didn't have any overalls, so we got all covered in paint. It was a good way to put together something to wear onstage, as we didn't have the back-up of the Sex boutique. We had to adapt what we could find in the second-hand shops, which was really horrible. We used to take jackets around to the car spray shop in the railway arches around the corner and say, "OK Pete, give us a spray."

'We weren't very good that night, because we'd been up very early unloading the scaffolding and building the stage. We were mean to the Buzzcocks, because we were the London crews, and we looked at them sitting in a row, thinking "You measly berks from the north." Now I really like those Buzzcocks records; they were also very good that night. It shows how mean we were: we didn't think of them as part of our scene. There was no solidarity.'

Everybody agrees that the Sex Pistols played brilliantly that night: certainly up to the standards then requisite for a professional Rock band. By now Steve Jones had perfected his role as the 'Guitar Hero' so mockingly painted on his battered stage speaker, and was accompanying his bursts of cluster chords and feedback with suitably pained expressions and macho movements. Lydon's customary rage was amplified by a collision with his microphone: a tooth cap was knocked out and the pain resulted in a blinding performance.

But, for all their shock tactics, the Sex Pistols were making conscious moves towards the music industry. The usual shambles was missing. If they sounded better than their rival colleagues, this was the result of stage management. 'The Buzzcocks and the Clash got no fair crack of the whip on the PA whatsoever,' says Roger Armstrong, 'miserable little sound like a transistor radio, then for the Sex Pistols they suddenly switched the PA on. It was so funny, these people putting something new together, and here's the old tricks.'

'From the Screen on the Green onwards, there was a real sense of campaign, that something more coherent had to emerge,' says Richard Boon. 'There was a sense of time running out.' The race was on to make the statement, patent the angle before the shutters came down. The presence at the cinema of several A&R men and the Sex Pistols' own confidence made the prospect of entering the music industry and thus the mass media more tantalizing: the Sex Pistols began to relax into the roles, not of 'everykids', but of stars.

A week later, the group flew off to Paris to play at the opening night of a disco in middle of the Bois de Boulogne called the Chalet du Lac. 'It was so refreshing, that trip,' says Nils Stevenson. 'It was marvellous to get out again: the whole group was very close for the whole trip. Billy Idol drove over in his van, with all the Bromley people sleeping in the back. The group kept Siouxsie and all those people at arm's length. It had got a bit elitist already in that way.'

'There was seven of us,' says Simon Barker. 'Little Deb, Sioux, Steve, me, Billy and Michael, one of the twin hot-dog sellers. Sioux had her boobs bare, and her outfit with the swastika armband. We were walking to this club and suddenly these guys jumped out with knives, really hassling us. When we got in to the club, Siouxsie got punched by this guy who tried to grab her tits, and then it got so bad that we were moved to another part of the club for our own protection. We just waited in the dressing rooms until the promoter said it was safe for us to leave.'

'That was one of the places where John really had it,' says Jonh Ingham. 'On the Saturday afternoon, Caroline decided that we'd all meet at the Deux Magots, because that was where Sartre and company had hung out. It started out that there was her and me and the Stevensons. People just kept showing up: all the group that had come

(left to right) Nils Stevenson, John Lydon, Jonh Ingham: Les Deux Magots, Paris, 4 September 1976 (© Caroline Coon)

over. We're just growing, this amorphous lump, and John showed up and he minced, he came in with this great big grin on his face.

'He was in a great mood: wearing a beret and this baby red sweater that was ripped down the side so he could get it on and this crucifix safety-pinned on. In ten seconds about eight photographers exploded out of their tables and this big crowd grew around us. Instantly people just stopped. John was clearly in his element: it was fascinating that we could stop an entire restaurant and that a crowd formed instantly when he showed up. The fact that he was last, it was almost staged: it was brilliant and it was great theatre.'

For their appearance in front of designers like Castelbaljac and the French Punk rock aristocracy – magazine owner Michael Esteban, Marc Zermati and writers Yves Adrien and Alain Pacadis – Vivienne and Malcolm unveiled a new costume suitable for their status, confirmed by Esteban's *Rock News*, as 'Couturiers Situationnistes'. At the Chalet du Lac, the Sex Pistols stood on a floor lit in strips, like a sunblind: flanked by Matlock and Jones in brand new 'Anarchy' shirts, John Lydon threw his hunchback poses in an extraordinary garment later called the Bondage suit.

In McLaren's account, the change was gradual: 'We started wanting to get rid of the fetish gear because it was not representative. You couldn't really wear a rubber mask walking down the street. When I came back from working in America, I'd brought a pair of military fatigue trousers, American marine trousers. I liked the basic idea and feel, but I wanted them to be tough, new. We found a fabric called Black Italian: it was a polished black satin cotton which British Rail used for their waistcoats.

'That fabric became the basis for the design based on those trousers. I wanted to put the fetish elements in. The sense of making a trouser become tighter even though it's wide was good: it had that energy, that ability to contract itself. So we got the zips, not only on the back up to the knee, but also on the thigh. We also got a zip that went right through the trousers and half way up the back; that was another fetish element.

'Then the idea of putting straps between the legs came up. We didn't know how to do it so that you could still walk. Vivienne worked it out: we had buckles on the calves and a strap between the legs. Then we wanted something primitive, something that reminds you of Tarzan and babies at the same time. Like a nappy or a beaver tail. That's where we came up with those bum flaps. Towelling was the best fabric and we should definitely never have it any other colour than black. Dye it black: make everything black, black, black.'

'John wore the bondage suit for the first time at the airport on the way to Paris,' says Ingham. 'People freaked out because they didn't have reference points for it. There was a serious fashion consciousness through the early days of Punk. So it was great fun, here in Paris, where everyone still looked the same and wore that year's fashion, to be outstyling them and causing concern on their part because we were so completely over the top. But cool.'

The return to England was an anticlimax. While the group was away, the *So It Goes* clip had been aired. From those who hadn't seen the Sex Pistols and wanted to know what the fuss was about, the televised effect was deeply jarring. The group avoid the lens: forced to depart from set positions in order to comply with the television convention of showing the person making the noise, the cameras chase Lydon in a sequence of jerky motions that give the clip an intense excitement. When the camera finds Lydon, he gives it a fleeting finger before swooping out of sight. At the end, the singer stares, as if envisaging the future, while the song dissolves into feedback.

In their heads and on the TV, the group were already stars, but as often happens, the future was a little slow in coming. The group came back from two major showcases to more boring northern dates. Paul Cook had quit his job at the brewery in the anticipation of signing a contract, but nothing had yet come through. 'Shortly after Paris, things began to get very strained,' says Nils, 'they were fed up with Malcolm and with having no money. Malcolm came in for a great deal of criticism. John was being quite serious about splitting the group up.'

Siouxsie, Michelle and Steve Severin at the front of the queue, the 100 Club, 20 September 1976 (© Caroline Coon)

16

Self-preservation is what's going on today.

Candi Staton: 'Young Hearts Run Free' (#2, July 1976)

You're only twenty-nine
Still got a lot to learn
And when your business dies
It will not return

John Lydon for Sex Pistols: 'Seventeen' (July 1976)

It was central to McLaren's ethos that the Sex Pistols would sign with a major record company. For him, there was to be no choice: he was in competition not only with New York and Paris but with Bernard Rhodes and Andy Czezowksi, and now Acme's John Krivine, who was trying to get a group together with Tony James and Billy Broad, who had just changed his name, in a marvellous act of wish-fulfilment, to Billy Idol. The Sex Pistols were clear brand leaders and had to have the best label possible.

There was an alternative: England now had a tiny independent circuit and by August, they were sniffing around the heels of the Punk groups. 'We were going to sign the Damned,' says Roger Armstrong of Chiswick Records. 'We'd seen them early on at their first Nashville gig. Jake Riviera, Ted Carroll and I were all standing at the back after it had finished, and we all looked at each other, and said: "That was terrible, but it was great. Somebody's got to sign them." '

Armstrong and Ted Carroll ran a small label that had been born out of the expanding Rock On empire: in addition to the Golborne Road and Soho Market stalls, Carroll opened a shop by Camden Town tube in August 1975 which quickly became a mecca for Punk, 1960s and R&B fans. Carroll had begun the label in order to license the old, obscure records for which he was always being asked in the shops, but he found himself quickly immersed in the here and now: the first release on the Chiswick Label, in December 1975, was an EP by the Sex Pistols' former rivals the Count Bishops.

Through feedback from retail outlets, Chiswick not only knew what people were after but how they liked it presented. By the time of their third release, the 101'ers' 'Keys To Your Heart', Chiswick were making picture sleeves. 'I became aware of the demand for them when I was at Golborne Road,' says Carroll. 'There was a little French guy who came in with EPs and picture-sleeve singles – mostly British beat groups like the Stones and the Kinks. We were just starting Chiswick when Skydog came along from France, which was very much aimed at that market. They did two Flamin' Groovies EPs which had picture sleeves: they sold extremely well.'

Chiswick had the field to themselves until two Pub Rock entrepreneurs, Jake Riviera and Dave Robinson, started their own label in July 1976. In a previous company Robinson had been responsible for one of the more spectacular hypes of the hippie era, when, in 1970, he flew a planeload of journalists out to New York to see the unknown Brinsley Schwarz. Seven years later, this would have been hailed as a masterstroke, but in an era of authenticity, it was disastrous. As is often the case, hype had been laid over real talent and Brinsley Schwarz made several good records in an enervated English Country Rock mode.

As Pub Rock grew, Robinson became involved as a promoter and a producer: he installed a studio in the basement of a prime venue, the Hope & Anchor, Islington, and recorded every group that played there from 1973 to 1975.

Named after the American music industry slang for a flop record, Stiff Records was formed with a four-hundred-pound loan from Lee Brilleaux, singer with Dr Feelgood. In the same way as Punks wore their insults with pride, Stiff developed a self-mocking approach to marketing that referred to its small size and 'lo-fi' production. Their slogans played on the record buzzwords of previous years: 'Today's Sound Today' and 'Mono enhanced Stereo'.

Their first single, released in August 1976, was a fine example of Pub Rock on the turn. Nick Lowe's 'So It Goes' was cynical, but 'Heart of the City' was a hyperactive tribute to urbanism which owed much to the Ramones. The single cost £45 to make, had eyecatching graphics, and instantly connected with contemporary obsessions, proving that independents could catch events as they happened. In an era where speed was everything, these snapshots would prove invaluable.

Stiff's agility and their eye for the main chance enabled them to make the first Punk signing in September 1976. The Damned were coming up quickly, perhaps too quickly, with a velocity that reflected the group's abuse of drugs. 'We used to take sackloads of speed,' says Captain Sensible, 'as much as we could possibly get.' Despite Czezowski's connections, the Damned and their manager were not part of the 'inner circle': the Damned had neither the unified look of the Sex Pistols, nor their socio-political ideology.

'Us and the Stranglers were always shunned from the Punk in-group,' says Sensible: 'I admired them, because they didn't give a shit. You've got to be true to yourself. There was very little camaraderie among the Punk groups. When we talked to the press, it was all slagging, but we got on with most people: we were such hopeless slobs that we didn't threaten anyone. In London there was a certain snobbery, but out of town it was fine: we were very approachable. We'd always be drinking with the people who came to see us.'

All the other groups presented a coherent front, but the Damned pulled in all directions. At the back was Rat Scabies, an ugly redhead dressed in denim and very little else, pounding the drums like a young Keith Moon. Ray Burns, now called Captain Sensible, treated his bass like a lead guitar; his unpredictable antics distracted attention from the serious members of the group. Bryan James had the wasted, Keith Richard look, while Dave Vanian made up for any lack of vocal ability with an effective Hammer Horror image.

'The Damned, much as I love them, were just hell-for-leather destruction merchants,' says Captain Sensible. They were the Bash-

Street Kids of Punk: their lack of calculation and insistence on high-octane, hell-raising fun meant that their rapid rise was bedevilled by the impossibility of any planning. While the other groups were carefully considering their moves (or having them considered) the Damned went out there and pulled faces at the world as if there was no tomorrow.

In August, the Damned played the 'First European Punk Rock Festival'. Staged in Mont de Marsan in south-west France, the event was an attempt to reassert France's primacy as the European Punk arbiter. As usual, the politics were all-important: the headliners were Eddie and the Hot Rods, already, after the events at the Marquee, confirmed enemies of the Sex Pistols. After the altercation between Sid Vicious and Nick Kent at the 100 Club, the Sex Pistols were banned from the festival for 'going too far', and the Clash then withdrew in solidarity. The Damned had no such scruples.

'The whole thing was organised by Bizarre Records,' says Andy Czezowski. 'We were offered five pounds a day, hotels at the other end, and a hundred pounds if we played. So we jumped on the coach: we were the only Punks in a coach of groups like the Pink Fairies and Roogalator, so we cornered the whole back. It was a nightmare. Nick Lowe had a fight with Rat Scabies: this level of abuse went on all day until we arrived in the evening.'

'That was the day I got my name,' says Sensible. 'We used to go up to Laurence Corner for cheap clothes, and I got this shirt with epaulettes. I was pretending to be the pilot, and shouting: "It's alright! It's alright! Everything's under control! It's on autopilot!" I could have passed for a pilot and people were getting upset. And someone said: "Oh, it's fucking Captain Sensible." We called ourselves by wacky names, so we could keep signing on at the DHSS. I thought it would last five minutes: I didn't know I would still be called Captain Sensible at thirty-five.'

'It went on like that,' says Czezowski. 'They didn't sleep all night, all on speed, running round the hotels, climbing out of the windows, concierge going bananas to the point where he called the police about 2 a.m. So they finally go to sleep at 8 in the morning and they're supposed to be on stage at 12 a.m. All they wanted to do was sleep and there was this fearful argument. They did their barnstorming to about fifty people and a chicken. Afterwards: more speed, more pills, more drink.

'By this time the festival was a disaster. It grew from about fifty people to a hundred and fifty. The bullring could have held five thousand people. Once back on the coach, the daggers start to come out. Jake Riviera comes over and says: "Don't do your washing in public", and by the end of the trip he's virtually their manager. The whole thing was foul. So we bust up: Ron Watts took them over for the briefest time before Jake signed them up.'

McLaren would have spat as soon as sign the Sex Pistols to Stiff Records: these old Pub Rockers were the sort of people who had impeded the Sex Pistols' progress from the very beginning. There was a serious side to the insistence on signing with a major: 'We were accused of being in it for the money,' says Jamie Reid, 'but I think, as with any sort of subversion, which was the name of the game then, money ought to be used to create the possibilities of change.'

'Always announce your music in the most theatrical manner possible,' McLaren wrote in a retroactive manifesto. He was preparing his final media assault; the movement was to be born by Caesarian if necessary. The idea of a festival was good: if it could be done at CBGBs or Mont de Marsan, then he would make the English festival the way to secure England's lead. The 'Punk Rock Festival' was the climax of his campaign to woo the record companies.

'Malcolm needed people then and was gathering them,' says Sophie Richmond, who became McLaren's secretary in the week before the Punk festival. The next week, McLaren hired Stephen Fisher as his solicitor and co-director of Glitterbest, the Sex Pistols' management company – bought off the shelf for a hundred pounds and incorporated on 23 September. Fisher reflected the businessman aspect of McLaren's character; Sophie, together with Jamie Reid, represented his more thoughtful, politicized side.

The daughter of a career diplomat, she had worked with Jamie Reid on the Suburban Press after leaving Warwick University in 1972. By 1975 the press had been sold and Richmond was living in Aberdeen when she was asked to take the job. 'I'd been interested in pop, but not in the way that men are,' she says. 'Men start collections and develop an expertise. For women it's a more emotional and personal thing. With the Sex Pistols, I liked being part of a group of people that I didn't know, but you had something in common. There was a diffuse intimacy: you could talk about anything, and not feel out on a limb.'

The finalized bill for the festival ran over two nights: on 20 September the Sex Pistols, supported by Subway Sect, Siouxsie and the Banshees and Stinky Toys; on the 21st, the Vibrators with and

Rob Simmons, Paul Myers, Paul Smith, Vic Godard: Subway Sect in front of Paul Simonon's mural, the Clash rehearsal studio, September 1976 (© Sheila Rock)

without Chris Spedding, the Buzzcocks and the Damned as headliners. 'It was a good idea of Malcolm's,' says Simon Barker, 'because it gave the media the idea that Punk Rock was big enough to have a festival. Really it was just a couple of nuts down at the 100 Club, but people still go there just to see the place. It's like some Mecca.'

The air of urgency was such that groups were conjured out of thin air. 'There was a vacant space,' says Siouxsie, 'and it was being discussed at Louise's. Malcolm was saying, "We need another band," and I volunteered, "We've got a band." We hadn't. The next day we rehearsed with Sid on drums. Billy Idol said yes at the time but vanished. Marco Pirroni we knew, he was a friend of Sue Catwoman's: so it was him and Sid Vicious and Stephen. *The Cry of the Banshee* had been on a couple of nights before and we thought banshee was a great word.'

'That first afternoon, when people were first putting down their gear and sound checking,' says Jonh Ingham, 'Ron Watts was saying that there were going to be hundreds of people down that night and the place would be packed. People told him he was out of his mind, but he went out, came back and said there were about five hundred people outside. This was the first time I'd seen a Punk I didn't know in the street.'

First on were Subway Sect, a group formed by two Mortlake

residents, who retained some of the distance and insularity of this obscure suburb. 'I was walking with Rob Simmons past the Marquee one night,' says Vic Godard, 'when we heard this noise. We went straight in and saw Johnny Rotten in the audience, throwing chairs about. We loved their image, but we weren't that mad on the actual music. But the performance was brilliant. We'd been doing rhythm and blues stuff and this blew that right out the window.

'Malcolm paid for our rehearsal time when we first started, at a place called Manos in Chelsea. He wanted as many groups as he could get. When he first came to see us, he thought we were so awful that there was no way we could do it. So he booked us in there, eight in the morning until seven at night, all week, and paid for it. And we were supposed to be on the festival the next week. We had only about five songs, "Nobody's Scared", "Don't Split It", "Out Of Touch".

In contrast to the speed and blur of the other groups, Subway Sect were monotone, more rigorous – their stage demeanour was as drab as Eastern Europe, their music coming in at the oblique angles of a group like Television. 'We used to dye all our clothes grey in those days,' says Godard, 'in a big bath. We liked the colour. We got the twangy guitar stuff from the Velvet Underground: what I was trying to do with the songs was to change the way that Rock songs were written. To pare it down, take out all the Americanisms. I didn't mind what went into the song, as long as the language was different: no "Yeah"s and "Baby"s.'

The Banshees' first performance was marred by problems. 'We had an abortive rehearsal at the Clash's place on the Monday,' says Marco Pirroni. 'We realized there was no point in trying to learn any songs.' The Banshees were going to use the Clash's equipment until Bernard Rhodes objected to Siouxsie's swastika armband and the swastikas felt-tipped on Sid Vicious's T-shirt, not wishing the Clash's PA to be tarnished by such an association. So the Banshees used the Sex Pistols' equipment instead.

'We did a Velvet Underground thing for what seemed like hours and hours,' says Pirroni. 'It was horrible: Sid was doing Mo Tucker. I was doing "Sister Ray". I remember me and Sid looking at each other and we were fed up so we just stopped.'

'Boom splat, boom splat, that's how Sid went,' says Siouxsie. 'It captured the spirit of how to do things: it was a shambles but something much more memorable than doing something we rehearsed. Listening back to it I could hear "Smoke on the Water" in wafts, but it all fitted.

'It was taking the piss out of all the things we hated. Whether Marco with his feedback, or me wailing over the top of it singing "Knocking On Heaven's Door" or "The Lord's Prayer" and Steve trying to turn his bass on, and Sid with his relentless banging. We expected to be stopped by outside forces: we didn't envisage being able to get away with it. One of the songs was "She Loves You" and also "Young Love" by the Bay City Rollers. What song do you really hate? What would you like to throw in as a shock tactic? What can we mutilate and destroy?'

All the groups were improvising new ways of performing out of necessity and terror: the media spotlight on the festival was intense. The Banshees had taken the idea that anybody could do it – as Sid Vicious said, 'You just pick a chord, go twang and you've got music' – and in pursuit of this ideal, jumped off the edge of the cliff, but the Clash were more cautious. The group lacked confidence but had some fine new songs like 'London's Burning', a hymn to the inner city, and a trebly sound that nagged like an itch.

Part of that lack of confidence was due to the fact that the Clash were now a four-piece band. 'Our drug intake was financially limited,' says Joe Strummer, 'but Keith Levene was much more "pro" on the speed. Sometimes I'd see him with a bag of resiny balls, speed in a very pure form. He began to lose interest. He rang up when we were doing "White Riot", and he said: "What are you working on? 'White Riot'? Well there's no need for me to come up then, is there?" I said, "Make that never, man." Bernie was shocked, but Mick was pleased: Keith and he were in competition about who was going to be the lead guitar player.

'At the 100 Club we broke a string. It probably only lasted a few gigs, but we'd decided, in all purity, that you shouldn't say anything in between numbers. But when somebody broke a string, you'd have to chat. I always used to have a transistor radio with me, because there was those cool pirate radio stations. We didn't have spare guitars then, so I just switched on the radio and held it up to the mike. At the mixing desk Dave Goodman was hip enough to put a delay on it and it happened to be a discussion about the bombs in Northern Ireland. It wasn't set up: it was pure luck.'

'The Pistols were absolutely phenomenal that night,' says Jonh Ingham. 'I think that was one of their great feats; the place was going berserk.' The performance at the 100 Club was more efficient, less playful than even a couple of months before. There was less banter between Lydon and an audience which was, by now, not hostile but totally converted. 'I felt bored that it wasn't going any further,' says John Lydon, 'it was too minuscule. We could very easily have fallen in love with ourselves and stayed there and died the death. You've got to get out of there, you've got to preach to a wider audience.'

Whether consciously or unconsciously, the group were being groomed for the music industry. For all their polemic, the Sex Pistols were ambitious for pop stardom and to this extent, the new world looked much like the old world: original fans like Shanne Hasler were already turned off by their elite aura. If the first night was for the elite, the second was to make up the numbers. The French Punk band, Stinky Toys, were held over, as the club had emptied after the Sex Pistols and they had refused to play. The rest of the bill was taken up by outsiders.

The Vibrators were a good example of a group caught in the middle. A Pub Rock group who had played the London circuit for a while, they were easing their toes into water that was heating rapidly, but any shrinking back was construed as a disastrous failure of nerve. They wore leathers but they performed Beatles and Stones covers. This was the sort of thing that the Punk groups were self-consciously reacting against.

As Punk picked up speed, many hoped to hitch a ride. It was a question of timing: the new groups were no more opportunistic but they got their pitch wrong. The Sex Pistols and those closest to them demanded a commitment which was beyond many people's understanding. With their long hair and mildly risqué name, the Vibrators were passers-by as far as Punk taste-makers were concerned. Never mind that singer Knox had a line in catchy tunes: they lacked *moral* content.

The sense of lines being drawn deepened during the Damned's set, when the antagonism felt between the Sex Pistols and the group that had formed in their wake spilled over into violence. While the group thrashed through the Stooges' '1970', Sid Vicious expressed his opinions about the group by throwing a beer glass at the stage. It hit a pillar at one side, shattered and showered glass over the front of the audience. Several people were cut and a glass splinter hit a girl in the eye. Sid Vicious was pulled out of the crowd and, with Caroline Coon in tow, bundled into a police van. By the time he reached the station, he had been badly beaten up.

This was an appreciable deepening of the miasma of violence surrounding Punk in general and the Sex Pistols in particular. 'The violence was just for the yellow papers,' says Richard Boon, 'it was completely incidental, very localized and small scale.' Punk violence was theatrical, but at the same time McLaren and Westwood were complicit in inciting acts of violence, as at the Nashville or, three months previously, at the 100 Club itself.

It was partly the result of impatience, frustration and intellectual arrogance. Yet there was something deeper: McLaren and Westwood were genuinely interested in the teenagers who flocked to their shop but they also used them as experiments in social engineering, human guinea-pigs for their deeply held libertarian beliefs. McLaren had been an admirer of R.D. Laing and the *Oxford Street* film had located itself within the framework of a child's viewpoint.

Of all those who flocked to the pair's dream academy, Sid Vicious was the most vulnerable. At the same time uncontrolled and rigorous, unpleasant and witty, he was still a child, thrust into an arena in which he was encouraged to run wild. More than any of the group, he was easily identifiable as Punk's figurehead. He had invented the 'pogo'; he came out with the most identifiably 'Punk' statements. Sid was the most extraordinary Punk everykid.

Sid had been involved in both violent incidents at the Nashville and the 100 Club. The name that had begun as a joke was becoming an imprisoning self-definition, one that was soon to be shared by the public. There was no one who was prepared to check him. Sid was indulged: even today, people close to the group will deny that Sid was guilty. 'Sid was very disturbed,' says Caroline Coon, 'but I don't think he threw the glass: I thought the stuff was thrown by first-time Punks who had come to the festival, and thought that was what they had to do.'

A week later, Vicious was in Ashford Remand Centre, from where he wrote a letter which contains the material one might expect from a twenty-year-old locked up for the first time. Apart from some contrition, there are the horrors: 'I get so agitated in here that I can't sleep at all. When I do, I get the most awful nightmares.' Clues emerge about the material he was being fed: 'I'm reading that book about "Charles Manson" which Vivienne lent me, and am finding it quite fascinating.' But finally, there is a serious statement of intent: 'One of the things I believe in since being slung in here is total personal freedom.'

The result of the incident was that, although they were not there at the time, the Sex Pistols were banned from the 100 Club, along with other Punk bands. 'After that we could just not continue with that sort of threat,' says Ron Watts in *The Sex Pistols*. 'If it happened again, *we* could be in trouble.' This was the latest in a long list of bans that covered most of London's smaller venues: the Marquee, the Nashville, the Rock Garden in sympathy with Dingwalls, and now the venue that had sheltered them since the spring.

Despite Punk's shut-out from the 100 Club, the festival was a great success. Ingham and Coon were preparing big pieces for their respective papers. The London-only *Evening Standard* ran a large piece a couple of days later about the festival, announcing a new, apocalyptic cult with a 'harsh dogmatic attitude'. 'The group and their followers,' it concluded, 'have recently been attracting a great deal of interest from leading record companies.'

While the Sex Pistols went on a tour through Wales, attracting the hardest-core Punks yet, McLaren and his new team made a final push. Working out of Thurleigh Court, Sophie arranged tours, daily payments, printing, flyposting, appointments with the music industry. At the start of October, McLaren was confident enough of success to hire an office in Dryden Chambers, a Dickensian backwater. A stone's throw from the hubbub of Oxford Street, the building was occupied by several seedy tour operators and escort agencies.

After the Punk festival two record companies were in the running for the Sex Pistols' contract, Polydor and EMI. Chris Parry at Polydor was convinced about their 'very good mainstream Rock appeal', but he was having problems pushing the deal through his immediate superiors. EMI were late on the scene. The principal A&R man was Nick Mobbs, who, at thirty, was initially resistant, despite being dragged to see the Screen on the Green showcase by the younger Mike Thorne, who had stumbled across the Sex Pistols at the 100 Club. Quite separately, Terry Slater from EMI Publishing made moves to sign the group for a £10,000 advance against publishing rights. Despite the fact that they were branches of the same company, EMI Publishing and EMI Record Division were quite separate entities, in different buildings. In Manchester Square, EMI's General Record Division would be interested in Slater's decision to sign the Sex Pistols, but not swayed by it to the extent of signing the group for recordings. In his denim, granny glasses and long frizzy hair, Mobbs was unconvinced.

Chivvied by Mike Thorne and impressed both by the atmosphere and by newspaper coverage of the Punk festival, Mobbs cut short a trip to Venice to see Wings, in order to see the Sex Pistols play Doncaster on 27 September. The day after, McLaren went to see Mobbs, who had been up all night listening to the Goodman tapes. He was not convinced that the group would translate to record. McLaren then pressed the Larry Parnes button and came up with the sales spiel of his life.

'I tried to convince him that this music had to be taken outside his form of taste,' McLaren says. 'I said "If you don't help these kids then God help the industry, it's all washed up and over. If you can't sign something that's new and young and in front of your eyes you're living in the past and you might as well shut up shop."' Fired up, and with Mike Thorne in tow, Mobbs used rhetoric not very different from McLaren's to persuade his immediate superior at EMI, Bob Mercer, to authorize signing the Sex Pistols. Against his own taste, Mercer agreed.

It was a money upfront, damn the royalties deal. The worldwide contract was for an initial two-year period, with two further one-year options, exercisable by EMI. In return, the group got a £40,000 non-returnable advance against future royalties, which were payable to the group – or rather, under Clause 17, to Glitterbest in the first instance – at the rate of ten per cent. Of this advance, £20,000 was payable on signing, with £20,000 a year later. EMI paid for 'reasonable' recording costs, deductible against future royalties. The group and Glitterbest were to approve sleeve design, with the choice of producer a 'mutual' decision.

Once they had made their decision, EMI moved very quickly, drawing up, altering and signing the contract in just one day, 8 October. The deal happened so fast that Polydor Records, who had paid for the Sex Pistols to do some more demos at DeLane Lea Studios, first heard about it when Parry phoned McLaren up to tell him the Polydor contract (for £20,000 less) was ready for signing the next Monday. McLaren just told him that EMI had got there first.

The EMI signing was a coup for both parties. The record company had got the group most visibly identified with the new movement of the year. EMI needed a contemporary success: although they'd recently had Queen and Steve Harley, the record division was still coasting on the huge profits made by the Beatles back catalogue. If the Sex Pistols were successful, then it was excellent PR for EMI; if they weren't, then they could quickly be forgotten when the next thing

(left to right) Glen Matlock, unknown, Terry Slater, Paul Cook, Steve Jones, Malcolm McLaren, John Lydon, Steven Fisher at the Sex Pistols' signing to EMI publishing, October 1976 (© Doug MacKenzie)

came around and £40,000 could be easily written off: the music industry is a high-risk business.

For the group, it meant a regular wage, the chance to record with proper facilities, and a way out of the web of bans that threatened to stall their progress. It also vindicated their self-image as the Punk elite: it was all very well for the Damned to sign to Stiff, but with EMI's production and promotional back-up, there was every chance that the Sex Pistols would become Rock stars, able, if they still so desired, to act out their theatre of nemesis not only in the UK but also worldwide.

The real victor was McLaren. With little or no experience of the music industry, he had hoisted a group that had started only a year before as near rejects, no-hopers, into one of the music industry stories of the year. The quality of the group was irrelevant in the face of the reactions that they inspired. Signing to EMI was a vindication, not only for his hard hustling, but also for his wide-ranging and extreme theories about rebellious cultures. His ego and ambition expanded.

'When we started, we were all pretty much our own men,' says Paul Cook. 'We weren't McLaren's puppets as everyone believed. He was like another member: he'd throw ideas in. He was a good guiding figure, when all the publicity started coming in, he knew how to manipulate that. But once he knew that something was happening,

Malcolm was totally into the band. That was when he started taking it away. He started thinking the whole thing was his: I could see that then.'

One further step had also been taken, and it built a time bomb into the already shaky structure of the Sex Pistols. On the day of their appearance at the Punk festival, the four Sex Pistols signed a management contract with Glitterbest at Stephen Fisher's office. 'I wanted to get legal advice for it,' says Glen Matlock, 'but nobody else was particularly bothered. In fact John said to me: "I hope you've read it, because I'm going to sign it and if it's wrong it's your fault." I had read it, and I wanted to argue the toss.'

This was the first real business between McLaren and the group. The initial period of the contract was for three years, longer than the EMI contract, with options over the next two years. In return for managerial services, Glitterbest not only took 25 per cent – most managers make 20 per cent – of the Sex Pistols' earnings but also obtained covenants from the group that put every aspect of their professional life in its hands. Glitterbest's contractual control over the group was to be as complete as possible. The management received the money from the record company, out of which it was to take 25 per cent, while they were to take 50 per cent from any merchandising. Glitterbest would further the group's career and undertook to provide bi-yearly accounts, but, according to Clause 14, the group accepted 'that the name "Sex Pistols" was created by the Manager and that such name belongs to and is owned by the Manager'.

'I remember saying, "Don't sign it",' says Nils, who nevertheless witnessed the document, 'because I could see how heavily in favour of Malcolm it was. I'd always been led to believe that I'd get some percentage of the management, that I'd get some points out of it. I looked for my name and it wasn't there. Rotten was saying, "It's alright, if you don't want a part of it, I'm leaving", which was all nonsense. Then they signed with EMI and Malcolm was saying "Come on, boy, get in the picture", and I wouldn't.'

It's easy to see the Sex Pistols' mistake today, after fifteen years of legal activity over contracts like this one: signed without independent legal advice by three people under twenty-one. But then the events which the Sex Pistols and Glitterbest set in motion have resulted in a greater knowledge of the music industry's workings. At the time, just as McLaren went for money upfront, none of the group thought much beyond the next month, let alone three years.

Punk was of the instant, like all teenage phenomena, but in their eagerness, the group had fallen into a classic trap. 'We had no independent lawyers,' says John Lydon, 'we were told, "If you don't sign it tonight, there'll be no deal." At that age, you're naive, you don't think of these things. You just see: contract, the big time. You think of the hundred pounds you're going to get out of it, not how it'll be an albatross for the rest of your life.'

The return of Generation X, October 1976 (Jon Savage archive)

17

The last part of what I've written describes any 'fascist' regime anywhere – this was what its enemies called it. But this time of bland, insular conformity, with its nasty amalgam of church, royalty, industry, the respectable arts, and the formerly unrespectable arts (every variety of pop), together with official science and official medicine, was also an age of anarchy which grew worse every month.

Doris Lessing: *The Four-Gated City* (1969)

Fascism is the basic emotional attitude of the suppressed man of our authoritarian machine civilisation and its mechanic-mystical conception of life. It is the mechanic-mystical character of modern man that produces fascist parties and not vice-versa.

Wilhelm Reich: *The Mass Psychology of Fascism* (1933)

'That summer was such an extraordinary event,' says Sophie Richmond. 'I was out of the country a lot but as soon as you got halfway down Scotland, you noticed. Aberdeen was really lush, and then after that everything was brown. And it seemed that everything was getting out of control on a larger scale.' As the heatwave intensified, drought conditions prevailed: by late August, columns of smoke from small fires dotted the landscape like warning beacons. When the weather broke in early September, the apocalyptic mood did not.

It was a time of portents. England's crisis had become what Stuart Hall calls 'the articulation of a fully fledged capitalist recession, with extremely high rates of inflation, a toppling currency, a savaging of living standards, and a sacrificing of the working class to capital'. In June, unemployment reached 1,501,976, 6.4 per cent of the workforce, and the worst figure since 1940. The pound dropped below $2 to reach a figure of $1.70. By July, the Chancellor, Denis Healey, was told by the Treasury that he had to cut public expenditure to regain the confidence of the markets.

'The real state of the British economy,' states Philip Whitehead in *The Writing on the Wall*, 'was now less important than the impression of it held by those from whom Britain had to borrow.' After failing to stem the slide with a package of £1 billion cuts announced for 1977–8 in July, the British government were forced to apply to the International Monetary Fund at the end of September. Although this was a world banking body, the balance of power was held by conservative Americans, inimical to a socialist government.

When the IMF team arrived in England on 1 November, American monetarists came to dictate the policy of a centrist Labour government. Even the avuncular James Callaghan could not disguise the fact that the consensus that had governed postwar politics and social life was cracking up. This consensus, partly inspired by the century-long democratic ideal of American consumerism, was not only inadequate against the recession of the mid-1970s but also patently untrue: one had only to look at the decaying inner cities to realize that poverty and inequality, far from being eradicated, were visible as never before.

It is difficult to remember, after more than ten years of divisive, radical Conservative government, how prison-like that consensus view had become by 1976. Under economic attack, the 'social contract' was beset from all sides by a multitude of conspiracies against the English way of life, in which letter-bombs, the Angry Brigade, public-sector strikes and muggings were all seen as a concerted, even orchestrated assault by a multitude of minorities that threatened to swamp the majority. This was a society wallowing in a not entirely unpleasurable masochism and lashing out at scapegoats.

Political and social (even behavioural) extremism seemed very attractive as a way out of this *impasse*: one of the first shibboleths to be overcome was the upper-middle-class liberalism which had been nourished by the 1960s and was now entrenched in parts of the government, the public sector and in some sections of the media, which failed to reflect the new, harsh, urban reality. 'Liberal-baiting,' wrote Peter York in *Style Wars*, 'Doctor Martens . . . punk Swastikas . . . the Thatcher Government: might work, *try it. Try it. Try it.*'

4.10.76: In fashion at the moment: 50s SF/Sub SF illustration; Razor-blade pendants; 'Sex' gear: T-shirts: Brian Epstein S&M/Gay stud/ Cambridge Rapist Hood/Collage Marxist/Mao/Plain with tear/bloodstain/ safety-pin; legends: 'I hate true love'/'Chaotic Bass Is Here'; leather trousers; dyed hair; Basic look (if affordable): terminal decadence, up to the wearing of Nazi armbands; Worry: when they start living what they dress. How soon?

Punk announced itself as a portent with its polysemy of elements drawn from the history of youth culture, sexual fetish wear, urban decay and extremist politics. Taken together, these elements had no conscious meaning but they spoke of many things: urban primitivism; the breakdown of confidence in a common language; the availability of cheap, second-hand clothes; the fractured nature of perception in an accelerating, media-saturated society; the wish to offer up the body as a jumble of meanings.

The Punk festival and the Sex Pistols' signing to EMI were big enough events to increase the media coverage. In the first week of October, both *Melody Maker* and *Sounds* ran extensive features on the festival which propagandized the new generation. Caroline Coon uttered for the first time the incantation: 'Do it Yourself'. *Sounds* ran a six-page feature, not only giving the first 'history' of the Sex Pistols, but rounding up seven new groups and selecting various individuals – Mark P., Siouxsie and Sid Vicious – as exemplars of the new age.

Ingham's disquisitions on what the movement should be called – 'Welcome to the (?) Rock Special', ran the headline – were in vain as, with the name 'Punk' firmly in place, it hit first the music press, then the evening London papers, then the tabloids. These initial reports were not unfriendly: a mixture of fashion notes and mild titillation. On 3 October, the *People* featured Newport Punk rocker Mark Taylor with swept-back hairdo and a chain through his nose. On the 15th, the *Sun* gave Punk a double-page spread.

Again, polysemy predominates: safety-pins, a handcuff, leather, rips and swastikas. 'The result looks like Hell's Angels in a Clockwork Orange nightmare', runs the copy. At the centre of the piece are the Sex Pistols: 'Thousands of punks gather wherever they play,' claims Judy Wade with a piece of hyperbole that might have come from the lips of McLaren. 'We want chaos to come,' Lydon is quoted as saying, 'life's not going to get any better for kids on the dole until it gets worse first.' Whether or not Lydon actually said these words is irrelevant: they show exactly on what terms Punk would enter the world outside the music press playpen. The 'movement' had now developed, within six months, into a complex, ironic phenomenon containing a rich mixture of truth and hype. Most of those involved had always wanted to engage with the mass media, indeed sought self-justification by so doing, and they now had their wish. The movement's growth was accelerated by this free publicity, but it was a Faustian contract.

'I hadn't expected to see the idealism of my generation denigrated with such aggressive negativity,' says Caroline Coon. 'When these boys were slagging off hippies, I realized that they had grown up reading about hippies in the tabloid press, and what they were doing was spouting "the shock and the filth" of the hippies. So I said: "The gutter press did to hippies what they're going to do to you."'

Punk's idea was to play the media's accelerated jumble of signals back at them, like one of William Burroughs' tape-recorder experiments in *Electronic Revolution*. This involved not only contempt for the media, but enough engagement so that there could be some common ground. The media were already encoded in the heart of Punk graphics, songs, clothes and attitudes: they would now dictate the way in which Punk developed.

Punk began to develop a sociology of its own. The most visible examples of this process were the Clash. The Sex Pistols were located in Soho with a dash of Chelsea, but the Clash were rooted in North Kensington. The Sex Pistols uncompromisingly set themselves apart, while the Clash were warmer and more of the people; if the Sex Pistols implicitly and then explicitly advocated the destruction of all values, the Clash were more human, closer to the dialogue of social concern and social realism – more in the world.

I've been trying to go out recently, but I've had to stay in. And the only thing I've got at home is a TV that hasn't got any sound on it. So I'm staying in, right, and I just want to hear sounds, I don't want to see no visuals, I want to go out and see some groups. But there ain't anything to go out and see. I've seen it all before. So I have to stay at home and watch TV without sound and lip-read my way through it. I'd just like to protest about this state of affairs. So if there's any of you people in the audience who aren't past it yet, and if you can do anything, why don't you get up and do it, instead of, like, lying around?

Joe Strummer: stage rap, the Roundhouse (August 1976)

While the Sex Pistols had been put together the previous year – and reflected their time with a sound that was often muddy and sliding – the Clash were brand new that autumn, pin-sharp, straight off the product development line. 'We had group discussions,' says Strummer, 'Bernie would say, "An issue, an issue. Don't write about love, write about what's affecting you, what's important." We were strict. We'd look at everything and think: "Is this retro?" I painted this shirt which said "Chuck Berry Is Dead". If it was old, it was out.'

The Clash began as a classic Mod group: angry, smart, mediated, pop. They speeded up the heavily chorded, stuttering sound of the Who and the Kinks and added new variations: the massive, galloping beat of Terry Chimes, a minimum of guitar solos, and the plentiful use of 'drop-out' – where all the instruments drop away, just leaving the beat – borrowed from the dub Reggae that you could hear in Shepherd's Bush or Portobello Road markets. And with Joe Strummer they had a great front man: energetic, tough, humorous yet compassionate.

Early material included songs about love, school, the heat: 'How Can I Understand the Flies', 'Mark Me Absent', 'I've Got a Crush on You'. But 'London's Burning', '48 Thrills' and 'Protex Blue' were ambiguous celebrations of a new urbanism, as up against the wall of Monday morning, the Clash sped 'up and down the Westway, in and out the lights'. Here was a new map of London, drawn with an innocence and a relish that the Sex Pistols never had.

The big book that autumn was J.G. Ballard's *High Rise*. Set in the near future which is also the shadow of the present, it describes a closed world of techno-barbarism simultaneously recorded and replayed on video. The sheer physical presence of the tower blocks 'had a second life of their own'; the blocks themselves are vandalized in the pleasurable exercise of forbidden impulses. High rises were both graphically interesting – for their stark, grid-like shapes which feature in McLaren's Croydon Art School portfolio – and convenient as emblems of a harsh urbanism: they had already appeared, rising out of slum clearance, on the cover of Led Zeppelin's fourth album, unfavourably contrasted with the rural landscape. After Ballard's *High Rise* and *Crash*, it was possible to see high rises as both appalling and vertiginously exciting: for now, their clean, brutal lines were a perfect site for the Clash's frantic hypermodernism.

From his grandmother's nineteenth-floor flat on the Warwick and Brindley Estate, Clash guitarist Mick Jones had an eagle's-eye view of a whole stretch of inner London: Harrow Road, North Kensington and Paddington, dominated by the elevated Westway; and blocks like the massive Trellick Tower that looms over the whole of Portobello Road and Ladbroke Grove. This was their stretch, marked, where the Westway passes over the Harrow Road, by a graffito, 'THE CLASH', that remained there, fading slowly, for years after the group's vigorous life was over.

The Clash's urban hyperrealism was quickly overlaid by a more conventional sense of social relevance. The group poached a Subway Sect song, 'USA', to spice up their own 'I'm so Bored with You'. 'I'm so Bored with the USA' was a brilliant rant against the popular culture of the day. '*Kojak* and *Columbo* were big at the time,' says Strummer. 'That lyric's not bad even now, although it's caveman primitive: it says a lot of truth about dictators, "Yankee dollar talk to the dictators of the world".'

By the time of the Punk Rock Festival, the Clash were still playing 'Flies', with its sheet-metal drumming, but the songs about school and love went out and in came 'Career Opportunities', based on Mick Jones's experience at the Post Office during the letter-bomb scare, 'Janie Jones', and 'I'm so Bored with the USA'. Their set was framed by two brand new songs, '1977' and 'White Riot', written after the events of the Notting Hill Carnival.

Traditionally held on the Bank Holiday which falls on the last weekend of August, the carnival is one of the few places where England's blacks can relax on their own terms in an otherwise cold, often hostile climate. By 1975, the carnival had been marked by the worsening relations between young blacks and the police. But this year, the police changed their tactics, increasing their presence from just under 200 the previous year to nearly 1,600: the result was a mood of anger and resentment which grew over the two-day event.

'Coming down, coming down,' the crowd chanted spontaneously on the Sunday, repeating the phrase over and over again as they passed through Notting Hill's crumbling, narrow stucco terraces. The next day, it did. After 5 p.m. on Monday 30th, most of the visitors had gone, leaving a hard core of black youth. When the police moved in to make an arrest, all hell broke loose, in the first major riot mainland Britain had seen since the riots there in 1958: 456 injured and 60 arrests.

'It was a lovely day,' says Strummer, 'me and Bernie and Paul were under the Westway and we were grooving to the Reggae. About twenty coppers came through in a line and I saw this coke can go over and hit one of them on the head. Immediately, twenty more were in the air: then the crowd parted to get away from the targets and the women began to scream. The three of us were thrown back against the wire netting as the crowd surged back. I thought we were all going to fall in this bay underneath the Westway, but the wire held.

'I lost Paul and Bernie for a minute. Chaos was breaking out all over the Grove: Ladbroke Road was lined with rebels, and cop cars were speeding through, these Rover 2000s, and they were being pelted with rocks and cobble stones and cans as they came through, it was like a bowling alley. I ducked in the Elgin and said, "Gimme a couple of drinks here!" I downed one and took the second outside, and I saw Paul throw a plastic cone at a police motorcycle. He hit the front wheel of the bike but the guy managed to carry on.

'Then Paul and I were standing in Lancaster Road: we hadn't noticed that all the white faces had gone. Suddenly this young posse came up: "Hey man, what you got in that pocket there?" I had this transistor radio, but I had this brick in the other pocket, and I said: "Don't say that shit to me." They shrunk back because I was shouting really loud. That was when I realized I had to write a song called "White Riot" because it wasn't our fight. It was the one day of the year when the blacks were going to get their own back against the really atrocious way that the police behaved.'

30.10.76: I go to see my first proper punk group. I know what it's going to be like: I've been waiting for years, and this year most of all: something to match the explosions in my head. The group are called the Clash; everybody I talk to says they're the best.

Into a Victorian Hall, half empty with people standing in bunches. Hostile, insecure. Suddenly four men with brutally cut hair come on stage, bark into a microphone, start making an industrial noise. The noise coalesces with the speed into a perfect chaos. One song: a genuine cry, a child screaming in fear: 'Waa waa wanna waa waa.' Within ten seconds I'm transfixed, within thirty, changed forever.

With its wailing chorus, 'White Riot' expressed a desperate longing that a voice and a face should be given to the white dispossessed. 'Black men gotta lot of problems, but they don't mind throwing a brick,' sang Joe Strummer, 'White people go to school, where they teach you how to be thick.' And if 'White Riot' was a call for whites to organize in a riot of their own, 'What's my Name' cast the pop theme of adolescent identity into explicit class terms, in a short burst of loser rage.

This was an uneasy juggling act from a group of three art-school students, one of whom had even been to a minor public school. The Clash's first ever interview, in the fourth *Sniffin' Glue*, set them in their state-of-the-art pink and black studio, with an art-school interviewer, Steve Walsh: they talk about first consuming society in order to change it. 'We deal in junk, you know,' said Joe Strummer, 'what we've got is what other people have put in the rubbish bin.'

'They were really over the top that day,' says Mark Perry. 'I went along with Steve and they were complete prats. Paul had a gun, I don't know whether it was real, but they were trying to be heavy. And they had a go at me for liking Eddie and the Hot Rods. Those guys wear flares, all of this. To me that was bollocks. Mick Jones spent three years before Punk learning how to be a Rock'n'Roll star: he wasn't a hooligan. In that sense the early New York groups were more honest.'

'Like trousers like brain,' Strummer concluded. Despite the posing, the Clash saw it through: their Pollock spatters were at once very arty and very accessible. As much as Vivienne's designs for Sex, the clothes mirrored the group's ideology: not only could the clothes, in theory, be made by anybody, but they could be used to broadcast codes and slogans within the cultural resistance that was Punk. They dramatized the polarization that was the wish-fulfilment of their name, yet couched it in fashion.

'After the Pollock look we got into stencils and stuff,' says Joe Strummer. 'Bernie Rhodes was guiding and packaging. He used to watch us rehearse and say "This is good, this is bad." He was very creative, his input was everything. He'd read all the books, knew all the trends. He probably suggested that we write words on our clothing: I never knew much about that Situationist stuff, still don't today, but that's where it came from.'

As autumn deepened, the Clash's clothes announced apocalypse. The custom-painted look was replaced by prison numbers, stencilled group slogans like 'Hate and War' or phrases taken from Tapper Zukie's 'Rockers': 'Heavy Manners', 'Heavy Duty Discipline'. Another new song counted down the magical year: 'In 1977/Knives in

(left to right) Joe Strummer, Mick Jones, Paul Simonon, late 1976 (© Caroline Coon)

West 11/Ain't so lucky to be rich/Sten Guns in Knightsbridge.' 'Knives in W11' and 'Sten Guns In Knightsbridge' made it onto the shirts: the nightmare of the middle classes finally came amongst them.

The Clash had learned about more than instrument drop-out from West Indians: anybody looking for a music that reflected a society in crisis had to look no further than Jamaica and its latest rhythm. By 1975, Chris Blackwell's decision to market Bob Marley and the Wailers as Rock stars was finally paying off: not only were they having hits, but they brought Reggae into the open. Stimulated by dreams of crossover success and an expanding English black market, Reggae poured out of Jamaica.

Reggae had an authenticity and a spirituality lacking in the dominant white culture. The Wailers were all Rastafarians, an apocalyptic sect formed by Marcus Garvey in the 1920s. As Henderson Dalrymple says in *Music, Myth and the Rastas*, 'Rastas hold the view that black people are the true Israelites and they can trace their lineage beyond Solomon and Sheba. Most of their principles of living have much in common with the ten commandments, Genesis, Revelation.'

By 1976, Reggae had its own network of independent labels, such as Atra, while English record companies such as Virgin started their own labels like Front Line. At the same time as the music of dub became more enveloping, so the lyrics delivered apocalyptic visions. Most influential during this period were the productions of Joe Gibbs, not only the 'Africa Dub' instrumental series, but also remarkable albums by Prince Far-I and Culture, which set dense rants against minimal music.

Prince Far-I's *Under Heavy Manners* called for a strictness on the part of Rasta – 'heavy-duty discipline' – in the face of social disorder: 'Under Heavy Manners' was the phrase used by Jamaican premier Michael Manley when security measures were introduced in 1976, after a spate of politically inspired shootings. As Far-I chanted, a synthesizer made otherworldly sounds that resolved into the wail of a police-car siren. 'I can see with my own eyes, that it's only a housing scheme that divides,' sang Culture in the song that spelt out the deadline: 'When the Two Sevens Clash'. According to the prophecy, 1977 was the year that Rasta would be free, and Culture sang in the full belief that the world would be transformed.

Reggae transmitted the experience of England's most visible outsiders: those Rastas who, confronted with prejudice, totally refused to enter England's dream. The Clash had seen how Reggae had acted as a soundtrack for social resistance at the Notting Hill Carnival and, with their use of drop-out and stencilled slogans, they were attempting to create their own white Rasta in Punk – a new cultural resistance. The more thoughtful participants, like Mark Perry, believed in this resistance: 'I was very much into a working-class revolution, through music, through media, a general take-over by Punk sort of people.'

The Clash had picked up their own Punk 'everykid', their celebrity follower just like Siouxsie or Sid. Steve Connolly had just spent two weeks in prison for an outstanding fine: 'I got my travel warrant to London, came down and the Clash were playing at the ICA. I'd spoken to Joe just before at the 100 Club, and I mentioned to him that I needed somewhere to kip, and he said, "Come up to the studio." I said: "What if I hump your gear, can I stay?" Hence my career began.'

Steve works today for a PA hire firm. There is little trace of his Punk past except for a barely dimmed, ferocious stare which he uses sparingly. Better known as Roadent, he epitomized the moral authority and class rage which marked Punk that autumn: his comments are marked with a keen intelligence which he seems wary of displaying. 'My old man worked in a car factory and I got a scholarship to boarding school,' he says, 'so I've got that patina of middle-classness that Punk had. My father would come in pissed and I was the first target. That's why as soon as possible, I left: I hate my parents.

'I lived in a few bedsits around Coventry, slept rough. Lots of odd jobs. You could do that then, a couple of weeks in a car factory and you could afford to knock off and be pissed for three weeks. Going back to Coventry now I never realized what an intimidating atmosphere it has. We used to have to drink in a gay pub because we'd get the shit kicked out of us anywhere else. We were dressing with narrow ties, a bit obscure: when we came down to London, it was natural for me to click into a similar thing.

'Rehearsal Rehearsals in Camden Town: we stole electricity from next door, we had a one-bar electric fire, three sheets and one blanket and there was me and Paul and Joe staying there. Fortunately Joe didn't have a sense of smell, still hasn't. Lucky bastard. The sheets never got washed: we'd get turns with the sofa. It was uncomfortable but you don't remember things like that. We used to play silly games shooting each other.

'I liked the Clash on stage, a lot of movement; the same with the Sex Pistols: everything it stood for. The attitude was initially very individualistic: the Angry Brigade bombing Biba's because of manufactured lifestyle. I thought it was about being creative with the way you looked. There was a statement that "This is how I dress", and that was aggressive. There was this idea, look at this hippie advertising generation: Richard Branson, Habitat. *The Society of the Spectacle*: it's true.

'The Clash were the first band to steal fans from the Pistols: they were the construction to the Sex Pistols' nihilism. The two go hand in hand to a certain extent, and John and the Pistols decried the fact, but amongst the punters you couldn't just bang your head against the wall, you had to have some reason why you were banging your head against the wall. I'd already read bits about anarchy and I realized that destruction could be a creative urge. But that was the attraction, wasn't it, that you had to have a generation of destruction before a generation of creation.'

'Demand The Impossible' ran the Situationist slogan on the Sex shirt: like other pop movements before it, Punk made impossible demands. Yet by accepting them you made a leap of faith that suddenly made those demands seem possible. At this point, it was by no means certain that Punk would succeed. As the Clash played in London during October and November, they attracted a violence and

(left to right) Mick Jones, Joe Strummer, Terry Chimes, Paul Simonon, 'A Night of Treason', the Royal College of Art, 5 November 1976 (© Jonh Ingham) a hostility that were as much symptoms of the force with which they were trying to make a breakthrough as they were of their rhetoric.

5.11.76: Out of bed with the 'flu to see the Clash again. I know now that that song is called 'White Riot' and that it's 'about' the carnival riot. I understand. They play it two or three times to an abusive audience, a few fans and my tape recorder. At the end, not of a set but a set-to, the singer jumps off stage with a helper, who has been lurching with speed-brimmed eyes just a bit too close, and runs through the dispersing crowd to hurl himself at two long-hairs responsible for the heckling and the flying glasses. The crowd clears and circles. A messy and inconclusive fight starts among the beer-slops on the floor. People watch, hollow eyes: the PA plays the Stooges' vicious, vacant, 'No Fun'. Everything fuses together.

At the ICA on 23 October, the Clash had played well, but an incident at the side of the stage got all the press attention, as Shane MacGowan bit the ear of fellow fan Jane Crockford. Great copy, great pictures: delicious mutilation fantasies. Two weeks later, the Clash played in the sixties brutalist surroundings of the Royal College of Art: this time, the violence was directed at the group and resulted in a scuffle – involving Strummer, Simonon and Sid Vicious – that was not only an expression of genuine anger but a logical conclusion to the Clash's theatre of provocation.

These incidents occurred within the relative security of art colleges and art houses, playpens compared with the council estates which were Punk's desired locations. As Punk entered the real world during that autumn and winter, it was very possible to surrender to the rhetoric. And it was perversely pleasurable: any apocalypse seemed preferable to the slow death by suffocation that is all too often the emotional experience of living in England. It was a way of feeling something, perhaps the only way of feeling left.

'You could tell it was a different world,' says Mary Harron, who interviewed the Sex Pistols for *Punk* that autumn. 'There was violence in the air. There was violence in the streets. I'd come from a place where it was dangerous, and therefore in your club, you don't want aggression and violence. Your club was an absolute sanctuary and haven where there was friendliness. Backstage at the 100 Club, I saw these little teenage girls with swastikas, and my reaction was, "to us it's a cartoon, here this is being done for real".

'There was something electrifying about the mythology which the

Sex Pistols had brought with them. They were chaotic. It was wild, whereas everything had been more proficient in New York. There was a sense of chaos, and the New York scene was not about chaos. But the Sex Pistols created a sense of, "What the fuck is happening?" It had politics. American Punk had no politics at that stage. America at that point couldn't decide what was going to happen next: they had a liberal-ish government. The best thing to do was to disengage. In England, there was a nightmare coming to life, it was overpowering and disturbing. Something had been given permission to show itself, it was exploding out.'

If there was one symbol of this nightmare, it was the Punk use of the swastika. 'It was always very much an anti-mums and anti-dads thing,' says Siouxsie. 'We hated older people – not across the board but particularly in suburbia – always harping on about Hitler, "We showed him", and that smug pride. It was a way of saying, "Well I think Hitler was very good, actually": a way of watching someone like that go completely red-faced.'

After the thirties retro fad of the early 1970s, the Weimar period of *Cabaret* and Visconti's *The Damned* became an accepted metaphor for Britain's decline. One of the sensations of 1976 was a biography of Unity, the doomed Mitford, the headstrong rebel with her pet rat. During the late 1930s, Unity appeared at major Nazi rallies and penetrated Hitler's inner sanctum. The onset of war put paid to her dreams of uniting Germany and England: the day war was declared, Unity shot herself.

Unity's appearance in the media made it clear that much had been left out of the accepted history of the thirties: for a while, the British had shown a distinct penchant for fascism, whether through Oswald Mosley's British Union of Fascists or the policy of appeasement run by Lords Rothermere or Astor of Cliveden. Fascism seemed a possible British archetype, an inversion of the image that had been rammed down everybody's throats in hundreds of lying war movies: history could have gone either way, like in Philip K. Dick's *The Man in the High Castle*, where the Japanese and the Germans, winners of the Second World War, preside over a defeated USA.

The wearing of the swastika served notice on the threadbare fantasy of Victory, the lie of which could be seen on most urban street corners. That this fantasy was now obsolete was obvious to a generation born after the war and witness to England's decline: 'It was a joke,' says Sophie Richmond, 'like *Oh, what a Lovely War*. But when it came to people buying T-shirts with swastikas on, everybody got very alarmed. I was completely ambivalent about it: I defended it on some occasions, attacked it on others.'

'I thought Siouxsie and Sid were quite foolish,' says John Lydon, 'although I know the idea behind it was to debunk all this crap from the past, wipe history clean and have a fresh approach, it doesn't really work that way.' There was one final point to the swastika that goes to the heart of punk polysemy: the erosion of meaning itself. 'The political inhumanity of the twentieth century and certain elements in the technological mass-society have done injury to language,' writes George Steiner. What better way to display this lack of meaning by detourning a once loaded symbol?

Outside Punk's playpen, unpleasant forces were stirring, to which Punks themselves were not immune. 'The mid-seventies was the time of the National Front and International Socialist confrontations so one didn't want to be encouraging those thugs,' says Sophie Richmond. 'Malcolm always said of the "Destroy" T-shirt that he was making a general point about leaders, which was a bit too subtle for the average NF or even the average Punk. It was a pipe dream.'

As the economic crisis deepened, the scapegoat tactics used by British racists won a certain sympathy. After Enoch Powell's 1968 speech, immigration was a hot issue, exacerbated by successive waves of refugees: the influx of Ugandan and Malawi Asians was exploited by the National Front, which managed to present itself as an orthodox party of the far right. In the summer of 1976, at the height of the tabloid furore about the Malawi Asians, the National Front polled 18.5 per cent of the vote in the Leicester by-election.

Such extremist activity had already generated a response from the left, as an International Marxist Group (IMG) counter-march led to a pitched battle in Red Lion Square early in 1974, which resulted in the death of a student. The scene was set for public disorder: as Stuart Hall wrote, the National Front 'plugs itself into the territorial loyalties of those kids who are clustering on the football terraces. It begins to latch into working-class neighbourhood culture and it affirms the kids' feelings about their locality, their whiteness. It put Britain and British into the vocabulary of youth culture.'

This was the sort of imagery with which Punk was toying during the autumn of 1976. Pop culture itself was not immune to fascist flirtations: 'I think I might have been a bloody good Hitler,' David Bowie had said that February; in May, he announced his return to England with what looked like a Nazi salute at Victoria Station. In August, a drunken Eric Clapton made a speech in favour of Enoch Powell at a concert in Birmingham, his debt to black Blues guitarists or Reggae artists forgotten. The next month, a letter signed 'Rock Against Racism', calling for action against this 'racist poison', was published in the national music weeklies. In this climate, a song like 'White Riot' could be taken a different way: not as an admiring shout of solidarity in sympathy with the blacks of Notting Hill Gate, but as a racist rallying call. To those without a key to Punk's bewildering jumble of signals, its combination of cropped hair, emotive symbols and brutal, harsh music that seemed to eradicate almost every trace of pop's black origins, pointed one way.

'I first worked for the Clash at Lanchester Polytechnic in Coventry, on 29 November,' says Roadent (who had indulged in some Nazi posturing himself). 'The Clash supported the Pistols and they refused to pay us because they thought "White Riot" was fascist. Then the Pistols did "God Save The Queen", which was called "No Future" then, it was only the second time it had been played. The students called an emergency general meeting of the union and by order of the committee they decided not to pay these fascists.'

Punk was trafficking in taboos at the same time as it sought to illuminate and dramatize deep-seated contradictions with a sophisticated, ironic rhetoric. Unlike many historical avant-garde movements, it had the potential to enter the mass market and in November 1976, was poised to do so. But the mass market is notorious for simplifying complexities and steam-rollering irony and the idea of a youth movement with swastikas hitting 'the kids' was simply terrifying. Punk's countdown to apocalypse suddenly seemed very dangerous.

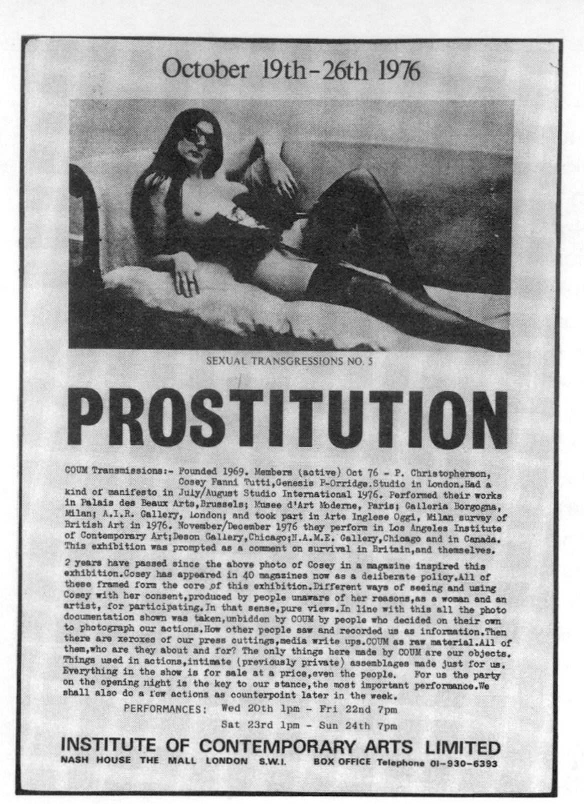

October 19th-26th 1976

SEXUAL TRANSGRESSIONS NO. 5

PROSTITUTION

COUM Transmissions:- Founded 1969. Members (active) Oct 76 - P. Christopherson, Cosey Fanni Tutti,Genesis P-Orridge.Studio in London.Had a kind of manifesto in July/August Studio International 1976. Performed their works in Palais des Beaux Arts,Brussels; Musee d'Art Moderne, Paris; Galleria Borgogna, Milan; A.I.R. Gallery, London; and took part in Arte Inglese Oggi, Milan survey of British Art in 1976. November/December 1976 they perform in Los Angeles Institute of Contemporary Art;Deson Gallery,Chicago;N.A.M.E. Gallery,Chicago and in Canada. This exhibition was prompted as a comment on survival in Britain,and themselves.

2 years have passed since the above photo of Cosey in a magazine inspired this exhibition.Cosey has appeared in 40 magazines now as a deliberate policy.All of these framed form the core of this exhibition.Different ways of seeing and using Cosey with her consent,produced by people unaware of her reasons,as a woman and an artist, for participating.In that sense,pure views.In line with this all the photo documentation shown was taken,unbidden by COUM by people who decided on their own to photograph our actions.How other people saw and recorded us as information.Then there are xeroxes of our press cuttings,media write ups.COUM as raw material.All of them,who are they about and for? The only things here made by COUM are our objects. Things used in actions,intimate (previously private) assemblages made just for us. Everything in the show is for sale at a price,even the people. For us the party on the opening night is the key to our stance,the most important performance.We shall also do a few actions as counterpoint later in the week.

PERFORMANCES: Wed 20th 1pm - Fri 22nd 7pm
Sat 23rd 1pm - Sun 24th 7pm

INSTITUTE OF CONTEMPORARY ARTS LIMITED
NASH HOUSE THE MALL LONDON S.W.I. BOX OFFICE Telephone 01-930-6393

The return of the repressed handbill, October 1976

18

I'm with you
You with me
We're going down in history
We're going down
We're going down
We're going down.

Iggy and the Stooges: 'Death Trip' (1973)

Hearsay: A new generation of performance artists has arrived. They use existing situations to actually affect society from the inside, to subliminally infiltrate popular culture aware of their perception as art but realizing their redundancy.

Genesis P-Orridge and Peter Christopherson: 'Annihilating Reality', *Studio International* (July/August 1976)

Two days after they signed to EMI, the Sex Pistols went into Lansdowne Studios to record their first single, 'Anarchy in the UK'.

'They were booked into the Deep Purple studio at Kingsway,' says Dave Goodman, 'but that never happened because the Polydor deal fell through. They couldn't finish the track at Lansdowne because they'd written slogans all over the walls, so we went to Wessex. We ran through the whole set: "No Fun", "Substitute", "No Lip", "Steppin' Stone", "What You Gonna do 'Bout it", "Did You no Wrong", and "Anarchy".'

'The idea was to get the spirit of the live performance,' says Glen Matlock. 'We were pressurized to make it faster and faster. We did about six run throughs while they were getting the sound together, and then we recorded it in two takes.' The result was rough and chaotic: over the bridge, Lydon puts on his Pied Piper act, shouting 'Follow me, little boys and girls' as the group thrashes away: the song ends with heavily echoed feedback, like an express coming to a stop. It was rejected.

'EMI didn't want "Anarchy" anyway,' says Goodman. 'They wanted a pop song, "I'm so Pretty", as they called it. Glen was going along with that but "Anarchy" was the strongest and that was what it was going to be. I was called into EMI, and Mike Thorne had gone in there with Glen and done their own mix of my production. They played me this acetate, and I just freaked. Then they went into EMI's eight-track and did about five or six tracks with Thorne.'

Despite the fact that the budget of £10,000 allocated to the single was almost used up, McLaren decided to find another producer: one mad idea was to use the reclusive genius of Pink Floyd, Syd Barrett, but when that came to nothing, Mike Thorne came up with Chris Thomas, an experienced producer who had begun his career working on the Beatles' *White Album* in 1968, and who had since produced Roxy Music and mixed Pink Floyd's *Dark Side of the Moon*.

Thomas was affiliated to Wessex Studio, a small studio in Highbury sited in the former Rank Charm School, and it was there that the Sex Pistols went to rerecord 'Anarchy' after fulfilling existing commitments around the country. It was not easy: there was conflict between Lydon and Thomas: despite the fact that Lydon's voice had been prominent among those wanting to rerecord 'Anarchy', he refused to sing and spent the time insulting the producer. Goodman was well known to the group, having travelled with them for the past few months, but Thomas came in as a perfectionist, and took hold of the Sex Pistols to give them a fuller, more professional Rock sound. Inevitably, he favoured the rhythm section and Steve Jones, with whom he began to develop the 'wall of sound' that would characterize all future Sex Pistols recordings.

As the one unconventional element in the group, Lydon felt rather squeezed. 'All those guitar overdubs,' he says, 'on "Anarchy", there were twenty-one guitar overdubs. That was Steve's first time, but it was all of our first times. There was one track left for the vocals, that was it. All I can presume is that Mr Chris Thomas didn't know how to bounce down, and neither did we. I don't think he was particularly interested. I had to do my bit in one go.'

There was pressure to get the single out, not only to comply with the demands of the Christmas market, but to keep up the Sex Pistols' own position as 'leaders' of the worldwide movement which McLaren was attempting to claim for the UK. Punk material was pouring into England through new distribution and retail centres like Bizarre, Rock On and Rough Trade. Rough Trade was the most closely tied in to the emerging market: unlike Bizarre, it had a storefront, in an old head shop one block away from the Portobello Road.

It was not only major-label material, like the second Patti Smith Group album, *Radio Ethiopia*, that was coming through, but also independent singles like Pere Ubu's '30 Seconds Over Tokyo', Television's 'Little Johnny Jewel', Wayne County's 'Max's Kansas City' and the products of Greg Shaw's BOMP label. From France came the Skydog catalogue, which made available relevant Flamin' Groovies and Stooges records.

The worldwide spread of Punk seemed to be confirmed by a forty-five from Australia, which contained the toughest, most brutal noise yet. The Saints' 'I'm Stranded' sounded as though it had been recorded in a wind tunnel, with the singer and the rhythm section hanging as gusts of guitar noise rushed past them. The lyrics, when they could be heard as the group plunged headlong into the heart of darkness, were full of the alienation and claustrophobia that were Punk's main concerns.

Through its centralized press, England was fast becoming the most efficient transmitter of the 'teenage news'. The Saints had been developing in near isolation for three years, but it took just one review in *Sounds* to make their career. In November the Damned released their first single, which was also the first record to come out of the Sex Pistols' generation. Stiff had moved fast, putting the group into a tiny, eight-track studio in October: the finished forty-five was out within weeks. 'We did that purely on cider and speed,' says Captain Sensible.

'New Rose' is a pure rush of enthusiasm, of people finding their power. There is virtually no tune and the words are nothing, but the group's relish is evident. The storyline – of the excitement of a new love affair – parallels the Damned's exultation in making noise. Beginning with a thunderous drum pattern from Rat Scabies, 'New Rose' resolves itself into a series of jerks and spasms, like a stormy sea, broken up by staccato drum breaks. Here was the first bulletin from an accelerated age: 'I'd better go, or it'll be too late.'

The Sex Pistols' pact with EMI was immediately seen as highly significant within the music industry. Nick Mobbs fielded the press calls with an excited rhetoric that could have come straight from McLaren: 'The Sex Pistols are the new people knocking at the door,' he said in the *Melody Maker*. 'They're knocking the Stones: the Stones are the Establishment to them. I think this particular group have a wider significance in that they're the start of a wave.'

Where EMI had jumped, many were preparing to follow. Throughout the autumn, there were the first signs of a contract frenzy, as, attracted by the press and the prospect of record-company interest, more groups sought to locate themselves under Punk's aegis. In October, the Vibrators were signed by RAK; one month later, UA picked up the Stranglers. Neither were strictly Punk, but nor were Eddie and the Hot Rods, then in the Top Thirty with their high energy 'Live at the Marquee' EP.

Another young group brought themselves to the attention of the press through a novel device. Formed by the teenage Paul Weller, the Jam had played in Woking and other south London hinterlands before reaching the London pub circuit in 1976: although they were genuinely teenage (unlike some of the other Punk groups), the Jam unfashionably paid explicit homage to the 1960s in general – wearing smart Mod suits and ties – and to the Who in particular. On 16 October, the Jam played in Soho Market, with electricity supplied by Rock On. The stunt had the required result: immediate attention. The Jam were young, fast and working-class but the reaction to them was equivocal. 'Sixties revivalists', *Sniffin' Glue* called them. Weller made the valid point that, at eighteen, the 1960s were new to him, but the smear of formal conservatism resulted in expulsion from the Punk elite.

There was now intense competition, not only between the Punk groups snapping at the Sex Pistols' heels, but amongst people fired up by the idea of pure novelty and speed. 'There was a period when there was this thing about wanting to be new,' says Jonh Ingham, 'there was more than just the Damned and the Sex Pistols by now. One night when Keith Levene was first doing the Quick Spurts, he was talking to me at Louise's: "The Clash aren't new are they? They're just the ultimate Rock'n'Roll form, aren't they?" '

'Keith and I used to work a lot on sounds,' says Viv Albertine. 'We used to talk about guitars all the time. We had this thing called guitar depression. It was about being depressed from learning to play your instrument: how you try to feed your personality through it. This sound we got was quite trebly, like a buzz-saw crossed with a wasp. It was just a matter of whacking all the treble up and distorting it. You had to be strict: there was no sign of a twelve bar in anything you did, except the Pistols.'

Albertine was working in a pool of musicians which included Keith Levene, Sid Vicious and Steve Walsh. Their group, the Flowers of Romance, rehearsed that autumn. 'It was a bedroom band, in Joe's squat in Shepherd's Bush,' Albertine says. 'We played Ramones songs, and couldn't keep time. Sid went from being a singer to also playing sax. It was a bunch of interesting looking people so we'd get interviewed and we'd never done anything and could hardly play.'

Vicious wrote some lyrics. With titles like 'Brains on Vacation' and 'Piece of Garbage', these scraps are a naked display of the ideas coursing through Punk. 'Kamikaze pilots/Want to die/Fredericks Hollywood/Husband and I', runs one verse: another song climaxes, 'Yer as bad as TV!' 'Belsen Was a Gas' was a distinctly queasy pun: 'Belsen was a gas/I read the other day/About the open graves/Where the Jews all lay/Life is fun and wish you were here/Was what they wrote on postcards/To who they held dear.'

'Sid was like a lot of psychotic people,' says Steve Walsh. 'I could never decide whether it was pathological or whether Sid was just a big baby. We slept in the same bed once after he'd been drunk on Special Brew and he pissed in it. He wasn't a typical hard man and he never pretended to be either. If the chance came for some serious violence he'd weasel out of it. Stab him in the back was his idea: there was nothing macho attached to it. There was a kind of worthlessness with him.'

Another new group, Eater, took the Punk concentration on the child even further, getting press from the fact that it had a manic fourteen-year-old drummer. 'When I first saw the band, they didn't aspire to Punk at all,' says Roger Bullen, 'they really wanted to be like the Velvet

Belsen Was a Gas

Belsen Was a gas,
I read the other day,
About the open graves,
Where the Jews all lay.
Life is fun, and
Wish you were here,
Was what they wrote on post-
cards to who they held dear

CHORUS Belsen was divine,
If you survived the train
Then when you got inside,
It's Aufiedersein.

Sid's handwritten lyrics, late 1976 (courtesy of Viv Albertine)

Underground. I was interested in being quite extrovert and over the top. So we became a Punk band in five minutes.' Bullen, much to the amusement of subheadline writers, became Dee Generate. Eater played their first date at their Finchley school: as the first Punk-by-numbers group, the most interesting thing about them was their youth. Singer Andy Blade played around with knives and scrawled swastikas on his clothes, while Dee spat and raved like his mentor Rat Scabies. It was a baby horror show. 'I was living in Surrey and going to school,' says Bullen, 'and I gained access to a kind of adolescent fantasy world. I could do all the things I wanted to do and I was praised for it. Suddenly I was given rewards for doing things that I wanted to do, that I thought were naughty.'

The children of the liberal consensus were turning against their parents, whether metaphorically or literally (as in the case of Sid Vicious and his hippie mother). 'Everyone was supposed to be seventeen,' says Mary Harron. 'It was a whole set of philosophical attitudes being set up by teenagers, who didn't know anything. At the time it was very exciting, because they had no sense of history or time.'

The Year-Zero behaviour of the Punks simultaneously railed at liberal *laissez-faire* and pushed it as far as it could go. Like any adolescent, Punk was attempting to find its limits, but in pop, anything was acceptable. In the outside world, however, there was by now a concerted campaign against the liberal freedom that the Punks exploited. As far as the tabloids were concerned, the 'freedoms of the sixties' had gone far enough and, with the COUM Transmissions 'Prostitution' show at the ICA in October, they served notice.

The 'Prostitution' show marked the first full public exposure of the radical theories centring around performance art. Parallel to Punk, it involved a merging of art and everyday life that is the archetype of the twentieth-century avant-garde. 'Our performances were about taboos,' says Genesis P-Orridge of COUM. 'I was getting more and more into the ideas of society's imposed conditions. So I'd deliberately try to break those taboos in a public situation where I was on the line.'

Born Neil Megson and brought up in Solihull, P-Orridge changed his name by deed poll in 1970. Obsessed by Warhol, he had worked with post-Fluxus English mixed-media artists, like David Medalla and Jeff Nuttall. The Fluxus idea was absurd, conceptual, witty, confrontational: early works included those by John Cage, LaMonte Young and Yoko Ono. P-Orridge formed COUM in 1969: 'The power of performance art was it could act like a magnifying glass,' he says. 'It was the reduction down to the critical moment between being dead and alive. Which is one only feels totally live but also under threat. That is expressed exactly in Punk at the beginning: the same edge.'

In May, the Sex Pistols had played at the Reading Fine Art department, with support from the Kipper Kids, a two-man performance group (both called Harry) who had a piece called 'The Boxing Match'. 'The basic gist was that there was one boxer and one referee,' says P-Orridge. 'The idea was that whichever Harry was the boxer had boxing gloves on and boxed himself. So he would be punching himself in the face, as hard as possible. Because the performance did not end until Harry Kipper the boxer had knocked himself out, it was a very bloody sight.'

'There were many ideas going into the Sex Pistols,' says Richard Boon, who organized that concert, 'many of which were implicit and many of which were explicit: ideas from the New York loft scene, and some of the difficult Italian and German performance art, and some of the British performance art, which were still in a very primitive state but had a lot of currency among the art-school crowd. There was a floating community of those people and it's not insignificant that they played at the Logan party.'

From that party on, throughout the year, Lydon often used live performances to launch himself into the void, stubbing out cigarettes on his forearm at the Lyceum, and entering into knife-edge provocation with the audience. This was a performance-art level of intensity in pop that had not been seen since the heyday of Iggy and the Stooges and, as Punk spread, it became one of the movement's hallmarks.

COUM Transmissions were also active in the growing 'mail-art' network, which had its most public expression in the San Franciscan magazine *VILE* and the Canadian tabloid *FILE*, house-organ of conceptual artists General Idea. Both printed pages of collages and fragments of mail, as well as providing indices of like-minded artists. By 1974, the artists had started to use xeroxes, because of the volume of correspondence. This then became the form itself: 'xerox art'.

In April 1976, P-Orridge was convicted of sending obscene material through the mail: the previous December, the Post Office had seized two postcards, one of which montaged Buckingham Palace and the Queen with images from a pornographic magazine. The same month, another mail artist, Pauline Smith, was harassed by the police for sending material relating to the 'Adolf Hitler Fan Club' through the post. It was not a good time to be examining taboos.

By the end of 1976, COUM were bored with the art world. 'The ICA show was a typical sarcastic rejoinder,' says P-Orridge, 'a fake final exhibition. In the installation we had porn mags like *Whitehouse* all museum-framed and dated. All of them had Cosey in them as a stripper and a model: that was part of her performance art, and the magazines were her documentation. Because we didn't do any of our own, that was our only rule. The documentation was the thing.

'Then there were four boxes on the end wall called "Tampax Romana"; that was a real Fluxus game. They were four cubes with glass fronts and one of them was an Art Deco clock with the insides taken out and instead one month of used tampons. It was called "It's That Time of the Month". Another was a Venus De Milo cast with a used tampax on each arm: here is the beautiful woman of art but she still has periods. And finally we had cycles of life: a box of maggots that turned into flies, and a twenty-eight-day cycle of tampons.

'We called the show "Prostitution" for obvious reasons, because art is prostitution. We thought the opening party was more important than the show. So we decided to invite all the most extreme people we knew and got lots of beer. No sherry, no wine; and let's have Rock bands playing and strippers and comedians who tell dirty jokes. All the art critics will hate it and go home and then we can have a good time. We decided to launch what we were going to do next, which was our group Throbbing Gristle.

'We knew John Krivine, who had this Acme Attractions group called Chelsea with Billy Idol, Gene October and Tony James. So we got Chelsea: we said to John, "They can't be called Chelsea for this, it's got to be something really naff", so we came up with LSD, because everybody hated hippies then. The band didn't want to play called LSD because they thought it was a horrible name. We said that that was the whole point! To annoy everyone.

'It went brilliantly. The stripper came and stripped. I got attacked by a guy from the *Evening News*. He came up behind me and smashed me over the head with a beer glass without saying a word. And I looked round and there he was with this glass. Then he went mad: he kicked somebody else in the balls, and then attacked three policemen outside with a brick. He got let off with a fine and then wrote this long vehement slag which triggered all the media off.'

Signalled by a threatening picture of Cosey Fanni Tutti in her working clothes, the opening on 18 October was chaotic, as Punk starlets mingled with journalists. 'The exhibition is on the theme of how the group is perceived by other people and how other people and the media distort it,' wrote Nicholas de Jongh on the day of the opening: the next few days saw this script brought to life beyond COUM's wildest dreams.

On 19 October the *Daily Mail* featured a trio composition of Debbie, Siouxsie and Steve Severin: 'These people are the wreckers of civilization.' Over the next ten days, the tabloids had a field day, until the Arts Council publicly repudiated their funding of COUM. On the 21st, questions about the show were asked in Parliament; the next day, P-Orridge went live on Thames TV's evening *Today* programme.

'It was depressing,' he says about the reaction which he had wanted to provoke, 'and odd. I would go down to the tube and there would be those newspaper posters saying "P-Orridge's Sex Show Scandal". I would look at it and think, "They mean me". After all that pressure for about ten days, I was just fed up. I didn't want to provoke any more: I could see the lie of the land. It would be an initial thrill and then an awful lot of counter-productive bullshit afterwards.'

The ICA show was the coda to a disastrous year in terms of the British public's perception of modern art. In February, open season had been declared by the Tate's purchase of Carl André's *Equivalent VIII*, a sculpture made out of fire-bricks. More attacks ensued on performance artists like Mary Kelly. This was not only an attack on public funding, but the beginning of the New-Right rhetoric about 'decency' and 'middle-class values' that came to dominate the social arena.

'All the animals come out at night,' says Travis Bickle in the big film of that autumn, Martin Scorsese's *Taxi Driver*. 'Whores, buggers, fairies, dopers, junkies. Sick. Some day a real rain will come and wash all this scum off the streets.' The shutters were coming down on the liberal dream and the artists who used that freedom to test society's limits found themselves public scapegoats as the New Right backlash began in earnest.

While the COUM scandal was passing through the tabloids, the Sex Pistols and Glitterbest were fine-tuning their relationship with EMI. On 12 October, they signed a two-year contract with EMI Publishing for an advance of £10,000, but almost immediately, a series of delays threatened to scupper the Sex Pistols' lead. EMI wanted 'Pretty Vacant': Glitterbest said 'No'. The record was to be released on the Harvest label, EMI's progressive subsidiary: 'No'. The artwork was usually done in-house: 'No'.

'Anarchy in the UK' was a strong idea and McLaren was ambitious for the Sex Pistols: the song was nothing less than a manifesto for the group's entry into public life. Lydon's ringing slogans: 'I wanna destroy the passerby'; 'Your future dream is a shopping scheme', are topped by a last verse that sounds like a scrambled newscast from a world beset by terrorist forces beyond the control of God or Government. 'Is this the MPLA?' leers Lydon in the final verse, echoing Tapper Zukie. 'Is this the UDA?' he continues, a second-generation Irish immigrant; 'Is this the IRA? I thought it was the UK!'

The presentation of the single had to be handled carefully. Group photos were rejected as clichéd by Glitterbest under their contractual veto: instead, they decided to use sleeves and posters to articulate the ideas behind the Sex Pistols. Reid and McLaren eventually came up with an idea devastating in its simplicity – a plain, shiny black bag. 'The idea was very anarchic,' says McLaren, 'to have no identity.' For the poster, Reid tore up a Union Jack souvenir flag and reassembled it with safety-pins and clips.

It was a difficult time for the group and their manager: attempting to

Jamie Reid's 'Anarchy flag', November 1976 (© Ray Stevenson)

make a nuisance of themselves at the same time as working within the industry to make sure they were heard. In contravention of industry practice, McLaren released details of the EMI advance to the press, but he was also working within the company for the group's success. Problems with production credits held up the single, while a dispute with the Ramones over billing held up a projected promotional tour.

The Sex Pistols' working practices were already chaotic, as concert dates were announced and almost immediately cancelled. The unofficial and specific venue bans placed upon them by promoters were still biting. During November, they only played three dates: one of them was at Hendon Polytechnic on the 19th where they performed a brand new song called 'No Future'. 'John was reading the words off a sheet of paper,' says Vic Godard, 'it was pretty shambolic. They'd obviously only just worked the song out.'

15.11.76: A tiny basement just off Leicester Square. Turn the corner, and you're in a circular hall, drenched in white light – one huge stage. Everyone is ready to act, to explain their novelty before the roving cameras. Mirrors, speed, self-recreation, identity-fuck, a sado-masochistic Pop group: the

Factory we've all been waiting for. The singer wears a filthy white shirt, round-collared with pin-holes, festooned with 'I survived the Texas Chain-Saw Massacre' stickers. It doesn't quite cover the burns on his arms. The group crash into 'No Fun' and 'Anarchy in the UK'.

People get up and dance on the stage and pour beer over each other, while the singer insults the audience and goads them to jump on each other. 'Got boring since we've been away, hasn't it?' Two girls are dressed in bin-liners and are tied up to one another with a dog-chain; the boy next to me has his face obscured by a Cambridge Rapist mask while cameras hover, kids wrestle by the stage. All the time, the cameras: the audience gets its own back by spitting on the director. On the way out, Clash are lurking, talking about record companies with Guy Stevens.

Tom Nolan, the EMI press officer, had no problem in getting coverage in the weeklies: it was more a question of orchestrating the requests. Three weeklies ran large pieces to coincide with the release of the single on 27 November: Caroline Coon and Barry Cain ran long pieces in *Melody Maker* and *Record Mirror* respectively, while Nick Kent opted to settle his scores with McLaren in the *NME*. This would be the last time that anybody got much sense out of them all for quite a while. More importantly, the group were getting some current affairs TV coverage. This was one area where EMI could use its clout. Every major record company has a TV plugger whose job it is to liaise with the closed world of producers and researchers. EMI's plugger was thirty-five-year-old Eric Hall (now the manager of 1990s footballing sensation Paul Gascoigne) who, although he had no great love for the group, could see that they had a good angle. Six months' weight of publicity finally paid off: the Sex Pistols weren't just a new group, but a social phenomenon.

On 12 November, the group appeared on BBC1's early evening show, *Nationwide*. The Sex Pistols were the leaders of new youth cult 'as big as the Mods and Rockers of the sixties'. Cartoonish fans like Sue Catwoman and Siouxsie fill the screen as the presenter runs down the new style: 'Punks wear vampire make-up, swastika armbands and leather trousers.' Even better was the studio discussion where Malcolm McLaren, Bakunin reincarnate, snapped: 'You have to destroy in order to create, you know that.'

On Friday 26 November, the Chris Thomas production of 'Anarchy' was finally released. A much cleaner, more mainstream version, it was by that stage so loaded with expectation that it was difficult to listen objectively. Things had happened so fast that to some, it was a disappointment, but Steve Jones's guitars held enough of the MC5's chaos to suggest a call to arms, while Lydon's final 'Destroy!' more than adequately broadcast the first part of Proudhon's credo.

Two days later, the *London Weekend Show* was broadcast (in the Thames region only). Presented by Janet Street-Porter, the programme remains the best single documentary about Punk, captured just before its fall. Filmed in the Notre Dame Roman Catholic church hall just off Leicester Square, the Sex Pistols look stilted but finally catch fire with a wonderful version of 'No Fun'. Vivienne Westwood jerks amid the hails of gob, while the pogopit at the front is distinctly polite. There are interviews with the Sex Pistols, the Clash, John Grey and the Banshees which sum up Punk's anarchic leanings.

What is remarkable about the documentary now are the obvious symptoms of psychosis: the almost autistic stares of the interviewees, the disturbed, rocking motion of the Clash, the lightning-quick mood shifts of John Lydon. There were many reasons for this, which are now readily understandable: individual disturbance, amphetamine use or simple adolescent obnoxiousness. But matched with an impoverished vocabulary that concealed both intention and intelligence, these blank stares dramatized the collective breakdown of a whole nation.

Punk psychosis was both a put-on and a paradox. 'What really impressed me through those first nine months,' says Jonh Ingham, 'was how intelligent the whole thing was. The Clash did a concert at a disco out in East London, there were only twenty people there, and bin-liners had just shown up a week earlier. Mick Jones and I were just falling about, saying: "It's so fucking stupid; what a great idea." "When it gets popular it's going to get really stupid," he said, and those were prophetic words.'

Against a backdrop of constant news stories about the bitter wrangling between the Government and the IMF, the Sex Pistols prepared to launch their single with a nationwide tour. Their management team hurriedly constituted a bill with the Clash and the Damned as support, with Johnny Thunders' Heartbreakers flying in as special guests from New York. Sophie Richmond, with help from Jamie Reid and Simon Barker, had to organize the PA, lights, transport, production and promotion for the nineteen-date tour – the venues of which were changing right at the last minute.

'It was a strain,' says Sophie, 'fitting yourself into an industry that was hostile and of course I knew absolutely nothing about how it worked. Practically everything about running a band, getting gigs and running that side of it seemed to pull up questions of principle all the time.' Throughout those two weeks, McLaren was convinced that EMI were not promoting the single properly. Unable to confirm his suspicions, he instead managed to extract more money to pay for the Punk package.

On the evening of 1 December the Sex Pistols got a break. An EMI group, Queen, pulled out of an appearance on the local London evening TV show, Thames' *Today*, presented by Bill Grundy. Eric Hall suggested the Sex Pistols as a substitute and had them accepted by researcher Lyndall Hobbs. McLaren wasn't sure: the group were rehearsing hard on a stage at the Roxy cinema in Harlesden and the Heartbreakers were flying in from America at that very moment, but when Hall arranged an EMI limousine, McLaren agreed.

'I met them at the studios,' says McLaren, 'we were in the waiting room where we were offered drinks. We were reading an article that appeared in *NME* that day – an interview with the Stranglers who were criticizing the Sex Pistols saying what a load of loathsome cunts they were, particularly Johnny Rotten. It really annoyed Rotten and Matlock; they were waiting and getting more and more bored. Eventually we were led up to the studio on the fourth floor.'

'I've got a feeling that Malcolm *was* geeing them up, stirring it a bit,' says Siouxsie, who had been brought in with Simone, Steve Severin and Simon Barker to add flavour to the proceedings. 'The group were trying to act nonchalant, but probably a bit nervous as well.' 'Grundy was wicked drunk in the artists' room before the thing,' says John Lydon, 'and extremely rude to all of us.'

The eight trooped into the harshly lit set: the 'fans' stood behind, while the group sat in front, from left to right, Lydon, Jones, Matlock, and Cook. The presenter was not well disposed. 'Grundy didn't want to interview us,' says Glen Matlock, 'not because we were gruesome, but because he felt he didn't know much about us. The producer said he had to do it so he thought his position was being undermined.'

'The thing that really started off the whole annoyance,' says McLaren, 'was the introduction to the show when Grundy was sitting in this chair and he was looking at a TV screen opposite him with the autocue. He was reading all his words and here were all the Sex Pistols sitting down and reading it with him and that really put him off. Jones especially coaxed him: "So we bring you to the *Today* news".'

'I was blonde then, with one eye and a star,' says Siouxsie: 'Very pert and very cheeky, very Larry Grayson. This horrible old man was trying to chat me up and I was going, "Well really! Ooooh!" '

'If you look at the media reports,' says Simon, 'it was like the Pistols had gone on there to do it. If you see it, that's not how it happened at all. If Grundy had said "Shock me" and Steve had done nothing, the Pistols would have been laughing stocks. Steve would have done it even if he wasn't in a pop group: John backs down, but Steve carried it out, just as if you'd said that to any football supporter.'

A transcript of the dialogue reveals its stilted, curiously archaic banality:

Grundy: I'm told that that group [he hits his leg with a sheaf of papers] have received £40,000 from a record company. Doesn't that seem, er, slightly opposed to their anti-materialistic way of life?
Glen: No, the more the merrier.
Grundy: Really?
[During this first exchange the camera shot is confused by waving arms, hands passing cups of coffee etc. Matlock tries not to giggle.]
Glen: Oh yeah.
Grundy: Well, tell me more then.
Steve: We've fucking spent it, ain't we?
Grundy: I don't know. Have you?
Glen: Yeah. It's all gone.
Grundy: Really? Good Lord? Now I want to know one thing. . .
Glen: What?
Grundy: . . . are you serious or are you just making me, trying to make me laugh?
Glen: No, it's gone. Gone.
Grundy: Really?
Glen: Yeah.
Grundy: No, but I mean about what you're doing.
Glen: Oh yeah.
Grundy: Are you serious?
Glen: Mmm.
Grundy: Beethoven, Mozart, Bach and Brahms have all died . . .
John: They're all heroes of ours, ain't they?
Grundy: Really? What? What were you saying sir?
John: They're *wonderful* people.
Grundy: Are they?
John: Oh yesss! They really turn us on.

Grundy: Suppose they turn other people on?
John: [whispered] Well that's just their tough shit.
Grundy: It's what?
John: Nothing. A rude word. (Pauses.) Next question!
Grundy: No. No. What was the rude word?
John: [a schoolboy] Shit.
Grundy: Was it really? God, you frighten me to death.
John: Oh alright Siegfried . . .
Grundy: What about you girls behind?
Glen: He's like yer Dad in' he, this geezer, or your Grandad?
Grundy: Are you worried or just enjoying yourself?
Siouxsie: Enjoying myself.
Grundy: Are you?
Siouxsie: Yeah.
Grundy: Ah, that's what I thought you were doing.
Siouxsie: I've always wanted to meet you.
Grundy: Did you really?
Siouxsie: Yeah.
Grundy: We'll meet afterwards, shall we?
[Siouxsie makes a moué.]
Steve: You dirty sod. You dirty old man.
Grundy: Well keep going chief, keep going. Go on, you've got another ten seconds. Say something outrageous.
Steve: You dirty bastard.
Grundy: Go on, again.
Steve: You dirty fucker!
Grundy: *What* a clever boy!
Steve: You fucking rotter!
[More laughter from the band and fans; Grundy closes.]
Grundy: Well that's it for tonight. The other rocker, Eamonn, I'm saying nothing else about him, will be back tomorrow. I'll be seeing you soon. I hope I'll not be seeing you [to the band] again. From me though, goodnight.
[Closing credits and perky signature tune: Lydon looks at his watch and Steve Jones gyrates his leather-clad hips.]

Viewed now, the *Today* clip is one long visual loss of control: all eight people slouch, grimace, look bored; hands fly across the screen at random; instead of waiting politely over the closing titles, the group bump and grind to the signature tune. And, rather than being the instrument of editorial objectivity, Bill Grundy loses his temper. Rather than dampening down an obviously volatile set of guests, he challenges them, with the inevitable response.

'When we went down to the green room,' says McLaren, 'there was Steve and Siouxsie getting hold of all the ringing phones and saying "This is Thames, get off the fucking phone you stupid old prat." The EMI chauffeur came whizzing through the revolving doors and said: "Come on boys, I've got to get you out of this straight away. There's going to be a storm."'

'Malcolm just grabbed me,' says Matlock. 'This limo was waiting outside, and we all piled in the back. Just as we were pulling off, a van load of police arrived.'

'I got a call in the office,' says Sophie Richmond, 'Eric Hall, sounding seriously worried, because he was obviously aware of the grossness of it in terms of TV convention. That was immediately after the broadcast, and then I had to go to Heathrow to pick up the Heartbreakers. We saw it on ITN while we were waiting for them. Malcolm may have been going, "Oh shit", but everybody else was exhilarated by getting all that attention. It was a kind of takeover.'

'We went out that night and people were pointing at us,' says Simon Barker, 'then we went up to the Hope & Anchor, and people were talking about it there as well. That's when I realized that it had gone out live. From that day on, everything was mayhem and madness, every single day.' 'It was hilarious,' says Steve Jones, 'it was one of the best feelings, the next day, when you saw the paper. You thought, "Fucking hell, this is great!" From that day on, it was different. Before then, it was just music: the next day, it was the media.'

Scandal becomes promo, December 1976 (Jon Savage archive)

19

Now all these tales [from Greek and German myth] are inspired by the same preoccupation. Cronos and Tantalus are fathers intent on destroying their offspring. The wicked queen, the hag, the giant and the giantess too are adults who try to destroy children, but in the end are destroyed by them. The common theme is generational conflict, between those who at present hold power and those who are destined to inherit it. And the means by which the adults try to retain power is, precisely, cannibalistic infanticide.

Norman Cohn: *Europe's Inner Demons* (1975)

In August 1989, Thames TV used the 'bloody battle' between Grundy and the Sex Pistols as a classic moment to advertise twenty-one years of programme making. On 2 December 1976, however, it wasn't quite such a glorious romp. About twenty seconds of, as the studio director Tony Bulley called it, 'a shabby and inconsequential item' had turned into a national scandal, with all the attendant farce: manic reporters, outraged posturing, and cries for action. The Sex Pistols' loud and dramatic shapes were replayed at them time and again.

On that morning, the headlines piled up. The *Daily Express* had 'Fury at filthy TV chat'; the *Daily Mail*: 'Four-Letter Punk Rock group in TV storm', plus a feature about 'The Bizarre Face of Punk Rock'; the *Daily Telegraph*: '4-Letter Words Rock TV'; the *Sun*: 'Rock Group Start a 4-Letter TV Storm'. Much of the problem was caused by the timing of the outburst, at 6.25 p.m., in the middle of, as the *Daily Telegraph* put it, 'happy family viewing'.

The right-wing Labour *Daily Mirror* – which had the most to lose from the IMF compromises – held the front page for its headline 'The Filth and the Fury': 'A pop group shocked millions of viewers last night with the filthiest language ever heard on British television,' ran the copy, alongside a transcript. 'Lorry-driver James Holmes, 47, was so outraged that his eight-year-old son Lee heard the swearing . . . that he kicked in the screen of his TV.'

'I've never seen Malcolm panic so much,' says Paul Cook. 'Some people believed that Malcolm had set it up, which doesn't compute at all,' says Ray Stevenson. 'I went into the office the following day and they were all shellshocked; they didn't know what to do. Steve didn't get over the shock for some time. Malcolm must have given him a telling-off after the Grundy show before he realized what the consequences were and how they could be used.'

'EMI wanted a meeting and it was ostensibly about the promotion of the single,' says McLaren. 'It was about the follow-up as well. That morning there were rattles on the door of Denmark Street from the press. Paul and Steve came rushing out: they ran off but were caught in the archway by Dryden Chambers. When we got to EMI they were completely surrounded by all the press: at all the windows of this building in Manchester Square there were people looking out and this herd of press outside with all their cameras.

'I met Leslie Hill, who told me that they were having problems with the workers at Hayes, who were going on strike and refusing to sleeve "Anarchy in the UK". "I'm going down to Hayes to iron out the problems," he said, "also, there's all this press outside. I don't know quite what I'm going to say: I'd rather not be in it, but there's nobody else." So he decided to call this press conference, and brought everybody inside EMI, and I brought in the Sex Pistols.

'They went to it tooth and nail. Leslie Hill was standing in the background and they asked the Sex Pistols what they thought of this and they just said that this was great. And this bloke said: "How did you judge whether this band can be a hit band, and what are you doing signing bands that are only out to cause trouble and swear on television, Mr Hill?" So he said that that wasn't necessarily true, that his advisers had said they were worthwhile musically.

'I suddenly realized, Jesus, you know it looked very heavy. But great because he'd been caught in it. Suddenly became part of the conspiracy. The press had their orders: "Follow them: everywhere today, the Sex Pistols had to be followed." I remember the *Evening Standard* arriving late and saying, "Where are you going now Mr McLaren? Where are the Sex Pistols? Where are they eating? Which café?" '

'At the time I thought, "Oh my God, we're doomed; this is the end of us",' says John Lydon, 'but it worked out all right. Ridiculous to hear of people kicking in their TV set; haven't they ever heard of the off button? It's the kind of thing you cannot plan, and when it happens, you make the best of it, you enjoy it for what it is.' 'It all made me sick,' says Glen Matlock. 'When we did this interview the next day, I burped, just burped, and went "Pardon me". Then it all came out: "Bass player belches", silly stuff.'

Grundy's culpability was the agenda for that evening's bout of headlines. Once Fleet Street gets hold of a scandal, an active editorial line has to be taken, tending towards some sort of 'action', real or symbolic, which 'resolves' the controversy. It is during this phase, as much as the initial burst of outrage, that boardrooms are persuaded to come to panic decisions. The *Evening Standard* had 'The Foul-Mouthed Yobs'; the *Evening News*: 'Grundy Goaded Punk Boys Says Record Chief'.

Print journalists have no great love for television journalists, who they believe steal their stories and are better paid. The *Today* team – producer Michael Housego and director Tony Bulley – had come unstuck on deadline fever; the decision to use the Sex Pistols was only taken ninety minutes before the show went on air. They were carpeted by Programme Controller Jeremy Isaacs. The next day, it was announced that Bill Grundy would be suspended for two weeks for a 'gross error of judgement'.

More interestingly, there were signs of a split between the two organs of EMI, the General Record Division, which handled the Sex Pistols, and Thames TV, 50 per cent owned by the parent company. Forced to comment at the press conference, Leslie Hill said that 'we feel that in many cases the media deliberately provoked this act; in no way does this affect the group's relationship with us'. The next day, EMI themselves were tabloid targets, as the scandal reached four front covers.

Much of the coverage the next day concentrated on 'results': TGWU action against the group, more concert bans, and Grundy's own retorts. In the right-wing tabloids, the music industry itself came under scrutiny: the results desired here were first, that the group should 'suffer' like Grundy and second, that the record company take some moral 'action'. However, this also revealed a Postmodernist view of scandal, as the media commented, almost instantaneously, on its own complicity in the processes of promoting outrage.

On the 3rd, the *Daily Mail* published an editorial entitled 'Never Mind Morals or Standards, the only Notes that Matter Come in Wads': 'The ultimate pedlars of the pop industry – slick, agile of brain, fast of mouth – know that the same three-chord product can be sold over and over again, as long as the package changes. Every financial year, the men who manipulate for money try to impose a fresh style. Increasingly, they capitalize on a basic tide of behaviour: young people's instinct to outrage the older generation.' This was a fabulous piece of hypocrisy, as well as the clearest articulation of the right-wing standpoint on the whole affair. As such, it was seized upon by Glitterbest who replayed it back to the world. This would become the standard view on the affair, reiterated at greater length by Ronald Butt in the *Times* the next week. What was forgotten, in the newspapers' irritation that neither McLaren nor EMI had expressed contrition, was that neither party had initially desired the publicity that Grundy had brought.

It was McLaren's cool insolence and EMI's commendable refusal to react that incensed the press. The dynamic of scandal works on fear and panic: if the intended victims choose to brazen it out, then the defeat of exposure is often turned into the victory of free publicity. Realizing this, the press turned on EMI itself: on the 4th, it was Leslie Hill's turn to be the object of attention, when his house was pictured, his neighbours canvassed and his family 'exposed' in the *Daily Mail*.

These arguments articulated deeper fears about Britain's future, as embodied by its youth. The moral panic that autumn was glue-sniffing: instant, cheap oblivion. The big fear, however, was unemployment. As the recession took hold, throughout the seventies, the seasonally adjusted figures rose inexorably: the figure of 2.7 per cent in November 1974 had doubled by December 1976. Of the 5.5 per cent who were unemployed, the 15–24 age group was the worst hit. It was these disturbing facts that Punk, with its nose for current affairs, dramatized.

The inevitable condemnations of Punk reflected its contradictory desires and its stupidities, but they were couched in terms so biased and based on an implicit definition of social acceptability that was so restrictive, that it was easy to reject them. If you did so, the whole thing collapsed like a pack of cards. If you were a Punk, you suddenly found yourself a scapegoat, an outsider. This realization – part delicious, part terrifying – radicalized a small but significant part of a generation.

The whole scandal ruthlessly unravelled the media play that had been going on within Punk at the same time as it exposed the workings of the music industry. It was very unusual to see the 'faceless' men of media boardrooms pictured in the press, and this is one of the origins of McLaren's radical reputation: it seemed that the Sex Pistols were an enemy within, entering the music industry in order to expose it, in a textbook example of 'demystification'.

The immediate result for the Sex Pistols was chaos. On 3 December, the four groups and their managers went to play the first date at the University of East Anglia Student Union in Norwich. It was cancelled on the day, by the Vice Chancellor, prompting a sit-in by enraged students. By then, six other dates had also been cancelled. On the 4th,

(left to right) Bernard Rhodes, John Lydon and Paul Simonon on the tour bus, 3 December 1976 (© Leee Black Childers) the tour was due to play Derby, but the Labour Council insisted that the groups audition before the Leisure Committee. McLaren decided that none of the groups should play, and issued a statement that the twelve councillors were 'too old to judge' the Sex Pistols' performance.

'It was like going on holiday but with guitars rather than a bucket and spade,' says Ray Stevenson. 'Leaving London there was a feeling that we were escaping from all the pressure, not realizing that it was waiting for us up there as well. All we could do was check into hotels and drink. You couldn't go out anywhere as you'd be accosted, so you were locked up with loads of alcohol. There were only so many pictures you could take of them drinking.'

The situation was rapidly degenerating. All the groups were travelling around on a bus and staying in expensive hotels paid for by EMI in expectation of sell-out concerts, but arriving for dates which might or might not have been cancelled by the time they got there. And the press were there, dispatched to keep the sensational front covers coming. At Derby, McLaren was approached by Wendy Henry from the *News of the World*, offering £500 for an interview: he refused before he realized that the cash might come in useful.

From Derby the bus went to Leeds, where a concert was scheduled for the evening of the 6th, after the cancellation of the Newcastle concert on the 5th. 'We suddenly realized it was going to be crazy with the press,' says McLaren, 'so the best thing was to keep on making more and more crazy ideas.' When the tour checked into the Dragonara Hotel in Leeds, the Sex Pistols gave the press what they wanted: 'This reporter said, "Go on, do some damage", so Steve and Paul kicked a few plants around,' says Roadent.

At this point McLaren went into overdrive and decided to push the already ridiculous situation to its limit. On the day of the Leeds concert, he 'refused to let the group appear' in front of Yorkshire TV's cameras, preferring to field the questions himself, with the group arranged behind like exotic, mischievous monkeys. On camera, the Sex Pistols giggle and stifle stagey yawns.

McLaren wears an Anarchy shirt, with a mohair sweater tied around his neck, and a quizzical expression. He delivers his comments in a fey Larry Parnes-ish voice. The interviewer opens: 'It's said that you're sick on stage, you spit at the audience and so on. I mean how could this be a good example to children?' McLaren replies, 'Well people are sick everywhere. People are sick and tired of this country telling them what to do.'

That night, the tour played its first date at Leeds Polytechnic. It was more of a media spectacle than a proper musical event. 'Because of the Grundy show,' says Roadent, 'people had started coming along to stare rather than to take part.' The Sex Pistols were determined to stoke the fire, as Lydon introduced 'Anarchy in the UK' with the dedication to 'A Leeds councillor, Bill Grundy, and the Queen – Fuck you!' The concert went from bad to worse as most of the audience, confused by the commitment the group demanded, either stood still or walked out.

'There was this pent-up volume of gob,' says Julien Temple who was travelling on the tour with his video camera, 'because everyone had read about spitting at Punk groups. It was volleys of gob hitting, and they were leaning into it: John looked fantastic with all this snot and gob over his hair. The Damned were on first, then the Clash, then the Sex Pistols: that was where the ranking of those bands was confirmed. The Damned were like this Radio One Punk group, and the Clash were very well-meaning in a Labour sense. The Sex Pistols were absurd anarchist theatre.'

Under stress, McLaren's latent Debordism came out. It became *his* show. At Derby, Councillor Leslie Shipley said that the other groups could play even though the Sex Pistols were banned: the Clash and the Heartbreakers showed solidarity, but Rick Rogers, the Damned's road manager, intimated that the group would play even if the others couldn't. After the bus arrived in Sheffield on the 7th, McLaren threw them off the tour. 'I sacked the Damned, a) because they were no fucking good and b) because Bernard wouldn't open for the Damned because he thought his band were much better. As far as I was concerned, after they had considered playing at Derby, they couldn't be relied upon. I remember Bryan James coming up to the room where I was with Leee and Bernard and he said, "Come on Malcolm, we're all in it together." And I said: "Well, we're in it together but I don't think you're going to be in it." '

'We thought the Damned had let the side down,' says Glen Matlock, 'but there was quite a bit of rivalry between Jake Riviera and Malcolm.'

'That was one of the saddest things,' says Sensible. 'Jake didn't trust us, and put us in a different hotel: I was fuming in Mrs Bun's B. & B., not knowing what was going on. I wouldn't have played: it would have split the ranks. Of course, after Grundy, they didn't need us anyway, they were news. We came out of it looking like a bunch of tossers, which we were, but not in that sense.'

Instead of the scheduled Bournemouth date, the tour went to Sheffield, chasing a concert that fell through at the last moment. By this stage thirteen out of the nineteen dates had been cancelled, and frantic readjustments were being made. Most commercial radio stations were refusing to play the Sex Pistols, and only John Peel stuck it out at the BBC. Record chains like Boots were considering whether to continue stocking the single, while small retailers who were selling it well complained about the lack of stock coming from EMI.

While the groups were in Sheffield, the situation with EMI blew up. Hill had proved patient, if not actually sympathetic, but his superiors had not. A warning shot was heard as early as the 4th, when EMI Chairman Sir John Read said about the Sex Pistols: 'Their style of attack on our society is something I greatly resent.' After the Dragonara incident, the *Daily Express* contacted Lord Shawcross, a former Attorney General and an EMI director, who said: 'I think we are being taken for a ride.'

On Tuesday the 7th, EMI's Annual General Meeting was chaired by Sir John Read: to his irritation, it looked as though the day would be dominated, not by the EMI Group's performance for 1975–6, but by the Sex Pistols. There were already internal EMI memoranda about the group circulating. Bob Mercer had written to Leonard Wood, Group Director of Music for EMI: 'It is worth making the comparison with the early Rolling Stones when they aroused similar outrage amongst media and the older generation.' But this was before Grundy.

The day before the AGM, Leslie Hill composed a much more terse, yet still sympathetic memo to John Read. This outlined the details of the group's contract and future plans: a second single for release in February 1977, and an album for April. Hill goes on to suggest that the press had inflated the problems. For Hill, it was a very difficult time, caught between the supportive General Record Division and his more conventional superiors on the corporate side of EMI. His own inclination was that it was worth persevering with the group.

There was little doubt which way the EMI board – which also included Shadow Chancellor Sir Geoffrey Howe – would jump. On the 7th, Read stated: 'Whether EMI does release any more of their group's records will have to be carefully considered. I need hardly add that we shall do everything we can to restrain their public behaviour, although this is a matter over which we had no real control.' 'Obviously irritated', Read openly discussed the possibility of terminating the group's contract with reporters after the meeting.

The Sex Pistols' retort to this paternalistic representative of the establishment, as reported in the *Daily Mail*, was 'Tell him to go fuck himself.' If there was a moment that sealed their fate with EMI, that was it. The same day, 'Anarchy in the UK' reached number forty-three in the chart. It was selling between 1,500 and 2,000 copies a day, a twentieth of what a Queen single would sell, but quite respectable for a first release, particularly for one with distribution problems that outweighed any hype.

More dates were being cancelled all the time. The next day, the tour bus drove to Manchester, where the groups were due to feature at the Electric Circus. 'EMI were phoning me up then saying, "Come on Malcolm, you'd better come home, this is going to be a disaster",' says McLaren. 'I refused. They were still paying but they refused payment at that point, saying they couldn't support us any longer. I decided to carry on, because I knew if we carried on, the publicity would, and we would turn round the story to "Would EMI drop the Sex Pistols?" because we were not crawling out.'

'It was a blind keeping going,' says Sophie Richmond, 'because if we cancelled this, then we'd disappear: so to go round the country creating a flurry registered that we were still there.' Holding the fort in Dryden Chambers, Sophie had to deal with the group's dwindling finances – rescued by a cheque from EMI Publishing which arrived on the 8th – and the fall-out from the cancellations. Worst of all, she had to field worried phone calls from the parents of the group.

'I'd told my family I was going to be on TV,' says Glen 'and my cousin, who was about seven at the time, was watching. So I phoned up a couple of days later, to test the water, and I got a right earful. I wasn't enjoying being on the road, and on top of that I got my mum going, "You don't think of us, why didn't you change your name." Because she worked at the Gas Board: "There's the girls at work, they're all calling me Mrs Sex Pistol." I had that going on every time I called home.'

It was a strange situation for all the groups. Neither the Clash nor the Heartbreakers had any record-company support. Although they had bread and board through the existing block hotel booking, if they didn't play, they had no money. 'All the way through December, we existed on twenty pounds a week,' says Leee Black Childers, now the Heartbreakers' manager. 'We still had solidarity,' says Joe Strummer, 'but we felt pretty small just then, because the Sex Pistols were front-page news, and we were just nothing, we were bottom of the bill.'

At the Electric Circus, it became obvious that the Sex Pistols were beginning to buckle under the pressure: just before the concert, they had been thrown out of two hotels. Any concert was a release of tension, but, as Richard Boon says, 'They were really sloppy. The Sex Pistols were still good, but with John the playfulness had gone. Some of the sharpness was there, but something had happened. Life was being made very hard for them.'

The Sex Pistols had now entered the vicious circle of media feedback subject to the law of diminishing returns. They were having to come to terms with a world that was almost universally hostile. 'The audience spends all its time spitting and throwing beer over the band,' wrote Sophie in her diary. 'Can they cope? I don't know. The audience don't seem to be able to react spontaneously and neither does the band – stilted reactions due to expectations produced by newspaper coverage. It makes me hate their guts.'

That Friday, McLaren went into EMI for the first time since Sir John Read's comments at the AGM. 'You could have cut the atmosphere with a knife,' he says. 'I noticed an in-house memo on Tom Nolan's desk, signed by Leslie Hill, which said that the Press Department were no longer allowed to speak on any subject concerning the Sex Pistols. That was from the top. Meanwhile Nolan was collecting piles and piles of press cuttings, he'd never seen anything like it in his life.

'John Bagnall [EMI A&R man], who had been artistically into it to the extent that he'd started to wear safety-pins in his V-necked jumper and his jeans started to be rolled up, had changed. His jeans were flared again. He was wearing high-heeled shoes and his hair was more Beatle-ish than before. Nick Mobbs wasn't really available for comment; Mike Thorne was out. Leslie Hill wasn't available for comment either: he was in trouble after the press stories about his house in Gerrard's Cross.'

EMI's policy about the group was in some disorder. The directors and the board wanted to get rid of the group, not only because of all the press but to absolve Thames TV of any responsibility. The Sex Pistols were convenient scapegoats. Leslie Hill and his managers were very concerned about the pressure, not only from the board, but from the threat of industrial disruption during the early December sales peak. But they also knew that sacking the Sex Pistols would damage EMI's effectiveness in the music industry.

If the Sex Pistols could have been demonstrably controlled, then a crisis decision might have been averted, but the public comments of the group after the AGM meant this was impossible. Instead of controlling his group, Malcolm McLaren was augmenting the madness. In the *Daily Mail* he seemed to be trying to drive a wedge between sections of EMI: 'It seems a case of Sir John saying one thing to so-called respectable shareholders,' he said, 'while another division of the company quite rightly thinks something else.'

By the end of that week, the press coverage had died down. EMI was in temporary disarray and had taken no action: there was a respite. On the following Monday the group had a meeting at Dryden Chambers to decide their own policy: they all decided to continue what was left of the tour. McLaren returned to EMI to try to get some more money for the Caerphilly concert the next day: he suspected that EMI were planning to drop the group quietly in the New Year after all the fuss had died down. They would thus be able to get rid of the trouble without being seen to give in to the press.

Every concert that could now be played was a minor miracle. There were very few venues in the country that would still have them. This was an extraordinary situation, which was beginning to resemble a witch-hunt out of all proportion to the original offence. The Sex Pistols had not been convicted of breaking the law, nor had such a thing even been suggested. They had not been dropped by their record label and the remarks of censure that EMI had made were general, not specific.

By this stage, the concerts themselves were secondary to the state of affairs: the Sex Pistols would never again play a date in England that was not surrounded by some scandal. From now on, they were a total spectacle. It had a disastrous effect on the group: from then until their demise in January 1978, they added only four new songs to their repertoire and their approach to their audience and their music remained the same. They were flies in the amber of notoriety.

At Caerphilly, the town seemed to have decided that a mixture of Genghis Khan and Satan was about to land in their community: shops and pubs were closed and shuttered. The previous week, two Labour councillors had attempted to get an injunction stopping the concert: when that failed, they led a carol-singing protest in the cinema car-park whose participants outnumbered those at the concert inside. 'I think they're very bored people who just need something to entertain their lives,' was Lydon's response, 'and we're the excuse.'

It was Lydon who suffered most from this notoriety. Steve Jones had started all the fuss, but he was only the guitarist and had a boring name: Lydon had the face and the pseudonym that captured the

John Lydon crucified, early 1977 (© Barry Plummer)

imagination. 'When I first met him,' says Debbie Wilson, then one of his closest friends, 'he was really skinny, young, sweet-looking, and quite naive. Then he got more old-looking, quite bossy, and quite nasty. It was fear, I think, fear of fame. You'd go places and he'd get recognized: he was frightened.'

In the short term, the group were kept busy just surviving in the bear-pit, as Punk finally began to hit 'the kids on the estates'. The Electric Circus, for instance, was surrounded by large, decaying, thirties council blocks. 'That second night was just a riot,' says New Order's Peter Hook; 'there were so many football fans and lunatics throwing bottles from the top of the flats. It was really heavy, a horrible night. Punk had been completely underground until Grundy: after that it was completely over the top. There were so many of the punks getting battered.'

Inside, the Sex Pistols seemed exhausted in comparison with the Clash: 'The difference between the two Clash performances at the Electric Circus was remarkable,' says Richard Boon. 'They were glowing. The Pistols had been on the road for most of the year and the Clash hadn't, and really benefited from practical experience.' As the Clash grew in public, so did the mistrust between the groups: 'On the tour it was OK,' says Nils, 'but in London the two groups wouldn't hang out together. With the Clash, it was like, the foe.'

The first issue of the magazine *Anarchy in the UK* went on sale in Manchester, brought up from London by Debbie Wilson and Tracey O'Keefe. It contained a mixture of Ray Stevenson's photos, Jamie Reid's graphics, and a special page from Vivienne. Planned well before the scandal, its extremist phrases now seemed only too apt, as the rhetoric of the Sex Pistols was reaping the response it had sown. In the middle of boardroom rows, tabloid front-pages and universal council bans, Vivienne's slogans like 'There is only one criterion: does it threaten the status quo?' looked, not silly, but extremely relevant.

After a final date in Plymouth on 22 December, the Sex Pistols and their tour returned to London exhausted, broke, homeless and with an uncertain future. That week, 'Anarchy in the UK' had reached number twenty-seven in the *NME* charts, but the group was running up debts that would eventually reach £10,000. There was still very little indication from EMI about what was going on.

Christmas, with its two-week shutdown, was looming. McLaren made one last push: 'I threatened EMI with a forty-eight-hour ultimatum, which was that they must come out into the open and say that they would support the Sex Pistols. And we wanted this statement to come from the Managing Director, if not from John Read himself.

'We were not willing to suffer his insults saying he might censor the Sex Pistols or any other pop music. We gave the news to Caroline Coon and Jonh Ingham, and the rest of the music press. It left us in a state where we didn't seem to be in a position where we were going to be promoted too much. At that point, there was no message coming through from EMI, and it didn't look like it was [going to]. Just before Christmas, EMI delivered a hamper from Fortnum & Masons to Dryden Chambers, and that was all.'

'We're so vacant': John Robert Burns at Leeds, 6 December 1976 (© Leee Black Childers)

20

Everyone is a prostitute
Singing a song in prison
Moral standards the wallpaper
The wall's a bad religion

Media TV what's to speak?
Take my decisions
How to find your inner self time
On the television

No one knows what they're for
No one even cares
We shout publicity hand-outs
Nobody's scared

The language we use is what we want
Does it help project the false?

Subject-to-object journeys mean
That a word loses course

We're talking in clichés
Betray yourself for money
Having is more than being now
Nobody's sorry

Subway Sect: 'Nobody's Scared' (September 1976)

I'm seventeen years old and haven't got one qualification at all. In my opinion, 'they' do not determine the level of your intelligence correctly. You can be on the lowest social level and have the most important asset – *common sense*; or you can have every piece of paper in the world and be the thickest, most pigheaded dunderbag on this planet.

Arcane Vendetta: *These Things* (November I976)

25.12.76: A party at Jonh Ingham's Victorian stucco house in Cambridge Gardens. In the kitchen downstairs, members of the Damned, the Clash and the Sex Pistols sit around a large table: the gathering is dominated by Roadent, whose furious scorn turns him into the living embodiment of obnoxiousness. Halfway through the evening, the Heartbreakers arrive, and install themselves in a tight corner near the telephone, which Johnny Thunders uses to make hour-long calls to the United States. Not collect.

The party settles into a series of small groups, staring at each other with a barely veiled hostility. In one corner, the Heartbreakers. In another, the Clash; in another, a couple of Sex Pistols. The sofas in Ingham's living room are arranged like battle-lines: Steve Walsh and I find a space in some no-man's land near the book-shelves and try to have some arty conversation. The evening drags on.

About 11 o'clock, the hissing and staring is interrupted by some real violence: a Frenchman bursts into the room, screaming that his fur coat has been stolen (it has, by Steve Jones) and he throws a knife into the door. The musicians' hard-man poses disappear until he has been bundled out and, afterwards, the atmosphere is more friendly: it could hardly be less.

The Grundy scandal had done more than damage the Sex Pistols' career development: it had broken for ever the fragile Punk unity that had existed even a few months before. Ambition replaced friendship, and stupidity intelligence as the groups queued to strike the simple, brutal poses now required by reporters. After the tabloid headlines, this new movement needed to be explained, but the explanations were flavoured by the news-peg of scandal on which they were hung.

Before Postmodernism, Style Culture and pop spread throughout Fleet Street, there was nobody to explain Punk from within: the reports were shaped by the images of nightmare which Punk conjured up. 'Punk rock lyrics certainly go along with terrifying the bourgeois,' said the *Observer*, while quoting one of McLaren's more extravagant statements: 'They are England's next generation and we will be proud of them. It's a class war; they want to destroy society.'

Throughout 1975 and 1976, a large, amorphous group of teenage stylists and social outcasts of all ages, sexes and sexual persuasions had gathered around the Sex Pistols and Sex, and around the other groups and shops on the King's Road strip as well. This was a milieu of some complexity, reduced within the twenty seconds of the Grundy interview to white, male Rock. A Rock movement of considerable energy, hostility and an unsettling politics, but Rock nevertheless.

'A lot of people who had been on the scene disappeared as soon as Grundy happened,' says Jonh Ingham. 'It became stupid very quickly and no one with any snazz wanted to be associated with something like that. They were into it for the clothes and the elitism and as soon as it became Rock'n'Roll they didn't want to know.' The Soul-boy crossover for instance, was wiped out overnight, as the unconvinced returned to their cavernous discos in the hinterlands.

'Bill Grundy was the end of it for me really,' says Marco Pirroni, 'from something artistic and almost intellectual in weird clothes, suddenly there were these fools with dog collars on and "punk" written on their shirts in biro. It had been like the Warhol scene, film-makers and poets and artists and God knows what. Then there was Sham 69: Jimmy Pursey leaping about like an idiot, and his band with long hair, flares, and Hawaiian shirts.'

Yet there was another side to this process of definition. All pop movements have started with elites – and none, to that date, more self-consciously than Punk – but there is always a point where the elite loses control. That point is reached when the mass market and mass media take over, a necessary process if that movement is to become pop. Within this transaction, simplicity is inevitably imposed on complex phenomena, but there is also a fresh burst of energy released with unpredictable, liberating results.

Punk was a living exemplar of the subcultural process: the dispossessed gain cultural access, but at a price. Pop music is the site of this sale and the record companies are the auctioneers. Definition is a vital part of this, not only pinning down Punk, but opening the floodgates of commerce. As the trade magazine *Music Week* stated: Punk 'might be THE NEXT BIG THING so long awaited'. For the next few months, any male Rock group with the requisite stance had an interested hearing from the major record companies.

The full musical impact of Punk would take a few months to appear: it takes time to form and develop a coherent sound live, let alone in a recording studio. The most immediate cultural impact of Punk was in the media. Mark P. had been one of the first people fully to articulate the 'Do it Yourself' ethic and in *Sniffin' Glue* 5 he had laid down the gauntlet: 'All you kids out there who read "SG" don't be satisfied with what *we* write. Go out and start your own fanzines.'

30.11.76: In the lunch hour, I sit on the bog attacking bits of paper with Pritt glue in a very real fever – got to do it now, now. 'It' is a fanzine. I need to give voice to those explosions in my head. Cut-up bits of the NME, *60s pop annuals, Wilhelm Reich and 'Prostitution' handbills, are slashed together around a long improvised piece about violence, fascism, Thatcher and the impending apocalypse.*

'In wartime only the clandestine press is free,' writes Greil Marcus, paraphrasing A. J. Liebling. At the end of 1976, the mainstream media were closed to Punk. Fanzines used the freedom they gained from this exclusion: the people who put them together could say whatever was on their mind, without worrying about censorship, editorial lines, subbing, deadlines – except the deadline of pushing your product into an arena that was still being defined. The result was a new language.

The most interesting fanzines were verbal and visual rants about whatever took their collator's fancy. Here, even the idea of authorship was at issue, as fanzines were produced anonymously or pseudonymously by people trying to avoid discovery by the dole or employers. In this they were closer to the submerged English tradition of pamphleteering – filtered through the psychedelic left or the pro-Situs – than anyone wished to admit at the time.

8.12.76: Up to see the Damned at the Hope and Anchor, clutching a few copies of London's Outrage, *hot off the xerox – a time-consuming and furtive procedure. The group are great: high-energy rubbish, with a lot of humour. Talk to a nice man from the TLS – identifiable by his camera – who is disappointed when he finds out that I'm not working class. I'm bemused until I realize that he has his script.*

Upstairs I manage to sell a few copies. There are two other fanzine writers with their products: Adrian with 48 Thrills, *and Shane with the original of* Bondage, *laid out on tatty bits of A4 paper. It looks fun and as I have access to free photocopying, I agree to xerox it: the next few lunch hours are spent dodging solicitors and injury from the rusty razor blades that festoon Shane's masterwork.*

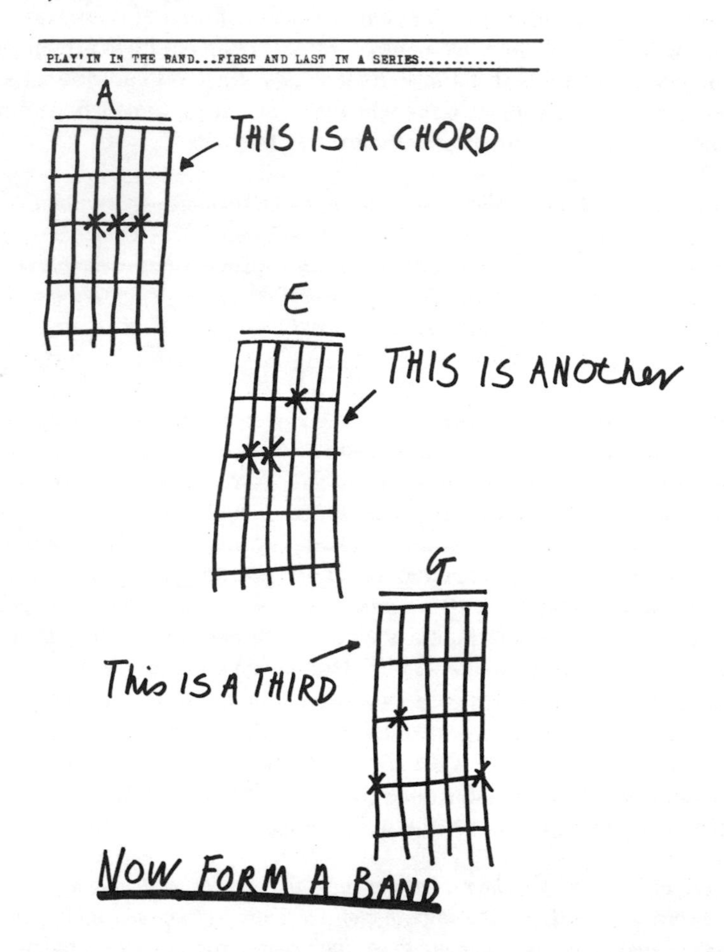

'This is a chord,' wrote the assemblers of *Sideburns*, a 'Strangler-zine', in December 1976, displaying an A, an E and a G: 'Now form a band.' Brilliant! Then there were *More-On*, by Crystal Clear and Sarah Shoshubi, with Pop-Art visuals, *London's Outrage*, *48 Thrills*, Arcane Vendetta's *These Things*, *London's Burning*, Jonh Ingham's Clash cut-up, inspired by Dawn Ades's *Photomontage* and Tony D.'s *Ripped and Torn* from Glasgow.

In fanzines, the leap of faith necessary within any pop movement was combined with a political critique that, although it now seems naive, was powerful then. 'There isn't any public decency,' wrote Shane MacGowan in *Bondage*, 'People only know what's decent by being told by ITV and the rest of the media and EMI too.' The same politics began to appear in the music press, as younger writers were hired to write as from within, in prose as extreme as the music.

The abdication by the established media from any sensible coverage of Punk was a boon to the music media. With their weekly deadline, the four major papers could explain Punk as soon as it happened, and, through their national distribution and good sales, have considerable influence. Even the black-and-white of Punk's graphics (and of its polarized mind set) fitted the papers' inky format.

Melody Maker and *Record Mirror* had their own Punk correspondents: Caroline Coon and Barry Cain. *Sounds* hired Jane Suck as resident, flaming Punk. It was the *NME* which had to make the biggest adjustment. Despite its brilliant analysis of pop culture's decadence – in a June article by Mick Farren, called 'The Sinking of the Titanic' after Bob Dylan's apocalyptic 'Desolation Row' – none of its writers could report on Punk as from within: figures like Farren – an early-seventies 'White Panther' – and Nick Kent were exactly the type of father that Punks wished to kill.

Change came from two directions. In July 1976, the bi-monthly *Street Life* had collapsed after sixteen issues, but not before leaving a mark: 'It encouraged this idea that there was more to pop or Rock, that there were other concerns, other interests, other politics,' says Angus MacKinnon, *Street Life*'s assistant music editor, who joined the *NME* that summer. 'In 1975: a paper that reviewed books, movies: a good issue would give *Q* or *Rolling Stone* a run for its money. It was hinting at a useful framework for the *NME* to inhabit by default, for the next few years.'

In August, aware of the need for new blood, *NME* Editor Nick Logan had placed an advert for 'two hip young gunslingers'. The two selected perfectly fitted the media image of Punk: Tony Parsons was twenty-one, from the East End, and had written *The Kids* for NEL, a Richard Allen-style novel which showed ambitions beyond that format. Julie Burchill was even younger, at seventeen, and – doubly unusual for the music press – female and working-class. They joined the paper in October: their brief was Punk and the *NME*'s expanding media section.

Nobody fully understood it that New Year, but the mixture of elitism and access, of aesthetics and social realism, that had made Punk so powerful was on the point of fracture under the impact of money, fame and attention. No group embodied these contradictions more clearly than the Sex Pistols. They were supposed to be the 'real', unreconstructed voice of the working class, but they were as heavily packaged as Slik.

The group were being clothed in the range developed for the new shop at 430, which had much greater input from Vivienne Westwood: now that they were paying their way, she could reinvest the profits in a change again intended to alienate the existing clientele. 'Vivienne wanted to go high fashion,' says Jordan, 'she made these proper outfits that locked together. She wanted to create a total image around the shop. People said it would never work.'

'The interior of Seditionaries was high tech, more pristine, more spartan,' says McLaren. 'The wall bars were kept but they were polished and placed in the centre. On the walls there were these huge photographs of Dresden being bombed in the war. Then I thought of a fun thing: Piccadilly. We put it upside down. Then to still have that bomb look we just bashed a hole through the ceiling.

'David Connor built this lovely little table with a live rat in a cage. For the front, we had the glass milked so you could have light coming in. It was a frosted white light so you couldn't look in. We wanted to keep the street outside and the photographs separate. Outside we just had a fluorescent light. Onto the glass we screwed in a brass plaque that said "Seditionaries".

'We had a grey industrial carpet that was rugged and good. We had nuclear chairs, sixties tacky futurist chairs in fluorescent orange. We had a label with black lettering on white with the "A" anarchy symbol and "For soldiers prostitutes dykes and punks". The bondage trousers, which had been designed at the end of Sex, really took off

(opposite) Michael Collins and Vivienne Westwood in Seditionaries, early 1977 (courtesy of Jane Withers)

with Vivienne's spider-man jacket. She carried on the straps and the zips that had been on the trousers across the jacket.

'Vivienne had this wonderful idea for the T-shirt which was to be done in muslin. I designed the "Destroy" image, the swastika with the cross upside-down and the broken head of the Queen and then the big word "Destroy"; they went on those marvellous T-shirts with the extra long sleeves that you could pull back with dog clips. They were all elements that we were taking from the fetish things and we were adapting them.'

Seditionaries opened just before the New Year. With input from Ben Kelly, who later designed Manchester's Hacienda Club, it was a futuristic, self-contained environment that put together all of McLaren and Westwood's obsessions – Sex, Royalty, England's atrocities – in an extreme environment. 'People were terrified of entering that shop,' says McLaren. 'You couldn't see in, so once you were in you were totally on edge. You were being watched. That was the point.'

The group were, of course, modelling the designs but there were signs of a crack in the Sex Pistols' image, especially now they were expected to pay for some of the clothes. Glen stuck close to his Mod roots, while Steve and Paul began to favour a more stripped, Ramones-style, Rock'n'Roll look. It was left to John Lydon to be the figurehead for the new, exclusive look, at the same time that he was playing the unemployed 'everykid' of England's nightmare.

The shop at 430 was becoming autonomous. Although McLaren had moved back to live with Vivienne, he was now involved with the Sex Pistols twenty-four hours a day, and would continue to be so for the next two years. In the meantime, Westwood had almost complete control over the shop and, increasingly, the last word on the designs. Throughout 1977, her reputation increased, as the Seditionaries clothes were used in endless glossy magazine spreads without any reference to the Sex Pistols.

The firestorm that resulted from the bombing of Dresden in 1945 is the most sensitive issue in any examination of English conduct in the Second World War. Its use as a basis of the shop's design indicates McLaren's increasing ambition to take on the Establishment. The Sex Pistols were as much a part of this ambition as Seditionaries, but they would stumble: human beings are not as malleable as store interiors and the group could not react quickly enough to their lightning-fast change in circumstance.

The Sex Pistols went from being cult figures to national scapegoats within the space of half a day. Under this blinding searchlight, a further contradiction was exposed: 'What was wrong with the Pistols,' says Nils, 'was that they were too good for their purpose. John's lyrics were incredible, for instance. The group became the style of the time because they were so good: instead of demystifying it and showing that anyone could do it, they proved that anyone couldn't.'

Lydon was a 'factor X' that McLaren had not bargained for, and from this time on, relations between them became more strained. Lydon had always been isolated within the group, but now he was further isolated by the level of public attention he received, which at the same time inflated his ego. There was more at stake now: the fight for control had begun.

The extraordinary events of December caused multiple problems for everybody in the group and for Glitterbest. These are recorded day by day in Sophie Richmond's diary: it is a depressed, and often depressing, account of very hard work. Sophie, until the autumn of 1977 the only woman in the office, was always deputized to do the mundane jobs – the only high points were provided by alcohol and the rare joy of seeing the group perform.

There was still no official word from EMI. McLaren had been in constant touch with Mobbs over the holiday, but, although Mobbs was totally in favour of the group, the decision lay with Leslie Hill. Conscientious to a fault, Hill canvassed opinion through the many divisions of EMI, and strongly resisted the pressure from Leonard Wood and Sir John Read, but they finally prevailed. A discussion on Christmas Eve killed the contract: the problem was how best to dress the corpse. Although it had gone against the grain to give in to press harassment, Hill had little choice. From his superiors came worries that the international reporting of the incident would jeopardize the business of other EMI branches: Sir John Read told Hill that the Sex Pistols' front-page appearance in the *Los Angeles Times* might damage sales of the 'EMI-scan', the brain scanner into the development of which the company had poured millions of pounds.

From the record side came a volume of complaints from packers, other managers and artists, all adding up to one message: the trouble that the Sex Pistols had caused and still threatened to cause far outweighed the prestige that they bestowed on the Record Division. Dissolving their contract might do considerable harm to EMI's reputation in the pop marketplace, but they were too hot for EMI to handle.

There was a burst of activity immediately after Christmas. Help came from an unexpected source: a music-industry hustler called Miles Copeland (the middle son of former CIA head Miles Copeland Sr). Copeland's record company, BTM, had folded in 1976. As a fervent believer in the free market, Copeland was unhampered by the fits of press moralizing surrounding the Sex Pistols. They seemed to him a perfect way to get back into business.

According to contract, EMI Holland were just releasing 'Anarchy in the UK' and the group were scheduled to promote the single on a Dutch TV show called *Rock Circus*. Copeland suggested three live concerts, two in the Paradiso, Amsterdam's famous drug club, and another in Rotterdam. The best thing was to keep the Sex Pistols working and with his pragmatic approach, McLaren had no problem in accepting Copeland's offer.

McLaren and the group prepared to go to Holland with the sure knowledge that their days with EMI were numbered. The people who made the decisions were still away on the Christmas break, but a final meeting was arranged for the 12th. McLaren continued to issue inflammatory communiqués to the music press who were covering every inch of the story. The only official statement from EMI had been Sir John Read's shareholders' speech of the previous month.

EMI's hand in this game of bluff was called on 4 January when the group, distinctly hungover, passed through Heathrow Airport on the way to Holland. It was an early start and the sight of the Sex Pistols looking green was enough: by early afternoon the hostile *Evening News* had broken yet another front-page story. Under the headline 'Revolting!', it told of how the controversial Punk-Rock group 'vomited and spat their way to an Amsterdam flight'.

A brief survey of the piece reveals a thin piece of muckraking: a KLM check-in girl who supplied the main quotation of the story 'would not reveal her name'. According to an internal EMI memo written by Hill the next day, it was also untrue. The Sex Pistols had been accompanied to Amsterdam by an EMI representative, Graham Fletcher. Hill checked the story with him twice: Fletcher repeated that the Sex Pistols hadn't vomited or spat on people that day. They hadn't even used the KLM check-out desk as they were late. But it was not enough. People do not read retractions but the headlines and first paragraphs of newspaper stories. The same day Robert Adley, MP for Christchurch and Lymington, sent a letter to Sir John Read stating that EMI was 'financing a bunch of ill-mannered louts who seem to cause offence wherever they go. Surely a group of your size and your reputation could forgo the dubious privilege of sponsoring trash like the Sex Pistols.' This was the final straw.

On the 5th, while the Sex Pistols were playing, rather distractedly, at the Paradiso, there was a flurry of phone calls between EMI and McLaren. As it was announced in an EMI press release the next day, the parties 'mutually agreed to terminate their record contract'. There was no information about the terms. The next day, Hill got on a plane to Amsterdam to work out the final details with McLaren, since under the terms of the contract, EMI were still legally bound to the group.

McLaren had seen this coming and had nothing to lose. He went for broke with a sequence of extraordinary interviews with the press, who continued to dog his movements. While most newspapers carried small reports giving the satisfactory – if a little tardy – 'result' of the scandal, the *Guardian* and the *NME* sent reporters out to Holland. As the Sex Pistols played their last show with Glen Matlock in the Paradiso, McLaren denied that the contract had been terminated.

'It's been very nice,' he said, 'someone's decided behind our back to mutually terminate the contract.' This was now ostensibly about the terms of severance but in fact McLaren was hyperventilating on the oxygen of publicity. In spite of Leslie Hill's conscientious behaviour, and his continued support for the group (when many others in his position would have given up long before), McLaren said one thing to EMI – agreeing to the termination of the contract – and another to the press 'talking unstoppably, like a man possessed'.

McLaren also attempted to orchestrate more scandalous headlines for the group's return on 8 January. 'Everything that Malcolm planned fell flat on its face,' says Simon Barker, 'and everything he didn't plan made headlines. He couldn't have planned that Steve was going to be really hungover, but when they came back, he made loads of us go to meet them. I went with Viv, Steve, Simone and Siouxsie, but there were only about three press people. No one was really interested.'

The press had won. After their own complicity had been put under scrutiny, they were more cautious in dealing with the group. Anything that too obviously smacked of manipulation was out. A genuine scandal was fair game however, and the next week, they had another when the very visible Lydon was picked up in Soho for amphetamine possession. The resulting headlines confirmed EMI in their desire to get the whole mess over as soon as possible.

While the Sex Pistols went into the studio – now rapidly becoming a haven – to record some demonstration tapes with Dave Goodman, the severance deal with EMI was finally hammered out. The Sex Pistols got everything: the £20,000 balance of the record advance, and most of the £10,000 advance from EMI Publishing, who were forced to fall into line with their parent company in releasing the group. Gentlemanly to the last, EMI issued a statement 'wishing the Sex Pistols every success with their next recording contract'.

The EMI Record Division's immediate future was troubled. After the departure of the Sex Pistols, the company lost confidence and staff over the next two years: 'If they'd stayed,' Mobbs told the *New Statesman* later, 'they'd have been successful internationally and EMI would have been re-established as a progressive company – a forerunner of the punk/new wave explosion, instead of not being part of it at all. It would have made a huge difference to its profitability.' In the second half of 1978, EMI's General Record Division lost £14.6 million.

As for the Sex Pistols, their recording future was assured. McLaren was already talking to other record companies, including Polydor and A&M. There was little doubt that the Sex Pistols would get another contract quickly: 'If you can't sell records after this publicity, you never will' was the attitude of the music industry. But no other company would be quite like EMI, with its place near the heart of the British establishment that exercised such a fascination for McLaren.

The Sex Pistols had hurled themselves at the corporate wall and, superficially, they had come out on top. Emotionally and creatively, however, they were at a virtual standstill: of the six songs taped in Gooseberry Studios, the only new composition was a splenetic rant about 'EMI'. In the January version, Lydon barely bothers to sing, merely reciting a list of legal points, but his customary scorn has been given extra moral authority. Had they not already issued a warning to the music industry in the lyrics of 'Seventeen'?

Even though the Sex Pistols had got their money, McLaren was locked in overdrive. 'I'm out to see Sir John Read and puke all over his face,' he told *National Rockstar*; 'I would like that satisfaction. Just put him in a room with me and the band on our own.' All the energies of both group and management were now concentrated on reacting rather than initiating: it was almost impossible to do any long-term planning, and when it occurred, it was usually sensationalistic.

The Grundy scandal made the Sex Pistols, but it also killed them. They were now frozen in time, leaders of a movement which had been wrested out of their control. It also froze Punk itself: 'If it had just been allowed to go its own merry way,' says Jonh Ingham, 'it would have grown very slowly throughout 1977, it would have snowballed, and it would have ended up being more intelligent.' The spites had now been let out of Pandora's box, but they flew on damaged wings.

'The residue of the impotence that everybody felt at the end of hippie was implanted into those kids,' says Caroline Coon. 'The politics being fed to those kids was that old-fashioned anarchy. That was the undoing of the Punk movement, they chose a philosophy that annihilated them. I went rushing to *Release* and said, "Look up the law on offensive weapons, because I think the government is going to use the fact that punks are wearing razors to annihilate the movement." But very quickly it was obvious that they weren't going to be any problem to the government at all.'

Joe Strummer, the Roxy, 1 January 1977 (© Ray Stevenson)

I want to tell it to you black brother and sister, then maybe you will understand, that this here 1977 nah go well dread, yah. Cause you know Garvey's words must come true. All brutality and war must come to a halt, war and trouble and fire are natty's fault. Equality and justice must stand, and all righteous men must stand too y'know . . . *When the two sevens clash!* . . . So you see that Marcus Mosiah Garvey's words must never be despised, and I hope Babylon the wicked shall now realize, there will be brimstone and lightning and thunder.

Bo Jangles: 'Prophesy Reveal' (1976)

Hopefully bands will emerge from other parts of the country to make Clash and the Pistols look weedy. Those bands themselves have a few aces up their sleeve. Also there is the possibility that we are witnessing the last death throes of youth and Rock'n'Roll. It could just become so boring, unexciting and predictable that no one will want to know, and will go on to do things for themselves.

'Punk Is Dead (Long live punk)', *Anarchy in the UK*, 2 (1977)

1977: rarely had a year been so apotheosized. Like 1966, the double numerals had been seen as a portent by apocalypsists of all types, from David Bowie to the Reggae artists whose tongues were to be heard wherever Punks gathered. It was not only the year of the Queen's Jubilee, but the year that Marcus Garvey prophesied that the Rastas' apocalypse would occur: when the chosen Jamaicans would be free to return to Africa. For Punks, it was to be the year that Britain faced up to the present and to the future.

The New Year was heralded, not by the Sex Pistols, but by the Clash's performance at a new club in Covent Garden, the Roxy. The Clash embodied this polarized New Year, in which, as Culture sang, 'the two sevens clash'. They were the true victors of the Anarchy Tour: benefiting from the publicity but not embroiled in controversy, they were *the* group to watch. To celebrate, Strummer specially customized a white shirt with a massive '1977' on the front.

From the New Year on, Glitterbest, and especially McLaren, developed a bunker mentality. Where once he had been generous and supportive to new groups, he now kept the Sex Pistols separate, held back from their now large ready market, clearly distinguished from the other Punk groups with whom they had once shared stages. At the very moment when he lost control, he sought control as never before over the movement that he had helped to generate.

Glitterbest attempted to give their view of things with the second edition of the *Anarchy in the UK* broadsheet. The notes for the unpublished magazine remain the clearest articulation of their philosophy: 'No one is interested in the truth. The fact that what is happening is fluid, spontaneous, changes day to day, living by your nerve ends, chaos. That's the day to day lives of the bands and managers involved and in some ways it was a major factor in the firing of the SPs by EMI.'

Much of the Glitterbest editorial is a rant against everybody in their immediate sphere, like 'respectable' Punk bands: 'In a small way the establishment has been threatened, so they tie you up with labels for historical/sociological analysis and package you for commercial exploitation. The nature of the rock industry, those who control what we listen to when, where and how much we play all make it very difficult for bands like SPs. What these bands can do is inspire fans to think and act for themselves.'

The problem was that, after the massive burst of publicity, there was a rush of people wanting to get on the Punk bandwagon: agents, promoters, journalists, record companies, old Pub Rockers. The Sex Pistols' bandwagon was careering at a pace too fast for most, but Punk in general was becoming commercialized under the slightly less tainted name, 'New Wave', a term that McLaren had used months before but which he now used with contempt.

The Sex Pistols could have played the Roxy on New Year's day but McLaren refused to allow it. As a location it was fine, but it was run by impure elements. 'Just as Billy and I were getting pissed with Chelsea,' says Tony James, 'Gene said he knew a place, Chaugerama's, where we could do a gig. He knew the owner. So we went down, booked a date, changed the name to the Roxy Club, and invited loads of journalists down. We got rid of Gene October, and played the first night as Generation X.'

The group's manager at the time was Andy Czezowski. 'We went to look at the club,' he says. 'It was dirty, dark, dingy, no style. They had red lights, red velvet seats and leatherette. It was run by this guy who we called the one-armed bandit, Rene Albert, a Swiss barrister. It was a local rent-boy hangout, and they knew they were going to lose their licence for noise pollution. I came along and offered them money: fifty pounds in advance, and we supplied all the booze.

'We completely repainted it. To get the premises I had to put a deposit down which I didn't have, so we borrowed the money off Barry Jones, Bruce Oldfield's half-brother. He wasn't rich but he did have a guitar, which he hocked. We printed up the hand-outs and off it went. They got their money, and we got enough money to take the guitar out of hock, and put it back in for the second show.

'Then I wanted the Sex Pistols to do a date but by this time Malcolm was pushing the fact that they were banned by the GLC and by everyone the world over: this wasn't entirely true but it was a nice story. He wasn't prepared to let me put on the Sex Pistols and the whole show. He didn't want someone else actually doing something and getting credibility for it: he would have felt like he had lost the whip.'

The Roxy was a basic toilet in a great location, on Neal Street in Covent Garden. At the time the whole area was a mass of run-down fruit and vegetable warehouses – the famous market had moved to Nine Elms in 1975. The dereliction outside soon spread inside: the Roxy had a small upstairs reception room and bar, while the main action happened on the downstairs stage and dance floor, surrounded by bench seats and mirrors, perfect for posing. After two Punk events, the ceiling had been punched out and was all over the floor.

After the Clash and the Heartbreakers played there, the club was off the ground. 'The 1st January launched a "permanent Saturday night" at the Roxy,' says Andy Czezowski. 'Then the Damned came along: they owed me money from my brief spell of management, so I said, "If you play the first night for nothing, then I'll take the cash you owe me, and we'll book you in every Monday for a month." We got 50 per cent, and it was a stormer, it was the biggest night we had.'

The Roxy provided a theatre to test the reality of the 'anyone can do it' Punk ideal, as the New Year saw the first real rush of groups directly inspired by the Sex Pistols. It was a bear-pit, where inexperienced groups had to make their impact on a difficult audience composed of their peers and competitors. The quality of their performance was instantly reflected, not only by the club's mirrors, but by the hostile reactions, or worse, silence, from the floor.

But all of this paled before the demands of the instant. 'We had no idea that it would work, but we gave it a try,' says T.V. Smith. 'By the autumn of 1976, we had a band. We didn't know there was a movement starting at the time, it was every band for itself. Punk groups were such a tiny proportion of what was happening. There was an urgency because we wanted to do it: even if no one else was going to do it, we were.'

The Adverts were typical of the groups that leapt into the space opened up by the Sex Pistols. On 28 February, they played their second Roxy date. They were a nondescript guitarist and drummer supporting a static female bassist, and a nervous, thin-faced singer who, despite the Rotten-like moves, obviously had something to say. Ignoring the audience, the Adverts launched themselves into the unknown.

The group was put together in the last months of 1976 by two Torquay art students, T.V. Smith and Gaye Advert. Fired by seeing the Sex Pistols, they moved to London. 'There was no strange reason for the name Adverts,' says Smith, 'it seemed like something that everybody could relate to, that was ironic. We almost called ourselves One Chord Wonders. I worked very hard on the lyrics and also thrashing out the demons as soon as you hit the stage. The demons we were exorcizing were the demons of living with yourself, that takes in everything around you – the political atmosphere, the social atmosphere, struggling with your own personality.'

(left to right) Laurie Driver, Howard Pickup, T.V. Smith, Gaye Advert: the Adverts, summer 1977 (© Barry Plummer)

I knew my youth couldn't last forever
I knew some chords so I got the band together
Sick of sleeping and beating up my mother
Forget those luxuries, I've got myself another buzz.

Now you don't see me, now you do
Pretty soon you're going to see what punks can do.

I stole some tunes from the radio
I lost my nerve but it didn't show
I found some friends with a little faith
Less money and no taste.

Now you don't see me, now you do
Pretty soon you're going to see what punks can do.

> But you've got to work at it, what a drag
> You've got to work, work, work, work
> You can't lag behind, lag behind, lag behind
> I want to get this gig over
> And I don't want to see it again
> But I don't want to go until it's over
> And I don't want to die in pain, die in pain.
>
> 2-3-4! I knew my youth can't last forever
> I'll sing the words until I can't keep the band together no more
> Oh! to do the quickstep on a Saturday night
> And hunt like brave man with a flashlight.
>
> Now you don't see me, now you do
> Pretty soon you're going to see what punks can do.
>
> **The Adverts: 'Quickstep' (April 1977)**

The songs of groups like the Adverts tapped the collective unconscious for the first few months of 1977, as the possibilities that had been built into the Sex Pistols were acted upon. Punk had become a style, but its elements – the stiff rhythm sections, overamplified guitar and harsh, almost characterless vocals – set up a terrific contrast between this rigid, strait-jacketed formula and the raging emotions that were being expressed.

The Grundy scandal made music-making an accessible and a highly charged activity. 'We wanted lots of snot-nosed bands about, undermining the establishment,' says Smith. The impact of Punk on the news, instead of on the entertainments pages, made it possible to sing about anything – except love. Singing about love only reinforced pop's 'private' status in society: Punk was public, determinedly *in* the world. Of all the groups of this period, the Adverts were always the most tentative – scratchy guitar, skittery rhythm section often out of synch – and they were capable of soaring or dissolving into dreadful lapses of tempo. Yet this very sense that they were overreaching their capabilities, walking the high-wire, allowed their music to express the urgency and freedom of the times.

'I wonder what we'll do when things go wrong,' mused Smith on 'One Chord Wonders', written in twenty minutes, 'when we're halfway through our favourite song, we look up and the audience is gone.' Here was Rozanov's definition of nihilism echoing out of an empty stage: 'The show is over. The audience get up to leave their seats. Time to collect their coats and go home. They turn round . . . no more coats and no more home.'

This was music by and for outcasts. 'The early songs, like "Bored Teenagers", were very personal,' says Smith, 'I was very alienated, but isn't every teenager? The TV and everything would like the teenager to feel that he's part of the same world, buying the same things, and listening to the same records, but it isn't like that. Thank God it was out in the open then.'

Here also was the everlasting present that had always been pop culture's ideal state and which now found its perfect expression. As Richard Boon wrote later: 'History was burning up. Every second a palpable threat to *being*, a serried, serious hazard to health and *becoming*, a spur to action.' The best records of that time remain those which retain the flavour of this intensity. Time seemed to be accelerating and the only way to freeze the instant was with a snapshot. 'That winter,' Boon continues, 'something that had been striving to give birth to itself was beginning to retreat, and there was a feeling that if there was nothing else, there should be a record. The Buzzcocks' phenomenon was desperately unskilled with no industry experience at all, and no resources. It just seemed worth documenting the activity, perhaps as the end result, perhaps the only result.'

In February, the Buzzcocks released their first record, 'Spiral Scratch', on their own label, New Hormones. 'There were no record labels up in Manchester then,' says Howard Devoto, 'it's the question of ambition. A lot of people in our situation would have realized, hey, there's something happening here. But we had some other sort of wherewithal, which made us borrow money from Pete's dad, book a recording studio and have records made.'

The picture sleeve of 'Spiral Scratch' shows the four youths crowding to get into the picture, as if it were their last. 'There was a feeling amongst the group and myself that the record could illustrate part of the "do it yourself", xerox/cultural polemic that had been generated,' says Boon. 'I took the cover picture on the steps of some statue in Manchester Piccadilly with a polaroid, which was a joke: a very Walter Benjamin, art-in-the-age-of-mechanical-reproduction sort of joke. It was instant replay.'

The recording details were on the sleeve. 'What was put on the back was true,' says Devoto, 'I sang the vocals live, and we did one overdub on a couple of them. It took about three hours, with another two for mixing.' Produced with a hint of ambience by Martin Hannett, the four songs (despite Devoto's reservations about his 'mickey-mouse, fake Cockney' voice) summed up the new aesthetic in phrases that leapt out like the distorted treble of the guitar from a speaker.

'I'm living in this movie, but it doesn't move me,' Devoto gabbled in disgust. The Buzzcocks spoke of life as a nagging itch, of 'whining in the dining room', of friends who 'keep me pissing adrenalin'. The keyword 'boredom' had been relocated to England's recession: 'Now I can stand austerity but it gets a little much, when there's all those livid things you never get to touch.'

'I thought Howard's lyrics were very funny,' says Boon. 'The period of Buzzcocks with Howard was difficult for people to digest because there was a lot of confusion about the ideas. The humour in Punk has been lost: "Boredom" was satire, taking the piss out of the whole scene. It was deceptive. Boredom had been a feeling in currency by the time it became a word in currency.'

Yet the Buzzcocks' glee at finding their voice turned facetiousness into liberation: 'Boredom' was broken in half by the siren sound of a perfect, two-note guitar solo. 'I just played the two notes and we all fell about laughing, so we kept it in,' says Pete Shelley. 'I'd been in these sub-Heavy Metal bands before, so really Punk evolved from sub-Heavy Metal played badly. That's what it was, fast riffs and singing over the top.'

The implications of 'Spiral Scratch' were enormous. There had always been independent record companies, such as Joe Meek's Triumph or Andrew Loog Oldham's Immediate, but they were, in the main, small companies trying to be big, like Island or Virgin. Chiswick and Stiff were releasing Punk-related material, but not as if from within: what was so perfect about the Buzzcocks' EP was that its aesthetics were perfectly combined with the means of production.

'It was the first independent record that people really wanted,' says Geoff Travis of Rough Trade. 'We must have ordered hundreds of them, and it was that which got us thinking we should become distributors. I thought the scam aspect of the Sex Pistols signing to EMI was brilliant, but my romantic notion of building my utopia was to avoid the record industry completely. With the power of the Sex Pistols and the Clash, they would have sold records out of the back of a lorry. They didn't need to be distributed through the majors.'

From the New Year, Rough Trade became a centre for small labels, Reggae pre-releases, and fanzines. Perhaps most importantly, the

Buzzcocks' record struck a permanent blow for regionalism. In the Liverpool Beat Boom of the early 1960s, groups had to go to London just to record, let alone become successful. By 1977, both Liverpool and Manchester had small but active musical communities that were proud of their autonomy, and 'Spiral Scratch' cemented this: here was a record, produced and manufactured by a local group, which had as big an impact as any that came out of London.

'In the latter half of 1976 there was a degree of alienation within the Sex Pistols,' says Boon, 'and we were removed from whatever changes were happening down in London. It was still important to retain a link but local interest became paramount. We were trying to find places to play and to make events, so we approached the Electric Circus, a Heavy Metal venue in a derelict cinema, to create and support the little audience that there was in Manchester.'

In early 1977, Manchester started to develop as England's second Punk city after London and, as the capital quickly became Punk-saturated, its most creative site. Largely due to the Buzzcocks, it was less macho and elitist than the capital. 'People were throwing in all these ideas,' says Pete Shelley, 'it wasn't only the freedom to make the music you wanted, but it was also that other people with other ideas were coming in. It was like going to college. People were being Bohemian rather than trying to conform. During that time, gay bars were the places where you could go and be outlandish with your dress and not get beaten up. It was about that time that I started to go to the Ranch, a gay bar, two or three times a week. Everyone used to drink Carlsberg Special out of the bottle with a straw. It was a very bisexual time really: a lot of the clientele was under-age boys but then there were a lot of girls there. It was almost like a youth club with alcohol.'

'In Liverpool you went to gay clubs like the Bear's Paw,' says Jayne Casey, singer in the city's first Punk group, Big In Japan. 'At that time I had my head totally shaved and used to wear rubber clothes from Sex. Liverpool was going through a very straight time just before Punk: you couldn't believe this was the city that all these things had happened in. People were very aggressive to you if you looked weird. Pete Burns and I nearly caused a riot one Saturday in Birkenhead: a crowd followed us and started battering us really badly.

'In 1975 I opened a second-hand clothes shop in a building in Mathew Street called Aunt Twackey's. It was started by this guy called Peter O'Halligan, who took over this warehouse, very near where the Cavern had been, and called it the Liverpool School of Language,

Music, Dream and Pun. I was selling second-hand American fifties clothes from the rag yards. Roxy Music were still going and all the girls from Kirkby used to come in and buy fifties' ball-gowns.

'In September 1976 Eric's opened just down the street. Roger Eagle came into my stall and said, "Here's some free tickets for this club I'm opening next week." We went down and it was either the Runaways or the Stranglers. It started off as a Punk club: it was like a door opening, and it took off instantly. The Sex Pistols played in October, and that was the most exciting thing you'd ever experienced. It wasn't so much that they were the greatest thing you'd ever seen, but that people were coming together.'

Just as in Manchester's Electric Circus, future members of pop groups gathered in the Mathew Street basement: Jayne Casey, Pete Burns of Dead Or Alive, Ian McCullough of Echo and the Bunnymen, Pete Wylie of Wah!, Julian Cope of Teardrop Explodes, Holly Johnson and Paul Rutherford of Frankie Goes To Hollywood. 'We'd all come from these repressive backgrounds,' says Casey, 'and we'd all discovered the Velvets and Warhol and Burroughs and the *Leaving the 20th Century* book. It was an instant bonding, and very deep, because we'd all arrived at the same place individually.'

'I'd go on the bus to Eric's and have a kettle as a handbag,' says actress Margi Clarke, 'the money to pay the fare was in the kettle. We thought we were brilliant, the height of fashion. Holly Johnson would wear tampax earrings and the top of a Cadbury's Milk Tray box on his head. I used to have a necklace made out of a piece of wood and I'd thread it through an apple. If I fancied anyone, instead of going, "Do you want a light?", I'd say, "Do you wanna bite?" '

Despite its extravagance, or maybe because of it, Liverpool failed, initially, to produce a strong Punk group. 'Liverpool is far more violent than Manchester,' says Casey. 'You'd walk down the street then in Manchester, and the crowds would part for you, as if you were diseased, but they wouldn't comment. In Liverpool, you'd get some scallies having a go as soon as you got off the train, and you experienced the difference every day. Musically, Liverpool is eccentric, and the Manchester musicians are all like New Order. Holly and I preferred Manchester music then.'

In the face of hostile councils and promoters, venues were all-important. From February onwards, Manchester's Electric Circus and Liverpool's Eric's became alternatives to London, pulling Punk groups in from all around the north of England. 'There was nothing going on in Newcastle,' says Pauline Murray, 'there was nowhere to play. In the sixties, there'd been the Club-A-Go-Go and the Animals, but it was all dead by 1976 . . . So we used to go to Manchester and Liverpool. We met people like the Fall, and the Buzzcocks. It was starting to link up by then. We'd formed Penetration after seeing the Sex Pistols. I'd never attempted to be in a band or anything before: I'd always gone to see them. Robert Blamire and I met Gary Chapman in the autumn, we were eighteen, and we started to practise two nights a week. We called ourselves Penetration after the Iggy Pop song, and played our first concert at the Middlesbrough Rock Garden in October 1976.'

Musically, the first Penetration followed the basic Punk guidelines – skittery rhythm section, James Williamson guitar – but with an added innocence provided by Pauline's cool voice and the clear belief that things could be changed. In anti-media rants like 'VIP', eco-songs like 'Duty Free Technology', or simple celebrations of seizing the time like 'NeveRr', one can hear the urgency and the unsustainable, all-important, naiveté of the moment.

Distance from London gave these non-metropolitan groups room to grow as they were shielded from the worst aspects of the signing frenzy in the capital. During the first few months of 1977, the spotlight was on Punk: just as with Rap and House in the late 1980s, the music industry was forced to respond to pressure from 'below', or, more accurately, from the people who actually made the music and its culture. The time span between forming a group and obtaining a record deal was becoming ridiculously brief. Groups were covered by the press on their first performance and signed on the next. The experience of the Adverts was typical: 'On our second gig at the Roxy, we got our manager, Michael Dempsey,' says T.V. Smith, 'and very quickly afterwards, Jake Riviera wanted to sign the band to Stiff. He said: "Sign with me and I'll make you poor." And you know what? He did. It was so easy to get a record deal that we didn't really notice it.'

It was also easy for the press and the A&R men those first four months of 1977: all they had to do was pop down to the Roxy, which was now Punk's focus much to the disgust of Glitterbest, who maintained that the club 'kept Punk off the streets'. 'I'd get in about 7.30,' says Don Letts, installed as the resident DJ. 'The club was open until about one: I just sat there and played the records I liked. At that point there were practically no Punk records, so it was almost all Reggae. Most of the groups were awful.'

Malcolm McLaren and Vivienne Westwood inside Let it Rock, December 1971 (© David Parkinson)

(Top, left to right) Simon Barker, Marco Pirroni, Sue Catwoman and Sid Vicious in 'Sex', October 1976 (© Bob Gruen)

(Below left) Siouxsie and the Banshees in Rehearsal, February 1977: *(left to right)* Fenton, Dixon, Siouxsie, Steve Severin (© Ray Stevenson)

(Below right) John Paul Getty III and Jordan in 'Sex', early 1976 (© Kate Simon)

(Top) The Final Frame: Sex Pistols at the Nashville, 23 April 1976 (© Joe Stevens)

(Below) Malcolm McLaren and John Lydon at EMI, 8 October 1976 (© Bob Gruen)

(Top left) McLarens Flower Picture in its commercial setting, Clapham Common, April 1968 (© Malcolm McLaren)

(Top right) Don Letts in Acme Attractions, early 1976 (© Sheila Rock)

(Below left) The Jackson Pollock Clash in Rehearsal Rehearsals, October 1976: *(left to right)* Joe Strummer, Paul Simonon, Mick Jones (© Sheila Rock)

(Below right) Pop sociology and exploitation as part of the product: Generation X handbill, January 1977

(Top) Sex Pistols at the Babalu Club, Finchley Road, 5 May 1976 (© Ray Stevenson)

(Below) Sex Pistols in May 1977: *(left to right)* Sid Vicious, Steve Jones, John Lydon and Paul Cook. Sid is hiding a spot. (© Barry Plummer)

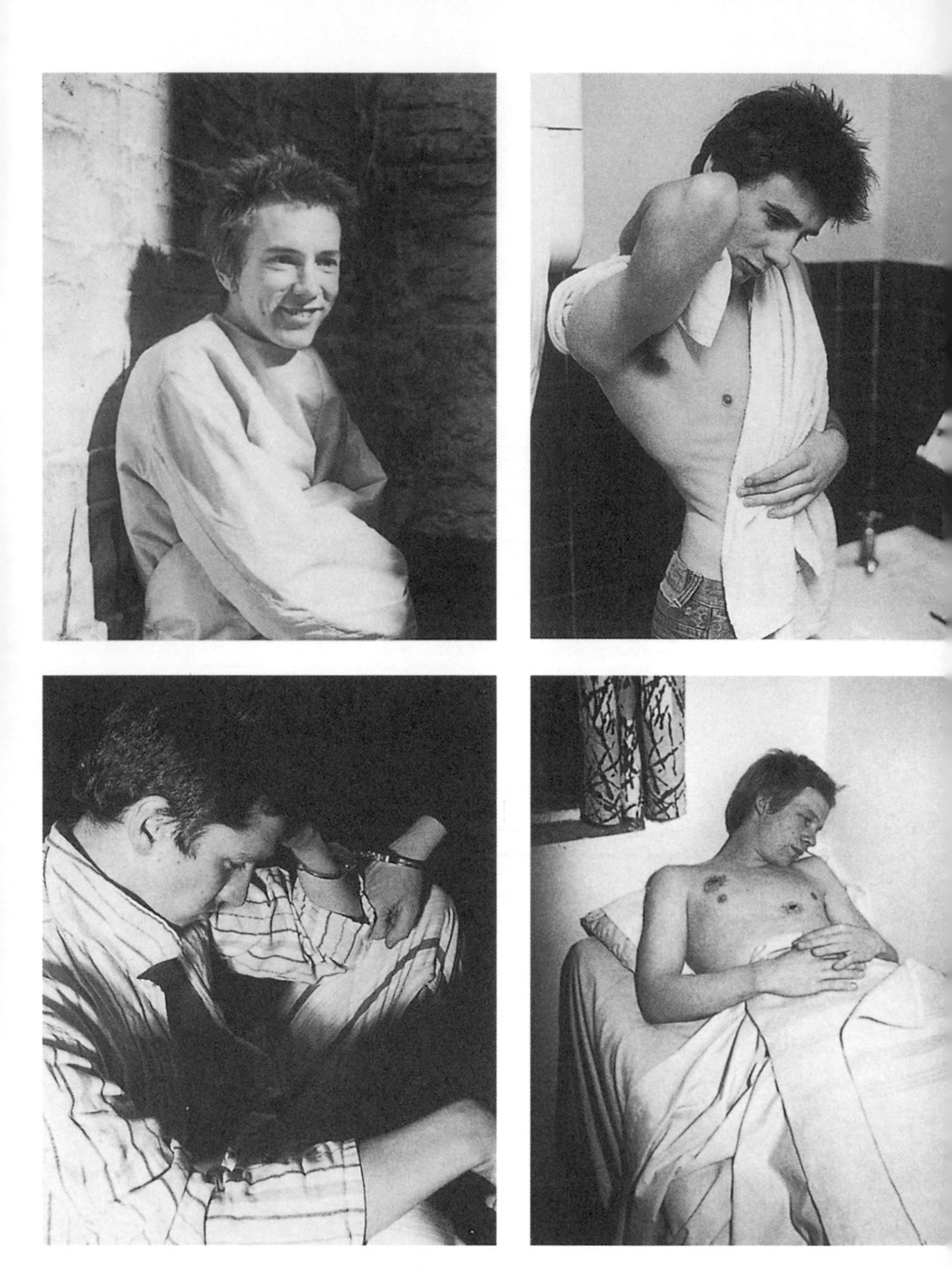

Sex Pistols as hopeless boys, early 1976: *(clockwise)* Johnny Lydon, Glen Matlock, Paul Cook, Steve Jones (© Peter Christopherson)

(Top) The Clash, Camden Town, March 1977: *(left to right)* Paul Simonon, Joe Strummer, Mick Jones (© Kate Simon)

(Below) The Buzzcocks, Collyhurst, August 1977: *(left to right)* Steve Diggle, Pete Shelley, John Maher, Garth (© Kevin Cummins)

(Top) US publicity: Warner Brothers poster, November 1977

(Below left) Sid Vicious during the *My Way* shoot, April 1978 (© John Tiberi)

(Below right) John Lydon surrounded by his past and present, late 1979 (© Sheila Rock)

The Damned had built up their following at the Roxy from a small crowd to a crush of 400 people within a venue supposed to hold only 100. Other groups came from all over the metropolis and the country: the Cortinas, five teenagers from Bristol; Wire, four art students from Watford and Hornsey; Slaughter and the Dogs and the Drones from Manchester; the Lurkers from Fulham; Marco Pirroni's Beastly Cads. 'We didn't know how to be in a band,' he says, 'in those days there was no question of being creative. What you concentrated on was stopping and starting at the same time.'

The Roxy had an instant self-consciousness: it was obvious to everyone that the space would not last long and that history was up for grabs. It was also where the dream of access turned sour, as many of the groups that came up displayed a lack of imagination and a reliance upon formula that were shocking only because they had happened so quickly. Within a month, Punk had been shrink-wrapped: a rubber-band rhythm section, with 1! – a fussy drummer and 2! – a bassist playing repeated single notes in the manner of the Ramones, 3! – a guitarist who turned up his amp to eleven and tried to keep up and 4! – a singer who barked angry lyrics (about media, TV, fascists and the like) in such a garbled fashion that only slogans were decipherable. Punk's accessibility seemed to suggest that anyone could do it: the Roxy proved that not everybody could.

English Punk was now open to every charlatan, poseur and genius attracted by the prospects of media attention and a record contract. Early on the bandwagon were a whole clutch of rejects from Max's Kansas City, summoned by Leee Black Childers: 'I called Cherry Vanilla and Wayne County and said, "Sell the furniture, get over here quick!" What we were doing in New York wasn't getting anywhere. Here, because of your media, it was a whole lifestyle.' More than ever, London was the best springboard to American recognition, and despite a strong undercurrent of envy, competition and hostility, New York still had a mystique that was perpetuated by the flood of releases that arrived in the first three months of the New Year. All were gratefully received in the absence of home-grown product: there were the Talking Heads' first single, 'Love Goes to Building on Fire', Blondie's first album, Television's 'Marquee Moon' and the Ramones' 'Leave Home'.

'In February, Miles Copeland came sniffing around,' says Andy Czezowski. 'He had his agency and his brother had one in New York, so he decided to pay for bringing over Cherry Vanilla and Wayne

County to do a big date at the Global Village. He thought he could take over the scene. The club pulled out, and he came back to me cap in hand: he'd paid for the air-fares, he was set up, and the only place was me. We did some deal: I guaranteed him £100 a night . . . We had Cherry Vanilla and Wayne, Barry did the hand-outs, and Cherry was backed by the Police. I could have her if I booked the Police.'

Although enthusiastically received by a *Sniffin' Glue* now subsidized and housed by Copeland, none of these acts had much to do with the new age. All had something to recommend them, yet their appearance showed how Punk's original rigour and genuine novelty were already being dissipated by commercial pressures.

Back in the Glitterbunker, this activity was viewed with some alarm. McLaren hadn't entirely given up his affiliation with the Clash and the Heartbreakers. As late as 18 January, an all-night meeting was held, with a view to setting up an umbrella, super-Punk organization, but each passing week only reinforced the fact that the Sex Pistols had to go it alone. The Clash were too close, too ambitious for the crown, while the Heartbreakers, with whom Glitterbest had most sympathy, were too desperate. For all his sophistication, Childers was inexperienced in band management, and unable to cope. 'They brought heroin to the Punk scene in England,' he sighs, 'when we arrived it was a very innocent scene, drugwise, and it changed extremely fast.' The group scored within twenty-four hours of arriving in the country.

The Heartbreakers arrived at the point when Punk was turning into Rock'n'Roll and they pushed it on its way. 'Born to Lose' was one of their song-slogans: although deeply imbued with a New York glamour and the loser ethic, their pounding, traditional Rock'n'Roll made them seem more macho than the English groups. Before the inevitable downturn set in, Childers hastily signed the group to the lunatic Track Records: unlike the Sex Pistols, he did not have the security of a record-company pay-off.

During February and March, the music industry moved in. The independents were the quickest: 'There were a few smart people around,' says T.V. Smith, who saw that there was something happening that was going to be exploitable in a commercial way. 'The smarter labels like Stiff would come and see what was happening before the big boys heard about it.' Stiff got the Adverts; Miles Copeland's Step Forward label, fronted by Mark P., got the Cortinas, the Models and Chelsea, while Chiswick got nothing.

'We nearly signed the Jam,' says Roger Armstrong. 'We had a studio holding time to record "In the City". When I got round to Ted's flat, he said, "They've just cancelled; they're signing to Polydor this afternoon." Chris Parry had been pursuing Bernie at a ferocious rate for the Clash, and Bernie was playing him off against CBS. CBS signed the Clash one day, and Parry turned round and signed the Jam the next. In early 1977, there were quite a few A&R men in the majors who had to have their own Punk band.'

The reactions of the other companies were more hesitant: majors like RCA, WEA and Phonogram were cautious, while EMI was temporarily out of the running. Decca hardly existed. Chrysalis, like Phonogram, had Punk bands through licensing deals, but were cautious: the other great sixties independent, Island, contented itself with Ultravox, an intriguing mismatch of Punk and Brian Eno, before signing a distribution deal with Stiff in February 1977.

The company making the strongest overtures was Track, who were flinging money at Punk from their offices in Carnaby Street. For two months, fanzines like *More-On, Sniffin' Glue* and *Ripped and Torn* ran adverts for the company. Track had been the premier English independent in the late 1960s with an extraordinary roster that included the Who, Jimi Hendrix, Arthur Brown, John's Children and Thunderclap Newman. By 1977 however, the company had entered its terminal phase.

'I quickly realized that I was dealing with madmen,' says Childers. 'But I stuck with Track because they had done it so easily. They supplied rehearsal facilities for Siouxsie and the Banshees and Sid's Flowers of Romance. They were doing what Miles was doing, except Miles hung on longer, and he made a fortune. Track thought it was going to be sudden, like the Beatles, but the Heartbreakers were not the Beatles, and neither Sid nor Siouxsie appeared to be sane.'

The big coup was the Clash signing to CBS, an American-owned company with an English branch able to take independent A&R decisions to develop UK talent for the world market. In 1976, its market share was 16 per cent of singles – second only to EMI – and 9 per cent of albums – third behind EMI and Polygram. In 1977, its Managing Director was Maurice Oberstein: because of A&R man Dan Loggins' hostility to Punk, he took a greater part in the Clash signing than usual. 'When the Sex Pistols and the Clash came along, there was a level of hysteria within the music industry, that this is a music we shouldn't be involved in. There is an inherent fear of the unknown. I had done fifteen to twenty years in the music business before Punk ever came along, managed to survive every trend, so strangely enough, it was easier for older, more experienced record people to contemplate taking on Punk than the contemporaries of Punk in the record companies. They found it very odd.

'It seemed perfectly natural: I'd seen Elvis and the Beatles on Ed Sullivan: suddenly there was another bunch of screamers. The record companies are in business to make money, and I saw the potential that these artists had to be on our label rather than some other label. We failed to sign the Sex Pistols and we ended up by signing the Clash. Our attitude towards them was that they had a uniqueness. I wasn't interested in looking at the Clash as a social phenomenon: we were just making records.'

The Clash's signing to CBS, for an advance of £100,000, was an important moment. 'I remember being upset,' says Mark P. 'I was talking to people like Geoff Travis and Roger Armstrong, and I knew that bands didn't need CBS. There were enough small record shops coming up. I had it all worked out for them: an EP of '1977', 'White Riot' and 'Career Opportunities', put it out themselves, it would have broken it wide open. It was a blow that they got signed; the music business hasn't really changed, but if a band as big as them had done that then it might have been a lot different.'

With hindsight, now that pop groups have to be as much businessmen as noise makers, the Punk groups seem to have been fantastically naive about the industry. Considering their ideas about freedom and autonomy, this naivety seems both wilful and magnificent. The Clash never thought that they would not sign to a major company, yet had no part in the negotiations: 'We were completely in the dark,' says Strummer, 'we let Bernie handle everything. We were really the people we were supposed to be. What did we know about record companies and contracts?'

Despite their fieriness, the Clash were a little more assimilable than the Sex Pistols. 'They weren't particularly difficult,' says Oberstein, 'all I did in the beginning was to take a gamble that they had a sound and a noise that they wanted to make. And they simply went into the studio without our A&R man, with a producer and engineer of our choice, and made an album, that was their album. I could see that our approach to making a good album wasn't necessarily making a good Punk album.'

'The whole first album was done in two weekends,' says Roadent, 'working only in the evenings, at lightning speed. All the songs the Clash knew were done, and there was this album that was about fifteen minutes long, so they did Junior Murvin's "Police and Thieves", which was a brave attempt at the time. With all the other tracks they kept things short, but as "Police and Thieves" was different it didn't seem to go on too long.'

To celebrate their signing to CBS, the Clash reemerged after a two-month hiatus with a one-off concert at Harlesden's kung-fu fleapit, the Roxy. In contrast to the 'anything goes' atmosphere of the Neal Street Roxy, the Clash and their manager decided to keep this 'night of action' strict. Only inner-circle Punk groups played, while the Clash unveiled their new equipment, their new drummer, Topper Headon, and their new look: as Strummer says, 'Painting dead men's clothes had gone as far as it would go.'

11.3.77: Up to Harlesden clutching the handbill for directions, and squeaking in the 60s drainpipe vinyl trousers I just bought in Brighton for £3. Inside the cavernous, damp cinema, Geoff from Rough Trade is playing reggae and tall Steve from the shop is looning about. The place is not full when the Slits come on: obnoxious 14-year-old singer, fabulous drummer, the other two not there. Really *untogether: crybaby noise. Their first gig.*

Subway Sect next, in black and white. The guitarist plays rhythm as lead, a la Velvets 'Live 69', guitar held as high as Gerry and the Pacemakers. Trebly, dustbin lid sound with an immobile singer. Not much applause. All I can think of, when the Clash come on, is that they jettisoned their great Pollock look for a more militaristic uniform of zippers and epaulettes. It makes them look like rock stars.

The next day, the Damned's first album, distributed by Island, entered the LP charts in the thirties. Within an industry where LPs were more important than singles, this was a sure sign that Punk's success was no publicity-driven fluke. The next week, the Clash released their 'White Riot' of police sirens, broken glass and apocalyptic shrieks: the most radio-unfriendly record conceivable, it nevertheless went into the Top Forty in the first week of April.

Anarchy in the UK, issue 2, ended with a dedication to 'Che, Durruti, the Watts Riots, the Weathermen, the Angry Brigade, the '72 Miners' strike, the Levellers et al, Black Power, the Women's Movement, Gene Vincent'. Staggered by the rupture they had made, Glitterbest wanted to push even further, to turn the Sex Pistols' violence into revolutionary activity. Yet now that it was in the hands of the music industry, Punk was a long way out of Glitterbest's and McLaren's control. So, almost, were the Sex Pistols.

The official signing to A&M Records, Buckingham Palace, 10 March 1977 (© David Hill)

22

> Accounts of the mechanics of sharping, and especially of simple confidence tricks, often seem absurd because they fail to convey the psychological adroitness that is the real core of the business. What the sharp most hoped to see in his prey's face was not stupidity but loneliness.
>
> **Kellow Chesney: *The Victorian Underworld* (1970)**

The events of December and January had left the group and the management company drained, angry and paranoid: the Sex Pistols were enmired in indecision and enforced inactivity. Between the end of the Anarchy tour and the 'Secret Tour' almost nine months later, the Sex Pistols played only three concerts in Britain, all of which were stunts of one type or another, all of which were nearly impossible to see, and one of which was terminated early.

In the enforced layoff, the resentment between Glen Matlock and John Lydon came to a head. 'Glen was a mummy's boy,' says Lydon, 'the best musician out of the lot of us, but too bogged down into the

Beatles.' This was untrue, but in Pistolspeak it meant that Glen was too accommodating for the Sex Pistols' new career as music and media industry scourges. For McLaren and the group, it came to a head during a meeting on 27 January with Warner US, where Glen, according to McLaren, 'acted like a squirm'.

'They had the hump with me because I wasn't pulling my weight, because I was angry,' says Glen. 'I remember Steve, Paul, Malcolm and I had a talk. They said: "What's the problem?" I said: "Look, I just hate John's guts." As far as I was concerned, the press had gone to his head. On top of that the stuff I wanted to write – melodies mainly – wasn't really falling in with what the group wanted to do.

'Steve and Paul went away for a short holiday, and I was just pottering around. When they came back, I heard they had started trying out Sid on bass, and people were going, "Aren't you worried?" I wasn't, because I was planning my new group and EMI were already interested. Malcolm called me up and we had a meeting. He said: "Look, I want you to go back in there and kick down the doors and say you're the bass player." I said: "Look, I'm not interested any more." He said: "If that's what you feel, that's fair enough." But within a week he'd sent the *NME* a telegram that he sacked me. [Matlock pauses.] I had to sign a release when I left. I'd get my share of song royalties, but I asked about the stuff I'd played on. Malcolm said that they were going to rerecord everything. I wasn't too sure about it but I was skint: he had a cheque sitting there. I'm still pretty green about it: I needed to pay the rent, so I had to sign.'

'He had been growing apart from them for some time,' says Simon Barker, 'you can see it in the photos: at the start he always used to wear clothes from Sex, but then his hair and his clothes got really neat. He was letting the side down.' Musically too, Matlock's harmonies were unwanted, and in the January demos his work is too funky for the monolithic noise the Sex Pistols were now aiming for – a wall of sound that would act both as a barrier and a shelter.

Matlock was also the most traditional musician in his friendships with members of other Punk bands, like Mick Jones. This made him suspect and vulnerable within the group, as Lydon, anxious to assert his dominance and independence of McLaren, made his move: 'It was John who insisted that Sid was in the group,' says Julien Temple. 'It was John who got rid of Glen. Sid was John's protégé in the group, really. The other two just thought he was crazy.'

The changeover was badly handled: it took a month for the news to be made public, by which time insiders knew anyway. McLaren was busy with record companies and there was some internal argument: the group had to record, and Vicious's bass playing was rudimentary. There was even some talk of pulling in Paul Simonon from the Clash. Matlock was kept on to do an audition session on 3 March, for which he was paid, along with the agreed settlement fee of £2,966.68. Like all victims of a scission, Matlock was insulted and vilified on his departure. Future exchanges in the press were marked by spleen on both sides. There is a sense in which Matlock has never recovered from this dreadful month.

There were other scissions. Nils Stevenson was also out, after being squeezed out of the EMI contract. 'I'd started managing the Banshees,' he says, 'I had them rehearsing in Denmark Street during the Anarchy Tour and Malcolm was so pissed off that they'd been in the studio. I'd kept it quiet but he found out when they got back. Malcolm offerred me £300 for the year's work: I took it, I was broke.' His brother Ray also left shortly afterwards, in a dispute over money.

Nils was replaced by John Tiberi, an Anglo-Italian with a face like a Red Indian. Tiberi had worked as a photographer in Soho before getting caught up in the libertarian politics of the late 1960s: in the early 1970s, he went to prison for cheque fraud. On his release, he began working with the 101'ers, from whom he got the nickname Boogie and little else. When Strummer left to join the Clash, Tiberi did not follow. A natural conspirator, he was immediately attracted by the Sex Pistols' set-up. 'They seemed like the band Joe had been in: mixed up about their motivations. I had a lot of loyalty, and when I went to see Malcolm, I found a place for that feeling, wanting to join up. It was after Grundy, it was a lot to do with that. Malcolm had dexterity and savvy: he was a bit of a magician. When I joined, the main thing was Glen leaving. The first thing I had to do was to go off and buy a car with Glen, a light blue Sunbeam Alpine, which was very non-Punk.

'It didn't make sense to me, getting rid of Glen, but everybody said they didn't like him, and that was it. The obvious thing was class. Malcolm didn't offer any defence: he must have thought it was all right to get this other guy in the group. Sid was a drummer, wasn't he? It was kids fighting with each other, it was good stuff. They had enough songs for an album, and if they needed more, perhaps they could get Glen in as a songwriter. But Glen got proud.'

'The band wasn't a band,' says Sophie, 'it was a name for four people operating. They didn't rehearse, they couldn't bear to be in the same room together half the time. John moaned about Steve and Paul a lot. It was a real effort in spring 1977 to get them to go to Denmark Street to write new tunes. Glen could write tunes and they couldn't. They could produce words and chords, but not tunes, and they were finished as a creative unit once he'd gone.'

Sid Vicious had got what he had wanted for nearly eighteen months now, ever since his friend had been selected for the Sex group instead of him. 'Sid had sacked me from the Flowers of Romance,' says Viv Albertine, 'because I couldn't really play. Then he got asked to be in the Pistols and I remember him asking me whether he should do it or not. He knew if he did that, then he would be giving up something of himself. We all reckoned that they were the best, so it was too much to turn down.'

'I was with him a lot through the last days of the Flowers of Romance,' says Leee Childers. 'They would have done fine. They were a combination of the Ramones and the Sex Pistols, very much the 1-2-3-4! syndrome. We had one of those perverted English relationships that I have since found out are very common. This father-son, I love you very much, why don't I sleep with you and kiss you, but not fuck each other, relationships. Then he joined the Sex Pistols and then Malcolm became the father figure.

'We know he had a psychotic side, but he was also a very sentimental person. He was taking pills, but then we were all doing that, and it was nothing when you're with the Heartbreakers. No shooting up until Nancy showed up. If the Heartbreakers brought heroin to England, then Nancy brought it to Sid. When the Heartbreakers were around, he wasn't interested. Suddenly when Nancy came, bang. That was the power of love. Her world was smack.

'On the day she arrived, I ran into her in the little alley that runs from Carnaby Street to Regent Street, and she came running up and said "Hi", and I just said, "Go away. Leave England". I'd known her for years in America. She was a total junkie prostitute. That doesn't mean I didn't like her, I liked her fine: she didn't actually mean any harm. She hung around Max's, she fucked for drugs, she'd give people drugs if they would fuck her, all combinations.

'Here she was, and she was looking for Jerry Nolan. I was keeping him on the drum kit, and the last thing I needed was Nancy Spungeon, with her bag full of drugs, so I told her: "Over my dead body you will see Jerry Nolan." And she turned around and she walked away. She wasn't hurt. Almost immediately I heard that she

Nancy Spungeon at Notre Dame Hall, 21 March 1977

had found Sid and hooked up with him. A cold chill ran down my spine when I heard, and from that day on, Sid was no longer the person that I knew.'

Nancy Spungeon's early life is recalled by her mother's book, *I Don't Want to Live this Life*, which remains the best account of the appalling impact of Punk on the public at large. Born and raised in suburban Philadelphia (in a place called, with hideous irony, the Main Line: in the late 1980s, this was the location for the cult TV show *Thirtysomething*), Nancy was an intelligent child who was also hyperactive from birth. Her parents first took her to therapy at the age of three when she used to go into uncontrollable rages; by the age of eleven, she was undergoing intensive psychiatric therapy.

During her teens, Nancy ran away from school several times and twice tried to commit suicide, but still obtained enough grades to enter the University of Colorado. At seventeen she ran ran away to New York and that was the last her parents heard, other than demands for money. 'She was a fairly typical suburban girl who worshipped rock stars,' wrote Richard Hell about their brief affair, 'she had an exceptionally large drive to be where the action was . . . Nancy just wanted to be somebody (not necessarily herself). And you've got to hand it to her, she made it. She would do absolutely everything to get what she wanted. There was really nothing between us.'

From the New York scene in which Hell was somebody, Nancy got more than simply a taste for the heroin-drenched, 'Rock'n'Roll' lifestyle which was exactly what most of those in and around the Sex Pistols were reacting against.

Although he wasn't yet officially a member of the group, Sid performed his first duty as a Sex Pistol on 13 February, sarcastically handling a transatlantic phone interview with Los Angeles DJ Rodney Bingenheimer. 'Sid referred to this girl they had discovered who licked out toilet bowls,' says Malcolm McLaren. 'That was Nancy. She had come to the shop looking for Jerry Nolan and ended up at Louise's and then Linda Ashby's place where she met John and Sid.'

'Nancy came to London specifically to get a Sex Pistol for a boyfriend,' says Simon Barker, who lived in Ashby's St James's flat. 'She tried to get John, who wouldn't have anything to do with her, then she got Sid. John hated her. I hated her as well: she was a New York hustler, you could see through her right away. She gave Sid a habit and sex. He didn't have to go looking for it, it was on a plate. He told me he thought she was the most beautiful woman he'd met in his life, and he didn't want to have sex with anyone else.'

Sid had gained his first proper relationship but he was driving a wedge between the Sex Pistols at the very moment they had been reconstituted. 'Sid and Nancy met as soon as he joined the group,' says Sophie, 'and he thought he was a big star as of that day. Steve and Paul were fairly ambivalent about him right from the start. And although it was John who got Sid into the group, as soon as Nancy was on the scene, they were no longer friends.'

McLaren had encountered heroin before with the New York Dolls, and hadn't known what to do about it then. This time, he wasn't aware of it, obsessed by the very thing he ostensibly hated, playing off one record company against another and endlessly discussing the politics of A&M, CBS or Virgin. 'Bernie gave me a lecture which I mainly agree with though Malcolm won't,' wrote Sophie, 'about how scrappy and nasty things have become, about not becoming obsessed with business wheelings and dealings.'

The search for record companies was not proving difficult. McLaren had made it a condition of his final negotiations with EMI that Leslie

Hill help the group to find an equivalent contract. True to his word, Hill got a response from two companies: CBS and Virgin. McLaren wasn't interested in Virgin at this time, but he wanted to find out more about CBS, who in turn were anxious to have a Punk band and were then courting the Clash. McLaren began dealings with Maurice Oberstein and Norman Stolman.

By that time, A&M Records were also in the running. On 19 January, McLaren had attracted the personal attention of Derek Green, A&M's English Director. The Sex Pistols would be an odd choice for A&M, a label best known at that time for sustaining 'album acts' – like Supertramp or Peter Frampton – over a long period of time. The label was a tight, family concern based in Los Angeles and run by two American music-industry veterans, Herb Alpert and Jerry Moss.

Green was very excited by the recent demos that McLaren played him: three versions of 'Anarchy' and a rough dub of 'No Future'. Then thirty-two, he had been at A&M since the early 1970s, and he was bored. In the Sex Pistols' music he heard echoes of the sixties rebellion that he had grown up with, and he wanted the group badly. He was also enough of a barrow boy himself to be intrigued by McLaren's taunting way of using his personality in negotiation.

McLaren was also fascinated. Part of him was like Odd John in Olaf Stapledon's science-fiction novel, wandering child-like through the entertainment industry, asking questions whose answers only revealed his elders and betters to be as foolish as he had expected. The Sex Pistols' notoriety opened the door to the industry directors and chairmen whose personal quirks fascinated him. This curiosity far outweighed his business sense, which was increasingly buttressed by Stephen Fisher's expertise.

By the second week in February, the bidding had come down to two companies: CBS and A&M. McLaren couldn't decide: the advantages of CBS were in the company's size and access to the means of distribution; the disadvantages were its style, the deal offered, and the fact that the Clash were signing to the label. A&M were smaller, and although distributed by CBS, they were offering more money. The chain of command was also less byzantine. All Derek Green had to do to get a decision was call Jerry Moss.

McLaren and Stephen Fisher flew to Los Angeles on 13 February to see Moss, check out other record companies, meet the Sex Pistols' US representative Rory Johnston and make the first murmurings about a Sex Pistols film. McLaren cut a bizarre figure in the Californian sun, his black bondage suit a dramatic contrast to Los Angeles beards and BMWs, and his abrasiveness got him into trouble at the Whisky-A-Go-Go, where he had a fist fight with Johnny Ramone. During his trip, on 15 February, McLaren's grandmother died alone in her Hove flat.

On McLaren's return, matters came to a head. At issue was the advance, the publishing rights and the number of songs to be delivered to the company over the contract period. It was a confusing time: McLaren was already, as Sophie Richmond put it, 'into creative management', coming up with ever-more ambitious schemes – such as a Sex Pistols film – while the group were still getting to grips with their new member in a series of rehearsals and studio sessions.

Despite constitutional ill-health, Sid Vicious was earnest about his bass playing, although he could play only one riff: indelibly etched into his brain during long nights in Davis Road, it was more of a rhythmic pattern than a sequence of notes. David Bowie had used this exaggerated, almost burlesque bump and grind in 'Hang On To Yourself' and the Ramones stole it for 'I Don't Wanna Go Down to the Basement'. It would now mark any Sex Pistols performance in which Sid was involved.

The first single for A&M had already been decided: McLaren had decided to pull out the song that John had written the previous autumn to exploit current-affairs interest in the Queen's Silver Jubilee, a country-wide jamboree to celebrate Elizabeth II's twenty-five years on the throne, which was planned for the weekend of 4–5 June. Although there was already some media interest in March, there was little indication that the Jubilee would be a success.

'I thought about it for weeks and then it came out in one go,' says Lydon. 'In the kitchen at the Hampstead squat. The music was worked out with Steve, we'd sit with an acoustic guitar and just thrash out ideas, no, no, yes, that'll do. Steve always had a set of the lyrics before anyone else. It was very little to do with the music then, I couldn't play a referee's whistle. But how far can you take that kind of approach? You fast run out of subjects. You can really only say that once, and then move on to new territory.'

Under the working title of 'No Future', the song had frequently been rerecorded, until it was wound up to the right pitch of hysteria. In March, it all finally came together: announced by a multi-tracked guitar fanfare, backed by Paul Cook's crisp drumming, 'God Save the Queen' declared itself very quickly. 'God save the queen,' enunciated Lydon very clearly in the spaces between Steve Jones's guitar, before filing his 'R's to points: 'The fascist regime. It made you a mo*rrr*on – a potential H-Bomb.'

Despite the chaotic circumstances that surrounded it, 'God Save the Queen' was perfectly honed. Chris Thomas's production was so clear and full that it gave the group an instrumental authority, which, for once, worked with Lydon's unconventional vocals. As the group slides, with a queasy chord change, into the final 'No Future' chant, Lydon's inability to keep tune with the massed guitar and vocal harmonies gives 'God Save the Queen' a unique vulnerability.

The title caused a severe disagreement between McLaren and Lydon. 'I actually called it "God Save the Queen",' says McLaren, 'and he tried to hit me because he wanted it to be called "No Future". I said, "That sounds like an ad for a bank. 'God Save The Queen' sounds big, it's something we're supposed to sing after the pictures have closed down in the fifties. No one is going to expect a group like the Sex Pistols to be singing the national anthem. That's the title of the song." I told Jamie to put that on the sleeve.'

A&M worked up cover roughs which showed the group in front of Buckingham Palace with sentries clutching signing-on cards. Glitterbest, however, planned a brilliant campaign that drew on all aspects of Jamie Reid's experience. The A&M single was to be released without a picture bag, but a whole series of images had been worked out for accompanying media: handbills, posters, adverts and stickers which were already being handed out. It was Reid's first integrated campaign. 'I must have done literally hundreds of different images around that official Cecil Beaton portrait. I did two days of sessions with photographer Carol Moss until I came up with the safety-pin through her mouth. There was no point in beating about the bush; you use the same tactics that you know are going to get thrown back in your face from the likes of the *Mirror* and the *Sun*. The safety-pin image wasn't banned at A&M, although the one where she has swastikas over her eyes was.'

The 'official' signing was set for 10 March. The day before, the real signing was carried out at the offices of Rondor Music, A&M's subsidiary publishing company. The deal, which did not include publishing, was for two years with a yearly advance of £75,000, for eighteen 'sides', or single tracks. This meant that McLaren could use the eight tracks already cut during the previous six months, while A&M could exploit the group as a singles act. That day, Derek Green met the group for the first time. In his deal-frenzy, he had deliberately avoided meeting the Sex Pistols in case they put him off. It was to prove a costly override of his instincts. Green wasn't particularly smitten with the four Sex Pistols but thought their behaviour was all part of the image. He was however more concerned about the fact that Sid Vicious had replaced Glen Matlock in the group and nobody had told him. Nobody pretended that the signing of the Sex Pistols to A&M was anything but a shotgun wedding.

The next day was farcical. A limousine picked the group up at nine in the morning, and whisked them off to Buckingham Palace where, with A&M's full cooperation, the group were to perform the signing in front of the Palace. The limousine circled the central island twice, the group rushed out, put pen to paper, flicked a few victory signs with the Palace carefully placed behind them for the shots, jumped into the limousine and disappeared, just as a policeman began to harass the gathering.

Next stop was a Beatles-style press conference at the Regent Palace Hotel. All the music press were there, many journalists from the nationals, German and American TV, Australian radio, and a lot of drinks. The group began attacking the alcohol like ratings on twenty-four hour leave, particularly Sid Vicious, who swigged vodka throughout. Lydon handled most of this sullen conference, which only took off when they all insulted *Sounds*' Vivienne Goldman.

The nationals were more exercised by the recent EMI signing of the Rolling Stones, who were involved in a scandal which threatened the Canadian Government. There was also a disinclination to play the Sex Pistols' media game. Such was the illusion of the group's power at this stage, that they were, as conference photos show, at their most threatening when they were most manipulated. By the time the music-press reports came out, the group were off the label.

The group hadn't been slow in grabbing as many bottles as they could to shove in their pockets after the conference, says McLaren. 'Having still all these bottles of booze, the band were by now almost catatonic. There was a fight between Paul and Sid in Wessex Studios, where Thomas was mixing the single. Gathering them up and chucking them into the limousine, we headed on towards A&M Records in New King's Road. Before arrival there was a huge outburst.

'Paul got the worst end of it and suffered a bashed-in nose and Sid's shoes were thrown out of the window, his foot now cut. Rotten's watch, that had been bought by his mother for his birthday the previous week, was smashed. He was totally furious. Steve, who had tried to stop the fight, being the toughest, was totally pissed and completely helpless. The fight was about who was the toughest; who was the most Sex Pistol.

'When we arrived at A&M Records, they all got out, Sid without any shoes, Paul with a black eye and blood dripping down his shirt. Steve was carrying bottles in his jacket and in his inside pocket, and the same went for Sid who was now totally catatonic himself. On arrival at A&M he slumped down into the executive chair in the Promotion Office and passed out, not without Rotten stealing a daffodil from the vase on a nearby table and throwing it into his lap.

'We were there for a promotional meeting, a) to discuss the single "God Save the Queen", what was to be on the B-side, to approve the A-side mix, b) to be introduced to all the people who were to work happily with the band and promote them and c) to join in what was possibly to be a celebration signing of the act in the afternoon. Well, there was no celebration and as for them listening to the mix, no one could because they were incredibly drunk.

'Steve Jones meanwhile dashed away upstairs and we had no idea where the hell he was. Sid was woken up with wine in his face thrown by Cook or Rotten, I can't remember which. Sid barely came round and was sent into the promotional room where the secretaries gazed at him with horror. He looked down at his foot, and he lifted it up and said: "My foot's bleeding, can you find a fucking plaster for me, you bitch!" He rushes into the toilet and all we hear is a smash. The toilet bowl is broken and Sid suddenly pulls himself up from the toilet bowl, he stands back a couple of paces and bangs his elbow and goes through the window as well. Then he was last seen bathing his feet in the toilet bowl: we hurried him out and downstairs into the basement where we chose the B-side.

'Green, in an incredible hurry to try to get the band out of there whisked through the demo tapes saying, "This one will do, let's just choose one." The group disagreed. Eventually Green said, "It's got to be 'No Feelings'. Come on, we've got to go now," and hurried us upstairs and there we were confronted by the limousine driver who quarrelled and refused to take us back and was sending in a bill for damages. They had to quickly call two mini-cabs.

'We later found out that Jones was so drunk that he went into the women's loo instead of the men's loo and saw these girls and started to have a go. At Denmark Street, there was a TV crew all set up and Sid by then was totally out to lunch. They all collapsed on Steve Jones's bed. Sid looked up at the cameras and said: "I've had the greatest time of my life. This is my first day and as far I'm concerned it's great being in the Sex Pistols." He then went out like a light.'

Green's public response to the Sex Pistols was to place no restrictions on the way the group behaved. As he told the *Melody Maker*, 'What they've done in the past is nothing in comparison with everyday life. Just look at what's going on in films, books, television and the theatre.' As far as personal behaviour is concerned, the music industry was (and still is) a kind of playpen, with licence granted to pop stars to act in a manner larger than life.

The Sex Pistols were supposed to be bad but they were stretching the limits of the playpen. Although Green had expected a certain wildness, the spectacle at the New King's Road offices was both excessive and squalid. McLaren was not obviously a manager in the sense that the music industry expects: someone who is able to discipline their group when necessary. McLaren was plainly unwilling, and/or unable, to do either. Despite these misgivings, the selected mix of 'God Save the Queen' went to the press that Friday.

The same day, Lydon had a date with Marlborough Street Magistrates Court, when he was fined £40 for the possession of amphetamine sulphate. Even that was within the parameters of pop star behaviour. 'He prefers going into a pub and having a few drinks,' said his counsel, and that night, barely checked, Lydon and his gang went to the Speakeasy to put this preference into practice, and test the wall-fittings in the music industry's most celebrated romper room.

'We'd go down to the Speakeasy and there were all these rock biz types who'd had their nose put out of joint,' says Wobble. 'It was a bit like when we Punks were put out by the Blitz scene in 1978, "Oooh it's not like the old days." They'd get a bit paranoid and comments would be passed, then glasses would be passed, if you see what I mean. If I went out and did the same things now I'd get killed, but then, people didn't know how to take Punk Rock and they were quite frightened.'

'Steve and Paul had begun to frequent the club noted for old hack singers,' says McLaren. 'Who arrives but John and Sid and a couple of their friends. Also in attendance were a group called Bandit, escorted by the ex-cop who comperes the *Old Grey Whistle Test*, Bob Harris. Wobble confronted him and said "Why don't you play the Sex Pistols on your programme?" He said: "We don't want the Sex Pistols on the programme, does that answer your question?" Of course it didn't to Wobble who was quite drunk and arrogant.

'The band who Bob Harris was with started to insult the Sex Pistols and the insults flew backwards and forwards for a number of minutes. After that, it seems that Sid was then insulted and pushed out of the way: he grabbed hold of his beer glass and went straight for Bob Harris's friend and said "You're just an old cunt." Bandit then set upon Sid and at that point one of Rotten's friends said to Harris, "We are going to kill you."

'On Monday morning I had a letter sent to me from Harris's lawyers and his management, a man called Philip Roberge who was a partner with Dee Anthony, who controlled the most successful artist on A&M, Peter Frampton. The news travelled fast and on the Monday afternoon I received a call from Derek Green saying what did I think of this kind of behaviour, that the Sex Pistols had threatened the life of a very good friend of his, Bob Harris. The threat was being taken seriously and their solicitors were going to sue us.

'Well in the same way as EMI, being used to being confronted with these situations, I still used the same ploy, which was obviously going to sound more grotesque. I suggested that "Boys will be boys" and everybody knows the Speakeasy is a place for all kinds of fights and brutalities. I said that I would try to carpet the boys, but I couldn't tell them that their behaviour was out of order because at three in the morning anything can happen. It was left at that.'

Green was finally appalled. This wasn't a bit of show aggro, but real violence. The consequences of rushing into the deal now came home to him: if he'd met the group, or done any research into their history, he would have seen that the Sex Pistols had left a wake of violence behind them from the very beginning. He hadn't signed 'the new Rolling Stones' but a bunch of psychos with a 'satanic' manager who would exploit their worst characteristics. As 25,000 copies of 'God Save the Queen' were being pressed, he panicked.

Green had signed the Sex Pistols against the wishes of most of his staff: his enthusiasm had convinced his superiors in America. Unlike Leslie Hill at EMI, he had no shareholders and no board to worry about. It was all up to him and his conscience. Green drove to Brighton on the morning of Tuesday the 15th, thinking hard. His reputation was on the line: it would be very embarrassing to get rid of the group he had signed himself, yet he knew that he could not support a group serious about its violence.

As soon as the time zones permitted, he called Jerry Moss and explained that, although he personally didn't want to work with the

Sex Pistols any longer, he thought A&M should stick with them because they would be successful. In what quickly became a choice between the Sex Pistols and Derek Green, Moss didn't hesitate, telling Green to get rid of them immediately. One hour later, Herb Alpert confirmed the company's commitment to Green and backed him up in his decision: something else would come along.

Green then drew up a terse, four-line statement: 'There is no longer any association between A&M Records and the Sex Pistols. Production of their single "God Save the Queen", which had been tentatively scheduled for release later this month, has been halted.' Then, at 2 p.m. on 16 March, he called McLaren and Stephen Fisher to a meeting at the premises of A&M's lawyers, where he presented them with his decision. Now it was McLaren's turn to be shell-shocked. He immediately tried to negotiate, but Green insisted that he would be releasing the statement to the press at 6.30 and the matter had to be agreed by then. A formula was quickly arranged whereby the Sex Pistols would be immediately paid £25,000 – the balance of the first advance having been paid the previous week – leaving Glitterbest and the group £75,000 richer for one week's drunken activity. In return, A&M washed their hands of the group by destroying almost all of the 25,000 newly pressed singles. They also destroyed the metal masters. The Sex Pistols were now music-industry pariahs.

'The following morning A&M released their press release,' says McLaren. 'I had the *Evening Standard* phone me up in the morning and I said, "I'm too tired, I won't be able to speak to you now." So he said he'd call back: "Promise that you won't speak to any other paper. I'm going out now and I'll ring you back in half an hour." I said, "OK, fine." Between eight and half-past eight I was thinking, "What am I going to say? What's going to be the best thing?"

'I got the clue from Stephen who said, "All we seem to be doing is going in and out of doors collecting cheques." So I took that idea and expanded on it, and when he called back I said, "It appears like we are some contagious disease. I just keep going in and out of doors and people keep giving me cheques." It was great news: a photograph of the cheque by Richard Young appeared in the *Evening Standard* that evening and we hit the newspapers in the morning. Incredible.'

'A mountain got created out of a molehill,' says Tiberi. 'The guy's injuries amounted to a black eye. It was just so clichéd, after Sid's other trouble at the 100 Club. But all Malcolm's plans were scuppered. This time around it wasn't funny. That interview with the cheque was heartfelt: ''What the fuck are you doing, you're supposed to be making hit records, and you keep on giving me money.'' He was beginning to act desperate. The Jubilee was coming up, the single had to be out, and the calendar wasn't on our side.'

John Lydon outside number 430, summer 1977 (© Bob Gruen)

Youth, after all, is not a permanent condition, and a clash of generations is not so fundamentally dangerous to the art of government as would be a clash between rulers and ruled.

Reverse of 'White Riot' sleeve (March 1977)

Can't we envision, isn't it encumbent upon us to imagine what an *intensive* life would be? Being alive means to be lively, to be quick. Being lively means being-speed, being quickness. Being-liveliness. All these terms challenge us. There is a struggle, which I tried to bring to light, between metabolic speed, the speed of the living, and techological speed, the speed of death which already exists in cars, telephones, the media, missiles.

Paul Virilio and Sylvere Lotringer: *Pure War* (1983)

On the Friday that the *Daily Mirror* put the Sex Pistols on their front cover once again – 'Punk group's £75,000 for nothing' – the other main story was 'Jim's Showdown': 'Now the Government is fighting for its life.' The IMF gamble looked set to fail: left-wing Labour MPs and ministers refused to accept the Government White Paper which outlined the IMF cuts. In Parliament Mrs Thatcher called for a vote of confidence which, if the Government lost, would result in a general election.

That particular crisis was ducked by the Government but their power to command a majority, and thus, effectively, to govern, was only retained through a last resort: a pact of convenience with the thirteen MPs of the Liberal Party. The political and social order seemed to be breaking up, and nothing symbolized this more than the Punk Rockers now visible on the streets of large urban centres. Through a mixture of conjuring and existential truth, Punk insinuated itself into the national psyche as the true face of England.

Throughout the spring, Punk hardened fast as the Burroughsian spiral took effect: record; instant playback; fast-forward. The scape-goating of December had had two results: a theatrical amplification of the 'outsider' role, and an increasingly extravagant rhetoric. With the Sex Pistols out of control, and countless groups snapping at their heels, it seemed as though Punk was crashing through barrier after barrier, that anything was possible.

'Malcolm and Vivienne focussed things so cleverly and so clearly,' says Jordan, 'it was their clarity that got it going. Clean lines, hard edges, bright colours.' Nowhere were the changes within Punk more visible than on the street which had given it birth, two years before. The King's Road was now attracting international attention as the Punk centre: apart from Seditionaries, a slew of new outlets marked the six-month changeover from the retro styles of the 1970s to something more in tune with the new age.

Sartorial control of Punk slipped away from McLaren and Westwood as the floodgates opened. In April, Zandra Rhodes unveiled a collection 'inspired by Punk Rock', featuring 'torn clothes, chains and safety-pins'. 'We had a period at the beginning where it was lovely and peaceful,' says Debbie Wilson, 'it was quite upmarket, then we'd have these working-class lads in, saying: "Have you got a T-shirt for five pounds?" It was so weird because we were dressing people off the street and international designers at the same time.'

In the first week of March, John Krivine opened his answer to Seditionaries, BOY. 'We closed Acme Attractions and moved upstairs onto the King's Road,' says Don Letts, 'I saw that as the epitome of selling out: catering to what the punters wanted. The intimacy had gone. A lot of shady deals went on in that basement. BOY was a box with a window onto the street, and you couldn't do anything. It was like being an animal in a cage.'

BOY was to Seditionaries what Acme Attractions had been to Sex, the more commercial rival. McLaren and Westwood had bondage suits, parachute tops and swastika T-shirts, but John Krivine had T-shirts with dried animal blood, with mock-up death pictures of Gary Gilmore (the mass murderer voluntarily executed that January) and jewellery made out of hypodermic syringes and contraceptive packets. On the walls were framed newspaper front-pages, each with 'Boy' in the headline, like 'Boy of 12 on Murder Charge'.

This was mediated Punk, dressed up in the usual extremism: 'Punk is finished,' Krivine told the *Evening News*, 'these clothes are about survival in London in 1977. They are about what happens every day on the streets.' BOY was notorious for its window of forensic cultures, small dishes of a simulated burnt Boy leg or hand, as if, while vandalizing, he had been caught in a fire. Made by Peter Christopher-

Peter Christopherson's window display, BOY, King's Road, March 1977 (© Sheila Rock)

son, these were so realistic that the police removed them within days of their going on display.

The Punk promenade was simple. In spite of its length, the King's Road is served by one only tube station, Sloane Square. That would be the starting point, with BOY, nearly a mile down the road. There were benches outside the Duke of York's Headquarters, where it was possible to sit and frighten passers-by. It was another mile to World's End, with Shades, in the Antique Market, for lurid sunglasses and fifties jackets.

Just before Seditionaries on the Sloane Square side, Beaufort Market had shed its antiques trade to become a rabbit-warren of tiny stalls. Upstairs there was Nigel Pennick's Smutz, with its rips, chains and crudity a faded copy of BOY, while downstairs were Caroline Walker, selling fifties suits, Dave Fortune from Robot selling winkle-pickers and a bizarre stall run by a teenage girl, sporting op-art clothes and prominent teeth braces, with the name of Poly Styrene.

'Take a cheap plastic bag,' she says, 'stick a lot of plastic flowers on it and things that nobody would be bothered to buy, then all of a sudden they become very very trendy and people want them. I had little lattice plastic bags and see-through Mary Quant shoes from the sixties: I used to buy up old stock. Anything different. Some of the things were vile but they were so vile they were cute. That was the whole thing: it was meant to be an extreme version of tack.

'I just wanted to do something that was fun. I wasn't planning on doing a huge big business out of it. Because in those days you were a teenager and it was more the fact you were doing something. I did the shop until the music started taking off: it was a great wardrobe for the music. We would walk into the shop and put something on and have my photograph taken and I'd be in the newspaper the next day and then be on stage.'

A striking woman with a surprisingly loud, gutsy laugh, Poly was born Marion Elliot, the daughter of a Somali father and a 'typically English' mother. After working in the fashion industry at a young age, she 'became a complete drop-out' and followed the hippie trail of the time. At eighteen, she had her first brush with showbiz: 'I did one single under my real name Marion Elliot: "Silly Billy". It wasn't me, it was acting. On my nineteenth birthday I saw the Sex Pistols on Hastings Pier. I just saw this tacky sign with "Sex Pistols" written all over it. The name was like a Freudian joke. They were just incredibly young and fresh looking.

'It's a question of peer pressure, isn't it? You see other people in your own age group doing things and after that you get all sorts of things together to compete. I liked the way they were writing about their surroundings: it was definitely a change in consciousness. It was painting the world to be ugly, which it is from a certain point of view: there are some horrific things that are happening so why whitewash everything?

'I just put an ad in *Melody Maker*: "Young punx who want to stick it together". And then they just appeared. I was writing new songs every week, about what I saw around me so it would be historical. Some songs are timeless: they can apply to any generation. I was

Poly Styrene outside the Beaufort Market, World's End, spring 1977 (© Falcon Stuart)

trying to do a diary of 1977: I wanted to write about everyday experiences.

'My thing was more like consumerism, plastic artificial living. Especially as I had done that whole way of travelling around and living in harmony with nature. There was so much junk then. The idea was to send it all up. Screaming about it, saying: "Look, this is what you have done to me, turned me into a piece of styrofoam, I am your product. And this is what you have created: do you like her?"

'One of the first songs we did was "Oh Bondage Up Yours!" It was about being in bondage to material life. In other words it was a call for liberation. It was saying: "Bondage? – forget it! I am not going to be bound by the laws of consumerism or bound by my own senses." It has that line in it: "Chain smoke, chain gang, I consume you all": you are tied to these activities for somebody else's profit.'

With a solid rhythm section in the then-fashionable accelerated mode, and a sax player, the sixteen-year-old Laura Logic, whose unrestrained playing merged perfectly with Poly's high shriek, X-Ray Spex began a residency in the basement of the Man in the Moon pub, right next to Beaufort Market. With a name taken from ads in the back of *True Detective* magazines and two aggressive frontwomen, X-Ray Spex were an immediately attractive proposition: within three concerts, they had made their first record.

16.4.77: Roxy Ratpack, Saturday nite. Find a friend and stick close: sink or swim. A club full of 'Wild Boys' outtakes and budding SS officers – (Sunday Times *headline Sunday April 3 'National Front Woos the Young') – plenty of new faces as the music, fashion and attitude is spread by word of mouth and publicity. The soundtrack for this B-movie is five bands, all of which use as a base Punk Rhythm 1 – the drill-Ramones variant.*

First on are Smak. No style, no music, no presence, and lyrics half-digested platitudes. And they try to 'shock' – Yecch. X-Ray Spex, of all the bands on tonite, seem to have the most potential for mass appeal. The sound is basic but full and driving, and best of all, well mixed. Poly buzzes around stage taking hecklers in her stride and forestalling most obvious criticism with her songs: 'I'm A Cliché', 'I Can't Do Anything'. Most are converted, even Ari from the Slits, who came to pull mike wires.

Record, instant playback, fast forward. By the time that X-Ray Spex played the Roxy for the first time in April, the club was almost history. 'There was a decline after the first three months,' says Don Letts, 'in the last month it did fizzle out, basically because the best groups were starting to make it big and we were getting the dregs down there.' The process is caught by Letts' documentary *The Punk Rock Movie*, shot in the Roxy, as, caught up in the general sense of empowerment, the DJ picked up a Super-8 camera.

The film graphically shows the full effect on Punk of the 'shock–horror' publicity as the media's script was replayed for real. Keith Levene is shooting speed in the Roxy toilet. An unknown fan sensuously slashes his stomach with long passes of a razor-blade. Dee Generate, on April Fools Day, gets up from behind his drum kit to slash at a pig's head with a cleaver, while the rest of the group performs Velvet Underground feedback.

'Eater didn't really know what they were doing,' says Dee Generate. 'The pig's head was my idea; that was one of the last concerts we did. That night, the Millwall came, smashed the place up and beat everybody up. By that time I wanted to go back to school and do my O Levels: anything was better than being involved in something that was straight off the football terraces. I'd lost interest in that part of it.'

16.4.77: Next are Wire: they short-circuit the audience totally, playing about twenty numbers, most around one minute long. The audience doesn't know when one has finished and another is beginning. I like the band for that . . . good theatre. Image-wise they look convincingly bug-eyed, flash speed automatons caught in a '64 Mod time-warp.

There seems to be some scheme of things, but this is buried in the poor sound and the limitations of the format. I caught the words to two: 'Three Girl Rhumba' and '12XU', a song about sexual paranoia, which was the best of the set. There were glimpses of genuine originality. The audience only really got interested when the bass player blew his stack at a heckler.

'They were very chaotic evenings,' says Bruce Gilbert, 'there wasn't a lot of time to think about it. The Buzzcocks were very nervous but looking very composed in comparison to how they were at the 100 Club. It was obvious that they'd been working on what they were doing, they'd been editing, which was why we felt some sympathy with what they were doing. It was that quality of being self-contained. The chances to play were so few and far between.'

Wire had been formed by four art students from Watford and Hornsey. They were slightly older and their style more considered than most: guitarist Gilbert had worked with tape loops; drummer Robert Gotobed had played with R&B group the Snakes. 'After we'd rehearsed for four days a week, twelve hours a day,' says Graham Lewis, 'we weren't inhibitied. We could write songs about what was going in England: about media and perception. We were struck by the quality and distortion of information. Colin Newman was writing a lot of the music then: it was a deconstruction, a piss-take of Rock music. The structures were Rock'n'Roll, taken apart and put together in different ways. This is how they go, but not quite. They *swerve*.'

'When the text ran out, it stopped,' says Gilbert, 'we hadn't thought of the songs as being any length. That's how long they were, and when they stopped, another one started.' The result was a series of brilliant disquisitions on love, Punk Rock, the media and mundaneness transcended.

16.4.77: By the time that Johnny Moped came on, one riff was beginning to merge into another . . . So Moped didn't grab my attention too much. In fact, he's fun: one of nature's loons, he prowls around like a shabby tiger, sawn-off leather jacket and forehead full of hair. He's one of the audience up on stage – the distance between them is minimal – and they love it.

'You could write a book about the Mopeds,' says Roger Armstrong. 'You had Slimy Toad, the guitar player who was a very good musician, good at flash, Jazz–Rock guitar playing, Fred Berk who wrote very funny pop songs, like "Darling, Let's Have Another Baby". Then you had Johnny, a very sweet guy, with a history of instability. He was very strange offstage, but you put him onstage and he was transformed. It was really street Punk, ripped flares, dad's old jacket with safety-pins in it, long hair.'

16.4.77: Four bands into the punkathon, numb-out. All the better that the Buzzcocks are so good. They sing and play because they have something to say. It isn't particularly high-flown, brief jottings of everyday small incidents of boredom, frustration and despair, as the supermarkets and motorways spread. Their image/music mesh is good too – the flat Mancunian accent and laconic dryness fitting the lyrics and cheap as a siren guitar sound.

That night, all the groups were recorded by Mike Thorne for a live album to be released on EMI Records, recovering from the Sex Pistols debacle. 'There was this madman who said, "I'll sign you up for a record if you let me do the production",' says Andy Czezowski, 'we miked up the toilets and got all the conversations about the meaning of Punk and people shooting up. That was quite good to eavesdrop on.'

By the time the record came out in the middle of June, the Roxy *was* history. 'We were completely washed out by Rene Albert,' says Czezowski, 'The whole thing was ropey. At the time he had a friend who had just come out of prison for manslaughter, called Rod; Rene showed him around this place packed with kids, and he thought, "I'll have some of this". I think Rene Albert flogged it to him – so we were out – and from that point on it went downhill.'

Now that the music industry had decided to take Punk seriously, the only way it could market it was as a type of Rock. This in turn set up a whole sequence of demands on the Punk groups and those who interpreted them. At the same time as Punk advertising increased, the music press went Punk crazy. With its new writers, it could fulfil its function as an interpreter to the industry and those outside the Punk enclaves around the country, curious but not committed.

In order to be marketed as Rock, much of Punk's original complexities were stripped to the bone. A good example of the transaction on offer was Tony Parsons' brilliant fixing of the Clash early in April in an *NME* front cover. Gone were any hints of the group's art-school background or Strummer's public-school past, as the Clash's image was taken dead straight: these were 'the lads', ex-skinhead Maoists from a new brutalist landscape. On the album sleeve, photographed from below, they glare with righteous ferocity.

This album, released in early April, was the first major Punk statement. In the fourteen songs, the Clash forsook the 'sheet-metal' sonic experimentation of their early performances for a solid, polite production which highlighted the songs' words and thus their message. Apart from the white Rasta tunes – 'White Riot' and 'Police and Thieves' – the most clearly identifiable subject was blue-collar hedonism and aggression, epitomized by the interjected 'Oi!' of 'Career Opportunities' and the terrace chants of 'What's my Name'.

The 'sound of the Westway'; the 'Tower Block syndrome'; Punk fixed forever as social realism: here were McLaren's pronouncements of the previous December replayed. The fantasy contained some truth: it was also great propaganda and the *NME* weren't the only ones pushing it. *Sounds* published their 'Images of the New Wave': on the cover was rabid superfan Shane MacGowan; inside were pictures of office blocks and an anti-fascist editorial.

The music press hires young writers because of their exploitable enthusiasm but, within the confines of the weekly deadline, places intense pressure on those writers to make their names. Finding an angle takes a while: it usually involves either finding new groups to praise, or ripping apart selected targets. The process begins with enthusiasm, peaks very quickly, and then goes into a steep spiral: a cycle of eighteen months to two years. As the main interpreter of Punk, the music press failed to match the diversity of the original fans, whose experience was ignored. Because it is young men rather than women who usually develop pop expertise, the music press is a male-dominated atmosphere. This reflects the music industry at large, which, despite its air of Bohemianism, is often a haven for outdated gender and sex attitudes that contravene the experiences of both musicians and their audiences. If Punk was to be lads' Rock, then lads would write about it.

For a young woman like Jane Jackman [Jane Suck], attracted to Punk by the images of sexual freedom propagated by performers like Patti Smith, the reality of the music industry was a shock. 'If you're a woman you mean nothing in the music press. You are the lowest of the low, and no-one will support you. And if you're a lesbian, and I was the only out lesbian in the music press, then you're really on a limb. You can't screw your way into favour: you've got nothing to give.'

An orphan, Jane was brought up in Weston-Super-Mare where she listened to the Beach Boys and wore skinhead clothes. 'I wrote from when I was twelve, compulsively, but journalism happened by accident. I read a Jonh Ingham piece in *Sounds* and it was the first time something lifted me out of my chair. I wanted to be part of it. I'd read *Sounds* and think "This is crap: I could do better than this." Then Alan Lewis published a piece of mine about the Roxy and wanted something from me every week.

'It was a joke. Punk was tolerant, it took in groups of people who were alienated, but there weren't enough of the kind of people involved with Punk to change the music press and industry for the better. My recourse was to start taking speed: once I started injecting I didn't have to worry about my sexuality. I became asexual, I think many people were, it was an incredibly asexual movement.'

As far as the music industry was concerned, it was business as usual. Punk was an oddity to which they had to respond but, apart from the Sex Pistols, most of the groups were easy enough to deal with: a bit surly perhaps, but delightfully unconcerned with the small print which would eat into those impressive sounding advances. The records didn't cost much to make and had guaranteed sales and guaranteed publicity. In spite of a couple of hiccups, it was almost fun.

'In 1977, we probably signed about a dozen Punk or New-Wave bands,' says Maurice Oberstein. 'That would represent no more than 10 or 15 per cent of the acts that we signed. It wasn't a special direction that we would concentrate in: we were always a multi-faceted music company. We had soul artists, we had a special enjoyment for Heavy Metal: we signed Judas Priest at the time, we signed Barbara Dickson, we were across a full spectrum of music.'

As Punk novices, the majors had one big problem: how could you tell whether a Punk group was a good Punk group? And, if you did put money into one, how could you market it, bearing in mind you weren't quite sure why you'd signed it in the first place? For those who didn't trust their ears, like Chris Parry at Polydor, or who didn't have their own Punk advisors, like Miles Copeland, there was only one answer: the gimmick.

The concept came from the collectors' subculture. Stiff and Chiswick had guaranteed a small minimum sale through specific marketing and attention to detail – picture sleeves, badges and slogans. Stiff quickly became the market leader with their eye-catching graphics and crazy scams: the first two thousand Damned albums, for instance, featured a picture of Eddie and the Hot Rods inserted 'due to record company error'. It was the first of many Stiff stunts.

'We quickly found out about the cynical attitude of the record business, even with Stiff,' says T.V. Smith, 'although they were doing it in a mocking way, it was still a big shock to see the cover of our first record, and there was a big picture of Gaye's face. It suddenly hit home – we've got a good-looking girl in the group and that's what's going to happen. We didn't think it was an issue. It cheapened it for all of us, that people would find a gimmick in what we'd hoped would avoid all gimmicks.'

The majors were quick to take note: sales in the first two weeks of a release are usually all-important, as they will feature on the chart, which will then increase airplay and push sales onto another level. Punk was not an airwave favourite, so gimmicks were a perfect way to achieve swift sales, and accorded with the music industry's gut belief that Punk was just a gimmick anyway. An early, influential example was WEA's marketing of Television's 'Marquee Moon' on a 12" single, pushing this non-radio cut into the Top Forty.

The 12" single was just coming through from America. There, DJs had found that the new, orchestral, extended Disco format worked much better on larger discs, with the increased playing time and better sound quality. Until 1976 these 12" records were only available to DJs as promotional items. The first general English release, the Who's 'Substitute', was quickly followed by a rush of Disco and Reggae releases, sonically well suited to this format. Punk was not.

Marketing devices always work on a law of diminishing returns: as everybody else catches on to a gimmick, the stakes have to be raised in order to retain exclusivity. Simple 12" singles were soon swamped by coloured vinyl editions and special products like Phonogram's 12" for the Ramones' 'Sheena is a Punk Rocker', which had an extra track and serrated cut-out badge. They were sold in a numbered, limited edition just like a work of fine art. The effects of this short-term solution were far-reaching: they permeate the multi-mix, multi-format music industry of today. Creatively, it helped to unlock a new generation of sleeve designers but their impact would only come later in the year: in the early summer, these music industry ministrations only reinforced the extent to which the record companies were asserting control over Punk.

What was selling was Rock. Following *Damned Damned Damned*, the new sensation was the Stranglers' first album – a cleverly arranged stew of appealing psychedelic tunes masking vicious lyrics – making the Top Five. The same week, *The Clash* entered the album Top Twenty. A couple of weeks later, the Jam became the first New-Wave group to play on *Top of the Pops* with their first single 'In the City'. Their album entered the charts shortly after.

McLaren and Rhodes' carefully formulated definitions of Punk now meant nothing. 'Punk' was now 'New Wave' and could mean acts as diverse as American visitors Talking Heads, Television or Blondie, whose April/May tour showed that the illusion of any Punk unity of style or of milieu – either in London or New York – was becoming unsustainable. Blondie were a pop group with Mod threads; Television were a Rock group, exuding a religious solemnity. Neither had much in common with the Sex Pistols.

The important groups were those who sold. The Stranglers and the

Jam were thrust into prominence on a level with the Clash and perhaps higher than the Sex Pistols. Yet there were problems with this: both groups occupied a New-Wave sector which was commercially useful but caused ideological headaches. The Stranglers were rightly criticized for the puerile sexism of their lyrics, while the Jam's Paul Weller, exasperated beyond endurance by Punk pieties, stated in May that he would vote Conservative in the next election.

Punk was politically riven as it interacted with the world outside. If the Jam and the Stranglers were going to coast in the slipstream of the Sex Pistols, then it was not surprising if they were judged on the same radical criteria and found wanting. Despite the element of novelty in both groups, there were also strong traces of stylistic and/or ideological conservatism which made them a satisfactory bridge between the mainstream and Punk's all-out assault.

More serious was the row which embroiled the Sex Pistols in early May. Under the banner headline 'Rock's Swastika Revolution', John Blake disinterred the swastika paranoia of six months before in the *Evening News*: 'Frequently [the National Front] have turned up to cheer the Sex Pistols.' McLaren immediately fired off a blistering letter unequivocally decrying 'that scummy organization', but the damage was done.

The stakes had been raised: that month, the Front had attempted to delineate their hopes for a 'Rock for Racism'. This was in direct response to the SWP-backed 'Rock Against Racism' movement which, after nine months' campaigning, held its first large event on May Day, featured Aswad and Generation X. The fierce opposition between these two organizations would eventually overtake all of Punk's anarchism. On the point of fragmentation, Punk found itself fighting on fronts which, secure in Louise's, it had not even known existed.

During May, the Clash spent their CBS money on a month-long jaunt that, although nobody knew it at the time, was the last great Punk tour. Featuring the Jam and the cream of the inner-circle Punk groups, the 'White Riot' tour covered twenty-seven dates around the country: 'It was the first proper road show,' says Pete Shelley, 'because the Anarchy tour hadn't managed to do that. Its notoriety went ahead of it like a leper's bell . . . The Clash played everywhere with the Slits, the Subway Sect and us. It was great, everyone got on with one another, it was actually working. There was something there, and it was outside the established music business.'

Despite the way that it was conceived, in the spirit of Punk unity, contradictions became apparent early in the tour, when the Jam left over a dispute about the way that both headliners were being asked to spend money in supporting the other groups. The lads went wild on the tour just like Rock groups always do – 'You could throw things all over the place, get the fire extinguishers out,' says Vic Godard – but it was women who caused the real mayhem. 'Every morning,' says Viv Albertine, 'the coach driver had to be bribed to let the Slits onto the coach. Everywhere we went, we had to almost be strapped to our seats, every hotel we had to be smuggled in. We were not being nice little girls . . . If we'd been men, it would have been: "Oooh aren't they great, you know, like the Stones or the Pistols." Because we were women there was this constant sexuality. The coach driver had to be bribed, but because his sexuality was disturbed by this contradictory image of these pretty women with wild, matted hair. Ari's sexuality, only fourteen, a skirt that didn't hide her bum. He must have found it so threatening and so exciting at the same time.'

It was the Slits' first tour, and the first date at Edinburgh was the first time Albertine had ever been on stage. 'I was so forceful that I ended up by playing with them,' she says, 'but when I walked out on stage the first time, I didn't know how to play. I had a lot of bottle, but you need a fucking lot of bottle to do that.' Yet even this worked for the Slits as, in front of the Clash's riot backdrop, they enacted their theatre of female power, a message rammed home by Palmolive's cataclysmic drumming.

The 'White Riot' tour was the first outbreak of pure Punk mania. 'The crowds were very excitable,' says Pete Shelley, 'it was like good-natured vandalism.' 'They would have clapped anything,' says Vic Godard, 'anyone could have done anything and they would have gone mad. They liked us best when everything went wrong, when the amps didn't work.' Yet the fabric of existing theatres could not deal with this unleashed fury. However good-natured, Punk *looked* scary and it resulted in damage to venues built for staider times.

'Standing in the lobby at the Rainbow during the breaks between sets,' says Jonh Ingham, 'all you could hear was the sound of plastic glasses being ground under people's heels: that was the sound of sulphate.' While the Clash roared through 'White Riot', the audience rushed to the front and smashed up the front few rows of seats, which were then flung to the very front of the stage. The ensuing press headlines ensured continuing council bans.

At the forefront was the GLC, which, under a Conservative regime, was operating a restrictive application of its 'Code of Practice for Pop Concerts'. With fifteen sections, the GLC Code contained a web of rules which, if infringed, would result in a concert ban. From January onwards, when Hugh Cornwell of the Stranglers wore a T-shirt which spelled 'Fuck' on stage at the Rainbow, promoters like John Curd and Harvey Goldsmith had non-stop battles with the council.

Small venues were opening all the time, yet any attempt to put on a large-scale Punk or New-Wave concert, or a Sex Pistols concert on any scale, was thwarted. In July, the Chairman of the GLC Arts Committee, Bernard Brook Partridge, denied there was a blacklist, but offered the following indication: 'There are one or two groups that give the industry a bad name – the Bay City Rollers, the Sex Pistols, the Stranglers. I *do* distinguish between something which is distasteful and something which is in bad taste and is in breach of the code.'

This was a highly charged situation that backed up Punk's extremist fantasies. As one promoter put it at the time, the operators of the code were 'middle-aged and frightened': there was a real sense in which Punk's accurate record of England's tensions hit the desired chord – a clash, not between generations, but between rulers and ruled. If Punk was the true voice of the present, what did that make the people that opposed it? The holders of true power, who, provoked, were beginning to test their strength.

Sid Vicious and John Lydon, West Berlin, March 1977 (© John Tiberi)

24

Power is the ability to define phenomena and have them react accordingly.

Huey Newton, quoted in Bobby Seale, *Seize the Time* (1970)

After the Sex Pistols' sudden removal from A&M, the immediate task for Glitterbest was to organize a concert for Tony Potter of NBC News who was filming a documentary about the group. Few people at the time were aware the depth of hostility towards the Sex Pistols. McLaren tried to find a venue to take the group and, with no record company support, faced a near total ban. In desperation, he went back to the Roman Catholic priests at Notre Dame Hall who agreed, on the condition that admittance was kept to just fifty people. Chaos ensued.

'I was told they were playing in three hours, phone a few people,' says Simon Barker, 'I passed it on, and this was about three o'clock, and at 5.30 there were about five hundred people outside Notre Dame, and they wouldn't let anybody in. Sophie talked to these priests: I think they let in about 150, and then we had to come and face all these people. I said to Malcolm, "It's your fault, you think it's really funny that people have to sit outside, but it's crap, they want to see the group play." He was really careless.'

Inside, the atmosphere was as spectacular as the LWT filming had been. The most notable element was the début of Sid Vicious in front of a live audience: any deficiencies he might have had as a bass player were made up for by his performance. Sharing stage announcements with Lydon, he was already showing the barely controlled aggression which would rule his persona from now on. This persona was not true to Sid's real personality: 'There was this illusion that Punk was all midle-class art students', says DJ Jay Strongman, then an art student himself. 'But there was a hard core of thirty hard-nut East-End guys, always in the latest Vivienne creations. That night, Sid came out of Notre Dame and someone shouted: "You've sold out!" He turned round and said: "Who said that?" He saw it was the twin hot-dog sellers, Michael and John, and he immediately backed off. There he was pretending to be a hard nut, and when he came across the real thing, he was very apologetic.'

The next day, the group left the country for Jersey, on the instructions of McLaren, who was worried about a possible backlash. Just before they left, Lydon gave a quick interview to Caroline Coon, which was emblazoned on the front of the *Melody Maker* in bold type: 'A record company is there to market records – not dictate terms.' Coon caught the mood: 'It's as if the group, unable to insult the Establishment without incurring severe retaliation, have turned on themselves and their own.'

Hooked on adrenalin, McLaren was simply moving faster than the institutions that were his opposition – the media and the record companies – and this speed and adroitness gave him time to outwit his enemies. 'Malcolm milked situations,' says Paul Cook, 'he didn't instigate them: that was always our own doing. There was never any blueprint, as people now believe that Malcolm sat down and planned it in advance.' The power of McLaren's account of events means that people are inclined to accept as fact events which he himself will admit are embellishments of the truth. 'During the course of the A&M affair,' McLaren says, 'I noticed on Derek Green's desk a telex from Rick Wakeman in Switzerland which said: "Dear Derek, I have just gone out and bought eleven razor blades and 115 safety-pins." Green said it was just a piss-take, but of course we established in the press that it could possibly be blackmail on behalf of some of the artists.'

McLaren's increased visibility at a time when the group was absent meant that he was the object of suspicion and frustration felt by fans and press alike. By remaining centre-stage, and continuing to issue inflammatory statements, he gave the impression that he was in control, but this sleight of hand also made him appear responsible for events – like the fact that the Sex Pistols were unable to play live – which were outside his control.

The Sex Pistols had now received £125,000 in six months. Although the group were given an immediate rise from £25 to £40 a week, they would never see their full share. McLaren spent the money on keeping the Sex Pistols organization going. Although Lydon had already sent in a demand for some accounts, the group were too busy struggling for their day-to-day existence to worry. They did not notice that McLaren, while acting in their immediate interests, was developing an agenda of his own.

In his unfinished *Oxford Street* film, McLaren had laid down an inchoate manifesto for the group: now that the music industry had been, to some extent, mastered by the Sex Pistols, his ambition extended beyond music into feature films. Here was a whole new industry for him to play within: here was the perfect way to control the promotion of a group so enshrouded in myth and scandal that traditional music-industry methods no longer worked. But, just like Andy Warhol earlier in the 1970s, McLaren seriously underestimated both the expense of the feature-film making process and the toughness of the film industry – in comparison to which the music industry was child's play. His head had been turned just as much as John Lydon's: he was the manager of an eighteen-month-old pop group, taking on two media industries at once, with a small team and a group that was badly in need of reassurance rather than new horizons.

After the EMI sacking, McLaren began to assemble news and performance footage of the Sex Pistols for a possible short film. 'Malcolm asked me to get hold of these bits of footage from the Anarchy tour to make a show reel,' says Tiberi. 'He had this idea to sell the group as a visual act. We were very aware of the group's potential to get fired from record companies, and TV was a new direction. That's why I was there, knocking on the door.

'*Number 1* was all re-filmed. It was very early days in home video technology. The only place we could get the Grundy programme was from a Country and Western promoter whom Sophie had phoned up to record it. Julien Temple did the refilming, he shot the video image on to film and edited it into chronological order at film school, overnight, and we showed a cutting copy the next night. It was very stirring stuff, propaganda-oriented.'

The brilliance of *Number 1* was in replaying the media's curses with a mocking laugh. The twenty-five-minute short tells the story of the scandals from the group's side, cutting supercilious youth presenters, pompous chat-show guests, mealy-mouthed academics, with simple, stark footage of the group playing and talking. It closes with 'God Save the Queen' playing over speeded Pathé footage of Royal Circumstance Past. The final shot pans from the glittering coach to sweepers . . . shovelling horse shit.

The idea for a feature film, tentatively titled 'Rock Around the Contract', had first been acted upon just after the EMI sacking on 10 February, when John Lydon and McLaren went to visit Peter Cook, a possible screenwriter. Cook was shy but cautiously interested. When McLaren went to Los Angeles for the A&M negotiations three days later, he used the time to canvass some film companies: when he returned, Gerry Goldstein was put on the payroll to develop the idea.

Immediate problems pushed the film into the background. Whatever impression McLaren gave to the world at this point, the truth was that everything was out of control. When the group were hurriedly whisked to Jersey, for an enforced holiday, the trip ended in farce: according to McLaren, 'Jamie was sent to look after them. On arrival they were not allowed into the hotel and ended up with police escorts, being searched and suffering a great deal of discomfort. They were given twenty-four hours to leave the island. They managed to get a hotel for the night. After that morning, they went out and wherever they went, they had police outside. They did a short TV interview and they were then contacted by a couple of local gangsters who drove them to a quieter part of the island. On his return, Rotten was furious; he said that Jamie didn't seem in control of the situation. He was refusing to go back home and they all stayed in a hotel in Lancaster Gate except Steve.'

The next day, at Tiberi's suggestion, the Sex Pistols flew off to Berlin. 'Rotten was a precocious little shit then,' he says, 'it was trying to think of what this little shit wanted to do. We stayed at the Hotel Kempinski, the equivalent of the Connaught, and there was nothing much to do. Got in touch with the local record company, German EMI. Hired a VW and bombed around the wall, all around those towers. Sid was a real tosser for not having a passport: if he had, we'd have crossed over. I couldn't imagine leaving him behind.

'The band loved it: they didn't have a stage to play on, but they had fun. Getting into fights with film crews. It had got out of balance, as far as John and Sid were concerned the whole thing was getting top-heavy. It was very removed, but it did connect with Malcolm pushing in rehearsals to write new songs. The only one really interested in it was John: he found East German TV in the hotel room, he was knocked out by that. He was a grammar-school boy really.'

In London, McLaren was suffering a tremendous backlash from the record companies. 'The Sex Pistols had come up with a novel idea. They didn't necessarily have to make any records, they didn't necessarily have to play anywhere, but what they had to do was to create a tremendous outrage and con every record company from the fact that they are the enfants terribles of the scene and they are out to destroy things. If they do that sufficiently well, they can enjoy as much notoriety as they would ever be likely to create at any ordinary Rock'n'Roll concert. Nothing was having the effect the Sex Pistols were having without having any product on the market: they were the biggest group in England and becoming important in Europe, and an incredible enigma in the US. They perplexed everybody in the record industry to the extent that every door was shut.'

McLaren tried Decca, Pye, Polydor, even EMI again. Larry Parnes offerred to set up his own label for the Sex Pistols. As far as McLaren was concerned, the whole point was to sign for another large advance. 'How long was it going to take and how much longer would the band put up with the fact that they were banned? There was very little for them to do except write tunes, a ridiculous task in the light of them not having anywhere to play them and certainly nowhere to record them.

'We went back to CBS. What it was this time, was that they were prepared to sign us, but not only would we have to stay outside of the building and meet in Soho Square, but, as we had enough money from the two advances, that they would sign us for no advance. I thought, "We aren't in the business to sign acts for nothing", even though we had made by now what amounted to about £125,000. What were we going to do?'

Another showcase was arranged at the Screen on the Green, on 3 April: the cinema was almost the only place in town – apart from the now despised Roxy Club – which would have them. 'One person that really needs a medal is Roger Austin,' says Jordan, 'he was a benefactor, and somebody who doesn't want any credit for it either.'

Even then, an elaborate rigmarole was necessary to avoid trouble with an ever-vigilant GLC: the free concert didn't begin until midnight, and entry was remarkably difficult.

9.4.77: It must be conceded that Malcolm McLaren has a first-class media brain with a perfect instinct for theatre. He can now have his cake and eat it – the media hype around the Pistols is so entangled that people will now believe anything. Always there are two or three different explanations for any given event or stroke pulled.

After a longish wait, the audience of 350 get to watch a home movie collage of Pistol happenings. It's disturbing, cheap and nasty: the sight of Rotten filling the screen is chilling (someone's been watching Privilege). McLaren's shop gets plugged, the straight media is fooled, ritual bogey figures are there to be hissed at. Us and them.

More waiting, frustration and boredom. A good atmosphere for the Pistols to operate in. They've improved, even tho' the material is familiar – 11 songs plus two encores, the only newish material being 'EMI' and 'God Save the Queen'. In fact they seem frozen in time . . . but now to the audience, musical and stylistic considerations are all but irrelevant. The Pistols have become symbols, the songs anthems, inviolate from criticism. Just to see them is enough.

This replay of the previous summer's concert only served to reinforce the difference between the two occasions. The group were supported by a rough cut of *Number 1* and the third appearance of the Slits, who were untogether but explosive. The Sex Pistols were muted, only coming to life when Lydon stretched out both arms, prophet-like, during the final 'God Save the Queen'.

The next day, according to McLaren, the Sex Pistols were turned down by five record companies. Within three days, Sid Vicious was in hospital with hepatitis: he had played the Screen on the Green stoned and afterwards went off to score heroin with Keith Levene. When he turned up a couple of days later looking ill, there was an unpleasant confrontation between him and McLaren where, after he admitted that he was using heroin, he was told that he had to leave Linda Ashby's flat and stay with his mother. But Anne Beverley had a new boyfriend, so Sid was put up by Goldstein for a few days.

'When we eventually pushed him into a hospital,' says McLaren, 'he was looking so ill it was unbelievable. We kept it under wraps as much as possible – it must never be known that the Sex Pistols take drugs. We couldn't afford to look as though we were ever out of control and everybody was sworn to secrecy. It was kept quiet as a dormouse.'

Sid's month in the hospital effectively kept the group out of the public eye for that time. At the same time, McLaren's business options were narrowing: 'CBS dropped out on 31 March, but Jean Fernandez from Barclay Records in France kept on phoning us up. He had heard "Anarchy In The UK" and thought it was amazing. Stephen Fisher said that Barclay had a terrible reputation: they didn't pay anything and were effectively pirates. Meanwhile Branson kept on phoning us up: I tried to get rid of him. He offered meetings, and we went to one. We didn't decide anything: hopefully we'd get another record company.

'Meanwhile, having got interested in this mad Frenchman from Barclay Records, I decided to phone up every company worldwide. The idea might be this time to not sign with one company in the UK. Sophie started sending out telegrams to Durium in Italy, to Spain and Greece, to Metro Records in Germany, to RCA Germany and Inelco in Holland, Wizzard in Australia and Sonet in Sweden. There were trickles of interest. We eventually decided, after all the efforts, to sign with Barclay in France.'

At the same time, McLaren and Gerry Goldstein were proceeding with the film, looking for backing and scriptwriters. Their lack of experience translated into a frenetic tour of the English film world. After some meetings with experienced producer Sandy Lieberson (whose credits included *Performance*), Peter Cook dropped out: the next pair to be canvassed were Graham Chapman and Johnny Speight who, in the middle of April, bashed out a draft script. This was quickly rejected as 'too documentary'.

The promotion plans for 'God Save the Queen' continued apace, in anticipation of signing a record contract with Virgin. A TV advert was also filmed. Very brief, it featured John Lydon glaring into the camera, with the words: 'You thought you'd got rid of us, but we're back, on Virgin Records'. Jamie Reid continued to develop various poster and sleeve ideas: he added a Union Jack to the background of the Queen's head poster and designed a single sleeve in the official Jubilee colours of blue and silver.

The result of all this frenetic activity was that McLaren was spending less and less time with the Sex Pistols. They were all twenty-one or under, and none was living at home. 'Malcolm didn't do much to help,' says Paul Cook, 'he was a bad manager in that respect. Someone said to me that he's a band breaker, and it was true.'

Just at the point where the group were becoming isolated and needed more emotional support, McLaren withdrew, and the day-to-day handling of the group was taken over by John Tiberi (live and studio work) and Sophie Richmond (domestic details, appointments etc). Sophie began arranging taxi-cab accounts, flats for the group and generally behaving as a surrogate mother. 'The differences started to develop then,' says Tiberi, 'John's idea of independence meant independence from the others and he got that when he moved home.'

In turn, everyone was neglecting the hospital-bound Sid, except for Nancy. Sid was feeling more lonely and vulnerable than usual: of the group, Steve and Paul visited him infrequently, and his former best friend John Lydon never. Only Sophie went regularly, and her time was circumscribed by office work. During this month, Sid came to rely totally on Nancy: after he left hospital on 13 May, they were inseparable.

On the 8th, McLaren, Stephen Fisher and Jamie Reid flew to Paris where they signed a production deal for £26,000: this covered not only France but Zanzibar, Switzerland and Algeria for a two-year period. They returned to face the moment of truth: whether to complete the contract negotiations with Virgin. McLaren resisted until the last moment, but Fisher insisted that the Jubilee was bearing down like an express train and the marketing for the single was too far down the line.

'Malcolm was trying to get them to just do one single,' says Tiberi, 'but they wouldn't have it: they wanted to take advantage of the situation to get a long-term contract. Then I saw Branson as a daring person: he talked about getting behind the concept. Malcolm was very concerned about the Jubilee deadline, but I now think Virgin was a mistake. They had the group worked out wrong. And it seems a shortsighted way of looking at the group to see them having to meet deadlines.'

Virgin was different from both A&M and EMI. It was a young independent which was the brainchild of one man, who had stamped his own personality over the company. It then had no shareholders, no American parent company, no middle-aged management and board, not even much industry standing. Virgin had nothing to lose: in Richard Branson, McLaren now had to deal with a company head younger than him and equally ruthless. Branson's appearance belied his character. McLaren scorned him as a 'hippie' but severely underestimated Branson's energy and determination. Despite the long hair and air of woolliness, Branson had never really lived the hippie lifestyle: the image and the products were an accident of timing rather than of true inclination. For Branson, drugs and trips east had taken second place to determined, ceaseless business growth, with the burning ambition of the driven.

'All the way through school Richard was crucified by people, he really was,' says Johnny Gems, who was with Branson at Stowe, 'it was because he was dim, a cartoon character. But you don't need brains to make money. He was vilified, so he had this tremendous desire to show the world that he was a winner and that's what gives him his demonic energy.'

Within a few months of leaving Stowe in 1967, Branson began his first business venture with Gems: a magazine to cater to the newly self-aware student generation. Still in his teens, Branson already showed a sound grasp of how to plan a business. By 1970, he was seeking to expand. 'In April, the Conservative Government announced a relaxation of the recommended retail price on records', says John Varnom, who had started with *Student* a few months before, 'Richard got the idea of selling records at cut prices and started Virgin Records.'

Virgin was very much a family, and most of Branson's immediate associates – like Nik Powell and Simon Draper – were also close personal friends. Varnom was the black sheep, bound to his upper-middle class, home-counties boss by a mixture of love and hate. As Mick Brown writes in Branson's authorized biography: 'He admired Varnom's breadth of learning. Furthermore, the fact that Varnom was so impishly resistant to Branson's powers of persuasion both disconcerted Richard and constituted a sort of challenge.'

Branson had placed the ads but had no records: when the mail-order money started pouring in, he got Varnom to call up the record companies and get the required records at a discount in return for mentioning them in *Student*. 'The mail order paid for its own advertising but it never made any money,' says Varnom, 'when the November 1970 postal strike happened, we managed to get a shop open at 24 Oxford Street and that did amazingly well, very quickly.'

There were some hiccups – including a fine for £28,000 incurred when the Customs and Excise caught Virgin faking exports (exported records could be sold cheaper when illegally imported, minus VAT) –

but Virgin expanded rapidly, opening new shops in Notting Hill Gate, Manchester, Newcastle and Brighton. The selling attraction was that one could go into a Virgin shop, smoke dope, stay all day, and nobody would bother you. 'They were hippy hovels,' says Varnom, 'we used to highlight this in the copy.'

In 1972, Virgin opened a recording studio at the Manor, in Shipton-on-Cherwell, near Oxford. One of the first releases was Mike Oldfield's *Tubular Bells*, the record that made Virgin. Consisting of two long suites of Philip Glass-type 'process music' with more than a whiff of English pastoralism and whimsy, *Tubular Bells* sold phenomenally well, remaining in the charts for over four and a half years. Its success catapulted Virgin into the major league, but it was not followed up.

'The label did quite well for a while,' says Varnom, 'and then it seriously began to lose money. The roster was vast. We had a lot of German music, like Tangerine Dream and Faust, and I called it "Kraut Rock" in a piece of mail order copy: that became a genre. Then we had Hatfield and the North and Henry Cow. I think there was a serious bit of intellectual snobbery going on there. Then in 1974 they bought Vernon Yard and Al Clark joined as Press Officer.'

In 1975, Virgin began releasing Reggae on the Front Line label, but artists like Linton Kwesi Johnson were not the big sellers that Virgin needed. It also carried with it a volatile business subculture with which Branson did not know how to deal. In March 1976, three men connected with a Reggae label, Atra, that Branson was distributing, broke into Branson's house to demand £5,000. By the end of 1976, things were getting a little desperate.

'As it turned out,' says Al Clark, 'a whole lot of options to renew came up at the same time. One memorable night at Richard's house in Denbigh Terrace, it was clear that if the company didn't change gear, it would just trickle along. We discussed all the people we would commit to for some time longer, or decide that it wasn't happening. It was a very turbulent evening, involving a lot of bridge-burning.'

The Sex Pistols had already been passed over twice by Virgin. 'In the summer, Richard was quite interested,' says Varnom, 'but Simon Draper said: "We sign the Sex Pistols over my dead body." So there was a delay.' In the New Year, Leslie Hill had arranged a meeting between McLaren and Branson as part of his attempt to prise the Sex Pistols gracefull out of EMI: McLaren still had plenty of options and refused to deal coherently with Branson.

By May 1977, time had run out. Branson instinctively knew that the

Sex Pistols were the perfect thing to rejuvenate a floundering company and, if he could succeed where EMI and A&M had failed, in taming the Sex Pistols, then it would make his name. As far as McLaren was concerned, he was under no illusion: he disliked Branson, both for his style and his class. 'Just as Lydon looked at McLaren and thought, "I'll have you",' says Bernard Rhodes, 'so Malcolm looked at Branson and thought the same.'

On 12 May, the Sex Pistols – through Glitterbest – signed to Virgin Records for an initial payment of £15,000 to cover one Sex Pistols album. McLaren insisted that the sum be paid, not all at once, but in twelve instalments, as individual tracks were delivered. One month later, a further £50,000 advance was paid for Virgin's right to release Pistols' product in all world territories including those covered by the Barclay/Nippon Columbia deals, and America.

'Richard had problems straightaway with Malcolm because Malcolm was as cunning and as smart,' says Varnom. 'Richard doesn't appreciate this. There was this political line from Malcolm and Jamie to bugger about with the company if they could. So Richard's back was put up to begin with and things just got worse and worse.'

'Malcolm and Richard were so similar,' says Clark, 'and in Richard, Malcolm had met his match. He didn't like that.'

'As soon as we signed,' says McLaren, 'there was this incredible argument. They were terrified that they were going to be the third company to be taken for a ride and refused to put Virgin Records on "God Save the Queen": their way out would be that they were not involved but were just distributing it. We made sure they put their name on the record label so we looked like any other artist.'

On 16 May, Sid Vicious finally made his signature on the Virgin contract: his presence in hospital had made the whole signing process low-key. Glitterbest were not anxious to draw attention to his absence. Immediately, there was another row. It had been decided to release 'God Save the Queen' on 27 May, with the aim of having the song in the Top Ten in Jubilee week. Production of the single had been started, from new metalwork, straight after the signing, but, on the 17th, the CBS pressing-plant downed tools in protest against the single's content.

Branson started to panic and McLaren, seeing his chance to get out of the Virgin contract, began to court Chrysalis. He was still totally unconvinced about the Virgin signing as, at this stage, was John Lydon. Although Branson was as enthusiastic as the other companies

Directors

M.McLAREN
S.FISHER

Registered Office,
23 Great Castle St,
London, W.1.

GLITTERBEST LTD

40 DRYDEN CHAMBERS
II9 OXFORD ST
LONDON W.I.

OI-734-II37
OI-734-II38

NO FUTURE

1/ God save the queen – And the fachist regime
It made you a moron – A potential H bomb

God save the queen – Shes not a human being
There is no future – In Englands dream
Dont be told what you want
Dont be told what you need
No future no future no future for you
God save the queen – God save window been
God saves ——— human beings

2/ God save the queen – tourists are money
Our figure head – Is not what she seems
God save history – save the mad parade
Lord have mercy – All crimes are paid
When theres no future how can there be sin?
We are the flowers in the dustbin
We are the poisen in the machine
We are the romance behind the screen
God save the queen – we mean it man
We love our queen – God saves

Repeat 2'nd verse
End on NO future etc . . . .

had been, he suddenly seemed vulnerable to industry pressure, despite his intention to bring the record out on a double-thickness flexi-disc, thus bypassing the usual pressing plants. After a flurry of phone calls, CBS resumed pressing, after yet more publicity. The next day, the platemakers refused to make plates for the printing of the 'God Save the Queen' sleeve: another flurry of phone calls ensued. On the 23rd, Tiberi and Temple arranged for a promotional film to be shot at the Marquee, for showing on *Top of the Pops*. The shoot was chaotic: Lydon was behaving like a prima donna and Vicious was still ill, yet somehow the atmosphere of madness worked well – the footage was both electric and humorous.

'God Save the Queen' had already proved ridiculously difficult to manufacture: it now began to prove equally difficult to promote. John Varnom and Jamie Reid came up with a wide-ranging campaign, costing over £5,000, that included: 1,000 double-crown posters for use on London buses; 3,000 quad-sized posters for flyposting; 6,000 stickers; 3,000 streamers; transfers; T-shirts, as well as TV, radio and press advertisements. Also mapped out was a detailed campaign for individual retailers and small chains.

This cross-media campaign immediately encountered serious obstacles. Thames and LWT rejected the TV advert and the radio stations refused the radio advert. The single was banned from the airwaves. The BBC refused to play it on the grounds of 'gross bad taste' (although John Peel played it twice) while the IBA instructed all commercial radio and TV stations not to broadcast the single, as it was in contravention of Section 4 (10) (A) of the IBA act, being 'against good taste or decency, likely to encourage or incite to crime, or lead to disorder'.

The record went on sale on the 27th, but Woolworths, Boots and W.H. Smith all refused to stock it. The despised music press leapt into the breach: with a 'Single of the Week' across all four weeklies, the Sex Pistols made the cover of the *Record Mirror*, the *Melody Maker*, and the *NME*'s 'Special Gratuitous Sex Pistols overkill issue' (the news, reviews, gossip, features and letters sections).

Despite a surprising and unprecedented attempt across the media, music and retail industries to prevent its appearance, 'God Save the Queen' sold 150,000 copies in five days, enough to send it into the charts at number eleven. The Sex Pistols were vindicated: with this

(*opposite*) John Lydon's handwritten lyrics (Jon Savage archive)

first true hit they finally reasserted their position as Punk's most important group and, more importantly, formed a rallying point around which a statistically small but significant section of the population voted with their pockets and their dreams. The world took notice.

Sex Pistols' promotion, June 1977 (© Caroline Coon)

25

On the radio the only talking I can find is the BBC World Service, famous for its role in The Resistance. Every other station is pop music. This is a change. Twenty-five years ago there would be nothing but the Jubilee. Now it is hard to break through the layers of pop music.

Mike Thomas: *Nothing to Declare: A Scene from an Exile's Chronicle* (June/July 1977)

The national idea, with the flag as totem, is today an aggrandizer of the nursery ego, not the annihilator of an infantile situation. And the numerous saints of this anti-cult – namely the patriots whose ubiquitous photographs, draped with flags, serve as official icons – are precisely the local threshold guardians whom it is the first problem of the hero to surpass.

Joseph Campbell: *The Hero with a Thousand Faces* (1949)

The Sex Pistols released their single at the moment when it could make the greatest impact. Nobody connected with the group, least of all John Lydon when he scribbled the words in a Hampstead squat, could have foreseen the effect that 'God Save the Queen' would have, just as nobody could have foreseen just how successful the Jubilee would be. At the moment when the world's press came to England to cover the official fantasy, here was its negative image, its shadow.

'Most symbols of the British nation seemed at a discount,' states Philip Whitehead in *The Writing on the Wall*. 'The celebration of Elizabeth II's Silver Jubilee as Queen of Great Britain and Northern Ireland seemed a chancy affair at such a time. In the event the British and two-thirds of the Northern Irish decided that one way to confront a future that might not work was with the trappings of a past which had worked.'

To those who were unconvinced, the Jubilee seemed an elaborate covering of the social cracks – with fading Coronation wallpaper. Out of the morass of mid-1970s pluralism emerged the old spectres thinly disguised with a fresh lick of paint. Here was the blind superiority that had characterized the English world-view after the Second World War; here was a concentrated dose of all the unappealing traits – snobbery, insularity, xenophobia – that rendered England's continued claim to be a world power meaningless. Here was Jack Warner in a new haircut and a flared suit – the embodiment of a repressive consensus against which nobody could argue.

Some 90 per cent of the population accepted what Tom Nairn calls 'the Glamour of Backwardness'. It would have been surprising if they had not: the extra two days' holiday was enough for most people. There was nothing else in the media: bonfires and bunting covered the country. The souvenir industry went mad, with everything from mugs and scarves to bras. In London alone, up to 4,000 street parties were held, while a crowd estimated at 1 million saw the procession from Buckingham Palace to St Paul's Cathedral on 7 June.

What was being celebrated was an edited, English version of what it was to be British. The United Kingdom was not only bereft of Empire but also divided within itself: Welsh and Scottish nationalism were at a peak, while the Civil War in Northern Ireland had spread onto the mainland with the post-1974 IRA campaigns. England itself was becoming ungovernable, but the Queen's speech contained the sentence, 'The Commonwealth can point the way for mankind.'

The Sex Pistols appeared with all the force of a hand-grenade tossed into an arrangement of gladioli. 'God Save the Queen' was the only serious anti-Jubilee protest, the only rallying call for those who didn't agree with the Jubilee because they didn't like the Queen, either because like John Lydon, they were Irish, or, much more to the point, because they resented being steamrollered by such sickening hype, by a view of England which had not the remotest bearing on their everyday experience.

The Sex Pistols leapt into the abyss that had suddenly opened but very few followed them. What seemed terrifying about the Jubilee was its sheer unanimity: the only critical press coverage was in the *Morning Star* and the *New Statesman*, while anti-Jubilee festivals at Alexander Palace and Blackheath were damp squibs. There was a brisk trade in 'Stuff the Jubilee' badges but that was all. Any dissenting voice was shut out.

What was so great about 'God Save the Queen' was that it was confident, clear, unapologetic – so much so that it gave a voice to everybody who hated the Jubilee, and there were many more of them than would ever be officially acknowledged. That June, the song's phrases could be taken at face value and yet they contained a number of time-bombs.

God save the Queen: the fascist regime . . .

'A modern democracy,' wrote Norman Mailer in *The Presidential Papers*, 'is a tyranny whose borders are undefined; one discovers how far one can go only by travelling in a straight line until one is stopped.' In the 1970s, the limits of European democracies were tested by armed guerillas: in Italy, Autonomia; in Germany, Baader/Meinhof; at any airport, the PLO; in England, the IRA and the Angry Brigade. Paul Theroux's *The Family Arsenal* depicted urban terrorists drifting anonymously through an apocalyptic London.

Surrounded by the same Situationist rhetoric that had led Detective Inspector Habershon to the Angry Brigade, the Sex Pistols seemed, for a moment, to be urban guerillas themselves: unpredictable, deeply destructive, everywhere. What had initially begun as the fight to get established and to spearhead a new pop generation had quickly become an all-out assault on the music industry, then the media, and now the very figurehead of the English system herself.

The Sex Pistols' considerable, but ill-defined conviction lent moral authority to their attack on the status quo. 'We were most powerful up to six months after getting our product out,' says Jamie Reid, 'because people didn't know about our background. They didn't know which direction we were coming from. In the same week we would be accused, quite seriously, of being National Front, mad communists and anarchists. It's pertinent to English politics: they like to label you really fast, and anything that can't be labelled is a bit dangerous.'

In the remorseless Jubilee hysteria, the phrase 'the fascist regime' didn't seem like the usual posturing of pop politics, but, in view of the reaction to the song, an all too accurate point. 'If this country isn't a fascist regime,' stated Al Clark at the time, 'which it clearly isn't for most people, then one of the first principles of democracy is that the band should be free to sing that line on radio and TV.' They weren't, so what did that make England?

It made you a moron, a potential H-Bomb . . .

In these phrases, you can hear the struggle of postwar youth culture, reacting against those who whose world view was shaped before the event which broke the history of the twentieth century in half: the Hiroshima atom bomb. 'The people who had not yet reached puberty at the time of the Bomb were incapable of conceiving of life *with* a future', writes Jeff Nuttall in *Bomb Culture*. What we call youth or pop culture is often a shorthand term to describe the accelerated perception triggered by this philosophical and spiritual black hole.

By 1977, the Second World War was in some ways still not over. The economic system under which we live – commodity capitalism – is a direct product of the Second World War American economy adapted for 'peacetime'. The fast turnover, instant obsolescence, mass production are expressed not in armaments but in consumer throwaways. As Paul Virilio says, 'It's the absolute identification of production with destruction.'

God save history, God save your mad parade . . .

This pop intensity can also serve as a description of its own means of production: the relentless motion of novelty. There was a distinct sense then in which pop culture was the spearhead, the sugar on the pill, of the economic system to which, in the 1960s, it had appeared to offer some critique and some alternative. Yet when its own economic origin was so tied in with war and destruction, the claims of pop culture to be autonomous seemed distinctly shaky. It was this contradiction, as well as many others, with which the Sex Pistols would struggle until their demise seven months later. 'The Sex Pistols damned Rock'n'Roll as a rotting corpse,' writes Greil Marcus, 'as a monster of moneyed reaction, of false consciousness – and yet, because they had no other weapons and were fans in spite of themselves, the Sex Pistols played Rock and Roll.'

Here was the rub. In the sound of 'God Save the Queen', the Sex Pistols acted out McLaren's original fantasy of bringing the existential intensity of fifties Rock'n'Roll up to date: there was the flash of leather and loud noise; there was the return of the repressed, threatening violence; here was the ultimate statement of pop's everlasting present, just at the moment when the masses were celebrating a past.

> *There is no future, in England's dreaming! No future for you, no future for me, no future for you!*

'Music is prophecy,' writes Jacques Attali in *Noise*: 'its styles and economic organization are ahead of the rest of society because it explores, much faster than material reality can, the entire range of possibilities in a given code. It makes audible the new world that will gradually become visible; it is not only the image of things, but the transcending of the everyday, the herald of the future. For this reason, musicians, even when officially recognized, are dangerous, disturbing and subversive.'

'God Save the Queen' was shocking, not only because it said the present was a lie but also because it prophesied a dreadful future. In a country submerged in nostalgia, this was a serious breach of etiquette. 'No Future' was both a matter-of-fact statement and a terrible warning which had multiple applications, not only for the crumbling postwar consensus, but for the whole idea of youth culture and for the group themselves. With hindsight, the Sex Pistols can be seen as the last gasp of youth culture as a single, unifying force – that sixties ideal which all those concerned with the group both hated and loved. They reasserted the primacy of pop as the divining rod of the times at the very moment when they predicted its loss of power in the 1980s, weakened by power politics, cynicism and demographics. Within one year of Conservative government, the unemployment figures doubled: worst hit were the nineteen to twenty-four age group, the classic 'teenage' consituency.

In the 1960s, youth had been celebrated, not only as a market but also as beatific principle. With its economic *raison d'être* removed, youth became a problem, until it was actively penalized. By the mid

1980s, the late-fifties promise of teenage consumer equality had been reneged upon: it was seen to have referred not to age, but to a style of consumption which was now taken up by an older age group who had been trained to consume teenage products and could still afford to do so.

Nevertheless, as the *Record Mirror* noted, 'simply by stating "No Future" the Sex Pistols are creating one'. There was humanity couched in the multiple contradictions of 'God Save the Queen'. 'Punk was truth couched in deceit,' says Jamie Reid. Deliberately masking their feelings – for fear of being pinned down, and because they were the product of a movement that denied feeling – the Sex Pistols offered optimism disguised as cynicism, and unleashed powerful emotions from behind a blank, sarcastic façade.

You didn't have to understand this to react emotionally to the record. What was extraordinary about John Lydon was the power he wielded for a period of about two years to conjure up the demons of the time. It is a power which he could never analyse. 'I don't think there's any great talent in what I do,' he says, 'I hit the nail on the head sometimes. If anything, that's when instinct takes over: you can't work out those moments.'

'The formal conditions of apperception that are based in instinct,' wrote Jung in 1935, 'give the world of the child and the dreamer its anthropomorphic stamp. These are the archetypes, which direct all fantasy activity into its appointed paths and in this way produce, in the fantasy images of children's dreams as well as in the delusions of schizophrenia, astonishing mythological parallels. It is not therefore a question of inherited ideas but of inherited *possibilities* of ideas.'

'The Sex Pistols seemed to be the heirs to the Diggers and the Ranters,' says Julien Temple. 'Rotten's lyrics had that millennial feel. He hadn't read the texts but he spoke in that language: it was staggering. It wasn't to do with Malcolm, the anger and the energy were totally his. That was the best thing about the Pistols: the English Revolution was a very strange, surreal time when people were excited beyond all expectation. That's what they were tapping into.'

'God Save the Queen' pushed a submerged version of English history to centre stage. Its utopian heresies fell within the boundaries of revolutionary millenarianism defined by Norman Cohn: 'It is characteristic of this kind of movement that its aims and premises are boundless. A social struggle is seen not as a struggle for specific, limited objectives, but as an event of unique importance, different in kind from all other struggles known to history, a cataclysm from which the world is to be totally transformed and redeemed.'

This is the struggle of much twentieth-century vanguard art and pop culture: it would be as wrong to claim that this sensation was exclusive to the Sex Pistols and Punk as it would be to say that it was in the same 'tradition'. Each generation has the power to restate an archetype in a new language. Like Reggae, Punk drew from the millenarian well, but it gave the draught a peculiarly British flavour.

Figures like Lydon had already appeared in the world as demonic harbingers of destruction and disorder, such as Pinkie in *Brighton Rock*; a conflation of Dickens characters like the Artful Dodger, Sim Tappertit, Uriah Heep or the title character from *Barnaby Rudge*; and Abiezer Coppe, the mid-seventeenth-century Ranter, who foretold an apocalyptic collapse of values and delivered utopian heresies with a scourging moral authority. Lydon was not to know this: why should he?

In his studies for the *Titus* trilogy, a specific allegory of the English psyche written throughout the 1950s, Mervyn Peake describes the seventeen-year-old revolutionary Steerpike: 'Limb by limb it appeared that he was sound enough, but the sum of these several members accrued to an unexpectedly twisted total. His face was pale like clay and save for his eyes, mask like. These eyes were set very close together, and were small, dark red, and of startling concentration.'

In the summer of 1977 the nineteen-year-old Polystyrene screamed in a voice pitched so high that it was like talking in tongues: 'I clambered over mounds and mounds/Of polystyrene foam/Then fell into a swimming pool/Filled with fairy snow'. The music continued at the same manic pitch, until the shredding voice reappeared with the final verse: 'The X-Rays were penetrating through the latex breeze/ Synthetic fibre see-through leaves/Fell from the rayon trees/The day the world turned Day-glo . . .'

This 'world turned upside down', a distant echo of the 1646 Ranter-inspired broadside ballad, could not have been written without Punk and Reggae's chaos of symbols, their respective invocations of 'the antichrist' and 'Babylon'. The Sex Pistols' language of revolutionary millenarianism represented the other side of their careless use of the swastika. They embraced the struggle between authoritarianism and freedom which was now to be acted out in the country about which they spoke so passionately.

'The musician, like music, is ambiguous,' writes Attali. 'He plays a double game. He is simultaneously reproducer and prophet. He is an integral part of the sacrifice process, a channeler of violence; simultaneously *excluded* (relegated to a place near the bottom of the social hierarchy) and *superhuman* (the genius, the adored and deified star).'

Like the Ranters and the Situationists, the Sex Pistols were chanting about nothing less than the age-old vision of utopia, that had been written out of history but was now claiming its time.

> I do not blame the Oxford undergraduates. If you are dragged suddenly out of the real world into a mouldy imitation of a past life, what can you do but become a ghost yourself? What is there for you outside but the world of the dole queue and Punk Rock? But the real energy, fire, restlessness of youth comes from that dole queue and is sung by a dionysiac Punk Rocker.
>
> **Stanley Reynolds: *Guardian* (4 June 1977)**

The Sex Pistols were triumphant. 'What we started was right,' said Paul Cook that June, 'and it made the BBC and the Top Thirty look redundant.' Yet the Sex Pistols' moment of greatest success seemed double-edged, a sensation echoed in the interviews they gave in the week or so after the release of 'God Save the Queen', where, as well as the expected chest-thumping, the group expressed a disenchantment with Punk and hinted at their own demise.

By the time of the Jubilee weekend, 'God Save the Queen' had sold over 150,000 copies. Virgin and McLaren sought another publicity angle for publicity, and decided to hold a promotional stunt on the River Thames, as a mocking precursor to the Queen's own river progress through London on the 9th. 'I had to go down to Charing Cross Pier,' says John Varnom, 'the day before the *Mirror* had carried a front-page story about the single, coining the immortal falsehood about calling the Queen a moron. Virgin Records had also been mentioned. The Captain was very anxious. 'It's not one of those punk bands, is it? Aren't the Sex Pistols on Virgin Records?' I ignored the questions and told him that the whole affair was in aid of a German synthesizer band who were heavily influenced by Wagner and Bach. His boat was called the *Queen Elizabeth*, so we had a huge streamer made which proclaimed, "QUEEN ELIZABETH WELCOMES SEX PISTOLS".'

The national press had played down the Sex Pistols' record and its success during the previous week, but on the Sunday, two stories raised the pressure. In the *Jubilee People,* there was a picture of Jamie Reid's 'Queen' T-shirts, with the caption 'Punk Rock's own *nasty* little bit of Jubilee fun'. The *Sunday Mirror* was more explicit: one of Jamie's stickers was reproduced alongside quotes from a 'far from amused' Buckingham Palace and an 'angry spokesman for the Silver Jubilee Appeal': 'Every citizen must be hopping mad.'

At 7.30 on Jubilee night, the Sex Pistols cast off from the pier into a fraught situation. 'It was really tedious,' says Lydon; 'It was like patting yourself on the back, playing to a captive audience who have to pretend they like you. Selfish rubbish is what that was.'

'It was touch and go,' says Jordan, 'John was in a terrible mood. Here was this anarchist group, the Sex Pistols, with people like Richard Branson on the boat that he didn't think should be there. In the end, he was furious: he just got to the limit.'

7.6.77: the Sex Pistols gather themselves onto what passes for the stage (the top deck of the Queen Elizabeth) at about 9.30 p.m. The weather's lousy – moving clouds form undifferentiated volumes of grey overhead – and the whole set-up is decidedly artificial. The boat is full of people staring at each other. The group look fed up and everybody else is paranoid – a state encouraged by the amphetamine sulphate which the sycophants are lining out in the bar.

Banners have been unfurled down the side: one reads 'QUEEN ELIZABETH, THE NEW SINGLE BY THE SEX PISTOLS "GOD SAVE THE QUEEN" ' *– distinctly low profile. The record is already a hit but more important is the whiplash kick that it has given to the Sex Pistols' already careening momentum: the sense of hysteria that has been building for the last seven months is reaching its peak and nobody, least of all those involved, knows what is going happen.*

This Monday is the 25th anniversary of the Queen's accession. For the past month or so the whole country has been inundated with Jubilee hype. This is a testing ground for what will become a media commonplace hereafter: news-led anniversaries, and a volume of royal trivia as relentless as the glare of an interrogation light. The shadows in which punks have run, if not free, then as wild as could be possible are being obliterated. Everything is overexposed: there's nowhere left to move.

It's as though the nation has been taken over by the spirit of Jack Warner – that embodiment of the postwar consensus with his stoicism in the face of austerity and his homilies: 'Mustn't grumble'; 'Have another cup of tea'. This collective forelock-tugging marks an acceptance of England's stasis which the Punks totally reject, but the really scary thing about it is that the resentment which always lurks behind English phlegm is now directed against anybody who is different, who dares to disagree.

Punk throws this difference and the decay that is being denied back in the faces of the public. This is very un-English, particularly now. Suddenly, dressing at all Punk has ceased to be a style option and has become a dangerous game: if you're not randomly assaulted on the street, there is always the fear that you might be turned in by the thought police. Indeed in its present patriotic decay, England already seems to have passed into that mythic future so furiously fetishized in Punk songs: 1984.

Although we're all outcasts or have, at least, temporarily cast ourselves out of England's current state of grace, the Queen Elizabeth *is hardly brimming with solidarity. Any group identity formed by the Sex Pistols and their followers in the 100 Club days last summer has long disappeared: torn apart by the volume of publicity they have received and by the group's inevitable withdrawal into Rock stardom.*

At this point too, the violence that has always been a part of Punk since the beginning is turning inwards. Much of this violence seemed more theatrical than real, but as the internal and external pressures increase, there's a collective bad temper that could explode at any time. Last night at Country Cousins Judy Nylon stubbed out a cigarette on Bryan James's teeth in some unnamed revenge: this in the middle of a party for the Ramones and Talking Heads, Americans bemused by the maelstrom swirling around them.

In the current overlit landscape, Punk's thorough immersion in the apocalypse has as much to do with its own situation as any external reality. Things have happened so fast that total exhaustion beckons. The extraordinary parabola that the Sex Pistols have described in England's stagnant air has reached the zenith of its curve and everybody senses it in the pit of their stomach. Mixed with the physical sense of alienation experienced by most on board, the result is a claustrophobia so tight that you can barely speak.

And yet simply being on this boat is an act of faith in itself – a decisive, foolhardy act, like putting your head above the parapet. So the question remains: why we have pinned our faith on one young, ill-tempered pop group? Because they're the ones who've put themselves on the line, articulating, with as much courage and wit as they can muster, what many of us feel yet have hardly managed put into words. Their reward is to live every aspect of their life in a no-man's-land, lit by the flares of prejudice.

The four Sex Pistols bunch up against the Jubilee bunting like fugitives up a blind alley. By this time we've been up and down the Thames: down to Beckton, up to Chelsea Bridge and back down to Westminster. They stab at their equipment, to be rewarded with a hail of feedback. Cook and Jones are trying to get things started; Sid looks distinctly out of focus. None of them are exactly ecstatic but Rotten is murderous: what a shitty situation. More feedback squalls. And then, as the Houses of Parliament heave into view, the four finally find the key: as they launch into 'Anarchy in the UK', all present lock into the HERE and NOW.

stols on the *Queen Elizabeth*, 7 June 1977 (© Dennis Morris)

The Sex Pistols play for their lives. Rotten pours his all resentments, his frustration, his claustrophobia into a cauldron of rage that turns this petty piece of theatre into something massive. From our vantage point a few feet away, the world is reduced to a pair of glassy eyes and a snarling mouth, framed by red spikes. The audience is so close that the group are playing as much to fight them off, yet at the same time there is a strong bond: we feel what they feel. We're just as cornered.

The vortex that the group has set in motion begins to spin faster and faster. Rotten baulks at the start of 'No Feelings' but is drawn in despite himself; during this song and the next, 'Pretty Vacant', the group fuses with the audience. As Rotten vomits up 'and we don't caaaare!' in what can only be described as a secular exorcism, two police launches begin circling the Queen Elizabeth, *like demons invoked by our collective, extreme negation. During 'I Wanna Be Me', Lydon shrieks the bridging 'Now!' as if total concentration on the moment can banish ALL THIS, for ever and ever and we can crash through to the other side.*

Things spin out of control; the motion of the vortex sucks everything in to a smaller, smaller space. As the police launches circle ever closer, the Sex Pistols tear into 'No Fun' to stave off the inevitable. Suddenly everything explodes: there is a scuffle; in the gap that instantaneously opens up, Roger Austin's face contorts in anger and pain. As the police launches move in for the kill, the Queen Elizabeth *slides inexorably towards the massed policemen on the landing stage and Lydon intones 'No Fun' in impossibly flat tones, in a numb mantra: 'NO FUN I'M ALONE! NO FUN I'M ALIVE! I'M ALONE! I'M ALIVE!'*

So here we are in the here and now, ten o'clock on the Thirteenth of June, in the Year Of Our Lord 1977. It's like that moment in 'The Day Of The Triffids' when the sailor and girl are walking hand in hand through the deserted streets of London, alone with their sight in a world of the blind. Because England's dreaming – and for all our fragility – it seems as though we're the only ones left awake.

By the time the boat docked, the situation was chaotic. The captain had switched off the power: John Lydon continued screaming 'No Fun', while Paul Cook kept up the rhythm pattern. None of the audience made any move to leave, but the captain was adamant and so were the police. For about half an hour, there was a stand-off as the tension mounted; night fell on the boat and the serried ranks of police. Some people began trickling off but a hard core of fans, friends and the curious remained. The police began to manhandle members of the audience down the gangplank, as insults and inanimate objects were thrown at them. They lost patience and a struggle developed between the police and those trying to reach the Embankment.

The four Sex Pistols were highly visible targets and had already been in enough trouble with the law: 'They would have really got it,' says Debbie Wilson. It was important to Glitterbest to get the group out of the way. There was an almost unnoticed stairwell on the right-hand side, and, while everybody else was making a lot of noise, Tiberi and Sophie got the group and the equipment off the site.

Both sides overreacted. As people were pushed up the stairs, some, like Vivienne Westwood, on the point of being trampled, resisted the police pressure and were arrested. When Cherry Vanilla's piano player, Zecca, went to help her, he was arrested too. 'I stuck very close to Malcolm,' says John Varnom, 'we reached a high point, from which short steps descended to the pavement. It was at precisely this point that Malcolm raised his fist and, in full view of about five or six police, screamed: "You fucking fascist bastards!" It was a direct invitation, and it was not declined.'

Luciana Martinez, Jimmy Lydon, Kenny Morris, John Varnom (with beard), Malcolm McLaren, Al McDowell: on Charing Cross Pier, 7 June 1977. The author is bottom right (© David Wainwright)

'It was really vicious in the police van,' says Jamie Reid. 'Near my feet Debbie and Tracy were on the floor being sadistically kicked by these burly policemen who obviously got a perverted pleasure out of it. Very macho. Especially with Debbie who's so vulnerable but childishly provocative. I remember thinking they must both be made out of rubber to put up with it but the drink helped. We all got pretty knocked about without feeling it a lot.'

7.6.77: We go to Bow Street Police Station. No message. No bail. No press. No, not an IPC card. 'There are people who we'd like to arrest but we don't know who they are.' A direct hint. Buzz off. And don't wait on the pavement. No help. And then the seven of us REALLY slip into 1984: we move to this pub where everybody is enacting this weird ritual which involves wearing of red/white/blue hats and 'singing' arcane folk lore.

The next day, only one of the nationals, the *Mirror*, picked up the story and it ran it small. When the eleven arrested – who included all of Glitterbest except Tiberi – were bailed on various charges including assault and using insulting words, the London evening papers reported the fact without any mention of the previous night's events. Glitterbest wondered whether they would have got more press coverage if the band had been arrested, but, on the night, humanity had prevailed.

Yet there were other, delayed reactions. 'I thought there was doom coming after the boat trip,' says Jordan. 'You got this feeling that it had snowballed too quickly. John was being really obnoxious to everybody. I don't think he could quite handle it. Nobody believes how difficult it is to carry on something like that. Anyone can sing, but to sing with conviction those powerful words every night, words that were black and white, not clouds and rolling hills. I think he'd lost that need to do it.'

By the end of Jubilee week, 'God Save the Queen' had sold 200,000 copies. The *Daily Mirror* had predicted that the single would be number one in Jubilee week despite all the efforts to stop it. There then ensued one of the murkier episodes in the history of the Sex Pistols. 'It seemed clear that the music business was disapproving,' says John Varnom, 'in all probability, the BMRB, the British Market Research Bureau, juggled the national chart positions so that "God Save The Queen" did not make number one. It was pipped by a Rod Stewart single. But Virgin's sales out of stock exceeded the sales figures on the

Rod Stewart single. Richard even contacted the BPI directly over the discrepancy. He was very keen for a number one. The industry quite definitely was not. It wanted to bury the Sex Pistols.'

'Rod Stewart was distributed by CBS, like us,' says McLaren, 'CBS were saying that we were selling two records to every one of Rod Stewart's so we were far and away the biggest winner.' Today, the *Guinness Hit Singles* shows Rod Stewart's 'I Don't Want To Talk About It' at number one for that week, but it was on a dying fall – its last week at number one. The man responsible for the charts was then the head of the British Phonographic Institute, John Fruin. Also Managing Director of WEA Records, he lost his job in 1981 after irregularities were uncovered about the chart placings of several WEA acts.

'Branson's suspicion that the chart had been fixed was lent weight by an anonymous phone call,' writes Mick Brown, Branson's official biographer, 'alleging that, in the week that the Sex Pistols might have been expected to reach number one, the BPI had issued an extraordinary secret directive to the BMRB, that all chart-return shops connected with record companies be dropped from the weekly census of best-selling records. Virgin, the store where most Sex Pistols records were being sold, was struck off the list. A week later, the decision was reversed.'

After the Jubilee holiday was over, the nationals resumed their coverage of Punk, writing about Punk in general terms, as a movement 'sweeping teenage Britain', and pointing to the Sex Pistols as ringleaders of a 'sick', 'sinister' conspiracy against the English way of life. The punitive stage of this overrunning scandal was about to begin: as Labour MP Marcus Lipton stated in the *Daily Mirror*, 'If Pop music is going to be used to destroy our established institutions, then it ought to be destroyed first.'

'PUNISH THE PUNKS', ran the headline in the *Sunday Mirror*, and the British public took the instruction to heart. The attacks were now not just verbal but also physical. The first to be victimized was Jamie Reid, the next day: he was attacked just around the corner from his Borough flat and his leg and nose were broken by unknown assailants. The next Sunday (of the second *People* story) it was the turn of Public Enemy Number One, John Lydon.

'Chris Thomas and I were in the Pegasus, just around the corner from Wessex Studios,' he says, 'and as we left, we were attacked in the car park by a gang of knife-wielding yobs, who were chanting, "We love our Queen, you bastard!" Normally I'd say they were National

Front, but a third of them were black. They were just lads out for violence. I got some bad cuts from that. It severed two tendons, so my left hand is fucked forever, and as I'm left-handed, I can't close the fist properly. I'll never play guitar: there's no power to it. I jumped into the car and someone jumped after me with a machete and cut me from there [he points to his thigh about a foot down] . . . to there [his knee]. I had on extremely thick leather trousers at the time, thank fucking God, because it would have ripped the muscle out and now I'd be a one-legged hoppity.'

The two incidents made the morning editions on the 21st: they were put down to the feud between Teddy Boys and Punks. By the afternoon, the evening papers were reporting a third attack, on Paul Cook. 'It was along the Goldhawk Road,' he says, 'I had Teddy-Boy shoes on. These young Teds came up: "Oi, what you got those shoes on for, Punk?" "I like them, why?" Then they followed us: I got a bit of a hiding, hit with some metal. We were marked, everyone knew our faces. It was a nasty period.'

Here was the ultimate application of the violence which had hung like a miasma about the group, from the very first incident in the Nashville. For the previous fourteen months, the Sex Pistols and their management had initiated and cultivated a violence which, within the confines of the music industry, had been unpleasant but effective. Now it had been let loose in the world outside and it rebounded on the Sex Pistols, particularly on John Lydon, who suffered another attack three days later.

McLaren, who had abdicated day-to-day control of the group to Sophie and Tiberi, tried in vain to deal with a situation which he failed to understand. 'There was great pressure in the band,' he says, 'they were staying first in the Portobello Hotel, but had got thrown out. They ended up at the Chelsea Cloisters, whereby they were getting increasingly paranoid, particularly Rotten, who was by now blasted out on speed, living with Wobble, Grey, Nancy and Sid all together.'

Under the stress of being national scapegoats, relations between Lydon and McLaren went into a nosedive from which they never recovered. McLaren was unable and unwilling to give the group the emotional commitment – even nursemaiding – that they now more than ever required. 'He's hopeless at dealing with people,' Lydon says, 'He couldn't care less about you. "Hello? I'm having a nervous breakdown." "Go away, I'm busy scandalizing you in the press!" '

'He broke them,' says Wobble. 'I suppose he did the business for them, but John felt bitter 'cos he found it hard to get dough out of him: it was always money. During the Jubilee we went up the West End and this whole coachload of geezers saw us, and it got very nasty. It was lynching time. John and me and John Grey ended up in some restaurant, barricaded in. John felt that with Malcolm setting up all this publicity, he wasn't on the fucking streets, he was in limos and taxis, and John's on the streets.

'I'd go round to Chelsea Cloisters and he'd be saying, "This isn't my scene," but he wouldn't come out. I can understand that paranoia a bit more now. He was very young to be on the cover of all those magazines. Normally when you get these young parcels crack big in the music game, they've generally got a big machine around them, protecting them. He didn't have that, he had to fend for himself. It damaged him but he's got to work these things out for himself.'

Amphetamine abuse exacerbated the problems. On 27 June, Sophie Richmond had a midnight call from Sid Vicious saying that they should all get out of the country because things were so bad. The next morning, she got a similar telephoned blast of misery from John Lydon. This time, McLaren acted quickly: a tour of Scandinavia was arranged straightaway. Sophie arranged accommodation for Sid, Nancy and John Lydon.

But the damage had been done: this was the moment when the Sex Pistols split in real time. According to Sophie Richmond, 'The rest of the week dissolved into flaming rows of who was doing precisely what to whom and why. By the end of the week everyone was emotionally drained. The band were at a point where they had to decide whether to patch it up and keep going or split and then what? I think that "Then what?" pushed them back, but the impetus seemed lost.'

John Lydon, in the air above Sweden, July 1977 (© John Tiberi)

26

Here as elsewhere in twentieth-century cultural history, images of autonomy obscured its eclipse.

Richard Wightman Fox and T.J. Jackson Lears: introduction, *The Culture of Consumption* (1983)

REVOLT is understandably unpopular. As soon as it is defined it has provoked the measures for its containment. The prudent man will avoid the definition which in effect is his death sentence.

Alex Trocchi: 'Invisible Insurrection of a Million Minds' (1966)

During that third week of June, the Sex Pistols finally reached the edge of the abyss that they had always been seeking, and backed away from its terrors. In hiding, torn by rows, they were in no position to capitalize on the considerable but nebulous social power that they had. Here at last their rhetoric came up against realpolitik: they were, after all, not armed revolutionaries, but just a young pop group, vulnerable as scapegoats to street violence.

'I've never known so much national hatred focused on a pop group,' says Al Clark, who was dealing with Fleet Street at the time. 'For a few weeks the band seemed to me to be sitting targets for anybody with a grievance. They had conveyed the image of being indestructible, hard, and they became targets for the same sort of people who walked up to Robert Mitchum in bars in the 1950s and wanted to try it on. They were treated as though they had no feelings.'

The Sex Pistols' subsequent career was a long, slow retreat from the climax of that Jubilee fortnight, although they would always carry a trace of the power they had had at that time. For Lydon, that fortnight meant claustrophobia and stark terror: for Glitterbest, it meant vindication. Just as Lydon, until his departure, would be continuously facing into the abyss, Glitterbest would spend their time, until their final dissolution, justifying and refining the politics which had gained them their triumph.

' "God Save The Queen" was the band's peak,' says Jamie Reid. 'Just afterwards things started coming apart. I said to Malcolm, "Wouldn't it be great to just disappear? Just be a hit and run".' This would have been possible for the members of Glitterbest, who all had other skills, but the group had nothing except their notoriety and now their chart success. 'God Save the Queen' had, if nothing else, made the Sex Pistols a pop group.

This retreat was inevitable, but that inevitability made it no less shattering for all those in the Sex Pistols and those who had been touched by them. For a brief while, their unprecedented success had unified a fragmented Punk movement, but, when that moment disappeared, disillusion set in. As the attacks from outside increased, Punk began to split from within, as those whom Punk had united rediscovered their mutual antagonism.

The same sense of disillusion was to be found in the society with which Punk was now so closely intertwined. Jubilee hype had raised expectations to an unrealistic level, but the week itself was something of an anti-climax. For those thousands who had believed in the mystical power of the monarchy, or just in a good piss-up, the hangover set in with a vengeance. The political and social tensions which the Jubilee had held in check also returned, with greater intensity.

'A solitary laser beam hung flickerless over London like a single wire of an imprisoning flesh,' wrote Jan Morris in her travelogue of London that summer. 'Didn't they feel it too, I asked my friends? Didn't they sense, in the condition of their city that night, some symptom of disintegration? It was like someone who had sufferred a breakdown, I said, whose personality is split, splintered or possibly in abeyance. London is in flux more than usual now, and out of the uncertainty, ugly things are sprouting.'

In the weeks immediately after the Jubilee, the newspapers were full of stories about the mass-picketing of Grunwick Film Processing Laboratories. A dispute about union recognition had been exacerbated by the National Association For Freedom, intent on polarizing public feeling about union power. On 11 June 11,000 pickets battled with 4,000 police. In the ensuing press coverage, NAFF won the propaganda battle: the front-page pictures of a young policeman lying in a pool of blood on 23 June was another image to add to England's nightmare.

There was no better metaphor for the times than Punk, as the mass media began to take up on the Punk discourse which it had already so influenced. In the last week of June, the *Daily Mirror* ran an editorial with the headline 'Punk Future'. Referring to that month's dole figures, it stated, 'Punk rock is tailor-made for youngsters who feel they only have a punk future. Is it any wonder they turn to anarchistic heroes like Johnny Rotten? A brave new generation of talent and purpose is turning sour before our eyes.'

Just as Johnny Rotten was flashing across the mass media as a subversive phantasm, hundreds of Punks began to act out England's nervous breakdown on inner-urban streets. Summer is always a good time for youth visibility, but the Punks that began to throng the King's Road strip were different from the previous Mods or Skinheads, neither obsessed with clothes nor with violence, but preferring to act out, in Sophie Richmond's phrase, 'lives of noisy desperation'.

The very English phlegm which had served as a powerful physiological metaphor for denial and needless stoicism was now, literally, expelled in torrents as, inspired by the Damned, Punk audiences covered their objects of desire with sheets of saliva. McLaren had moulded his children to his own 'harsh orality', in Vermorel's phrase. Although it was a gesture of contact rather than abuse, Punk musicians were at best inconvenienced, at worst infected, by this bodily waste.

Like termites, the punks emerged out of the Sloane Square station Underground. The London tube was a key location in Punk songs, being both a cheap mode of transport and a metaphor for Punk's drive to the subconscious. 'Down, down to the underground,' shouted Lydon in 'I Wanna Be Me', or, as Poly Styrene screamed so gleefully: 'Let's submerge!' Hidden, yet omnipresent in London's centre, the tube's rapid, occluded transits were perfect for those who wished to burrow beneath the culture.

Blinking in the Sloane Square sunlight, the Punks wore what was for insiders a degraded uniform. Everything was artificial and deliberately askew, from the dyed hair rubbed with KY or Vaseline, to the ripped and torn jackets. The leather jacket on the outside symbolized protection and aggression, whilst the T-shirts underneath were graffitied, like walls, with whatever came to mind. On the legs were the bondage trousers of claustrophobia and babyish incapacity.

With their syphilitic, archaic language – 'vile', 'poxy', 'bollocks' – and this costume which theatricalized poverty, the Punks were the Postmodern children of Dickens. Inspired by amphetamines and the style which amphetamines had suggested, their gestures were jerky, violent and unpredictable, their demeanour was loutish and loud, and their faces as white as zombies'. Dramatizing catatonia, the Punks showed up the rest of the public: they were not narcotized by England's dreaming, and they flaunted the fact.

Punk's visibility and hints of violence added to its effectiveness as a scapegoat. The instruments of the backlash were the Teddy Boys whose revival had, by this summer, resulted in their virtual takeover of boroughs like Hammersmith. They had already been associated with the attacks on Cook and Lydon, and now they decided to mass-market the process. One of their first targets was the shop that had reneged on their fashions.

'When the Teddy-Boy season started,' says Debbie Wilson, 'it was horrific. They smashed in the windows at least four or five times. We really were hated up there: we used to hide in the cupboards. Vivienne got off on the violence because people were rebelling against something they didn't want. Her attitude was, "Don't be scared, stand up for yourself", and we'd say, "Viv, there's a six-foot-two girl out there waiting to beat the shit out of me." Vivienne would say, "Now don't you worry." Viv's political views were really hard to cope with because they were not real.'

From the early summer, the King's Road had been the scene of skirmishes between Punks and Teds which became pitched battles as the publicity started to mount. Punks had originally combined the costumes of Mods and Rockers and had then put the history of the battles of 1964 into their manifestos: the Punk/Ted battles were quickly slotted into this self-conscious discourse, epitomized by a *Daily Mirror* cover of 2 August, which predicted 'WAR ON THE SEAFRONT' for the coming bank holiday.

'This huge Ted came up to me in the King's Road,' says Marco Pirroni. 'He was handing out leaflets for the big fight down at Margate. He said: "There's a fight down on the beach, Punks versus Teds, come down, it'll be good." He talked to us for ten minutes, and we were going, "How can you be really friendly to us now, but want to kick the shit out of us down there?" He couldn't really justify it, but we ended up having tea with him.'

Punk meant violence: that was the equation. When the Vortex, the 'new Roxy', finally opened in July, it was marked by the amphetamine aggression typical of that summer. 'At the Roxy, people didn't have to look like a Punk,' says T.V. Smith. 'They could do what they wanted. After the Vortex opened, there was this feeling that you should like this and you shouldn't like that. It was very unpleasant. It's difficult to explain: things degenerate. This was a fast-moving movement, and it went through its cycle very fast.'

The same month *Harpers and Queen* published its long piece about Punk, the first in the mainstream media to show any insight. 'It will be photographed and reported around the world,' wrote Peter York, 'no matter that it drew on American antecedents, the British style, British clothes, British music, are light-years ahead.' Within a week, *Time* ran a cover story captioned on the cover, 'Punk's primal scream'. It announced the worldwide spread of this disturbing new mutation.

A hand spins a blue globe blotched with a black cancer, written on the carefully deleted countries are sinister messages.

NEGATIVE WORLD STATUS
NO REASON FOR EXISTENCE
OBSOLETE

A hand turns the pages of a book with scrubbed-out images of sexual bondage which resemble the stockinged and balaclavaed features of bank robbers and terrorists.

Derek Jarman: 'The World's End', scene 4 of *Jubilee* (1977)

Jordan as Amyl Nitrate: promo picture for *Jubilee* (© Jean-Marc Prouveur)

While McLaren was in Hollywood attempting to start the Sex Pistols' film, an independent British director went ahead and shot a feature. 'The genesis of *Jubilee* was a Super-8 film with Jordan,' says Derek Jarman. 'It was to do with whatever she wanted to make, but it grew during the course of 1977. I had started collecting fanzines and that excited me, and it got amalgamated with writing the script. Jordan brought Adam [Ant] along. I'd seen him on the street, with FUCK written on his back in what I thought was eyeliner, but Jordan told me he'd had it carved in with a razor-blade.'

'The Sex Pistols had taken a run at this wall and smashed a big crack in it,' says Adam. 'It was just a case of going through.' After various vicissitudes, including a suicide attempt, Adam formed a group, named, in the punning style of the time, the Ants. 'I just entered into the craziness. It was scary: I used to wear rapist hoods, and just attack the audience. That was just the way it was. The audiences then, there was an element of danger, but there was excitement: it was like parachuting for the first time.'

When Jarman put them on the stage of the New Victoria theatre, Adam and the Ants were only two months old. With Adam in full bondage regalia, they played 'Deutscher Girls' and 'Plastic Surgery': sludgy songs, but great performances, sick and twisted. 'They were hectic,' he says, 'it was a hectic time. I dislocated my knee during that performance. There were a lot of people standing round, very scared of the group. It was pandemonium.'

Jarman's outsider status led to some minor infelicities, like the scene when the script requires Ian Charleson to break into social realist clichés: Adam Ant burst into unscripted giggles which Jarman kept in the finished film. But with its persistent air of disillusion and warning, *Jubilee* captured the mood of Punk England better than anyone could have predicted, not the least in its locations: it remains one of the few places where you can see the 1977 London landscape.

The plot revolves around the Candide-like figure of Adam, a young musician (just as in 'real life') entering the media industries, with the sharply expressed, but not always sincere, distaste of the time. The violence of the music is set against the cynicism of most of those involved with those industries, and against a landscape reminiscent of J.G. Ballard. Adam is a victim, but Jordan, in twinset and pearls, crosses with her Punks to the side of the oppressors.

'*Jubilee* set out to be prophetic,' says Jarman. 'I thought Punk was an understandable and a very correct disgust with everything, but it wasn't focussed. Youth seemed to get it right, but, in its funny way, it did end in repression with Margaret Thatcher's England. *Jubilee* told that parable and at the time, it was fantasy, based on complete supposition, but in time it came true. Everyone had signed up, including Adam, who became an old-fashioned pop star.'

With 'God Save the Queen' still in the Top Ten, the Sex Pistols rush-released another single. There were several factors: the Sex Pistols had finally signed to Virgin for Europe on 8 June, for £75,000 without publishing, and new product was necessary for the imminent Scandinavian tour. McLaren also wanted to keep up the Sex Pistols' momentum, and to deflect the group's attention from his extended absence while he was negotiating the film.

The group had written a new song during the Berlin trip, 'Holidays in the Sun', but it wasn't ready. McLaren and Reid decided to go with 'Pretty Vacant': it was catchy, already very popular with the fans and lyrically uncontroversial. It could not on the face of it be banned. 'We wanted to test whether they would play any record,' McLaren says, 'I had to prove to myself that it was the group that was successful.'

'Pistols keep it clean,' ran one headline, and this time, the Sex

Pistols had no trouble: Virgin went so far as to play an acetate of 'Pretty Vacant' to buyers at the multiple chains, who gave it a clean bill of health, as did the IBA and the BBC. Virgin planned a similar campaign of flyposting and radio adverts like those prepared for 'God Save the Queen', and this time, they were broadcast on commercial radio.

'Pretty Vacant' was one of the Sex Pistols' earliest songs and the most obviously anthemic, with its simple, but dramatic, repeated-chord opening and its inclusive chorus line: '*We're* so pretty, oh so pretty, vay-cunt!' There is a hint of overproduction in the final release – Chris Thomas leaves no holes in the sound and Lydon's voice is becoming mannered – but the song's swaggering, sardonic swing gave an illusion of release and power.

Unused artwork for *Pretty Vacant*, July 1977 (© Jamie Reid)

Despite the haste with which it was planned, 'Pretty Vacant' was a charged, complicated package, from the Situ picture sleeve through to the searing, ridiculous version of 'No Fun' on the B-side. The song still resonated: a good description of the group's status (vacant, or a blank slate), a rallying call for new Punk converts, a nice put-on (we're not as stupid as you think we are) and a great chorus ('vay-cunt') with which to annoy parents.

The day after the single was released, McLaren flew out to Los Angeles. He had two items on his agenda: an American record deal for the Sex Pistols and a firm deal for the film. By now the former was subordinate to the latter: it had been one of the considerations in releasing 'Vacant' that its sure success would increase record-company interest and thus raise money for the film. McLaren wanted serious money from the heart of the media's integrated circuit.

The film was in the usual McLaren-inspired state: great idea, great hustle, where's the product? In early June, McLaren had formed a separate company to deal with his film interests, called Matrixbest. In the middle of that month, the film was reported as going ahead, to begin shooting in August, for screening at Christmas, with Johnny Speight as scriptwriter and Russ Meyer as director. A pair of independent producers, Michael and John Goldstone, were brought in.

After Speight dropped out at the last minute, McLaren knocked out a treatment with John Varnom and it was with this barely coherent document that he went to Hollywood. Meyer's interest had been roused by a screening in April of *Sex Pistols Number 1*: 'He seemed very interested but was tied up in shooting,' says McLaren. 'When I told him the budget would be £150,000, he exploded and said "That ain't much". I told him pictures didn't cost a lot to make in England. Little did I know.'

Meyer was an odd choice for McLaren: a choice based, not on serious thoughts about compatibility, but on gut reaction and fantasy. McLaren liked the *idea* of Meyer: he was not liberal, being what McLaren later described as a 'redneck war veteran'; at fifty-five he was significantly older, and his stock-in-trade was frankly exploitative, if humorous, soft-porn movies of a similar sexuality to the *Carnival* magazines McLaren had sold in Let It Rock.

Meyer's principal claim to fame then was *Beyond the Valley of the Dolls*. According to scriptwriter Roger Ebert, Meyer had conceived the film as 'a satire, a serious melodrama, a Rock musical, a comedy, a violent exploitation picture, a skin-flick, and a moralistic exposé of "the oft-times nightmarish world of Show Business".' The estate of novelist Jacqueline Susann, upon whose novel the film was loosely based, sued on the film's release.

McLaren's initial meeting with Meyer was not favourable: Meyer hated the treatment. A script written by McLaren and a screenwriter called Rene Daalder came to nothing. Before he signed, on 13 July, to direct the Sex Pistols' picture for £30,000, Meyer insisted on his own scriptwriter. 'McLaren in person turned out to be pleasant,' wrote Roger Ebert at the time, 'and very sure of what he wanted: "The movie should end with the Sex Pistols inspiring an anarchist revolution that sweeps England".' Ebert was not a soulmate, but he was a professional: within a week, he had completed the script.

McLaren had worked fast and well: by the time he left Los Angeles on 29 July, he had locked much of the film into place. During the time that he had been away, however, the Sex Pistols had been going through their acelerated changes. It was a crucial time for the group, and during that month, the balance of power between Glitterbest, Virgin and the group had shifted considerably. Lydon and Cook were still recovering from the shattering events of June. Glitterbest were understaffed, with Reid out of action with a broken leg, and Sophie working flat out.

In this state, the Sex Pistols were more vulnerable to the suggestions of their new record company. The most independent member of the group was John Lydon, and it was on him that Virgin began to work. A row was building up over the promotional film that had been filmed on 5 July. 'Pretty Vacant' was shooting up the charts and the film was the principal promotional tool that Virgin had. It was the first test of power.

'Malcolm was away and we wanted to get them on *Top of the Pops*,' says John Varnom, 'we took Rotten out to a Greek restaurant and put this thing up of "It's going to be right next to Cilla Black and Des O'Connor: it's going to be fantastic". So he said: "I never thought of that, right, OK", which was fine. I was doing Virgin's press and radio promotion and arguing their case: it had to be argued.' Lydon also agreed to do an interview with Capital Radio.

On the day that the group were flying to Scandinavia, the row came to a head. From Hollywood, McLaren called Lydon with the furious instruction that the film should *not* be shown. Phone calls to Virgin ensued, but McLaren was powerless: Branson claimed that he couldn't get the film back from the BBC. He was hardly likely to take

McLaren's side: Glitterbest had connived with the mass-importation of 'Anarchy in the UK' by Barclay, in direct competition with Virgin.

When it went on the air the next day, the clip showed the Sex Pistols as much more of a Rock'n'Roll band than they had ever been. 'Malcolm had visibly lost interest in the style of the band,' says Adam Ant, 'he'd realized it was all over.' Shot close-up in a studio with dazzling lights – just like the staging of *Top of the Pops* itself – Lydon sported sunglasses, a new yellow thatch, and a Johnny Thunders sneer. Completing the image, Steve Jones was wearing the old working-class symbol of a handkerchief knotted on his head.

'The "Pretty Vacant" video is fantastic,' says John Varnom. 'It's such a funny song anyway, and delightfully subversive. If you're politically subversive you can be dismissed by people of another political colour, but if you're subversive in a way that affects the whole of the value system, it's difficult for people to pin you down. It was a very, very strong statement on *Top of the Pops*, but it did dissipate after that.'

Glitterbest were even more furious when Capital Radio's Tommy Vance show was broadcast on the 16th. Lydon had obviously had enough of McLaren's public control and now made his own power move: 'It's fashionable to believe that Malcolm McLaren dictates to us but that's just not true. What really amuses me about Malcolm is the way they say he controls the press: media manipulator. The point of it all is that he did nothing: he just sat back and let them garble out their own rubbish.'

Even worse for Glitterbest was the way in which 'Johnny Rotten' came across: according to the *Sunday Times*, 'a mild-mannered liberal chap with a streets of Islington accent'. Lydon had had enough of being dehumanized: just as earlier he had irritated McLaren by turning up to a photo session dressed as a Teddy Boy, he now chose records for the show by Neil Young, Peter Hamill, Doctor Alimentado and Captain Beefheart – McLaren still splutters about this one. 'I like *all* sorts of music,' Lydon said disarmingly.

The interview – reported verbatim in the music press – enabled a wider audience to relate to Lydon and put him within some sort of recognizable Rock context. This was exactly what Glitterbest wanted least: McLaren had a Year-Zero approach to pop culture which, as the script he was working on displayed, was hardening. For him and for Reid, this was a 'shit' interview, because it established Lydon as a 'man of taste', and thus 'lost his and the band's threat'.

The two weeks of Scandinavian dates, by contrast to almost everything else in the group's lives over the past few months, offered a breathing space. Away from the rows and the attacks, the Sex Pistols relaxed into doing what they were supposed to do: 'they wanted to be a pop group,' says Tiberi. The thirteen dates in three countries went off with an amount of fuss that was, for the Sex Pistols, minimal.

To suit their new status the group went not only with an expanded entourage including John Tiberi, Roadent and photographer Dennis Morris but also several journalists, as McLaren's fiat – 'We don't like giving interviews about ourselves' – was countermanded by Al Clark. 'The record company insisted that all the papers came over,' says Roadent, 'and John insisted that if they came over there they had to pay for themselves, not to let the record company pay. Consequently they had weeks of double-page spreads: having had to pay for themselves, they wanted to get their money's worth.'

During this tour, the Sex Pistols found themselves functioning as a Rock'n'Roll band and they thrived on it. Sid was happy to be on the

John Lydon, Paul Cook, Sid Vicious in Sweden, 2 July 1977 (© John Tiberi)

road and playing live for the first time: he was not using heroin. Throughout the trip, they were bona-fide pop stars: getting constant press, and attracting hordes of fans wherever they were. 'In terms of playing, the group took full advantage of it,' says Tiberi, 'they were really good. It had been a long time . . . It was a simple tour, but all the gigs were strange. We flew right up North for a bizarre gig in a saloon, not a nightclub. There were places where there was no stage, like those photographs Dennis Morris took, with some punk going mad and John six inches away from his face with a microphone. It was totally different from the 100 Club. At that point they hadn't played anything bigger than a 400-seater cinema. We filmed a Swedish gig and it was the biggest they had done, in a college.

'There was this fanatical Teddy-Boy element in Stockholm, the Raggare, who were a problem. They broke up the gig, outside, and the police put the group in a van, blue lights flashing, drove through town to the hotel, then they went away. The hotel had to barricade the doors, as these guys were coming through the gardens, bashing at plate-glass doors. We couldn't go out, but Steve had to, to find some girls. It was like the Beatles in *Help!*'

> Here we all are in the latest craze
> Stick with the crowd, hope it's not a passing phase
> It's the latest thing to be nowhere
> You can turn into the wallpaper
> But you know you were always there anyway
> Without the new wave
> What about the new wave?
> Did you think it would change things?
>
> **The Adverts: 'Safety in Numbers' (August 1977)**

By August, Punk, or its commercially defined variant, New Wave, had become big business. That month, the Roxy album went into the Top Thirty, as did *My Aim is True*, the first album by Elvis Costello; Phonogram released a compilation called *New Wave* with a cover showing a black-clad Punk spitting Colt 45 at the camera; featured on the album was a track by the Irish R&B group the Boomtown Rats, 'Looking After Number One' which, when released as a single, just failed to make the Top Ten.

The signings were reaching their peak as companies invested in out-of-town groups – Manchester's Buzzcocks signed to UA and Slaughter and the Dogs to Decca, Edinburgh's Jolt to Polydor, Surrey's New Hearts and Bristol's Cortinas to CBS, Swindon's XTC to Virgin. Punk/New Wave had become a stereotype – a fast, Ramones-style strait-jacket, played by four men between twenty and thirty, usually wearing some leather, a ripped shirt, a school tie, and a blank/angry expression.

Within the lapse that occurs between media time and real time, many groups were having hits just at the moment when Punk was over. Indeed, success in conventional pop terms became a lifeline out of waters that were becoming increasingly choppy. Punk's superheated, sickly motion was acted out by the Saints, last November's critical raves, who arrived from Australia into an English music scene that had changed immeasurably within seven months.

'By the time we got here the initial spirit had already died out,' says guitarist Ed Kuepper, 'it was very contrived. There were too many people following slavishly after. We had problems because we didn't look New Wave.' Despite strong performances, the Saints were rejected on stylistic grounds: they had long hair, the singer was slobby, they played *oldies*. In turn, the Saints were unimpressed: 'Not everybody wants to look the same,' they sneered on 'Private Affair'; 'Not everybody wants to think the same.'

In July, EMI released the Saints' third single, 'This Perfect Day', a song which speeded up the Rolling Stones' 'Paint it Black' riff into pure extinction. 'This Perfect Day' is almost too fast: the group nearly come off the rails before singer Chris Bailey brings everything to a grinding halt in an extraordinary cluster of negatives – 'Don't need/No one/To tell me/What I don't/Already know!/I need nothing/Don't want no one/I don't need nothing/nothing at all!'

EMI marketed this uncompromising slab of Hard Rock with a gimmick, as a 'limited edition' 12"-pressing with an extra track added by error, which 'has been consequently withdrawn from future release consideration'. The song entered the Top Thirty a couple of weeks later, putting the group on *Top of the Pops* the same week as the Sex Pistols finally appeared on the programme with 'Pretty Vacant': even hard-core Punk was finally crossing over.

In August, the Adverts, just over nine months old, released their first record through a new deal with Anchor records. Like 'This Perfect Day', 'Gary Gilmore's Eyes' made few apparent concessions to the mainstream, but its 'wake up!', 'Pretty Vacant'-style guitar/drums introduction, and the sense of excitement caused by the acceleration of the tempo during the performance, caught the enlarged Rock audience for Punk. The mass audience was also intrigued by this bit of ramshackle horror. In September, 'Gary Gilmore's Eyes' went into the Top Twenty.

Just as T.V. Smith was writing a song critical of the New Wave, he became a New-Wave pop star. ' "Gary Gilmore's Eyes" seemed to go, right from the very first moment,' he says. 'In popularity terms, that was the high point. Suddenly everyone liked us, we were on television. The only trouble was, it then froze: that was what people wanted from us. We hadn't frozen, we'd only just started, and a band that should have developed into something extraordinary was hampered by public expectation.'

The first date of the SPOTS tour, Wolverhampton, 19 August 1977 (© Kevin Cummins)

27

A MASKED HORSEMAN rides through the streets of contemporary London, past landmarks of the past and present. He is dressed entirely in red, rides a black horse, and carries a black flag: Red and Black are the international colours of anarchy. He rides past such familiar places as the Tower, Harrods, Trafalgar Square, Piccadilly Circus, the Victoria Embankment, the Prince Albert Memorial, and what is now left of Covent Garden.

Roger Ebert: *Anarchy in the UK*, second draft, July 1977

After a final concert at a car-race meeting in Linkoeping, the Sex Pistols flew back to England on 30 July. Their public profile was higher than ever, as the Scandinavian stories filtered through the music press. All were sympathetic and humanizing, yet they trapped the group: 'It's very tiring to be that much at the heart of things,' says Al Clark, 'with everybody waiting on your next move.'

For about a year, the Sex Pistols had been moving faster than lightning; now they were caught. Throughout that time their career had consisted of a ritual dance with the media. Vital to this had been the ducking and weaving motion that McLaren had inspired, and the impossibility of pinning them down to any concrete position, whether political, aesthetic or social.

This evasiveness was impossible to keep up. 'This summer,' wrote Charles M. Young in *Rolling Stone*, 'the Pistols have been careening into overexposure in their homeland. Taking Punk lyrics at their literal word, the dailies regularly proclaim the movement the end of Western Civilization.' The pressure was maddening everybody: Glitterbest were becoming ever more doctrinaire, while the Sex Pistols were pop stars.

'John became very difficult', says Sophie Richmond. 'I couldn't grasp the extent of his paranoia about being on the streets, and I didn't have any idea about how vulnerable he was feeling. Nobody took much account of the fact these were four kids who were young, they didn't have a lot of experience and suddenly they had shot to fame and how were they dealing with it? It's the kind of thing that middle-class people can spend three years with an analyst for.

'Steve and Paul were quite realistic and once they got their flats they were easy. Sid started to become impossible, and John made everything as difficult as he could, partly to get attention. He always had me running around: I'd go off and deliver his wages to him – they had gone up to £50 a week by the time Russ Meyer was around – and Malcolm would say, "Make him come to the office". I saw this pretty much as wanting attention from Malcolm.'

There was another problem: nothing ages one faster than living a life in newspaper headlines. The Sex Pistols project had been, in part, an explicit engagement with the processes and politics of mass media. So far it had had an unprecedented, unexpected success. But as the Sex Pistols teetered on the high wire, the media were waiting for a fall. Events were now moving so fast that they were instant history. *Record, instant replay, fast forward*.

In August, the first meetings were held about a Sex Pistols book, to be written by McLaren's old art-school associate, Fred Vermorel, and his wife Judy. Everybody cooperated except McLaren, still fearful of being pinned down. The result was a brilliant piece of editing: Sophie Richmond's insider diary, press quotes, and transcripts of the interviews that caught the group just at the time that they were becoming embalmed in public opinion and in their own roles.

Having a book written about them was a sure sign that the Sex

Pistols were already history, and the film script hammered the point home. Just like the later *Great Rock'n'Roll Swindle*, the Ebert script *Who Killed Bambi*, throughout its seven drafts, returned always to the same obsession: McLaren's retelling of the whole Sex Pistols story, from the Nashville fight through to the Jubilee – a history of fifteen months. The second draft opens with each Sex Pistol delivering one of their by now famous slogans to the camera, amongst a parade of the dispossessed. Intercut with sexual adventures of polymorphous perversity, the plot presents a battle to the death between the group and the forces of oppression, the industry mogul 'Proby' (who exhibits many McLarenesque tendencies) and a Mick-Jagger-type pop star 'M.J.' It ends with the group victorious and McLaren's question: 'Will success spoil Johnny Rotten?'

It is difficult to tell from the script – as Meyer was a very visual director – but, just like Alex Cox's later *Sid and Nancy*, *Anarchy in the UK* seems an uneasy mixture of fiction and all-too-recent fact. *Beyond the Valley of the Dolls* had worked because its setting – the Los Angeles music industry – was so obviously fake. The Sex Pistols, in contrast, were strongly connected with English current affairs. Could Meyer and Ebert deal with such an intrusion of reality? Some of the group thought not. When the script, which even Glitterbest thought 'wooden', was presented to the group in early August, the reaction was divided: Steve Jones liked the sex, Paul Cook didn't mind, while both Sid Vicious and John Lydon were vehemently negative. Lydon in particular was furious at being presented with a *fait accompli* which had McLaren's name all over it, as producer and story originator: 'I hated that film right from the start,' he says.

His life had been rewritten by somebody he'd never met, under the instructions of a manager with whom he was already sparring. There was, as always, an element of the spoilt child in Lydon, but Glitterbest did not have a highly charged public image, unlikely to be improved by scenes like number 40: 'INT. JOHNNY ROTTEN'S BEDROOM – MORNING. The room is very plain and bears very little sign that it is his, aside perhaps from the odd Nazi poster.'

The project came up against the wall that has divided pop and film since *Help*. Pop's power relies on an authenticity that, if not social, is existential: 'We know what we *feel*.' McLaren's models for the film were the rupturing of *Blackbord Jungle* and the sleazy, cartoon flash of *The Girl Can't Help It*, but those were products of pop's first innocence, now lost forever. Pop was self-conscious, burdened by its history.

The archetypal pop film, the Beatles' *A Hard Day's Night* had been made at the very moment that pop gained its self-conscious authenticity. Dick Lester's documentary approach retained this crossover between authenticity and artifice, deftly highlighting reality without requiring the group to act, and containing sequences of pure visuals for songs like 'Can't Buy Me Love'. His subsequent *Help* added elements of fantasy which made the Beatles prisoners of the script.

The most successful films using pop stars had used performers in full command of their image: *Performance* and *The Man Who Fell to Earth* cast Mick Jagger and David Bowie in plots which were extrapolated from the blurring of identity and the sense of alienation consequent on pop stardom. None of the Sex Pistols had this distance from their personae: 'I hate films', Sid Vicious told Judy Vermorel, 'because people have to act parts in them. Play people who they're *not*.'

The film became even less likely to work when Meyer and Ebert arrived in England on 11 August. The Sex Pistols and Glitterbest were in disarray: the source of trouble was now the rerecorded album. For lack of anything else to do, Steve and Paul would spend days and days perfecting their 'wall of sound' with producer Chris Thomas. Lydon stayed away unless absolutely necessary, but Sid made efforts to lay down bass tracks. When McLaren heard the results of the most recent sessions, he hated them.

The album was overcooked. Endless overdubs had created a sound that was fuller and more technically proficient, but that had never been McLaren's interest: he felt that the new tapes, when compared to the versions cut over the previous year, lacked life. He also wanted new material, not the same old songs worked over again. After a few rows, he threw himself back into the film.

Into the middle of this confusion dropped Charles M. Young of *Rolling Stone*. This was arranged, not by Virgin, but by Glitterbest: US representative Rory Johnston had advised McLaren that some good press could affect the film negotiations. *Rolling Stone* was the biggest Rock paper: one long article there could preclude the necessity for any others. On his arrival, Young was given the run-around for two days, finally meeting up with Meyer, Ebert, Lydon and Reid over dinner at Wheelers.

Young describes this as a climactic meeting of mutual incomprehension: Meyer and Ebert were treating Lydon like a slide specimen, dissecting his dialogue, while Lydon resented being put under a microscope by people for whom he had no respect. 'A tosspot is even lower than a jerk-off,' he told Meyer, 'A weed is a pansy. If you don't know that, it's just an indication of how fuckin' stupid you Americans are.' If there was a moment when the film died, this was it.

The next day was the first date of what would be known as the 'SPOTS' or 'Secret Tour'. After the dates in Scandinavia, the group and John Tiberi wanted to keep playing live, particularly since Sid's claim to be a musician had been made more plausible by his performances. McLaren wanted the group out of the way: in his day-to-day improvisation, any activity was better than none. The Sex Pistols needed to seem like a functioning group.

'The group didn't know what they were going to do next', says Al Clark, 'Would a tour be a sell-out? Would they do individual dates and pretend they were banned everywhere else? Would they get banned everywhere else? Steve and Paul were the most stable, but they suffered the most. They wanted to be in a performing band and by that summer the Sex Pistols weren't a proper group at all. Even when they did dates, they were more like missions into enemy territory.'

With John Jackson at booking agents Cowbell, McLaren cooked up a new wheeze: the group were still banned by many councils and booking agents: so why not play unannounced concerts at tiny clubs? Even better, why not make it like a treasure hunt? Announce the possibility of dates around the country under assumed names in the press and let speculation take its course. Two days before the tour was due to start, the *Melody Maker* got hold of the story: the stage was set for chaos.

SPOTS (Sex Pistols On Tour Secretly) opened on the night of Friday the 19th at Wolverhampton's club Lafayette. The tiny venue was beseiged by fans eager to see the group's first public date for nearly nine months. 'There were coachloads from Manchester,' says Roadent, 'bouncers were standing on the front monitors, holding onto the ceilings to balance themselves, and nobody could see the band: a brilliant atmosphere where everything is threatening and exciting.'

The group were gleeful at being able to play in front of an English audience and let rip. 'For the first time,' wrote Charles M. Young, 'I saw Johnny Rotten crack a smile – only a brief one, but unmistakably a smile.' McLaren was not so happy: after the previous evening's dinner, he had realized that the relationship between Lydon and Meyer was so bad that the film might have to be abandoned. Meyer hadn't seen the need to make the trip, but McLaren himself went up to Wolverhampton for his first view of the group live for four months. He loved the chaos,but found the Sex Pistols themselves disappointing, particularly Lydon. Despite entreaties, McLaren refused to go backstage. In turn, the group got upset at McLaren's lack of emotional commitment. 'An emptiness set in,' says Jamie Reid. It was now obvious that the interests of group and manager were quite separate.

Shrouded in rumour, the group headed north. The venues were arranged at the last minute: Doncaster as the Tax Exiles, Scarborough as 'Special Guests', and Middlesborough. 'It was strange out of London,' says Barbara Harwood, the group's driver for the tour, 'suddenly it was off to these corners of Britain. There wasn't much to do. There was just us, instead of us with all our friends, with places to go and things to do. We'd arrive, plug in and away we'd go.'

'That tour was real good,' says Steve Jones, 'there were a lot of fans, queueing up around the block, and they went nuts when we played. It was like how it should have been, a band playing to an audience which dug you. This was playing to fans who wanted to come to see us. All I was interested in then was getting my dick sucked and getting drunk. If we'd done a good gig and there was plenty of birds around I knew there was no problem. I was just a sex fiend.'

'A long time had passed,' says Pauline Murray, 'you didn't feel so close. We went to see the Sex Pistols at the Middlesbrough Rock Garden, which is a small club renowned there for its violence. It wasn't the same; it had gone back down again. It was lacking in the original fire: it had a different sort of energy, more violent. They weren't making a message, it was more a barrage. It seemed disconnected somehow. It was still great, but odd, like they didn't know where they were going.'

After the initial enthusiasm, the chaos of the tour became gruelling. 'Nowhere was big enough,' says Dennis Morris. 'It was soul-destroying, more so for John. Steve always had a laugh, Paul was always in the background, but for John, because he never had proper microphones, his voice would go after about the second number. It was hurtful for him, because he wasn't trained. He was beginning to make plans. He was really into the space of Reggae music, not thrash.'

For Sid Vicious, it was a turning point. 'He got tougher,' says Barbara Harwood. 'Malcolm used to say that Sid was a natural talent. He had that childlike rebelliousness, but he was really soft underneath. But there was this sex and drugs and Rock'n'Roll' image, and I didn't know which was in charge. When we were in Plymouth I got a sense that the image was in charge of him: he got in a real mess, and he wanted me to go away with him for a bit.

'He was asking me about why I was interested in homoeopathy, why I was driving the band. Why I didn't take him away and sort him out? It was a weird conflict, knowing that he needed the whole persona that he had, and that both he and the band depended on that, and here he was wanting to get himself together. It was all so momentary, standing looking over the sea. I couldn't possibly afford what he was asking me to do: it was more than I could give him. I had kids back in London.'

'Sid broke down at the last gig in Penzance,' says Dennis Morris, 'he went back to the hotel and he couldn't eat anything. The audience was real close, and expecting a lot. I felt the crowd destroyed him. Penzance was a good gig, but it was one number then literally twenty minutes before the next. That's when Wobble turned up and everybody realized something was going down, because John was being really friendly towards him. It was the start of something new.'

The Sex Pistols returned from these six dates to the same old nothing. The problems they had had before the tour were still there. The film was the central issue on which everything else hung – even the album, which was the only thing that could occupy them: until it was resolved, the Sex Pistols' career was stalled. Momentum was lost, and they became an increasingly exotic side-show, preserved behind glass while style wars raged around them.

Now is the time of departure. The last streamer that ties us to what is known parts.

We drift into a sea of storms.

Derek Jarman: scene 46 of *Jubilee* (1977)

In the middle of August, everyday life superseded art. For a year now, Punk had celebrated riot, whether in the Clash's slogans, lyrics and LP sleeve, or the Sex Pistols' calls to urban insurrection. Outside events now overtook Punk's aestheticized apocalypse, when, six weeks after the worst of the Grunwick dispute, the National Front planned to hold a march through the predominantly working-class, black borough of Lewisham – in a deliberate act of provocation.

The National Front had gained power throughout 1976 and 1977: in March 1977, they beat the traditional third party, the Liberals, in the by-election at Stechford, Birmingham. They also polled a significant number of votes in the GLC elections that summer. Suddenly, they seemed a real threat. Despite the fact that trouble was inevitable, the

Lewisham, 23 August 1977: sleeve for Sham 69 / *Don't Wanna*, October 1977 (© Harry Murlowski/ Jill Furmanovsky)

march was allowed to go ahead (unlike Sex Pistols concerts). The result was riot 'live' on the streets of south London, as over 5,000 protestors battled with 4,000 police and 1,000 NF marchers.

'Like a lot of people,' says the *NME*'s Angus MacKinnon, 'I didn't think the Front march was a good thing. On the day, I arrived at New Cross and couldn't get any further. It was about eleven o'clock and there were already a lot of people there, most were trade unionists. It said in the papers the next day there were three thousand, but it must have been twice that number. They said it was the standard rent-a-mob. It wasn't. Many had come from all over the country, for the same reason as myself: enough was enough.

'We were contained up by the New Cross area. The Front was a small march: there must have been about a hundred and fifty of them, all ages. A few skins, a lot of older people whose politics were not only unpleasant, they were unpleasant to look at. Odd, the physiognomy of English fascism. They were eventually escorted onto the main street which goes towards Greenwich, and as they came out, there were mounted police, and things started to get very scary very quickly.

'People started picking up bricks and stones. Some of the NF had sticks already, they threw bricks back at us. Someone close by went down with a brick in their face, the police horses came towards us. Police horses are very frightening indeed, the crowd were surging forward and back. Basically the police were saying, you have to clear away, these people are going to march. The crowd got very angry and there was a lot of brick-throwing.

'The general idea was to go down the hill. There was no traffic or anything, the whole area had been sealed off. We got to the bottom, and there was a pitched battle going on. The Front had long since disappeared, they'd had their pathetic little meeting in a church hall, and now there were people rushing everywhere, more policemen than I'd ever seen before. There were baton charges, orange smoke everywhere. People throwing things through shop windows.

'Because it was Saturday there were people down there trying to buy things, and it was just impossible. Marchers and police up and down Lewisham High Street, and over it all was this enormous pall of orange smoke, very thick, acrid, and very unpleasant. I slipped down the side of the High Street to get away, and then we were stuck, seven or eight of us in a cul de sac at the back of a supermarket by the delivery bay, huddled in absolute terror.

'Right down the end of the High Street, we were rounded up and put by a police bus to be shunted off. We weren't, only because someone started throwing stones and bricks at the police bus, which withdrew. We were denied the dubious pleasure of being detained at Her Majesty's Pleasure for rioting. There were no buses, so I walked all the way back to Pimlico, five or six miles, got back about seven or eight in the evening, and was very, very frightened.

'I read about it the next day and was made incredibly angry. Did the police over-react? Or was it a real social disorder? I think it was. I was talking to this policeman who was seconded from Hampshire, who was very threatened. I bumped into him again later on, looking very much the worse for wear. We just looked at each other and I thought, "Oh my god, he's had a bad day, he's going to hit me," because it was people like me, supposedly, who had been the trouble, but he just came up and said, "What a terrible, terrible day. I've never had a day like this in my life." '

Lewisham was an immediate propaganda success for the National Front. As a Camerawork survey showed later that year, the message given in the media coverage was of the police valiantly attempting to mediate between 'extremists backed by an artillery of bottles, bricks, tins'. The recurring image was that of a young policeman with blood streaming from a head wound: as planned, the Front were upheld as fighters for the right to free speech and free assembly.

The events at Lewisham also helped to break Punk apart under the weight of its own contradictions. In superseding Punk's rhetoric with reality, it showed the apparent lie behind the antinomian heresy: freedom was not in the mind or the imagination, but to be fought for in the here and now. The Clash had initiated the discourse in their *NME* interview of April and, triggered by an incendiary Parsons/Burchill piece also in the *NME*, it would dominate the coverage of Punk during the next few months.

The National Front had 'won on points' in the nationals, but Lewisham saw Rock Against Racism and the Socialist Workers Party winning hands down in pop culture (the two had been closely affiliated since RAR's inception the previous year). After the success of confrontational tactics at a Front march in Wood Green in April, both were active in organizing the opposition at Lewisham – although many people needed no organization to express their hatred for the National Front's policies and physical presence.

After Lewisham, as David Widgery writes, 'The SWP made the decision to broaden the base of the anti-fascist movement by initiating the Anti-Nazi League.' In July, RAR began publishing a broadsheet, *Temporary Hoarding*, which resembled *IT*, with smart fanzine visuals: all montage and typed headlines. In issue 2, the magazine had a coup when Sophie Richmond pushed Lydon into an interview: 'I despise the National Front. How can anyone vote for something so ridiculously inhumane?'

The SWP took up the struggle from the IS (International Socialists) and the IMG (the International Marxist Group), both of which had been active in the Red Lion Square demonstration: more recently, SWP members had swelled the Grunwick picket. The SWP were committed to smashing capitalism and to instituting their working-class revolution: their hardline struggle and workplace-orientated politics, expressed in tough, macho language, made them perfectly in tune with the times.

This conjunction of music and politics was quickly gaining a commercial imprimatur. The same week that the music press carried their reports on Lewisham, they announced the signing of the Tom Robinson Band to EMI Records for nearly £100,000. The TRB – who were affiliated to RAR, Spare Rib, the National Abortion Campaign, and Gay Switchboard – offered the perfect chance for EMI Record Division, still bruised by the events of December, to claw back some radical chic.

Robinson had recorded for Ray Davies' Konk label with soft rockers Café Society: as well as a business headache, he'd picked up Davies' music-hall inflections and knack for lyrical reportage. Despite Robinson's considerable courage in coming out as the first openly gay singer, the TRB were an orthodox mixture of Rock clichés and dragging tempi. Conservative music was cloaking radical politics, but to many that seemed necessary, to halt Punk's uncontrolled acceleration of the last year.

Punk had ruthlessly thrust itself into the world and now the world was coming to claim it. Many would have argued that it was the original irresponsibility of the Punk elite that had made this insertion of politics into popular culture necessary, but there was something else besides politics at stake. August saw the start of a vicious class and ideological battle between the opposing tendencies united by the Sex Pistols: the arties and the social realists. The arties had a continued interest in experimentation; the social realists talked about building 'a brick wall' and extolled the virtues of Punk's latest sensation, the *ur*-Punk Sham 69. Punks had focused attention on working-class culture, albeit cloaked in art-school rags, but somebody was bound to take them literally. 'I was very conscious of class then,' says Mark P., who released Sham's first record, 'Jimmy was refreshing, because I'd spent a lot of time with people with ideas and Jimmy was the bit that was missing. He was going to take it down to the gutter again.'

Lead singer Jimmy Pursey was Joe Hawkins from Richard Allen's book *Skinhead* come to life. With his second Sham, he stripped the Ramones style down to brief, inflammatory guitar riffs and piledriver drumming, over which he roared direct, accusatory lyrics of class rage. In that late summer, Sham stormed out of the Surrey wastelands with all the force of a fist in the face, triggering the return of the subculture that had been lurking below Punk: the Skinheads.

Sham made the cover of the final *Sniffin' Glue*. Mark P. had turned the magazine over to Danny Baker, who wrote in a language that was untroubled by doubt or possibility: the style of a door being firmly shut. In the same issue, Mark P. committed *auto-da-fé*: 'I want you to burn *SG* 12 and burn it good.' 'When Danny came into the Glue,' he now says, 'he had a better way of putting the revolutionary ideas than me, restating the Deptford stance. But I didn't want the magazine to continue: I was fed up with packaging the anger.'

Mark P. was collaborating with Alex Fergusson and Genesis P-Orridge on his Zappa-esque Alternative TV, whose song about impotence, 'Love Lies Limp', was packaged as a free flexi-disc in the *Sniffin' Glue* which also carried all that tough talk. As A&R man with Miles Copeland's Step Forward Records, he also signed up Sham 69, whose first single was packaged with a picture from the Lewisham riot. On the one hand he was proud of his class roots, on the other he was too intelligent for the dumb stereotype.

Punk had disseminated explicit ideas about working-classness and 'common sense'. Within pop, this had been exciting, but in the world outside, these fantasies were essentially conservative. 'I was playing at being a hard nut and in the Punk scene, I could get away with it,' Mark P. says 'but to Jimmy Sham, I was some toffee-nosed record man. I enjoyed the scam, but I remember Jimmy refusing to go on one night, because all the kids were there, and we were saying, "But Jimmy, they're The Kids," and he said, "Yeah, but they're horrible".'

'The working-class thing was something that the media interfered with,' says Richard Boon, 'it played on that lowest-common-denominator thinking that the gutter press likes to impose on the working class. Some of the working class may be Hersham Boys, but it's dangerous for those role models to become established. The threat posed by earlier Punk was that intelligent young working-class people would throw off the shackles of oppression! and step into history!'

The insertion of organized Left politics into Punk threw up many contradictions. In the split between the 'arties' and the 'social realists', neither was right: their mistake was to turn an emotional response to a specific situation – the increased visibility of the National Front – into a cultural principle. If one thought the TRB's music was terrible did one think the politics were terrible too? Of course not, but the two were suddenly indivisible; 'Which side are you on?'

Punk's language of possibility had come up against the brick wall that, despite the Sex Pistols' attempts, had not been demolished. On one side, its language was to become increasingly inward-looking and impenetrable; on the other, increasingly hectoring and absolute. As was bound to happen, Punk's own moral authority – born out of a peculiarly sharp view of oppression – was lost in intolerance.

Any fascist ambiguity in Punk was fueled by the way that the style had bled Rock dry of all black influences: one way to overcome any taint of white supremacy was to affirm visible links with Reggae. By the autumn, there was a crossover between Punks and the new generation of English Reggae groups. Bills like the Slits with Steel Pulse, or Generation X with the Cimarons (an RAR benefit) paved the way for a thorough working out of the connections between these two gnostic cultures.

This connection informed what was probably the Clash's greatest single. With the Sex Pistols absent, the Clash had become the standard-bearers of the whole Punk movement, embodying its contradictions. As their design became more militaristic, Joe Strummer's voice became more and more vulnerable; at the same time as they became more of a Rock'n'Roll band, they hired the smokiest, most mysterious Jamaican producer of all, Lee Perry, to produce 'Complete Control'.

The genesis of the song lay in a spat between the Clash and their record company: in June, CBS had released a weak track, 'Remote Control', as a single, against the Clash's wishes. Not only did it flop, but it raised the question of the 'artistic freedom' promised by the contract. A trifle, but the Clash used it as a springboard from which to issue their bulletin on the progress of a unified Punk movement just at the very point when it was about to splinter. Much more than the Sex Pistols ever could, the Clash had integrated Reggae into their music: their earliest tracks showed a through knowledge of dub drop-out, while their 'Police and Thieves' on *The Clash* was a risky but successful fusion of Punk and Reggae. Perry did not produce 'Complete Control' to alter the group's by now thundering Rock'n'Roll thrust but, with his use of endless, deep echo, he gave the song a grandeur which turned petty plaint into parable.

The song begins with the trademark Punk fanfare of guitar and bass drum, before Joe Strummer settles into his story. Like a general reviewing past campaigns, he begins with the recent tribulations of Clash, rebel Rockers, but halfway through, the song splits. In contrast to the swaggering choruses, the music becomes almost tentative; Perry's murk deepens. Suddenly Strummer emerges, almost cracking: 'All over the news spread fast/They're dirty, they're filthy/They ain't gonna last'. He starts ranting. The song slides towards its climax, which is like the wave of a crowd roar round a football stadium. As

Strummer, still ranting furiously, is swamped by the noise, the pay-off comes: 'Total control,' Mick Jones repeats, 'C-O-N control,' but this is subverted by the song's pure exuberance. Unless you have a lyric sheet, it sounds like 'see you in control' and, instead of a piece of cynicism, 'Complete Control' becomes a hymn to Punk autonomy at its moment of eclipse.

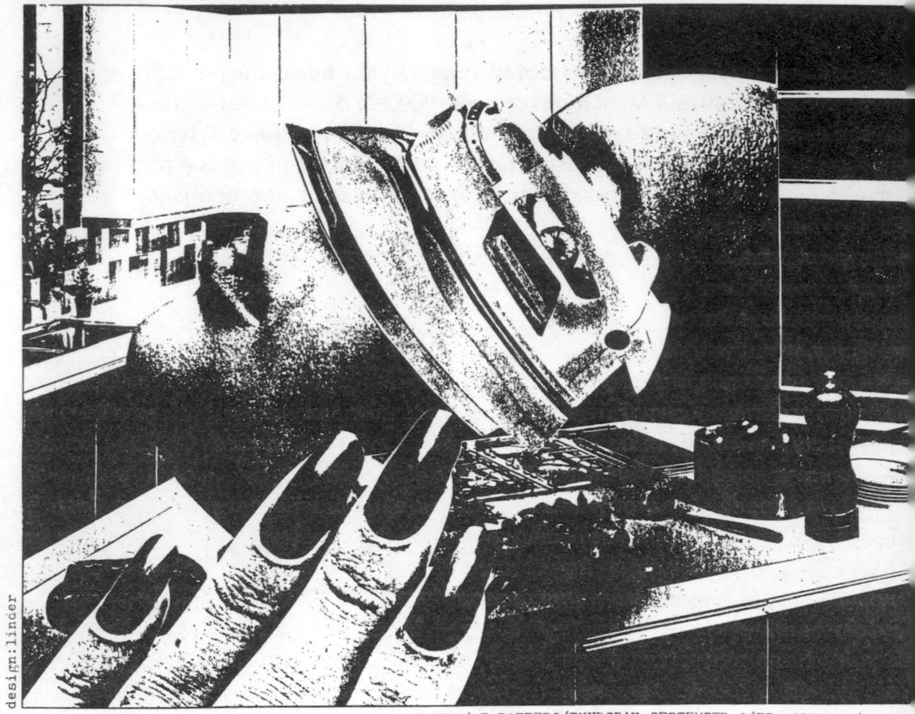

28

The mode shifts: dust settles/favourite beat combos the country wide deal with scope and personnel/fever subsidy/no sweat: traditionally new – next year's Damned reformation rumours already.

Richard Boon: *Girl Trouble 6b: A Focus on Industry*, (October 1977)

WE HAVE TIME TO GROW OLD THE AIR IS FULL OF OUR CRIES
BUT HABIT IS A GREAT DEADENER

***Gunrubber*, issue 6 (August 1977)**

By the autumn, the accelerated motion of Punk culture and New-Wave business had reached the point of burn-out in London. Groups like the Jam and the Stranglers were releasing thin second albums, whose formulae seemed to mock the possibilities that were still present. Others, like Generation X, found it difficult to translate the sounds in their heads onto record. As the pace mercilessly exposed any weaknesses, early frontrunners, unbuttressed by success or a sympathetic record company, found the going very tough.

'It was the old syndrome with the Heartbreakers,' says Leee Childers, 'taking the money that's on the table, rather than playing cool and collecting later.' Caught in a spiral of drug abuse, the group overrecorded their first album, *L.A.M.F.*, until it sounded like mud. 'The result was a very predictable disaster, when they were doing the greatest songs in the genre. The only way to record that kind of music was to go in, do it, and get out again – like the Adverts.'

For the Damned, speed was not enough. 'I wanted to work with someone from the Floyd,' says Captain Sensible, 'I suppose it was Syd Barrett. We ended up with the drummer, who had nothing to do with the Floyd we liked. After our second album was so appalling, I lost all respect for Bryan James. I thought: "I can write better than this." Because the album was a turkey, Stiff got rid of us: they thought we'd run our course: if I was them, I'd have done the same.'

In October, the Adverts released 'Safety in Numbers': 'It was becoming apparent what was going to happen,' says T.V. Smith. 'We had a lot of internal tensions. The rhythm section hated each other. Gaye had a big speed problem. Laurie went through a little heroin phase. Then we had this tension from outside: when "Safety in Numbers" wasn't a hit, suddenly we were one-hit wonders. It's a terrible feeling to think that the public perceived the band as having peaked, when you'd just started.'

10.9.77: Fanzines are the perfect expression – cheaper, more instant than records. Maybe THE medium. A democratization too – if the most committed 'new wave' is about social change then the best fanzines express this. Perhaps most importantly outside saturated London, they provide a vital function as a base/coordination point of the local scene. And that means Ilford as much as Glasgow. Eventually new impetus, reinterpretation will come from there.

Many of the early groups were faltering, and the structural changes which they had helped to initiate arrived too late to benefit them. The whole 'do it yourself' polemic of the year before was finally bearing fruit, stimulated by the opportunity given to the independent retail network by the Sex Pistols' bans that summer. By the late summer, each major city throughout the UK had its own independent record shop or Virgin branch, selling punk records, badges, fanzines and operating as a clearing house for local information.

'The Glasgow Punk fanzine was *Ripped and Torn* by Tony D.,' says

Edwyn Collins, then a teenage art student. 'Tony let us do an article on Glasgow record shops and their attitude to Punk. The best shop was called Graffiti, where Glasgow Punk bands, like the Jolt and Simple Minds, then called Johnny and the Self Abusers, hung out. Glasgow had peculiar licensing laws, so there were no Punk concerts in the city. We'd all commute out to Paisley to see Generation X and the Buzzcocks. The audience used to average about forty.'

When *Sniffin' Glue* imploded, the fanzine racks at Rough Trade and Compendium Books were fuller than ever before, as, like the groups which were flooding the clubs, dozens made their stab at immortality. The result was an explosion of information, as dozens of fanzines from all over the country – like *Revenge* (Grimsby), *Chicken Shit* (Glasgow) or *Hanging Around* (Edinburgh) – charted Punk's diaspora in scrawled, montaged, xeroxed pages. Punk was as much about graphics as it was about print. The layout techniques of the original *Sniffin' Glue* – hand-written captions and typewriter headlines – had already been assimilated by the music press and the high-rise imagery of early 1977 had been thoroughly coopted by the music and fashion industries. Fanzines went further into the vanguard art that seemed, to many art students at least, the root of Punk. Many used the form to comment on the printing processes of xerox and litho themselves.

This graphic experimentation was not conducted in a vacuum. Punk was saturated in coded information. After McLaren and Rhodes, young managers like Al McDowell, who was now handling Glen Matlock's new group, the Rich Kids, thought in terms of a total package: 'It was important to make an impression with what we were doing. There was a lot to do with the poster mentality, grabbing you from a distance, and screen prints – the simplicity that came from that medium.' Apart from badges, which were booming by that summer, the principal focus for all this activity was the single sleeve, which, since its inception by Stiff and Chiswick, and its quick acceptance by the Sex Pistols, had become both a manifesto and a major selling-point.

Apart from Jamie Reid, another important innovator was Barney Bubbles, the shy obsessive who did so much to create Stiff's early success by his witty lettering and unblinking, monochrome portraits of the motley crew that constituted the label's early roster. Like Reid, Bubbles was older than most of the Punk designers: he had worked at UFO and done sleeves like Hawkwind's *In Search of Space*. His experience quickly led him away from a surreal mundaneness to an inspired pastiche, performed with a wit sadly lacking by the time the process became industrialized in the mid-1980s: his cover for the Damned's 'Music for Pleasure' borrowed from Kandinsky's 1924 *Yellow Accompaniment*, while his design for 'Your Generation' by Generation X was pure Rodchenko.

'We set up our own design company after the Rich Kids signed to EMI,' says Al McDowell. 'We called ourselves Rocking Russian after Barney's sleeves. There were several of us: David Dahlson of *Don't Flex*, Clint Hodder and Neville Brody, who was doing a London College of Printing project on fanzines. We did graphics, T-shirts, even released records quite a while later. We had no idea what we were doing, businesswise. There was a feeling that you just did things and money came in and everything would be all right.'

'Hawkwind were very influential on the way I worked with the Buzzcocks,' says designer Malcolm Garrett. 'They were completely divorced from the music industry: this family unit with Barney Bubbles and the dancers and the lights. When you went to see them you entered this whole experience, even without the drugs. By the time I was working with Buzzcocks, I was trying to ensure that all the bits and pieces looked part of a whole: nothing in the posters, badges or sleeves looked like it was done by someone else.'

The Buzzcocks incorporated art-student designers Linder and Malcolm Garrett into a total look: they regarded their music, not as an end in itself, but a focus. For Linder, graphic work was a logical extension of her social life. 'Punk was cutting out the question: "Can I do this?",' she says. 'I began to do bits of collage, quite naturally. I took lots of photographs and wondered, what could I do with them? I started to get bored, and went from collage to montage, using scalpels, glass cutting. I'd always loved magazines and I had two separate piles. One you might call women's magazines, fashion, romance, then a pile of men's mags: cars, DIY, pornography, which again was women, but another side. I wanted to mate the "G-Plan" kitchens with the pornography, see what strange breed came out. I did it all on a sheet of glass with a scalpel, very clean, like doing a jigsaw. Rising above it all. The first one I did like that was for a Buzzcocks concert at Rafters: "Cosmetic metal music: manicured noise".'

Montage is a twentieth-century notion, capturing the pace of technology both in method and in image. Linder's images for Buzzcocks complemented them perfectly, with their concentration on gender and the domestic: more critical than celebratory, more Heartfield than Hamilton, they were the dystopia to the Independent Group's first, innocent embracing of the American consumer utopia that was just about to arrive in England. Twenty years later, consumerism seemed as much a prison as a liberation.

The Sex Pistols and the groups they inspired had fulfilled many of the Independent Group's pop prophecies, right down to the violence implicit in the 'pop!' bubble, shot from a gun, in Eduardo Paolozzi's *I was a Rich Man's Plaything*. Now they were into the 'expendable' and 'transient' phase of Richard Hamilton's definition. Linder's dark, claustrophobic air caught Punk as it was folded in on itself. Things were happening too quickly: an event, like the closing of the Electric Circus club in Manchester, which at any other time would merit a shrug, now seemed of cataclysmic importance.

15.10.77: Warsaw look young and nervous. Desperate, thrashing, afraid of stopping/falling: 'What are you going to do when the novelty's gone/

The Electric Circus, Collyhurst, Manchester, 19 August 1977: Paul Morley in the centre (© Kevin Cummins)

You'll be back in the gutter where you came from' ('Novelty'). The Prefects take some getting used to: as ever, the sound is terrible, but they're young (19), rough and powerful. In the surroundings, their bleak/bitter approach makes sense.

Even more so the Worst. They look as though they've stepped out of the industrial waste, blinking in the spotlight. No 'image'. They play not as though their lives depend on it, but because it does. John Cooper Clarke begins reading: small and skinny, reminiscent of 1966 Bob Dylan, he declaims his poetry of wit and warmth fast. The audience claps to his rhythm. It's hard to imagine this in London because up here there is no distinction between art and life.

The Buzzcocks are on home ground and here they are the stars that they will be soon. They haven't sacrificed their intrinsically understated and warm approach: in an age of hectoring, that merely adds to their strength . . . they end with 'Time's Up' and encore with 'Louie Louie' – remember the 'gotta go now' refrain? John the Postman and several others get up on stage to help, and then the audience goes berserk and rushes the stage . . . the plugs are pulled, lights turned off, 'This could be the last time' plays . . .

At the moment when a subculture becomes visible and thus gains power, there is great tension between the enjoyment of that power and the commercialization that, simultaneously willed and despised, is bearing down like an express train. Since the previous summer, the Mancunian Punk subculture had developed in a degree of isolation, away from the capital's weekly media spotlight: Manchester's proud regionalism seemed to offer greater potential.

'You didn't need bondage trousers and spiky hair to be a Punk in Manchester,' says Malcolm Garrett. 'It was more a question of your attitude. Everybody got their clothes from the Salvation Army or the antique clothes market. Coming to London to see the Ramones in June, I was astounded at how fashion-oriented it was. It was more-home made in Manchester: people aren't as cool there as they are in London. There, everyone is on the guest list: in Manchester you get dressed up, you go out to have fun, and you get wild.'

More than Liverpool or Glasgow, Manchester was an ideal Punk community, having, to some degree, put the ideals of autonomy into practice. 'The reason Manchester happened was that they had undisputed talent in a number of fields,' says Garrett, 'the music, the management, the journalists, designers and photographers. The local media were very supportive: the *New Manchester Review* and Granada's *What's On*. There was a professional infrastructure, but it was so small that it was like a village community. You felt you were in control.'

Local independent labels included Tosh Ryan's Rabid, which released the first records by Slaughter and the Dogs and John Cooper Clarke, the Buzzcocks' New Hormones, and Valer. The city had new groups, poets, graphic artists, clubs, clothes shops and fanzines such as Paul Morley's *Girl Trouble* and Pete Shelley's *Plaything*, which, with their one-page, A4 format and clipped prose captured the movement's acceleration on the point of implosion.

'Local activity was seen to be important and was more commonplace,' says Richard Boon, 'although still open to the same mutations as in London. The Drones had been like the Bay City Rollers. They were operating on the media definitions: these were the shapes to throw, and they threw them. It was pretty thoughtless. But there were also groups like the Fall beginning, and Warsaw, the group that was to become Joy Division – also tacky and captivated by the media interpretations of Punk.'

'Ian Curtis had "Hate" written on the back of his jacket,' says Peter Hook, Joy Division bassist. 'He stood out in the crowd. Our first concert was supporting Buzzcocks in May: playing wasn't important, getting up and making a noise was. The playing would just come. It was incredibly naive, but that is what you gathered from the Pistols. The air you gave off was the important thing: how you had the cheek to get up onstage I don't know, but everybody was in the same boat, so they weren't bothered.

'The last night of the Electric Circus was so bad: we really had to fight to get on. The Drones wouldn't let us in the building. The next night was the Buzzcocks, and Richard Boon had told us we could play and then on the night mysteriously changed his mind. In the end Ian just had a blue fit at him. The whole period was intensely frustrating. We were heavier, musically and in personality, than Devoto or Shelley. Because you were different, people treated you differently.'

In the end, the last night of the Electric Circus marked the Buzzcocks' coming-out ball with the music industry. Their first UA single, released in November, was as compressed a package as any released by the Sex Pistols. Malcolm Garrett set one of Linder's more eye-catching montages – a naked woman with mouths for nipples and an iron for a head – against an electric yellow background and lettering which ran at right angles. Inside, the Buzzcocks, with sympathetic production from Martin Rushent, showed how Punks could harness speed.

'Orgasm Addict' finally admits the laughter that is too often banished from sex, with Devoto's packed, polymorphously perverse lyrics set off perfectly by Shelley's casual swearing, heavy breathing and simulated orgasms. The tension between Shelley's ludicrous, camp squeals and the group thundering behind him is terrific. The images flash past you like scenes from a humorous porno loop, there is a brief guitar stutter, Shelley shouts out the title phrase, and it's all over – in 1 minute 59 seconds.

The radio wouldn't play it, of course, but once the groups had got used to the recording studio, the battle to get Punk heard was almost won. This access was bought at a price: 'People like Richard didn't start off as managers,' says Shelley. 'Their input was creative, but when you hit the music industry, people who've been doing particular things aren't going to see themselves wearing different hats. Once we were in the music industry, people had become more diversified, there was nothing to pull them together again.'

> Bending too fixedly over hideousness, one feels queerly drawn. In some strange way, the horror flatters attention, it gives to one's limited means a spurious resonance. I am not sure whether anyone, however scrupulous, who spends time and imaginative resources on those dark places, can, or indeed, ought to leave them personally intact. Yet the dark places are at the centre. Pass them by and there can be no serious discussion of the human potential.
>
> **George Steiner: *In Bluebeard's Castle* (1971)**

> Monopoly capitalism will construct its own ministry of leisure over Western Europe: Butlins camps or rarified Belsens all along the Costa Brava.
>
> **'Work', *King Mob Echo, 6* (1969)**

During September and early October, the members of the Sex Pistols coped with the delays according to their characters. Steve and Paul spent time in the studio and played out whenever they could – like the opening date of Johnny Thunders' tour. The more vulnerable pair, Sid and John, retreated further into their respective bunkers: Sid with Nancy and drugs, John with a household of friends (Debbie, Wobble and John Grey) to buttress him against a hostile world. It was about this time that his relationship with newspaper heiress Nora Forster began.

The stakes were now immeasurably higher: the film was becoming dangerously out of control. In July, the budget had been estimated at £250,000: £125,000 would come through Sandy Lieberson at Twentieth Century Fox; £50,000 from Richard Branson, and £50,000 had been agreed with impresario Michael White. The final £25,000 would come from McLaren and the group, out of the most recent advance money. A production manager was brought in to work out a budget: his final figure of £400,000 came as a shock to all concerned. Even with revised figures, there was still a £75,000 shortfall. The film was now dependent on the American sales of the album. McLaren tried to negotiate with Arista and Columbia Pictures, hoping to get one company's backing for the film in place of all the smaller investors.

A further casualty of McLaren's single-mindedness was Glitterbest's relationship with Virgin. 'The first major row centred on who had the Pistols for America,' says John Varnom. 'The Pistols' contract quite clearly stated that the Pistols would go with Virgin provided Virgin matched whatever other offers Malcolm got. Malcolm, on the other hand, wanted to do a deal with a different company in every territory. What really annoyed Branson was McLaren's flat refusal to treat the contract as anything to do with the matter. There had been a good deal of painful negotiation before the UK deal was worked out: the US clause was an important one to Richard. Now he was being told that the clause was useless, simply because Malcolm proposed to ignore it. Virgin could do nothing or they could sue. And obviously, they couldn't sue. They would have looked just like EMI or A&M. Branson felt outflanked and hated it.'

The album negotiations and film preproduction continued through September. With Virgin out, the field was narrowed down to Warners, Arista, Columbia and Neil Bogart at the disco label Casablanca. McLaren alienated Arista's Clive Davis, and Columbia Pictures President David Begelman was sacked on the fraud charge recounted in *Indecent Exposure*. That left Warners, who were unsure about the film, and Casablanca, who likewise couldn't come to a decision.

Warners eventually agreed £200,000 for the film and £50,000 for the album on 10 October. Four days later, Arista Music signed their North American publishing rights. The film was by now in pre-production: locations were being scouted and Dickensian sets were being built at Bray Studios. The majority of the £11,000 a week needed for this was being funded by Branson, but McLaren had already put in over £50,000 from Glitterbest's account.

McLaren was worried. Apart from the rumblings within the group itself, faced with a severe eight-week shooting schedule that would keep them all on set until Christmas, there was trouble because the film companies were unsure of the group's physical or mental ability to stand up to this rigorous schedule. The members of the group had to undergo medicals, which they passed, but the question mark remained: could they actually do it? Worst of all, the costs continued to soar. At a final budget meeting on 7 October, the figure had almost doubled to £741,000: £150,000 was to come from Fox, £200,000 from Warners, £150,000 from Michael White with an additional £25,000, £165,000 from Virgin and £51,000 from Glitterbest. But at the end of that week, McLaren's hand was still on the wheel: although the final budget hadn't been sealed by contract, filming was to begin the next Tuesday.

The Sex Pistols album was also in chaos, with three different versions of every track available. The title and the cover concept had been decided, however: initial versions had been called *God Save Sex Pistols*, and Jamie Reid had worked up some proofs in dayglo yellow and dark red. There were to be no picture of the group, just cut-out lettering with a crude finish reminiscent of screen-prints. During the summer, the album became known as *Never Mind the Bollocks*, a phrase supplied by Steve Jones.

The confusion suited McLaren, who was stalling as much as he could for the American deal, but Virgin were frantic. On 20 September, Richard Branson spent a long night selecting versions and track listings: he wanted all the hits on the album, although most of Virgin, Glitterbest and the group were against the idea. The problem was that there were no new songs, except 'Holidays' and the just-completed 'Bodies'. The group were not playing and not rehearsing.

To keep up some momentum, 'Holidays in the Sun' was pulled out of the hat as a fourth single. Glitterbest and some of the group felt that it was lacking in impact and goosed it up every way they could; the song was remixed, given more overdubs and jackboots were added in time with Paul Cook's opening drum rhythm. McLaren and Reid then worked up another campaign with a video (never shot) that would be a 're-creation of the TV ads used by the *Sun* and the *News of the World* to advertise holiday features'.

This was the heyday of the Sex Pistols' graphic image: most other media were closed to them. Under pressure, Reid went public with his Situationist connections. The front cover of the sleeve was detourned from a holiday brochure produced by the Belgian Travel Service, which had cartoon illustrations of a typical family on a typical holiday. Rein inserted the song's lyrics into the cartoon bubbles in the same way that the original Situationist strips had done with forties detective comics.

For the reverse, he pulled out an illustration from Suburban Press, called the *Nice Drawing,* and simply added the 'Satellite' lettering readymade from the 100 Club poster of the previous year. For the music press ads and large, 4ft by 2ft posters, Reid took a graphic he had contributed to Chris Gray's 1974 translation of Situ texts, *Leaving the 20th Century,* adding speech bubbles and an old Suburban Press sticker: 'Keep Warm This Winter, Make Trouble'.

'Holidays' is the sound of a group collapsing in on itself. Written just after they had been thrown off A&M, the lyrics record John Lydon's paranoia and feelings of uselessness, suddenly pitched into the alien environment of Baader/Meinhof 'Wanted' posters and Turkish ghettoes, and dominated by the concrete Berlin Wall which it was then inconceivable to cross. As written, 'Holidays in the Sun' is a brilliant rant sparked off by a Situationist trope, set to one of Steve Jones's most readymade riffs. 'A cheap holiday in other people's misery,' sneers Lydon over the opening chords; 'I don't want a holiday in the sun/I wanna go to the new Belsen/I wanna see some History/Cos now I gotta reasonable economy.' Lydon distractedly attempts to confront the reality behind his apocalyptic rhetoric, 'World War Three' live: 'I looked over the wall and they're looking at ME!'

The recording is the Sex Pistols' most compressed. First, there was Lydon's general state of mind in the studio: 'I'd be sitting there all day, screwed up,' he says, 'dreading the moment when I'd be called down, and with all that energy and adrenalin and fear, I'd just let rip. The most I could do it would be four times in a row, and by then I'd be completely hoarse.' Like 'Bodies', this was recorded after the June attacks, with Lydon bunkered and near breakdown: the result is hysterical.

The Sex Pistols' career had crashed through barrier after barrier, but here they hit the wall at high speed. For the first half, the song has a structure: in each verse, Lydon throws out his polarities – 'Belsen', 'the Communist call' – but the verse/chorus pattern holds. As Lydon comes up to the break, he stares down the wall as hard as he can, and it stares back, unblinkingly. The breakdown of the lyrics spills into the performance, as the song cracks apart and with it, the Sex Pistols themselves.

If 'Holidays' has a location at all outside Lydon's burning skull, it is West Germany. In 1977, the West German state was under its most concerted attack from the urban guerillas that had taken their original inspiration from the same late sixties roots as Punk Rock. This hard-core nihilism had gone, not into pop, but into urban warfare. From the early 1970s young urban revolutionaries calling themselves the RAF, the Red Army Faction, had killed dozens of people.

West Germany in those days was full of 'Wanted' posters. The portraits of young, almost Bohemian RAF members – ideal, in their black and white blurriness, for an album sleeve – stared down from every public place. The country had the quiet, edgy feeling of a state under siege. Ever since the four core members of Baader/Meinhof had been imprisoned at Stammheim prison to await trial, they had become a focus for an RAF second wave, which killed judges, kidnapped politicians, and blew up the German Embassy in Stockholm.

In May 1975, their trial began in a specially constructed 'fortress' at Stammheim. After Meinhof's suicide in May 1976, the trial was conducted with extraordinary security. In April 1977, the Federal Prosecutor was murdered. After the remaining three defendants were sentenced to life, the RAF shot the banker Jurgen Ponto in his own house. The ringleader was Suzanne Albrecht, a friend of Ponto's family. Here was the ultimate poison in your machine.

The struggle entered its terminal phase while the Sex Pistols were preparing 'Holidays' for release. Incarcerated in Stammheim for crimes which they had always admitted, the prisoners felt the reality of the 'omnipresence of the state' that had been their rhetoric. Their every twitch was monitored by a vast, burgeoning bureaucracy. They compared themselves and their situation with the 'Auschwitz and Buchenwald' that had been in their heads since birth.

On 5 September, Hanns Martin Schleyer, the head of the German equivalent of the CBI, was kidnapped by the RAF and held hostage. An intense manhunt began, but all that was seen of Schleyer was his image on a series of videotapes and polaroids, sitting in front of an RAF symbol. The manhunt and the negotiations dragged on for the next month, under conditions of extraordinary polarization: 'There's sadism bursting out everywhere,' noted RAF member Gudrun Ensslin with satisfaction.

On 13 October, a Lufthansa jet was hi-jacked by Palestine sympathizers. It came to rest in Mogadishu, Somalia, where on the 16th and 17th, it was stormed by West German commandos. The next night, Ensslin, Baader and Raspe died in their cells at Stammheim: it was never established whether this was suicide or murder. On the 19th, Schleyer's body was recovered after forty-three days. The RAF communiqué that announced the location of his corpse spoke of the 'fascist drama'. On the 20th, 'Holidays in the Sun' entered the English charts.

At the words 'the Berlin Wall', Lydon's voice explodes and, as the break climaxes, he starts to gibber: for the rest of the song, he hardly stops. The structure disappears as he fights to keep up with the juggernaut riff (or vice versa) 'Claustrophobia . . . there's too much paranoia . . . there's too many closets: when will we fall?' As the song judders to a halt, Lydon keeps hurling himself at the wall of death, screaming: 'I don't understand this bit at all: please don't be waiting for me'. This polite request is one of the most terrifying admissions in all pop, issued by someone who has jumped into the abyss. As the song folds in on itself at the end, it speaks of many things: Lydon's fury and terror at finding that autonomy has turned into another form of bondage, that revolutionary fantasy paled before the reality of Stammheim and that, despite the weaponry of their name, the Sex Pistols were just pop musicians. This was not just failure, but annihilation.

There was no respite on the B-side. 'Satellite' was one of the Sex Pistols' oldest songs: rerecorded until it had as many layers as ancient Troy, it was now a million miles removed from the world of Shanne Hasler and student discos. With layer upon layer of guitar sound, 'Satellite' is so complete that you can hardly breathe. As the riff churns, Lydon mutters, almost to himself: 'I can't take no more – you'd better stop'. He whoops, yells, bashes the microphone: after the last chopped chord, he is still screaming.

Whether intentionally or not, Lydon had allowed himself no way back from this single. Confusion greeted its release, as might be expected with a record of such complexity, and the single did less well than Tom Robinson's equivalent of 'Pretty Vacant', '2-4-6-8 Motorway'. Faced with political strife and Punk break-up, the Sex Pistols came out with a complete statement of extremism's psychological wasteland.

The record itself was overshadowed by its concentrated promotional campaign. The ads made public for the first time in England the link between the Sex Pistols and their Situationist references. Within days, the Belgian Travel Service threatened legal action against Virgin for breach of copyright: the artwork was pulped, but not before thousands of covers had been released and there had been more free publicity. It seemed that the group couldn't make any move without attracting some legal attention.

The week that 'Holidays in the Sun' was released, the film collapsed. Because not enough had been done to satisfy the film's backers that the completion clauses could be met, no finance had come through. For Meyer, no pay meant no play and, after one day's shooting, on the 11th, he walked off location, never to return. On

Richard Branson, Virgin, Notting Hill Gate, October 1977 (© Barry Plummer)

hearing this, Twentieth Century Fox pulled out: the shooting schedule was scrapped, actors and technicians stood down, and the film was put on hold.

Shortly afterwards, *Never Mind the Bollocks – Here's the Sex Pistols* was finally released. The chaos surrounding the film had spilled over into the album with which it was so closely interwined. By late September, a final track listing and running order had been put together by John Tiberi, but right up to the moment of rush release, on 28th October, rows were going on between the group and Virgin about what should go on the album. Glitterbest took advantage of the confusion to insert some confusion of their own. In late October, a Sex Pistols bootleg entitled 'No Future U.K.' was released under the fictional group name of 'Spunk'. These were recordings made from the Goodman tapes of July 1976 and January 1977 which McLaren preferred to the finished album, although Cook and Jones were embarrassed by the quality. In fact, Glitterbest owned the tapes – as they had paid for both recordings outside any contract – but the release was in breach of the Virgin deal.

Worldwide release of the album was scheduled for 10 November. Glitterbest had already shipped tapes to Barclay and, as a further delaying device, insisted that Virgin add 'Submission' to the eleven tracks already pressed. In the last week of October, Virgin learned of Barclay's plan to import copies into England ahead of the release date, and a furious Richard Branson ordered that the album was rush-released in whatever form, with or without 'Submission'.

The Sex Pistols album had been announced as far back as June. Events had moved so quickly that, by the time it came out, it was almost an afterthought, a 'greatest hits' collection. The Sex Pistols were embalmed: the endless rerecording means that everything is fixed, there is no space. 'It was too produced,' says John Lydon, 'too clean. It still sounds like that now, too nice. It reminds me of a West Coast band, the way everything fits so nicely into place, note perfect.'

It is difficult to listen to *Bollocks* all the way through, but individual tracks show the Sex Pistols at the height of their power. 'I thought it sounded great,' says Paul Cook, 'I still do. Me and Steve would go in and do the guitar and drum parts, which is pretty unorthodox, it's usually bass and drums, but we knew the songs so well that we could do without the bass. We got them done quickly. Chris Thomas was professional; he seemed to know how we wanted to sound.'

Bollocks has Steve Jones stamped all over it. His massed guitars dominate the older songs, giving them a life often denied by Lydon's increasingly mannered vocals: if the overproduction swamps '17' or 'Submission', then it also gives others, like 'New York', coherence. The newer 'EMI' is immeasurably better than the January version, with some extraordinary morse-code overdubs during the final verse. The only all-new song is 'Bodies', put together in the studio. Announced by the usual Cook/Jones fanfare, John Lydon starts his story, sparked by a fan letter: 'She was a girl from Birmingham/She just had an abortion . . . ' There is no tune, just relentless punk, as Lydon enters into insanity. Like many of his songs from this period, 'Bodies' has no fixed narrator, being told in both third and first person; it has an almost schizoid viewpoint.

Lydon starts screaming again, trying to convince himself that he is not part of the same humanity that lets this horror take place, that he is not subject to bodily processes like sex, birth and death, that he isn't the baby itself. Unlike on 'Holidays', however, he is in control of himself. The song suddenly folds into a false ending: into the silence, Lydon leaps with the first of five, percussive 'fucks' – a deliberate irruption of male aggression, all the more powerful for its precision.

'Sex Pistols in a new "four letter" storm' ran the *Sun* headline on the day that the album was released. With 'Bodies', the title and the already banned 'God Save The Queen', the album was banned by Boots, Woolworths and W.H. Smith. The advance orders of more than 150,000 were enough, however, to send it straight into the charts at an unequivocal number one. It was a near repeat of 'God Save The Queen', but unlike June, this time it was a full stop. The group would never record together again.

Malcolm McLaren, after Cruickshank, 25 December 1977 (© Malcolm McLaren)

29

This is '77, nearly heaven, it's black, white and pink, just think there's more to come, hum hum hum hum it's so obvious. Well it's alright just listen, can't wait for '78, God those r.p.m., can't wait for them, don't just watch, hours happen, get in there kid – and snap them.

Wire: 'It's So Obvious' (1977)

Steve Walsh: OK, so what's your raison d'etre?
Subway Sect: WE HATE ROCK.
Steve Walsh: You can't say that – it's such a negative reason!
Subway Sect: Yeah, but there's nothing to get enthusiastic about.

Subway Sect interview, *Zigzag* (September 1977)

In the autumn of 1975, British Punk had begun at 430 King's Road: just over two years later, a host of other shops presided over its spread. In London, Rock On and Rough Trade were augmented by other independents like Beggars Banquet and Small Wonder. Just as Rock On had done, all were beginning their own independent record labels,

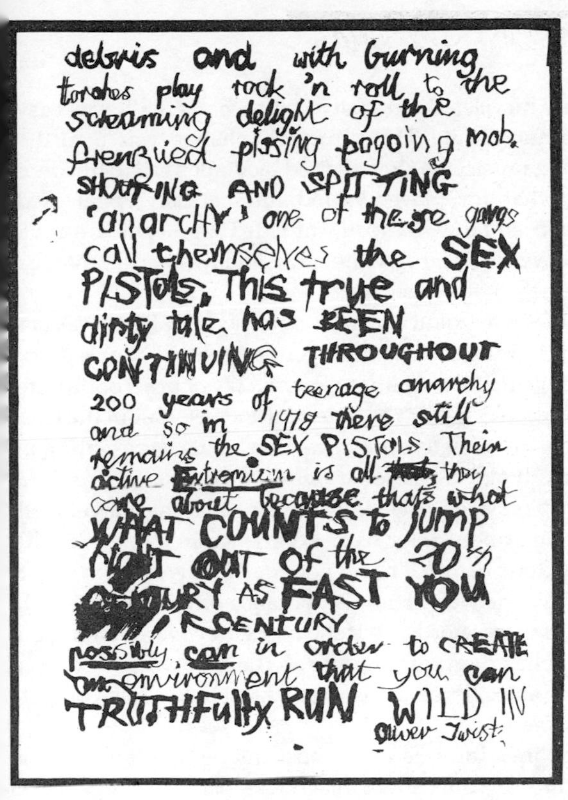

debris and with burning
torches play rock 'n roll to the
screaming delight of the
frenzied pissing pogoing mob.
SHOUTING AND SPITTING
'anarchy' one of these gangs
call themselves the SEX
PISTOLS. This true and
dirty tale has BEEN
CONTINUING THROUGHOUT
200 years of teenage anarchy
and so in 1978 there still
remains the SEX PISTOLS. Their
active Extremism is all they
come about because that's what
WHAT COUNTS to jump
right out of the 20th
CENTURY AS FAST YOU
CENTURY
possibly can in order to CREATE
an environment that you can
TRUTHFULLY RUN WILD IN
Oliver Twist

as a result of their closeness to the fast fluctuations of consumer demand.

'Punk was the last time you could have a label like Chiswick or Small Wonder,' says Roger Armstrong, 'make a record for nothing, press enough up and guarantee you'd sell a few thousand.' During the first half of 1977, the independent labels were slow to get off the ground, but by the autumn they had combined to form an alternative, countrywide distribution system.

The independent labels and shops promised some degree of autonomy from the music industry, and after the Buzzcocks' example, this went hand-in-hand with a promise of decentralization. This was given form by the 'Small Is Beautiful' discourse of E.F. Schumacher who, in the face of vast, ecologically destructive multinationals, proposed a new kind of technology that was small scale, accessible: a tool rather than a master.

The independents began as a classic example of supply-side economics, but they quickly developed an ideology. 'Xerox music is here at last,' the Desperate Bicycles chanted on their second EP: 'It was easy, it was cheap, go and do it.' This structural change was a further inspiration to young musicians already fired by Punk's call to freedom. If you knew that what you played would automatically be released, then you could relax and do what you wanted. That meant you could extrapolate on the weird shrieks, white noise and hysterical rants that had been part of the original package.

The beginning of what would become known as post-Punk was also informed by often hidden, but definite gender politics. 'Punk didn't do much to challenge male sexuality or image,' says Lucy Toothpaste, whose fanzine *Jolt* explicitly dealt with feminist ideas. 'But in the early days it did give a lot of women confidence. Boy bands were getting up on stage who couldn't play a note, so it was easy for girls who couldn't play a note to get up on stage as well. By the time that they developed, women were singing about their own experience in a way which I don't think they'd done before. I never got one Punk woman in any of my interviews to say she was a feminist, because I think they thought the feminist label was too worthy, but the lyrics they were coming out with were very challenging, questioning all the messages we'd been fed through *Jackie* comics. Punk made women feel they could compete on equal terms to men.'

These sexual politics informed the most interesting 'inner-circle' Punk groups. 'Punk became more macho as people's Rock'n'Roll tendencies started to sneak back out again,' says Viv Albertine of the Slits, 'but there were those who stuck with questioning. The whole thing was about looking at things with a fresh eye, and sexuality had to be looked at, there were so many problems in there that had to be solved. And that meant stepping back. We all worked on each other's guitar, bass, singing, everything. It was painful, but we were very strict with each other.'

The difficulty for groups like the Slits and Siouxsie and the Banshees was how to translate an often obnoxious but proud attitude into a new form of music. No woman had made these noises before. For the Slits, the result was a maelstrom of over-amped guitar and sheet-metal drumming and, amid the chaos, musicians creating their own order. By the autumn, the 'armed playground chants' of songs like 'Love and Romance' and 'Vindictive' had become full-blown streetfights, anarchic and threatening.

Siouxsie and the Banshees played off Siouxsie's dominatrix-style hauteur against three pretty-boy musicians. By the late autumn, they

(left to right) Tessa Pollite, Ari Up, Palmolive and Viv Albertine: the Slits, winter 1977 (© John Tiberi)

were playing songs full of awkward twists, casual brutalities, mass-media trash, and the intense excitement of ambition outstripping ability. 'We weren't musicians,' says Siouxsie, 'talking about breaking down walls and actually doing it are quite different things. In our naivety, we started making this noise that was ours.'

For a male group like the Subway Sect, the idea was to work, not with power, but weakness and introversion. To them, failure was more interesting than chart success. 'Subway Sect were so literary,' says Geoff Travis, who released their second, ironically titled single, 'Ambition'. 'Vic is the great lost soul of the era: his nihilism is more extreme than anyone's. He seemed to have seen through the circus which he was being enticed into, from day one. He saw all the contradictions and didn't want to be a pop star.'

'I thought the Sex Pistols were the end of Rock'n'Roll,' says Vic Godard. 'But as it turned out, they weren't. Nor were the Clash. Steve Jones had obviously learned to play from the New York Dolls, but we wanted to sound like the Velvet Underground or the Seeds, nothing remotely heavy. We never used ordinary guitars, a Gibson or a Strat: we used Fender Mustangs because they have a trebly, scratchy sound. We became quite purist. Our guitarist refused to allow any macho, Rock'n'Roll attitudes on stage.'

As the autumn deepened, the oblique, often harsh noises of these groups – and others like Manchester's the Fall, with their female organist – offered a sense of possibility that had been squeezed out elsewhere. Although those caught in the adrenalin rush could not see it, Punk was now an outmoded definition, liable to result in stylistic and/or social conservatism, whether in the *ur*-Punk of Sham 69, the social-realist rock of Tom Robinson, or the New Wave of the Jam, the Stranglers or the Boomtown Rats. All this had happened within a year. Acceleration was the problem. Time, and perception itself, seemed fragmented as in a Ballard or Burroughs dystopia. This couldn't last: the social realists had already shown that the security of commitment was one viable option for split psyches. There was another solution, proffered by the alienated synthetics evident in two of the autumn's number one records – Donna Summer's 'I Feel Love' and 'Magic Fly' by Space.

If Punk was jumping the rails during the last third of 1977, it was Kraftwerk's 'Trans-Europe Express' that brought everything to a halt, with a screech of metal on metal. 'From station to station/Back to Dusseldorf City/Meet Iggy Pop/And David Bowie', they sang, imitating the emotionless, precise speech of translators or robots. A complement to the disco music pouring into America from Giorgio Moroder's Munich Machine, their 'motorik' – music for autobahns – had already been picked up by style barometer David Bowie for *Station to Station*, a Top Three album in early 1976.

3.11.77: Bowiedream: Moss Garden/very humid/odiferous/jewel encrusted/ until arrival of J. J. Burnel plus Finchley Boys/leaning behind the tailfin/of 60's Ford Zodiac/I shot

This was the hidden soundtrack of 1977. During Punk, David Bowie had disengaged himself from both England and America, relocating to Berlin. Influenced by Kraftwerk and Neu, he produced four LPs in one year: his own *Low* and *Heroes* as well as Iggy Pop's *The Idiot* and *Lust For Life*. When Iggy played his first concert in Britain since the King's Cross débâcle of 1972, at Aylesbury in March 1977, Bowie was there, an anonymous but obtrusive figure at the keyboards. The concert was a stand-off: the gobbing audience had come to see blood and psychosis, while Iggy, temporarily, was into health and self-discipline. His new material was a more distanced exploration of his founding nihilism couched, not in the slashing, ubiquitous rhythms of Punk, but the repetitive, measured groove and deceptive simplicity of motorik. From *Death Trip* to *Lust for Life* had taken only five years, but it was a long journey.

Just when Punk, having reached burn-out, was shifting into the death trip that would claim many, Iggy's hard-won, if sardonic, optimism had a big emotional impact. These two records, his most successful in this country, broadcast a musical language that Punk had silenced. Iggy spoke of a new urban psychogeography: 'I am the passenger/I stay under glass', he sang, 'I see the bright and hollow sky/Over the city's ripped backside'.

This new, oblique language was founded on disengagement and/or acceptance. It had been Punk's project to dissolve the boundaries between art and everyday life: Lewisham marked its failure. Once the failure had sunk in, some turned to 'everyday life', to work out Punk's politics and sociology, while others turned to 'art', to work out its emotional and perceptual implications. If the latter was what you wanted, then Brian Eno was the model.

A founder member of Roxy Music, Eno had shuffled some of the same vanguard art cards as Punk, but they had turned up in a very different order. If Punk was in the world, then he was, determinedly, apart from it: 'In the insulated setting in which works of art are conceived and perceived,' writes Rick Poynor in *More Blank Than Frank*, 'artists and their audiences can experiment with ideas, attitudes and behaviour that might, in real life, have disastrous consequences.' Eno's public persona was austere, intellectual, remote.

By 1976, Eno was making synthetic, entropic instrumental music. It was this approach that David Bowie used for *Low* and *Heroes*. Recorded in a decaying ballroom right by the Berlin Wall, both albums consisted of two contrasting sides: the first would contain skewed but conventional songs, the second synthetic, instrumental moods. The songs on *Low* were abrupt, almost autistic, but the instrumentals were depersonalized, utterly remote. Only on the title song of 'Heroes', his own Berlin Wall song, did Bowie inject some overt humanity into the mix.

Framing 1977, both records had a huge impact. For every person who saw the necessity of getting *into* the world, of becoming politically active and thus translating the original commitment of Punk into a fierce, organized protest campaign, there was another who wanted to get *out* of the world: to disengage, to sort out the turmoil within their own heads, whether in a more protected musical environment, or in inner space itself. Both approaches were now utterly separate.

'I was rigorously apolitical,' says Howard Devoto, whose new group, Magazine, were the sensation of the autumn. One of their first, and strongest, songs was 'Shot by Both Sides', where, over a stinging riff, Devoto delivered a classic restatement of the outsider position that had been such an important part of early Punk and which was now lost in the necessity of taking sides. 'That's where the title came from, a socialist friend saying "You're going to get shot by both sides".'

Magazine made their début at the end of October with a brief, unannounced set on the last night of the Electric Circus. Such was Devoto's reputation that within days, they were signed to Virgin Records. Magazine (the name had been chosen because Devoto liked the double meaning contained in the word – guns and media) were definitely post-Punk: extravagant, musicianly. The tempi were slower than Punk and, to compensate for his nervousness, Devoto assumed a glacial stage demeanour and a measured, often forced, vocal style. He resembled Eno even in his cropped, receding hair.

This split between art and social realism worked both ways. 'Orthodoxy had arrived,' says Bruce Gilbert of Wire, a patient man, whose first LP, *Pink Flag*, showed the influence of Eno in its offhand, opaque brevity. 'The openness had gone. It was a matter of getting the outfits right, and the photographs. The political pose had become formalized, and with it, perception. After we had been described as "Grey and mesmerizing", people's imaginations just closed up. We were used as an example of what was coming up: Industrial, Ice Warriors, New Psychedelia.'

The new mood was remote, yet as confrontatory and chilling as anything in Punk – now seen as the new Establishment.

'Throbbing Gristle's studio was in a factory next to London Fields in Hackney,' says Genesis P-Orridge, 'which is where a lot of the plague victims were buried. Through the concrete walls of the basement were thousands of dead bodies, so we nicknamed it Death Factory. But we always saw the Death Factory as a metaphor for industrial society as well. When we'd finished producing the tapes, I went outside at Martello Street as a train passed on the railway line, and there was a transistor radio blaring round the corner, and a sawmill cutting up wood, and a dog barking, and I just said, "We haven't invented anything. We've just put down what's here all the time." That was when I suggested we should do muzak for factories, using the actual noise of the factory, but making it rhythmic and acceptable in itself, instead of trying to drown it out with disgusting popular music.

'In October we decided to do an album ourselves. We borrowed the money to do it, and made 785 copies. My estimate was that it would take three years to sell, that it was far away from what was going on. It was very nihilistic, and sarcastic: I had this T-shirt which said "Rock'n'Roll is for arse-lickers". But suddenly they'd all gone. Throbbing Gristle existed. We hadn't thought of becoming part of the music business: we were a comment on culture, and hypocrisy and double values.'

26.11.77: Somewhere in all there the 'New Musick'. Think of it rather as texture. Sublimity. Nuclear nightdreams. Thought sleep. How's this? 'The absolute destruction of all the values it believed in, the total loss of its position in the world, has put the UK in a psychotic position. One sign of that is a total inability to face reality.' Oh. Now I'm blinded I can really see . . .

Late in the year, *Sounds* attempted to put these new ideas together over a two-week piece entitled 'New Musick'. This was what any music paper would do: find a bunch of disparate phenomena, note them, and lump them together with some dreamed-up name into a trend. But the spreads made some accurate connections, with articles about Electronics (Eno, Kraftwerk, Throbbing Gristle, Pere Ubu, etc.), post-Punk (Siouxsie), Dub (King Tubby, etc.) and Disco. In this scattershot approach lay the future.

As a unified movement, Punk was dead. but it had made enough connections to inform the next decade of pop. 'Although it had tailed off by the end of the year,' says Roger Armstrong, 'that was the starting point for the vast majority. When Punk had its first fling, it didn't sell a lot of records, but it got very young teenagers into it. Kids develop their tastes in a very short period. Your sense of what's happening when you're thirteen is very heightened. You're watching from outside and you're dying to get in and do it.'

So strong, they say you're acting like a star
So strong, they say not everything is wunderbar
Too long, you want money and girls urgently
Too long, too much too soon, you wait and see

You have fun and experience
Nothing he does ever makes sense
Sid is only curious
John, don't take it serious

The Slits: 'So Tough' (1977)

After its instant success, *Never Mind the Bollocks* was the only new album in a Top Five dominated by TV-advertised repackages, though the album would itself have been advertised on TV if it were not for official hostility. Virgin had prepared a £40,000 radio and TV advertising campaign which was provisionally cleared by the IBA, but the adverts were refused by the TV and Radio Associations. As a spokesman said: 'It's not the ads but the product itself we object to.'

Virgin and Glitterbest were forced to find other avenues. 'We did window displays at the Virgin stores,' says John Varnom, 'in Notting Hill Gate every single album in the store was *Never Mind the Bollocks*. It was everywhere. Then they got banned.' During the second week of November, plain-clothes police visited the London Virgin branches and Small Wonder Records: the shops were advised that they faced prosecution under the 1899 Indecent Advertisements Act. In Nottingham, under instructions from the Chief Constable, police visited all the record shops displaying the album, and seized window displays and copies of the album sleeve. When the manager of the Virgin shop, Chris Searle, replaced the display, he was arrested, on 9 November. Richard Branson had encountered this Act before, when he was prosecuted in 1970 for a leaflet produced by his Student Advisory Centre. He asked the QC who had then acted for him, John Mortimer, to act for the defence in the action due on the 24th.

After a whistlestop Sex Pistols radio tour around the northern half of England, Lydon arrived in Nottingham for the trial. As in many confrontations between past and present, the agenda of this Magistrates Court was set by a statute that was antique; the formal courtesy of its language cloaked a struggle as savage as any the Sex Pistols had encountered that year. Using Mortimer seemed like using a sledgehammer to crack a nut, but it was not just the album's title that was on trial. The prosecution had to establish that printed matter 'of an indecent nature' was exhibited to public view. This case ostensibly hinged on the word 'bollocks', but the prosecuting QC, perhaps hoping to fatten his thin case with prejudice, quickly widened the matter at hand to the poster's size, and the juxtaposition of the words 'bollocks' and 'Sex Pistols'. The lack of impartiality of the police witness was exhibited by his statement that a million people would have the album 'inflicted on them'.

Mortimer brought on some expert witnesses: Caroline Coon, who neatly sidestepped the prosecution's smears on her character, and James Kingsley, Professor of English Studies at Nottingham University, who asserted the proud history of 'bollocks' as a good, upstanding Anglo-Saxon word, used in records from the year 1000 and quoted in Eric Partridge's definitive *Dictionary of Slang*: 'I would take the title to mean "Never Mind the Nonsense here's the Sex Pistols".'

'One wonders why a word,' Mortimer stated in his summing-up, 'which has been dignified by writers from the Middle Ages in the translation of the Bible to Dylan Thomas and George Orwell, and which you may find in the dictionary, should be singled out as criminal because it is on a record sleeve by the Sex Pistols. It was because it was the Sex Pistols and not Donald Duck or Kathleen Ferrier that this prosecution was brought.'

That the case had social implications was reinforced by the bench's final statement: as the chairman said, 'Much as my colleagues and I wholeheartedly deplore the vulgar exploitation of the worst instincts of human nature . . . we must *reluctantly* find you not guilty on each of the new charges.' For many people, the Sex Pistols were an anathema, not only because of what they did, but because of the way in which they had been represented.

The true nature of the case was shown by the national press headlines the next day. Ever since the summer, it had been open season on the Sex Pistols. The *Sun*, a newspaper popular with policemen, had been hammering away at *Bollocks* since the album's release, and their front cover of 25 November contained, above the news of a Tory by-election victory at Bournemouth East, its own verdict. 'Astonishing,' it roared. 'That gives Johnny Rotten and his foul-mouthed Sex Pistols the chance to put up two fingers to the world.'

Lydon's public reply was suitably triumphant – 'Bollocks,' he repeated, very definitely – but the album's legal vindication couldn't disguise the tensions within the group, Virgin and Glitterbest. Even the case was embarrassing, as the Sex Pistols had benefitted from the very liberal consensus that they ostensibly despised. 'Virgin had an over-educated view of it all,' says Tiberi, 'the *Bollocks* case misconstrued the whole point of it. Winning the case was not the image this group wanted.'

By this stage, McLaren was barely interested in the Sex Pistols or their music but was obsessed with trying to keep the film alive. 'Christ, if people bought the records for the music, this thing would have died the death long since,' McLaren told the press that November. He alighted on a director/writer team, Jonathan Kaplan and Danny Opatoshu. Both were ex-students of Martin Scorsese and carried the recommendation of exploitation king Roger Corman.

They arrived on 5 November and immediately set to work writing an untitled treatment. 'John liked them,' says Julien Temple. 'Jonathan Kaplan had the idea of a kind of Punk Woodstock with a festival in the middle of winter on a housing estate and it was a great idea, but Malcolm didn't like it, for some reason.'

Realizing that the group weren't actors but Rock musicians, Kaplan and Opatoshu sought to write not a script, but a loose treatment that would allow the group to improvise off scripted dialogue that would be performed by professional actors. It adhered to the general theme of the Meyer movie – Sex Pistols against the music industry – and was handed in on 22 November.

McLaren disliked the pair and did not take the project seriously. Despite the fact that the Sex Pistols agreed to the treatment, Michael White was not prepared to back it and McLaren sacked Kaplan and Opatoshu – nothing had been agreed in writing. When the group heard of Kaplan's departure, they refused to work with any other director. McLaren was back to square one, and Kaplan reworked the idea into *Over the Edge*, one of the first 'brat-pack' movies.

Worst for McLaren had been that one of the pair had been over-involved with Sid Vicious. Immured with Nancy, Sid was rapidly becoming uncontrollable: in early December the pair made the front page of the *Sun* for smashing up a hotel room. Vicious felt himself in an impossible situation: he was the newest member of a group that he at once hated and thought was the best in the world, and they were so inactive that he wasn't sure whether they (or he) existed.

Glitterbest had long decided who was the problem, and had already attempted to solve it in their own idiosyncratic manner. 'It was completely mad,' says Sophie Richmond. 'The idea was to put Nancy on a plane to America with a one-way ticket. We didn't get as far as Heathrow. She was terrified of getting on a plane without drugs. It resulted in me and Nancy standing in the street arguing; I then called the office and said that I couldn't do it. Malcolm and Boogie came down, and had no more success than I did.'

'They were all wearing those light blue raincoats from the shop,' says Roadent, 'the Glitterbest uniform. When Nancy saw Malcolm and Boogie arrive she ran down the street: the three of them followed and caught her. I stayed with the cars: all the doors on both cars were wide open where everyone had run out. From twenty yards I could see these four people all screaming at each other: in those coats they looked like a little Mafia gang.'

Realizing he was defeated, McLaren lost his cool and finished by screaming at Nancy that she was messing up Sid and the group: 'Stay out of my sight!' If the intention had been to amputate Sid from his drug source, then the attempted kidnapping had the opposite effect: it pushed Sid and Nancy back closer than ever before, and planted in Sid's brain a hatred of McLaren which he would never shake. Glitterbest were treating the symptom rather than its deep-seated cause.

'Sid was the archetypal "Hope I die before I get old",' says Roadent. 'He was cruising for it. There was a lot of wit and humour in him and he just went downhill. He became sullen and bitter, and it was purely his getting involved with drugs. Malcolm had nothing to do with it. The man's got his own life. If Malcolm had been selling him the smack you could maybe say it was his fault, but Sid had always liked drugs a lot, then Nancy introduced him to smack, and he liked that. Malcolm tried to help him, a lot of times.'

McLaren's itch for chaos was bearing bitter fruit. Sid Vicious had been the most vulnerable to the bizarre Sex experiments in social engineering and, like Frankenstein's monster, was threatening to run out of control as a massive, highly public, responsibility. McLaren did care, but he hated having to be responsible: he had a genuine affection for Sid Vicious, but was rendered helpless by his own inadequacies.

In the end McLaren took a time-honoured course, and got the band playing to pretend that they still existed. With dispatch, Cowbell arranged a ten-day tour of small clubs in Holland starting 5 December. 'We had to get the band out working to keep Sid away from dealers,' says Roadent, 'so we went off to Holland. There's a lot of drugs in Holland. Everyone would take it in turns staying up all night with Sid to try and keep him away from smack.'

Sid wasn't the only problem. The group had always claimed they hated each other: now the element of truth behind the joke was coming out. 'Paul and I grew up together,' says Steve Jones, 'Sid was alright, he was a laugh. He didn't care about anything. John was the only one you used to resent. He was a bit stupid sometimes: he'd let his trip go a bit too far. He'd do it with us, the band.'

'Sid was fucking up onstage, and John was taking the thing a lot more seriously,' says Roadent. 'Steve and Paul had always taken it seriously, and they were getting everything they wanted out of it.

They were the workmen. There was a real antipathy towards Sid from John. John wanted to do what he went on to do afterwards: he felt he had this mission to change the world. I don't think he did at the beginning, it was just a laugh, but he liked the power it gave him.'

With the total collapse of the film, Glitterbest and Cowbell attempted to put together an ambitious tour to capitalize on the world-wide interest shown in the group. Holland was just the start: the group would go to America at the end of December, travelling from there to Finland, Sweden, Germany, France, Yugoslavia and Spain before returning to England in March to play, in a circus tent if necessary. There was even an idea of their going to Russia.

These plans were almost instantly thrown into chaos. The subsequent highlighting of McLaren's 'Machiavellian' qualities obscures the enormous amount of prejudice that was directed against the group by this stage. Fearful, as one promoter put it, of 'adverse publicity combined with the notorious reputation' of the Sex Pistols, most of the councils and leisure corporations which were approached to put on Sex Pistols concerts refused point-blank.

A 'Never Mind the Bans' tour was quickly put together for the group's return from Holland, in the towns which would allow the Sex Pistols to play under their own name. Jamie Reid's poster illustrated the letters of rejection, as well as details of the eight confirmed concerts and petitions being organized by fans to pressurize local councils. After the tour, the group would leave for their opening date in America at Pittsburgh, on 30 December. None of this turned out as expected.

The Dutch tour had been bad, but the opening date of the English tour was worse. The Sex Pistols were to play the gymnasium at Brunel University in Uxbridge, twelve miles outside London. It was the Sex Pistols' first London date since April: for many, it seemed as though they had perished and been brought back to life as zombies. 'When they played the whole place erupted, a lot of violence from the audience,' says Dennis Morris, 'it was directed towards the band.'

Tired from so much adversity, the Sex Pistols simply couldn't handle success. 'It was a fiasco,' says John Lydon. 'We were in that big hall, which was jam-packed, nobody really knew why anybody was there, least of all us. I was very confused by the sheer popularity of it. I thought, "This is horrible, it shouldn't be like this". I'd seen us as a small clubby band. We were way ahead of ourselves. We didn't know how to get past the first twenty rows.'

The tour proceeded in the usual chaos. Of the original eight dates, Wolverhampton, Birkenhead, Bristol and Rochdale were cancelled through illness, or police and council pressure. The few concerts that they did play, such as the Links Pavilion at Cromer on the 24th, were marked by an atmosphere that was a mixture of relief, exhaustion and seasonal celebration. The party mood continued on Christmas day, when the group played at Ivanhoes Club in Huddersfield. As well as the evening show, the Sex Pistols played – outcasts to outcasts – an afternoon party for over 500 children under fourteen: the sons and

John Lydon, Steve Jones, Sid Vicious, Paul Cook, acting in character, Holland, December 1977 (© Syndication International)

daughters of striking firemen, laid-off workers and one-parent families. It was a rare moment of solidarity from the group, and one which had a considerable impact on the local community.

'Everybody was kids that afternoon,' says Barbara Harwood, who organized the party. Away from London, Lydon was always more relaxed and able to mock himself: during the kids' performance, he dived headfirst into the cake and a food-fight ensued. Sid Vicious sang the Heartbreakers' 'Chinese Rocks' and 'Born to Lose': he was less happy about the audience. 'He just couldn't deal with them,' says Jamie Reid, 'his usual persona didn't work in front of children, who thought he was being a fool.' After the concert, John Tiberi filmed Sid and Nancy's protracted attempts at having sex.

As the year ended, the Sex Pistols were mentioned in all the end-of-year round-ups throughout Fleet Street and the music press, whose circulation they had done so much to boost. *Vogue* presented John Lydon as one of the 'Successes of the Year', while the *Investors Chronicle* put the group on the cover as 'Young Businessmen of the Year': 'They certainly got to grips with the principles of business, taking a total of £115,000 from the likes of EMI and A&M Records.'

The year 1977 had been dread: Grunwick, Mogadishu, Stammheim, Lewisham – the Jubilee already seemed like a pathetic scrap of bunting hung up amidst this list of apocalyptic locations. The Sex Pistols were a symbol of the year: Johnny Rotten's face was an archetypal image to be set against that of Margaret Thatcher, the Lewisham policeman, the burning 747, or on the cover of Dennis Browne's *Datsun*, placed next to L.R. Hubbard, Gudrun Ensslin and Elizabeth II.

On 29 December, the Sex Pistols were embroiled in another front-page controversy. On the day they were due to leave for America, the US Embassy refused to grant visas because of the group's criminal convictions. These were numerous but petty: Steve Jones had thirteen charges of theft, breaking and entering, etc; Paul Cook, theft; Sid Vicious, various assaults; and, most seriously from the American point of view, John Lydon's amphetamine conviction. Amid rumours in America of political pressure, from the White House downwards, Warner Brothers' attorney Ted Jaffe got to work. Two days later, the Sex Pistols were granted permission to enter the country by the State Department, but only on condition that Warners posted a surety of $1 million on the group's behaviour. The delay meant that they had to cancel the northern half of the tour: they would travel straight to Atlanta, in President Carter's home state of Georgia.

This would be the Sex Pistols' greatest test, to which all concerned looked forward with mixed feelings. 'Everybody knew that something horrible was coming up,' says Jamie Reid, 'Malcolm was trying to wriggle out of going, but Sophie told him he had to face up to his responsibilities.'

'John had a problem with Malcolm and with the rest of the group at that stage,' says Julien Temple, 'but when I saw him the night before he went, he still thought he was going to conquer America.'

Calendar for the Weirdos, Los Angeles, 1978 (Jon Savage archive)

30

Following are the birthdates of the Sex Pistols. Keep them on file somewhere as people are starting to ask us these strange questions.
Johnny Rotten: Jan. 31, 1956
Steve Jones: Sept. 3, 1955
Paul Cook: July 20, 1956
Sid Viscious (sic): May 19, 1957
I hope none of you [try] to figure out what signs these geezers were born under because, take it from me, they wuz all born under a bad sign.
Bob Merlis: Inter-office memo, Warner Bros Records (28 October 1977)

I the Emperor proclaim
Us the masters we rule the game
Inclination – somethin' to dream on
Deprivation – we are sons

Rip them down
Hold them up
Tell them that
I'm your gun
Pull my trigger
I am bigger than . . .

The Germs: 'Forming' (June 1977)

In early November, *Never Mind the Bollocks* was rush-released in America. The album was so popular that crowds were reported outside Aquarius Records in San Francisco. In terms of publicity and notoriety, the Sex Pistols looked set to repeat their English experience in America. The media were immediately won over: the general consensus – with a few hostile exceptions – was that America was ready for it, whatever 'it' was.

In the deluge of publicity that followed the album's domestic release, several things were made clear. The Sex Pistols were a high-profile signing for a waning company, thought to be losing its prestige acts to its deadly rival, CBS; the novelty and guts of their music constituted a possible shot in the arm for an American music industry just then flagging under the weight of reissued styles; and they were the spearhead of the new Punk style in the US, which would stand or fall by their success or failure.

Punk was such an international sensation that it would have been suprising if the media weren't primed, but how ready was the rest of the country? In the first week of 1978, America's hottest musical attraction were the Bee Gees, riding the crest of *Saturday Night Fever*: the soundtrack album was reaching the peak of its slow climb to number one, with its single 'How Deep is your Love' already at that slot in the pop charts. Disco had finally been codified in the market-place after four years of pop success.

The late 1970s now seem as far away as the 1920s. The cultural mood of the time saw sixties hedonism flowering to an extraordinary degree. You can read it in Andy Warhol's diaries. What they lived in smart New York, many aspired to: as California's Governor Jerry Brown stated, 'even a superficial reading of history indicates there has rarely been a period of such self-indulgence on such a mass scale as there is in America today.'

Disco's sensurround rhythms and gay-derived insistence on pure pleasure fitted straight into this cultural imperative. Its mass access made it a subject of scorn and envy for the Punks, who were competing for similar industry resources: in the race between Punk and Disco as to what would be the next big thing in the US, Disco was streets ahead. 'When Disco broke very big, with *Saturday Night Fever*,' says John Holmstrom, 'people said to us, "Punk is dead, Disco is what's happening now".'

Yet many of the qualities of Disco that were so derided were mirror images of those qualities that were celebrated in Punk: an annihilating insistence on sex as opposed to puritan disgust; a delight in a technology as opposed to a Luddite reliance on the standard Rock group format; acceptance of mass production as opposed to individuality. It was the difference between *1984* and *Brave New World*: between a social realist dystopia, and a nightmare all the more realistic because accomplished through seduction.

In *Saturday Night Fever*, John Travolta decides that the only way that he can transcend his boring life is to become the best dancer in the city. To achieve this individuality, however, he has to negate his own personality: the dancing steps required of a Disco champion are so formulaic that to excel he must become an automaton. This was the true blankness to which the Punks never came close. The hedonism propagated by Disco was more immediately subversive of established morality. If, through *Saturday Night Fever*, Disco succumbed to its own prophecy as its machine-like rhythms became industrialized, Rock had already arrived at that situation. Warner Brothers' 1970 success with the cross-media marketing of the chaotic Woodstock festival set the pattern which would emerge during the 1970s: 'It was the beginning of the end,' says Country Joe MacDonald, a Woodstock star, 'the music industry learned to market million upon million of records by safe hippie groups.'

The true beneficiaries of this process were not the first blazing hippies – like Country Joe and the Fish – but survivors like the Rolling Stones, Paul McCartney and Wings, the Californian school of cocaine country-rockers like the Eagles and Linda Ronstadt, or soft-poppers like Peter Frampton. The whole process was brought to its height by Fleetwood Mac, whose *Rumours* stayed at number one for thirty-one weeks in 1977 with sales of 7 million.

'The country picked up on the conservative end of the hippy thing,' says *Punk*'s John Holmstrom, 'which was typified by the culture of the early 1970s, the Allman Brothers, who eventually had links with government. I think there was some government tinkering, too. They didn't like what happened in the 1960s and they wanted to make sure it didn't get resurrected with Punk. Carter said during a jazz concert or similar on the White House lawn that he wanted to stop Punk.'

If Punk was, to any small extent, an assault on the power structure, then America would not be as easy to crack as England had been. 'It appears to me that the establishment music people don't want it to happen here,' said radio consultant Paul Drew in November 1977, 'which I find similar to what happened with Elvis in '57 and the Beatles in '64. That doesn't mean it's not going to happen, but it appears that the establishment is against it. The industry seems to be saying "Yecch".'

The most important medium in America then was radio. After the demise of the Ed Sullivan Show, there was no concentrated, nation-wide TV exposure of pop until MTV in 1981. There was almost no centralized press as in England. The main waveband was FM, the Rock format, which, originated by Tom Donahue in 1967, had done much to break the first generation of hippie groups, but just as that culture had passed into the mainstream music industry by 1977, FM radio was locked into a marketing-led, conservative format.

In signing the Sex Pistols, Warners had put themselves out on the line, and they were seeking industry support. They were not going to get it. When Bill Drake, the publisher of the country's most influential radio bulletin, was asked about New Wave, he said: 'People tell me they don't think it will amount to much.' If you spun the FM dial in any major American city during that time, it was as if the seventies had never happened. All you heard was a continuous loop of the Beatles, Cream, Fleetwood Mac, the Beatles.

This was borne out by the experience of the Ramones and Talking Heads as they played around the country to packed crowds at the end of 1977. There was then no college radio network, and despite this grassroots success, their albums were stalled in the lower reaches of the Billboard 200. 'In England, Punk's not a passing fad,' said radio consultant Lee Abrams, 'but here, it doesn't look like it will happen with the same kind of impact, because the social climate is different. It's more positive here.'

The predominant high-school experience of the day was Led Zeppelin, with a seasoning of the Rolling Stones and their clones, Aerosmith: Hard Rock that had passed its original moment of inspiration, but which still held claims to the community that is the central American pop experience. In comparison, Punk offered an individualist negation which could be marketed in England – which was what many people, secure in a community, wanted to feel – but which in a more diffusely populated country, had little attraction.

In 1976, as *Rolling Stone* noted, 'kids destroyed schools to the tune of $600 million in the US'; this indicated that there was a vast reservoir of untapped anger which could have been a fertile breeding ground for a new white pop movement. But in a vast country consisting of so many markets and with such a conservative music industry, Punk was shut out. The only way for it to develop was like R&B in the 1950s, or garage bands in the 1960s: city by city, state by state.

'In Georgia we were so far away from everything that to me the Sex Pistols were just the same as Ultravox,' says Peter Buck, now guitarist in America's most successful Post-Punk group, REM. 'For two years, from 1976 to 1978, you'd buy everything that came out. You had no idea what it was and the odds were that it would be pretty good. We came out of that era when we didn't realize that every city had groups. Punk meant to us that you didn't have to follow the rules, that you could write your own songs, and that you could make records on your own label.'

Throughout 1977, musicians throughout North America were blending similar archetypes of negation and freedom with their own regional flavour, in what was an almost hopeless defiance. The knowledge that they were shut out gave them a degree of inward-looking self-destructiveness. It also allowed them to assume strange shapes. The impetus came from two sources: first-hand experience of trail-blazing tours by the Ramones or the Damned, and the vanguard art of the day. Just as the first UK Punk groups had come out of a Bohemian, arty milieu, in much of North Ameria, Punk came out of a post-Fluxus mixture of the mail art and xerox art end of performance art. One of the leading exponents, the conceptualists General Idea, were based in Toronto while Vancouver's Image Bank enshrined the access principle with a sophisticated, cut-up media aesthetic that was laid out in their 1973 manifesto, 'Now is the time to attack the Problem of Nothing'.

In America, 'Nothing' was more omnipresent and thus more difficult to engage. Unlike in England, the media were monolithic: easily able to stifle unwanted information. Yet the media dominated the music that was, or became, associated with North American Punk, whether in New York's deadpan Talking Heads, or the perceptual packaging games of groups like the Residents, who cut up existing records into a virulent, gleeful blast against the sixties Rock culture 'which has brainwashed the youth of the world'.

The space opened up by Punk gave isolates like the Residents a new arena, but more groups formed in direct response to the Ramones, the Sex Pistols and the Damned. Punk was fixed into an international teenage archetype of obnoxiousness, confrontation and the simple celebration of the present and the future. Groups like Toronto's Diodes opened their own clubs, made their own fanzines, and blasted out snappy songs about 'Plastic Girls' and 'Death in the Suburbs'. 'We were aware of what was happening in the world and we didn't want to be left out,' says their singer, Paul Robinson, 'we wanted other countries to know that we existed.'

The hardest-core American Punk developed in Los Angeles and San Francisco. Both had dozens of groups playing increasingly confident Punk mutations, with their own styles, hierarchies and clubs like the Masque in the basement of the old Cecil de Mille building on Hollywood Boulevard. Early West-Coast forty-fives remain among the best in the Punk genre, while the magazines *Slash* (Los Angeles) and *Search and Destroy* (San Francisco) further developed the Punk aesthetic with an intelligence, obnoxiousness and passion no longer to be found in England.

'*Slash* started as a bluff,' says its editor and principal writer, French-born, self-styled 'street scum', Claude Bessy. 'We were pretending there was an LA scene when there was no scene whatsover. The magazine was it. For the first time I could say whatever came into my head; I was having a whale of a time. Then all these disaffected loonies started focusing on the mag and decided "We can be it, too". Within a few months, there was a snowball effect: suddenly there were more bands than we knew what to do with.'

One of the first Los Angeles Punk groups were the Germs, a mixed gender group of teenage sybarites fronted by the seventeen-year-old Bobby Pyn, later known as Darby Crash. Pyn took the Iggy route, assaulting the audience and cutting himself in chaotic performances. Their 'Forming' forty-five was the first from Los Angeles: like 'New Rose', it described not only its subculture but the idea that groups could learn in public. As the riff churns repeatedly at the song's end, Pyn delivers a critique of the group's performance: 'The drums are too slow, the bass is too fast, the chords are all wrong, they're making the ending too long - Aaah I quit!'

For English people dazzled by the Los Angeles sun, it is difficult to realize that this fantasy city can harbour oppression all the more cruel because it is masked by image and wealth. 'The disaffection was enormous,' says Bessy, 'there were a lot more closet art weirdos out there. They had this incredible sense of humour. They were really proud of looking like shit on the streets.' They formed groups like the Screamers or the Weirdos, who accompanied songs like 'I'm Plastic' with costumes that looked as though they were wearing all the items from a thrift store at once.

Screamers handbill, May 1978 (© Gary Panter)

'While most people were walking around in shorts,' says Bessy, 'Punks were wearing white make-up and long overcoats. People on the street would be incredibly aggressive. Stoned-out hippies would physically attack you. The media totally ignored it: the record companies and media were all hippies who had made it, and they were very hostile. That's when it got good, actually. We decided that it was our party, nobody was interested, so let's go wild. It definitely seemed like we were going to be rejects forever.'

San Francisco Punk was informed by the city's beatnik past. 'People here had been rebellious and nurtured their lifestyle of rebellion for a much longer period,' says *Search and Destroy* editor Vale, a Japanese-American who had worked for years at prime Beat bookstore 'City Lights'. 'It was more complex as a result, there weren't any role models. Most of the first Punks were dissident artists, refusing to use a canvas and oil paints, inventing their own collage posters, with much hardcore imagery. In August 1976 the Ramones played a low-rent club in North Beach called the Savoy. There were about twenty people there, of whom I was one. I was astounded: minimalist structure, a lot of anger and vituperation coming from the band, pure negative energy, but very disciplined. Then there was a totally different look that we hadn't seen before – black leather motorcycle jackets, ripped up T-shirts that were too small, saying things like, "Let God kill 'em all": unpleasant messages.

'The only other people in the audience were these interestingly dressed people who had been living in New York through this period, and they were the Nuns, who started the first Punk band in San Francisco. They were all very striking: it was easy to remember them. At the end of '76 I went to the first Nuns show. And that was all there was, for about three months. There were all these Heavy Metal bands playing the Mabuhay, Soft Rock, Glam Rock bands. Then the Damned came from England.

'I started working on *Search and Destroy* in January '77. Our approach was really minimalist, we felt that that was the new philosophy. It wasn't just going to be a documentation, it was going to be a catalyst. We felt that the music was the fun part but that it was an entire lifestyle, you don't spend your entire life playing music on a stage, so we gave book lists, we tried to encourage people to read, we listed films like the *Texas Chainsaw Massacre, Pink Flamingos*, that weren't really in the average canon of cinema then.

'It was a free-form climate in which people could meet, communicate and encourage each other. We made links with LA right away, but we felt that there was a difference between the two cities. Here you had Crime and the Nuns, these people were political. You felt that the cultural scene there in LA was more social and style. You had the Dils coming along pretty soon after, and they were expressly political – so much so that they eventually moved to San Francisco. In LA it was much younger.

'A lot of the posters borrowed graphics out of war or porno magazines. *Finger* magazine was a great inspiration to me with *Search and Destroy*. It was an incredible, reader-written magazine on newsprint, stapled: all these people sent in their photos and the kinkiest stories. The most incredible, accidental poetic language. They did a parody of Patty Hearst, with a slavey-looking girl posing as Patty with a fake Symbionese Liberation Army banner. They showed things like sex with amputees: everything that was taboo.

'I soon realized that Punk was total cultural revolt. It was a hardcore confrontation with the black side of history and culture, right-wing imagery, sexual taboos, a delving into it that had never been done before by any generation in such a thorough way. The Punks were the first to examine the Vietnam war after the 1960s, reading *Soldier of Fortune* magazine: there was a lot of Burroughs in Punk. The Nuns did a song called "Media Control", right off the bat: the hippies had no media awareness, but Punks did.'

Punk hit America as a rush of claustrophobic nihilism, in tiny clubs, but the group that would transcend that claustrophobia was Cleveland's Pere Ubu. After travelling to the 'Heart of Darkness', founder member Peter Laughner left to form his own group, in what became a vertiginous downhill slide, on methedrine and cognac. In June 1977, he died: 'They said his spleen exploded in his sleep,' says his then room-mate Adele Bertei, 'but he had made a tape of his songs, a little biography on the night before he died. I think he took a methodically planned overdose.'

'Peter's death was the end of an era for me,' wrote Lester Bangs that September, 'an era of the most intense worship of nihilism and deathtripping in all marketable forms. It may be time, in spite of all indications to the contrary from the exterior society, to begin thinking in terms of heroes again, of love instead of hate, of energy instead of violence, of strength instead of cruelty.'

'Peter was dark,' says David Thomas, 'he wanted to be dark, and it killed him. This is why the death of Peter Laughner was an influence as much as anything else, in that it soured us to the Romantic vision of things.' For Pere Ubu, Laughner's death marked a change in direction from 'the destructive illusions essential to certain popular Rock and art aesthetics' to 'a disciplined, pragmatic optimism'.

Living within a dying industrial city, the group celebrated their environment with a sense of wonder, as Thomas has explained: 'In the Flats where the coke cars line up on the railroad tracks and the gas flames come out from under the ground, it's just acres of flame coming out of the ground, and green smoke. The Clark Bridge is surrounded by blast furnaces. The sky goes green and purple. It wasn't only Cleveland as a particular location, but to get a perspective you need to be able to see these views.'

'We understood the relation of sound to vision,' he now says. 'You'd go by the steel mills and there was this very powerful electrical feeling, combined with a particular sound in the air that conjured up a whole set of visions with it. The original idea was to make sound stimulate the imagination: we always saw what we did in very visual terms. In the end, we almost transposed the guitar and bass functions. We were aware of this.'

To suit this new urbanism, Ubu translated their first garage Punk into dreamlike textures that were punctuated by unearthly synthesizer blasts. The synthesizer's primary use had previously been used mainly to mimic other instruments; Allen Ravenstine set it to harsh bursts of rhythmic oscillation or machine-like noise, blowing like the winds from the Mid-West. Like the Ramones, Ubu often let the bass – not the guitar – carry the melody, in sinuous, loping lines that would have a great influence on post-Punk groups like Joy Division.

In the first home of American Punk, New York, nihilism was given a more extreme cast by a new musical movement. 'Punk was just petering out when I arrived from Cleveland,' says Adele Bertei who was organist in the Contortions, 'people like Patti Smith had all got major deals, and they weren't playing at CBGBs any more, and in the aftermath came people like Lydia Lunch. She really intrigued me, she was so over the top.' After Lunch's Teenage Jesus and the Jerks came gender-integrated groups like Mars, DNA and the Contortions, punching out a dissonant, squalling, hostile noise.

'We were all feeling that nihilism, because culturally, musically, America was so stale,' says Bertei. 'We were screaming out, coming out of this void. As a fairly illiterate kid growing up in reform schools, Patti Smith turned me on to Rimbaud and Burroughs and Brion Gysin, it opened my world up. To me, Punk was a throwback to the kind of music on Lenny Kaye's *Nuggets* album. But we were all listening to Coltrane and Bird and old Stones, and James Brown too. Stirring it up and spitting it out again.

'We played at CBGBs and it was incredibly successful, and people started inviting us to performance spaces like Artists' Space, that Downtown scene. I played organ, and I'd never played in my life, so I played it like a percussive instrument, what I later found out was called "clusters" in jazz, five or six keys together. It was on an AceTone, a sixties organ with a screechy vibrato. We worked the sound out together: it was very much about counterpoint, and space.

'No Wave was when women started playing instruments in bands. It was liberating: we were just like the boys, finally, we could do what the fuck we wanted to do, without any sexist bullshit. There was a woman in DNA, there were two women in Mars, Conny Burke and Nancy Arlen, and Lizzy Mercier was around. We'd wear tight black jeans, Doc Martens, T-shirts and leather jackets, and very short hair. The Contortions' guitarist, Pat Place, and I used to shave our eyebrows, and we were constantly cutting at our hair, chopping it away. It was a very defiant look.'

Despite the black references, nothing sounded whiter, less funky, than this maelstrom. The No New York movement was very confrontational, taking nihilism as far as it could go – further even than the Sex Pistols or the San Francisco groups. Yet it was also doomed to wither, away from the glare of mass exposure: 'It was quite an explosion,' says Bertei, 'but no record companies would come near us. We resented that people like the Sex Pistols could get these big deals and we didn't get any interest.'

Sex Pistols, San Antonio, 8 January 1978 (© Joe Stevens)

31

Oh I believe
The end is coming
I'm standing on the edge
I'm watching two sunsets
The water is on fire
I know! I know!

They all hold their breath
As they watch the last sunset
And their dreams have finally come
At the end of the world.

The Avengers: 'End of the World' (14 January I978)

In this world of mine, nothing lasts:
It's got to . . . blow up!

The Dils: 'Blow Up' (October 1977)

The Sex Pistols arrived in New York on 3 January like the men who fell to earth. Strangers in a strange land, they were in a unique, contradictory position: although they had had no major hit, they came not as underdogs but as international celebrities backed by one of America's largest labels. As far as Warner Brothers were concerned, the Sex Pistols were Rock-stars-to-be, a position they had not yet achieved in England, where they were hamstrung by notoriety.

Now they were too high-profile to be other than a success or a spectacle, despite McLaren's attempts at sabotage. The tour had been arranged at short notice and McLaren's negotiations with Warner Brothers had been tough. His view of the American music industry had been formed by his six months with the New York Dolls when, excluded as an untried outsider, he had learned to hate Los Angeles and particularly New York, the incestuous capital of the American music and media industries. When it came to planning the Sex Pistols' first American tour, he deliberately avoided these centres as much as possible, keeping the press at bay. The Sex Pistols were to swing through the Deep South that McLaren had found so romantic in early 1975. There they would be playing to 'real people' in a situation that would ensure fresh confrontation. Both the group and the press covering the tour would be forced to see – and master if they could – the real America, not the illusory sophistication of the seabords.

This was a quixotic though inspired idea typical of McLaren, and it failed to convince either the group or Warner Brothers executives like Bob Regehr, who knew how to make Rock groups successful in the US and knew that this was not the way. McLaren made Warners agree to the schedule and extracted from them airline tickets out of America valid for whatever destination the holder required: the group had only been admitted on a two-week visa, and Warners were happy to comply.

But in turn McLaren underestimated the American record company: Warners were not EMI or Virgin, gentlemanly players in a small market, but had serious muscle in the largest, roughest and most corrupt music industry in the world. Warners had invested time and a lot of money in getting the Sex Pistols into the country and with a $1million bond hanging over their heads, the Sex Pistols were 'damn well going to behave themselves': the moment that they landed, three days ahead of McLaren, they were whisked into special care.

'Warners were very concerned about the surety,' says Tiberi. 'They took over the minute we got there. We got off the plane, did the immigration thing like normal people, and then this ferret, Noel Monk, comes along and all the luggage came through customs straightaway on a trolley. Warner Brothers had started to talk. The first night, I was saying to Rory, "This is going to fall apart, they don't understand any of it." Rory said, "Don't worry, I'll speak to them," but Malcolm fell into line.'

'To be honest, we needed an American tour manager,' says Rory Johnston. 'I didn't have much experience of touring then, and Boogie was completely out of his depth. The guy that Warners brought was a bit heavy-handed, but he was doing a difficult job. We were doing difficult things, touring the south, a lot of publicity, dealing with Sid who was completely out of control, everybody hating each other, Malcom not really stamping his authority on the band.'

'When he did arrive,' adds Tiberi, 'he had no great control over the situation. Neither did I. We were looking a bit silly. It pissed me off, because the performance suffered. Warners started pumping all the stuff we didn't need, like luxuries. They were sycophantic with the pop stars and heavy with me. The group could look after themselves, but Warners weren't going to look after the individual parts, like Sid.'

On the 5th, the Sex Pistols embarked on their journey to the end of the night with a plane ride to Atlanta. The tour had been planned by someone with no concept of America's distances: within the next nine days, the group had to travel back and forth across six states in the middle of a hard winter, accompanied not only by a circus of pressmen from America and Fleet Street, but by various local sheriffs, alerted by inflammatory lyrics and scandalous press. The surety hung like a millstone around their necks.

The first show, at Atlanta's Great SouthEast Music Hall, was held in a shopping mall. It was not a concert but a trial. *Never Mind the Bollocks* was stuck at number 108 in the Billboard charts but that was the least of the group's worries: the five-hundred-strong audience paled before a horde of journalists, TV crews and members of both the Atlanta and Memphis Vice Squads. Nobody quite knew what to expect, although most expected the worst: they got the worst, but not in the way that they were expecting.

The Sex Pistols did what they always did when they were under intense scrutiny: they stank. Steve Jones's guitar was out of tune, the rhythm section's timing was out and John Lydon's voice was hopelessly flat. There was no murder, no vomiting, no mutilation: just four pale twenty to twenty-one year-olds trying either to get on with the big beat or to confound the expectations of spectacle. 'Aren't we the worst thing you've ever seen,' John Lydon asked the audience, 'you can all stop staring at us now.'

The general verdict was that the show was a grave disappointment, but it was already irrelevant: by the time *Newsweek* and *Time* came out the Sex Pistols would have much more than one bum gig on their minds. Much more to the point, Sid Vicious completely disappeared after the show: 'He went AWOL to get a feel for America,' says Tiberi, 'Sid found these fans that were straight out of Ziggy Stardust. He just showed up again in the morning.'

Before the group's departure, Sid Vicious had built up a considerable dependency on heroin: in America, cut off from his usual supply, he was detoxing and desperate. He was uncontrollable and had to be watched twenty-four hours a day, with the added threat of Vice Squad officers waiting to pounce. Tiberi refused the job: 'Sid had his private life, and it wasn't a case of me looking after him, shaking his willy and putting it away afterwards.'

The next day, the Sex Pistols flew to Memphis: on the way, the plane was struck by lightning. Those in the party who did not take this as an apocalyptic portent – the tour was already generating its own mythology – at least regarded it as a sign that in future they would travel by bus. Soon after they arrived at the local Holiday Inn, Sid disappeared again, looking for drugs. When he was eventually found wandering stoned by the poolside, he was given the first of many beatings by the Warner Brothers security.

'The security didn't take any shit from Sid at all,' says Joe Stevens, who was covering the tour for the *NME*. 'He was nothing, even though they were paid to take care of him. If he tried to get out of his bunk, they'd push him back in. If he started stealing things, they'd beat him up, but not to the point where he couldn't work. John was in a state of misery: first time in the US, on a coach with Sid and these gun-toting hippies.'

'Sid became infantile,' says Bob Gruen. 'Those guys filled a tub, put him in the tub, washed him like a baby. If someone treats you like a baby, you regress. On the second night of the tour, he went to some girl's house with Noel Monk, he takes 500 mg of something strong, and he asks to see Noel's knife. He wants to see how deep a cut he can make, and he makes a half-inch gash in his arm. After that, the roadies wouldn't let him out of their sight.'

The atmosphere, already bad, was becoming immeasurably worse.

'That American tour was so heavy with paranoia,' says Paul Cook. 'Malcolm wasn't helping: he was saying that people were following us around and that we had to be careful. Sometimes there were policemen with guns standing at the side of the stage while we were playing, two on each side. I got the feeling someone was going to get killed at any time, it was really heavy. And there was that stupid film crew following us around. There's so many loonies just waiting to latch on to you.'

One person embodied the mood of the tour: the black-clad figure of *High Times* publisher Tom Forcade, who joined the tour unannounced and uninvited. A former Yippie, he carried a conspiratorial air with him like a shroud. 'He went along to make the film *DOA*,' says John Holmstrom. 'It all happened because Lech Kowalski came to talk about making a movie on the tour. An hour later they were in a helicopter on their way to Kennedy, making a movie. That's the way Tom was about things. Tom saw Sid Vicious get beaten up by the bodyguards the night before, so he wants to get them some bicycle chains, so the Sex Pistols can get away from their bodyguards. He wanted to infiltrate their organization: he felt they were on the same political wavelength. Tom was one of the original Yippies, him and Abbie and Jerry. He was into the MC5: *High Times* had got its name from the MC5 album. Tom figured that if this was the new youth movement, he wanted in on it: he loved the music as well.

'I joined the tour in Memphis. The FBI were supposed to be there, but I think some of them thought that Forcade was FBI. The Pistols didn't like him: they didn't figure out that he had *Punk* on the tour. Forcade had told us not to let anyone know that we were involved with him at any time. He was very paranoid. A lot of bad rumours went round about Tom, that he was CIA. But he wasn't. Tom was not a nice guy – he was very moody – although his motives were good.'

'When I arrived in Memphis,' says Joe Stevens, 'the band weren't speaking to each other. Jones and Cook were hanging out together: they'd go bowling. Rotten would have nothing to do with McLaren, nothing at all. And Sid was cold turkey in the lobby. I began rooming with McLaren: he didn't want the British press to know where the gig was, so I'd give press briefings in the lobby, whispering the information.'

On the 7th, the group and their considerable entourage made the journey from Memphis, Tennessee to San Antonio in Texas, stopping off at Austin on the way: their last free day for the next five. The next day, they arrived in San Antonio, a working-class southern town. 'It was impossible to get an interview with the Pistols,' says Holmstrom, 'but Roberta Bayley had come down with us by then, and she knew Malcolm and we had dinner together. Malcolm was just telling us his plan for the tour, which was brilliant. I was asking a lot of questions, like "Why tour the south, why not the north?" Malcolm and Tom must have had a lot in common. He spoke of creating an environment where the Sex Pistols philosophy would thrive. He knew if they came down to the south, it would be much rowdier audiences, that there might be a violent episode that would get the band some press.'

'That show in San Antonio is one of the best Rock'n'Roll shows I've ever seen in my life,' says Joe Stevens. 'It had violence, good music, fantastic. Rotten was in top form, the boys had put it out, the kids were going completely nuts. I'd never seen Sid play with the Pistols in England: he had this area of stage where he would cavort, throw things around. Rotten was used to having the cameras on him, and he could see the cameras going to Sid's area of the stage. Sid was stealing his limelight.'

The Sex Pistols were structured around the guitar and drums of Cook and Jones, so Sid Vicious's bass experiments made no difference. Throughout the trip, Cook and Jones concentrated on getting on with the job at hand. The biggest change was in the other two. Lydon had hit the brick wall: in the footage of the tour, he plays out a mesmeric pantomime of claustrophobia, in poses that twist into the hurricane that is partly of his devising. Curiously inward, many of these gestures seem to scream: 'Let me out of here!'

Sid, on the other hand, had hit the wall many times and kept on coming back for more. America is a country which responds to loud, simple forms: Vicious was the most understandable Sex Pistol. Cook and Jones had normal names and stayed out of the way. Lydon as Rotten was weird and sarcastic, alternating between withdrawal and a brief, flaring egotism. That left Sid Vicious, with a violent, cartoony name which he was determined to live up to. Unlike the others, he was prepared to go all the way.

'They were under rein for the first two shows,' says John Holmstrom, 'and if there were any riots they weren't at Atlanta. By the time they reached San Antonio, a lot of people dropped off the tour and they were themselves.' The venue was Randy's Rodeo, a big ballroom, which on the night, held about 2,200 rowdy Texans. The staging was minimal: just pure white light – a flare on a war-zone. As soon as the group came on stage, the audience pelted them.

'They were throwing everything they could get their hands on,' says Rory Johnston. 'Hot dogs, popcorn, beer cans. The audience was fighting among themselves, Indian guys and Mexicans fighting with the cowboys. This bottle of Jack Daniels comes flying over the column, and there's a little sheriff standing there all done up in his guns, and the bottle smacks him in the head. He staggered back and I saw him go for his guns. I thought, "Fuck, he's going to shoot somebody!" I was the first person he was going to see, I thought he 'd probably shoot me. I ran.'

This was a confrontation for which the script had long been written, whether by Roger Ebert in the film *Anarchy in the UK* or the Sex Cowboys T-shirt that Lydon wore onstage under his tartan bondage suit, and Sid completed the circle: 'You cowboys are all a bunch of fucking faggots!' The audience erupted. When a young Texan tried to express his disagreement physically, Vicious clubbed him with his bass guitar, and all hell broke loose: the lights went off and the show was stopped for several minutes.

'That was insane,' says Roberta Bayley, 'all these rednecks throwing bottles. When Sid hit the guy over the head with his bass, you definitely felt there was going to be a riot. There were very few people there who cheered for them, it was definitely macho Texans who had come down to check out what this shit is. Nobody knew what Punk was. It was totally strange. I thought the Sex Pistols were amazing, but I wasn't getting up close, even to shoot pictures, I thought, "This is too frightening."'

'It was very hostile,' says John Holmstrom, 'but if you wanted what Punk Rock was supposed to be, this was the ultimate show. The bass incident happened very early on. The audience seemed ready to kill the Sex Pistols as soon as they came out. Malcolm had mentioned this as the place he wanted, he was hoping there would be this kind of incident. They were throwing full beer cans at the Pistols. I saw Sid take a full beer can right in the mouth, he took it and dared them to throw more, and they realized they were for real. They they started throwing things for fun. Johnny got a pie in the face. After the show you couldn't see the stage for the beer cans piled on it. I've never seen such a mess, and the Pistols loved it, they came out and talked to the press for the first time. There was a great headline the next day: "Pistols Win the San Antonio Shoot-out". That's what it was like.'

There was no let-up. An overnight drive lay before the group's concert the next day at the Kingfish Ballroom in Baton Rouge,

Louisiana. Their arrival was heralded by their appearance on nationwide television in *Variety '77*, an end-of-the-year showbusiness round up. The situation was unreal: at the time of the transmission, the objects of this media hysteria were stuck in a tiny bar in the Deep South, fighting boredom, head colds, and themselves.

For Sid Vicious, San Antonio had been a legitimization of his attitude. He was the only one who had stood up to the cowboys. The spiral that would end in his death had begun. 'I was sitting with him at the soundcheck,' says Roberta Bayley. 'He said, "I wanna be like Iggy Pop and die before I'm thirty," and I said "Sid, Iggy is over thirty and he's still alive, you got the story wrong".'

'Sid fell in love with his ego and it was the end of him,' says John Lydon. 'I tried desperately to keep him away from drugs: he was on the bus at all times. The tour itself was very, very bad: not being talked to, being ignored, being stuck in my room, with nowhere to go, nothing to do, it was very, very boring.' Jones and Cook had each other and McLaren: Lydon's only friend was Vicious and the more Lydon withdrew, the more Vicious hogged the limelight. The more limelight Sid got, the more uncontrollable he became. More problematically, Lydon was busy trying to short-circuit the audience's expectations. Most Americans had got their idea of Punk from the July NBC news report which had broadcast clips of the Sex Pistols and their followers throwing loud and dramatic poses. The Sex Pistols had become victims of their own history: Lydon's response was to insult and confound the American audiences by refusing to conform to the violent image. But if he was not prepared to offer it, Sid was.

By the fourth concert, in Baton Rouge, the Sex Pistols were trapped. Even when they tried to counter the audience's habit of throwing things by asking for more 'presents', the audience threw money. During the set, Sid started having sex with a blonde who came up on stage. During the encores, Lydon and Vicious collected more than fifteen dollars: a tidy sum when their daily pay was twenty-five dollars each, but a Pyrrhic victory in the group's battle with their public.

Things had reached breaking point: the first to crack was not Vicious but the heart of the group. Jones had been uncharacteristically quiet: after the concert, he flatly refused to travel on the group bus.

'John and Sid were obviously the most striking,' says Paul Cook, 'so they got the most attention and they needed the most looking after. Steve and I could always go off and mingle. We didn't like the Vietnam Vets who were looking after them and Sid was driving everyone mad, so me and Steve started flying. Otherwise it was driving in the bus for ten hours at a time.'

'I travelled on the bus from Baton Rouge up to Dallas,' says Sophie Richmond, who had just arrived from England, 'after that I didn't take the bus. It was too male, god! Sid and John, all the Warner Brothers guys. But that journey was the nicest bit of the tour for me: it was snowing, driving across America, great articulated lorries overturned by the side of the road, stopping to buy souvenirs, little keyrings with guns. Sid was ill, and John was pissed off with Sid, Malcolm, the band and everything.'

At the Dallas soundcheck, Lydon attempted to get the group to rehearse a new song. 'We had major rows because I was writing differently,' says Lydon. 'I wrote "Religion" during the tour and Malcolm said, "Ooh no, that's bad for the image, can't do things like that." I wanted to get them away from three-chord Rock'n'Roll into something more spicy. But they wanted to do what Malcolm wanted them to do. He would give this, "Waay, we're all mates and he's the odd one." '

Sid Vicious and Glenn Allison, Atlanta, 6 January 1978 (© Bob Gruen)

Vicious's behaviour was becoming so extreme that, like a living poltergeist, he attracted disturbance wherever he went. 'One night, we stopped at 3 a.m.,' says Gruen, 'the guards were all sleeping, and I said "Come on, let's get a burger." Some cowboy is sitting there with his wife and they start talking with Sid, who sits at their table with his steak and scrambled eggs. The guy says, "Sid Vicious? If you're so tough, can you do this?" He sticks his cigarette out in the palm of his hand, flicks the ashes around.

'Sid is eating, and he says, "Yeah". He cuts his hand as he's eating, and the blood drips onto the plate with the steak and he keeps eating. The guy grabs his wife and kid and goes screaming out of the restaurant about how weird Sid was. I thought, well, you started it, man. But it was a lesson to me that even in the least likely circumstances, something odd would happen to these guys. Nobody stubbed cigarettes in their hands in front of *me*.

'Joe Stevens told me a funny thing later. Sid really liked my engineer boots from New York, and while I was sleeping, Sid took a big hunting knife and held it to my throat and said to Johnny and Joe, "If I kill him, I could have his boots." Johnny didn't say anything, he just watched him to see what he would do. Sid changed his mind, apparently: he didn't kill me. When I woke up, he was wearing the boots.'

At the Dallas Longhorn Ballroom, (a former topless bar once owned by Lee Harvey Oswald's killer, Jack Ruby) Sid went out on stage with a magic-marker message scrawled over the scars on his naked chest. Like a gladiator, he was now stripped to the bare, fighting essentials. The message read, such was his desperation and need for drugs: 'GIMME A FIX'. The Sex Pistols were adept at playing around him – at Dallas, three out of Sid's four bass strings were broken – but his antics now dominated the group.

A car-load of Punks had made the journey from Los Angeles with the express intention of causing mayhem: when one of them, Helen Killer, headbutted Vicious on the nose, he refused to staunch the blood but let it flow all over his face and chest, like an Indian donning war paint. When it had dried, he broke a beer bottle and slashed his chest. 'He's not playing a lot,' says Gruen, 'The band's going, "Hey! Sid!" ' But it was no good: as the wait between each number stretched into minutes, Lydon spat: 'Look at that: a living circus.'

'The whole thing was just bizarre,' says Bayley. 'They had no protection. I don't think anyone except John was intellectually

Sid Vicious and Helen Killer, Dallas, 10 January 1978 (© Bob Gruen)

advanced enough to see it the way Malcolm saw it. I don't think Malcolm gave a shit: he was throwing them to the wind. It wasn't causing the stir that he had wanted it to. They didn't reach the media, they were still doing that 'Punk Rock comes to town' jokey article. America is a big place to try to make an impact.'

After another journey through the worst snow for several years, the group reconstituted in Tulsa for the penultimate date of the tour, at Cain's Ballroom on the 11th. Tulsa was right in the middle of the American badlands, a highly religious, 'dry' (alcohol-free) city on the southern rim of the Great Plains, the site of Larry Clark's famous 1964 photo-essay of terminal speedfreaks from which Coppola derived the setting and the mood for his 1983 teen-angst classic *The Outsiders*.

Cain's was a perfect backdrop for the Sex Pistols' nihilism: a decaying, 600-seater ballroom the walls of which were hung with sepia-tinted portraits of country archetypes Hank Williams, Tex Ritter and Bob Wills. The group went on stage at 11 p.m.: they played without any major brawls, but despite the enthusiasm of the audience, their performance paled before the general air of dread.

In America, people were sick everywhere. At Tulsa, the group were picketed by a Baptist pastor: 'There is a Johnny Rotten inside each of us and he doesn't need to be liberated, he needs to be crucified.' 'We pulled into a truck stop,' says Gruen, 'and there was a real Okie with his fifteen-year-old daughter. As we were getting back on the bus, he said, "Would you take my daughter with you? Let her see a bit of the world." He wanted her to have a shot at something famous, because he'd seen these guys on TV.'

After the concert, the group did not see each other for three days: their next date was in San Francisco. Cook and Jones flew on with most of the entourage, McLaren, Sophie, and John Tiberi, and the *Punk* contingent, while Lydon, Vicious, Gruen and Stevens stayed with the coach. Disaffected from McLaren's half of the group, Lydon and Vicious had developed what they thought was a close relationship with Monk and the other bodyguards, Glen Allison and D.W. who were the only people to show any interest in them.

'An awful lot happened on that tour, and by the end there was a difference in everyone,' says John Holmstrom. 'They'd never done a tour where they had to deal with so much. Tom wasn't helping things by making the movie. Every time they'd go to a gig, they'd find a camera crew there, so they'd chase them out, to find there were more cameras. The security wouldn't let Johnny talk to anybody, Steve and Paul didn't have much to say, and no-one was trying to keep Sid from killing himself.

'There were so many hassles, with the hotel people, within the group, between Warners and the group. There was also a rift between Warner Brothers and the bodyguards, because the bodyguards had their own agenda for what they wanted the Sex Pistols to do, which was different from what Malcolm wanted them to do. The Sex Pistols were using the bodyguards as a way to keep Malcolm away from them, and to keep other people away from them. It was a very political situation.'

By the time the McLaren troupe checked in at the MiYako Hotel in San Francisco on the 13th, they had been banned from American Airlines and the Holiday Inn chain. They arrived to the news that they had been banned from their next destination, Finland, where they were supposed to play on the 18th, at Helsinki's Worker's Hall. They had finally been refused work permits, after an argument that split the nation, on the 12th.

The arrangements for the Sex Pistols to visit Finland had been made without fuss in December. On 3 January, a very hostile editorial appeared in the *Helsingin Sanomat*, which stated that every member of the group had been charged for drugs and fighting; that they put safety-pins through their cheeks; that their most important instrument was a mechanical distorter which produced a sound like spitting; and that Finnish children's money was being demanded for the sound of crows cawing.

As in Britain, the hostile press triggered nationwide outrage: the response to the article was to turn youth organizations right across the political spectrum against the Sex Pistols. By the 5th, the Sex Pistols' work permits were in the balance. As the volume of press mounted, hostility to the group spread across all classes: the concert was cancelled. This sparked off a vigorous, nationwide debate about discrimination, but it was too late to save the tour.

The Sex Pistols were due in Stockholm on the 19th: this suddenly left a gap of five days. 'Warners had contracted to get the group out to the destination of their choice,' says Joe Stevens, 'so when McLaren has this brainwave: "Why don't we go to Rio?", Warners had to cover them. McLaren had a really bad head cold; they had to bring in an acupuncturist to treat the congestion. So I spoke to Biggs in Rio: we arranged a hotel where the group could play in the lobby.'

Mclaren's latest idea polarized the class attitudes within the group. Ronnie Biggs had played only a minor part in the infamous, £l million Great Train Robbery of August 1963, but had become a folk hero after a series of escapades. In November 1974, he had been arrested and only narrowly avoided deportation to the UK. 'He's just a regular south London guy who got involved in something and got all the publicity,' says Paul Cook, 'because he got away. He's had the light shining on him and the British love people like that.' Lydon did not.

The rest of the 13th was taken up with preparations for the concert at Winterland, an enormous, tubular twenties barn run by Bill Graham, the legendarily tough entrepreneur who, keeping his head while all around him lost theirs in 1967, now had full control of live music in San Francisco. He had hated the Velvet Underground and didn't like Malcolm McLaren: the feeling was mutual, as the pair started to argue about every aspect of the arrangements for the sold-out show. In a deliberate slap in the face to the idea of musicianship and professionalism, McLaren wanted the stage open to any group that turned up, and broadcast the invitation on radio. This was not what Graham had in mind. It was his town and, as could be expected, he got his way: the concert would open at 5.00 p.m. and would show movies and feature leading Bay Area Punk bands until the Sex Pistols came on at midnight, a time set to coincide with a live simultaneous broadcast on the local radio station, K-SAN FM.

Sid Vicious and John Lydon arrived in San Francisco early on the 14th. After a trip to a sex store, where they both bought leather garments and studded accoutrements, they went to a K-SAN interview: in comparison with the no-holds barred interview given by Cook and Jones the previous day, the pair from the coach were restrained, with Lydon in particular serious and definite. 'I don't like Rock music, I don't know why I'm in it,' he said, 'I just want to destroy everything.'

Neither checked into the MiYako with the rest of the party. As far as the bodyguards were concerned, their job was over. Sid Vicious hooked up with some local punkettes: 'Warner Brothers knew it was the last gig and they were starting to give him some leeway,' says Joe Stevens, 'they just let Sid go to Haight Ashbury with these girls, and watched over him. Sid was well out of it at the gig: it was the only one he did smack on.' Lydon meanwhile had had plenty of time to think. At the same time as he was pulling away from the group, he was being ignored.

'Sid and John turned up at the soundcheck,' says Tiberi, 'I don't think they had booked into another hotel by then. But after the gig, John did. This was the biggest gig they'd ever done and Mr Warner Brothers, Bob Regehr, turned up. He's in the hotel, talking to Malcolm about the gig, Rock'n'Roll rapport. Essentially the issue of where Rotten is is not part of anything. Nobody's paying any attention.'

Until San Francisco the tour had been a qualified success. There had been no arrests, no deaths. Although the album was slipping in the Billboard charts, expectation was still high: 'We'd originally been booked to play a five-hundred capacity place,' says Paul Cook, 'but because of all the publicity it was the Winterland with five thousand people. It was alien to us, because we'd never played in such a big place.' This was the big test, not only of the Sex Pistols but of the whole Punk movement.

'It was so weird,' says Legs McNeil, 'I was hanging out with the Ramones in LA, so I watched them come across America, as they toured I watched the kids skin their heads, in that week. The audiences changed overnight. The kids there got it off the TV, Telly Savalas saying, "And next the fabulous Sex Pistols", on some award show, every five minutes. The Ramones were great. It was "Rocket to Russia", and it looked like they were going to take off too, but then along came the Sex Pistols and ruined the Ramones too.'

'We knew Lydon would try to make fun of San Francisco,' says Vale, 'that he would spit on them metaphorically if not literally. We knew that he didn't come to praise but to destroy. You had the Winterland as setting for this psychodrama, which is this huge cavernous hall, a former ice-skating rink, the very opposite of the intimacy of Punk that we had experienced. There had only been one year of Punk in San Francisco, which was very personal: this was a totally alienated situation.

'You had the very thing which the Sex Pistols set out to critique, you had a spectacle, and I don't know if there is a way you can defeat expectations by being a band playing on a stage about ten feet above the audience, with bouncers, burly jock-like characters hired to stop people getting onto the stage. That was unheard of at the Mabuhay, anyone could go onstage any time they wanted. There was an oppressive, police-state kind of atmosphere.'

The evening opened with sets by the Nuns and the Avengers, a local band, managed by Rory Johnston, whose single 'Car Crash', a fine restatement of the 'Too Fast to Live' ethos, had just been released. Before the Sex Pistols came on, *Sex Pistols Number 1* was shown. Several hours after the show opened, the Sex Pistols came on to an atmosphere where expectation and frustration had reached fever pitch. The Sex Pistols came out on stage, saw their future, and hated it.

'In America, what fucked it up was that they treated us like Rock stars,' says Steve Jones, 'they didn't know any different. They treat anyone who comes over in the same way. At Winterland, I had a cold, Sid wasn't playing a note and he wasn't even plugged in half the time. Me and Paul just wanted to play. I kept cutting out, strings breaking left right and centre. And all these people thinking, "It's great: what's going on?" '

'You couldn't decipher anything,' says Vale. 'There was a terrible PA set up. It was inadequate. The sound people were probably third-string Bill Graham technicians who were in contempt of the musicians. To me it was someone screaming something in an English accent, which is hard, by the way, for Americans to understand. The audience was mostly hippies, with a few hundred Punks in front, standing. Everyone else was lining the walls of this huge venue.

'Everyone I knew had a feeling of let-down. They came over, but they were already passé; but there were some hardcore punks whose attitude was, "Wow, our idols are here". We'd already heard all the songs and read his interviews, and it was exactly what I thought it would be. It was a zombie performance, people who were already dead, reanimated for a while, going through their motions. They were media-saturated, they'd run out of message to deliver.'

'I just speed: that's all I need': as a root manifesto, it had served the Sex Pistols well. Their collective speed had enabled them to stay defiantly alive in the face of the media speed of death. At Winterland, where Lydon, as Greil Marcus wrote, 'hung onto the mike like a man caught in a wind tunnel', the combined gusts of expectation and media presence threatened to blow the group off the stage. Huge holes are revealed in their sound, and the air rushes out as from the lungs of a dying man. Just listening to rough recordings of the event is a dreadful experience. Cook and Jones are playing for their lives: Jones has to carry the whole weight of the group's manic drive. Vicious is not so much out of tune and rhythm as on a different planet: the reports of his flailed bass punctuate the songs like far-off explosions. It is Lydon who acts out the group's sensations: as the gusts howl round them, one can hear him lose faith in both his persona and his performance.

As the Sex Pistols run through the same songs that they had played at the 100 Club, seemingly aeons before, Lydon comes to the realization that those songs, repeated so many times, describe so accurately what he is going through RIGHT NOW that they might have been written for this very moment: 'I've had enough of this'; 'You won't find me just staying static'. He begins to slip out of role. 'I'm an abortion', he sings on 'Bodies', and then, very abruptly, in his speaking voice: 'What does that make you?'

There are two awful moments. After six songs, the Sex Pistols played the only material which could be described as remotely new – Sid Vicious's 'Belsen was a Gas' – and even that was old. As originally written for the Flowers of Romance, the song was a one-line, very sick joke. Taken up by the Sex Pistols late in 1977, it seemed to confirm the group's very worst, most naive aspects: a fetish with Nazi imagery and the holocaust that, lacking any overt morality, showed the Sex Pistols succumbing to their nihilism.

But nobody listened to what the Sex Pistols had to say, or, perhaps, nobody could. As supplemented by Lydon, the song's cheap laugh – at the Gestapo's pretence that the travellers on the trains to the camps were on their way to a holiday – is transformed. He sings the first three verses straight. 'Be a man, hah!', he sneers in the bridge, before launching into a vocal improvisation which begins as scat singing, slips into a forced, mocking laugh, and then breaks out into a full-blown shriek of terror and disgust. Lydon is trying to force himself to

[...]st Sex Pistols' group shot, backstage after the Winterland concert, 14 January 1978 (© Joe Stevens)

be sick but the vomit will not come. As the song hurtles towards its conclusion, he begins a deadly countdown: 'Be a man/Kill someone/ Kill yourself/Be a man/Be someone/Kill someone/Be a man/Kill youself!' Propelled by the percussive 'Kill's', there is a whistling as the Sex Pistols reach terminal velocity. On the very last word, the group cuts dead, so that the audience, stunned, fails for a few seconds to cheer. The rushing silence is like a black hole: within it, the group implodes.

After 'Belsen', there was no way back. In 'Anarchy in the USA', nihilism becomes affirmation: 'Don't know what I want' becomes 'I know what I want and I know how to get it.' The group go off, but the crowd demands an encore: the Sex Pistols reassemble around their standard, 'No Fun'. Lydon has made a decision, but he hasn't yet realized it. 'This is no fun,' he announces; this is not a song introduction, but a statement on his situation. As Jones pulls out an ultimate version of the Stooges' razor chords, he intones the Sex Pistols' mantra of nihilism.

After a couple of verses, Lydon's voice goes. Assuming an impossibly deep, aged voice, he tries to force himself through this physical barrier, any barrier, to blast himself right out of here – but it is no good. He suddenly stops: 'Oh bollocks, why should I carry on?' Cook and

Jones continue the riff: he *has* to carry on. For the remaining minutes, Lydon doesn't speak to the audience but to himself: 'There's no fun in being alone/This is no fun/It is no fun at all.' He sits on the stage and looks emptily at the crowd: there is no performance, there is no audience, there is no Sex Pistols.

'The Winterland show was the worst Rock'n'Roll show I've ever seen,' says Legs McNeil. 'The sound was terrible, the place was too big, nobody was having any fun on that tour, everyone was completely miserable. You can't blame the Sex Pistols for Malcolm doing his job, but they destroyed Punk. The Ramones had a mystique, and the Sex Pistols blew away that mystique. The Ramones were much smarter: that wasn't their style. They hated the Sex Pistols.

'I went backstage and watched. Sid was sitting there going, "Who's going to fuck me tonight?" I was really jealous that they were paying attention to Sid, but of course he was a Rock star. Really beautiful teenage girls . . . and Sid didn't look like he even knew how to undress them! Then there was Paul and Steve, going, "Who's got the can opener?", looking like they could have been working a gas station and been happy all their lives.

'And Annie Leibowitz there to take a picture. *Rolling Stone* does a Punk story! They got Johnny Rotten in the bathroom being an obnoxious asshole. It was so pathetic. She wanted a picture of the whole band and nobody would get up. That was real funny. The Ramones would do that for the press, then they would drop it and have a good time, but the Sex Pistols didn't seem to know who to trust. All Americans were all Americans, there was no distinction.

'You felt like asking them if they wanted to split for a beer, but the Sex Pistols never dropped the pose. I didn't wanna be around them, that's all I knew. The only funny guy was Malcolm. I told him he should go try and get Nixon reelected. He said, "Who are you?" They were so obnoxious, so British. It seemed like they were into class, and Punk wasn't about the class system, they were being totally arrogant without humour.'

'We could only get one person backstage,' says John Holmstrom, 'I sent Legs and I'm sorry, because he just came back and said, "Ah, it sucks back there." Nobody was kissing his butt. The Sex Pistols were picking up all the girls but we ran into Malcolm right afterwards. He started talking about breaking up the group, and how this wasn't the way he pictured it. He'd lost interest, he felt they'd become just like Led Zeppelin, a group with an uncritical audience, and there was nowhere to go but down.'

'My next clear memory is getting out of Winterland,' says Tiberi, 'and that was the beginning of it. It came from John, who said: "I don't want to stay with the rest of them." Noel Monk gives me the address of the motel in San José. I'm getting mixed signals, they don't really want me to know. Malcolm wasn't letting on as though he'd noticed: Regehr was swanning the whole thing. John and Malcolm started acting up on each other.'

Sometime during that long day, Lydon had acted on his decision. The overt cause was the trip to Rio, about which he had not been consulted and with which he violently disagreed. But when he took a stand, nobody listened. 'The fact that Rotten didn't want to cooperate was more icing on the cake to McLaren,' says Stevens, 'because he was fed up. He didn't want to be a manager anymore. He should have done something to rescue the situation but he couldn't take the step. Rotten picks up a girl at the party, takes her back to San José, calls the next day. I tell him that it's 7 a.m. departure the next morning at San Francisco airport, Pan Am, for Rio. It looked like it was going to happen, because this kid wasn't having any effect on changing all these plans. Next morning, Steve, Sophie, me and Cook get into a taxi to the airport. We never saw Sid, we never saw Rotten, but we saw the flight take off. We drove back and we knew something deadly was going to happen.'

'The problem was that we were due to tour Sweden straight after,' says Paul Cook, 'and nobody fancied it. It was just getting too much: we didn't know how much longer we could carry on like that. We should have just cancelled it, rested up for a few months. There was no way that was going to happen. Then Sid O.D.'d: some girl turned up crying her eyes out, and me and Steve rushed over there. There was no way we could have toured with him in that state.'

'It was on the corner of Haight and Ashbury,' says Tiberi, 'it was a squat, a shooting gallery, and he was going blue on a mattress on the floor. I picked him up and walked him around and he was very lifeless. We drove him up to an alternative doctor in Marin County, who gave him acupuncture. This was in the morning: when I got back to the hotel, Rotten had arrived. When I went back to the doctor to pick Sid up, he looked like he'd never been in the Sex Pistols. Suddenly the whole weight of the thing had hit him.'

While Vicious collapsed on the corner of Haight and Ashbury, John Lydon was preparing his move. The night before, on the 15th,

Johnston and Tiberi had made the trip to San José to persuade him to go to Rio: Noel Monk refused to let them speak to Lydon, who now claims he was never asked. At five that morning, Sid called Lydon: although 'incoherent', his message was plain enough: he was disgusted with the group, and most particularly with his old friend.

'It got out of control,' says Rory Johnston. 'Malcolm let Rotten get so alienated for that critical moment. He didn't have to do that. Although Rotten might have hated his guts, he would have come round. He just felt abandoned, and Malcolm set it up for Jones and Cook to tell Rotten he was fired. Even if Sid was incapable of carrying on, Rotten and Cook and Jones should have kept it going. But all Malcolm was interested in was the film and Brazil, and Ronnie Biggs, the next buzz, which wasn't a very feasible proposition. It was going to be a novelty at best.'

Everybody's options were narrowing: the only thing that Lydon could do was to persuade Cook and Jones to side with him against McLaren. 'This is the emergence of Johnny Rotten as a man,' says Stevens, 'he is about to be barred from the group. He's years away from getting his own cheque book, but he could still do things on his own. This is the first time I'd seen him take charge in a foreign country. He shows up at the MiYako. McLaren is still crashed out upstairs: he'd lost all his energy.'

Unable to contact anybody, Lydon booked himself a room, before finally confronting Steve and Paul. 'John wanted to carry on,' says Steve Jones, 'he was saying, "Let's get rid of McLaren." I was sick of the band. I was saying, "I'm gonna piss off with McLaren: I'm going to Brazil to do something with Biggsy." Just to get away. My mind was made up, and Paul just followed. After the tour, we weren't talking to one another, there was a lot of needling going on between the band. It was horrible. It used to be a laugh.'

'The three of them have a talk,' says Stevens. 'Steve was saying: "That was a stupid thing, John; you should have come to Rio. There was a good move. A really good move. McLaren was topping us all." Cook agreed. I managed to get them upstairs to McLaren's room and that was the break up. They all scattered around: we ordered some beers and they could sense that McLaren wanted nothing to do with the band, and so Steve said, "I'm fucking pissing off."

'John just said to Malcolm: "You're always stitching me up, you've been stitching me up ever since you met me, stitched me up with people beating me up, telling lies about me to the press and now you want me to sit on a plane with Sid Vicious for hours. You're not talking to some idiot who coshed somebody on the train." McLaren said: "You're turning into Rod Stewart, we don't need you, go downstairs, find some cocaine." That was pretty much it. Bitter.'

'Malcolm couldn't control me,' says John Lydon, 'and that really upset him. All the time during the tour, he was plotting and scheming. I wasn't talking to Steve and Paul, they weren't talking to me. I was just as bad as them, don't get me wrong. I have my faults too: my faults are really quite intense. But I meant it at the end of the Winterland Show – "Ever get the feeling you've been cheated?" – because I felt cheated. I knew it couldn't go on. There just didn't seem to be any way of connecting it all, ever more.'

After these brief but final conversations, the Sex Pistols went their separate ways on the sunny morning of 17 January. Cook, Jones and McLaren drove off to Los Angeles before going to Rio. It was arranged that John Lydon should fly to New York with Joe Stevens, while, after collecting a fragile Sid from Marin County, Sophie Richmond took him to Los Angeles. Unable to contact McLaren, she spent a dreadful night watching Sid's every move, before Tiberi arrived the next day to take over.

'Rotten had just lost the best job he'd ever had,' says Joe Stevens, 'he was still a young lad; he'd never been to New York, and they didn't leave him with any money. Forcade rings up as soon as he gets to New York and says, "I can take care of that right away." All he has to do is to sign a release for the movie. Rotten has thirty dollars in his pocket. Forcade was offering him fifteen thousand dollars for signing the document: "No fucking way," John said, "I'll need that money at another point." He was so smart.

'He felt fucking awful. I said: "John, you're a Warner Brothers recording artist. Call Warners and then they could send some idiot down with some money. You could pay me back the fifty dollars you owe me and then we could go out and get comatosed." He said sure. We called Warners and we got stonewalled. They didn't want to have anything to do with Rotten at all then. They didn't know which one they wanted. They couldn't figure out which little dirtbag it was.'

On the day that he arrived in New York, the 18th, Lydon was the first to announce the group's break-up in an interview with the New York Post: 'I am sick of working with the Sex Pistols.' By the time the piece appeared the next day, another Sex Pistol was sick, of life itself.

'We went to a doctor who prescribed methadone pills, then we got on a plane for New York,' says Tiberi, 'a red-eye, probably, and Sid flaked out. He must have had something else, he just didn't wake up. We were in first class, too.'

Three days after his last overdose, Vicious now slipped into a drug-induced coma. His condition was so poor that on arrival in New York, he was immediately rushed to the Jamaica hospital, right next to the airport, where he was kept under observation. During the next two days, a raging blizzard prevented almost any motion in or out of New York. Of all the Sex Pistols, blown to the quarters of the world, he was the most completely alone.

'They really made a mess of things,' says Roberta Bayley. 'Breaking up was such a good idea, even if they didn't do it for all the reasons we could have wished they did it, but it was the best thing they could have done. It would have gotten awful if they had carried on. They broke up at a good point. Even the Beatles, it was the same thing. Sometimes with a group no matter how much you like them, the best thing they can do is break up.'

'If something happens in New York nobody pays any attention to it in America,' says Holmstrom. 'America hates New York. That's why it had to happen in London. America loves England, at least it did. The same way Jimi Hendrix had to go over to England before he could make it in America. When the Sex Pistols came over and did the tour and broke up, that was the official end of Punk Rock, because they were the only Punk Rock group in the world, according to America's perception.'

Transcript of phone call between Sid Vicious, in Jamaica Hospital and Roberta Bayley, in Manhattan (20 January 1978)

– *Sid? This is Roberta. Remember me from the tour? I'm the photographer, whose thumb you kicked in, whose thumb you broke?*
– I broke your thumb?
– *Nearly, you just broke the nail. How are you?*
– Did I do that? Oh yeah, I remember. Are you going to come visit me in hospital?
– *Yeah I would do, but it's snowing.*
– Oh . . .
– *I don't have a car and you can't go on the trains 'cos the winds are too high.*
– I'm lonely.

– *I'm gonna come tomorrow. You think you'll still be in tomorrow?*
– I'm supposed to be going back to London tomorrow.
– *Yeah, but the airports might still be closed.*
– Oh well then, in that case I'm getting out of here tomorrow, and I'm going to some girl's place that I know. I don't know, I've . . .
– *How are you feeling?*
– Weak.
– *Nobody's been up to see you or anything?*
– No.
– *Well, it's so miserable outside, I guess you can see it on television.*
– Yeah, I'm just sitting here on my own.
– *Oh fuck. I mean it's really far away where you are, you know I'd come right over there, I've got some great pictures to show you. How long you been in there, just last night?*
– Um, yeah.
– *What happened to everybody else? Who was on the plane with you?*
– Boogie. Are you a photographer?
– *Yeah.*
– Not a reporter?
– *No, I'm a photographer.*
– What happened was, I done 80 mg of methadone, right, and when you get about six or seven valiums, when you get high in the air, it has a much greater effect on you than it does when you're on the ground. You get pissed a lot quicker when you're in the air.
– *Yeah, you get drunk faster.*
– That's what happened.
– *So did Boogie just go back?*
– Yeah.
– *He's in London? He left you?*
– No he's still here.
– *Where is he?*
– I don't know.
– *Oh that's nice. And nobody else is in New York?*
– Oh yeah, there are people in New York but there's nobody to bother or [indistinct] whatever.
– *Fuck, that's really fucked up. I could call Bob tonight, you know Bob Gruen?*
– Oh no, forget it, I already called him.
– *What did he say?*
– He said he couldn't make it.

– *'Cos of the weather, right?*
– Yeah.
– *The highway to where the hospital is is shut off. So it's really fucked, and the trains go above, instead of going underground. So the wind's too bad.*
– What, so they just blow off?
– *I think they've probably stopped them, it's too dangerous, 'cos the wind's going to get worse tonight.*
– I wouldn't expect anybody to get on a train and come all this way just to see me anyway.
– *Oh come on, come on, do you have a TV at least?*
– Unh?
– *Do you have a TV set? A television?*
– Yeah.
– *Colour or black and white?*
– What I could do with is a decent something to read.
– *Yeah, magazines or something, right.*
– What I really want is a very, very large pile of Marvel comics.
– *Yeah, wow, I've got some great comic books.*
– So do I have, but Boogie's got them, the arsehole.
– *You don't have any way to get in touch with him or anything?*
– No, he said he'd call me later today and he hasn't bothered. He won't be bothering either. He's a cunt.
– *If people just come up there, they can just visit you, it's not a problem?*
– Yeah.
– *What happened with this group of yours anyway?*
– I left them.
– *It seems like everybody left them.*
– Well I don't think anybody really wanted to continue but no one had the guts to actually say it, so I just phoned John up and told him what I thought of him, and where I thought he was at, and erm, I mean I still think I'm pretty good, I think I was better than any of the others.
– *Well, with the attitude, yeah, but what are Steve and Paul gonna do?*
– I don't know, they'll probably try and get another band together and fail. John is completely finished.
– *That seems to be the general consensus.*
– Huh?
– *[Repeats]*
– Does it?
– *Everybody's just saying well, what can he do now?*
– Yeah, right.

– That no one can figure out anything that he can do now.
– He's finished as a a person as well, he's just not what he used to be.
– Maybe this will shake him up a little bit.
– Yeah, that's what I'm hoping, that that'll shake him up and then he'll be able to do something. That would be good if he could do that but otherwise if it doesn't shake him up and get him out of it, then as a person, not only will he not do anything but nobody will even want to know him. They'll say, 'Oh, didn't you used to be Johnny Rotten?'
– I guess everybody in England's going to be really upset about this.
– Yeah.
– How do you feel about it? Do you care?
– I'm glad that it's over 'cos it was like, I felt I was the only one putting any real energy into it. Did you see our show at Frisco?
– Yeah.
– Didn't you notice there that . . .
– It was a very weird show there.
– . . . John wasn't doing very much, was he?
– No. Steve was just sort of jumping around, I dunno the shows got worse instead of better.
– Yeah. I think the one we did at Dallas or something . . .
– San Antonio. That was the best.
– Was it? Was that the one where I got butted in the face?
– No, that was Dallas I think. I liked the one where you hit the guy with the guitar.
– Oh was that the one where I was going really nuts?
– Yeah, and John was jumping around a whole bunch and people were really throwing lots of beer cans. That was really exciting. I've got all these great pictures to show you of everything. Tons of stuff. We really should come up tomorrow, I'll fucking make Gruen come up.
– Yeah, can you do that?
– Yeah, we'll bring all kinds of stuff.
– Yeah, make him, make him come up. It'll have to be before nine o'clock though.
– In the morning?
– No.
– In the night?
– If you're coming up tonight.
– But if the planes go out tomorrow, then would you go out first thing in the morning, if they open up the airports?
– Well, I've said I would, so Sophie will have booked the ticket.

– But they may not be letting planes go up, that's the only thing.
– I hope they don't, in a way, cos I wanna stay in New York for at least one day.
– Yeah, you should. You really should, you should come into the city there's all kinds of people who want to see you and everything.
– Yeah.
– You've never been here before, you could have a good time, if you're healthy enough to do it.
– I can't drink, I can't, like the doctor said if I drank anything even remotely like the way I've been drinking for the past like however long it's been, I've got six months at the absolute outside to live.
– Oh well then don't drink. You asshole.
– It's like the drugs as well, the more I can't do anything, if I went out anywhere I'd just sit there.
– But you could just come around and, I don't know.
– If I went out anywhere I wouldn't be able to resist the temptation, that would be the trouble. I'll end up burning myself out.
– But what will you do if you go back to London? The same thing?
– Yeah, I probably will die in six months actually.
– You have to straighten out for a while.
– I can't straighten up, I just can't be straight.
– Yeah, you could, just as an experiment.
– Suppose I just didn't have to be? I haven't figured out yet quite how I'm going to do it. I haven't been straight in like four years.
– Just as an experiment you should do it and see what happens. There must be a way.
– Yeah well listen, please try and check Bobby out tonight.
– Tonight it's almost physically impossible but tomorrow for sure if you're still there.
– If the planes aren't running tomorrow I'll see you tomorrow.
– Can you phone out from there?
Yeah.
– Why don't you take down my number?
– Okay.
– So where is Malcolm? Has he gone back to England?
– Malcolm is in LA.
– He's still out there. What's he gonna do now?
– He'll take a rest for a while and then I don't know.
– Do something else?

– Yeah, I'm going back to London to get a group together with Johnny Thunders.

– Yeah, you should do, you'd be much better than Billy Rath.

– Huh?

– The other bass player, you should just kick him out.

– Yeah, right, he's just an arsehole.

– You'd be much better.

– Just think what that group would be like with me, Thunders, Nolan and Walter Lure.

– Yeah, amazing, really amazing.

– We'd be pretty good, wouldn't we? Particularly if I was healthy. That would be an incentive for me to get healthy as well.

– Well Johnny somehow manages to, he does do, I mean, I know he has a few bad habits but he somehow manages to stay pretty healthy in spite of it. I don't know how he does it.

– He never had hepatitis. I had hepatitis, and when I got out of hospital I really fucked myself up as badly as I could. I don't know why but everybody said, you can't do it, so I just went ahead and did it. It's my basic nature.

– Your basic nature is going to get you in a lot of trouble.

– My basic nature is going to kill me in six months.

– Well, you've just got to change it.

– Yeah, I will do as well.

– You can call me, later tonight, or else call me in the morning if you think you're still gonna be there. I'll call you back too.

– Yeah, okay. Thanks for calling anyway.

– Call me if you're bored, okay. We're worried about you. Take care of yourself. Bye.

– Bye.

John Lydon and Vivienne Goldman, Jamaica, February 1978 (© Kate Simon)

32

Only those movements which were able to cease, to stop by themselves before dropping dead, have existed! The autonomists, if they shut down operations, if they tip their hats saying, 'We've done our thing, we're leaving the stage, we can't do more', show that they're not Stalinists, that they aren't inscribed in history.

Paul Virilio and Sylvère Lotringer: *Pure War* (1983)

Negation is not nihilism. Nihilism is the belief in nothing and the wish to become nothing. Negation is the act that would make it self-evident to everyone that the world is not as it seems – but only when the act is so implicitly complete that it leaves open the possibility that the world may be nothing, that nihilism as well as creation may occupy the suddenly cleared terrain.

Greil Marcus: 'Artforum' (November 1983)

'When the news came through,' says Roadent, 'the crew of the PA and the lighting company had got onto the plane to fly to Stockholm, all the equipment was over there and then I was told to cancel the tour, to get what money we could back, and the crew were paged off the plane. We went down to the 100 Club and all these people were crying. We bought three bottles of blue label vodka between three of us, me and Jamie and Sue Steward, and celebrated.'

The first public report in England of the break came on 19 January with the front page of the *Sun*, just then serializing the Vermorels' *Sex Pistols* book. At the moment of its dissolution, Punk had finally attained some degree of tabloid respectability. That afternoon, Glitterbest heightened the drama: 'The management is bored with managing a successful Rock'n'Roll band. The group is bored with being a successful Rock'n'Roll band. Burning venues and destroying record companies is more creative than making it.'

'We made up this press statement which the Guardian printed,' says Roadent. 'We very quickly withdrew it on Malcolm's orders, he was worried it was libellous. Malcolm had an idea he could get it back together, but everybody over here knew that it was the end. We were humouring Malcolm, he was paying our wages and he said to keep it quiet, so we did. I don't know how he took it: he waits until he sees reactions before he lets his reactions be known.'

By the third week of January, Lydon, Vicious and McLaren were all back in England. If there were any doubts about the group's break-up, then subsequent interviews with both Lydon and Vicious quickly dispelled them with the bitterness that would be the hallmark of the year. 'I'm so glad I'm out of that group,' Sid told Chris Salewicz. 'I won't work with any of them again,' Lydon told Caroline Coon, 'and that's no great pity.'

McLaren kept busy. His immediate task was to organize a film crew before joining Cook and Jones in Rio. He was also tinkering with an idea for a film with the Slits, a treatment full of a violent, social realism and loathing for the media industries. But, despite his almost perpetual buoyancy (even if Lydon *had* left, there would always be another angle) McLaren fatally underestimated the forces ranged against him in the first few months of 1978. The most obvious warning was in Glitterbest's increased burden of litigation, arising from the Sex Pistols' chaotic business affairs and McLaren's autocratic, Debordian style. Russ Meyer had initiated proceedings for his unpaid wages, while Ray Stevenson was in dispute over Glitterbest's attempt to stop his photo book, *The Sex Pistols File*.

During 1976 and 1977, McLaren had got away with his wilder schemes because of the power of the Sex Pistols: once Lydon, who, in most people's eyes, *was* the group, had left, the enemies he had made clustered in readiness. Of these, the most immediately powerful were the record companies to whom the Sex Pistols were still contracted: Warner Brothers US and Virgin Records. If the group had split up, there were some hard decisions to be made.

Virgin would not finally commit themselves until well into 1978, but, according to John Varnom, 'There was an immediate groundswell in Virgin which was really Simon Draper's cast of thinking about who was the talent in the band. You then got the first inklings that this could be a good thing for Virgin. If they are split up, then Malcolm no longer has any power in the band, so you can ignore him, and we can get hold of Rotten.'

On 3 Feburary, Richard Branson paid for Lydon's trip to Jamaica, ostensibly to act as A&R consultant for a new spate of Virgin Reggae signings. As pressing a motive was the opportunity it gave Richard Branson, who also made the trip, to win Lydon's confidence. Surrounded by his friends Don Letts and Dennis Morris, and journalist Vivienne Goldman, Lydon spent three weeks in the sun, unashamedly smoking ganja with assorted Rastas for Kate Simon's camera.

The event was not without its inevitable element of farce. McLaren was still obsessed with the film, and arranged for John Tiberi to go to Jamaica. McLaren was still hoping for a reconciliation but if this was not to be, Tiberi was to film Lydon and confront him with the line, 'Who killed Bambi?' It was not successful. 'I had several pieces of blank paper which Malcolm had signed to make false promises to John,' says Tiberi, 'I didn't consider it worthwhile. It wouldn't have worked. John was taking the piss, very arrogant.' Reduced to skulking behind bushes, Tiberi was, at one point, thrown in the pool by Lydon's entourage.

The week that Lydon went to Jamaica, Bob Regehr came to London for a meeting with McLaren. Warner Brothers had gone out on a limb to sign the Sex Pistols and in return they now had nothing but a mess. Of the original deal, there was a shortfall of the £200,000 film advance: Regehr wanted to know what was going to become of his money. McLaren stalled, but Regehr got the impression that he was a manager who, instead of trying to patch up divisions, was only making them worse.

In the second week of February, McLaren joined Cook and Jones in Rio. During their seven-week stay, the pair recorded two songs with Ronnie Biggs, a reworking of 'Belsen was a Gas' and a new song called 'A Punk Prayer', a distinctly libertarian plea that tolerance should be extended even to archetypes of evil like Myra Hindley and Martin Bormann. And so that nobody could accuse them of being bleeding hearts, they filmed a promotional clip with American actor Jim Jetter playing Bormann, in full Nazi regalia.

In the third week of February, McLaren went from Rio to Los Angeles, where Bob Regehr was attempting to arrange a reconciliation between Lydon and McLaren. Warners had paid for John Lydon to fly out with his mother: on his arrival, Lydon flatly declared to Regehr that he had no intention of working with the Sex Pistols and asked that the company fund his as yet unformed new group. McLaren had some hope that Lydon would come round: he still wanted to use the Warners money on the Sex Pistols film. Regehr got the pair together one morning at the Continental Hyatt House Hotel, but the result was a disaster. Lydon wanted nothing to do with McLaren: when asked at least to give his cooperation for the film, he imposed content stipulations which McLaren rejected. The meeting ended in some hostility.

McLaren had completely underestimated the depth of Lydon's rage, which had finally been brought to boiling point by Tiberi's presence in Jamaica. If the June 1977 beatings had already scarred Lydon, then the events of early 1978 implanted in him a bitterness that still marks him: he still cannot speak of McLaren without vitriol. It's as though he felt that his soul was stolen: to make the point, he arranged a symbolic death. From now on he was known not as Johnny Rotten, but as John Lydon.

As late as the beginning of March, McLaren was still writing to Warners that 'his first priority was to keep the four Sex Pistols together as a recording and performing group'. But after that last encounter in Los Angeles, the parties were irrevocably split: if Lydon thought that McLaren had stolen his soul, then McLaren – in the true schismatic style – began to vilify Lydon as an 'enemy within', a traitor who had gone over to the hated music industry, a *collaborator*.

Lydon had only one recourse, and he hired the best. 'Everything was withheld from me, all monies, everything,' he says. 'I was literally stranded. That was the situation and the only way around it was the courts. Initially Malcolm threatened court action against me, then he claimed that the name "Rotten" was his property, and that was an impossible situation. Enter Brian Carr.'

Now a music industry lawyer renowned for his aggressive negotiating, Carr still remembers his first meeting with 'this Punk dressed in a top hat, a morning coat, and second-hand clothes and orange hair'. On 29 March, just as Cook and Jones were returning from Rio, Lydon sent a solicitor's letter to Glitterbest asking them to furnish him Sex Pistols accounts, as contracted, for the two quarters up to 30 September 1977 – the opening salvo in what would be an eight-year battle.

> We demanded more. We did not quite know how to say what that more was; but many of my friends and I did not find any solution in the merely negative, in the *rage at having been deceived* and in the denial of all previous values. And so we were driven more and more to the Left.
>
> **George Grosz: *A Little Yes and A Big No* (1946)**

> All over people changing their votes
> Along with their overcoats
> If Adolf Hitler flew in today
> They'd send in a limousine anyway
>
> **The Clash: 'White Man in Hammersmith Palais' (June 1978)**

'Everything happened in what, two years,' says Paul Cook. For that period, the Sex Pistols had pulled the whole of popular culture into their nihilistic slipstream and their demise only reemphasized their power. With their death, so died Punk as far as many people were concerned. 'Everyone around that scene was slowly falling apart,' says Debbie Wilson, 'once you've been involved in a close-knit thing and suddenly you're pushed off, there's a terrible aftermath.'

For anybody who had lived through 1977's hyperintensity, 1978 was unremittingly grim. If 1976 had been a year of amphetamine rush and 1977 the year of the full-blown sensation, then 1978 was the year of the classic comedown and its attendant psychoses of paranoia, extreme hostility and aggression. The bitter invective that was breaking out between Lydon and McLaren paralleled the mood within Punk, particularly in London, throughout 1978.

The Sex Pistols' split might have been a totally logical conclusion to the group's whole career, the ultimate act of denial in keeping with their ethos, but it also left business unfinished. With their performances and records, the group threw down a gauntlet, not only in the confrontation with power, but in the statement of several, uncomfortable, existential truths that very few people could follow through.

The Sex Pistols had said 'No' so forcefully that the world had been forced to listen. For those who chose to see things that way, they initiated an intense process of questioning everything in their lives, a process which still continues. They left the creation that was to follow destruction unstated and unresolved: as very few people had the courage to see nihilism through, this negation curdled into the nullities of dogma, cynicism or self-destruction. Despite the Clash's efforts, the Sex Pistols had remained the undoubted figureheads of Punk: nobody had come up to the challenge of their preeminence. Their demise merely made official what many people already thought: that the heady days of 1976 and 1977 were over. The Sex Pistols had imploded with a great deal of negative force: within pop itself, the most immediate effect was to disperse the detail that had been encoded into the Sex Pistols like spores on the wind.

McLaren and Westwood had researched the history of postwar youth subcultures in their various shops at 430 King's Road, but for the Sex Pistols they had thrown up all these styles – Ted, Mod, Zoot, Rocker, Skinhead – into the air and collaged them together with rips, safety-pins and sexual provocations. As these styles began to unravel within popular culture, pop's linear time was shattered forever: there would be no more unified 'movements', but tribes, as pop time became forever multiple, Postmodern.

There were symbols clashing everywhere. As noted in Dick Hebdige's *Subculture*, pop now had a past and a set of semiotic codes, which early in 1978, translated into the frantic plunder of the past which continued throughout the next decade. In February, the *NME* printed a page full of new groups, dressed in the styles of 1958 (Whirlwind: Ted), 1963 (Pleasers: Beatles), 1965 (Jam: Mod), 1970 (Skrewdriver: Skinhead), 1973 (Adam: Glam) and 2008 (Devo: SF futurism). Explaining and interpreting the codes each week was the music press, now set in the febrile motion which has still not deserted it: forever searching for 'this week's big thing'. Punk had been very good for the three weeklies because its complexities had needed interpretation for a wider audience. Although the burning need for explanation had subsided, the complexities remained: as you read about apparent polar opposites Tom Robinson and Devo, you realized that every group now came with a ready-made manifesto.

The music press took on the internal bickering that beset what remained of the Sex Pistols and Punk, just like a bad marriage. In February, for instance, there was a new style about which to hyperventilate: sparked by the success of the Jam, 'Power Pop' hoped to feature the return of beat groups, like the Pleasers or Glen Matlock's Rich Kids. Within a week it had been denounced, as was Blondie, then having a Top-Two hit with their cover of Randy and the Rainbows' 1963 'Denis'.

Punk was now tearing itself apart. The year 1978 was marked by a high level of violence, directed both internally and externally. Theatrical violence became actual violence as Punk finally went countrywide and reached those 'kids' that had been the object of its rhetoric. 'It was a once-a-week thing,' says Graham Lewis, 'they all got dressed up and expected to have a riot inside. Outside, they expected to get beaten up because they were Punks. Wire had a real riot at the Newcastle Guildhall. The stage was two steps up from the audience. Skinheads in Newcastle then weren't sixteen year olds, they were guys in their late twenties, working in the shipyards, wearing steel-toecap boots, and they were serious about their violence. This psychopath got up while the second group were on, and placed the drummer's teeth down his throat. We played, there was an encore, we came back: it was one of those frozen moments.

'This bloke walked through the crowd, chose someone, indiscriminately, hit him, and the whole place went up, a hundred and fifty people just beating shit out of each other. We stopped: there was nothing to play to anymore.'

There was a delightful bloke at the front with a coat hanger wrapped very tightly around his head,' says Bruce Gilbert, 'next to the two blokes with LP covers with eye holes cut out, looking like the Ku Klux Klan. Extremism, mutilation.'

Newcastle was a specific location for violence, but one group became notorious for carrying it around with them where ever they went. 'Skinheads are back!' Jimmy Pursey had yelled in November, and he reaped his reward as the goonsquad often associated with that subculture wreaked havoc at several Sham concerts, most notably at the London School of Economics on 4 February, where they chanted 'Sieg Heil', posted Nazi stickers and did £7,500 worth of damage. Fascism was breaking out all over.

'The National Front got big in Liverpool at one point,' says Jayne

Casey. 'Early in 1978 the Swinging Apple opened: it was a Punk club that was quite NF, and that crowd hated Erics. Roger Eagle wouldn't allow any of that element into Erics – he was and still is a great expert on black music – and there was a big split between the right-wing kids who wore swastikas and the Erics kids, who listened to dub. Those right-wing kids were just carrying on the politics of their parents, but it got very violent.'

Punk had wanted to break down the boundaries between art and life, to live in the present and the future, as opposed to the idealized past, but in 1978, it hit the brick wall of England's decline. The present was grim and the future suddenly looked worse. Punk had been the product of the gaps that had been opened up in the social sphere, whether in inner city collapse or the political stasis of the Callaghan Government. But this stasis was finally breaking up.

Callaghan had somehow staggered through 1977, but at the cost of the Government's credibility. Under Mrs Thatcher, the Conservatives had captured the imagination of many voters with an individualistic, tough rhetoric that, to some degree, was the mirror image of the libertarian, anarchist ideas thrown up by Punk. In collaboration with the National Association for Freedom, Mrs Thatcher had redefined the word 'freedom' for the New Right. As delineated in the influential 1977 document called 'Stepping Stones', this involved the dismantling of working-class power structures to facilitate free enterprise.

Punks and Mrs Thatcher were the symbiotic opposites of the time. Punk seemed uncannily predictive, its apocalypse restated by politicians and activists on the hard Right and on the hard Left, as its warnings of 'No Future' came true. By the summer of 1977, unemployment was up to 1.6 million, 6 per cent of the workforce: the public service cuts demanded by the IMF began to bite, and the polarizations of the time found their expression in street violence.

The new politics was of division. On 30 January, Mrs Thatcher gave an interview on Granada Television, where she made 'impromptu' remarks on the subject of race. 'People are really rather afraid that this country might be rather swamped by people with a different culture.' Within the context of the time, this was saying the unsayable, but suddenly to say the unsayable was possible, even desirable. In its pandering to prejudice, this speech struck a chord in a nation no longer tolerant, scared and seeking a scapegoat. As Philip Whitehead writes, 'it cut deep into the working-class vote', and that also meant the Labour vote. Racism was now not simply the preserve of extremists, but at the heart of England's political agenda.

25.3.78: It is maintained by this writer that everyone involved with Rock'n'Roll as a mass medium has an enormous responsibility in our unstable and worsening political situation – with various forms of totalitarianism threatening – and that this responsibility is not always, is in fact rarely realized or undertaken.

Punk had been almost too successful in disinterring some of the culture's demons which were best left undisturbed. During the previous two years, it had used many symbols of totalitarianism – specifically, the swastika – within a context that at first was mainly aesthetic and theatrical. It is impossible to get irony as a concept through to the mass market and, with Punk's successful entry into the social domain, it became obvious that there was some facing up to do. Punk's libertarian politics had been deliberately vague, and its anarchist flourishes were all too easily being coopted into a different kind of individualism. There had long been hostility between anarchists, believing in 'the flux of never-ending change', and the more rigid, schematic approach of Hegelians and Marxists, contradictions which had been contained within the SI and Punk but which were now, under intense pressure, exposed.

Like all millenarian movements, full realization for anarchists was always out of reach: in Herbert Read's phrase, 'a point on the receding horizon'. Very few Punks had the rigour or the courage fully to investigate the ideas contained in their subculture, as one of the few groups to take up the gauntlet thrown down by 'God Save the Queen' and 'Anarchy in the UK' explain: 'Our anathema was no future,' says Penny Rimbaud of Crass, 'we said, "We're not going to have all these young kids thinking that there isn't. We'll go out and show that there is a future".'

'Germany got Baader-Meinhof,' stated Crass on a 1978 poster: 'England got Punk, but they can't kill it.' Just at the moment when Punk was dying, Crass gave it new life by making the first, and only, concerted attempt to work through the nihilist archetypes of the time. From the spring of 1978 on, they issued a series of rants, broadsheets, slogans in a bewildering array of media – music, graffiti, logos, magazines, books, posters, films – whose effect was to lay one of the foundations for the resurgence of British anarchism.

But for the SWP and RAR, 'Coming sometime maybe' was just not good enough. As far as the Left were concerned, the day of reckoning was now: there was the immediate threat of fascism and further, the possibility of assuming power in England's collapsing consensus. To the horror of serious Punk ideologues like Jamie Reid, the SWP made their move to claim Punk for the Left: 'The socialist movement will inspire it,' a member stated that winter, 'direct it. Give it muscle. Only we socialists have an alternative!'

Early 1978 was the time of RAR, not only because some public show of solidarity seemed necessary to dissociate Punk and its culture from any taint of racism, but also because its amphetamined politics filled the black hole left by the Sex Pistols' demise. Since Lewisham, both organizations had grown considerably, with several well-publicized demonstrations, adaptations of Punk catchphrases – 'Nazis are No Fun' – and high-profile concerts.

On 24 February, RAR held a concert at the Central London Polytechnic, which featured Sham 69 – the group then most associated with the National Front – with Southall Rastas Misty. Despite being well attended by members of both sides, the concert passed without any major trouble. Emboldened, both the ANL and RAR decided to hold a joint demonstration, set for 30 April, which would begin with an assembly in Trafalgar Square and march to Victoria Park in Hackney.

This carnival caught the mood of the moment. Following the *NME*'s lead the previous year, the music papers were now carrying regular features about RAR and ANL. In March, for instance, *Sounds* ran an eight-page feature which delineated the recent history of institutionalized racism and gave pop stars' opinions on the National Front. Caroline Coon went into the bearpit and interviewed Martin Webster, then National Activities Organizer for the National Front.

On the 30th, 100,000 people gathered in Victoria Park to hear sets by the biggest names of the day: X-Ray Spex, Tom Robinson, Steel Pulse and the Clash. Although the music was indifferent, the event was a spectacular success. It was barely reported in the next day's papers, but, nevertheless, it gave the unequivocal message that, should National-Front activists attempt to capitalize on the mood mobilized by Mrs Thatcher, they would be opposed by a hefty segment of the day's youth.

'Rock Against Racism were very good at politicizing the people who came along to the gigs,' says Lucy Toothpaste. 'There would always be leaflets, and our magazine, *Temporary Hoarding*, which took up issues

Tom Robinson in Trafalgar Square, 30 April 1978 (© Barry Plummer)

to do with racism, fascism and sexism. Many people who came along didn't have any political persuasion, but they responded to the statements made by musicians, that it was necessary to challenge people who were putting forward racist ideas.'

The carnival eradicated for ever the miasma of fascism that still hung over Punk. It also expressed a burning need for affirmation in a culture by now embittered. The success of Victoria Park was followed by two more well-attended carnivals that summer – one in Manchester in July, headlined by Buzzcocks, the other in Brockwell Park, near Brixton, headlined by Sham 69 and Elvis Costello – which were supported by scores of club concerts around the country.

Just at the time Punk was spreading nationwide, RAR provided a local infrastructure. An RAR concert guaranteed an audience and thus made local concerts viable: many groups – like the Ruts (Southall), the Gang of Four and the Mekons (Leeds), and the Special AKA (Coventry) – and many towns benefitted from the opportunity and support given by this organized decentralization. 'Punk wouldn't have had so much impact outside London without the anti-fascist movement,' says journalist Steven Wells, then a teenage New Waver, 'but then the anti-fascist movement would not have had much impact without Punk. In Leeds, where the Young National Front were really strong, some of the early Punks had formed fascist groups like the Dentists and the Vents. Punk was apolitical in that context: many people saw it as fascistic even though Martin Webster came out against it. RAR caused Punk to make real contact there: the time when most people see Punk as being diluted was the time when it was gaining substance.'

The problems began, however, when the central organization of RAR tried to codify what was a specific response to a particular social issue into a post-Punk aesthetic. There was already considerable suspicion between RAR and Punk groups: at Victoria Park, Joe Strummer wore a Red Brigade T-shirt, a type of politics with which RAR wasn't happy. 'Camp,' David Widgery calls it in *Beating Time*, a book full of insults for the groups who supported RAR. For members of the RAR inner circle like Widgery, it was 'their revolution' and it would be done their way. There was some tension between RAR headquarters in London and those who worked for *Temporary Hoarding* and local groups, who were trying to set up an open, nationwide structure. But the absolute fiats of the RAR discourse, at least as presented by its most articulate exponents, captured the overwhelming drive of what was left of the Punk subculture of 1978.

'Just whose side are you on,' asked Tom Robinson on *Up Against the Wall*, a compendium of the radical obsessions then current. Howard Devoto, himself an object of this polarized discourse on the release of 'Shot by both Sides', stated flatly: 'My Mind ain't so Open'. This was the language of doors being closed, of nothing more to be learned: an absolute mind-set that brooked no argument. You could read it every week in the *NME*.

The diaspora continued. Many went 'social realist' and fully assumed the RAR discourse: in July, Sham had a Top-Ten hit with an adaptation of a South American freedom song, 'If The Kids are United'. Reggae groups became fixtures at Punk clubs, while new groups like the Ruts continued the fusion of the two styles. Others, like the Rich Kids or Generation X, went pop, appearing regularly on the Punk generation's version of *Ready Steady Go*, *Revolver*, which began at the end of May.

For many of those who had been involved at Punk's beginning, the only recourse was to go their own way. 'The whole of Punk for me was the Sex Pistols', says Jordan. 'Once they had stopped, I went straight into Adam and the Ants, to something that was overtly sexual or Siouxsie and the Banshees, who were asexual. There was a time when the Ants played with the Banshees and they were great concerts, real value for money. They were vying with each other.'

After his February residency at the Marquee, Adam began to capture a new generation of younger, harder-core London Punks: at the time, however, his popularity was ignored by almost all the media, except for pure-Punk magazines like *Ripped and Torn*. Damned through his association with the film *Jubilee* – which was released in February to uniformly hostile reviews – and Germanic songs like 'Deutscher Girl', Adam was persuaded to play an RAR concert in June.

Caught by the backlash, the Banshees also made a public disassociation from any previous carelessness: early in 1978, they premiered a new tune called 'Metal Postcard', a song which, they took pains to make clear, was sparked off by the John Heartfield collage 'Guns and Butter'. 'It took a long time to live down the Nazi thing,' says Severin, 'from us having worn swastikas and that line in "Love in a Void". In the first year nobody wanted what we were offering.'

13.5.78 'I was minding my own business when my string snapped . . .' ('Suburban Relapse') their most fully realized mix. Very English: paraquat parties behind the privet hedges, the pebble-dash prisons that keep the occupants in just as much as they keep the outside world out. English emotional and physical isolation turning ever inwards into psychosis, unnameable perversions in deep closets . . .

Integration for the industry was a problem for the Banshees, but unlike groups like Subway Sect, they had a manager who had absorbed some of Malcolm McLaren's allure and some of his tactics. 'Nils Stevenson was hyping it up something rotten,' says Severin. 'There weren't queues of A&R men, and he was making great play of the "greatest unsigned band".' He set the graffiti campaign, spraying "Sign the Banshees" on all the record company headquarters.'

By spring, the Banshees were full of controlled hysteria. Fronting Kenni Morris's massive, cymbal-less drumming, and the counter-pointed guitars of John McKay and Steve Severin, Siouxsie dramatized breakdown. 'It goes back to pre-Grundy, everything being more complex,' says Severin, 'all those bands that were taking things from the Ramones that fuelled an imaginary torture. It was coming straight out of suburbia, looking for somewhere else to go.'

Punk had been taken up so quickly that the more experimental inner-circle groups were finding survival tough. They had to contend with a culture not only newly hostile to experimentation, but which had also fragmented on exposure to the music industry. Many record companies were now looking for the 'next big thing' after Punk: if you had not signed, survival was doubly tough because the original Punk community had gone. 'It all fell apart,' says Viv Albertine, 'when everyone became a working band.'

That spring, the Slits recorded 'FM', whose storyline found the group so bathed in media that they surrendered their humanity to electronics. 'My head is like a radio set,' sang Ari over a background simultaneously experimental and threatening, 'my nightmares don't project my dreams.' At the song's end, the group record a sweep over the radio band: out of the atmospherics comes the Union Gap's paedophiliac song 'Young Girl'.

It is hardly surprising that the music industry was not ready for a cosmopolitan group of aggressive, politicized females: without a strong manager, with a mixture of outrage and preciousness, the Slits withdrew even further. 'The blokes in the record companies are not the sort you would associate with, totally naff human beings, and there you are trying to deal with them,' says Albertine. 'We got offered contracts quite early, and we didn't want them.'

Of all the original Punk groups, the Buzzcocks and the Clash were now in the most interesting position. Shelley used the security of a record deal to continue Punk's fervid momentum through five 1978 hit singles. On their forty-fives, the Buzzcocks sang about various kinds of love, but their first LP contained songs about ecology, autonomy and the wish to destroy pop that, such was the speed of events, had become obsolete between the time of writing and recording.

The Buzzcocks were now pop themselves, though with some remaining ideals. They played incessantly throughout the year. 'One of the big things about Punk was the social obligation,' says Shelley, 'we got our first gigs in London through Malcolm: the 100 Club Festival, and later the White Riot tour. We had the Slits and the Gang of Four for the Another Music tour, Penetration for Entertaining Friends, and Subway Sect for the Love Bites tour.'

These ideals were laudable, but often misapplied, in a subculture now become as conservative as that against which it had originally revolted. In April, Sheffield electronic group Cabaret Voltaire got bottled off stage at their first London appearance at the Lyceum, a venue notorious for its hostile audiences. Another Lyceum victim was the young, Bristol based Pop Group, who ended up ankle deep in cans after two and a half minutes.

On Punk's avant-garde side, electronics and Captain Beefheart were the new gods for the first post-Punk generation. The spring's big tour was the first visit by Pere Ubu, whose thorough grasp of technology and mature aesthetic was a revelation to the teenage group who supported them. The Pop Group came out strongly with baggy, fifties-style clothes and the first convincing fusion of Punk with black American Funk. The name 'James Brown' was whispered.

In denying black musical forms, Punk had got into trouble: now they had found one way out of the impasse. If the Pop Group translated the Punk archetype into different forms – 'We were all teenage Rimbauds,' says bassist Gareth Sager, 'dedicated to creating hell on stage' – the Leeds-based Gang of Four applied funk rhythms carefully to aesthetic ideas taken from rigorous vanguard artists like Art and Language. Their jarring, visceral polemics were given particular urgency by the high level of fascist activity in Yorkshire.

'There was terrible violence,' says Gang of Four guitarist Andy Gill, 'pitched battles between students and British Movement members on the University campus. We could see the struggle between the SWP and the BM capturing the straying youth. We were sympathetic to the SWP, we had done some benefits, but we didn't make our own approach in those broad political terms. It was more to do with living in a late capitalist society: we also were very concerned about the spectre of Thatcherism, and what it was going to do to the people in this country.'

The Sex Pistols had ripped the heart out of any remaining 'movement'. Lacking a centre, everyone lost power. The 'arties' lost their contact with the social mix which had given the original Sex Pistols so much of their bite and the result was laboratory pop. The social realists claimed an aesthetic radicalism, but in damning the 'arties', they lost contact with the forms and the ideas which could make their political radicalism resonate beyond the slogans of the day.

The possibilities which had seemed so tangible the previous year had disappeared as though they had never existed. In reaction, the several discourses became ever more bitter, always on the verge of ideological violence. This process was caught, as ever, by the Clash, still the lightning conductors for their generation, and even more so with the Sex Pistols gone. For the first few months of 1978, they met these contradictions head on, and grew yet further in power.

They hired an American producer, Sandy Pearlman, and at the same time they continued to fuse Reggae with their increasingly powerful Rock attack. They were still attempting to maintain their social radicalism, even when they were on trial for trying to bring down pigeons with air rifles. The event was attended by their now customary entourage of lads, liggers and Rock'n'Roll poseurs. Now fully-fledged Rock stars, they released their most moving record to date.

The narrative of 'White Man in Hammersmith Palais' has Joe Strummer attending a Reggae all-nighter: not only is he the only white present, but he finds that the cultural baggage he brings to the event is confounded. He has come for 'roots rock rebel', while everybody else has come for entertainment. Here is the perennial problem of the kneejerk white approach to black culture, which holds that what is, in fact, pop and highly mediated, is 'authentic', the voice of struggle. The song moves from confusion to despair as Strummer realizes that unitary rhetoric pales before the reality of state power. But, like all great pop records, the music subverts the song's lyrical message: at the time Strummer realizes the limits of his well-intentioned rhetoric, the group's music is their most full, sympathetic fusion of Punk and Reggae to date, with its dub-like space, the slightly phased hi-hat and the plaintive, melodica-style harmonica.

As the song continues, slow and measured, Strummer piles on his agony at the death of the culture which has given him his strength. No pop performer has sounded more completely alone as, at the song's close, he searches in a hostile dance-hall for that very commodity that, in 1978, was in short supply: 'Oh please mister, just leave me alone: I'm only looking for fun. Looking, looking, looking . . .'

Poly Styrene, summer 1978 (© Pennie Smith)

Shame on you child/The way you dress
The state of you/Oh what a mess
Your hair is natty dread/Your shoes are Ted
And you yoused to be a Skinhead

Identity/Identity/Identity is the crisis can't you see?

When you look in the mirror/Do you see yourself?/Do you see yourself?/ On the TV screen/ Do you see yourself?/In the magazines/When you see yourself/Does it make you scream?

Identity/Identity/Identity is the crisis can't you see?

When you look in the mirror/Do you smash it quick?/Do you take the glass?/And slash your wrists/Did you do it for fame?/Did you do it in a fit?/ Did you do it before?/You read about it.

Poly Styrene for X-Ray Spex: 'Identity' (June 1978)

Not all of today's youth are killer kids, but this generation born between 1955 and 1962 face a life-and-death conflict in their collective psyche. Uranus in Leo square Neptune in Scorpio translates to mean self-will vs self-loss – an arrogant desire for freedom coupled with a simultaneous longing for death.

'The Cruelty of Today's Youth', *Horoscope Magazine* (October 1977)

Time slowed down. 'When we got back from Rio we were still poncing about, making the film,' says Steve Jones. 'We were still getting dough, but I was a miserable sod: I started getting involved with smack, and I just didn't have time for anything. All the excitement of the early Pistols until we split up, and there was this big hole. I just felt terrible, and smack just filled that hole.'

McLaren and Westwood's experiment in social engineering had helped to unleash a wave of negation across the world, but the nursery demons were now clustering around in force, like the spites from Pandora's Box. Nowhere was this more obvious that within the Sex Pistols' inner circle, as 'Search and Destroy' played through to 'Death Trip'. 'It was a sick scene,' says Wobble, 'There was an unhealthy vibe with a lot of the personalities. My antennae were up then. You know that Dennis Potter play where the grown-ups are playing kids, *Blue Remembered Hills*? It was like that. When you put emotional cripples together, you get something very powerful. It can be good or bad, and it can be directed either way. It had to burn out, it was the same energy of a four-year-old asserting itself on the world, when it throws a tantrum. It wasn't going anywhere else.'

'We weren't these manipulable kids any longer,' says Debbie Wilson, 'we were all getting personalities of our own. It was really easy for Malcolm to dominate kids, but when you start getting older, he couldn't really handle that. Malcolm started pulling out when John started asking for real things and all of us, in the shop he must have started thinking, "Let's get down to some younger people," and he did.'

No one more emphasized the process than McLaren and Westwood's favourite child, Sid Vicious. 'He would do anything that John wouldn't do,' says Julien Temple. 'He was more malleable as a Sex Pistol, but he hated Malcolm with a vengeance, even though Malcolm liked him so much as the ultimate Sex Pistol. Malcolm couldn't control John intellectually, but he could control Sid, although not physically, or as a junkie. When Sid became a junkie it was all over.'

Holed up in Pindock Mews in London's drug central, Maida Vale, Sid Vicious and Nancy Spungeon rapidly became enmired in heroin hell: Vicious was returning to his old habits with redoubled force, now that there was nothing to stop him. Lech Kowalski's *DOA* filmed them both just after Vicious's return from America: lying in bed, extremely stoned, they are trying to do an interview, but Sid is so exhausted from his recent escapades that he keeps falling asleep. It's an appalling scene. Nancy tries to wake him by repeated nagging but Sid is not only verbally but physically incapable: he cannot string more than a sentence together. At points, he burns Nancy with a cigarette, and plays with a large hunting knife. Nancy meanwhile is quite lively, proving herself aware of their self-mythology. 'Sid and Nancy,' she dreamily declares, 'we were partners in crime, we helped each other out.'

No one has been more vilified than Nancy but almost everybody will agree that the pair were totally dependent on each other, albeit in a private world. An important part of this world was the mythology of self-destruction: 'Sid always used to say he didn't want to live past twenty-one,' adds Wobble; 'often people talk that way, it's the old James Dean thing, but when you assume something, you can become it, and it becomes dangerous.'

McLaren still had high hopes that Sid would become the reconstituted Sex Pistols' front man, but he underestimated the severity of Vicious's condition. McLaren still wanted to keep the group going without John Lydon: he had developed the attitude that the idea, the brand name was more important than the personalities. He was also going full ahead with his plans for a Sex Pistols' documentary called *Four Stars are Born*. Temple had been filming constantly and now had a considerable backlog of material. He was not McLaren's first choice but there were several factors in his favour. 'I could provide cameras for free,' he says, 'also I had quite a close relationship with Malcolm. From the beginning of '78, we had this scheme, to take them to the four corners of the world. We wanted to do Johnny Rotten in Delhi, we did Steve and Paul in Rio, and then we did Sid in Paris.

'We went in March. We stayed in an eighteenth-century hotel on the Rue de Rivoli, and we were there for three weeks. We started out trying to get Sid to sing "Je Ne Regrette Rien", and he just wouldn't do that at all. And then Jean Fernandez from Barclay Records came up with the idea – partly because they owned the publishing for Claude François – to do "My Way", which made a lot of sense. It was definitely his idea, and so the next task was to get Sid to do it.'

'After the split, I'm the only guy who can look after Sid,' says John Tiberi, 'I didn't want to go but Malcolm is very difficult to say no to. Sid was all we had left of the Pistols at that point. He wasn't too sure about "My Way" but we worked it around him. The development of the scene was worked out between Julien and myself and Malcolm, and Sid. But when it came to the actual shooting, Sid worked it out himself. We did a rehearsal, and it was great, and he did it again, exactly the same. He had a great intuition about cameras: he understood perfectly.

'Sid was the Sex Pistols, because he was their number one fan, and that was the greatest thing about having him in the group. Once he

Sid and Nancy, partners in crime (© LFI)

was in the group it was like, ''Oo-er, never thought it was going to be like this, where's the chicks?'' Sid was getting demoralized, because the dream was broken. Not only the dream of being a pop star, but this thing, with which he was in love, as a fan, as a guy at the 100 Club with or without a beer glass. That's his PR. Rather than the group dying, the audience dies.'

'We eventually filmed it in a totally empty theatre in Paris, on a set that was built for Serge Gainsbourg,' says Temple. 'We wanted him in a kind of destroyed version of dinner dress, and as long as he could wear his trousers and his boots he didn't mind anything. He had trouble doing it again and again, he sweated. He loved the idea of shooting the audience: we wanted him to shoot his mother. We saw Sid as the first monster child of the hippy generation.'

In Paris, Vicious was operating under a cloud of junk and methadone. He was only the most obvious example of the drug abuse that, like a mirror image of hippie, was sweeping through inner-circle Punk disillusion. 'It was a logical way for Punk to go,' says Al McDowell. 'Junk is a drug which is absolutely right for those ageing rockers, it's the only way to make you think you're still great.'

This psychic predisposition coincided with changes in the patterns of supply. A 1985 report prepared for the British Journal of Addiction stated that, '1978-9 was a watershed year for heroin use in Britain. Political events in Iran contributed to a substantial increase in supply on the British market. This increase in availability led to a fall in price, which, combined with a decline in existing subcultural taboos against heroin use, filled existing demand and seemed to encourage experimentation.'

While the Paris farce was in progress, Tracey O'Keefe fell seriously ill. 'I'd been kicked out of the shop,' says Debbie Wilson, 'because John had left the band, and I stuck up for John. So I lost control completely. When I tried to contact Vivienne to find out what was wrong, she wouldn't tell me, and refused to let me see her. At the end of May I got a phone call from Johnny saying that Tracey had died: from leukaemia. It was very sudden. She was eighteen.

'She got slightly into heroin in the end, when she was dying, which I thought was a bad thing. It became a morbid time. Tracey took it very very hard, when the Pistols broke up, and I think partly the reason she got into heroin was that she took the whole thing to heart, got very upset by it. I went off with some mad guy who I had a bad time with for two years, and John got more withdrawn and into himself.'

While Cook and Jones busied themselves with recording and playing with Johnny Thunders, Lydon retreated into his lair at 45, Gunter Grove, just above the intersection with the New King's Road. 'I had to do it,' he says simply.

'John became a recluse,' says Debbie, 'he'd hide away from the world then he'd call up in the middle of the night and say you've got to come round. He couldn't handle being at home on his own. He was really frightened of himself.'

'It got quite poxy at times,' says Wobble. 'People had quite a tenuous grasp on reality, and we'd make up these problems. Group therapy going on, with some people doing heroin, some doing speed, some doing both. We'd be up for three days on end, talking paranoia, conspiracy theories and shit. Everyone secretly knowing it's a lot of bullshit, but just getting off on the whole trip.'

Wobble was now the bass player in John Lydon's as yet unnamed new group, announced to the world in an *NME* cover feature on 27 May. 'I was on the dole, squatting, and all I was doing was reading the papers about the band splitting up. John called and said "Come round, I want you to be in my band, with Keith." I'd had offers to be in bands before, but unless I could be in something really good, I didn't want to to do it.'

Public Image sprang initially from Lydon's desire to avoid the Rock'n'Roll thrash of the Sex Pistols. He was obsessed with the space of dub, while Levene had refined his guitar playing into a barrage of ringing noise. This was post-Punk, definitely experimental. 'I wanted to do something which was true power,' says Wobble, 'not choppy rhythm guitars out of time, loud. When you're thinking about music you're thinking about something supposed to have a lasting effect. That bass will be reverberating for years.'

Membership of the group also demanded participation in the communal life at Gunter Grove. Here Lydon, although he had gained his sanity and perhaps his soul, participated in the sickness of the time for which he was still a powerful symbol – as Gunter Grove picked up and amplified instability. 'Poly Styrene was often there,' says Wobble. 'She was a strange girl who talked of hallucinating. She freaked John out. It must have damaged a lot of people, that scene, for what good it did.'

X-Ray Spex had been through a lot very quickly. After a one-off single for Virgin, 'Oh Bondage! Up Yours!' which was a deserved press sensation if not a hit, the group had signed to EMI records at the start of the year. By this time, Poly was a star, with her dayglo clothes, multi-racial background, teeth braces, and surreal songs which wittily commented on that very process of consumption and packaging that she was at once celebrating and transcending.

Along with other women, like Siouxsie and the members of the Slits, Poly challenged for her generation the perennial pop demand that female performers be submissive and even conventionally beautiful, and she was loved for it. That was not enough. By the end of April, when 'The Day the World Turned Dayglo' made the Top Thirty, X-Ray Spex played the Victoria Park Carnival. Already, image had become a prison: Poly came on in a head-dress which she tore off – to reveal a bald head.

'I shaved it on John Lydon's balcony,' she says. 'It was dark round there. It was macabre, he was pretty nocturnal. There were lots of little horror pictures on the wall and he would talk about ghosts and there were crucifixes upside down on the wall. He was just toying with the darker side of his character: he was a bit of an actor really. But Punk had become too negative, which was to do with a lack of vision, on the part of the people who were the so-called leaders of that particular generation and also the music industry.'

Poly confronted all this on a new song, 'Identity'. Frustrated by the demands of image on a female performer in the music industry, the demands of a Punk audience that wanted 'ramalama' while she wanted to move on, and by her inability to reach transcendence, Poly threw everything into the recording of that song, so much so that it becomes, not a comment upon identity, but a desperate cry for help from an identity on the point of disintegration.

By the time the song was in the Top Thirty, Poly was in serious trouble. 'It was on tour in Doncaster,' she says, 'and I was still awake in the hotel room at three in the morning. All of a sudden I looked out of the hotel window and I saw this sort of energy. It was bright, bright, luminous pink, and it had a disc shape. It was faster than the speed of light. I was inside a window but the radiation effect hit my body. I was suffering afterwards, and my body kept going hot and cold.'

The result was that, at twenty-one, Poly Styrene quit her Punk identity. 'I didn't know why I'd seen this thing,' she says, 'it hit me so much as an omen that I just didn't want to play music anymore. It was horrible: I had a kind of breakdown. I wanted to take a break and rethink what I was doing, everything that I was involved in, because I saw it in a superstitious way, that I shouldn't continue. The only way I could resolve it was through mysticism, and that took some time.'

> Two sides to every story
> So somebody had to stop me
> I'm not the same as when I began
> I will not be treated as property
>
> **John Lydon for PiL: 'Public Image' (October 1978)**

At the end of June, the Sex Pistols released their first record since the split. Although it bore the group name, Lydon had had nothing to do with it: one side of the double 'A' was taken up by the 'Punk Prayer' recorded with Biggs in Rio, while the other featured Sid Vicious's 'My Way', his opening Sinatra pastiche quickly giving way to a classic thrash with queasy strings overdubbed by Simon Jeffes of the Penguin Café Orchestra.

The single was delayed because of the controversy that was now inevitable on any Sex Pistols release, thanks to Glitterbest's determination to push Virgin as far and as hard as they could. As far as McLaren was concerned, if Virgin refused Biggs as the new lead singer of the group, then he could cancel the contract and take the Sex Pistols elsewhere, just as he had done at EMI and A&M. There was one point on which Virgin baulked: as part of their policy of provocation, Reid and McLaren changed the title of the single several times, from 'A Punk Prayer' to 'The Biggest Blow' to 'No one is Innocent', before eventually preparing artwork with the title 'Cosh the Driver' – a reference to the fatal assault that occurred during the Great Train Robbery. It is doubtful whether these were seriously intended for use, but they had the desired effect, that of annoying Virgin.

The single was a big hit, rising to number six in July: it sold more copies than either 'Holidays' or 'Queen'. Glitterbest felt vindicated: there was a strong demand for the Sex Pistols' product even without John Lydon. This was a vote of confidence in the continued strength of the project. Glitterbest were full of plans for the future, which involved, if not the destruction of Rock'n'Roll, then at least its deconstruction.

'One of the things we were aware of was the need never to remain still, to remain stagnant,' says Jamie Reid. 'After three or four records have come out there begins to be a typical Punk fan, who identifies with the band in the way that fans always do. I don't blame them: it's a fact of life. When Rotten left and we put in Ronnie Biggs, they couldn't understand. It seemed like a good idea to us, but the fans wanted a classic Rock'n'Roll format.'

It quickly became clear however, that Glitterbest had misunderstood why the record sold: the real hook was not the idea, nor Biggs, but Sid Vicious's legendary destruction of a myth. 'I didn't like the Biggs single,' says Al Clark. 'I liked "My Way" a lot. Now there was an icon that needed demolishing – possibly the most narcissistic song of all time. Then the play element took over, what could we do next to get up people's noses, now there isn't a group?'

Despite Cook and Jones's valiant attempt to promote the record, the press outrage looked contrived. There was a germ of a brilliant idea in the Biggs single, but it was vitiated by its execution – for all their many qualities, neither Cook nor Jones had Lydon's moral conviction – and its context: a limit had been called on outrage as a guiding principle. Now that Conservatives and the National Front were saying the unsayable, it didn't seem so attractive.

Despite the obvious potential for a south London villain in a culture dominated by Sham 69, it was hardly feasible for Biggs to continue as the Sex Pistols' lead singer. Biggs was still on the wanted list in England, such a public embarrassment that police inspectors and freelance kidnappers made several attempts to spirit him home to serve the rest of his sentence. There was also the question of the contract, which was hardly favourable.

McLaren had taken his usual 25 per cent manager's commission and despite Biggs's hope that 'there will be no rip-offs or other forms of Foul Play; don't forget I've got a lot of mates in London', very little was ever sent to Rio. After throwing a few thousand Biggs's way, McLaren had other projects to spend Glitterbest's money on. There was also the dubious legality of the whole enterprise: Virgin could not send cheques, so all dealings were done in cash.

From the late spring, McLaren threw himself into the film project that Temple had finally sold him. Although he was initially reluctant, McLaren quickly became very enthusiastic: here, if nothing else, was the chance to tell his side of a story that had ended and which, in the instant replay of the time, was becoming myth. Thinking faster than the opposition, McLaren realized that he could scoop the telling of the full Sex Pistols' tale, which was already in dispute.

All the footage was there: from Derek Jarman's first Super-8 of the Logan party to 'My Way'. The next stage was to think up an overriding idea. The new film was to be called *The Great Rock'n'Roll Swindle*: using the phraseology of the right-wing critics who had castigated the Sex Pistols for 'exploitation', McLaren presented the group's story as a carefully planned exercise to embezzle as much money as possible out of the music industry 'in reprisal for what the industry has stolen out of Rock'n'Roll'.

What the industry had stolen was best exemplified by the film's opening, relating the history of the group, over scenes of the 1780 Gordon Riots. In this context, the 'Liberty Riot' displayed the impulse to spontaneous, untrammelled freedom that was buried deep in English history. The Sex Pistols had tapped this same impulse but they they had been seduced by capital: just as in the French Revolution, the former leaders were to be ceremonially executed.

There was no question that the Sex Pistols were over, except as a vehicle for propagating McLaren's ideas. Vicious and Cook both end up dead while Jones is effectively washed up, castrated. Having refused to appear, Lydon is only glimpsed in the archive footage: elsewhere, he is the subject of McLaren's denunciations. Dressed in a rubber outfit, talking to Helen, or throwing Sex Pistols' products into the fire, it is McLaren's finest hour. Here he achieves what he always wanted: to be the Sex Pistols' front man.

This is a role into which he had to be coerced. Much of McLaren's power had been gained by being elusive, by disappearing when any trouble occurred, by not being accountable. But now his ego had taken over, and there was no choice: the budget, such as it was, would not allow the use of actors, and there was nobody that could take on any of the duties of the front man within the group. Now he was to be the figurehead, just at the time when opinion was turning against the Sex Pistols as a whole.

As McLaren becomes the dominant presence in the film's scenes, they show the contradictions in his character. With Helen as a magical talisman, McLaren presents himself as a mixture of Dr Frankenstein and Larry Parnes – a 'fetish Lucifer'. The self-portrait he paints is deliberately unflattering: the first time we see him is whispering sinister sibilants, totally encased in rubber. Never has McLaren displayed more clearly that element of his personality which he both despised and yet celebrated for its marginality: his Jewishness.

The structure of the script is like a stress nightmare: McLaren is always running, always one step ahead of his pursuer, Steve Jones, who, like a drowning man, is trying to piece together the memories of the Sex Pistols and his own identity. 'Farce is about the chaos of mixed identities,' wrote Michael Watts, and the script caught the fragmentation both of the Sex Pistols and Punk. Steve Jones, the petty crook, is dressed in the Burberry of the *film-noir* Private Eye, wandering through the streets of Soho.

If Jones is McLaren's shadow, then the rest of the group are treated in cartoon form. As mentioned, Lydon is evident only in the documentary footage. Vicious is there for the Rock-rebel flavouring and Paul Cook is passive, 'Slave Cook'. He croons his song 'Silly Thing' in a cot, while elsewhere he is assaulted by a homosexual, generic Virgin New-Wave group called the Blowaves. In an echo of real life, he is assaulted by Teddy Boys at the top of a tube escalator.

The film's central device is the Ten Lessons, a self-mocking yet powerful statement of authorship. If the author is God, then McLaren's adaptation of the Ten Commandments in an epigrammatic form that exemplifies authorial power, reemphasized that *he*, McLaren, was the group's creator – just as it said in the management contract – and that he had stage-managed every event from day one. The Ten Lessons read as follows:

LESSON ONE: HOW TO MANUFACTURE YOUR GROUP
LESSON TWO: ESTABLISH THE NAME SEX PISTOLS
LESSON THREE: HOW TO SELL THE SWINDLE
LESSON FOUR: DON'T PLAY, DON'T GIVE THE GAME AWAY
LESSON FIVE: STEAL AS MUCH MONEY FROM THE RECORD COMPANY OF YOUR CHOICE
LESSON SIX: HOW TO BECOME THE WORLD'S NUMBER-ONE TOURIST ATTRACTION
LESSON SEVEN: CULTIVATE HATRED, IT IS YOUR GREATEST ASSET
LESSON EIGHT: HOW TO DIVERSIFY YOUR BUSINESS
LESSON NINE: TAKING CIVILIZATION TO THE BARBARIANS – USA
LESSON TEN: WHO KILLED BAMBI?

'That film was us preventing the whole thing from turning into a dreadful tragedy and turning it into a fantastic enigma,' McLaren says. 'That's what we tried to do, to lie incredibly. We did it quite successfully. The irresponsible nature of it all was the key to it, and we prevented it from becoming responsible for as long as we could hold out. So when we were accused of dastardly deeds, absolutely say Yes, because the last thing you want to say is No".

'You never wanted to be part of that New-Wave, Rock'n'Roll liberal tradition, looking like you were doing good things. That was never behind Eddie Cochran, or Elvis Presley. He was a Punk rocker, and so was Gene Vincent. So was Marilyn Monroe. They were Punks, they were anti-establishment, and they were gods. Marilyn Monroe is bigger than ever, and so is Sid Vicious. I don't see Johnny Rotten on a T-shirt on the Lower East Side: I see Sid all the bloody time.'

As the film developed, the script began to overtake its author. The Sex Pistols had already found their limits: hitherto protected by his agility and speed, McLaren was nevertheless beginning to hit his own brick wall. Just as Punk became more Stalinist, McLaren would take on the most fanatical elements of Situ politics and style as he slipped into the role of 'the Swindler'. He began to be trapped by those very hostile definitions he was attempting to detourn.

As it was eventually realized on film, the script's seamless blur of fact and fiction persuaded many people that what was in fact fiction was a truthful account. McLaren was attempting to burst the bounds of the group's history: in true Situationist style, he was trying to turn the instruments of power back on their institutions. It was an ambitious attempt, doomed to failure because of his own contradictions, railing at the industry with which he was still flirting: that summer he travelled to New York for a possible RCA consultancy job.

Uninterested in the film, Cook and Jones continued to record material: as well as new tunes like 'Silly Thing', 'Here We Go Again' and 'Black Leather', they dusted off four songs from the July 1976 Dave Goodman sessions and put them through their now perfected wall of sound. Retaining John Lydon's vocals but wiping most of the original instrumentation, the powerchord covers of 'Substitute' and 'No Lip' are a convincing update on the Sex Pistols' original power. This went on throughout May, June and July: by the time that McLaren and Temple had prepared a complete draft of the film script, on 9 August, there was enough for a soundtrack album. At least one third of the film had already been completed: this had used up Warners' £200,000. Producer Don Boyd put in £50,000 for a 7 per cent return; Matrixbest, £170,000 from record royalties and unused advances. Jeremy Thomas was brought in as executive producer.

The shooting began in the middle of August. One of the first scenes was the audition for the new Sex Pistols' singer at the Duchess

Theatre. This run-through the film's title song was the last time the three remaining Pistols would appear on the same stage together. 'All the Pistols were into finding a new singer,' says Temple. 'We tried a hundred guys. Eddie Tenpole came in during the lunch hour: he did this strange routine with a cigarette, and a dance, and he was serious. He was the one.'

The search was necessary because McLaren and Vicious had washed their hands of each other. 'He hated Malcolm,' says Temple. 'Sid would only do "My Way" if he got Malcolm to sign this note saying "Malcolm McLaren is no longer my manager", and Malcolm signed it.'

Tiberi and production assistant June Miles-Kington were the only people who could rouse Sid from his torpor to perform his remaining duties as a Sex Pistol: to record and film his versions of Eddie Cochran's 'C'mon Everybody' and 'Something Else'.

Already adrift, Sid and Nancy had started to float into uncharted seas, becalmed for weeks on end until rocked by sudden violence. Despite his physical problems, Vicious was now bent on living up to his name, with fights in Rock'n'Roll pits like the Speakeasy and Dingwalls, with Paul Weller, Jimmy McCullough and an unnamed marine who injured his right eye so that he could no longer open it fully.

One of the problems of heroin use is that, although the drug offers insulation from the stresses of everyday life, it does so by effectively embalming the user's body and emotions. Sid and Nancy were locked into permanent adolescence because of the drug which they had now been taking solidly for at least a year. While Nancy was able to hide her disintegration, Vicious began to lose his striking good looks: his face became skull-like, and he developed a paunch abnormal in a young man of twenty.

'Sid had completely gone off then,' says Poly Styrene, 'I saw him at John's, with a great big knife, playing with it. He was gone: it was quite a hellish planet.' In August, Sid and Nancy were shocked out of their stupor by the death, in Pindock Mews, of a friend, twenty-two-year-old John Shepcock, who overdosed on cocaine. The pair were so stoned that they took several hours to realize that the body with which they were sharing a bed was a corpse.

Realizing that enough was enough, Sid and Nancy attempted to take the methadone cure, registering themselves on the legally obtained opiate which is used to stave off the worst aspects of heroin withdrawal. But methadone is as addictive as heroin, with withdrawals that can be much worse. The dose that Spungeon and Vicious were given at their private hospital, Bowden House in Harrow-on-the-Hill, was one of the highest prescribed in such cases. They had swapped one prison for another.

In August, Vicious finally overstayed his welcome at Gunter Grove. When he turned up in the small hours with Nancy, he was denied admittance and started kicking the door in. Versions of the story vary, but one of Lydon's cronies, either Paul Young or Wobble, rushed down the stairs and attacked both Sid and Nancy with a sharp instrument – probably an axe. While Nancy hid the injuries behind sunglasses, Sid took this as the final blow.

The pair decided to go to New York, Nancy's adopted town, which in 1978 still held some of the druggy allure propagated by generations of musicians. To add to their fund, the pair fronted a concert at the Electric Ballroom in Camden as the Vicious White Kids with a band of Steve New, Rat Scabies and Glen Matlock. In the last week of August, Sid filmed the kiosk sequence eventually cut from the *Swindle*: the next day, he departed with Nancy for New York.

John Lydon had not been idle. Determined to free himself from Malcolm McLaren, he busied himself with collecting affidavits and data for a legal showdown with Glitterbest. 'He hadn't produced any accounts whatsoever, and I hadn't received any money,' says John Lydon, 'he was claiming that he owned the name and that I didn't deserve any money because I broke contract. That wasn't true, so it went to court.'

Throughout May and June, Lydon tested the water with his lawyers and Virgin. One of the planks in his case was that the partnership that had been the Sex Pistols had dissolved in San Francisco: McLaren's management not only caused the break-up but was now invalid. Lydon obtained affidavits from Joe Stevens and Noel Monk which laid out his view of events: that he was not contacted about the trip to Rio until the very last moment. The partnership had dissolved and now Lydon wanted contractual confirmation.

A Public Image single had already been recorded and was ready for release: a startling counterpoint of Wobble's impossibly deep bass, Jim Walker's kinetic drumming and Keith Levene's scything guitar, it featured Lydon shouting his identity and his fury to the world. In a mirror image of McLaren's own attempt to claim that he alone had created the Sex Pistols, 'Public Image' was a definite assertion by

Lydon that he was the Sex Pistols and that, once he had gone, they would never return.

By September, Lydon had clear advice that he could go ahead with his new project: by now managing himself, he signed a new contract with Virgin Records, to whom he was in no small degree indebted. 'In my view, we could have had better,' says Wobble, 'if we'd held out a bit. It wasn't too clever. I think it was for eight LPs. You get your recording advance, it's just like the old companies, it still goes on now. There was grief from the start.'

There was one last delay: the group's image-maker, Dennis Morris, had decided on a picture sleeve which was a folded simulation of the *Sun*, right down to the headline typeface. Inside were several examples of Gunter Grove humour at which printers baulked. The single was finally scheduled for release in the second week in October, but by then, the squabbling had turned to tragedy.

Anne Beverley with her son, after his release from Riker's Island, October 1978 (© Joe Stevens)

34

> If the hero, like Prometheus, simply darted to his goal (by violence, quick device, or luck) and plucked the boon for the world that he intended, then the powers that he has unbalanced may react so sharply that he will be blasted from within and without – crucified, like Prometheus, on the rock of his own violated unconscious.
>
> **Joseph Campbell: *The Hero with a Thousand Faces* (1949)**

On their arrival in New York, Vicious and Spungeon checked into the Chelsea, the West 23rd Street hotel that had long been celebrated as a residence for artists and Bohemians. By the late 1970s, the cheapness of the rent (£17 a night for a double room) was somewhat offset by the hotel's decay: the Chelsea had been declining for years and, as *Rolling Stone* stated, 'the first three floors of the twelve-storey building have been reserved for junkies and other low-life types.'

Sid and Nancy had come to America to start a new life. They would get off drugs; Nancy would manage Sid into stardom; they might even get married. They quickly found that, if London had been unsympathetic, New York was brutal. Not only did the general public take Vicious at name value – Sid was embroiled in constant fights at the Spring Street methadone clinic – but the pair also encountered the hostility that had always marked relations between New York and London Punk.

Although not yet twenty-one, Sid and Nancy were imprisoned by their notorious past. Vicious came with all the baggage of an ex-Pistol: a member of the group that had stolen the thunder from New York Punk. His image had become larger than life, not only in his own behaviour, but in the expectations of others. When he played Max's in early September, many came expecting to see the rabid star of the infamous Sex Pistols' tour: what they got was a young man, old before his time, sleepwalking through several Punk archetypes.

Vicious played with a back-up group which comprised the New York Dolls' rhythm section, Killer Kane and Jerry Nolan, with Mick Jones guesting on guitar. The concert of 7 September was taped: the group rush through nine songs – all covers, except 'Belsen Was A Gas'. Although there are a few lapses, Sid proves that he had a perfectly adequate voice and attitude to carry off material like 'Steppin' Stone' and 'No Lip' but there is another, disquieting factor.

The songs, consciously or not, add up to one logical conclusion of Punk nihilism: from externally directed to internally directed violence. As Sid puts all the strength he can muster into 'Search and Destroy' and 'I Wanna Be Your Dog', you can hear him talk of a life taken over by Iggy's script. 'I'm so messed up,' he sings, with complete authenticity: 'Somebody gotta help me please; somebody gotta save my soul.'

The concerts were by no means a disaster, but they did not augur well: withdrawn from the world, Sid could not project himself on stage and Nancy spoiled everything through her aggression. 'They alienated all the press,' says Joe Stevens, 'who went to Max's to get free drinks and fuck the waitresses. People like Lenny Kaye, other big shots, used to live in that night club and all of a sudden this little broad from Philadelphia is giving the shit at the top of the staircase. It was like trying to get in to the White House.'

As far as the American music industry was concerned, Vicious was in the same state as the Heartbreakers whose lifestyle he had emulated. Warners were not remotely interested, and any attempts that Vicious made to form groups foundered on Nancy's behaviour and his own severe dependence on methadone: he could not stay more than a few days away from the clinic without withdrawal. The move had not brought freedom but increasing bondage: as Sid said that September, 'the world has put us under house arrest'.

After a week-long visit to Nancy's parents in Main Line, Philadelphia (which, in Deborah Spungeon's account, was a complete nightmare) the pair began to fall apart. Their non-stop rush to oblivion was taking its physical toll: both were now weak and constantly ill. The drugs that they were taking were among the most debilitating in the pharmacopoeia: not only street heroin and prescription methadone, but Tuinols (barbiturates) and Dilaudid (the synthetic morphine which was often given to cancer patients). These were not drugs that got you high, but which blotted out the world.

On top of the effects of these drugs, neither had recovered from past illnesses and overdoses: Vicious had nearly died at least twice that year, while Spungeon was suffering from a serious kidney complaint. There was also the nature of their relationship: Nancy was the stronger of the two, provoking Sid into regular fights and beatings, which might once have had sexual connotations but were now just the way in which they confirmed their interdependence.

Spungeon was noticeably fading that early autumn. Before she had been a party girl, but now New York acquaintances noticed that she was uncoordinated and extremely depressed. 'Mildly suicidal' is how Max's manager Peter Crowley described them. 'She and Sid worked on each other all the time. One would talk about getting depressed and get the other going. I saw Sid within three or four days of Nancy's death and we tried to talk about his career. But he couldn't pull himself out of all the self-destructive talk.'

Because of the confused circumstances of Spungeon's death, and the confused minds of the material witnesses, it may never be possible to piece together what actually happened on 11 October. In the early evening, Sid and Nancy were seen sitting in the Chelsea's lobby with a punk girl: all three went upstairs to room 100 until midnight, when the girl left. Nancy then started making phone calls within the New York area, looking for a way to spend the money Sid had just received from Max's Kansas City and from Virgin.

At 1.30 a.m. Nancy got through to dealer Rockets Redglare, a police informer and methadone addict. Nancy asked for forty Dilaudid capsules at forty dollars apiece, which Redglare was unable to get: he took them a small amount of the drug and stayed until either 4 or 5 a.m. Nancy gave him a few hundred dollars for the next day. As Redglare left, he saw another dealer arrive, one Steve Cincotti.

Cincotti, who had a history of mental illness, would later sell a sleazy version of the story to the *New York Post*: that night he sold them Tuinol.

Redglare's police testimony conflicts with the account given to journalists immediately after Nancy's death by Neon Leon, a black guitarist who lived down the hall. In this version the pair came over at midnight: Sid showed him a five-inch knife that Nancy had bought him on Times Square, to protect himself from frequent beatings. Then Vicious gave Leon his leather jacket and his newspaper clippings, repeatedly saying that he was nobody, that he had no self-confidence. A few days after telling his story, Leon disappeared.

If you believe Leon, the last contact the pair had with the outside world was when they phoned him at 4.30 p.m. to ask him for some pot. According to Redglare, Cincotti was still in the room after that time, although he left soon after. What happened next will always be a blur. In an account given by Vicious shortly before his death, he woke up from a Tuinol stupor in the light of morning to find a trail of blood leading from a soaked bed to the bathroom.

Stumbling across the debris of the room, he found Nancy lying under the sink with a hunting knife sticking out of her side. She was wearing only a black bra and black bikini briefs, which were soaked in the blood that was all over the floor. Vicious went into complete shock – from which he would barely recover for the rest of his life. As the realization of what had occurred sank in, he panicked totally: the only person who had ever cared for him was dead, by his knife, and he couldn't remember a thing.

Some time between 5 a.m. and 9 a.m. – the police were never able to fix the exact time – Nancy Spungeon died on the bathroom floor of room 100: the cause was internal haemorrhaging due to a single knife wound in the lower abdomen. Vicious admitted to stabbing Nancy on arrest: 'I did it because I'm a dirty dog.' Handcuffed, he was taken to the Third Homicide division on 51st Street. By the time that Nancy's body was taken out of room 100 at 5.30 p.m. on the 12th, Vicious had been charged with second degree murder. He was oblivious.

As soon as the news was known, crowds gathered outside the Chelsea. Many were in time to see Nancy's body being removed. The immediate reports assumed Vicious's guilt: radio reports and local television news emphasized his violent relationship with Spungeon, his inability to give an account of events and his embodiment of a nihilistic culture that was regarded with puzzlement and hostility by most Americans. Sid had finally turned into a fully-blown scapegoat: a media monster from the id.

McLaren was alerted early in the afternoon of the 12th, by a *New York Post* reporter. He called Sid's mother, Mrs Beverley, and Joe Stevens, and then flew over straightaway. 'The legal people that handled Warners problems in America were Prior, Cashman, Sherman and Flynn,' says Stevens, 'they were showbiz lawyers. The next day, McLaren and I show up in court for the bail hearing, we just made it: this entertainment lawyer got Sid Vicious out on $50,000 bail, after he's been accused of killing an American citizen. Fishy.'

On his appearance in court that day, the 13th, Vicious was 'disconnected', unable to comment about anything. While he was forcibly undergoing cold turkey in the hospital wing of Riker's Island, McLaren started barnstorming. Prime among his concerns was raising money for a long court case: among his plans were a projected record and concert appearance by Sid once he was out on bail. After a day of phone calls, McLaren got a promise of bail money from Virgin Records, to arrive on Monday the 17th.

On Sunday the 16th, Anne Beverley arrived in New York, armed with a sleeping bag, her curious patience, and a reported $10,000 contract from the *New York Post*. Her visit to Rikers' Island was the first time she'd seen her son for a while. 'After Simon and Nancy got entrenched together,' she says, 'there was nothing I could say. Simon was loyal. If you tried to point out that so-and-so wasn't a good person to hang around with, he would stick up for them through thick and thin. He was like that all the more with Nancy. After she died, all my friends were really good, they forked out whatever they could afford, and I was on the first plane I could catch, because when you're in that kind of trouble, you need somebody with you. Malcolm did everything, he really was wonderful. I was just there. Simon was very down. Perhaps I was the most unfortunate person for him to be with. If I love someone, I can hold them, stroke their hair, but I can't talk, because I'm so frightened of saying the wrong thing, I don't know why.'

That same Sunday, Nancy's body was buried in Philadelphia. The next day, Virgin telegraphed the bail money to McLaren, who was unhappy at being beholden to Richard Branson, but had no choice. By the time he was released on bail on the morning of the 17th, Vicious was still in no position to defend himself, still traumatized by Nancy's death and the rushed withdrawal on Riker's Island. He was immediately whisked away from the prying eyes of the media.

With Sid facing a sentence of a maximum of twenty-five years, minimum seven, McLaren worked immediately to counter the general presumption of guilt. He accused the police of 'railroading' Sid and hired a firm of private investigators to look into the possibility of third-party involvement. There were so many gaps in the police's knowledge of events, and one of their first admissions muddied the waters still further: the room had been robbed during that night.

In the lack of any firm evidence, three separate theories emerged. The first was that Sid had killed Nancy in a squabble over drugs or in one of their many violent, insensible fights. The second pointed to third-party involvement, through Cincotti, unnamed thieves, or some Puerto Rican dealers with whom Nancy had had a recent argument. This was feasible: where had the $1,500 gone, if not all to Redglare? The third favoured a botched suicide attempt.

And the horror did not stop: on the 22nd, Sid Vicious tried to commit suicide. In anguish at Nancy's death, he was completely unable to control himself: after taking all his supply of methadone by Sunday morning, he began to suffer unbearable withdrawal symptoms. He slashed himself so badly that he was admitted to the psychiatric ward of Bellevue Hospital. To many, this added to the possibility that Sid was the survivor of a suicide pact gone wrong.

'Long afterwards I found a suicide pact note,' says Anne Beverley, 'in his handwriting, in his pocket. I think I'm trying to tell myself that I didn't find it until afterwards, because if you had tried to take your own life, by yourself, alone, and it doesn't come off, it's no longer a criminal offence. It used to be. But it is still a criminal offence if you make a suicide pact with another person: if you survive and they don't, it's manslaughter. So although I knew what happened, there was no way I could say anything. On the night in question, he told me he dropped nine Tuinols, which should have killed a horse. And I really do think Nancy stabbed herself. She wasn't a well person, she was always getting bladder infections, she had kidney trouble and was in a pain a lot. If you're intent on doing something like that, it's quite easy to do. If she told me once, she told me fifty times that she would die before she was twenty-one. It was a fixation.'

'They were staying at the Seville, a welfare hotel on Madison Avenue,' says Joe Stevens. 'The courts are getting really picky about Sid: they keep his passport, he's got to go for urine tests. He hates staying with his mum. McLaren and I get a call in the middle of the night from Ma Vicious. "Get here right away please. Sid's done something to himself." So we go flying uptown, get into the hotel room and there's Ma Vicious doing circles, spinning, and there's Sid on one of the two beds in the corner near the window.

'He's opened up one of his arms, but he's done it up the arm instead of across the wrists. He's mangled his arms. I'd been out the day before on an assignment with my micro cassette recorder and camera, so it was still in the bag. I took it out of the trunk. We thought Sid was close to death. McLaren goes over to the bed and says, "What did you fucking do this for? We're going to get you out of jail, you stupid cunt. You didn't kill Nancy now, did you?"

'Sid is lying there going, "Get me something to finish me off. Get me some smack." So Malcolm says to Sid: "Don't worry, I'll get you some quaaludes." What he's really doing is calling an ambulance. Ma Vicious hadn't done that yet. He calls Bellevue Hospital, quite close to the Seville, leaving me on the second bed, my bag between my legs, so I get the tape, lean over and say: "Why the fuck you wanna do that?" I thought I was talking to the soon-to-be-late Sid Vicious.

'He just said: "I want to be with my Nancy, I want to be left alone. I don't want to talk to any more New York City policemen. I don't want to be alone with my mum." I asked what happened with him and Nancy. He said: "You know how the Dead Boys poke each other with the knives through the leather jackets? Nancy slapped me in the nose just after I'd been punched out by the bellhop." He was loaded: when you're on Dilaudid, you don't like to be touched, a big problem, your skin is paranoid.

'He said: "She smacked me on the nose just where I'd been punched, and I took the knife out and said: 'Do that again, I'm going to take your fucking head off,' and she stuck her belly right in front of my knife." So it was a combination of him pushing, her pushing. "She didn't know. I didn't know that we'd done anything really bad. She crashed out on one bed. I crashed out on the other. I woke up first and decided to get some methadone. Took a forty-five minute taxi ride."

'He was guilty of negligence. While he was out, she got out of the bed, filled up the entire room with blood, crawling around. The way we guess, she sees herself in the mirror and collapses. The last thing she saw, according to the DA's office, she was face up, she was looking at the pipes under the sink. When I saw her body in the bag, she was still in the same position. The murder guys said that to me.

'Sid said he stuck her, but Sid and I both knew what she meant to him. She cashed his cheques. Sid didn't need to put out of commission the person who was keeping him afloat. The reason they had the fight was, she couldn't score drugs. They cashed a cheque for $1,300 from Virgin, but she was so obnoxious that she scared away Rockets Redglare. He was pretty obnoxious himself, but he didn't get along with Nancy, so even with all that money she couldn't score.

'While they were waiting for Rockets, Sid decided to go down to all the junkies' rooms, he was banging on doors and somebody complained. The bellhop, who was black, decided to kick ass. Sid made some stupid insult, and the guy whacked Sid in the nose. So when he returned to the room, he said, "What did you get?" "Oh, I never want to see that fat cunt again." "Never mind that, what did you buy?" Then they had the fight, and that argument is what caused her death.'

The blistering, almost psychotic nihilism encountered everywhere – no fun, no feelings and the savage dreams of mayhem – even in those closest to you – becomes the language of cash registers. Bourgeois society has bred its monsters. It objects to them at the same time as it makes money out of their denunciations.

Anonymous: *The End of Music* (1978)

Then like a load or rats from a sinking ship
You slag us down to save your hip
But don't give me the benefit of your doubt
'Cos I'll bite it off and spit it out.

The Clash: 'Cheapskates' (November 1978)

The most terrible thing about Sid and Nancy's self-destruction was that it was entirely expected, as a logical conclusion, not only to their individual life trajectories, but to the culture whose sickness they embodied. 'Everybody was glad it wasn't them,' says Legs McNeil. 'Many people thought at some time they could have gone out that far. No one has ever understood Punk, no one knows why it was, and when Sid killed Nancy, it was just more of it. Leave us alone.'

In London, Punks were, according to Nick Kent, 'harangued by passers by cracking jokes about "stabbing your girlfriend up".' From many of Sid's former friends and colleagues, harassed by the press, the initial reaction was negative: 'Don't care,' said John Lydon in one of the interviews to unveil Public Image, 'I don't see why I should have any feelings about it at all.'

Lydon went on to modify his comments, but humanity was in short supply at that point. The week that Nancy died, adverts had appeared for the Public Image single which referred to Sid and Nancy's injury at Gunter Grove: in a parody of a Smirnoff advertising campaign then current, the copy read 'I was wild with my chopper until I discovered PIL'. This was unfortunate timing, but indicative of the reflex sweeping London Punk – of which the 'Public Image' single, for all its brilliance, was part.

On the King's Road, where the first post – *Taxi Driver* Mohicans were appearing, Vivienne Westwood brought out a T-shirt which explicitly commodified Sid: 'She's dead, I'm alive, I'm yours.' Sid was now an object. 'You care about some people more than others,' Vivienne said at the time, 'more about Sid than Nancy. I also was aware that some people would think it was a bit sick, and I did it for that reason too, because I like to upset people.'

This only reinforced Lydon's sour view of McLaren's motives for flying to New York. A proposed Sex Pistols' reunion concert to raise funds for Sid was firmly vetoed. Depite Lydon's later expressions of concern, the only people who actually did anything about Sid's predicament were McLaren and the Clash, who, after a personal intervention from Anne Beverley, agreed to play a London benefit on 19 December.

Nancy's death marked the limits of Punk's negation: from now on, petty nihilism flourished in all its forms. All who had been remotely connected with London Punk were tearing each other apart. 'The year of complete control – getting flash Yank producers in to ensure the big dollar markets,' wrote Paul Weller. According to John Lydon, his new single was 'a slagging of the group I used to be in'. Dreams of possibility were replaced by cynicism, or survival.

Punk had been, if nothing else, a concentrated restatement of adolescence within culture, whether in an all-consuming anger, frustration or in the 'everlasting present' that is the hallmark of the teenage experience. 'I've got no time,' the Saints had boasted: through its very velocity, Punk had appeared to burst the bonds of time, but now it was imprisoned. For many, the clock had stopped. Some did not survive. The Saints, for instance, were used up after three albums in two years. 'That first blur of anger was something you can only do when you're about seventeen,' says Ed Kuepper, 'you make a decision that you want to survive.' Others, like the Adverts, continued as best they could.

'What was happening inside the band seemed to be reflected outside,' says T.V. Smith, 'it felt like autumn.'

'It came and went so fast,' says Roger Armstrong, 'that the groups all went to the roots of whatever they'd got into it for in the first place. You listen to the second Clash album, and they'd moved on. The Buzzcocks found their pop sensibility pretty early. And Siouxsie with that swirling, psychedelic thing. The bands that obviously suffered were the thrash bands. In the case of Moped, one album is what they had in them. It was too bizarre to keep going.'

Survival would now depend, not only on the quality of material and the strength of individual psyches, but on successful interaction with the music industry, something which many groups had never thought about when they first made noise. One of the surprises of the year was the success of Siouxsie and the Banshees, whose first single, 'Hong Kong Garden' made the Top Ten in September. 'It seemed totally logical,' says Severin, 'we just got the timing right.'

The Banshees' first album, *The Scream,* was very Ballardian: a cool, malevolent sweep through a landscape of decay. Together with Siouxsie's trademark make-up and hairstyle, this was a new English Gothick. Protected by a strong manager and a reasonable record deal, the group had mastered the initial stage of success: they now, suddenly, had to plan for longevity. 'There were new pressures,' says Severin, 'there didn't seem to be any reason why things were going wrong, except there was nothing to bounce off.'

'About the future I can only reminisce/But what I had is what I'll never get': one of the big songs that autumn, performed by Buzzcocks and Penetration, was Pete Shelley's bittersweet 'Nostalgia', a song about escaping time, which was trapped by the way its title fitted the regret of the moment. Caught between the past and an age yet to come, the Buzzcocks and Penetration tried to keep their ideals alive within an indifferent music industry.

Their very timeliness had taken them unawares, as they struggled within an industry where Punks were not seen as a long-term investment. 'We were so naive,' says Pauline Murray. Like many groups that epitomized the moment, Penetration were finding it hard to adapt. The style that had sounded great on eight-track now sounded lumpy on sixteen or twenty-four tracks. Badly advised by a 'Rockist management' and their record company, Penetration were now expected to go through the motions of a Rock group, which had not been the point.

The Buzzcocks had converted Punk's momentum into a frantic work-rate of tours and records, but that autumn, time caught up. 'There was a change,' says Pete Shelley, 'because during that year we took off. At the beginning, we were playing the Roundhouse, and it built up to the Lyceum, then the Hammersmith Odeon. It was unnerving. When we did the "Love Bites" tour I was convinced by Richard Boon not to leave the band. It was all getting too much.'

The independent sector that the Buzzcocks had done so much to inspire began to provide a real alternative to a mainstream music industry in manic overdrive. 'Rough Trade was very committed to supporting independent endeavour,' says Richard Boon, 'and established a network for disseminating that information. They expanded the mail order, they established links with sympathetic retailers round the country, and began the Cartel distribution network.'

'We always saw distribution as a political thing,' says Rough Trade's Geoff Travis. 'If you only have W. H. Smith selling books, then you only get a certain kind of book. If you set up a viable system that sells other kinds of literature, then you give people a chance to decide for themselves. When we started our own record label it was my taste and my politics which informed it, and it wasn't Punk but post-Punk – Cabaret Voltaire, Metal Urbain – and women's music: Kleenex, the Raincoats.'

For many musicians, the independent sector offered space to grow at their own pace and still be heard. In a mutually beneficial symbiosis, the music press found the independents a fertile seam to mine. Independent releases were often given lead reviews; there was an 'alternative chart'. At a time when London was bitter, the messages from around the country and around the world still held some hope of forward movement and accounted for a high proportion of Punk sales.

The independents' ideologies were as various as the styles they recorded. Some just released records by whatever groups walked through their door just to get something out, without much thought beyond turning over 2,000–5,000 copies so that they could go on to the next one. In this way, they often acted as unofficial A&R men for the majors, or major minors, very pleased to have somebody filter all this disparate information.

In Northern Ireland, Terri Hooley's Good Vibrations enabled a new generation of Belfast groups to record: their biggest find, however, was Londonderry's Undertones, whose wonderful 'True Confessions' EP was taken up within a month of its release by Sire Records.

Edinburgh's Fast label was something else: a mixture of rigour and the new obsession with the packaging process. Cutting-edge records by the Mekons, the Human League and Gang of Four illustrated the variety of approaches on offer: electronics, DIY, rigour.

The north and north-western network resulted in another label, Factory, based around the Manchester club of the same name. The first product – a collaboration with Liverpool label Erics – was a double, seven-inch, plastic-wrapped 'Factory Sampler', which featured Cabaret Voltaire, Durutti Column, and Joy Division. This was the start of the independents' heyday. 'By 1979, Rough Trade had had some success with Stiff Little Fingers,' says Tony Wilson, Factory cofounder, 'and the political identity had arrived. The point was to keep your major group – ours was Joy Division – on your indie label: not to sell to the majors.'

Many new independent groups took on the dialectical process that had begun with RAR, recognizing RAR's importance in local infrastructures. In London, a clutch of groups clustered around Rough Trade: the post-Slits; rigorously feminist Raincoats; PragVec, formed out of the agitprop Derelicts; the revived Red Krayola, or Scritti Politti, whose first record, 'Skank Bloc Bologna', detailed the exact cost of producing a record yourself.

Despite the apparent liberation of their rhetoric, many of these groups painted themselves into a corner: there were so many things you could not be – sexist, racist, entryist, Rockist – that the negatives overpowered any potential *jouissance*. Apart from brief bursts of Scritti Politti, the music was no fun at all. And, for a while, just like the rhetoric of RAR, the organization that had inserted the Left discourse into Punk, the ideological rigour of these groups brooked no disagreement.

The hostility between the 'arties' and the social realists had now been long established: during the year, the arties subdivided into the rigorous, the pop-obsessed and those carrying on the examination into the darker side of humanity. Hostility broke out between these subdivisions: a concert played by Throbbing Gristle at the London Film Co-op in July ended in a pitched battle between the group on stage and several members of the Slits and the Raincoats. It was a complete clash of ideologies.

As the year deepened, the nihilist techniques of the age, whether inside Punk or out, fed back. The result was self-destruction or cynicism. In November, just before a concert at the Crypt, P-Orridge took so many pills that he overdosed after the performance ended. 'I pulled back, just,' he says, 'I completely lost my memory for twelve months just after that: I was so burned out by the drugs. The overriding feeling was one of failure on every level.'

Already, Punk communities in San Francisco and Los Angeles were being stifled by the lack of mass-media interest. In New York, the ultra-negative 'No' groups – Mars, DNA, Teenage Jesus and the Jerks, the Contortions – had their first compilation record released in November, to little avail. 'Things started to go sour for me when I started hearing all the racist bullshit,' says Adele Bertei. 'James Chance flirted with it: it was, let's outrage as much as we can, to the point where you're sacrificing your morals to shout racist abuse. James would leap into the audience and get the shit beat out of him, but towards the end of that masochistic syndrome of his, there was one gig we did at the Paradise Garage which really got out of hand. They didn't want to pay us what they had agreed to pay us. James completely freaked out, took a beer bottle, smashed it in the hallway, took the broken shards and proceeded to dig at his face, while we were trying to control him.

'Finally we got the glass out of his hand, but it was real. Not a put-on performance anymore. This kid is really disturbed, to do this. He was already unstable, very nervous, but it just got worse and worse. Then a lot of smack started to flood the Lower East Side. All of a sudden it was everywhere, and James and his girlfriend, Anya Phillips, started getting into it. Outrage: "How Far Is This Gonna Go?" That aggression against society began to implode.'

'We never felt part of any of that stuff,' says Pere Ubu's David Thomas. 'I've said before that I thought that the New-Wave movement is the worst thing that ever happened to music in America: it wiped out a generation of musicians. All the interesting groups that came out of that period, like Devo and Talking Heads, had been working prior to that window of 1977, in isolation and without any hope of commercial success. These were important things.

'When you're young there comes this splitting of the road: you'll see it in any American High School. You have the geeks bending off – you've got pens in your pocket and you play chess at lunchtime and you make films – or you go off to the mainstream. The geeks know they're geeks, and that everybody despises them, and they plough ahead nonetheless. New Wave presented the face of hardcore geekdom, but without any substance: it was a template. Once you have a template to mould yourself to, you're out of isolation. All these people suddenly had something to copy, and at that point, it doesn't matter what you're copying, you're still copying.'

London's cynicism was captured by Tony Parsons and Julie Burchill's *The Boy Looked at Johnny*, which, published in November, came off not as an 'obituary of Rock'n'Roll', not even a celebration of Tom Robinson or Poly Styrene, but a case study in amphetamine psychosis. 'After reading through ninety pages of BP's unrelenting vituperation,' wrote Simon Frith that year, 'I was much more upset about their unconscious obsessions than by their conscious arguments. Theirs is an aggressive, neurotic normality.'

During that year, the hardline rhetoric of RAR had solidified into its own nihilism. RAR and the ANL had defined themselves negatively, in reaction to the National Front. There were flaws in their own rhetoric: as Martin Thom pointed out at the time, 'the use of terms like rats, scum, plague, vermin, disease make racists appear inhuman, outside society and history.' This rhetoric of impurity exactly paralleled that of the fascists themselves.

The Parsons/Burchill book fell into the same trap. 'Theirs is a language of physical decay,' wrote Frith. 'BP seem compulsively disturbed by baldness, disease, frailty. Faggot is another ubiquitous term of contempt.' This is the discourse described by Peter Sloterdijk: 'Here, a mannerism of rage makes itself felt that gives the great dead ego a pedestal from which the nauseous, incomprehensible world can be despised.' In the hands of Burchill (Parsons bailed out) it would prove a powerful media reflex.

11.11.78: It's hard when you define a period so accurately. The Pistols broke up and neatly avoided the issue. Here, the Clash seem locked in time, stranded in their conception of what the problems are, where solutions are to be found, and what problems face their audience. They have an audience which is loyal to the point of fanaticism: they often seem to relate to each other on the basis of mutual reinforcement. Trapped in this circle, the Clash's solution is Rock'n'Roll. From being radicals, they become conservatives.

'The sport of today is exciting/The in crowd are into in-fighting': if it was happening, the Clash sang about it. Their delayed second album, *Give 'Em Enough Rope*, was finally released in November, heralded by an extraordinarily paranoid press conference and uniformly bad reviews. As Punk's heart, the Clash could do no right once the heart had gone out of Punk. This was unfair. If the world itself wasn't falling apart, then *their* world was.

The Clash had been set up to organize a Punk community which had largely disappeared, except in the enthusiasm of their young audiences. They could not but help fall victim to the disillusion of the time. The year had been a difficult one: there were business disputes with Bernard Rhodes, and the perennial second album problem: how to come up with new, relevant material, yet translate their social power in recorded terms. *The Clash* took a week; *Give 'Em Enough Rope* took over three months.

The Clash had been a concept album of trial and tribulation in Ladbroke Grove, but *Give 'Em Enough Rope* was about global oppression. The Clash posed in military gear in front of a world map underscored by National Front marchers: inset boxes on the map depicted what was happening country by country: Son of Sam (America); Neutron Bomb (America); Red Brigade (Italy); Baader/Meinhof (Germany); Aboriginal genocide (Australia); Pol Pot (Cambodia); British occupation (Northern Ireland).

This was confused, to say the least. Yet the Clash were adept at recognizing their contradictions, and expressing them musically. Here high-gloss production is still fighting amateurism, and the whole monolith is given humanity by Strummer's ranter persona. When the group take off together and he launches on one of his rants, like 'The English Civil War', the Clash retain the suspension of disbelief that was now necessary not only for the group to carry off a rhetoric that was bursting at the seams, but just to keep together.

Give 'Em Enough Rope was a powerful but baffling record: the film to which it was effectively the soundtrack was not released for another year. If, in 1979, *Rude Boy* was embarrassing, today, it is a visual record of a lost era. Opening with mute shots of the clichéd high rise, the film quickly takes you on a tour through a society in terminal crisis: SWP and NF graffiti, huge embattled marches, Mrs Thatcher making inflammatory calls for law and order.

This is the backdrop against which the Clash are attempting, throughout 1978, to Rock'n'Roll at the same time as they raise a generation's consciousness. The contradictions of the time are embodied in the film's principal character, Ray Gange, a real Clash acolyte, 'the typical fan': one of those adolescent males who hangs out with Rock groups. He hangs around long enough to become their road manager, but is fired because he is such an idiot.

Not much of a story, and the device is often laboured, but there are some emotional kicks, partly because of Gange's very ineptitude, the actual documentary footage, and the decidedly non-fictional, hostile reactions of group members towards him. The Clash have problems of their own without having to worry about carrying a passenger. Throughout, they are embattled by police, bouncers, fans, and their own contradictory position: Rock stars or politicians?

'What the hell is wrong with you,' Strummer screams in frustration onstage: 'You're just doing what you're supposed to do.' *Rude Boy*'s achievement is to present the Punk subculture at the point of its disintegration. As the film carries on through the year, the Clash solve their dilemmas by becoming progressively less open, more 'professional'. And, the film says, such is the greatness of the Clash, that their struggle was a microcosm of England at that time.

The cautious optimism of the early part of the year – based on economic projections – had, by late summer, collapsed into a defensive posture on the part of the Labour Government. A June vote of confidence was narrowly retained by 287 to 282. The forthcoming election was delayed for two reasons: Callaghan wanted the economic situation to be seen to get better, and he was worried by the Tories' improvement in the opinion polls, stimulated by one advertising campaign of the summer, which, over an image of the unemployed that could have been on a Punk album sleeve, stated: 'Labour Isn't Working'.

Callaghan decided to use the time finally to set a seal on the social contract of regulated public sector pay-rises, but, at the party and union conferences, the unions and the Labour Left rebelled. From November, when the Government met a Commons defeat in its attempt to block a proposed Ford pay rise of 15 per cent, open season was declared. As the winter deepened into one of the harshest for years, the social fabric of the country, that part most affected by the many public sector disputes, began to deteriorate.

On 8 January, all the country's docks were closed. By the 11th, when Callaghan was reported by the *Sun* to have come back from a holiday in the sun with the words, 'Crisis, what crisis?', it began to seem as though England was ungovernable, as though Babylon was really falling. Suddenly, the rhetoric of Punk and Reggae wasn't quite so far-fetched. Yet it was almost too descriptive: as it became clear that the country had to make a choice, which side would the Punks be on?

'Face front we got the future/Shining like a piece of gold.' Strummer is recording 'All the Young Punks' in the studio, 'But I swear as we got closer/It looks more like a lump of coal.' This is the nub of *Rude Boy*: the future is coming up fast and, for all their humanity and their courage, the Clash are impotent. 'The reason the left wing is better than the right wing is that it's not just the many slaving for the few,' says Strummer. 'My idea is to become one of the few,' Gange replies. 'I want to be a capitalist.'

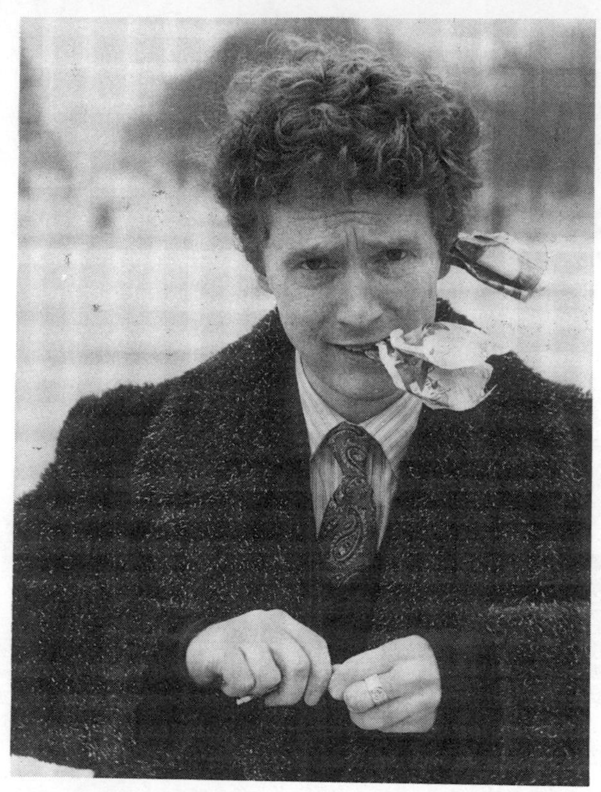

Malcolm McLaren, during the filming of *The Great Rock'n Roll Swindle*, August 1978 (© Rex Features)

35

Those who hate fervently must once have loved deeply. Those who want to deny the world must once have embraced what they now set on fire.

Kurt Tucholsky: 'Dada' (20 July 1920)

Boredom is no longer my love. Rage, perversion, madness, whose every impulse and disaster I know – my burden is set down entire.

Arthur Rimbaud: 'Bad Blood' (1873)

On 10 November, John Lydon started High Court proceedings to wind up the Sex Pistols partnership. The case was adjourned until a hearing date could be fixed: there was some delay in serving notice on Sid Vicious, then in Bellevue. Shortly afterwards, the date was set for the second week in February. Like most court actions, number 1152 in the 1978 List was entirely unnecessary if one applied logic, but logic was the last thought in the minds of the two protagonists.

Lydon and McLaren had not spoken to each other since that weekend in February, but the constant back and forth of press reports, lawyers' meetings and London gossip had inflamed their already intense hostility over the year until it had reached the stage where Lydon could announce on LWT's *Weekend* show that he would like to see McLaren dead. Each man hates another for what is inside himself, and nowhere was this truer than in the mutual loathing between the pair.

Even in dispute, the similarities between Lydon and McLaren were evident. Each was insisting that it was he who had created the Sex Pistols, and he alone: 'Egomaniac traitor,' Lydon called McLaren on *Low Life*; 'collaborator' was McLaren's epithet. McLaren took on the characteristics of the swindler Lydon had branded him; Lydon dressed up Public Image in a poor imitation of Seditionaries, as if to say that even this was his idea.

The extent of this antipathetic symbiosis puzzled the other parties in the case. 'We took a neutral position, which was where we were, between Malcolm and John,' says Paul Cook. 'We weren't interested in court cases, we didn't get into it for that. It wasn't in our make up, to sort business problems out. We were still involved with Malcolm on the film. John hated Malcolm. He really wanted to take him on, and there was this clash all the time.'

The Sex Pistols were still nominally in existence, but with Sid tearing himself apart in New York, things had slowed right down. Any new product was now pegged to the film, scheduled for release in January. The skills of Cook and Jones were in demand: late in 1978, Steve Jones flew to America to do some production work with the Avengers and ex-Runaway Joan Jett, the start of a sound that would dominate American Rock when Punk finally broke there in the mid-eighties.

The people now most enthusiastically committed to keeping the concept of the Sex Pistols alive were Glitterbest. 'The thing in the office,' says Julien Temple, 'was that the *idea* of the Sex Pistols was not to be a Rock band and make millions and go on forever. We were all very charged up about that idea, which wasn't easy to do because John was really important, but I felt that the idea of destroying the group in the most spectacular way possible would be done better together with Malcolm.'

Much of the paperwork had been done, but until the tortuous legal process was invoked, there was still a chance that the Sex Pistols would settle out of court. Richard Branson wanted Public Image and the Sex Pistols to coexist peacefully on Virgin: he sent money for Sid Vicious's bail and put up another £150,000 to continue *The Great*

Rock'n'Roll Swindle. This increased his control over both the Sex Pistols – extending their existing record contract – and the film.

Until the end of October, the agitators were not Virgin, but Warner Brothers America, who were instituting proceedings to sue for their £200,000 film advance. 'Bob Regehr had sent John £12,000 to buy the flat in Gunter Grove,' says Joe Stevens, 'then when they flew me over to do depositions in the summer, John had an account at Barclays, and Regehr sent him monies for the case.' Regehr had made his decision: days after Nancy's death, Warners dropped Sid and the other two Pistols from the label. Their relationship with Glitterbest was also severed.

But, despite the vitriol that appeared later on film and in court, McLaren was trying to engineer his own escape, just as he had at Croydon ten years previously. During October, McLaren and Stephen Fisher were involved in 'completely confidential' negotiations with James Ware, Virgin's lawyer, for a Virgin buy-out of Glitterbest. The asking price was, as Steven Fisher wrote to Ware on the 31st, 'a minimum of £500,000', which was reasonable for a company which only showed a £6,568 profit for the previous nine-month period.

Events overtook the plan. McLaren's own mounting mania made him impossible to deal with. 'During the time that Sid was being tried, or in gaol,' says Julien Temple, 'Malcolm had a permanent red "M" on his forehead. I think he was very wired, deranged. I think the whole Sid thing was far more complicated in his head than he let out. He did feel responsible in some ways. I don't think he did anything wrong, but he did feel very humanly about it.'

McLaren's unreasonableness forced the oncoming court case. 'Cultivate hatred: it is your greatest asset' was the seventh lesson of *Swindle*, and McLaren was determined to put it into practice. In true Debordian mode, he would expel everybody from the Sex Pistols faction until he was the only person left. Stress brings out personal extremes: in McLaren's case, what emerged were persecution mania and self-destruction.

The film was not going well. The film industry involves a much higher level of investment and thus the backers have more control than in the music industry. There, as Michael Watts wrote, McLaren's 'ideas were subjected to a practical scrutiny that they did not often survive'. Film production involves a collaborative process which it took McLaren a long time to understand: 'He was forever changing his mind,' Julien Temple said then, 'but the basic problem was in him not knowing how to translate an intellectual idea into film.'

About two-thirds of the film had been shot, including the startling Gordon Riots sequence, and McLaren's tap dance to 'You Need Hands', with Helen the dwarf, in the closed part of Highgate Cemetery. But the whole project was coming apart: 'I remember one day telling Malcolm that there was no money in our account,' says Sophie Richmond, 'the script changed throughout the shooting, according to what could be done. And where was the material for the *Swindle* album going to come from?'

Worst of all, the nightmare with Sid continued. Within a few days after his suicide attempt, Sid was discharged from Bellevue, but not before the judge in charge of the case called for a psychological examination to be made. The next court hearing was adjourned until 21 November. Sid found another disturbed girlfriend, Michelle Robinson, an actress who had also lost a partner: with her, he reentered New York night life.

Robinson was in court holding Sid's hand on the 21st, when District Attorney Al Sullivan said: 'He cultivates an image of antagonism and has a flagrant disregard for constitutional authority.' The judge allowed bail to stand at $50,000 provided Sid reported to New York Homicide and the methadone clinic. This involved daily appointments, something Sid was not good at: he was left in the control of his mother, who was not very good at controlling herself.

On 9 December, Sid went to Hurrah's, a new disco. At about 2.30 a.m. he got into a fight with Todd Smith, Patti's brother, whose girlfriend (the guitar player in Skafish) Sid had molested. Smith threw a few punches at Sid, who retaliated with a broken bottle. Smith was taken to hospital with a head wound needing five stitches. The next day it was back to Riker's Island and cold turkey, for Sid's abuse of drugs had not ceased. When the next court hearing was held, on 12 December, Vicious was right in the middle of his detoxification. Judge Leff decided to keep Vicious in custody while reports were prepared. The next hearing was set for 31 January: until then, Vicious would have to continue his Riker's Island detox. 'There was a guy who took care of him there,' says Joe Stevens, 'the people read about his murder case and they left him alone.'

That week, John Lydon and Public Image released their album, a primal sound of rage and claustrophobia. Most of the material had some bearing on the Sex Pistols' 'divorce', whether 'Public Image', 'Attack' or the excoriating, almost sub-judice 'Low Life'. The first song, 'Theme' was slow, monotonous, druggy. 'It goes on and on and on,' Lydon intoned as though being slowly suffocated. He tries to vomit it out, but it's no good: 'I wish I could die.'

The events of the time overshadowed the record's real achievements. Lydon had performed an astonishing feat: reinventing himself with a totally new sound that was every bit as powerful – musically – as the Sex Pistols. Freed from the Rock'n'Roll format, Lydon used his voice like a muezzin, high wailing over the top of a constantly shifting, loose yet extremely powerful, wall of sound from Levene, Wobble and Walker, that fused Reggae, Rock and Funk. No instrument, including the voice, was highlighted for very long: each musician was equal in the mix and, as they each tried out new approaches to their instruments, the tension was terrific. And if that wasn't enough, the cover was a dizzying spoof on image and marketing. 'John said, "Why don't we go to the opposite, I'm fed up with all this punk thing",' remembers Dennis Morris, 'hence that sleeve. John was *L'Uomo Vogue*, Wobble was *Time*, Keith was *Mad*, and the drummer Jim, was *Him*, the gay magazine'.

25.12.78: Public Image Limited, Rainbow Theatre, London. This, as expected, is mainly Rotten's show. Except now there is a new element of whining and self-justification: he whines about the Pistols, the press, the audience, Glitterbest, etc, more than is necessary. It sits ill with the traces of his previous persona, and subtracts from PiL's still fragile freedom. And its all about him*: pointing at himself, megalomania rampant, I wanna be MEEEEE!*

Much of *Public Image* presaged the future, but Lydon was trapped by a past from which he would not be able to escape for many years. He had engineered his getaway from the Sex Pistols at a considerable cost: without any time to recover from the previous two years, he had been forced to fight for his very existence. Despite support from Warners and Virgin, he felt completely alone – and was wise to feel so: irritated by the album's abrasive production, Virgin haggled over its release while Warners US baulked completely.

McLaren's mania began to increase in parallel to Lydon's. With Temple, he was now frantically working to get the film finished before the deadline, but much still remained to be done. Right through the winter, Temple continued to shoot odd days on a miniscule budget: with McLaren so often away, the scenes began to reflect his own obsessions with an English tradition, in the use of Irene Handl and the *Carry On* feel of the final cinema sequences with Eddie Tudorpole, renamed Tenpole Tudor.

'I had a huge bust-up with Malcolm just before the court case,' says Julien Temple. 'Like everyone else I had sided with him. We were in this horrible old Soho tenement, and we had this big screaming match where he wanted to sack me from the film but to keep me on as a sort of slave where he wanted me to bring trims when ordered but never to open my mouth again. He said he'd raised me from the gutter, which was a funny line. He just wanted to take control.'

McLaren was fatally distracted by the ongoing nightmare in New York. Sid was due in court on 1 February, the week before the Glitterbest/Lydon case was to be heard. Lydon had spent at least nine months preparing his case: just as would happen seven years later, McLaren left the pulling together of his affidavits right to the last minute: the last, by John Tiberi, was taken on 2 Feburary. By this time, the last act of the tragedy had been played.

The plan had been that McLaren should go to New York with bail money and meet Vicious out of court. Sid would then travel with McLaren and the remaining two Pistols to Miami, where they would cut an album of standards like 'Mack The Knife' to raise money for Sid's defence. During this time in Riker's, Vicious had detoxified and had healed physically. There were enough inconsistencies in the prosecution's case to offer hope of acquittal. The plan was completely destroyed by the Lydon court case. Mired in lawyers' meetings, McLaren was not able to devote much time to Sid. Unable to leave the country, he decided to send Barbara Harwood, who, inspired by Sid, was now training to be a homeopathic doctor. 'I worked out what remedies Sid was going to need,' says Harwood, 'the same day I got back to the office and Sid's mum rang to say that she was sitting in Sid's room, he was dead, what should she do?'

On the 1st, Sid's lawyer, James Merberg, made an impassioned plea which worked all too well: Sid was out by lunchtime, a day ahead of schedule. Waiting for him were several members of the New York junkie set and his mother, who had already bought some heroin to give to her son. In the pictures taken that day, Sid looks healthy but there is a deep vacancy in his eyes: time had not healed the severity of Nancy's loss. Without her, he felt like nothing. He had nowhere to go.

'We got back to Michelle Robinson's flat in Greenwich Village,' says Anne Beverley, pausing before taking the plunge. 'I'd invited about eight people. I was going to do a spaghetti bolognese in celebration of Simon getting out. Simon had had a fix early in the day, supplied by this guy called Martin, which had so little in it that it didn't do anything. Then later on this Martin said he could get some more. I argued with Simon, but he wanted some more.

'He was a well-known person. If I had said no, he would have just gone and got it himself. If he did that, he was going to get nicked, because he was Sid. So I had to go along with it. What are you gonna do, put a collar and a lead on somebody? So Martin left. I cooked the meal, the guy came back, we all had the meal. They all went out into the bedroom, and a quarter of an hour later they all walked back in, and Simon had a rose pink aura around his whole body.

'I went, "What?" I said, "Jesus, son, that must have been a good hit." He was elated, quietly so. Elated on the inside, coming out, creating the aura. I've never seen anything like it. Five minutes later he went back into the bedroom and someone said, "Simon's collapsed". He was sliding down the bed, what should I do? Should I take him to the hospital, which was just up the road, or do I sit it out and hope he comes round?'

She pauses, and breaks down. After above five minutes, she continues. 'We put him on his side. Hope he slept it off. He came round. "Oh fuck, I was so worried about you." "I'm fine, mum, I'm alright." He didn't want to go for a walk, and he had to report in the morning, so they went to bed. I slept on the couch in the sitting room. That night, after they'd taken it, I said, "I'll have the rest of it, I don't want you taking anymore," and I put it in my back pocket. I don't know how he could have got it: it must have been a relapse.'

'They cleaned him up beautifully in Riker's,' says Stevens, 'vitamins, sleep. He was completely detoxed. I hadn't visited him on this one: he's bottling people, come on! The next day, I leave the apartment, I'm walking past a cafe and they have an FM radio on, and I hear, "Sid Vicious found dead in girlfriend's Greenwich Village apartment. Stay tuned for further details". So I go down there.

'There's a cop outside and he says, "Get outta here" but Michelle gets me in. I didn't take any pictures. Ma Vicious is freaking out, Michelle was taking time out from freaking out, then going back into it again. I said to Michelle, "You know Hendrix died: with all those people, the story starts to change after awhile. So why don't we get the facts down now? Who knows, the truth might stick." So we go into the bathroom and she tells me everything.

'I tell the same thing to Ma Vicious, "Be straight with me, I won't fuck you." She said, "Let's go in the back room where it's quiet." In the back room there's a little table lamp, the bed all rumpled, and she starts talking. At this point I don't have much room on the bed so I push something away, and it's Sid's foot, they just put a sheet over him. And there she is, telling me how she bought the smack.

'So what happened was that the party's going on, when the dealer arrives. He says "There's a problem with the smack: it's nearly 100 per cent." Five weeks before it's unheard of, but something has happened to the smack scene in that time. The dealer says, "Please, just take a little bit." So Sid takes a little bit, but he puts in a little more. Then he turns blue, but survives. In the middle of the night, he gets up, goes to ma's purse, grabs the packet, shoots up a whole load, goes back to bed and dies.'

'I'm glad he died, in view of what happened,' says Anne Beverley. 'Nothing can hurt him anymore. And where could he have gone, from where he was at? He was in a corner. It would have come out that it was a suicide pact, which made him guilty of manslaughter, and sorry, here's five years, you'll be out in three. Three years in a hard nick in the States? He couldn't have done that, because he was not a hard man, he was too sweet and soft. He would never have survived. The rug was pulled out from under his feet.'

The news was a numbing blow on emotions already badly bruised. 'The call came into the office on Friday,' says Barbara Harwood. 'Malcolm and Jamie and I went to French's, and got maudlin, blaming ourselves. I blamed myself. Each of us blaming ourselves and telling each other we weren't to blame. "Oh, it's not your fault. What could we have done that would have made any difference?" I cried all weekend.'

If cynicism had greeted the death of Nancy Spungeon, then the reaction to the death of Sid Vicious was all the more terrible because it seemed so *expected*, which was another way for everybody involved in the culture to shake off their own responsibility. As can be imagined, Fleet Street went to town on the story, which made the front page of all the tabloids on 3 February. It was a God-given story: Sex'n'drugs'n'-Rock'n'Roll'n'knives'n'death.

It was all pre-packaged, this story of 'the inadequate youth who turned a tasteless pop gimmick into pathetic real life'. John Simon Ritchie had been turned into an object, right from the time that John Lydon had thought up his name, Vivienne Westwood had programmed him and McLaren had encouraged him. During the previous two years, the Sex Pistols had been through inhuman pressures: McLaren, Lydon and the others were surviving, albeit scarred, through luck, a strong self-preservation instinct, and a bedrock emotional stability.

John Simon Ritchie lacked all three: his mother was unable to prevent the damage of her own youth being inscribed on him from the earliest age. The pressures that had severely damaged all those around him were too much for John Simon Ritchie: as Sid Vicious, he had not, as Dick Hebdige noted at the time, 'done it his way'. Whether his final rush to oblivion was a reflex or one last act of volition we shall never know. And the whole exploitation process – recently revived to bring life – now commodified death: within three weeks, the next Sex Pistols record was to be released, Vicious's cover of Eddie Cochran's 'Something Else'. It would sell 382,000 copies, nearly double 'God Save the Queen'. And so the grisly James Dean archetype – linking youth, speed and death with sex, just like the 1988 Levi's advertisement which fictionalized Eddie Cochran's life – was given another lease of life.

There is another reason for Sid Vicious's entry into myth. From the days when Richard Hell and Tom Verlaine transformed themselves, Punk was infected by a Rimbaldian script: live fast, disorder your senses, flame brightly before self-immolation. In this script, Rimbaud's final days as an arms dealer are as much a void as any death. Sid Vicious went for this as hard as possible: his protracted demise, now world-wide news, was the ultimate statement of Punk's inbuilt drive to failure.

McLaren was very upset. Exploitation masked real emotion: 'You acted beyond the formal role and relationship you had with him,' wrote Sid's psychologist, Stephen Teich, to McLaren the next day, 'clearly out of a sense of humanity and concern for somebody you cared for. His loss is even greater on the personal level than on the public one. From beginning to end, Sid as a person was seen through the warping influence of dollar signs in the eyes.'

'Malcolm liked Sid,' says Stevens. 'They had their battles, but Sid had a sense of humour that penetrated with McLaren. John knew Sid was a real pussy and that he had stitched him up into a name and a lifestyle that wasn't going to help him grow up and get out of his miseries. He was always trying to live up to the hype and Rotten knew he'd stitched him up with that, and he felt some guilt, although he never confessed that to me.'

This is where McLaren hit his personal brick wall: five days later, while the remains of Ritchie were being cremated in New York, he had to attend court for the first day of the action brought by John Lydon against his two companies and the other three Pistols. There was no time, no room in the law for grief. Almost catatonic, he had to attend in an arena where his brilliant, airy ideas and fancies were to be dissected in the cold, deliberate language of intention and fact, and would be found wanting.

The hearing, which began on Wednesday 7 February in the Chancery Court, had been triggered by money. John Lydon had been incensed that McLaren was effectively using royalties and advances that he, as one of the Sex Pistols, had earned, on trying to continue a group which no longer existed. His money was also being used for a film in which he had never wanted to participate, over which he had no control, and which was likely, moreover, to vilify him. He had had no satisfactory accounts nor had he been paid what he was due.

Lydon's case was that the Sex Pistols partnership had been dissolved in San Francisco on 17 January, and that the Glitterbest management contract had ceased to stand as from that date. He was therefore pressing for an injunction that would halt the whole Sex Pistols enterprise, before redistribution of assets in recognition of the partnership dissolution. These assets included not only the name itself, but also the copyrights both before and after the split.

Lydon hinted at various possible avenues of argument in his affidavit. There was the possible conflict of interest in the constitution of Glitterbest itself, run only by their manager and their lawyer; there was also the question of whether the original contract was valid. Then there were hints of mismanagement by McLaren, centring around first, his preventing the group from playing live during 1977 and second, his use of Glitterbest money on the Matrixbest *The Great Rock'n'Roll Swindle*.

McLaren's reply detailed all that he had done for the group managerially, which, when totted up over several pages, was undoubtedly impressive: film contracts, record contracts all over the world, all worth hundreds of thousands of pounds. On the main issue, McLaren was consistent: the partnership had not dissolved in San Francisco; all that had happened was that the plaintiff had left, and he had been left holding the baby – i.e. several contracts which had to be fulfilled.

When the case finally came to court, it became clear that the underlying issue was the authorship that McLaren had claimed in the original management contract. Who 'was' the Sex Pistols, their singer or their manager? The Sex Pistols had been a collective effort, but now they were reduced to a bitter struggle between two intransigent people who were also egomaniacs: the age-old struggle, endlessly repeated in the law courts, between manager and performer.

In this struggle, Lydon seemed very much alone, the sole plaintiff against Glitterbest, Matrixbest and the two Sex Pistols. Virgin had not swung completely behind him even at this late stage, but he had three powerful factors on his side: detailed planning; public sympathy for the performer as opposed to the manager; and Glitterbest's complete inability to account for the group's earnings. Of course, they couldn't: they had spent them on the film. And he had a powerful QC, John Wilmers, who made mincemeat of McLaren right from day one. The film was McLaren's weak point, and Wilmers hammered at it ruthlessly. When the *Who Killed Bambi* script was read out in court, the judge took it as an accurate record of what went on. It was easy to present McLaren as an evil Svengali, a character out of some Victorian melodrama, of the sort that McLaren himself was attempting to portray in scenes from *The Great Rock'n'Roll Swindle*. Once this had been suggested, nothing could change the judge's mind.

Here McLaren's initial lack of generosity told badly against him: it was easy for John Lydon to say that the contract had given McLaren 'too much control' over the group. After all, he along with two other Sex Pistols, had been under twenty-one at the time and – as would later become a deciding factor in these cases – they had not obtained independent legal advice. 'McLaren signed them up at an early age,' says Joe Stevens, who appeared as a witness for Lydon, 'he was impatient and had no time for what he had started.'

By Friday, McLaren was admitting to John Tiberi that 'We won't be in great shape; on Monday, they'll get a receiver for the partnership, but not for the Glitterbest company. They won't be able to determine whether the management of the group is void except by going to trial, which means that the case will go on, maybe for months. Whether they decide to go ahead and spend another £100,000 is questionable, so the other side may want to come to a settlement this weekend.'

But, as the details piled up, it became increasingly obvious that McLaren would lose this round. According to Wilmers, Glitterbest had received £434,000 in the period between September 1976 and

March 1978, and most of this money – from royalties and record advances – had been spent on the film. Virgin and Lydon were now controlling the case in court, and on Tuesday the 13th, the last nail went into McLaren's coffin as Paul Cook and Steve Jones, furious at the alleged misuse of £90,000 owing to them, changed lawyers and changed sides.

'From the beginning, Malcolm had put the advances and the artist's royalties into the movie,' says John Tiberi, 'it could be construed that he was playing around with other people's money, but it was all to make the group more money. It was taking advantage of things that had to be filmed when they happened, to record the group's career. Virgin were putting the skids on the group's money and that could have been more likely to be construed as interference in the group's career than anything Malcolm had done. Branson told Steve and Paul, "He's spent your money on this film, and I can't afford to pay you unless you come in with me."'

The next day, Mr Justice Browne-Wilkinson delivered his verdict, restricting himself to the Sex Pistols' financial matters. Of the £880,000 the Sex Pistols had earned, £343,000 had been spent on the film and only £30,000 was left. The only asset available to the Sex Pistols and Glitterbest was the film and its soundtrack: the only way to rescue any money out of the dispute was by the exploitation of these assets and a third-party receiver was appointed to administer them.

The rest of the judgement showed that Browne-Wilkinson had no wish to enter the Sex Pistols' labyrinth. As to whether John Lydon's contract with McLaren was invalid, or as to who owned the name, he made no judgement, but suggested that the parties concerned should come to some agreement after the finances had been sorted out. Although McLaren was now not in control of the group, the judge suggested that he should help to exploit the film, subject to the right of the Receiver to remove him if necessary.

But McLaren was gone, flying that very day to Paris. Although the result of the court case was inconclusive – so inconclusive that it would take another seven years and nearly £250,000 in legal fees to resolve – it had taken the Sex Pistols away from his control, into the hands of City accountants: chaos into cash. It was, effectively, a resounding defeat for McLaren and what he and Glitterbest had kept at bay for a year had come to pass: the Sex Pistols were over.

In a sequence of bitter interviews, he laid out his situation. Now broke, with over £50,000 of personal debts, he was off to Paris to sign a contract for an LP of standards, including 'Je Ne Regrette Rien', which might offset some of these debts and his legal fees – an estimated total of £100,000. He regarded the court case as a victory for Virgin Records and the music industry in their struggle to gain control over the Sex Pistols.

This view was supported by John Varnom, who had taken the side of Glitterbest to the point that he had been fired by Virgin in December 1978 for uncontrollability. Varnom called down a plague on Virgin's house in his affidavit: in his view, Lydon had agreed to take on the court case to reassert his control over McLaren, a course of action which would also benefit Richard Branson and Virgin Records, who had already decided to destroy McLaren.

Branson has always specifically denied this. Right up until the weekend he had been in favour of settling the case: an agreement whereby Lydon was paid £100,000 by Virgin in respect of his claims foundered only for tax reasons. He had continued to fund the Sex Pistols, Sid Vicious and the film right up until the last minute. He expected to have his hand bitten by McLaren: that was part of the game which he enjoyed playing.

In return, he got an increasing amount of control over what was still hot property, and the industry kudos of appearing to tame the untameable Sex Pistols. But his patience boiled over when he telexed McLaren in Paris on 22 February with the offer of £20,000 on his first single. 'Please stop believing the conspiracy theory,' he wrote, 'there was and is none.' When McLaren waved the telex about as proof that he was being bought off, Branson declared war.

24.2.79: *Always, the approach to media was hard, realistic, not liberal; the trashiness and superficiality inherent in most forms of media was understood and worked on. The Sex Pistols and Glitterbest realized that to use any medium to its fullest extent for your own ends you have to accept the medium and confront it on ITS OWN TERMS.*

In the third week of February, Virgin exercised their new influence over the Sex Pistols by rush-releasing *The Great Rock'n'Roll Swindle* soundtrack and the first single from the double album, 'Something Else'. As ever, Virgin were forced to bring forward the release schedule to avoid imports coming in from the French label. Everything was done in such a rush that the album was released in two different sleeves, and with two different track listings.

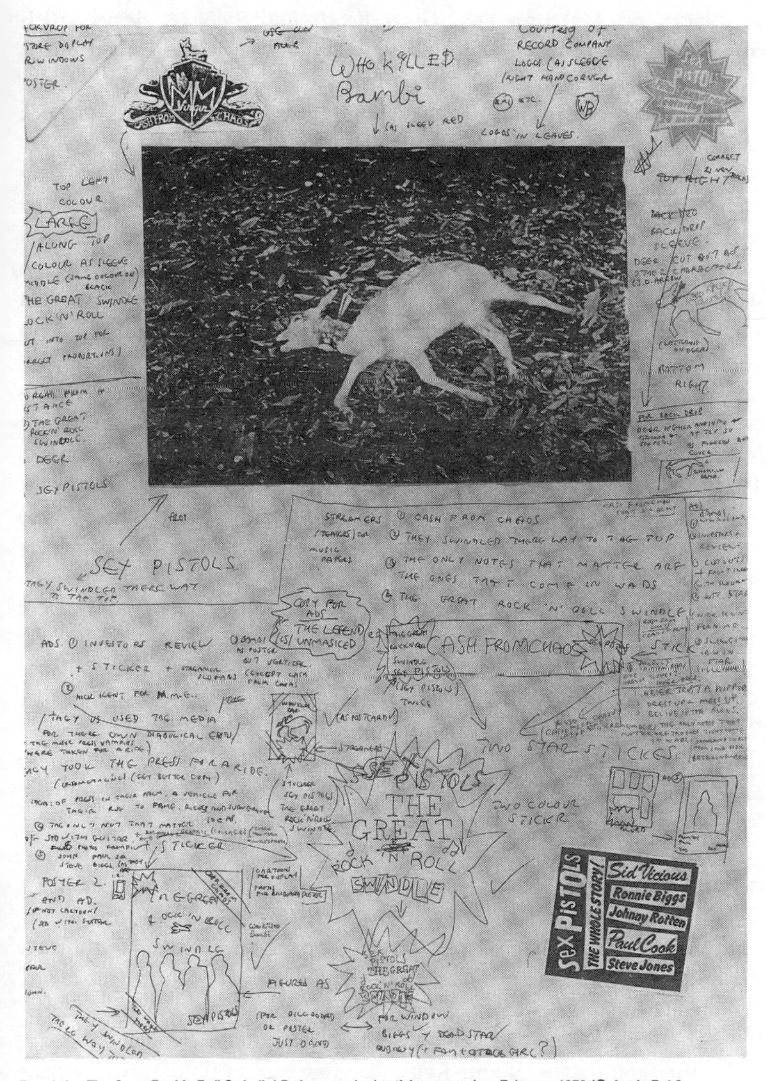

Rough for *The Great Rock'n Roll Swindle* LP sleeve and advertising campaign, February 1979 (© Jamie Reid)

Surrounded by the bitterness of the court case and disillusion with Punk, the album was badly received. It seemed a travesty of the Sex Pistols' former glory, and only emphasized that glory was now long gone. Lydon's smears had hit home, and were reproduced in a series of attacks on McLaren. *The Great Rock'n'Roll Swindle*, despite the contributions of Cook and Jones, was very much McLaren's parting shot to an industry which he now loathed.

Of the twenty-one tracks on the album, seven are by the original Lydon Pistols. Then there are the two Sid Vicious singles, plus a cover of 'C'mon Everybody'; the two tracks cut with Biggs, and sundry Cook and Jones pop tunes and rugby songs. There remain the hardcore McLaren tracks, which at once hark back to the first primal energy of Rock'n'Roll (Steve and Paul are as good as that) and reflect on the distance between then and now, in a series of vicious attacks on the modern music industry.

The point that anyone can be a Sex Pistol was not quite true, yet not quite false. McLaren had recorded new versions of Pistols songs: the orchestral 'EMI' and 'God Save the Queen', Jerzimy's busked 'Anarchie', and the Black Arabs' brilliant disco medley. New vocalist Tenpole Tudor squeaks his way through 'Rock Around the Clock', the slogans of 'Who Killed Bambi?' and the title track, which ends with a rant against the pop stars of the day: 'Mick Jagger, white nigger; Elton John, hair transplant'.

Ideas still crackle from the record. Many are as good as any McLaren had come up with: *The Great Rock'n'Roll Swindle* celebrated disposability at the time when Punk's spontaneity was turning into Rock solemnity; it transgressed the Sex Pistols' place, already installed, in Rock history; it used the forms of pop to launch a massive critique of the greed, egomania and sheer confidence trickstering of the music and media industries. At the same time it eulogizes Tin Pan Alley in 'Cash from Chaos'.

You can hear what *The Great Rock'n'Roll Swindle* film might have been; a chaotic, sprawling carnival that redrew the map of London. 'The whole eighties cult of Soho came from the Sex Pistols,' says Julien Temple, 'Malcolm had a great sense of history.' And the film's opening images of ragged Punks in the Gordon Riots reemphasized the covert but powerful English tradition of disorder, already highlighted by 'God Save the Queen' with results that still reverberate.

'In the end,' says Jamie Reid, 'it was our fault that we didn't articulate our ideas well enough.' Despite McLaren's libertarian intent, *The Great Rock'n'Roll Swindle* became swamped, as his wish to destroy what he had created fused with the cynicism of the time. Instead of relieving the Punk culture from the burden of history and wiping the slate clean, the record was subverted by the very processes which it was intended to subvert.

Images of products abound in the *Swindle*: in the 'Quality Street' lettering of the film's title, and the various items of Sex Pistols merchandise: 'Gob Ale', 'Sid Vicious Action Men', Anar-kee-Ora' and 'Rotten Bars'. This is a comment on the taming of the Sex Pistols' raw innocence by the product-orientated music industry, but what emerged from the record was not the destruction of the music or pop industries but their reinforcement, such importance did McLaren attach to them.

Despite its self-mockery, McLaren's attempt at escape from assimilation foundered on his authorial voice. He and Westwood had planned a hype which had become a real culture, through the collective effort of the people with whom they worked. The burst of freedom that ensued could never have been predicted. In stating that this was no accident, but just the calculation of one author, McLaren unconsciously replaced freedom with a programmatic cynicism, which would infect English popular culture throughout the 1980s.

The rest was a mess. Despite the court's instructions, it was inconceivable that McLaren, who had returned to London, would continue to work in a subordinate role on his film, and on 15 March, he sent a blistering letter to the receivers, complaining about the cut: 'a pathetic scrapbook butchered about by people with no direction. Stop it now!' Within a day, he had carried out his threat to walk off the film.

Temple saw his chance. 'After the court case I was totally in charge of completing the film, with the receivers,' he says. 'That was based on my response to Malcolm saying, "You're a slave from now on." I said "Fuck you, it's you or me, I'm gonna finish the film by any means that I can, in the way that you would fight Johnny Rotten." Malcolm's tactics were very Leninist: total victory or nothing.

'It took a long time to edit, because it was three years of random shooting. The only things that we cut out were the kiosk thing which was a funny idea, but we had extras reacting to Sid which was very phoney, so that didn't work. The Blowaves thing was very anti-John. I think one of the interesting things about the film was the absence of John anyway. The basic idea of that piece was that John was gay. Then we had a lot of legal problems.'

One of the major problems was caused by McLaren, who used his connection with Barclay to hold up the release 'My Way'. The film would not come out for another year, when it was an immediate, if unpromoted, success. (It has still not been properly released in the

US.) The appointment of the receiver had put the exploitation of the group's assets and back catalogue into a limbo from which it never recovered.

And then there were three. McLaren had now alienated or disowned all his group and most of his staff. Tiberi had left to take over his father's antique shop in Pimlico. Cook and Jones were in Rock'n'Roll limbo, and were attempting to come to terms with the fact that it was all over: 'I just didn't want to know about anything,' Jones says. 'What do you do,' asked Paul Cook, 'after you've been in one of the most important groups ever?'

'It was very horrible towards the end,' says Sophie Richmond, 'Malcolm and Jamie off fighting with Virgin the whole time, and no band. There was quite a lot of animosity from Malcolm towards me, but I felt that my responsibility at that stage was to get everything neat and tidy so that the band could proceed with their lives. I didn't see any other way, now that it was all in the hands of the courts. I came out of it in June thinking, what do I do next?'

And then there were two. Jamie Reid was still supporting McLaren, and continued to supply Virgin with a constant stream of single sleeves, posters and streamers, as befitted a project where packaging and media campaigns had to make up for the fact that the group did not exist. Many of the graphics are among the Sex Pistols' most explicit articulations, like the 'Viciousburger' sleeve for 'C'mon Everybody', an update of the Situationist 'corpse' metaphor, or the message on the reverse: 'The media was our lover and our helper.'

Reid became consumed by the extremity of the time: his artwork contained constant attacks on Virgin, in the use of swastikas and in personal vituperation of Branson himself. It was bitter, and even the dogged Reid gave up after nine months: 'In the end I was producing more and more imagery that Virgin were rejecting, and I was left feeling more and more isolated. It was a dreadful time: it took me years to get over the scars of the Pistols.'

And then there was one. 'Malcolm had done a deal with Eddie Barclay,' says Johnny Gems. 'Then Richard sent Malcolm this thing to sign that declared he would never get involved in the music business ever again. It was delivered to his flat in Clapham. He was there with Vivienne and the messenger waited there so he could sign it, and take it back. He didn't, he just tore it up. After that, he went to Paris for a year. All he had were some friends but not very much money. He was in a terrible state, mentally.'

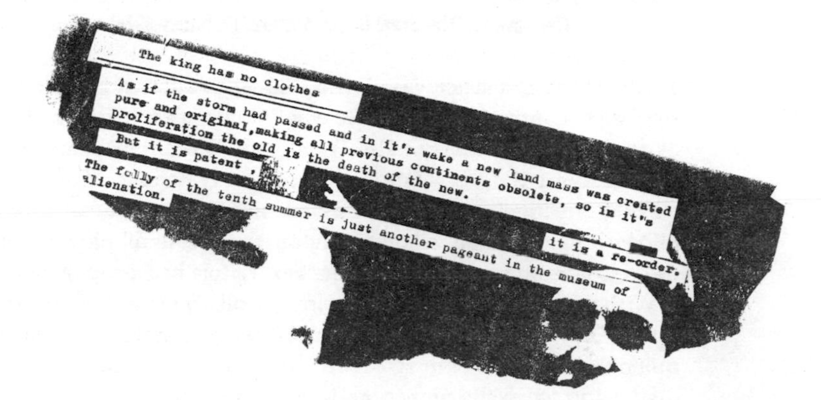

Anonymous flyer, Manchester, summer 1986

36

The Great British mistake was looking for a way out, was getting complacent, not noticing the pulse was racing – the mistake was fighting the change, was staying the same. It couldn't adapt so it couldn't survive, something had to give, the people take a downhill slide into the gloom, into the dark recesses of their minds.

I swoop over your city like a bird
I climb the high branches and observe
Into the mouth, into the soul
I cast a shadow that swallows you whole
I sweep, I climb, I cling, I suck, I swallow you whole

Bring out the drip-feed, they're losing their world, they're losing their hard boys and magazine girls, advert illegal, TV as outlaw, motive as spell. They'll see the books burn, they'll be 45l, it's people against things and not against each other, out of the pre-pack, into the fear, into themselves. They're the great British mistake – the genie's out the bottle, call in the magician, they didn't mean to free him, devil behind him, devil in the mirror, chained to the right hands. They're the great British mistake – they'll have to come to terms now, they'll take it out somehow, they'll blame it all on something. The Great British Mistake – when will it be over? How can they avoid it?

The Adverts: 'The Great British Mistake' (February 1978)

The Sex Pistols' last act was played against a nationwide backdrop that seemed to confirm the substance of what two years before had seemed like apocalyptic fantasy. The 'Winter of Discontent' seemed to be tearing apart the very fabric of society. 'Watching all the rubbish, wasting my time', Lydon had cackled: and there, as the sacks of refuse piled up, six feet high, all over London, was the final, physical proof of the self-lacerating disgust that the Sex Pistols had propagated.

With the Conservatives soaring in the polls, and Callaghan paralysed into inactivity, the four largest public-sector unions brought out 1.5 million employees on strike in February: the result was severe disruption across the country and a public relations disaster. There were Punk-style tabloid headlines like 'The Road to Ruin' and 'No Mercy'.

The strike continued through March, while the Clash's 'English Civil War' was in the Top Thirty. The Government was powerless to stop the rot: 'We were engaging in what I called occupational tribal warfare,' said Peter Shore, then in the cabinet, 'as though every separate group in the country had no feeling and no sense of being part of a community but was simply out to get what it could.'

A vote of 'No Confidence' was announced for 30 March. The Government's majority was so slim that it was forced to rely on support from all the minority parties, from the Scottish National Party to the Welsh National Party and the Ulster Unionists. Despite their devolutionary policies, the Government could not please everybody: when the result of the long and tense debate came through, it had lost by one vote. An election was called for 3 May.

It was a bitter campaign, marked by severe clashes like the anti-National Front demonstration in Southall, where a schoolteacher was killed by a blow to the head from a member of the Special Patrol Group. ANL and RAR mounted a 'Militant Entertainment' tour to head off the National Front at the polls but, to a degree that the Front itself did not realize, Mrs Thatcher had undercut their vote with an election package that carefully synthesized the fears of the middle and working classes.

The Conservatives promised to curb union power, restore incentives, strengthen defence, and uphold the role of law and the primacy of the family. This struck a chord amongst the people who felt swamped by left-wing union activists, decaying cities, and all the archetypes of youth culture decay, whether Rastas or Punks.

Despite the fact that the 'originals' were now long dispersed, Punks – in their second or third generation – were visible on the streets as never before. On the day after the Commons vote, about 2,000 gathered to protest about the closure of Beaufort Street Market, just around the corner from the shop that had spawned them four years before: in the ensuing fracas, at least seventy arrests were made.

The Conservatives won the election by forty-three votes: by 4 May, Mrs Thatcher was in Downing Street. It is tempting to apply hindsight, and claim that England changed overnight: it did not. What is now called 'Thatcherism' – that application of market forces, jingoism, a hard-line morality and the explicit disenfranchisement of the dispossessed – only began once she had routed the opposition within her own party. In 1979, she still needed to stand for a more traditional, paternalistic Conservatism.

The Conservatives' victory did mark an end to the period of social unrest which Punk had charted so intimately. The postwar consensus was now over. 'Try it': now people had. The very freedom which Punk had not only sung about, but enacted in every possible sense, was now hijacked by the New Right to mean something quite different: an inequality that was not only institutionalized but installed as a ruling cultural and social principle.

Punk was over. Humpty Dumpty had fallen off the wall and there was no way of piecing him together. All the strands that it had been the extraordinary achievement of the Sex Pistols to combine had unravelled that spring: into pure music, subculture and the music and media industries. These are trails that have continued to hang in the sky ever since, longer than anyone could have possibly imagined or wished.

Punk was beaten, but it had also won. If it had been the project of the Sex Pistols to destroy the music industry, then they had failed; but as they gave it new life, they allowed a myriad of new forms to become possible. When Punk entered the music and media industries, its vision of freedom was eventually swamped by New-Right power politics and the accompanying value systems, but its original, gleeful negation remains a beacon. History is made by those who say 'No' and Punk's utopian heresies remain its gift to the world.

Appendix 1

Diary 13.1.86: A mild winter Monday. The High Court buildings are almost deserted. The Sex Pistols' case has come up on the Witness List with no prior warning: number 229/84, Lydon v. Glitterbest Ltd. Action and Counterclaim to 264/85, McLaren & ors. v. Lydon & ors. Already, a complicated sequence of passions is reduced to a file note; just one item in an old, deliberate process which, although decisive, is a world away from the events at issue. What is being resolved here today is the ten-year relationship between John Lydon and Malcolm McLaren: a relationship so intense that it not only sparked the Sex Pistols' success but also contained their destruction.

The scene outside Court 35 is pure theatre. The legal purpose of the action is to resolve the eight-year dispute between John Lydon and Malcolm McLaren; the two are so obsessed that the other ex-Pistols are pawns, or mere bit players. The original action, in February and March 1979, was so long and the parties so intransigent that the judge threw his hands up in the air and appointed a third party to run Glitterbest and thus the Sex Pistols' affairs. An accountant was put in charge of chaos.

The receiver collected the money but he didn't stoke the pot. The situation wasn't serving anyone and in 1984 Lydon initiated an action which has now finally come to court. This then is the opportunity for a final resolution, important enough for the two principal characters to fly in from Los Angeles to this uninviting, Dickensian setting. Outside the court, there is hardly anyone: a couple of court reporters and Mrs Beverley sitting patiently. She looks as if she has had plenty of practice.

McLaren comes into focus, looking like a scarecrow, with wild, curly red hair and a dark suit, cloistered down one end of the Victorian Gothic hallway with a gaggle of gowned counsel and suited solicitors. Just before the session begins, at eleven o'clock, Lydon sweeps in, wearing a large, fifties white overcoat and baggy grey flannels, his hair screwed up into orange rasta balls: a star's entrance. Ignoring McLaren, he occupies the space nearest the court with his entourage of lawyers, exchanging a few words with Anne Beverley and entering quickly when the court is opened.

Inside, a series of parallel pews face Mr Justice Mervyn Davies. Lydon signals his confidence by sitting in the front row, right in front of the judge like a classroom swot; the next two rows are taken up by the lawyers with their thick orange folders. McLaren and his solicitor, Howard Jones, sit to one side near the back. The only other Sex Pistol to attend, Paul Cook, arrives a few minutes late and slips quietly into the back of the court, with a movement as spare as his dress. The man who started the Sex Pistols, Steve Jones, is somewhere in Los Angeles.

After some shuffling of papers, a stocky, florid QC with red hair falling over his ears to the regulation length, opens for Lydon. Andrew McDonnell starts as he means to go on, unweaving the threads of an eight-year mix-up with infinite patience. The detail is fascinating but the progress deliberately slow: by lunch, McDonnell has only reached Glen Matlock's departure in the group's story and everybody, except Lydon, is beginning to look restless. Cook disappears.

At lunch, the PA reporter thinks they'll settle but McDonnell continues nonetheless. Lydon is alleging, as he did in 1979, that McLaren mismanaged him and, instead of paying him money due from group royalties and advances, spent it on *The Great Rock'n'Roll Swindle* film; his case centres on whether the group's original contract with Glitterbest, a company bought off the shelf comprising McLaren and his lawyer Stephen Fisher, was ever valid and whether the partnership at will of the original group ended when he left. This takes two-thirds of the day.

By the time that his submission is read out, at about 3.15 p.m., McLaren is frantic. All the old wounds of the 1979 action are being reopened, and the arid vista of a long court case stretches before him. The submission is brief: one phrase, however, sticks in the mind. 'McLaren put together the violent and aggressive Punk style; it was his original literary work.' After a brief, non-committal submission from Jones and Cook, the day winds up with a summons for directions: how does the judge want to treat the two separate actions?

The pedantic legalese depresses everybody, including the judge: 'What a grim day,' he says as he folds up his papers. But it's a good tactic: 'Horrendous,' mutters McLaren as he leaves the court and it's certain that if the case lasts two months, as at this rate it might, McLaren will have no stomach for it. On the second day, it looks as though they will settle: there is a flurry of dark, gowned movement between the flocks of lawyers as they get down to some serious horse-trading.

When court begins, Lydon resumes his position at the front of court; McLaren hovers outside in the hall. McDonell rises and, after the usual flummery, states that 'heads of terms are being negotiated – subject to contract' for a final agreement and will the judge grant a delay for 'the rest of the day extended to Thursday?' He hopes it will not be a waste of the court's time. The judge clearly has no relish for a long case either: he tells McDonell, in appropriate language, to get on with it. The case adjourns after ten minutes.

16.1.86: More people are collected outside the court, waiting for the kill. The PA reporter had heard earlier in the morning that they wouldn't settle: now it looks as though they will, if the level of activity among the lawyers is anything to go by. Unlike McLaren, who is busy courting the press in the centre of the hall, Lydon is lurking in the gents. As I pass, he snickers, loud enough for everybody to hear: 'There he is, looking like a pervert and all.' I see his point: McLaren has come to court in a black velvet, Little Lord Fauntleroy knickerbocker suit.

The exercise is becoming expensive: at a rough estimate, each day in court costs £10,000, which means £30,000 gone, this week alone. Court starts just after noon: there is one more hitch, however. As McDonell explains, with an actor's sense of how to milk a scene, the number of parties involved means a delay in getting all the signatures required. Can we come back after lunch? In The George over the road, Lydon sits supping halves with Joe Stevens, the man who bailed him out that dreadful week eight years ago when the Sex Pistols split apart in America. Lydon is tired, polite, but confident: revenge is a dish best served cold.

Soon after two, everything is over. With a flourish, McDonnell announces the agreement: McLaren is to hand over to the group the two companies Glitterbest and Matrixbest, in return for which he can discontinue his 1985 claim against the group with no costs. This is a complete defeat: McLaren entered this round of negotiations hoping at least to obtain his film *The Great Rock'n'Roll Swindle*, which was taken away from him and, the way he tells it, so cruelly butchered. Now he has nothing, and he is nowhere in sight.

Outside, Lydon poses for pictures and puts on his press act. He knows that in a case of this type, which centres on the oldest and most bitter struggle in the performance world, the struggle between performer and manager, between the person who has the idea and the one who gives it life, that the public and the courts will always support the performer. The papers do the rest: the figure of £880,000 which is in the receiver's pot is bumped up to £1 million. 'Lots of lovely money and it's all mine.'

McLaren returns my call the next day, obviously upset. After an initial hesitation, he doesn't stop talking: 'The whole thing was like two old men arguing over tomes. It was the end of an era. I have to look to the future rather than the past: I asked my counsel whether there was any chance of wrapping it up by Friday and he said: "No chance. There's no way he'll negotiate." He had ten days of witnesses lined up to give evidence: people like his brother, people from the American tour. It was insane: if he really feels I shouldn't have anything, then I'm better off giving it to him.'

McLaren repeatedly calls Lydon by his now rejected stage name. 'It was very sad to see Rotten with such pent-up fury. The guy was exactly the same: no change between '78 and '86. He just wasn't willing to give up. Paul Cook said something very shrewd: ''Whatever we try, Rotten will take you. You see Rotten loved you. You didn't pay enough attention to him.'' And it's true; I was more involved with Sid. ''He still has a feeling for you.'' It's a huge problem. Publicly displayed, damaged psychology. I never thought about it sufficiently. I was always thinking about event after event and not in terms of personal relationships.

'There was no way I'd stand in court for six weeks over the Sex Pistols. We could have struck a deal and gone home happy. But he doesn't want me to be happy. He hated the movie, and he didn't want me to exploit it in any way. The movie *I* made; I was the central character. They got the movie along with everything else. I remember just before the judgement in 1979 I was the untouchable: I left on a plane for Paris and I thought, ''This is it. This is really the end.'' It's constantly nagged at me for eight years. Now I'm shot of it.'

Appendix 2

23.6.96: Just before the Sex Pistols take the stage in the waning light, a curious hush falls: a myth is to be made flesh. The setting for this historical psychodrama is an instant, ugly festival site on the SE side of Finsbury Park – John Lydon's old manor; the boisterous 30,000-strong crowd has been warmed up by punks past and present, from Iggy Pop and the Buzzcocks to Skunk Anansie and the 60ft Dolls. The heart quickens as the central questions approach: how will the Matlock Pistols make the near twenty-year transition from the last time they played together onstage? Will they stink, like they always did at important shows? Will this be a zombie performance, or will they return to articulate – and it's fair to say, from being in the audience, that all here are in accord on this – our discontents yet once again? Can they conjure up any of the centrality to the culture that they had in 1977?

The debates have raged in spectacular form during the past few weeks, but now is the moment of truth. What *is* exactly going to happen? The sharp choice of Baccara's 'Yes Sir, I Can Boogie' (Euro Disco: the enemy in 1977, but perfect in 1996) segues into the introduction, performed with commendable brevity by England Euro 1996 Squad footballer Stuart Pearce. Here is a clue, but without any delay, a banner is unfurled, made out of those December 1976 tabloid front pages that made the Sex Pistols perennial public enemies: 'The Filth and the Fury', 'The Foul Mouthed Yobs'. As the noise swells, the four Pistols come crashing through the backdrop, fists and feet first, ripping the whole thing down: a classic pop entrance. The last time I've seen anyone do this was late

80s teen sensations Bros. It's so camp, so Richard Allen, that I start to laugh: this is going to be fun.

'Thank you for coming to our little party', shouts Lydon – very polite – and they're off, into the rollercoaster ride of 'Bodies'. Although we think we're in a safe zone near the edge of the crowd, my friend Paul Tickell and I (sober fortysomethings both) are swept up in a wild melee of flying liquid, shoving and leaping bodies, thousands of mouths screaming out the percussive 'fucks' in a communal release. I get hysterics, can't stop laughing: this is I wanted to do in 1977 but couldn't; for an instant, time is suspended and the original, wild chaos returns in a surge of gleeful energy. Things settle as the Sex Pistols speed through 'New York', 'Seventeen' and 'No Feelings'; the tone of the event becomes clear as Lydon mildly admonishes the crowd: 'It's only uncle Johnny and the boys here – FAT, FORTY and BACK!'

If the audience is expecting Lydon's trademark hostility and provocation, they're in the wrong time. Lydon knows all too well the destructive implications of the credo he expressed in Public Image Ltd's 'Rise': 'anger is an energy'. When he sang those words in 1986, the audience at the Brixton Academy took him at face value and battered him. You only need to look at the Sex Pistols' clothes to realise that threat is not high on the agenda: Lydon in a buttoned up, Nehru check jacket, silver straight-legged pants and an absurd corona of blue/yellow spikes, Steve Jones in gold lamé and leopard-skin with blonde highlights, Matlock in his understated Mod cool. This is showbusiness, and is meant to be: as the band crash into 'Satellite' – one of the Sex Pistols' best loved songs – Lydon addresses the crowd with a cajoling 'it's singalongaJohnnytime'.

As everyone realises that this is not an embarrassment and begins to relax, several differences between 1977 and 1996 become clear. The Sex Pistols are – as they always were – a great pop/rock band, with Matlock's melodic, endlessly pumping bass, Cook's driving, heartbeat drums and Jones' delinquent guitar – but now you can hear them through a decent PA without any distracting hysteria. (The hysteria was once the point, but cannot be recaptured within this context.) The changes are most evident in John Lydon: his defensive posture of yore has been replaced by the sharp self-mockery and florid gestures of the vaudevillian. As he chatters his way through 'Submission' he delivers a line which shows what he wants out of the occasion: 'and the crowd went wild'. The 1996 Sex Pistols are converting the rejection they once suffered into pantomime: 'We're the Pistols', Lydon sings, 'nobody likes us, and (cue thousands of audience throats) we don't CAAAARE'.

As the group tear into 'Pretty Vacant' with the crowd in their pocket, it hits me: this is really new. If you were a Sex Pistols fan in 1977, *you could not do this.* The group have only ever played in the UK to audiences of a few hundred people – ie about 1% of this gathering – who were quite capable of harassing and attacking them; if the audience didn't, then football hooligans, outraged nationalists and serried ranks of police would. It wasn't just the group: if you wore Punk clothes and gathered together in clumps of more than two, then you'd get attacked as well. Being a Sex Pistols fan was like being in a hermetic sect: you could safely express it in public only through secret, coded signs. The national hysteria after the 1977 Jubilee was such that, despite having three top ten singles and a number one album, the group could not relax into their success: instead they slid into a fabulous yet debilitating disaster – a blocked ritual that has haunted everyone concerned ever since, none more so than the four musicians onstage.

Reformations have become a 90s phenom – a result of the upward age expansion of the pop demographic: the Eagles, Madness, the Velvet Underground. Last year, the Beatles sold more records than they did in their heyday, with their three Anthology volumes of outtakes and reconstructions. For their 23 US dates, due to start in a month's time, the Sex Pistols will go head to head against costume rockers Kiss. In these reformations, there are only ever two reasons: unfinished financial and/or emotional business. The level of embarrassment depends on a finely-tuned relationship between the two. This tour is the first major public Sex Pistols event since they successfully went to court to get control over their affairs in January 1986, and they are keen to stress both their autonomy from Malcolm McLaren and the base motive. This is, after all, the Filthy Lucre tour – a phrase taken from a hostile Daily Mail editorial at the time of the Grundy scandal: now that's cynicism squared. As ever with punk, the Sex Pistols relish putting their worst face first.

Yet another motive can be found in John Lydon's statement from the pre-tour press conference in the 100 Club in March: 'The Sex Pistols never really ended properly, it just fizzled out. So there's always going to be a dot, dot, dot. So many have copied, imitated and fucked up what was pure and perfect that it's about time it was redressed. I don't give a shit if no one turns up, quite frankly it would be to my benefit as it's just for us as a band to say goodbye to each other properly.' Here is the nub: despite the presence of sundry Britpop and rock royalty (the Gallaghers, members of Guns 'N' Roses and Bush) this is not a contemporary pop event but an attempt to heal a nineteen-year-old wound. Both the group and the predominantly thirty/forty something audience felt cheated by British Punk's sudden, bitter demise: so many hopes dashed so quickly.

Despite their myth-historical status, the Sex Pistols are human beings – exactly what they accused the Queen of not being in 1977. The force and resonance of this accusation had the short-term effect of rendering the Sex Pistols and their followers as subhuman in the public's eyes. Punks have no feelings, right? Yet through the simple act of survival, the group and their audience at Finsbury Park can offer a parallel 1977. If the Sex Pistols only want to be loved now, then realistically, they must have – even at their vicious zenith – only ever wanted to be loved. Instead, they were hated, and what this is about is converting hatred into love.

As they careen down the home straight, through 'EMI' and the wild encores of 'Anarchy in the UK', 'Problems' and their ur-thrash, 'No Fun', the circle is completed: in becoming high quality entertainment, which is all they could possibly be, the Sex Pistols have laid to rest a collective burden. This is not infinitely reproducible (and will not be so on the long tours that follow) but here you can see it in the faces, as 1977 elides into 1996. What a relief.

Guy Debord: Society of the Spectacle (Black and Red translation, Detroit 1970)

Bibliography

For the truest, most immediate documents of Punk and this period of English life, there is no substitute for going through the archives of the weekly music press from 1976 until 1979: *Sounds*, *New Musical Express* (now *NME*) and *Melody Maker*. For the quite separate Fleet Street view, see the National Newspaper Library at Colindale.

All the interview quotes in the book are from interviews with the author, unless ascribed separately in the text. There are four exceptions:

Descriptions of the interior of 430 King's Road were taken from an interview with Malcolm McLaren by Jane Withers in 1988.

Extracts are taken from a long interview with McLaren by John Varnom in 1979: these deal with specific negotiations with record companies in late 1976 and early 1977.

The interviews with Jane Suck and Lucy Whitman were done by Liz Naylor in February 1990 for *Out On Tuesday*.

The Roger Bullen interview was done by James Marsh in 1987.

As with records, Punk's synthesis of postwar pop makes a massive bibliography possible, but not achievable here. For further pointers within the areas of pop culture and Punk, I would recommend the bibliographies contained in these books:

Simon Frith, *Sound Effects* (Constable, 1983)
Hall, ed., *Resistance Through Rituals* (Hutchinson, 1976)
Greil Marcus, *Lipstick Traces* (Secker and Warburg, 1989)

Sex Pistols

Fred and Judy Vermorel, *Sex Pistols* (Star Universal, 1978; reprinted Omnibus, 1987)
Glen Matlock, *I Was A Teenage Sex Pistol* (Omnibus, 1990)
Noel Monk and Jimmy Guterman, *12 Days on the Road: The Sex Pistols and America* (William Morrow, 1990)
Lee Wood, *Sex Pistols Day by Day* (Omnibus, 1989)
John Lydon (aka Johnny Rotten), *Rotten: No Irish, No Blacks, No Dogs* (Hodder & Stoughton, 1993)
David Dalton, *El Sid: Saint Vicious* (St Martin's Press, US, 1997)
Nils Stevenson and Ray Stevenson: *Vacant: A Diary of the Punk Years* 1976–79 (Thames & Hudson, 1999)
Sex Pistols, *The Filth and the Fury* (St Martin's Press, 2000)

Then all the picture books:

Ray Stevenson, *Sex Pistols File* (Omnibus, 1978)
Dennis Morris, *Rebel Rock* (Epoch, 1985, now Omnibus)
Bob Gruen, *Chaos* (Omnibus, 1990)
Anne Beverley, *The Sid Vicious Family Album* (Virgin, 1980)
Keith Bateson and Alan Parker, *Sid's Way: The Life and Death of Sid Vicious: The Official Biography* (Omnibus, 1991)
Paul Burgess and Alan Parker, *Satellite* (Abstract Sounds Publishing, 1999)

Other relevant books:

Craig Bromberg, *The Wicked Ways of Malcolm McLaren* (Harper and Row, US, 1989)
Mick Brown, *Richard Branson – the Inside Story* (Michael Joseph, 1988)
Alex Cox and Abbe Wool, *Sid and Nancy* (Faber and Faber, 1986)
Clinton Heylin, *Public Image Limited: Rise/Fall* (Omnibus, 1989)
Catherine McDermott and Edwina Ehrman, *Vivienne Westwood* (Philip Wilson Publishers, 2000)
Michael Moorcock, *The Great Rock'n'Roll Swindle* (Virgin, 1980)
Jane Mulvagh, *Vivienne Westwood* (Harper Collins, 1999)
Jamie Reid and Jon Savage, *Up They Rise – the Incomplete Works of Jamie Reid* (Faber and Faber, 1987)
Deborah Spungeon, *And I Don't Want to Live This Life.*
Paul Taylor, ed., *Impresario: Malcolm McLaren and the British New Wave* (MIT, US, 1988)
Fred Vermorel, *Fashion and Perversity: A Life of Vivienne Westwood and the Sixties Laid Bare* (Bloomsbury, 1996)
Jann Wenner, ed., *Twenty Years of Rolling Stone* (Ebury Press, 1987)

General Art, Culture and Social History
Dawn Ades, *Photomontage* (Thames and Hudson, 1976)
Christopher Booker, *The Neophiliacs* (Collins, 1969)
Christopher Booker, *The Seventies* (Penguin, 1980)
Kellow Chesney, *The Victorian Underworld* (Pelican, 1972)
Nik Cohn, *Today There Are No Gentlemen* (Weidenfeld & Nicholson, 1971)
Peter Everett, *You'll Never Be 16 Again* (BBC, 1986)
Simon Frith and Howard Horne, *Art into Pop* (Methuen, 1987)
Rose Lee Goldberg, *Performance – Live Art 1909 to the Present* (Thames and Hudson, 1979)
Charlie Gillett, *The Sound of the City* (Souvenir Press, 1983)
Paul Gilroy, *There Ain't No Black in the Union Jack* (Hutchinson, 1987)
Dick Hebdige, *Hiding in the Light* (Comedia, 1988)
Robert Hewison, *Too Much – Art and Society in the Sixties 1960–75* (Methuen, 1986)
Bevis Hillier, *Art Deco* (Studio Vista, 1968)
Bevis Hillier, *Austerity Binge* (Studio Vista, 1973)
Harry Hopkins, *The New Look* (Reader's Union, 1964)
Derek Jarman, *Dancing Ledge* (Quartet, 1984)
John Lahr, *Prick Up Your Ears – the Biography of Joe Orton* (Penguin, 1978)
Edward Leffingwell, ed., *The Rise and Fall and Rise of Pop* (MIT, US, 1988)
Catherine MacDermott, *Street Style – British Design in the 80s* (Design Council, 1987)
Colin MacInnes, *England, Half English* (MacGibbon and Kee, 1961)
George Melly, *Revolt into Style* (Penguin, 1972)
Richard Neville, *Play Power* (Paladin, 1970)
Jeff Nuttall, *Bomb Culture* (Paladin, 1970)
Guy Peellart and Nik Cohn, *Rock Dreams* (Pan, 1974)
David Pryce-Jones, *Unity Mitford* (Book Club Associates, 1976)
Hans Richter, *Dada: Art and Anti-Art* (Thames & Hudson, 1978)
David Robbins, ed., *The Independent Group: Postwar Britain and the Aesthetics of Plenty* (MIT, US, 1990)
Jean Stein and George Plimpton, *Edie* (Jonathan Cape, 1982)
Roger Shattuck, *The Banquet Years – the Origins of the Avant-Garde in France 1885 to World War 1* (Vintage, US, 1968)
Susan Sontag, *A Susan Sontag Reader* (Penguin, 1983)
Andy Warhol and Pat Hackett, *Popism – the Warhol 60s* (Hutchinson, 1981)
Nigel Whiteley, *Pop Design: Modernism to Mod* (Design Council, 1987)
Jon Wozencroft, *The Graphic Language of Neville Brody* (Thames and Hudson, 1988)
Peter York, *Style Wars* (Sidgwick and Jackson, 1980)

Subcultures
Richard Barnes, *Mods!* (Eel Pie, 1979)
Iain Chambers, *Urban Rhythms* (MacMillan, 1985)
Stanley Cohen, *Folk Devils and Moral Panics* (Paladin, 1973)

Henderson Dalrymple, *Bob Marley: Music Myth and the Rastas* (Carib-Arawak, 1976)
Stuart Hall and Tony Jefferson, *Resistance Through Rituals* (Hutchinson, 1976)
Charles Hamblett and Jane Deverson, *Generation X* (Signet, 1964)
Dick Hebdige, *Cut'n'Mix* (Comedia, 1987)
Dick Hebdige, *Subculture: the Meaning of Style* (Methuen, 1979)
Nick Knight, *Skinhead* (Omnibus, 1982)
Angela MacRobbie, ed., *Zoot Suits and Second-Hand Dresses* (MacMillan, 1989)
Geoffrey Pearson, *Hooligan – a History of Respectable Fears* (MacMillan, 1983)
Johnny Stuart , *Rockers* (Plexus, 1987)
Situs, Autonomists, Anarchists, Pamphleteers, Ranters, 1968

Essential collections of Situationist International writing:
Christopher Gray, ed., *Leaving the Twentieth Century* (Free Fall, 1974)
Ken Knabb, ed., *Situationist International Anthology* (The Bureau of Public Secrets, 1981)

Anon: *The Angry Brigade* (Bratach Dubh Documents #1191, 1978)
Anon: *Les Levres Nues – Textes de L'Internationale Lettriste 1954–1958* (France, 1978)
Anon: *Like a Summer with a Thousand Julys* (BM Blob, 1982)
Anon: (translation of pamphlet by Mustapha Khayati), 'Of Student Poverty' (Spontaneous Combustion, 1978)
Anon: 'Once Upon a Time There Was a Place Called Nothing Hill Gate' (BM Blob, 1988)
Anon: (Dave and Stewart Wise), 'The End of Music' (Box V2, 1982)
Stefan Aust, *The Baader-Meinhof Group – the Inside Story of a Phenomenon* (Bodley Head, 1985)
Jillian Becker, *Hitler's Children – the Story of the Baader-Meinhof Gang* (Granada, 1978)
David Boulton, *The Making of Tania Hearst* (NEL, 1975)
Block 14, *The Work of Art in the Electronic Age* (Middlesex Polytechnic, 1988)
Nick Brandt, *Refuse* (BM Combustion, 1978)
Gordon Carr, *The Angry Brigade* (Gollancz, 1975)
Norman Cohn, *Pursuit of the Millennium* (Paladin, 1970)
Crass, *A Series of Shock Slogans and Mindless Token Tantrums* (Exitstencil Press, 1982)
Colin Crouch, *The Student Revolt* (Bodley Head, 1970)
Guy Debord, *The Society of the Spectacle* (Black & Red, 1973)
— *Comments on the Society of the Spectacle* (Verso, 1990)
Nigel Fountain, *Underground – the London Alternative Press 1966–74* (Comedia, 1988)
Ronald Fraser, *1968 – a Student Generation in Revolt* (Chatto and Windus, 1988)
Jonathon Green, *Days in the Life – Voices from the English Underground* (Heinemann, 1988)
Clifford Harper, *The Education of Desire* (Anarres, 1984)
Christopher Hibbert, *King Mob* (Reader's Union, 1959)

Christopher Hill, *The World Turned Upside Down – Radical Ideas During the English Revolution* (1972: Peregrine, 1987)
Stuart Home, *The Assault on Culture* (Aporia, 1989)
Stuart Home, ed., *Plagiarism: Art as Commodity and Strategies for its Negation* (Aporia, 1987)
Andrew Hopton, ed., *Abiezer Coppe: Selected Writings* (Aporia, 1987)
Asger Jorn, *Fin de Copenhague* (Editions Allia, 1985)
Sylvère Lotringer, ed., *Italy: Autonomia* (Semiotexte 9, 1980)
Norman Mailer, *Miami and the Siege of Chicago* (Penguin, 1969)
Greil Marcus, *Lipstick Traces* (Secker and Warburg, 1989)
George McKay, *Senseless Acts of Beauty: Cultures of Resistance* (Verso, 1996)
George McKay (ed), *DIY Culture: Party and Protest in Nineties Britain* (Verso, 1998)
John Nicolson, *The Great Liberty Riot of 1780* (Bozo, 1986)
Point-Blank!, *Point-Blank! 1* (San Francisco, 1972)
Penny Rimbaud, *Shibboleth* (AK Press, 1999)
Nigel Smith, ed., *A Collection of Ranter Writings from the Seventeenth Century* (Junction Books, 1983)
Valerie Solanas, *S.C.U.M. – Society for Cutting Up Men Manifesto* (Olympia, 1971)
Peter Stansill and David Zane Mairowitz, ed., *BAMN – Outlaw Mani-festos and Ephemera 1965–1970* (Penguin, 1971)
Mike Thomas, *Nothing to Declare – a Scene from an Exile's Chronicle* (Bozo, 1984)
Vague #11916/17, *Psychic Terrorism Annual* (Vague, 1987)
Tom Vague, *King Mob Echo: From Gordon Riots to Situationists & Sex Pistols* (Dark Star, 2000), reprints of *King Mob Echo: English Section of the Situationist International* (Dark Star, 2000)
Raoul Vaneigem, *The Revolution of Everyday Life* (Rebel Press, 1983)
Gee Vaucher, *Crass Art and other Pre Post-Modernist Monsters* (AK Press, 2000)
René Vienet, *Enragés et Situationnistes dans le mouvement des occupations* (Témoins Gallimard, France, 1968)
George Woodcock, *Anarchism – a History of Libertarian Ideas and Movements* (Penguin, 1975)
Many of the pamphlets are still available from Compendium Books, 234 Camden High Street, London NW1 8QS.

The catalogue for 1989's travelling Situationist exhibit: *On the passage of a few people through a rather brief moment in time – the Situationist International 1957–1972* (MIT, US, 1989); the UK version, including King Mob material, is called: *An endless adventure . . . an endless passion . . . an endless banquet* (Iwona Blazwick, ed., ICA/Verso, 1989).

Fiction and Poetry

Richard Allen, *Skinhead* (NEL, 1970)
— *Suedehead* (NEL, 1971)
— *Teenybopper Idol* (NEL, 1973)
— *Glam* (NEL, 1973)

— *Dragon Skins* (NEL, 1975)
— *Punk Rock* (NEL, 1977)
J. G. Ballard, *The Atrocity Exhibition* (Jonathan Cape, 1970)
— *Crash* (Cape, 1973)
— *Concrete Island* (Cape, 1974)
— *High Rise* (Cape, 1975)
Alexander Baron, *The Lowlife* (Collins, 1963)
William Burroughs, *The Naked Lunch* (Calder/Olympia, 1965)
— *Junkie* (NEL, 1966)
— *Dead Fingers Talk* (Tandem, 1966)
— *The Wild Boys* (Calder and Boyars, 1972)
— *Electronic Revolution* (Expanded Media Editions, 1977)
— *APO–33 Bulletin* (Beach Books, 1965)
Albert Camus, *The Outsider* (1942: Penguin, 1985)
Philip K. Dick, *The Man in the High Castle* (1962: Penguin, 1976)
Charles Dickens, *Oliver Twist* (1837–9: Penguin Classics)
— *Barnaby Rudge* (1841: Penguin Classics)
Margaret Drabble, *The Ice Age* (Weidenfeld and Nicholson, 1977)
Paul E. Erdman, *The Crash of '79* (Sphere, 1977)
Gillian Freeman (as Eliot George), *The Leather Boys* (Blond, 1961)
Graham Green, *Brighton Rock* (1938: Penguin, 1970)
Hanif Kureishi, *The Buddha of Suburbia* (Faber and Faber, 1990)
(Comte de) Lautréamont, trans. Guy Wernham, *Les Chants de Maldoror/Poesies* (New Directions, US, 1975)
Doris Lessing, *The Four-Gated City* (Granada, 1972)
Colin MacInnes, *Absolute Beginners* (MacGibbon and Kee, 1959)
Wolf Mankowitz, *Expresso Bongo* (Ace Books, 1960)
Mervyn Peake, *Titus Groan* (1948: Penguin, 1969)
— *Gormenghast* (1950: Penguin, 1969)
Ruth Rendell (as Barbara Vine), *A Fatal Inversion* (Penguin, 1987)
Arthur Rimbaud, trans. Paul Schmidt, *Complete Works* (Picador Classics, 1988)
Thomas Sanchez, *Zoot-Suit Murders* (Secker and Warburg, 1978)
Jean-Paul Sartre, *Nausea* (1938: Penguin Modern Classics)
Mary Shelley, *Frankenstein* (1818: Penguin Classics, 1985)
Paul Theroux, *The Family Arsenal* (1976: Penguin, 1977)
Alexander Trocchi, *Young Adam* (NEL, 1966)
— *Cain's Book* (Jupiter, 1966)
— *Thongs* (Olympia, UK, 1971)
— *School for Wives* (Olympia, UK, 1971)
For essays and a history, see Peter Kravitz, ed., *Edinburgh Review* 70, 1985
Dave Wallis, *Only Lovers Left Alive* (Blond, 1964)

Politics

Corelli Barnett, *The Audit of War – the Illusion and Reality of Britain as a Great Nation* (MacMillan, 1986)
Stuart Hall, *The Hard Road to Renewal – Thatcherism and the Crisis of the Left* (Verso, 1988)

Richard Mayne, *Postwar – the Dawn of Today's Europe* (Thames and Hudson, 1985)
Tom Nairn, *The Enchanted Glass – Britain and its Monarchy* (Radius, 1988)
Philip Whitehead, *The Writing on the Wall – Britain in the Seventies* (Michael Joseph, 1985)
David Widgery, *Beating Time – Riot'n'Race'n'Rock'n'Roll* (Chatto, 1986)
Hugo Young, *One of Us – a Biography of Margaret Thatcher* (MacMillan, 1989)

Perception, Philosophy, Psychology
Jacques Attali, *Noise – the Political Economy of Music* (Manchester University Press, 1985)
Joseph Campbell, *The Hero with a Thousand Faces* (1949: Paladin, 1988)
Barbara Ehrenreich, *Hearts of Men* (Doubleday, US, 1983)
James Hillman, *Insearch – Psychology and Religion* (University of Dallas,1979)
C. G. Jung, *Psychological Reflections – a New Anthology of His Writings 1905–61* (Routledge & Kegan Paul, 1971)
R. D. Laing, *The Divided Self – an Existential Study in Sanity and Madness* (Pelican, 1965)
Friedrich Nietzsche, *Beyond Good and Evil* (1886: Penguin Classics)
— *Twilight of the Idols* (1888: Penguin Classics)
Martin Pawley, *The Private Future* (Pan, 1974)
Jonathan Raban, *Soft City* (Hamish Hamilton, 1974)
Paul Radin, *The Trickster* (Pantheon, 1972)
Wilhelm Reich, *The Mass Psychology of Fascism* (1946: Pelican, 1975)
Peter Sloterdijk, *The Critique of Cynical Reason* (Verso, 1988)
George Steiner, *In Bluebeard's Castle* (Faber and Faber, 1971)
Klaus Theweleit, *Male Fantasies – Women, Floods, Bodies, History* (Polity, 1987)
Paul Virilio and Sylvère Lotringer, *Pure War* (Semiotexte/ Foreign Agents, 1983)

Pop Biography and Criticism, including Punk Books
Isabelle Anscombe, *Not Another Punk Book* (Aurum, 1978)
Nina Antonia, *In Cold Blood – Johnny Thunders, the Official Biography* (Jungle, 1987)
Nina Antonia, *The New York Dolls: Too Much Too Soon* (Omnibus, 1998)
Lester Bangs, ed. Greil Marcus, *Psychotic Reactions and Carburettor Dung* (Random House, 1987)
Peter Belsito and Bob Davis, *Hardcore California – A History of Punk and New Wave* (Last Gasp, 1983)
Victor Bockris with Debbie Harry and Chris Stein, *Making Tracks – the Best of Blondie* (Dell, 1982)
Victor Bockris and Gerard Malanga, *Uptight – the Velvet Underground Story* (Omnibus, 1983)
Victor Bockris, *Transformer: The Lou Reed Story* (Hutchinson, 1994)
Victor Bockris with John Cale: *What's Welsh for Zen: The Autobiography of John Cale* (Bloomsbury, 1999)

Victor Bockris and Robert Bayley: *Patti Smith: An Unauthorised Biography* (Simon & Schuster, 1999)
Michael Bracewell, *England Is Mine: Pop Life in Albion from Wilde to Goldie* (Harper Collins, 1997)
Lloyd Bradley, *Bass Culture: When Reggae Was King* (Viking, 2000)
Julie Burchill and Tony Parsons, *The Boy Looked at Johnny – the Obituary of Rock'n'Roll* (Pluto, 1978)
Robert Christgau, *Any Old Way You Choose It – Rock and Other Pop Music 1967–73* (Penguin, US, 1973)
Alan Clayson, *Call up the Groups! The Golden Age of British Beat 1962–67* (Blandford, 1985)
Nik Cohn, *Pop From the Beginning* (Weidenfeld and Nicholson, 1969)
Caroline Coon, *1988: the New Wave Punk Rock Explosion* (1977: Omnibus, 1982)
Julian Cope, *Head On – Memories of the Liverpool Punk Scene and the Story of the Teardrop Explodes (1976–82)/ Repossessed* (Thorsens, 1999)
Deborah Curtis, *Touching from a Distance: Ian Curtis and Joy Division* (Faber and Faber, 1995)
Chris Cutler, *File Under Popular* (November, 1985)
David Dalton, *The Rolling Stones – the First Twenty Years* (Thames and Hudson, 1981)
Julie Davis, *Punk* (Davison, 1977)
Michael Dempsey, *100 Nights at the Roxy* (Dempsey, 1978)
Jim DeRogatis, *Let It Blurt: The Life and Times of Lester Bangs* (Bloomsbury, 2000)
Tony Fletcher, *Remarks – the Story of R.E.M.* (Omnibus, 1989)
Simon Ford, *Wreckers of Civilisation: The Story of COUM Transmissions & Throbbing Gristle* (Black Dog, 1999)
George Gimarc, *Punk Diary, 1970–1979* (St Martin's Press, 1995)
George Gimarc, *Post-Punk Diary*, 1980–1982 (St Martin's Press, 1997)
Marcus Gray, *The Last Gang In Town: The Story of the Clash* (Helter Skelter, 2000)
Anthony Haden-Guest, *The Last Party: Studio 54, Disco, and the Culture of the Night* (William Morrow & Co, 1997)
Todd Haynes, *Velvet Goldmine* (Faber and Faber, 1998)
Val Hennessy, *In the Gutter* (Quartet, 1978)
Gary Herman, *Rock'n'Roll Babylon* (Plexus, 1982)
Clinton Heylin, *From the Velvets to the Voidoids: A Pre-Punk History for a Post-Punk World* (Penguin, 1993)
Brian Hogg, *The History of Scottish Rock and Pop: All That Ever Mattered* (Guinness, 1993)
Stewart Home, *Cranked Up Really High* (Codex, 1995)
Barney Hoskyns, *Waiting For The Sun: Strange Days, Weird Scenes, and the Sound of Los Angeles* (St Martin's Press, 1996)
Barney Hoskyns, *Glam! Bowie, Bolan and the Glitter Rock* (Faber and Faber, 1998)
Mark Johnson, *An Ideal for Living – An History of Joy Division* (Proteus, 1984)
Roman Kozak, *This Ain't No Disco – the Story of CBGBS* (Faber, US, 1987)
Dave Laing, *One Chord Wonders – Power and Meaning in Punk Rock* (Open University, 1985)

Legs McNeil and Gillian McCain, *Please Kill Me: The Uncensored Oral History of Punk* (Grove Press, 1996)
Greil Marcus, *Ranters and Crowd Pleasers: Punk in Pop Music 1977–92* (Doubleday, 1993), published in the UK as *In the Fascist Bathroom: Writings on Punk, 1977–92* (Viking, 1993)
Dave Marsh, *Before I Get Old – the Story of the Who* (Plexus, 1983)
— *Fortunate Son* (Random House, 1985)
— *The Heart of Rock'n'Soul* (Penguin, 1990)
Mick Middles, *From Joy Division to New Order: The Factory Story* (Virgin, 1996)
Jim Miller, ed., *The Rolling Stone History of Rock'n'Roll* (Picador, 1981)
Steven Morrissey, *New York Dolls* (Babylon, 1982)
Per Nilsen, *The Wild One – the True Story of Iggy Pop* (Omnibus, 1988)
Lucy O'Brien, *She Bop: The Definitive History of Women in Rock, Pop and Soul* (Penguin, 1995)
Robert Palmer, *Dancing in the Street: A Rock and Roll History* (BBC Books, 1996)
Mark Perry, *The Bible* (Dempsey, 1978)
Mark Perry, *Sniffin' Glue: The Essential Punk Accessory* (Sanctuary, 2000)
Iggy Pop with Anne Wehrer, *I Need More – the Stooges and Other Stories* (Karz-Cohl, 1982)
Rick Poynor with Brian Eno and Russell Mills, *More Blank Than Frank* (Faber and Faber, 1986)
Joy Press and Simon Reynolds, *The Sex Revolts: Gender, Rebellion & Rock'n'Roll* (Harvard University Press, 1996)
Mick Rock, *Raw Power: Iggy and the Stooges* 1972 (Creation, 2000)
Roger Sabin, *Punk Rock: So What? The Cultural Legacy of Punk* (Routledge, 1999)
Patti Smith, *Early Work:* 1970–1979 (W. W. Norton & Co., 1994)
Don Snowden and Gary Leonard, *Make The Music Go Bang! The Early L.A. Punk Scene* (St Martin's Press, 1997)
James Stark, *Punk '77: An Inside Look at the San Franciscan Rock'n'Roll Scene, 1977* (Re/Search, 1999)
Dave Thompson, *David Bowie – Moonage Daydream* (Plexus, 1987)
Lynne Tillman and Stephen Shore, *The Velvet Years: Andy Warhol's Factory 1965–67* (Serpents Tail, 1996)
Tom Vague, *The Great British Mistake: Vague 1977–92* (AK Press, 1994)
Fred and Judy Vermorel, *Adam and the Ants* (Omnibus, 1981)
Eric Weisbard and Craig Marks, *The Spin Alternative Record Guide* (Random House, 1995)

Also worth looking at are any of the scores of fanzines from this period. As are any copies of:
Who Put The Bomp (1969–79).
Let It Rock (1972–6).
FILE (1973–82).
Street Life (1975–6).
Punk (US, 1975–80).
New York Rocker (1976–82).

Search and Destroy (US, 1977–80).
Slash (1977–82).

Individual articles of note include:
COUM Transmissions, 'Prostitution' (Rapid Eye, 1990)
General Idea/Image Bank, 'Pablum for the Pablum Eaters' (*FILE*, 5 May 1973)
John Holstrom, 'The Harder They Fall' (*Punk* 14 May 1978)
Jonh Ingham, 'Welcome to the (?)Rock Special' (*Sounds*, 9 October 1976)
Greil Marcus, 'The Cowboy Philosopher' (*Artforum*, March 1986)
Charles Shaar Murray, 'Are You Alive to the Jive of '75?' (*NME*, 7 November 1975). Now collected in *Shots from the Hip* (Penguin, 1991).
Charlotte Pressler, 'Those Were Different Times – a History of Cleveland 1969–75 Part 1' (*Cle* magazine 3, 1979)
Mick Watts, 'The Rise and Fall of Malcolm McLaren Parts 1–3' (*Melody Maker*, 16–30 June 1979)

Discography

If Punk was a summation of all postwar pop music up to 1976/77, then this discography must be – Sex Pistols apart – necessarily selective and thematic.

For the definitive discography, please refer to the astonishing, 736-page *International Discography of the New Wave*, edited by B. George and M. Defoe (Volume II, published by One Ten Records/ Omnibus Press, UK, 1982). Relevant individual discographies can be found in *Record Collector* (published monthly in the UK, 43–45 St Mary's Road, Ealing, London W5 5RQ). As for chart places and so on, see the various editions of *British Hit Singles* and *British Hit Albums*, edited by Tim Rice, Jo Rice, Paul Gambaccini and Mike Read, published by Guinness Books.

Other useful discographies and guides include:

Bob Christgau, *Christgau's Record Guide: Rock Albums of the 70s* (Ticknor and Fields, 1981)

Greil Marcus, ed., *Stranded*, (Knopf, 1979)

Greil Marcus, *Lipstick Traces*, (Harvard, 1990)

Jim Miller, ed., *The Rolling Stone History of Rock'n'Roll* (Picador, 1981)

Ira Robbins, ed., *The New Trouser Press Record Guide* (Charles Scribner, 1985)

There are now hundreds of punk and Sex Pistols sites on the web: you could do worse than to punch the name of what you want directly into the search engine. Here are some worthwhile general punk sites: www.allmusic.com (has details of Punk groups and how to buy them); www.punkbands.com (as billed, from the 1970s to the present day); Rockin' Rena's Women of 70's Punk (again, as billed: www.comnet.ca/~rena/index). All of these have good links to other related sites. Individual sites are included where possible under each group heading.

Every effort has been made in this amended discography to feature material that is actually available. One feature of recent digitalisation is that some records do not remain in print for very long, and there are still many unaccountable gaps. Websites of companies that feature punk material can be found under individual names: e.g., Rhino, Captain Oi!, Overground. There are also archive houses – most notably ebay.com – where you can find vintage material. Otherwise you're on your own. Welcome to the labyrinth!

1954–1962

One useful starting point for tracing Punk influences was the jukebox at 430 King's Road during the Let It Rock/ Too Fast To Live, Too Young To Die periods. Apart from the more obvious hardcore Rock'n'Roll records by Jerry Lee Lewis, Gene Vicent, Elvis Presley, Chuck Berry and Eddie Cochran, the following were either played or sold in 430: Max Bygraves, 'Fings Ain't Wot They Used To Be'; Boyd Bennett, 'Seventeen'; Randy and the Rainbows, 'Denis'; The Diamonds, 'Little Darlin''; Link Wray, 'Rumble'. One of the only LPs owned by McLaren was the soundtrack of *Oliver*.

In 1972–3, there were two very important Rock'n'Roll reissues: Elvis Presley's fundamental *Sun Collection* (RCA), the start of modern pop music, and *Put Your Cat Clothes On*, a collection of wild early Rockabilly (Sun/Philips). These inaugurated the flood that followed. Of particular relevance are the semi-legal compilations of bad taste Rockabilly and 50s pop unearthed in the wake of Punk: the *Born Bad* series (Vols 1–5: Born Bad Records, 1988; now on CD) and compilations like *Red Hot Rock A Billy 1955–1962* (Rock-A-Rolla A-Hillabilly Wing Dong Do, 1988).

Also of relevance are these early UK Rock'n'Roll recordings: Vince Taylor, 'Brand New Cadillac' (Columbia, 1959; re Chiswick, 1976); Billy Fury, *The Sound of Fury* (Decca, 1960, 1981; the Music CD *Best of Billy Fury* contains much of this album); Various, *The Joe Meek Story* (Decca 1977; the best available cross-label CD compilation of Meek's productions is 'The Musical Adventures of Joe Meek' – Kenwest 1994), with Screaming Lord Sutch's 'Jack the Ripper' and the Tornados' hits.

Classic Rock'n'Roll and 50s material is now available on CD throughout the world. Much has been remastered, but beware rerecordings! The best single overview can be found on the uncompromising Rhino 4xCD box set *Loud, Fast and Out of Control* (1999), which delivers as billed over 104 tracks, including 'Brand New Cadillac'. Otherwise, you could try (all CD unless indicated): Link Wray, *The Original Rumble* (Ace, 1989); Elvis Presley, *Sunrise* (RCA, 1999: 2xCD includes outtakes and alt. versions); *The Very Best of Sun Rockabilly* (Charly, 2xCD); Eddie Cochran, *Legends of the 20th Century* (EMI, CD 1999 – includes 'Something Else' and 'C'Mon Everybody' as covered by Sid Vicious); Soundtrack of *Oliver* (CD); Various, *The Sound of Sun* (Sun/ Charly, 1987); Soundtrack of *Oliver* (That's Entertainment, 1990). The soundtrack of *American Graffiti* (MCA, 1973) contains many Rock'n'Roll classics which would have been on the Let it Rock jukebox, and is a good document of the impact of the Rock'n'Roll revival on England between 1972 and 1974.

1963–1967

A mixture of smart, violent Mod pop and sixties American Punk was another important stylistic influence on 1976 and 1977. From 1972 on, a series of reissues mined these pop styles at the same time as Rock'n'Roll was being rediscovered and reissued. These would have been heard and bought by many Punk musicians on both sides of the Atlantic. This runs to 1967, after which hippie extravagance takes the stage: often fabulous, but not Punk.

The great grand-daddy of them all was Lenny Kaye's *Nuggets* (Elektra, 1972; re Sire, 1976) which included cuts by the Electric Prunes, 13th Floor Elevators, the Seeds, the Standells et al. Now a cliché of a particular kind of pop taste, it was a total revelation at the time. In 1998, Rhino released the original double album on one CD in a 4CD box set with ninety-one extra tracks from the same time, space and attitude. Includes hardcore punkers from the Sonics, the Bees, the Music Machine, We the People and the Chocolate Watch Band, among their more pop/soft-syke contemporaries.

Two important compilations mined the UK mid sixties in 1973–4: Andrew Lauder's *Merseybeat* (UA) and *The Beat Merchants* (UA) showcased the first Punk flush of post-Beatles pop from the North West, while Charles Shaar Murray and Roy Carr's *Hard-Up Heroes* (Decca) trawled hardcore British R&B. Some of this has a distinctly punkish slant: for example, the Addicts' 'She's My Girl' and the Birds' 'Leaving Here'.

Note also David Bowie's 1973 *Pin-Ups* (EMI, CD 1990), which put sixties Mod retro into the heart of UK pop culture with covers of songs by the Yardbirds, the Who, early Pink Floyd, and the Kinks. A similar pop taste can be seen in the early songs played by the Sex Pistols: a mixture of the Kinks, the Who, and the Small Faces – pure Mod punks – along with early psych material from groups like the Creation. This is the sound also achieved by the early, pre-record Clash.

You also have to acknowledge, although Punk bands never would, the considerable shadow of the Rolling Stones.

Suggestions for prolonging that everlasting NOW!:

Various, *Acid Dreams*, two CDs – *Acid Dreams Epitaph* and *Acid Dreams Testament* – of mid-sixties 'psychotic terror' (re-released in 1998 and 1999, Head CD).

Various, *The Sixties Explosion: Vol. 1 1961–67* (See For Miles, CD 1988). Covers some of *Hard-Up Heroes*. (Volumes 1–3, Timeless CD).

Captain Beefheart, *Safe as Milk*, (Buddah, 1967; now Buddha/BMG CD, 1999, with extra tracks and excellent liner notes).

The Kinks, *Are Well Respected Men* (PRT, 1987). Singles 'A' and 'B' sides, including 'All Day and All of the Night' and 'I'm Not Like Everybody Else'.

The Who, *My Generation: The Best of . . .* (Polydor, 1996). Includes such fundamentals as 'Substitute' and 'I'm a Boy', both covered by the Sex Pistols.

The Yardbirds, *The Ultimate Collection* (Charly, 2xCD).

The Small Faces, *The Decca Anthology* (Decca, 2xCD, 1996). The one Brit group that prefigures the early Sex Pistols. This 36-tracker includes the Sex Pistols covers 'Understanding' and 'Whatcha Gonna Do Bout It'; if you want to follow their subsequent career, the 1999 Castle Immediate anthology *Darlings of the Wapping Wharf Launderette* is group-approved and definitive. It includes 'Wham Bam, Thank You Man', played by the Sex Pistols in their earliest rehearsals.

The Rolling Stones, *More Hot Rocks* (London, 1986). Don't tell me that 'Fortune Teller' isn't Punk and that 'Have You Seen Your Mother Baby, Standing in the Shadow' isn't nihilist.

1967–1974

The seventies begin with the first Velvet Underground album. Everybody agrees but the records still sound great. *The Velvet Underground & Nico* (Verve, 1967, now remastered Polydor CD 1996). All the original four VU albums are essential: *White Light/ White Heat* (Verve, 1968, now remastered Polydor, CD 1996), *The Velvet Underground* (Verve, 1969, now remastered Polydor, CD 1996); *Loaded* (Atlantic, 1970, now Warner Special Products, CD import). Also available is Rhino's expanded 2xCD *Fully Loaded Edition*. The first three are also available on vinyl (expensive UK copies on Simply Vinyl; mid-price copies on US Polygram).

Many of these records were released in small runs during the late sixties: the Velvet Underground's UK reputation was boosted by the rerelease of albums 1–3 in Polydor's 1971 Head Hunters promotion. In 1974, Mercury Records released the 1969 Velvet Underground Live double set (now CD), while during 1976, semi-legal compilations like *Evil Mothers* (Skydog) and the *Foggy Notion* (White Label EP) plugged straight into the emerging Punk subculture.

Since Punk, the amount of Velvet Underground material available either legally (on albums like *VU* and *Another View*) or semi-legally has grown. Most of the group still record, and their history has been explored in several books and TV programmes like 1987's 'South Bank Show'. Trace them and the VU cult in magazines like *What Goes On* (published from 5721, SE Laguna Avenue, Stuart, Florida 34997–7828, USA).

In 1995, Polydor released a 5xCD box set, *Peel Slowly and See*, which contains all the four original albums plus many extra outtakes and an extraordinary disc (1) of 1965 demos, including 'Venus In Furs', 'Wrap Your Troubles in Dreams', and 'Heroin'. In 1993, the original four returned for a rapturously received European and British tour, the highlight of which was a sunset performance at Glastonbury 1993. Late in that year, Sire released a 2xCD (later just one) of tour highlights, *Live MCMXCII*.

Of the VU's early to mid 70s work solo, the following albums are highly recommended:

Lou Reed, *Transformer* (RCA, 1972, now CD) features the immortal 'Vicious', from where Sid got his name.

Lou Reed, *Berlin* (RCA, 1973, now CD). The harrowing song-cycle, featuring the infamous 'The Kids'.

Lou Reed, *Rock'n'Roll Animal* (RCA, 1973, now CD). Surprisingly entertaining sludge-metal versions of VU classics, among others. After which it's for fans only, apart from:

Lou Reed, *Metal Machine Music* (RCA, 1975, now CD). Epic fuck-you double album of feedback drones with great cover photos and the ultimate amphetamine manifesto: 'my week beats your year'.

John Cale, *Fear* (Island, 1973), *Slow Dazzle* (Island, 1974) and *Helen of Troy* (1975), all collected on *The Island Years* (Island, 2xCD 1996) – essential abrasive songs, the missing mutant Welsh link between the VU, Elvis Presley, Snatch, Roxy Music and the Modern Lovers.

Finally, one last apocalyptic blast:

Nico, *The End* (Island, 1974) features Cale and Eno on icestorm synth.

David Bowie is the link here, bringing the VU to a wider UK audience with VU homages like 'Queen Bitch' (1972) and covers of songs like 'White Light' and 'Waiting For My Man'. All his albums between *Hunky Dory* (RCA, 1972; now EMI, CD) and *Diamond Dogs* (RCA, 1974; now EMI, CD) are essential, i.e.:

Ziggy Stardust and the Spiders from Mars (RCA, 1972; now EMI, CD)

Aladdin Sane (RCA, 1973; EMI, CD)

The compilation *Best of 69–74* (EMI, CD 1997) should meet most of your requirements. If you can find them, discs 1 and 2 of the Ryko *Sound and Vision* boxed set (3xCD, 1989) contain a parallel Bowie history of these years.

Note also Bowie's productions of Lou Reed's *Transformer* (RCA, 1972; now CD) and Mott The Hoople's 'All the Young Dudes' on the CBS *Greatest Hits* CD (Sony); the original *All The Young Dudes* album has been recently reissued by Sony.

Most importantly, Bowie bankrolled (through his management company, Mainman) and mixed what is the most complete statement of the psychological paradigm that would be worked out during 1976–9: Iggy and the Stooges' *Raw Power* (CBS, 1973, re 1977; now remastered Sony CD 1998, with great new sound, extra Mick Rock photos and even better Iggy sleevenotes. If you like the photos, check out the Creation book *Raw Power: Iggy and the Stooges 1972* (2000)). If you have to listen to just two records out of this discography make it this one and *Never Mind the Bollocks*. *The Stooges*, produced by John Cale (Elektra, 1969, now CD), comes a close third with the first versions of 'No Fun' and 'I Wanna Be Your Dog'. See also *Fun House* (Elektra, 1970, now CD); note too the Rhino Handmade ltd edition 7xCD outtakes from these sessions.

The Stooges' cult continues in the many recordings that have surfaced since 1977, many of dubious legality and quality. Caveat emptor! The best is *Kill City* (BOMP, 1978; now, with seminal 45s 'I Got a Right' and 'Sick of You', Revenge, CD).

The Stooges also link the Velvet Underground with another important Punk prototype, Elektra labelmates and fellow Detroiters the MC5. Again, all the first three MC5 albums are essential, for their high-energy political rhetoric and unstable guitar sound:

Kick Out the Jams (Elektra, 1969; now CD)

Back in the USA (Atlantic, UK, 1970; now CD)

High Times (Atlantic, US, 1971; now WEA CD)

In addition, there is an important compilation, spanning the group's whole career, from 1966 to 1972 – lousy sound but great material: *Babes in Arms* (Danceteria, CD 1990). In 2000, Rhino released *The Big Bang! The Best of the MC5*, a near definitive compilation from the three albums with the explosive, punky 67–68 singles 'Lookin' At You', 'I Can Only Give You Everything', and 'I Just Don't Know'.

That unstable guitar sound – and perhaps you could trace it back through John Cale's VU viola to the sine-wave drones of LaMonte Young, which you can now hear on *Inside the Dream Syndicate Volume 1: Day of Niagara* (1965) (Table of the Elements 2000) – recurs on the fourth great Punk prototype, the New York Dolls. Yet again, their lifetime albums are essential, and were rereleased during 1977:

The New York Dolls (Mercury, 1973)
Too Much Too Soon (Mercury, 1974)

These are now only available on vinyl (Mercury UK). The bulk of these albums is available on the 20 track compilation, *Rock 'Roll* (Mercury, CD 1994).

Post-1977 releases of note are: *New York Dolls* (Kamera, 1982), 1972 demos with Billy Murcia; *Red Patent Leather* (New Rose/ Fan Club 1985), the February 1975 Hippodrome concert, with McLaren era songs like 'Teenage News' and the title track.

None of these American groups sold many records in the UK before 1977 and they played here rarely, if at all. The most successful high-energy American group during this period was Alice Cooper, whose hits 'School's Out' and 'Elected' filled the hard rock void. Their best record was *Love it to Death* (WB; now US CD); the compilation *The Beast of Alice Cooper* (WB; now UK CD 1989) includes 'I'm Eighteen' and 'School's Out' as performed by John Lydon at his Sex Pistols audition.

The most accessible high-energy American group were the Flamin' Groovies, who came to the UK after 1972. Singles like 'Slow Death' (UA, 1972), 'Grease' (Skydog, 1973) and 'You Tore Me Down' (BOMP, 1976) were very popular just pre-Punk, as was their 1976 album *Shake Some Action* (Phonogram/ Sire); after this, their sixties fetish became too obtrusive although the records were fine. Still available:

Teenage Head (Kama Sutra, 1971; now Buddha/BMG CD 2000)
Groovies' Greatest Grooves (Sire, US 1989). Compilation from 1971–80, including 'Slow Death' and 'You Tore Me Down'.

Before we leave the Americas, the Doors' influence on many of the above – and Punk – should be noted. This is the start of pop's fantastic voyage into the subconscious:

The Doors (Elektra, 1967; now CD)
Strange Days (Elektra, 1967; now CD)
Waiting for the Sun (Elektra, 1968; now CD)

Along with David Bowie, Roxy Music were the principal UK art stars of the time. All of their first four albums are essential guides to this period's emotional map:

Roxy Music (Island, 1972)

For Your Pleasure (Island, 1972)
Stranded (Island, 1973)
Country Life (Island, 1974)
All are now available on remastered EG/Virgin CDs (1999).

'Is there a future?' Roxy sang on 'Mother of Pearl', and other traces of Punk's musical and social discourse can be found in the Glam thump that was England's pop sound during 1972 to 1974. Examples: Sweet's 'Ballroom Blitz' (1973), Mud's 'Dynamite' (1974), and Cockney Rebel's 'Death Trip' (1974). This stuff is best found on various artists compilations like *The Best Glam Rock Album in the World . . . Ever!* (2xCD Virgin, 1998).

Good burlesque fun, and now rightly recognised as the huge influence on Punk that it was. After all, had not Hello sang of a 'Teenage Revolution' early on in that fateful year of 1976? Students of the period should try to resource the now out-of-print, obscurity-packed *The Great Glam Rock Explosion* (Biff, 1986), and should also rent Todd Haynes' great, flawed *Velvet Goldmine* on video or DVD – which captures the Glam spirit better than anyone wanted, or dared to remember.

Finally, a submerged but archetypal vein of Englishness:
Ranters
Richard Thompson, *Henry the Human Fly* (Island, 1972; now Hannibal CD)
Roy Harper, *Stormcock* (Harvest, 1971, now Science Friction, CD 1997)
Roy Harper, *Lifemask* (Harvest, 1973, now Science Friction, CD 1997)
Peter Hamill, *Nadir's Big Chance* (Charisma, 1975, now CD)
Squatters
Hawkwind, *In Search of Space* (United Artists, 1971, now EMI, 1996 CD remastered and with extra tracks, including 'Silver Machine'. An excellent package, faithful to the Barney Bubbles original, with many photos).
Hawkwind, *Epoch Eclipse: Best of* (EMI, CD 1999). The sound of Notting Dale, including 'Urban Guerilla'. Also the famous double live album *Space Ritual*, now on two CDs (EMI, 1990 with extra tracks and full photo booklet.
The Murray Head 45, 'Say It Ain't So Joe' can be found on the album of the same title (Island, 1975, now CD) but try and find the original 45 if you can as the rest of the album is not good: Island 6252 (1975).

1974–1976
Apart from the final flowering of Glam – see Sparks, *Mael Intuition – The Best of Sparks 1974–76* (Island, CD 1988) – this period sees the first Punk recordings from CBGBs New York and Cleveland. Almost all of these records were released on tiny independents and are only now being excavated.

The spiritual father, or elder brother, of the new, post-Glam mood could be Jonathan Richman. His first Modern Lovers cuts were produced by John Cale in 1972, and include the seminal 'Roadrunner', 'Astral Plane' and 'Pablo Picasso'. All of these plus several other naif songs like 'Modern World' are on *The Modern Lovers* (Home of the Hits, 1976, now Revola/Creation CD). There is also a CD compilation of Kim Fowley's demos from this time (Bomp

Records). Also recently unearthed, an excellent 1972 live recording, *Live at the Longbranch Saloon* (Last Call US CD), plus some tracks from 1971.

All of Patti Smith's pre-1977 releases are essential:

'Hey Joe'/ 'Piss Factory' (Mer, 1974; re Sire, 1978)

Horses (Arista, 1976; now remastered CD, 1996, with a bonus track of the classic live version of 'My Generation' mentioned below).

'Gloria' (Arista, 1976). Features 'My Generation' on the B side, with the 'I'm so young, so goddamn young' rap later immortalised by REM on the 1986 'Just A Touch'.

Teenage Perversity and Ships in the Night (World Records, 1976) is a bootleg of the Smith group's concert at the Roxy, Los Angeles 30 January 1976, featuring early versions of 'Radio Ethiopia' material, a guest appearance from Iggy Pop, and a great medley of 'Pale Blue Eyes' and 'Louie Louie'.

Radio Ethiopia (Arista, 1976; now CD)

Montage review of Television, 'Marquee Moon', February 1977 (© Jon Savage)

As is anything by Television/ Richard Hell:

The Neon Boys, 'That's All I Know Right Now'/ 'Love Comes in Spurts' (recorded 1973; re Shake, 1980)

Television, *Double Exposure* (no label), bootleg of abortive 1974 Eno demosplus a version of the Elevators' 'Fire Engine'; 'Little Johnny Jewel' (Ork, 1977 7", re WEA 1979 as 12" single) – this essential performance is still unavailable on CD, compilers note!; *Marquee Moon* (Elektra, 1977, now CD with extra

edits); *Adventure* (Elektra, 1978, now CD); plus medium-sounding double live CD from 1979, *The Blow Up* (ROIR), including their version of the 13th Floor Elevators' 'Fire Engine'.
Richard Hell and the Voidoids, 'Blank Generation' (Ork, EP 1976; Stiff, UK, 1977); *Blank Generation* (Sire; now CD plus extra tracks)
Richard Hell, *RIP* (ROIR, cassette, 1984) compilation includes Heartbreakers' demos like 'Hurt Me'
Various, *The Great New York Singles Scene* (ROIR, cassette, 1982) compiles the above Hell, TV and Patti Smith Ork/Mer singles along with other important but later works.

The Ramones' first album was astonishing on its release in April 1976. It remains one of the few records that changed pop forever, but all the group's first three albums are definitive. After which infinity beckons:
The Ramones (Sire, 1976)
The Ramones Leave Home (Sire, 1977). Original versions contained the cut 'Carbona Not Glue', pulled in favour of 'Sheena is A Punk Rocker' when the trademark owners objected. Both albums are now compiled, along with two early demos – 'I Can't Be' and 'I Don't Wanna Be Learned'/ 'I Don't Wanna Be Tamed' – on the indispensable Sire CD *All The Stuff and More Vol. 1* (1990).
Live at the Roxy (Dog and Cat Records, 1976)
Rocket To Russia (Sire, 1977). Includes 'We're a Happy Family' and 'I Don't Care'.

All the Ramones albums, including these first three, are individually available on Warners Mid-Price CD. *Ramonesmania* (Sire, CD 1988) is a good 30-track compilation, but has been superseded by the 58-track *Hey Ho Let's Go* (Rhino/ Warner Archives, 2xCD 1999), which collects all the essentials of the Ramones' 21-year career plus the long-lost 'Carbona Not Glue'. Also of note: *It's Alive* (Sire, CD): a hyper-adrenalined record of their 31/12/77 show at the Rainbow, Finsbury Park – 28 songs in 54.36!

The most successful of the CBGBs groups did not belong to the Punk hardcore. The first three Blondie and Talking Heads albums each remain powerful documents, although Talking Heads' chilly preppieisms – on songs like 'No Compassion' – can grate. In comparison, Blondie's 60s neologisms are a breeze.
Talking Heads, 'Love Goes To Building on Fire' (Sire, US, 1976). Also collected on *New Wave* (Phonogram, UK, 1977).
Talking Heads '77 (Sire, 1977; now CD)
More Songs About Buildings and Food (Sire, 1978; now CD). Includes 'Warning Sign' and 'Found a Job'.
Fear of Music (Sire, 1979; now CD)
Blondie (Private Stock, 1976; now Chrysalis CD)
Plastic Letters (Chrysalis, 1977; now CD)
Parallel Lines (Chrysalis, 1978; now CD). Contains the Punk/ Disco breakthrough, 'Heart of Glass'.

Two 1976 compilations of New York's enlivened club scene: *Live at CBGBs*

1977 Pere Ubu graphic (© ubuprojex)

(CBGB/OMFUG, US; Atlantic, UK). Great idea except none of the talented CBGBs groups are there. *Max's Kansas City* (Ram, 1976, now ROIR CD) features Jayne County and Pere Ubu. The only overall compilation I've been able to find is *Blank Generation – The New York Scene (1975–78)* (Rhino CD, 1993), which features most of the essentials over 19 tracks. The best document of CBGBs, if you can see it, is Amos Poe's out of sync but riveting film, *Blank Generation*.

The only Cleveland 45s to come out during this period were the first three from Pere Ubu on their own Hearthan label:
'30 Seconds Over Tokyo'/ 'Heart of Darkness' (Hearthan, 1975)
'Final Solution'/ 'Cloud 149' (Hearthan, 1976)
'Street Waves'/ 'My Dark Ages' (Hearthan, 1976)

All grow rather than diminish with the passing of time, and can now be found in a variety of formats: on 7 singles plus the fourth, 'The Modern Dance' (Hearthan, 1977), in *The Hearpen Singles* box (Cooking Vinyl, 1998); on *Terminal Tower – An Archival Collection* (Rough Trade, 1985, now Cooking Vinyl CD), and on disc 1 (1975–1977) of the 5xCD boxed set *Datapanik in the Year Zero* (Cooking Vinyl, 1996). Disc 5 of this great package includes pre-Ubu rarities like a 9-minute rehearsal of 'Heart of Darkness', a live cover of the Seeds' 'Pushin Too Hard' and a killer Rocket from the Tombs version of '30 Seconds Over Tokyo' – just hear Crocus shriek 'tora! tora! tora!' as the tape cuts. Also of note: 7 minutes of ghostly Allen Ravenstine EMS synthesiser, 'Home Life'.

The first full-length album, *The Modern Dance* (Blank, 1978), is a classic, and is still available (Cooking Vinyl), as is the fine second album *Dub Housing* (Chrysalis, 1978, now Cooking Vinyl); and the rest you can hear on the

Terminal Tower set. Pere Ubu reformed in 1987, and have recorded seven well-received albums for Polygram and Cooking Vinyl, beginning with 1988's *The Tenement Year* and ending with 1999's *Apocalypse Now (Live 1991)*. Their great official website is: www.projex.demon.co.uk.

A group that has to be heard to be believed is the Electric Eels, who played out some of the central Punk tenets (and attitude and fashion) to uncomprehending audiences years ahead of their time. Recorded in 1975: the killer 45 'Agitated' / 'Cyclotron' (Rough Trade, 1979), which can be found, along with the rest of this group's poorly recorded, maxed-out, hate-filled repertoire on two CDs: *God Says Fuck You* (Homestead US, 1991), or *Their Organic Majesty's Request* (Overground, 1998). You have to hear classics like 'No, No', 'No Nonsense', 'You're Full of Shit' and the epic 'Accident': 'there's no attraction like a fatal crash',

Also from CLE during this period: Eels sleeve-note writer (and Psychotronic editor) Michael Weldon's group The Mirrors had their one 45 released on Hearthan, 'Shirley'/'She Smiled Wild' (recorded 1975, released 1979). CLE chronicler Charlotte Pressler recorded a great single as Pressler/Morgan, 'You're Gonna Watch Me' (Hearthan, 1979), which can also be found on the Terminal Tower boxed set. A fuller picture of Rocket from the Tombs can be gained from the *Life Stinks* album (Jack Slack Records, 1990), which features David Thomas, Peter Laughner and future Dead Boy Cheetah Chrome. With early 1975 versions of Ubu tracks like 'Final Solution' and some Iggy covers, Rocket from the Tombs were right on the edge: poised between power ballads and a more troubled future.

Another cuspy 1975/6 moment – a fascinating period this, before the guidelines were drawn up – were Debris, from Chickasha, Oklahoma, who recorded and released their one and only album *Debris* on their own Static Disposal label in an edition of 1000 copies in April 1976. An intense mix of VU/Stooges abrasion, mainstream US rock, and synthesiser/'multi-stringed electronic exasperator' abuse, this record was re-released on the Anopheles label (US) in 1999 and is recommended to seekers of the arcane.

Reggae 1972–8

This list is by necessity very selective. A thorough history of Reggae has now been published by Lloyd Bradley: *Bass Culture: When Reggae was King* (Viking, 2000). See also Steve Barrow's sleeve notes for the flood of reissues that have come out of Trojan Records since 1986, which are an excellent starting point. In 1997, Barrow published *The Rough Guide to Reggae* with Peter Dalton, which is an excellent primer. Also of note is Penny Reel's *Deep Down with Dennis Brown* (Drake Publications, 2000): a typically idiosyncratic (and well-written) account of Dennis Brown's 70s career and the underground London reggae culture of the time (1972–79).

Thanks to patterns of immigration into the UK, Jamaican music featured in the charts from 1964 on – after Millie's #2 hit 'My Boy Lollipop' – and no more so than during the Ska and Reggae crossover of the late sixties and early seventies. Two CDs from Island Records' 40th anniversary series (1999) chart the story of Jamaican music from 1959 to 1969: *Volume 1: 1959–1964: Ska's The Limit* and *Volume 2: 1964–1969: Rhythm and Blue Beat*. For an example of this impact, 20 Reggae Classics (Trojan CD, 1987) collates hits like 'Red Red Wine' and '007 (Shanty Town)' from the period already fetishized by Bernard Rhodes on the 1974 'Sex' T-shirt, and which would fuel the most powerful youth subculture of 1979–80, Two Tone.

Despite this pop success, there was little career development within Reggae until Chris Blackwood promoted the Wailers as a Rock band after 1972. Their story is well known, but note the following Bob Marley hits from the Punk era:

'No Woman No Cry' (Island, 1975) #22

'Jamming'/ 'Punky Reggae Party' (Island, 1977) #9

'Rastaman Vibration' (Island, 1976) #18

Exodus (Island, 1977) #8 (both these albums now on Tuff Gong CD)

Also Peter Tosh:

'Legalise It' (Virgin, 1976, NOW CD) #54

And Bunny Wailer:

'Blackheart Man' (Island, 1976, now Reggae Refreshers CD).

Some of this was due to the usual shortsightedness (if not racism) on the part of the majors: the almost pandemic chaos within the Jamaican music industry didn't help either. The result of this is that until 1976–7, Reggae releases were haphazard, often hard to find – even if you lived in metropolitan centres – and rarely played on radio. One of the indirect effects of Punk's avowed debt to Reggae was to boost the release of JA material in the UK.

After the ubiquitous 14/6d 'Tighten Up' series on Trojan, (a selection from which is now available on *The Tighten Up Box Set*, Trojan 3xCD), the first important crossover Reggae product was Island's *The Harder They Come* soundtrack (Island, 1972, now Reggae Refreshers CD). Both the film and its music made a huge impact: not surprising, with songs like the Slickers' 'Johnny Too Bad', the Maytals' 'Pressure Drop', and the Melodians' 'Rivers of Babylon'. (These can also be found on *20 Reggae Classics*.)

One result of the film was pop success for Jimmy Cliff, and a strong fan base for Toots and the Maytals, who toured with Dr Feelgood in 1974 and released two mature albums of pop/reggae: *In The Dark* (Trojan, 1974) and *Funky Kingston* (Island, 1975); both are now available on Trojan CD.

The first appearance of the Dub technique in the UK charts was Rupie Edwards 'Irie Feelings' (Cactus, 1974) #9: the 'Irie Feelings' CD (Trojan, 1990) contains one fascinating origin of today's megamix music economy: twenty-two versions on the same rhythm track, Johnnie Clarke's 'Everyday Wandering'. From 1974 on, Dub became more audible – if not easily consumable – in the inner cities: one early crossover record was Augustus Pablo's 'King Tubby Meets the Rockers Uptown' (Island single, 1975).

Nothing could have prepared you for the sheer audacity and texture of early Dub records like Skin Flesh and Bones' 'Everlasting Dub' (High Note, 1975); they still sound terrific. The mystery was augmented by these records' customary packaging in plain white sleeves, with just the title stamped or handwritten, like 'Dub Sensation' by the Revolutionaries, which pits the infamous Sly and Robbie rhythm section against all manner of found noises. Look for anything by the Revolutionaries: 'Bamba in Dub' (Skynote Records, 1977) or 'Hordcore Dub' (OMLP, 1990).

My vote for the greatest dub album ever goes to: Keith Hudson *Pick a Dub* (Klik, then Atra, 1975, now Blood and Fire CD). Twelve cuts, all fantastic, especially 'Don't Move'/ 'In the Rain'/ 'I'm All Right'. Versions of 'I'm All Right' crop up on Trojan's compilation of Hudson's production work: *Studio Kinda Cloudy* (Trojan, 1988, now CD), which includes essential cuts like 'Satan Side' and 'Riot'. Hudson continued to record important albums like 'Torch of Freedom' (1976) and 'Rasta Communication' (Joint Records, 1978) for several labels, including Virgin, until his death in 1984.

A good case can be made for King Tubby (Osbourne Ruddock) as the inventor of Dub: he was certainly early the first to use such Dub trademarks as delay echo, slide faders and phasing. His story is told on the posthumous, essential compilation *King Tubby's Special 1973–1976* (Trojan Records, 1990): thirty hard-to-find cuts. Trojan have also rereleased several 1975–6 albums by the Aggrovators mixed by King Tubby: *Johnny in the Echo Chamber* (Attack, 1989) and *Dub Justice* (ATLP, 1990). During the last few years, there has been a comprehensive reissue programme by Blood and Fire of King Tubby's 1974–79 productions. All of these are great: *If Deejay Was Your Trade: The Dreads at King Tubby's*, *Dub Gone Crazy*, *Dub Like Dirt* and *King Tubby's Prophecy of Dub* featuring Yabby U.

Don't forget also King Tubby's infamous album-length compilation with Augustus Pablo's melodica on *King Tubby Meets Rockers Uptown* (Yard Music, 1974; now US CD) – most of this album is contained in *El Rockers* (Pressure Sounds, CD 2000). More essential albums by Pablo (Horace Swaby) include: *Classic Rockers* (Island CD, 1995), *Original Rockers* (Greensleeves, 1979; now CD), a compilation of sides from 1972–5, and *East of the River Nile* (1977, now US CD). For a comparison between King Tubby and the Upsetter, pick up Dr Alimentado's *Best Dressed Chicken in Town* compilation of 1973–6 sides (Greensleeves, 1978, now CD). Find if you can the battle of the producers on *King Tubby Meets the Upsetter at the Grass Roots of Dub* (Fay Music, 1976, now Studio 16 CD).

The full story of the Upsetter, Lee Perry, would fill a book. After setting up his Upsetter Records in 1968, Perry got a UK Top Five hit with 'Return of Django' (Trojan/Upsetter, 1969, now available on Trojan CD and vinyl, as are many classic albums). For the bridge between the soul-influenced style of the 45 and LP (Trojan, 1969) and his later dub experiments, hear: *Lee Perry and Friends – Give Me Power* (Trojan, 1988) which compiles 45s from 1970–73; *The Upsetter Collection* (Trojan, 1988, now CD), 'Open the Gate' (Trojan 2 CDs) – mid seventies cuts featuring the Heptones, Junior Murvin and the Diamonds, among others; and *The Upsetter Compact Set* (Trojan, CD, 1988) which collects three scarce albums from 1973–4. His 1970 Wailers' productions: *Soul Revolution 1&2* (Trojan, 1988, now CD).

As part of the more general digitalization of reggae that has occurred during the later nineties, many new compilations of seventies' Lee Perry have appeared. The best are: *Arkology* (Island, 3 CDs), which contains many classics from Max Romeo, Junior Murvin, George Faith, the Congoes et al.; *Voodooism* (Pressure Sounds), including the great 'Mash Down' 45 by Roots; *Produced and Directed by the Upsetter* (Pressure Sounds), rare 45s and mixes compiled by the late, great Roger Eagle.

Important Perry productions from then on include: Max Romeo 'War in a Babylon' (Island, 1976; now CD), George Faith's 'To Be a Lover' (Island, 1977); and Junior Murvin's transcendent *Police and Thieves* album (Island, 1976, now CD). Try also to find the non-LP 'Memories' on the 12" (Island, 1977). His big Island era LP is *Super Ape* (Island, 1976), while other productions from this period are collected on *Reggae Greats* (Island, 1978). His production of the Congos' *The Heart of the Congos* (1978) has been reissued with an extra mix CD and a booklet with copious notes (Blood and Fire); his own *Roast Fish, Collie Weed and Corn Bread* (Lion of Judah, 1978) is still available on Jamaican vinyl and is highly recommended.

The other great JA innovation of the early seventies was what was first called 'talkover' and what we would now think of as Rap. The practice originated in tandem with Dub: whereas previously DJs had shouted or grunted interjections, the newly spacious rhythm tracks gave them more room. The history of early talkover – with tracks like Scotty's 'Draw Your Brakes', Prince Jazzbo's 'Free From Chains' and Big Youth's 'Moving Version' – is told on these Trojan CD compilations: *Keep on Coming Through the Door, U-Roy and Friends: With a Flick of My Musical Wrist*, and Scotty's *Unbelievable Sounds*. All 1968–73.

By the mid seventies, these shrieking DJs had moved into the reggae mainstream and were picked up by Virgin's big investment in Jamaican music under the Front Line logo; see *The Front Line* sampler (Caroline 1976, now CD). More detail here. Important mid seventies talkover albums include: U-Roy's *Version Galore* (Trojan, 1974) and *Dread in a Babylon* (Virgin, 1976); Big Youth's *Screaming Target* (Trojan, 1976) and *Dread Locks Dread* (Virgin, 1975, Front Line, 1978); Dillinger's *CB200* (Island, 1976) includes 'Cocaine in My Brain'. All of these are now available on CD, as is a great collection of early to mid seventies' Big Youth: *Tell It Black* (Recall/Snapper 2xCD).

For the way in which talkover influenced a declamatory JA vocalese, hear these wonderful albums: Tapper Zukie, *Man Ah Warrior* (Mer, 1977); *MPLA* (Klik/Front Line, 1976/8) includes his seminal 'Rockers' 45; *Tapper Zukie in Dub* (Blood and Fire, 1995, CD) has dub versions of 'MPLA', 'Prophesy' and others. Prince Far I's *Heavy Manners* (Joe Gibbs, 1976) is essential, as are these other Gibbs productions that were coming through after late 1976: Culture's *Two Sevens Clash* LP (now Shanachie US CD) with its talkover 45, Bo Jangles's *Prophecy Reveal; Money in my Pocket* (Trojan, CD); and the peerless *African Dub All Mighty Chapter 3*.

Gibbs had his moment when Althea and Donna's 'Up Town Top Ranking' went #1 in January 1978 (issued in the UK by Lightning, 1977–8 along with most of the above Gibbs productions, now available on *300% Dynamite*, Soul Jazz, 2000).

Also recommended:

Burning Spear, *Garvey's Ghost* (Island, 1976); now with its full vocal 'Marcus Garvey', on CD)
Gladiators, *Trenchtown Mix Up* (Virgin, 1976)
Twinkle Brothers, *Love* (Front Line, 1976)
Aswad, *Aswad* (Island, 1976)
Rico, *Wareika Dub* (Ghetto Rockers, 1977)

Vivian Jackson, 'Pick the Beam out of My Eyes' (Grove Music, 1977)
Glen Roy Richards, 'Wicked Can't Run Away' (Grove Music, 1977)
Dr Alimentado, 'Born For a Purpose' (Greensleeves, 1977, now CD)
Roots, 'Mash Down' (VP, 1977)
Linton Kwesi Johnson: as Poet and the Roots; *Dread Beat and Blood* (Front Line, 1978, now CD) includes 'It Dread Inna Inglan'/ 'All Wi Doin Is Defendin'.
Paths of Victory (Island, 1979)

Some of these British artists – who regularly shared punk bills – can be found on the Pressure Sounds compilation of UK reggae, *Don't Call Us Immigrants* (CD, 2000).

For more information: the Trojan catalogue is available from Regent House, 1 Pratt Mews, London NW1 0AD. You can visit and buy direct from their website: www.trojan-records.com. During the last year, Trojan have been issuing a budget series (16 so far) of themed 3xCD box sets covering many styles, of which *Trojan Dub Box Set* and *Trojan Dub Box Set Volume* 2 are highly recommended. Essential catalogues are also available from: Blood and Fire, 37 Ducie Street, Manchester M1 2JW (website: www.bloodandfire.-co.uk); Pressure Sounds, PO Box 12757, London E8 1PZ website: www.pressure.co.uk).

1976–: Sex Pistols

Until their formal dissolution in the courts, the Sex Pistols officially released only five UK 45s and one album. The original group had a repertoire of only twenty-five or so songs: these have been stretched, in various forms, over fifty or more different records. The exploitation process that can be seen to have begun directly after the February 1979 case with Virgin's handling of *The Great Rock'n'Roll Swindle* has continued until the present day.

Much of this has had to do with the peculiar situation that was a result of the court action in January 1986, when Glitterbest, the Sex Pistols' management company, was taken out of receivership and vested in the three ex-Pistols – John Lydon, Steve Jones and Paul Cook – and Sid Vicious' executrice, Anne Beverley. Any piece of business to do with the Sex Pistols had to be agreed by these four, with the consequent logistical problems. The situation was complicated further by the four waiting for rights to revert to them – which occurred in 1991. In the meantime, several small entrepreneurs stepped into the vacuum. Jock MacDonald, Dave Goodman and Lee Wood were all involved with the many semi-official (if not in contract, then in part-performance) Sex Pistols LPs and CDs that emerged after 1986. Most are dispensable, and recently the ex-Pistols have put their foot down to stem this wash of inferior products. In this Gordian knot of contractual activity, there is one final struggle of note: in 1988, Glen Matlock recovered from Glitterbest PRS money owned since 1978.

After the reversion of rights, the Sex Pistols moved quickly to represent their material in the way that they saw fit, forming a company to replace Glitterbest called Sex Pistols Residuals and constituting Lydon, Cook, Jones and, until her suicide in September 1996, Anne Beverley. Beginning with the excellent 1992 20 tracker, *Kiss This*, the group has re-released all its recorded material. For the

1996 Filthy Lucre tour and the 2000 Julien Temple movie, *The Filth and the Fury*, they were represented by Anita Kamerada.

The Sex Pistols still have no official website – although there is the promise of one through Virgin US – but you can update on news, etc. on: God Save the Sex Pistols (www.sex-pistols.net/banner.html), the site run by the *The Filth and the Fury* fanzine. This contains right up-to-date material on the group and its individual members, and links to many other sites of note.

Thanks to Bill Forsyth of Minus Zero and John Pridige for their help with this part of the discography.

Official Recordings

The Sex Pistols had three recording sessions before 'Anarchy in the UK' was finished at Wessex. All the material from these has appeared on subsequent official and semi-official recordings. Their first release, however, was:

'Anarchy in the UK'/ 'I Wanna Be Me' (EMI, 1976, 2566: 11/76) #38. The first 2,000 copies were printed in a matt black sleeve with Chris Thomas credited as producer on both sides. In fact, 'I Wanna Be Me' dates from the Goodman sessions in July 1976, and after a legal flurry, the credit was changed on the second pressing. This also dropped the black bag for a standard EMI logo. The record was effectively withdrawn during December, and deleted during January.

Under their contract, EMI issued 'Anarchy' in Holland (EC 00606924), Belgium (4c00606924) and Germany (1C00606924) in December 1976. It was also released in New Zealand (EMI 2566) and Australia (EMI 11334). All were quickly withdrawn. In June 1977, it was released in France on Barclay Records (740.509), and both 7″ and 12″ copies were imported in large quantities, with a new Jamie Reid sleeve.

Apart from making endless albums, 'Anarchy' has been rereleased twice on 45: as part of Virgin's twelve-track *Sex Pack* of singles in 1980 and, together with 'No Fun', as a 7″/12″ single with a shiny black sleeve (Virgin, VS 609, 1983). The 12″ (VS 609-12) contains 'EMI'. These three tracks also exist on a 3″ CD, with the clipped ending of 'No Fun' (CDT 3).

As a 'rock classic', a brief snatch of 'Anarchy' was included on a 7″ made to promote the institution of The National Discography: introduced by Tim Rice, the record also contained music by Mahler, the Beatles, Louis Armstrong and others (MCPS, 1986).

'I Wanna Be Me' has been reissued on at least ten official and semi-official LPs.

In September 1992, 'Anarchy in the UK' was reissued on vinyl (Virgin VS 1431), 5″ CD (VSCDT 1431) and a limited poster-sleeve edition (VSCDX 1431). This was to promote the *Kiss This* compilation: it went to number 33 in the UK charts. In 1998, a drum 'n' bass cut-up of 'Anarchy' and 'Pretty Vacant' was released on white label by Pollution.

After more recordings with Dave Goodman in January 1977 and Chris Thomas in February the Sex Pistols' next single was ready:

'God Save the Queen'/ 'No Feelings' (A&M, AMS 7284). Withdrawn. 'God Save the Queen' had been chosen as the 'A' side, and the 'B' side, produced by Dave Goodman, was hurriedly chosen by Derek Green on the day of chaos (10 February 1977) that followed the Sex Pistols' press conference. Due for release on 25 February, some copies were pressed on the 14th and 15th, but all, bar a very few, were destroyed when A&M severed all links with the Sex Pistols on the 16th. The small amount of existing copies – up to one hundred – was augmented by another 35 or so copies on the eventual demise of A&M Records in December 1999.

'No Feelings' has been released and rereleased ad infinitum while 'God Save the Queen' quickly found a new home:

'God Save the Queen'/ 'Did You No Wrong' (Virgin, 1977, VS 181) #2. After all the delays and problems in manufacture, the single was released on 27 May 1977, just a week before the Jubilee weekend. It was also released by Virgin in Germany (Ariola 11308AT) and Mexico (Virgin 8106A, 'Dios Salve a la Reyna'), while under the other Glitterbest deals, it was issued in France (Barclay 640.106), India (West W8), Australia (Wizard, ZS 176) and Japan (Nippon Columbia YK 90-AX). There was also a bizarre Thai EP (Express Songs Records EXP0330: 'Queen' plus tracks from Bryan Ferry, the Ramones, and Boz Scaggs).

'God Save the Queen' appears on *Never Mind the Bollocks* (Virgin, 1977) as well as *Flogging A Dead Horse* (Virgin, 1980) and *The Very Best of Sex Pistols* (Nippon Columbia, 1979). It also appears on the 1980 *Sex Pack*. 'Did You No Wrong' appears on the Virgin/ Nippon Columbia compilations. There was also in 1988 a 5" (Virgin CDF37) and a 3" CD (Virgin CDT 37) of the two-sided single plus 'No Lip'.

Released quickly, the Sex Pistols' pop single:

'Pretty Vacant'/ 'No Fun' (VS 184: 6/77) #6. Again, a Chris Thomas 'A' side and a Dave Goodman 'B'. No controversy greeted this record on release, the only time this occurred in all the releases up until 1979. As with 'God Save the Queen', 'Pretty Vacant' was released in Germany (Ariola 11331AT) under the Virgin deal. Other territories: France (Barclay, 640.109), Australia (Wizard ZS184) and, eventually, the USA (Warners WBS 8516, with a new Jamie Reid sleeve cutting up Sir John Read, b/w 'Submission'). Also, a Thai EP: (EXP 0342 + Jam, Saints, Dave Edmunds).

'Pretty Vacant' has made all the compilations, as has 'No Fun' – a definitive roar through the Stooges' song from the first 'Anarchy' sessions in 1976. The more recent releases on Virgin CDs – like 1986's 3" (CDT 3) – chop off at least 30 seconds from the end of the song for no good reason.

'Vacant' was reissued in September 1992 as the second single from the *Kiss This* compilation, backed with 'No Feelings (Virgin VS 1448). It made number 56 in the UK charts. The other formats were sprinkled with sundry Goodman demos: 'Satellite' and 'Submission' on 12" (VST 1448), 'Seventeen' and 'Submission' and the released 'What'cha Gonna Do Bout It' on one CD (VSCDT 1448), 'No Feelings', 'EMI' and 'Satellite' on another CD (VSCDG 1448). Its still the same old material.

After more recordings and rerecordings for the album:

'Holidays in the Sun'/ 'Satellite' (VS 191: 9/77) #8. Written during the March

1977 Berlin trip, 'Holidays' was under consideration for release in June 1977 but was not felt to be strong enough without a lavish package and more overdubs. This package got the record into legal difficulties within a week of release, when the Belgian Travel Company, whose artwork Jamie Reid had detourned, insisted on the withdrawal (and destruction) of about 50,000 picture sleeves. The record then went on sale in a plain white bag.

Foreign releases: Germany and Holland (both 11643AT); Italy (Virgin, VIN 4013); France (Barclay, 640.116); Japan (Nippon Columbia, YK-97-AK). 'Holidays' makes all the usual compilations.

Then, after many attempts, came the album:

Never Mind the Bollocks (Virgin, 1977, V2086) #1.

Side 1: 'Holidays in the Sun'/ 'Bodies'/ 'No Feelings'/ 'Liar'/ 'God Save the Queen'

Side 2: 'Seventeen'/ 'Anarchy in the UK'/ 'Submission'/ 'Pretty Vacant'/ 'New York'/ 'EMI Unlimited Edition'

The permutations are many. From June on, Jamie Reid worked on a cover for *God Save Sex Pistols*: the same catalogue number but substituting 'Satellite' for 'Bodies'. On release some copies had a blank back sleeve and contained an eleven-track LP without 'Submission', which was inserted as a one-sided 7" 'freebie' (VDJ 24). 'Submission' was left off some back sleeves, while some export sleeves were printed with two 'Liar's and 'Belsen Was a Gas' supplanting 'Holidays' and 'Queen'.

The album was released by Barclay in France, and by Warners in the US: the latter (BSK 3147) had a red and green colour combo, and reversed the order on 'God Save the Queen' and 'Problems'. It also came with a new inner bag, in the same style as the many posters printed by Warners to promote the record. None of it did any good in the short term, although the record finally went gold in the US during 1987, the year that *Rolling Stone* voted it the second greatest Rock'n'Roll album of all time.

In 1979, Virgin released the album in a picture sleeve format with a photo taken from the 'Pretty Vacant' video session (VP 2086). It is now available in several formats: a straightforward mid price issue (Virgin CDVX 2086, 1996), and more expensive editions in a 21st anniversary book cover (Virgin CDVP 2086, 1998) and a card sleeve (Virgin VJCP 68050, 1999). In 1998, the album was reissued on vinyl (Virgin VP 2086), ironically as part of EMI's First Centenary celebrations; there was another 2000-only edition (same catalogue number) in pink vinyl. In 1996, the group released NMTB as part of a double CD (Spunk 1), with 21 extra cuts from the 'Spunk' sessions (7/76 and 1/77) and, uncredited, the three tracks from the 5/76 Spedding sessions – their first official release.

After that, nothing. 'Belsen Was a Gas' was mooted as the next UK single for the new year, but the group split up.

After some piecemeal recordings in Rio and London, the first post-Lydon single was released.

'No One Is Innocent'/ 'My Way' (VS 220: 7/78) #8. More chaos. The Biggs side has several titles: the 7" runs 'No One Is Innocent – a Punk Prayer by

Ronnie Biggs', while the 12", which also includes a drunken bit of chat between Cook, Jones and Biggs, substitutes 'The Biggest Blow' for 'No one Is Innocent'. The other title, 'Cosh the Driver', was not used. It is the side that is simply called 'My Way', however, that has gone down in history.

Foreign issues: Italy (VIN 45018); Greece (Virgin, 2097961); Japan (Nippon Columbia, YK-109-A); Australia (Wizard, ZS190 plus 12" ZS12190).

For the rest of the year, Cook and Jones worked in Wessex either to record new material for the forthcoming film soundtrack album, or to rework existing Dave Goodman tapes. The result was ready to go long before the court case of February 1979, but Virgin's assumption of control resulted in a rush release of the album in several permutations:

The Great Rock'n'Roll Swindle (VD 2510: 2/79) #7. There are two versions of the album. The first comes with the last paragraph of McLaren's 'Oliver Twist' handbill for the 25 December 1977 concert overprinted on the back sleeve in blue:

Side 1: 'The God Save the Queen Symphony'/ 'Rock Around the Clock'/ 'Johnny B. Goode'/ 'Road Runner'/ 'Black Arabs'/ 'Anarchy in the UK'

Side 2: 'Silly Thing'/ 'Substitute'/ 'Don't Give Me No Lip, Child'/ 'Stepping Stone'/ 'Lonely Boy'/ 'Something Else'

Side 3: 'L'Anarchie pour le UK'/ 'Belsen Was A Gas' (live SF)/ 'Belsen Was A Gas' (studio with Biggs)/ 'No One Is Innocent'/ 'My Way'

Side 4: 'C'mon Everybody'/ 'EMI (Orch)'/ 'The Great Rock'n'Roll Swindle'/ 'You Need Hands'/ 'Friggin' in the Riggin''.

The second comes without the handbill lettering, and with a red rather than white spine:

Side 1: 'The God Save the Queen Symphony'/ 'Johnny B. Good'/ 'Road Runner'/ 'Black Arabs'/ 'Anarchy in the UK'

Side 2: 'Substitute'/ 'Don't Give Me No Lip, Child'/ 'Stepping Stone'/ 'L'Anarchie pour le UK'/ 'Belsen Was a Gas' (live SF 14/1/78)/ 'Belsen Was a Gas' (studio with Biggs)

Side 3: 'Silly Thing'/ 'My Way'/ 'I Wanna Be Me'/ 'Something Else'/ 'Rock Around the Clock'/ 'Lonely Boy'/ 'No One Is Innocent'

Side 4: 'C'mon Everybody'/ 'EMI (Orch)'/ 'The Great Rock'n'Roll Swindle'/ 'Friggin' in the Riggin''/ 'You Need Hands'/ 'Who Killed Bambi'.

This version is more common. In 1980, Virgin released a 12 track single album (VZ168) with a full colour poster: this format has been reproduced by a *Highlights* CD released in 1992 (Virgin CDVUX 2510). The first CD issue of *The Great Rock 'n' Roll Swindle* (CDVD2510) contained 20 tracks, omitting the live 'Belsen was a Gas' among others, a situation soon rectified by the 24 track single CD (VDX 2510). The new 1999 reissue (VJCP 68057) restores the elusive 'Whatcha Gonna Do Bout It' to the full complement of 25 tracks.

There are several origins for these songs. Five out of the six Lydon vocals are taken from the October 1976 Goodman sessions for 'Anarchy', and retain the rejected 'Pied Piper' version. For the three sixties covers, Cook and Jones rerecorded most of the instrumental parts (the Goodman originals are on his semi-official *Pirates of Destiny* CD, now Castle Music ESM CD 609, 1999) leaving the Lydon vocals from the earlier sessions. The terrifying Lydon 'Belsen' is from the group's last show.

The later recordings fall into several categories. The March 1978 Rio trip produced two Biggs vocals, while Sid's 'My Way' was recorded on 3 April 1978 in Paris and mixed in London. Jerzimy's French 'Anarchy' dates from this period. The Cook/Jones pop songs, the McLaren orchestral songs – including his version of Max Bygraves' vehicle, 'You Need Hands' – and the Black Arabs were all completed by August 1978, leaving the Ten Pole Tudor material the last to be recorded.

As Warners had terminated the Glitterbest contract, they did not release the album in the US. Virgin released an export version (AVIL-212510) before cutting it down to a single album – losing both 'Belsen's, the Lydon demos, and most of the perv McLaren bits – on release of the film in May 1980 (V 2168). The first 15,000 contained a film poster.

In the same week, Sid Vicious's posthumous single appeared:

'Something Else'/ 'Friggin' in the Riggin'' (VS 240: 2/79) #3. This was the bestselling Sex Pistols single, with a great picture sleeve and an ad featuring the immortal slogan, 'From Beyond the Grave'. Foreign issues include: France (Barclay, 640.159); Australia (Wizard, ZS 313); Japan (Nippon Columbia, YK-122-AX).

'Silly Thing'/ 'Who Killed Bambi' (VS 256: 3/79) #6. Foreign issues: Portugal (VV45009ES; b/w 'Anarchy in the UK', both from the *Swindle* LP).

'C'mon Everybody'/ 'God Save the Queen Symphony'/ 'Whatcha Gonna Do 'Bout It' (VS 272: 6/79) #3. Death sells, as Levis noted when they used the same song for their early 1988 ad campaign to accompany a truncated 'biopic' of composer Eddie Cochran. Sid becomes a Viciousburger on the sleeve. The Small Faces cover finds a home, sleeved in the clearest articulation of the Reid/ McLaren manifesto: 'The media was our lover and helper.'

Barclay collected the three Sid tracks onto a 12" EP (740.509) whose blue sleeve shows the Sid Action Man lying in a coffin. Later in 1979, Barclay released the McLaren cuts: 'You Need Hands'/ 'God Save the Queen' (640.161), and the two soundtrack album 'Anarchy's (640.162).

'Some Product: Carri On Sex Pistols' (VR2: 8/79) #6 (now available on CD Virgin CDVR2 mid price and VJCP 68056 card sleeve).

Side 1: 'The Very Name "Sex Pistols"'/ 'From Beyond the Grave'/ 'Big Tits Across America'

Side 2: 'The Complex World of Johnny Rotten'/ 'Sex Pistols Will Play'/ 'Is the Queen a Moron?'/ 'The Fucking Rotter'

The demand for Sex Pistols product was considerable but the cupboard was nearly bare. Ever resourceful, John Varnom put together this collection of spoken word material, from Virgin ads, the 13 Febuary 1978 Cook/Jones interview with K-SAN, and an audio recording of the Grundy incident. The fact that this was stew out of bones was reflected in the title: it still sold.

'The Great Rock'n'Roll Swindle'/ 'Rock Around the Clock' (VS 290: 10/79) #21. Reid's "American Express" sleeve caused immediate legal problems:

when Amex complained, the sleeve was pulled. The same occurred for the German/ Dutch release (Virgin 100916-100). The reverse showcased several dead rock stars including Sid, who also cropped up on the following quickie:

Sid Sings (Virgin, V2144: 12/79) #30 (now available on CD Virgin CDV2144 mid price and VJCP 68058 card sleeve).

Side 1: 'Born To Lose'/ 'I Wanna Be Your Dog'/ 'Take a Chance on Me'/ 'Stepping Stone'/ 'My Way'

Side 2: 'Belsen Was a Gas'/ 'Something Else'/ 'Chatterbox'/ 'Search and Destroy'/ 'Chinese Rocks'/ 'I Killed the Cat'

Rough tapes of Sid's Max's Kansas City dates in September 1978 – featuring the old New York Dolls rhythm section of Arthur Kane and Jerry Nolan and Mick Jones on guitar – were tidied up and nicely packaged by John Tiberi. John Varnom recounted the scam in *Melody Maker*, while Jamie Reid designed his guitar swastika logo for the label. The material had already been bootlegged (Innocent Records, JSR 21) and has been reworked on *Love Kills NYC* (Konexion, KOMA 788020: 1985). In 1995, a record of 'The Vicious White Kids' 8/78 show at the Electric Ballroom was released (Receiver RRCD 180). If you must, other Sid live stuff currently available on CD includes: *Sid Dead Live* (Anagram CD PUNK86) and *Sid Vicious Lives* (Dressed To Kill REDTK 123, 1999).

Flogging A Dead Horse (V2 142: 2/80) #21 (now available on CD Virgin CDV2142 mid price and VJCP 68052 card sleeve).

Side 1: 'Anarchy in the UK'/ 'I Wanna Be Me'/ 'God Save the Queen'/ 'Did You No Wrong'/ 'Pretty Vacant'/ 'No Fun'/ 'Holidays in the Sun'

Side 2: 'The Biggest Blow'/ 'My Way'/ 'Something Else'/ 'Silly Thing'/ 'C'mon Everybody'/ 'Stepping Stone'/ 'The Great Rock'n'Roll Swindle'

Shamelessness is not a virtue.

'I'm Not Your Stepping Stone'/ 'Pistols Propaganda' (VS339: 6/80) #21. Just to have something, anything to put out when the film was finally shown. The 'B' side has John Snagge's voice from the film trailers. This really was it, apart from *Sex Pack* (Virgin, 6 x 45 SEX 1: 12/80):

1: 'God Save the Queen'/ 'Pretty Vacant'
2: 'Holidays in the Sun'/ 'My Way'
3: 'Something Else'/ 'Silly Thing'
4: 'C'mon Everybody'/ 'The Great Rock'n'Roll Swindle'
5: 'I'm Not Your Stepping Stone'/ 'Anarchy in the UK'
6: 'Black Leather'/ 'Here We Go Again'

This was an excuse to release the two Cook/Jones tracks which had already come out on the Nippon Columbia *The Very Best of the Sex Pistols* LP (YX-7247-AX). New picture sleeves were made for numbers 2 and 5 to replace the controversial Reid designs.

The need for a proper Sex Pistols compilation was met by the strong September 1992 *Kiss This* compilation, which contained the following 20 tracks and is recommended as a primer to the group: 'Anarchy in the UK'/

'God Save the Queen'/'Pretty Vacant'/'Holidays in the Sun'/'I Wanna Be Me'/'Did You No Wrong'/'No Fun'/'Satellite'/'Don't Give Me No Lip, Child'/'(I'm Not Your) Steppin' Stone'/'Bodies'/'No Feelings'/'Liar'/ 'Problems'/'Seventeen'/'Submission'/'New York'/'EMI'/'My Way'/'Silly Thing'. Note the lack of many post-Lydon recordings, a deliberate exclusion elaborated upon in Lydon's brief comments on the poster. Various formats: single CD (Virgin CDV 2702), double vinyl (Virgin V2702), and an initial box edition with a poster and a bonus CD featuring nine tracks *Live in Trondheim: 21st July 1977* ('Anarchy in the UK'/'I Wanna Be Me'/'Seventeen'/'New York'/'EMI (Unlimited Edition)'/'No Fun'/'No Feelings'/'Problems'/'God Save The Queen').

Lydon was very much at the helm when the group reformed for the 1996 'Filthy Lucre' tour – indeed it seemed as though part of his motivation was to celebrate the final outcome of his prolonged power struggle with McLaren (which, as the performer/icon, he was, eventually, bound to win). The Finsbury Park show was recorded by Chris Thomas and rush-released as *Filthy Lucre Live* (Virgin CDVUS 116, vinyl VUSLP 116): 'Bodies'/'Seventeen'/'New York'/'No Feelings'/'Did You No Wrong'/ God Save The Queen'/'Liar'/ 'Satellite'/('I'm Not Your) Steppin' Stone'/'Holidays in the Sun'/'Submission'/'Pretty Vacant'/'EMI'/'Anarchy in the UK'/'Problems'. A single was culled, namely 'Pretty Vacant (live), 'Buddies' (i.e. 'Bodies'): silver vinyl (Virgin VUS 113); CD issue with extra tracks 'No Fun (live)' and 'Problems (live)' (VUSCD 133). It went to number 18 in the UK charts (7–8/96).

The tour and subsequent live album were trailed by a whole mass of ephemera: press kits, prostitute phone booth cards, God Save the Queen mugs, a Never Mind the Sex Pistols Here's the Bollocks beer bottle and promo CDs (including 'Pretty Vacant', one track CD Virgin Records USA DPRO-11550, 'God Save The Queen (Karaoke) and press conference' USA Virgin CD DPRO-11549 and a Belgian reproduction of GSQ CD 8935942). There is an interview CD from this time: *Never Mind the Filthy Lucre* (Suck My Filthy SUCK 1, 1998). Also available: *Outspoken and Outrageous* (Ozit OZITCD 0060, 1999).

The following essential videos/DVDs are also available: *Live In Winterland* (PNE Video PNV 1925, VHS 1996) – the awesome last concert, *Live at Longhorns* (PNE Video PNV 1026 and Castle Music Pictures DVD CMP 1004), which contains the infamous Sid Vicious and Helen Killer blood meeting and a pretty good performance by the rest of the group. 'Look at that', Lydon spits at his friend; 'A living circus.' It is noticeable that *The Great Rock'n'Roll Swindle* film is now not available on any format: this was one of the major issues in the eight-year Sex Pistols litigation and it seems clear that, now Lydon is in charge, the film 'I loath, hate and despise' (JL 2/2000) will not be made available – an absurd state of affairs.

John Lydon's version of *The Great Rock'n'Roll Swindle* was premiered in May 2000: the Julien Temple, Sex Pistols-authorized, anthology *The Filth and the Fury* (for a discussion of the film, see the Introduction). A 'soundtrack' CD was issued by Virgin (Virgin CDVD 2909 2xCD). The usual Sex Pistols' biggies are complemented by an eclectic mix of other relevant heroes and villains, including the Who's 'Substitute', the Creation's 'Through My Eyes' and Sailor's 'Glass of Champagne'. This is a good primer for those fresh to the period, with some sharp quotes from the group themselves in the sleeve notes.

Despite all this activity, the Sex Pistols' catalogue remains in a poor state for a group of their stature, with many releases suffering from the lack of any discographical information and the endless reduplication of the same tracks.

Semi-official Recordings

Apart from questionable live recordings, of which there are very many, most of the material here comes from the Dave Goodman sessions of July and October 1976, and January 1977. All were done outside a record contract – apart from the October 1976 'Anarchy' session, which fell outside a contract after EMI's severance – and were thus owned by Glitterbest.

In practice, this has meant that these recordings have been released outside the Virgin contract either with the connivance of Glitterbest – as with *Spunk* in September 1977 – or with their tacit acceptance. Goodman now alleges that he paid out MCPS and publishing money for the post-1985 sequence of releases that he was involved with and that the cheques were accepted. This state of affairs now seems to have ceased, but the shops are still full of Goodman product.

There is little honour in this area of human activity: there is only so much material, which has been repackaged many times under different names. The result is a nightmarish labyrinth of poor quality material, much of which – but not all – is listed here. If you're sane, the only semi-official product you need to know about is:

No Future UK? (Receiver Records, 1989, CD RR 117, now RRCD 117 and vinyl RRLP 117. Also available as above on Virgin Spunk 1.)

This contains, in order: 'Pretty Vacant'/ 'Seventeen'/ 'Satellite'/ 'No Feelings'/ 'I Wanna Be Me'/ 'Submission'/ 'Anarchy in the UK' – all from July 1976: 'Anarchy in the UK'/ 'No Fun' October 1976; 'God Save the Queen'/ 'Problems'/ 'Pretty Vacant'/ 'Liar'/ 'EMI'/ 'New York' January 1977.

This was the basis of the first Sex Pistols semi-official product to appear in any quantity, *Spunk*, which was released just before *Never Mind the Bollocks*. This album has been repackaged up to five times with different covers and tracks – most notably in its current form as *No Future UK?* – while the individual songs have been spread over at least ten different albums. Stick to this one which, after *NMTB* and *Kiss This* is the most essential Sex Pistols product.

Because the Sex Pistols were such an object of fascination, and because records were so slow to appear, the bootleggers started early. The first one to appear was:

The Good Time Music of the Sex Pistols (PFP/No Fun 1 6/77). Ten songs from the Manchester Free Trade Hall on 4 June 1976 recorded on a tape recorder with the batteries running down. Still fascinating. Initial quantities (up to two hundred) came with a cover modelled on the Pretty Things' first album, with a photo of Ian from the Worst on the front. Next came the post-Glen live material:

Anarchy in Sweden (Gun Records, 1978, GUN 101). Nine tracks from the July 1977 tour with a safety-pin sleeve.
Gun Control: Live SF 14/1/78 (Bang, SP2900: 6/78)
Welcome to the Rodeo – live Dallas 10/1/78 (SP2800: 8/78, now on CD When Records WENCD 008, 1996). The Winterland concert is essential, dreadful listening. The two immediate songs of interest, 'Anarchy in the USA' and the live 'Belsen' had already been released on two separate 45 pressings, the better known as Rotten Role (SUK 1/2). Although professionally recorded, the Winterland material has not been fully released: in 1980, Warners US released 'Anarchy in the USA' and an edited 'No Fun' on the sampler *Troublemakers* (PRO-A-857). Both records have been re-pressed many times.

Indecent Exposure (Rotten, SEXB 005: 11/78, now on CD as *The 76 Club*, Yeaah Records YEAAH 10, 1999). Thirteen songs recorded by Goodman off the desk from the 24 September 1976 concert at the 76 Club, Burton on Trent. Good versions of early material like 'Substitute' and 'No Lip'. This was repackaged many times before, bizarrely, being reissued (minus two tracks) by EMI's Fame label in 1985: (FA4131491). This was reissued on CD a couple of years later, plus one of the missing tracks but with the order completely changed and silence between the songs. Avoid.

This same concert has also been released as *The Original Pistols Live* (eleven tracks plus an interview disc: Receiver Records 1985, RRLP 101) and *After the Storm* (four tracks plus New York Dolls' 1972 demos: Receiver Records, RRLP 102).

Bootlegs were also made during the late seventies of the 20 September 1976 100 Club Festival (SP 3086) and the 5 January 1978 Atlanta date (Odd 2). Neither was of good quality.

In the early 80s came a 45 of the May 1976 Spedding sessions: 'Sex Pistols – We Don't Care' (Rotten Boys RB13202); 'Problems'/ 'No Feelings'/ 'Pretty Vacant' – lousy sound, but considerable historical interest. These three songs have now been placed in the extra CD of the Spunk 1 package.

From here on in, it's Goodmania. The producer's penchant for reworking the Sex Pistols sound which he helped to shape was first displayed on:

The Friendly Hopeful's Tribute to the Punks of 1976 (Abstract 1981 ABS 004). A witty medley of Punk classics like 'Liar' and 'Boredom'. Goodman then tried it on with: 'Land of Hope and Glory' (Virgina Records, Pistol 76) 1984. The packaging of this 45 would lead the buyer to think that this was a Pistols' out-take: it wasn't. Then came another repackaging – nicely done, but in tiresome 'collectors' editions – of the July 1976 sessions on Lee Wood's Chaos Records:
'Submission'/ 'No Feelings' (Chaos, 1984, 7" DICK 1)
'Submission'/ 'Anarchy in the UK' (Chaos, 1984, 12" EXPORT 1)
'The Mini Album' (Chaos, 1984, LP APOCA 3)
– all of the 7/76 session bar 'Pretty Vacant'. (now available on CD: Dojo

DOJOCD 265, 1996). Other studio releases currently available on CD: *Early Daze (the Studio Collection)* (Dojo DOJOCD119); *There is No Future* (Essential ESMCD 783, 1999); *Wanted (the Goodman Tapes)* (Essential ESMCD 608, 1998)

These releases passed without any comment from the receivers then still in charge of Glitterbest. The flood really started after 1985. Of all the records released since then, only the following are of any interest:

Sex Pistols (SEX, 1986, 24). This is the tape of the Nashville concert on 3 April 1976, plus a couple of numbers from St Albans in February 1976. The earliest authenticated Sex Pistols' recordings.

Pirates of Destiny (Essential ESMCD 609, 1998). Lo-fi interviews interspersed with rough live material, but this contains several songs of note: the originals of the three October 1976 demos reworked on the *Swindle* album, and a brief snatch of Lydon attempting a version of the Creation's 'Through My Eyes'. CDR's exist of the 100 Club concert on 29 June 1976 referred to on pp. 176–7. OK sound; sensational performance.

Apart from these two, the sad story runs as follows:

Live Worldwide (Konnexion, 1985, KOMA 788017). Jock MacDonald's rag-bag of Burton and the Goodman demos. One track is not the Sex Pistols.

Never Trust a Hippy (Sex Pistols, HIPPY 1). Super lo-fi stuff from Sweden, Atlanta, and Newport, December 1977.

Anarchy in the UK (Sex Pistols, UK, 1). Nine songs from Stockholm July 1977, plus three from Winterland.

Where Were You in '77 (77 Records, 771). Fifteen songs from Newport, 23 December 1977) – a near complete show.

The Best of the Sex Pistols Live (Bondage, BOND 007). One side from Burton, the other from Winterland.

Power of the Pistols (77 Records, 772). One side from Halmsted 15 July 1977, the other from Atlanta.

Last Show on Earth (McDonald Bros, Corp JOCK LP1). One side of mistitled Goodman demos, the other sundry Sid.

10th Anniversary Album (McDonald Bros, Corp JOCK LP3). Yet more Burton/ Goodman demos.

God Save the Sex Pistols (Konnexion, KOMA 788031). Compilation, in set list order, of live tapes from Halmstad, Dallas, Winterland, San Antonio (8 January 1978), Baton Rouge (9 January 1978), and Brunel (19 December 1977).

Cash from Chaos (SPCFC, 102). The Goodman demos plus Stockholm/ Winterland/ Halmstad tapes.

Anarchy Worldwide (Sex Pistols, SPAW 101). Yet again the 7/76 demos plus sundry Swedish/ US tapes.

Two final Goodman specials:

We Have Cum for Your Children (Skyclad, US SEX 6C). The usual rag-bag of demos and live tapes plus TV rerecordings (plus one track that is not, nor will ever be, the Sex Pistols).

Live at Chelmsford Prison (Dojo DOJOCD 66). The nadir. John Tiberi's tape of the fourteen-song Chelmsford Prison concert (17 September 1976) augmented by Goodman in the studio: new chat is added between numbers to suggest that John Lydon is inciting the prisoners to riot. Insulting.

Other live CDs currently available include: *Alive* (Essential ESDCD 321, 1995); *Better Live than Dead* (Dojo DOJOCD 73); *Live and Loud* (Dojo DOJOCD 71); *Raw* (Emporio EMPRCD 716).

Covers and Related Material

Anonymous version of 'Pretty Vacant' on 'Top of the Pops' (Hallmark, UK, 1977).

Paul Jones, 'Pretty Vacant' (Polydor, 1978). MOR version.

Johnny Rubbish, 'Living in NW3 4JR (Anarchy in the UK)' (UA, 1978). Unfunny comic.

The Low Numbers, 'Belsen Was a Gas' (on *Saturday Night Pogo – a Collection of Los Angeles Bands*, Rhino, US, 1978).

The Bollock Brothers, *Never Mind the Bollocks* (Charly, 1983). Track-for-track version includes Michael Fagin on two songs.

The Kingswoods, 'Purty Vacant' (G.R.E.E.N: Australia, 1983). Great Bluegrass.

Frank Sidebottom, 'Anarchy in the UK' (Regal Zonophone, 1984).

P. J. Proby, 'Anarchy in the UK' (Savoy, 1985).

Anthrax, 'Friggin' in the Riggin'' (Island, 1987). Speedcore.

Megadeth, 'Anarchy in the UK' (Capitol, 1988). With hilariously misheard lyrics.

Joan Jett, 'Pretty Vacant' (Epic, 1990).

Sex Pistols' songs remain rock standards, as evidenced by Guns'n Roses' and Motorhead's 'God Save the Queen 2000', from the album *We are Motorhead* (Koch, 2000).

In 1977, Jonathan King released a crap answer record:

Elizabeth, 'God Save the Sex Pistols' (Creole, CR, 139).

In 1979, the Vermorels began to make use of the interview tapes from their Sex Pistols book, releasing:

Cash Pussies, 99% Is Shit (The Label 010). Sid's phrase cut up and set to music by Alex Ferguson.

The Sex Pistols – the Heyday (Factory cass Fact.30 10/79).

Fuller interview material with all four members of the group and McLaren.

Finally, Heathcote Williams' version of Nancy's death:

Nazis Against Fascism, 'Sid Did It' (Truth, 1979, Rec 1).

Post-Sex Pistols Recordings

For a fuller PIL discography, see later.

Glen Matlock was the first to leave the Sex Pistols and formed his Rich Kids – with Steve New on guitar, Midge Ure on vocals and Rusty Egan on drums – in September 1977. Their first record was:

'Rich Kids'/ 'Empty Words' (EMI, 1978, 2738) #24. Also on

Ghosts of Princes In Towers (EMI, 1978, 3263, now on Cherry Red CDMRED 157). Their one LP, including the forced second single, 'Marching Men'. The best song is the title track.

Then Matlock worked with Iggy Pop on *Soldier* (Arista, 1980, SPART 1117, now on Arista/BMG CD 251160), before forming the Spectres with Danny Kustow from the TRB. They released two singles: 'Stories'/ 'Things' (Demon, 1981, D1002) and a cover of Ray Davies' 'This Strange Effect' (Direct Hit, 1981). Since then, Matlock has played with various musicians like JC from the Members, and recorded Pistols-retro material like Gary Oldman's version of 'I Wanna Be Your Dog' on *Sid & Nancy: Love Kills* (MCA, 1986, MCG 6011) and the Goodman Chelmsford CD.

In 1990, Omnibus published his autobiography, *I Was a Teenage Sex Pistol* ghosted by Pete Silverton, which sold well. After a period working with Bernard Rhodes, Matlock joined the re-forming Sex Pistols and released a solo album shortly after: *Who's He When He's at Home* (Creation CD CRECD 191, 1996). Despite a near-constant downplayment by Lydon, Matlock remains the Sex Pistol who wrote the tunes: in 2000 he hosted two BBC Radio 2 shows on the history of punk, *Anarchy in the UK*, played at the June Ian Dury Tribute Concert and in August released his second well-received solo album, *Open Mind* (Peppermint), with contributions by Mick Jones, Steve New, Tony Barbour and Patti Palladin.

Steve Jones and Paul Cook remained as a unit after the February 1979 court case. Their sociability and continuous playing resulted in several 1978 extra-Pistols recordings: Johnny Thunders, 'So Alone' (Real, 1978, RAL 1) includes the great 'You Can't Put Your Arms Round A Memory' and his answer song to 'New York', 'London Boys'. The Greedies, 'A Merry Jingle'/ 'A Merry Jangle' (Vertigo) with Thin Lizzy. The Avengers, *The American In Me* (White Noise, 1979, EP WNR002). Jones produces and plays.

Their 1978 recordings as the Sex Pistols remained in the charts during 1979, and resulted in an instant Virgin deal for their new group, the Professionals, formed with bassist Andy Allen, later replaced by Paul Myers from the Subway Sect. There were three singles, including: '1-2-3' (VS 376), then one album, *I Didn't See It Coming* (Virgin, 1981, V2220, now card sleeve CD Virgin VJCP 68059). By then Jones had fled to the US to avoid a small heroin possession charge, but not before contributing to Generation X, *Kiss Me Deadly* (Chrysalis, 1981, CHR 1327).

Jones made two unsuccessful rock albums: *Chequered Past* (Capitol, 1982, ST 17123) featuring the Blondie rhythm section, and singer Michael Des Barres, and a solo *Mercy* (MCA, 1987, 42006). Jones has since worked in Los Angeles as a session musician, for Bob Dylan, Asia and Guns 'n' Roses among others. He is an outspoken campaigner against drug abuse. Steve Jones remains the elusive Sex Pistol: a crude public image – note his narration for *Hooligans: The Video* in 2000 – contrasted with the terse, thoughtful person who comes through in this book and in *The Filth and the Fury*. In 1999, he won a US Grammy for his production work on Buckcherry's self-titled first album (Dreamworks) and played on Mel. C's 'Be the One' (from *Northern Star*, Virgin CD) and the Joe Strummer and Los Mescaleros album. At the May 2000 press launch for the authorized film, he pissed out of a window and made the tabloids. Later that same year, he released a compilation of his work with the Sex Pistols, Andy Taylor, Iggy Pop and the Professionals called *Sticks and Stones*.

Paul Cook lives quietly in West London. His musical activities have included *Chiefs of Relief* (Sire, US, 1988, 9257031). After a spell with Bananarama, he worked with Vic Godard on *Revenge of the Surrey People* (Postcard Dubh 936CD, 1993) and with Edwyn Collins on the international hit single 'A Girl Like You' (#4 UK, 1995) and the albums *Gorgeous George* (Setanta CD, 1994) and *I'm Not Following You* (Setanta CD, 1997). He was involved in the promotion of *The Filth and the Fury*.

The biggest UK hit to be scored by anybody from within the Sex Pistols and Glitterbest after 1980 is Malcolm McLaren's 'Double Dutch' (7/83) #3. After his return from Paris in 1980, McLaren used material collated for a potential musical – sometimes called 'The Mile High Club' – in his new project formed out of Adam's Ants: Bow Wow Wow.

After one terrific single 'C30 C60 C90 Go!' (EMI, 1980, 5088) #34 – and two fine albums – *Your Cassette Pet* (EMI, 1980, WOW) and *See Jungle! See Jungle! Go Join Your Gang Yeah City All Over! Go Ape Crazy!* (RCA, LP 00273000 10/81) #26 – McLaren left Bow Wow Wow to their own devices. Drummer Dave Barbarossa then worked with Beats International and bassist Leigh Gorman with Soho, both of whom had dance hits in the early nineties. A readily available collection: *Aphrodisiac – The Best of Bow Wow Wow* (Camden/BMG, 1998).

McLaren's performing career began in earnest when he travelled in Africa and America with Trevor Horn preparing his ethno-musicological album (also planned as a film) *Duck Rock* (Charisma, 1983, MMLP 1 5/83, now on CD Charisma MMCD 1) #18. The record was trailed by 'Buffalo Girl' (Charisma, 1982, MALC 1 11/82) #9, which brought both rap and scratching to a wider audience. Even better was February's 'Soweto' (MALC 2) #32, the first time that township jive made the charts in any form. Mix/outtake records from this period are *Buffalo Gals – Back to Skool* (Virgin CDV 2822, 1998) and *Round the Outside* (Virgin CDV 2646).

Consequent records have had a high media impact, often outweighing sales. 'Fans' (Charisma, 1984, MMDL2 12/84) #47 was McLaren's audacious attempt to marry opera and hip-hop: the autobiographical content of songs like 'The Boys Chorus' was teased out in the South Bank Show profile by Andy Harries to coincide with the album's release. Other records like 'Would You Like More Scratchin'' (CLAM, 1 5/84) and 'Round the Outside! Round the Outside!' (Virgin, CDV 2649 12/90) are remix mania.

1989's *Waltz Darling* (CBS, 4607362, now Sony CD) was a courtly mixture of lush Victorian painting, Strauss waltzes and the hardcore black gay activity of Voguing, usually performed to a House beat. Of particular note is Mark Moore's remix of the 'Deep in Vogue' 12" (CBS, 1989, Waltz 1 4/89) which features the voice of leading Voguer Willie Ninja Field. Some of the music on this album has been reworked from and into adverts, like that for the British Airways 1989 campaign.

During the nineties McLaren worked in the global media/cultural industries: apart from adverts – his credits included Nike, Coca-Cola and Minute-Maid orange juice – he managed a female Chinese group, Jungk, and released a theme record about his beloved *Paris* (No NOCD 1000) in 1994, which featured vocals from Catherine Deneuve, among others. (Initial copies came with a bonus ambient disc.) Offcuts from this project came out as *The Largest Movie House in Paris* (No NOCD 12). He also worked on adaptations of *The Odyssey* and a life of Christian Dior, and began his autobiography.

In 1988, the New Museum of Contemporary Art in New York held a show about McLaren's life and ideas called 'Impresario'; curated by Paul Taylor, it was launched with a particularly bad-tempered panel discussion at the Fashion Institute of Technology. Since then, McLaren has become a fine art issue, being featured in a costume exhibition at the Metropolitan Museum of New York and a year 2000 installation at the ZKM, Karlsruhe, Germany, called 'The Casino of Authenticity and Karaoke'. In the year 2000, he ran a high-profile but unsuccessful bid to become London's mayor (backed by ex-Creation Records' Alan McGee). For details on this and other recent news, go to the official website at www.mclaren.com.

1976–7: UK

Street Rock

Figureheads of the post-Glam, dirty Pub Rock breakthrough were Dr Feelgood, whose *Down by the Jetty* (UA, 1974) is essential. Their third album, *Stupidity* (UA, 1976) went to number 1 just as Punk was breaking. Both are now available on CD (Grand Records).

Other nasty Pub Rock:

Kilburn and the High Roads, *Handsome* (Dawn 1975, now Essential CD) includes 'Upminster Kid"/ 'The Roadette Song', and the Chris Thomas produced 'Rough Kids'. Ian Dury had one of the biggest-selling UK albums during the Punk period with: The Blockheads, *New Boots and Panties!!* (Stiff, 1977). #1. Currently only available on CD as Repertoire import (a situation sure to be rectified after Ian Dury's recent death).

Also note:

'Sex & Drugs & Rock & Roll' (Stiff, 1977, BUY 17).

Labels like Stiff and Chiswick, which released early Punk material, also started out of this milieu. Handy CD compilations are: *A Hard Night's Day* (Stiff, 1997); *The Chiswick Sampler: Good Clean Fun* (Chiswick) and *The Chiswick Story* (Chiswick, 2xCD).

More on-the-cusp products:

Trevor White, *Crazy Kids* (Island, 1976)

Eddie and the Hot Rods, *Writing on the Wall* (Island, 1976); *Live at the Marquee* (covers of '96 Tears'/ 'Get Out of Denver'/ 'Gloria'/ 'Satisfaction') (Island, 1975) #43; *Teenage Depression* (Island, 1976) #35. Their big hit was: 'Do Anything You Wanna Do' (Island, 1977) #9. Available on a best-of CD: *The End of the Beginning* (Island). Early member Lew Lewis made a fine R&B single, 'Caravan Man' (Stiff, 1977).

Count Bishops, 'Speedball' ('Route 66'/ 'I Ain't Got You'/ 'Beautiful Delilah'/ 'Teenage Letter') (Chiswick, EP, 1975, now available with 11 extra tracks on Chiswick CD); 'Train Train' (Chiswick, 1977).

Nick Lowe, 'So It Goes'/ 'Heart of the City' (Stiff, 1976).
The 101'ers, 'Keys to Your Heart'/ '5 Star Rock'n'Roll Petrol' (Chiswick, 1976). Joe Strummer's first group. Note the sound of North Kensington captured on, 'Elgin Avenue Breakdown' (Andalucia/Virgin, 1981).

Punk First Wave

This includes the very first groups formed in response to the Sex Pistols or the existing groups who sped up their R&B modes: common throughout is the Ramonic style which became the standard definition of Punk.

The first UK Punk single was, by a whisker:

THE DAMNED

'New Rose'/ 'Help' (Stiff, 1976); their first album was *Damned Damned Damned* (Stiff, 1977, now available on Demon CD) #36. The first thousand were released with a picture of Eddie and the Hot Rods on the reverse. An essential document. Picks: 'Neat Neat Neat', 'Stab Your Back, 'Feel the Pain'. The first few singles are collected on *Neat Neat Neat* (Demon 3xCD box) and *Skip Off School to See . . .* (Demon). *The Best of the Damned* (Chiswick) has material from Stiff, Chiswick and Bronze, including the great 1979 single 'Smash It Up'. There is also a CD of their John Peel sessions (Strange Fruit).

Next Brits to release a record were the Sex Pistols. Then:

BUZZCOCKS

'Spiral Scratch' (New Hormones, 1977, ORG; rereleased 1979 when it reached #31; reissued in 2000 by Mute Grey Area, both CD and vinyl)

Then twelve singles and three albums, almost all essential:

'Orgasm Addict'/ 'Whatever Happened To' (UA, 1977)
'What Do I Get?'/ 'Oh Shit' (UA, 1978) #37
'Love You More'/ 'Noise Annoys' (UA, 1978) #34
'Ever Fallen in Love' (UA, 1978) #12
'Promises'/ 'Lipstick' (UA, 1978) #20
'Everybody's Happy Nowadays'/ 'Why Can't I Touch It?' (UA, 1979) #29
'Harmony In My Head'/ 'Something's Going Wrong Again' (UA, 1979) #32
'Are Everything'/ 'Why She's a Girl from the Chainstore' (BP, 1980) #61
'Strange Thing'/ 'Airwaves Dream' (BP, 1980)
'Running Free'/ 'What Do You Know?' (BP, 1980)

All non-LP 45s up to "Harmony in My Head" are collected on *Singles Going Steady* (IRS, US, 1979; EMI, UK, 1981, now on EMI CD). The final three were collected on *Parts 1–3* (IRS, Canada, 1981). Both collections can be found, as can the following three LPs, on *Product* (EMI 3xCD, 1989 and later reissue).

Another Music in a Different Kitchen (UA, 1978) #15: first few thousand in a grey 'Product' bag. Picks: 'Fast Cars'/ 'No Reply'/ 'Get on Our Own'/ 'Sixteen'/ 'Fiction Romance'/ 'Autonomy'/ 'I Need'/ 'Moving Away from the Pulsebeat' (this final track was released on a limited edition 12" disco 45).
Love Bites (UA, 1978) #13. Picks: 'Operator's Manual'/ 'Nostalgia'/ 'Just Lust'/ 'ESP'.
A Different Kind of Tension (UA, 1979) #26. Picks: 'I Don't Know What to Dowith My Life'/ 'Money'/ 'Hollow Inside'/ 'A Different Kind of Tension'/ 'I Believe'.

Bootleg: *Time's Up* (Voto, 1978; reissued by Document 1991 (CD) and in 2000 by Mute/Grey Area with detailed notes, unseen photos and enhanced with the super 8 footage of the group's first concert at the Free Trade Hall). Ten songs from the Buzzcocks first demos (1976), including: 'Boredom'/ 'I Can't Control Myself'/ 'Orgasm Addict'/ 'Drop in the Ocean'/ 'I Love You Big Dummy'. Devoto sings, the band squeal: the result is a pure 1976 product, right down to the lyric change in their Troggs' cover: 'This kind of feeling could *destroy* a nation'.

An early nineties' best of, *Operator's Manual*, is still available (EMI CD), as are their 'BBC Sessions' (EMI CD) and 'Chronology' (EMI CD, 1997), a collection of demos and outtakes, including Paddy Garvey's great 'Run Away From Home'. There are also a couple of live CDs from their heyday: *Live at the Roxy* (Receiver) from April 1977 and *Beating Hearts* (Pilot, 2000), featuring a Manchester show (27/10/78) with one from a year later at London's Rainbow Theatre.

In 1992, the Buzzcocks re-formed, with Pete Shelley, Steve Diggle and new bassist Tony Arbour, beginning a successful second career which has included albums *Test Trade Transmission* (1993). They supported Nirvana on their ill-fated 1994 European tour. Two more albums followed: *All Set* (IRS, 1996) and *Modern* (EMI, 1999, plus bonus CD of greatest hits). In 1999, Toyota used 'What Do I Get' in a major US TV ad campaign. The official and exemplary band website can be found at: www.buzzcocks.com.

All the Buzzcocks' releases were designed by Malcolm Garrett.

Coming up very fast in early 1977 were:

THE CLASH

'White Riot'/ '1977' (CBS, 1977) #38. Both this and these subsequent singles are essential:

'Complete Control'/ 'City of the Dead' (CBS, 1977) #28

'Clash City Rockers'/ 'Jail Guitar Doors' (CBS, 1978) #35

'(White Man) In Hammersmith Palais'/ 'The Prisoner' (CBS, 1978) #32

'Tommy Gun'/ '1-2 Crush on You' (CBS, 1978) #19

'English Civil War (Johnny Comes Marching Home)' (CBS, 1979) #25

'Cost of Living' EP ('I Fought the Law'/ 'Groovy Times'/ 'Gates of the West'/ 'Capital Radio') (CBS, 1979) #22

'London Calling'/ 'Armagideon Time' (CBS, 1979) #11

'Bankrobber'/ 'Rockers Galore' (CBS, 1980) #12

'The Magnificent Seven'/ 'The Magnificent Dance' (CBS, 1981) #34

'Should I Stay or Should I Go'/ 'Straight to Hell' (CBS, 1982) #17

#1 hit in March 1991 in tandem with a Levis ad campaign. Its 'follow-up', 'Rock the Casbah', made the Top Twenty in April 1991.

After Mick Jones left in 1983, the Clash regrouped for the last great Punk Rock 45: 'This is England'/ 'Do It Now'/ 'Sex Mad Roar' (CBS, 1985).

These LPs quickly followed 'White Riot':

The Clash (CBS, 1977) #12. Almost every one of the fourteen tracks is a zinger. Picks: 'Janie Jones'/ 'I'm So Bored with the USA'/ 'White Riot'/ 'Hate & War'/ 'What's My Name'/ 'Deny'/ 'London's Burning'/ 'Career Opportunities'/ 'Cheat'/ 'Protex Blue'/ 'Police and Thieves'/ '48 Hours'/ 'Garageland'.

The CD initially available on CBS was the version of the album as released in the US in July 1979: i.e. without 'Deny' / 'Cheat' / 'Protex Blue' and '48 Hours', and adding the 'Clash City Rockers' / 'Hammersmith Palais' and 'Complete Control' 45s with 'Jail Guitar Doors' and 'I Fought the Law.' Both the UK and US versions are now available.

Give 'Em Enough Rope (CBS, 1978) #2; now CD. A deservedly successful, but patchy record. Picks: 'Safe European Home' / 'English Civil War' / 'Tommy Gun' / 'Last Gang in Town' / 'Guns on the Roof' / 'Drug-Stabbing Time' / 'Cheapskates'.

London Calling (CBS, 1979; now CD) #9. A much more American record – in terms of mythology and sound – and as such acknowledged as the Greatest Record of the Eighties by *Rolling Stone* in 1990 (Rel, US, 1980). Picks: 'London Calling' / 'Brand New Cadillac' / 'Spanish Bombs' / 'Lost in the Supermarket' / 'Guns of Brixton' / 'Train in Vain'.

Combat Rock (CBS, 1982; now CD) #2. A return to form after 1980's sprawling *Sandinista*. Picks: 'Know Your Rights' / 'Should I Stay or Should I Go' / 'Rock the Casbah' / 'Straight to Hell' / 'Death is a Star'.

All these six albums – from the UK *The Clash* through to *Combat Rock* – are currently available on Sony/Columbia CDs.

Cut The Crap (CBS, 1985; now CD) #16. Much maligned on release in an England grown cold, but an ambitious and moving state-of-the-nation address with innovative use of rap rhythm and atmosphere. Picks: 'Dictator' /

Clash graffiti under the Westway at Royal Oak, February 1977 (© Jon Savage)

'Dirty Punk'/ 'Are You Red . . y'/ 'Cool Under Heat'/ 'Movers and Shakers'/ 'This is England'/ 'Fingerpoppin''/ 'Life Is Wild'. Despite having been in print for over ten years, this record is now unavailable, a piece of revisionism worthy of the Sex Pistols themselves. Almost everybody says this record is crap: it isn't. Try to find a copy to judge for yourselves and see if you don't think that 'This Is England' is the best song Joe Strummer ever wrote (or, at least, the last (1985) great Brit punk song). *Cut the Crap* rocks, and isn't that the general idea?

Instead we get all this stuff, mainly conceived from an American perspective: the Clash as superior, successful rock band. (At one time, they were much more.) There is *Super Black Market Clash* (Columbia CD, with the re-recorded 'Capital Radio'); *The Story of the Clash* (aka the rewriting of the history of the Clash, Columbia 2xCD); *From Here to Eternity* (Columbia) – entertaining through inessential live album from 1978–81, used to promo the compromised *From the Westway to the World* TV show/film in autumn 1999. If you want the definitive non-album plus outtake material, then go for the *Clash on Broadway* boxed set (3xCD Epic/Legacy), which contains a couple of the 1976 Guy Stevens demos among the usual classics and less familiar material. Useful lyric booklet and good sleeve notes as well.

Bootlegs: many live LPs, but the Clash were aurally always better in the studio. Only one essential:

The Clash (blank yellow label), which features December 1976 Guy Stevens demos of 'Crush on You'/ 'London's Burning'/ 'Career Opportunities'/ '1977'/ 'White Riot'/ 'Janie Jones', plus the contents of the very limited 'Capital Radio' EP (CBS, 1977) which includes 'Listen'/ 'Capitol Radio'/ Audio tape of the Tony Parsons interview.

Joe Strummer continues to perform and record with Los Mescaleros and released an album *Rock, Art and the X Ray Style* (Casbah, 1999). There is perennial talk about a Clash reformation but it seems unlikely to happen. For more details, an official website: www.westwaytotheworld.com.

After that, the Punk bands come thick and fast:

THE VIBRATORS

Bandwagon jumpers to be sure, but sometimes bandwagon jumpers have the most fun and have the best tunes.

'Pogo Dancing' (RAK, 1976) with Chris Spedding

'Whips and Furs' (RAK, 1976)

The singles have a certain kitsch value, but one album has all you need:

Pure Mania (CBS, Epic, 1977) #49

Pop/Punk like 'Sweet Sweet Heart'/ 'Baby Baby'/ 'No Heart'/ 'She's Bringing You Down'/ 'Bad Time'/ 'Stiff Little Fingers'.

Currently available on CD: *Best of the Vibrators* (Anagram); *The BBC Sessions 77–78* (Captain Oi!).

EATER

'You'/ 'Outside View' (The Label, 1977)

'Thinking of the USA' (The Label, 1977)

Both these 45s can be found on *The Complete Eater* (Anagram CD).

SLAUGHTER AND THE DOGS

The sound of Wythenshawe, or as they described themselves: 'a bunch of bastards from Sharston'. The glam/punk/scally crossover.

'Cranked up Really High' (Rabid, 1977)

'Where Have All the Boot Boys Gone' (Decca, 1977)

Do It Dog Style (Decca, 1978, now Captain Oi! CD). Stupid but irresistible: 'Quick Joey Small'/ 'You're a Bore'.

These two great singles and more can be found on *Cranked Up Really High* (Captain Oi! CD).

THE ADVERTS

'One Chord Wonders'/ 'Quickstep' (Stiff, 1977).

One of the best Punk singles; the great B side has been unavailable since the 70s.

'Gary Gilmore's Eyes' (Anchor, 1977) #18

'Safety in Numbers'/ 'We Who Wait' (Anchor, 1977)

'No Time to Be 21'/ 'New Day Dawning' (Bright, 1978) #38

Crossing the Red Sea with the Adverts (Bright, 1978, – now on Essential CD with the non-Stiff 45s) #38. Initial 250 in red vinyl. From Jane Suck's title in, a fantastic record. Picks: the whole damn thing: 'One Chord Wonders'/ 'Bored Teenagers'/ 'New Church'/ 'On the Roof'/ 'Newboys'/ 'Bombsite Boy'/ 'No Time to Be 21'/ 'Safety in Numbers'/ 'Drowning Men'/ 'On Wheels'/ 'Great British Mistake'. A *Radio Sessions* CD is available from Burning Airlines.

THE SAINTS

Australian adoptees who produced the fiercest rock of Punk and any time. 45s include:

'(I'm) Stranded'/ 'No Time' (Fatal Aus, 1976; re Power Exchange, 1976). Still astonishing, as is:

'This Perfect Day'/ 'L.I.E.S' (EMI/Harvest, 1977) #34. Initial 12" copies came with 'Do the Robot'.

(I'm) Stranded (EMI Aus, 1977; re EMI/Harvest, UK, 1977, Harvest; now on Captain Oi! CD).

Terrific: one of the few Punk albums that still stands proud today. Picks: '(I'm) Stranded'/ 'One Way Street'/ 'Wild About You'/ 'Messin' with the Kid'/ 'Erotic Neurotic'/ 'No Time'/ 'Kissin' Cousins'/ 'Story of Love'/ 'Demolition Girl'/ 'Nights in Venice'.

Eternally Yours (EMI/Harvest, 1978; now Captain Oi! CD). Picks: 'Know Your Product'/ 'Lost and Found'/ 'Private Affair'.

Prehistoric Sounds (EMI/Harvest, 1978). Losing fire, but contains the great 'Brisbane'. All three albums were collected on the essential Wild About You, 1976–1978 (Raven/Hot, 2xCD, 2000: contains detailed sleeve-notes and four out-takes).

Just to emphasize the Saints' polar punk position, Hot released a CD of demos from 1974 as *The Saints – The Most Primitive Band in the World*. Fierce billing, which they live up to.

THE HEARTBREAKERS

Authentic New York Punk = Loser Rock

'Chinese Rocks'/ 'Born To Loose' [sic] (Track, 1977)

Both tracks plus the next two 45s are on:

L.A.M.F (Track, 1977). A smudged classic, including 'All By Myself'/ 'It's Not Enough'/ 'One Track Mind'. The original remains unavailable, although Jungle have released a good remix CD, *L.A.M.F. (Lost* '77 Mixes). The Track single sides are available on: *Born Too Loose – The Best of Johnny Thunders* (Jungle, 2xCD). A live snapshot of the Richard Hell period can be found on *What Goes Around* (BOMP, CD).

SNATCH

Unheralded, female legislators of the Punk attitude.

'IRT'/ 'Stanley' (BOMP, US, 1977; re UK Lightning, 1978)

'All I Want'/ 'When I'm Bored' (Lightning, 1978)

'RAF' (Polydor, 1978) with Brian Eno

All these tracks were available on a 1983 collection of 1976/7 recordings, *Snatch* (Pandemonium). The extraordinary 'RAF' (told from the point of view of hijackees waiting for deliverance in a stinking plane: 'do you think anybody cares about *you*!') can be found on the Brian Eno *Vocal* 3xCD box set (Virgin).

JAYNE COUNTY

Formerly Wayne.

'Paranoia Paradise' (Illegal, 1977). Then the immortal ('If You Don't Want to Fuck Me . . .') 'Fuck Off' (Sweet FA Records, 1977). A young woman was arrested and fined in Liverpool for wearing the badge which promoted this immortal statement of intent: you can now hear it on *Rock'n'Roll Cleopatra* (RPM CD). Jayne's autobiography, *Take it Like a Man*, is a hoot and is highly recommended.

GENERATION X

'Your Generation'/ 'Day by Day' (Chrysalis, 1977) #36. The 'B' side is a fabulous tube song.

'Wild Youth'/ 'Wild Dub' (Chrysalis, 1977). The missing link between Heinz, Glam Rock and dub.

Find the A sides on *Perfect Hits* 1975–81 (EMI CD).

Generation X (Chrysalis, 1978, now on EMI CD) #29. Veers towards over-production but songs like 'Youth Youth Youth' survive. After this, obtuse mythologizing until:

'Dancing With Myself'/ 'Ugly Rash' (Chrysalis, 1981) #62. The foundation of Billy Idol's deserved success.

CHELSEA

'Right To Work'/ 'The Loner' (Step Forward, 1977). Hilarious lyrics but good timing. For the next ten years, I have to plead ignorance, but you can hear the first five on *The Punk Singles Collection 1977–82* (Captain Oi!). For an eloquent defence of Chelsea's sterling virtues, read Steward Home's distaff punk survey, *Cranked Up Really High* (Codex, 1995).

CORTINAS
'Fascist Dictator' (Step Forward, 1977).
'Defiant Pose' (Step Forward, 1978). The picture sleeve features a youth in the act of vomiting; the title has been appropriated by Stewart Home for his second novel (published in 1991). Guitarist Nick Sheppard joined the 'Cut the Crap' Clash.

THE BOYS
One great album collects 45s like 'I Don't Care' (NEMS, 1977):
The Boys (NEMS, 1977, now available on vinyl only, Get Back). Sped-up white-boy rock – brevity is a virtue: 'Soda Pressing'/ 'Sick on You'/ 'Cop Cars'.
Further research: *The Very Best of the Boys* (Anagram) and *The Complete Punk Singles Collection* (Anagram).

RADIATORS FROM SPACE
From Dublin. Hyperactive 45:
'Television Screen' (Chiswick, 1977).
Their first LP *TV Tube Heart* (Chiswick, 1977) is sketchy but *Ghostown* (Chiswick, 1979; re 1989) includes 'Under Clery's Clock', one of the few songs about homosexuality (that is not about prostitution) from this period. Most of this material is collected on *Cockles and Mussels – The Best Of* (Chiswick CD); *Alive-Alive-O!* (Chiswick CD) rounds up demos with a 1978 live concert.

JOHNNY MOPED
His infamous 'Starting a Moped' tape (Chiswick, 1977) is a great farrago of updated 60s Punk, moped noises and sheer oddity. Not so great over short bursts, Moped needs time to work his highly individual charm, and is heard best on the *Cycledelic* album (Chiswick, 1978). All of Moped's Chiswick recordings – apart from 'Starting a Moped' – can be found on *Basically – Studio and Live* (Chiswick CD), which also includes a live show from 1978.

MODELS
'Freeze' (Step Forward, 1977).

THE LURKERS
'Shadow' (Beggar's Banquet, 1977: diff coloured vinyl). Sub-Ramones Pub Rock, and all the better for it: an awesome thunder. Find it on *The Beggars Banquet Singles Collection* (Anagram CD). A strong case has been made for the *Fulham Fallout* album (Beggar's Banquet, 1978, now Captain Oi! CD). Some BBC sessions from 1977–9 are available on Captain Oi!

999
One great 45, their third: 'Emergency' (UA, 1978, *Independent Punk Singles Collection*, Anagram).

PENETRATION
Late to record, but pure Punk idealism.
'Don't Dictate'/ 'Money Talks' (Virgin, 1977).
'Firing Squad'/ 'NeveRr' (Virgin, 1978).
Find these essential singles on *Don't Dictate (Best Of)* (Virgin).

Moving Targets (Virgin, 1978, now on CD). The first 15,000 were on luminous vinyl. Lumpy production, but 'Nostalgia' and 'Silent Community' shine through. After this, a mess except:
Race Against Time (Clifdayn, 1979, now on Pilot CD) contains one live side (dispensable) and one side of demos from April 1977 and January 1978; 'Never Never' and 'Duty Free Technology' are wonderful.

X-RAY SPEX

Definitive Punk snapshots.
'Oh Bondage! Up Yours!'/ 'I Am a Cliché' (Virgin, 1977). 'Yama Yama Yama Yama Yama Yama/Boredom Boredom Boredom Boring Boredom'.
'The Day the World Turned Dayglo' (EMI, 1978) #23
'Identity' (EMI, 1978) #24
'Germ Free Adolescence'/ 'Age' (EMI, 1978) #19
'Highly Inflammable' (EMI, 1979) #45
Germ Free Adolescents (EMI, 1978, now with the first single on Virgin CD) #30. Has almost everything: 'Artificial'/ 'Obsessed with You'/ 'Warrior in Woolworths'/ 'Let's Submerge'/ 'I Can't Do Anything'/ 'Genetic Engineering'/ 'I Live Off You'/ 'I Am A Poseur'/ 'Plastic Bag' plus the middle three 45s. A great London record.

Compilations include:
The Roxy London WC2 (EMI/Harvest, 1977, now Receiver CD; re EMI, 1990) #24
Contains the past (Slaughter and the Dogs), the untalented (the Unwanted), the talented (X-Ray Spex, Buzzcocks), the odd (Johnny Moped) and the future (Wire). Heavy on atmosphere, and thus essential, but light on truly memorable moments. Individual performances from the April 1977 recordings have since been released on Receiver: Buzzcocks, The Boys, X-Ray Spex, although the Adverts album isn't from where it claims to be.

If you need one compilation from this area of human activity, then you are directed to the excellent *1 2 3 4: Punk and New Wave 1976–79* (Universal 5xCD, 1999): 100 squalling tracks from the USA and the UK, almost all singles, featuring all the big names and great noises by the Lurkers, Menace, 999, the Yachts, the Ruts, the Dead Boys, Snatch, the Au Pairs, the Only Ones – to name but a few. It's the closest approximation you could have to a punk disco during 1977–8: charlatans rub up against visionaries, bandwagon jumpers against punk purists, in an accurate record of the period's chaos.

For those who want to dig deeper, try *Short Sharp Shock – Independent Recordings UK 1977* (Overground), featuring a perfect Richard Allen rip-off cover and several fabulously obscure records by Anti Social, the Exile, the Jerks, Headache, and unsung classics like the Now's 'Development Corporations' and Blitzkrieg Bop's unanswerable 'Bugger Off'. Did you know that the Jerks debuted as Simon Snake and the Amputated Leg Band?

If you can find it, the CD of Greil Marcus's *Lipstick Traces* (Rough Trade, 1993) contains a wonderful 27 track segue between the Slits, the Orioles, Buzzcocks, Adverts, Kleenex, the Clash (stage talk), the Mekons, Liliput, Guy Debord, Gil J. Wolman, Benny Spellman and rare Dada/Futurist sound recordings by

Tristan Tzara, Richard Huelsenbeck, Raoul Hausmann, Jean-Louis Brau. The Slits' cut, 'What A Boring Life', is one of the few places you can hear that 1977 'guitar depression' overload ambience, and is unavailable elsewhere.

New Wave

THE STRANGLERS

'Get A Grip On Yourself' (UA, 1977) #44

Old-style aggression – i.e. bullying misogyny. The chart positions of the following LPs should be noted:

Stranglers IV (*Rattus Norvegicus*) (UA, 1977) #4

No More Heroes (UA, 1977) #2

THE JAM

Little Tories until they grew up.

'In the City'/ 'Takin' My Love' (Polydor, 1977) #40. A hyperactive riff stolen by Steve Jones for 'Holidays in the Sun', then a quality gap until:

'"A" Bomb in Wardour Street' (Polydor, 1978) #25

'Down in the Tube Station at Midnight' (Polydor, 1978) #15

These began the Jam's run of eleven Top Twenty hits – collected on:

Snap (Polydor, 1983) #2

All Mod Cons (Polydor, 1978) #6. A drastic improvement on 1977's rushed 'In the City' and 'This Is the Modern World' but, despite the 1978 singles and songs like 'Billy Hunt', still too many little-Englandisms.

Paul Weller continues to blight British music as a faux-hippie solo act.

BOOMTOWN RATS

'Looking After No. 1' (Ensign, 1977) #11. After which many hits, but please refer to Bob Geldof's spirited autobiography, *Is That It?* (Penguin, 1985).

THE POLICE

'Fall Out'/ 'Nothing Achieving' (Illegal, 1977). Should be noted as an early independent but after that it's straight pop. Fine, but not Punk.

ONLY ONES

'Lovers of Today' (Vengeance, 1977), 'Another Girl, Another Planet' (CBS, 1978). Two great 45s before the trad rock indulgences of drug abuse and overproduction took hold. Forgotten for years, now much mythologized, but the truth is somewhere in the middle: both the first album, *The Only Ones*, and a good compilation, *The Immortal Story*, are available (Columbia CD), but my preferred pick is *The Only Ones Live* (Mau Mau/Universal): 'it's frightening – you know I'm faster than lightning!'

ELVIS COSTELLO

The first solo album *My Aim Is True* (Stiff, 1977) contains great, bitter songs like 'Less Than Zero', 'Miracle Man' and the very timely 'Waiting for the End of the World'. But Costello gets better when he gets his group. Start with the virulent:

This Year's Model (Radar, 1978; now Demon, CD, 1986) #4. Picks: '(I Don't Wanna Go to) Chelsea'/ 'Pump It Up'/ 'This Year's Girl'/ 'Lip Service'/

'Hand in Hand'/ 'Night Rally'. Then go to: *Armed Forces* (Radar, 1978) #2. Initial quantities came with a free 45 which has 'Oliver's Army', 'Green Shirt' and 'Accidents Will Happen' (all three are now available on CD via Demon/ Universal). There is also a *Very Best Of* (Universal 2xCD). Then you can carry through the eighties, although the less committed can satisfy themselves with: *Ten Bloody Marys & Ten Hows Your Fathers* (Demon, 1984, now available on CD). Quite the best Costello compilation, including 'Girls Talk'/ 'Hoover Factory'/ 'Tiny Steps'/ 'Big Tears'/ 'Dr Luther's Assistant'/ 'Radio Radio'/ 'Clean Money'.

Compilations include:
New Wave (Phonogram/Vertigo, 1977) #12. Handy selection of US cuts by Ramones, Dead Boys (their best: 'Sonic Reducer'), the Runaways, Richard Hell, Talking Heads and Patti Smith. The European stuff is dodgier. Good cover picture of 'minimalist interviewer' Derek Gibbs spitting to camera. *The Sound of the Suburbs* (Columbia CD) covers some of this stuff with 18 tracks by the Jam, Tom Robinson, the Members and the Boomtown Rats, among others.

Punk 1977–8

The Second Wave
From the middle of the year, the Punk diaspora starts: in the UK this occurs through the split between the arties and the social realists, the promotion of new styles (as Strummer sang: 'All the new groups are not concerned/ With what there is to be learned/ They got Burton suits. Ha you think it's funny/ Turning rebellion into money') and the starting up of the independent sector. Outside the UK there is the international reaction to Punk's global media impact: you want a world full of weirdos? You got them.

SHAM 69
Were briefly the leaders of the social realist cadre. Their 45s, 'I Don't Wanna' (Step Forward, EP, 1977), 'Borstal Breakout' (Polydor, 1978), and 'If the Kids Are United'/ 'Sunday Morning Nightmare' (Polydor, 1978) #9 all match nifty riffs to colossal drumming and tersely dumb social comment. This is continued on album 1: *Tell Us the Truth* (Polydor, 1978, now Essential CD) #25. Picks: 'Whose Generation'/ 'Family Life' – after which the gumbieisms set in. By this time the damage had been done: Sham are the bridge between early Clash and 'Strength Through Oi!'.

TOM ROBINSON BAND
Not Punk but certainly social realists: '2-4-6-8 Motorway' (EMI, 1977) #5; 'Rising Free' b/w 'Glad to Be Gay' (EMI, EP, 1978).

Other examples of the Sham tendency include:
SKREWDRIVER, 'You're So Dumb' (Chiswick, 1977) and 'All Skrewed Up' (Chiswick, EP, 1977) – issued before the bad politics kicked in.
COCKSPARRER, 'We Love You' (Decca, 1977). Good version of Rolling Stones' sarkfest.

MENACE, 'Screwed Up' (Illegal, 1977) and 'GLC' (Small Wonder, 1978)
UK SUBS, 'C.I.D.' (City Records, 1978). Great 45.

By the middle of 1978, much of this discourse has been subsumed within the NF/RAR polarization – with serious results: Skrewdriver's Ian Stuart was, until he died in 1993, a leading light in international white supremacy. If this street Punk scene threw up later crossover groups like Southall's the Ruts, then the only serious attempt to influence its politics was made by:

CRASS

Their 'Feeding of the 5000' (Small Wonder, EP, 1978) was the first of a sequence of media (records, slogans, books, posters, magazines, films, actions and concerts) so complex that they deserve a book to themselves, and so effective that they sowed the ground for the return of serious anarchism and the popularity of CND in the early eighties.

It's also possible to trace the current popularity of the travelling lifestyle to Crass's huge success in the early eighties. For their links with the Stonehenge and Windsor festivals read the 'Series of Shock Slogans and Mindless Token Tantrums' booklet enclosed in *Christ – The Album* (Crass, 1982). Both these and other Crass albums are now available on CD (on the group's own label). In 2000 AK Press published the work of Crass designer and writer Gee Vaucher, *Crass Art and other Pre-Punk Modernist Monsters*.

After Punk had been fixed as social realism by the autumn of 1977, these original three 'inner circle' groups turned inwards and honed their music into something inspired by, but different to Punk. Their concerts during this period were terrific:

SIOUXSIE AND THE BANSHEES

'Hong Kong Garden'/ 'Voices' (Polydor, 1978) #7. A great double-sided record and a deserved hit.

'The Staircase (A Mystery)'/ '20th Century Boy' (Polydor, 1979) #24. Going public with their Glam roots.

'Mittageisen (Metal Postcard)'/ 'Love in a Void' (Polydor, 1979) #47. German pressing with pic sleeve of Heartfield's 'Guns and Butter' – the inspiration for the 'A' side *The Scream* (Polydor, 1978; now CD) #12. One of the more lasting records of the whole era. Picks: the lot, i.e., 'Pure'/ 'Jigsaw Feeling'/ 'Overground'/ 'Carcass'/ 'Helter Skelter'/ 'Mirage'/ 'Metal Postcard'/ 'Nicotine Stains'/ 'Suburban Relaspse'/ 'Switch'.

Join Hands (Polydor, 1979; now CD) #13. Curiously airless. Picks: 'Regal Zone'/ 'Placebo Effect'/ 'Icon'/ 'Playground Twist'. This version of 'The Lord's Prayer' is a case of trying to lock the stable door after the horse has bolted.

During the tour to promote this album, the group split under sensational circumstances. Subsequent releases throughout the eighties showcased a lighter psychedelic Gothic.

Those early thrash recordings can be found on a 7″ bootleg from the March 1977 session: 'Track Rehearsals' (KK Records, 1985) which includes: 'Captain Scarlet'/ 'Bad Shape'/ 'Love in a Void'/ 'Scrapheap'/ 'Psychic'. These should be more generally available.

Two 'Peel Sessions' EPs from 1977 and 1978 fill in the missing eighteen months, and capture the group as they were earning their spurs (Strange Fruit, 1987 and 1989). The material is mostly from the first album. All we need now is a release of their early rallying call, 'Make Up to Break Up'.

THE SLITS

No officially released material until the 1979 release of the 'Typical Girls' (Island) – The 12" includes their version of 'I Heard It Through the Grapevine' – and the album *Cut* (Island, 1979, reissued by Universal, 2001, with extra tracks). Strong songs like 'Instant Hit'/ 'SoTough'/ 'Shoplifting'/ 'FM'/ 'Newtown'/ 'Love and Romance' have been worked on slightly too long. These six songs, plus 'Vindictive', are much better heard on *Peel Sessions* (Strange Fruit, 1990) from the September 1977 and May 1978 sessions. The version of 'FM' here may well be their finest moment. (Both albums now available on CD.)

The vertiginous early recordings surfaced on *Retrospective* (Y Records, 1980) which includes the songs written about so eloquently by Greil Marcus in his book *Lipstick Traces*: 'Let's Do the Split'/ 'What a Boring Life'/ 'Vaseline'/ 'Slime'. Unavailable on CD, sadly, but Jungle have plugged a gap with the *In the Beginning* CD of live tracks from 1977, 1980 and 1981.

SUBWAY SECT

Totally essential 45s: 'Nobody's Scared'/ 'Don't Split It' (Braik, 1978); 'Ambition'/ 'Different Story' (Rough Trade, 1978). These are collected on *A Retrospective (1977–81)* (Rough Trade, 1984) with other zingers like 'Parallel Lines'/ 'Chain Smoking'/ 'Double Negative'/ 'Stool Pigeon'. There has been a flurry of reissues during the last few years: *We Oppose all Rock'n'Roll* (Overground, 1996) and *20 Odd Years: The Best of Vic Godard and the Subway Sect* (Motion CD, 1999). These contain singles and rare offcuts (in cassette quality) of songs like 'Exit/No Return' from the mooted 1978 'Gooseberry' LP, the bulk of which remains unheard.

ALTERNATIVE TV

Straddling both axes but going weird fast. Early 45s, 'Love Lies Limp', free with *Sniffin' Glue* 12 (Deptford Fun City, 1978) – one of the only pop hymns to impotence; 'How Much Longer'/ 'You Bastard' (Deptford Fun City, 1977); 'Action Time Vision' (Deptford Fun City, 1978). ATV's line up was never stable, and after playing Stonehenge '78 as part of a tour with Here and Now, the group broke up in March 1979.

Genesis P. Orridge recorded the early concert released as *Live at the Rat Club 77* (Crystal, 1979). Currently available on CD: *The Image has Cracked* – first album plus early singles As and Bs (Anagram) (vinyl album on Get Back); *Radio Sessions* (Overground). Mark Perry continues to record: his latest is the 7" of 'Unlikely Star' (Sorted records). You can also find all the Sniffin' Glue collected in *Sniffin' Glue: the Essential Punk Accessory* (published by Sanctuary Publishing, 2000).

ADAM AND THE ANTS

Initially managed by Jordan. Two tracks feature on the *Jubilee* soundtrack, 'Deutscher Girls' and 'Plastic Surgery' (Polydor, 1978); then there were 45s on the Decca and Do It labels before McLaren co-opted Adam's group. *Peel Sessions* (Strange Fruit, 1990) has the recordings from January 1978, July 1978 and March 1979. Songs like 'Xerox'/ 'Physical' and 'Ligotage' are good attempts to update Pop Art, but they weren't pop. After this, Adam has the hits, and very smart ones they were too.

JOHN COOPER CLARKE

Fine Martin Hannett recordings of the 66 Dylan look-a-like rapper: 'Suspended Sentence'/ 'Innocents'/ 'Psycle Sluts Pts 1&2' (Rabid, 1977); 'Disguise in Love' (CBS, 1978). Like the flower of Mancunian talent – Joy Division, the Fall, the Drones, Buzzcocks, Magazine and Brummies the Prefects – Clarke played on the last nights of the Electric Circus in October 1977: 'You Never See a Nipple in the Daily Express' and 'I Married a Monster from Outer Space' on 'Short Circuit' (Virgin, 1978).

MAGAZINE

Great first two singles and album: 'Shot by Both Sides'/ 'My Mind Ain't So Open' (Virgin, 1978) #41; 'Touch & Go'/ 'Goldfinger' (Virgin, 1978). Then: *Real Life* (Virgin, 1978, now CD) #29 includes 'My Tulpa'/ 'The Light Pours out of Me'/ 'Motorcade'. Also 'I Love You, You Big Dummy' (Virgin, 1978). The compilation *Rays and Hail: 1978–81* (Virgin) contains most of the singles plus the original 'Shot by Both Sides'. It is the best introduction to the group. In 2000 there were two new compilations: a one-CD best-of, *Where the Power Is*, and a three-CD career overview, with out-takes and rare singles, called *Maybe It's Right to Be Nervous Now*.

ED BANGER AND THE NOSEBLEEDS

'Ain't Been to No Music School''/ 'Fascist Pigs' (Rabid, 1977); includes Durutti Column's Vini Reilly on guitar. As Ed Banger: 'Kinnel Tommy' (Rabid, 1978). Football song. Also in this vein:

JILTED JOHN

Actor Graham Fellows in a tale of teen angst. 'Jilted John'/ 'Going Steady' (Rabid, 1978; re EMI, 1978) #4. Answer record by Gordon the Moron: 'De Do Dough' (Rabid, 1978). In 1996, Receiver released *The Rabid/TJM Singles Collection* (CD), with the above essential early singles by John Cooper Clarke, Ed Banger and the Nosebleeds, and Jilted John.

THE DRONES

If you must, the LP: *Further Temptations* (Valer, 1977).

THE FALL

'Bingo Master's Break out' (Step Forward, EP, 1978) with 'Psycho Mafia'/ 'Bingo Master'/ 'Repetition'
'It's the New Thing' (Step Forward, 1978)
'Rowche Rumble' (Step Forward, 1979)
These first three singles, plus tracks from the *Live at the Electric Circus* album, are available on *Early Fall 1977–79* (Cog Sinister CD).
Live at the Witch Trials (Step Forward, 1979, now Cog Sinister CD) has 'Rebellious Jukebox'/ 'Industrial Estate'/ 'Music Scene'/ *Dragnet* (Step

Forward, 1979) includes 'Psychick Dancehall'/ 'Dice Man'/ 'Your Heart Out'.

THE PREFECTS

Birmingham's finest. Late, terrific recordings by this hermetic, sarcastic group: 'Going Through the Motions'/ 'Things in General' (Vindaloo/Rough Trade, 1979); the 'A' side is also collected on:
Peel Sessions (Strange Fruit, 1987) includes 'Total Luck'/ 'Faults' and 'Barbarellas', their hymn to Birmingham's one Punk club. Both 'Faults' and 'Motions' are the sharpest songs to have been written about the performer/ audience divide outside 'One Chord Wonders': 'Perfection in itself is a fault/ We stumble and blunder for better results/ But who really wants to hear our defects/ You just want 1-2-3-4 Prefects'.

Missing in action: 'Bristol Road Leads to Dachau', written after the 1974 pub bombings, '625 Lines' and 'Agony Column'.

THE REZILLOS

Cartoon SF from Edinburgh.
'I Can't Stand My Baby' (Sensible, 1977)
'Flying Saucer Attack'/ 'My Baby Does Good Sculptures' (Sire, 1977)
Can't Stand the Rezillos (Sire, 1978, now CD plus extra tracks). Singer Fay Fife did nothing for the group's career on Sire when she went for Seymour Stein's wife Linda with a cream cake during a reception for this album.

SPITFIRE BOYS

'Mein Kampf'/ 'British Refugee' (RK, 1977). First Liverpool Punk band to record featured future Frankie Paul Rutherford.

DEAD FINGERS TALK

Burroughsian name, but more conventional, albeit well-placed humanism on their one LP: *Storm the Reality Studios* (Pye, 1978). Includes: 'Electric City'/ 'Nobody Loves You When You're Old and Gay'.

ULTRAVOX

Very early Punk/electronic crossover. Brian Eno produced *Ultravox!*(Island, 1977, now CD) with Burroughsian tunes like 'Saturday Night in the City of the Dead'/ 'I Want to Be a Machine'. The breakthrough came late in 1978 with the 'Systems of Romance', six months before they were scooped by Gary Numan. After which they got Ure'd.

WIRE

The jokers in the pack. These are essential:
'I Am the Fly' (Harvest, 1978)
'Dot Dash'/ 'Options R' (Harvest, 1978)
'A Question of Degree'/ 'Former Airline' (Harvest, 1979)
Pink Flag (Harvest, 1977; now CD)
Chairs Missing (Harvest, 1978; now CD)
154 (Harvest, 1979; now CD). Initial pressings came with EP: 'Song 1'/ 'Get Down (Parts I & II)'/ 'Let's Panic Later'/ 'Small Electric Piece'.

Outtakes from the EMI period, including the complete Roxy 4/77 set and never recorded songs like 'Love Ain't Polite' and 'It's the Motive', were released in 1997 as *Behind the Curtain* (EMI CD). For a personal selection of tracks, hear *On Returning* (EMI, 1989). Otherwise hear the lot.

Wire reformed in 1986, and have made three terrific LPs which continue the spacious, Euro vein begun in 1978. They still sound like nobody else: *The Ideal Copy* (Mute, 1987); *A Bell Is a Cup Until It Is Struck* (Mute, 1988); *Manscape* (Mute, 1990). Also great are these two soundtracks by guitarist Bruce Gilbert: *This Way to the Shivering Man* (Mute, 1989) and *Insiding* (Mute, 1991).

By the time that Wire's *Pink Flag* was released in November, several things were happening. Firstly, the influence of the following could be ignored no longer:

Disco

Almost no crossover during high Punk – more fool everyone – but these two records opened up previously hostile ears:
Donna Summer, 'I Feel Love' (GTO, 1977) #1
Space, 'Magic Fly' (Pye, 1977) #2
Sylvester, 'You Make Me Feel Mighty Real' (Fantasy, 1978) #8

Rhino's *The Disco Box* (4xCD, 1999) contains 80 first-rank seventies pussy bumpers, including the Sylvester/Donna Summer hits. Avoid at your own risk!

KRAFTWERK

Two of the most important LPs of the seventies:
Trans-Europe Express (Capitol, 1977; now CD)
Man Machine (Capitol, 1978; now CD) #9

The start of Hip Hop; see Afrika Bambaataa, 'Planet Rock' (Tommy Boy, 1982) – and much more.

ENO

Taking Tiger Mountain (by Strategy) (Island, 1974; now CD)
With Robert Fripp: *Evening Star* (Island, 1975; now CD)
Another Green World (Island, 1975; now CD)
Discreet Music (Obscure, 1975; now CD)
Music for Films (Polydor, 1978; now CD)
Ambient 1: Music for Airports (Polydor, 1978; now CD) – the coining of a new genre.

The first edition of *Music for Films* was a limited edition of 500 and contained an extra nine tracks. This was handed out to broadcasters and film-makers. Note that Eno's music was used in Derek Jarman's *Sebastiane* and *Jubilee*, and in the title sequence for BBC2's 'Arena'.

DAVID BOWIE

After the plastic soul of *Young Americans* (RCA, 1975) #2 – whose true impact on a generation of Soul Boys would not become apparent for another ten years – and the motorik of *Station to Station* (RCA, 1976) #5, Bowie made these two LPs in Berlin with Brian Eno:
Low (RCA, 1977) #2

Heroes (RCA, 1977) #3

EMI UK released these four records on CD during 1991, and again in 1999.

IGGY POP

As produced by David Bowie.

The Idiot (RCA, 1977; now Virgin America, CD) #30 – includes 'Sister Midnight'/ 'Nightclubbing'/ 'Funtime'/ 'China Girl'/ 'Dum Dum Boys'

Lust for Life (RCA, 1977; now Virgin America, CD) #28 – includes 'Lust for Life'/ 'Sixteen'/ 'Some Weird Sin'/ 'The Passenger'/ 'Tonight'/ 'Success'/ 'Turn Blue'.

Some of this material was covered by David Bowie 1983–5. Iggy's reputation as the Father of Punk resulted in a flood of reissues and repackages of old material. An Embassy reissue of *Raw Power* made the UK charts (1977) #44, while outtakes from 1971–2 were released on Siamese/ BOMP records. BOMP also released the 'lost' demos from 1975 with James Williamson on guitar: *Kill City* (Radar, 1978).

Iggy's parting shot to this era: *New Values* (Arista, 1979): 'I'm looking for one new value/ But nothing comes my way'.

Secondly, material from around the world was starting to feed back into the UK – a mixture of Punk and the synthetic, cooler approach coming from Germany.

France

STINKY TOYS

'Boozy Creed' (Polydor, 1977)

METAL URBAIN

'Panik'/ 'Lady Coca Cola' (Cobra, France, 1977), 'Paris Maquis'/ 'Clé de Contact' (Rough Trade, 1978), and 'Hysterie Connective'/ 'Pas Poubelle' (Radar, 1978). All collected plus ten others like 'Ultra Violence' and 'Futurama' on: *Les Hommes Morts Sont Dangereux* (Byzz, 1980). A great combo of sneering Punk and a galloping Rhythm machine. A Metal Urbain CD compilation, *L'Age D'Or*, is available on Fan Club, while they and other groups like the Stinky Toys and the Dogs are collected on *Les Plus Grands Succès Du Punk* (Skydog 2xCD).

LIZZY MERCIER DESCLOUDS

'Rosa Yemen' (ZE, UK, 1979) 'Rosa Vertov'/ 'Decryptated'/ 'Herpes Simplex'. Despite Metal Urbain's shrieks, the Paris/New York ZE label remains the most creative French musical response to Punk. Now as for print . . .

Australia

THE VICTIMS

'Television Addict'/ 'Flipped out over You' (Artists Records, 1978). Find this peerless 45 on Various, *Where Birdmen Flew* (Taz Devil) which collates thirteen early Aus Punk 45s like the Scientists' 'Frantic Romantic' and Radio Birdman's 'Burned My Eye'. Like the Saints, the latter moved to the UK, but the next real Aus import were the Birthday Party in early 1980.

Holland

SUZANNES

'New Disease' (De 1000 Idioten, EP, 1978) features 'Hippie'/ 'Teenage Abortion' and so on.

Switzerland

KLEENEX

'Beri Beri'/ 'Ain't You'/ 'Hedi's Head'/ 'Nice' (Sunrise, 1978); 'You'/"U' (Rough Trade, 1979). Two terrific singles by all-female group now collected, along with later recordings, on *Liliput* (Kill Rock Stars, 2xCD).

Germany

Was slow to react musically. Important groups like DAF and Der Plan did not make records until after 1979.

Canada

THE DIODES

Had one great LP, *The Diodes* (Columbia, Canada, 1977) featuring songs like 'Time Damage', 'Plastic Girls', 'Death in the Suburbs', and their version of 'Shape of Things to Come' (from the 1967 teen takeover movie, *Wild in the Streets*). This group still deserve a wider hearing. Their one great 45 was 'Tired of Waking up Tired'/ 'Child Star' (Epic, UK, 1978). This is now the title track of the 25 track *Tired of Waking Up Tired* (Epic Canada), which has all the singles, all of the first album, and some tracks from the scarce second album, *Released*.

THE VILETONES

Were fronted by Nazi Dog (Stephen Leckie), a true psycho-bud. Their titles tell the story: 'Screaming Fist'/ 'Possibilities'/ 'Rebel' (Vile, Canada, 1977), then the 'Look Back in Anger' EP (Razor, 1978) features 'Don't You Lie'/ 'Dirty Feelin'/ 'Back Door to Hell'/ 'Swastika Girl'/ 'Danger Boy', now available on *A Taste of Honey* (Other People's Music CD, Canada, 1994). Xeroxing sometimes degrades the image.

USA

Punk as media sensation opened up a space for several conceptual groups who had been working in near total isolation:

THE RESIDENTS

Anonymous polemicists and studio explorers. *Meet the Residents* (Ralph, 1974) had a Beatles cut-up sleeve and was reissued with a different sleeve after legal representation (Ralph, 1977, now on Euro-Ralph CD). A wonderful first album (with pieces like 'N-er-gee (Crisis Blues)') heralded the new mood so well that it remains timeless.

Three records killed the sacred cow of sixties nostalgia: *Satisfaction* (Ralph, 1976; re 1978). Unlike Devo, who pulled the same trick, no quarter was given to this warhorse – which meant that the Residents never became the New Traditionalists. *The Beatles Play the Residents and the Residents Play the Beatles* (Ralph, 1977; now on CD) ('Beyond the Valley of a Day in the Life'/ 'Flying'). Cut-up and looping of thirty Beatles' songs prefigure the late eighties sampling boom. *Third Reich'n'Roll* (Ralph, 1975) answers the question: what happened

The Residents, 1977 (© Cryptic Corporation)

when the hippies won? Other records like 'Duck Stab'/ 'Buster and Glen' (Ralph, 1978) and 'Eskimo' (Ralph, 1979; now CD) ditch the polemics for more structured pieces. These three albums are now available on CD (Indigo). Visit the Residents website at www.residents.com. For a sharp assessment of the Residents see Chris Cutler, *File under Popular* (November Books, 1985).

CHROME

Three albums of pysch/garage cut-ups: *The Visitation* (Siren, 1977); *Alien Soundtrack* (Siren, 1978); *Half Machine Lip Moves* (Siren, 1979). Some of these are now available on CD.

BOYD RICE

One extraordinary album coming out of nowhere and going straight back there: *16/33/45/78* (No label, 1977; re Mute, 1981). Loops and samples ten years too early.

SUICIDE

Performance art – electro-pop. First 45 'Cheree'/ 'I Remember' (Bronze, 1978). *Suicide* (Red Star, US, 1977; Bronze, UK, 1978) has six definitive early synth rockers: 'Ghost Rider'/ 'Rocket USA'/ 'Cheree'/ 'Johnny'/ 'Girl'/ 'Che' with the mandatory blood-and-guts piece, 'Frankie Teardrop'. *Alan Vega – Martin Rev* (ZE/Island, 1980) better produced, nasty synth rockers: 'Harlem'/ 'Mr Ray'/ 'Touch Me'. This has been reissued, along with the killer 12" 45,

'Dream Baby Dream' (Island, 1981) on *The Second Suicide Album* (Blast First, 1999) as part of a double CD with 14 extraordinary, ghostly rehearsal tracks from 1975. Highly recommended. An early version is included, plus other demos from 1974–9 on *Half Alive* (ROIR CD 2000).

For a document of the often fraught relationship between audience and performer during this period, try to find: '23 Minutes in Brussels' (Bronze, 1978) which ends in mayhem: the other '21 1/2 Minutes in Berlin' aren't so restful either. The Brussels debacle has now been reissued, along with the first album, the 'I Remember' 45 and a 1978 show from CBGB's, as *Suicide* (Blast First, 1998).

DEVO

'The de-evolution band'. Early terrific 45s: 'Jocko Homo'/ 'Mongoloid' (Booji Boy, US, 1977; Stiff, UK, 1977–8; '(I Can't Get No) Satisfaction'/ 'Sloppy' (BOMP, US, 1977; Stiff, UK, 1977–8). Then Eno: 'Q: Are We Not Men? A: We Are Devo' (Virgin, 1978, now CD). Devo continued with Warners over five albums until 1984; the earlier ones are the best, with overtly ironic cynical titles like *Freedom of Choice* masking great singles like 'Beautiful World', 'Whip It', and 'The Day My Baby Gave Me a Surprize'. These and many other tracks – including the last flash, the nineties 'Stuck In A Loop' – are on the recommended Rhino compilation *Pioneers Who Got Scalped* (Rhino 2xCD, 2000).

Rougher (and thus more interesting) recordings from 1976 can be found on *Hardcore Devo Vol* 1: 1974–77, *Live – The Mongoloid Years* and *Hardcore Devo Vol* 2: 76–77 (all Rykodisc CD). Devo material from throughout their career is also available from the Rhino Handmade site – www.rhinohandmade.com. CDR's exist of the *Live in San Francisco* bootleg, taken from the Mabuhay 9/77 (UK Records, 1978), has an astonishing 15-minute segue of 'Smart Patrol'/'Mr. DNA'/'Gut Feeling'/'Sloppy' which trashes everything else they ever recorded. As Sleepers' guitarist Michael Belfer said about this show: 'it was like acid, but in a good sense.'

THE CRAMPS

Rockabilly recast for a sicker age. Essential first two 45s: 'The Way I Walk'/ 'Surfin' Bird' (Vengeance, 1978); 'Human Fly'/ 'Domino' (Vengeance, 1978). Both are collected, plus terrific later cuts like 'Love Me' and 'Garbageman', on: *Off the Bone* (IRS, 1983, now EMI CD). Their first album was *Songs the Lord Taught Us* (Illegal, 1980; now EMI CD plus 5 outtakes) includes such classics as 'TV Set'/ 'Sunglasses after Dark'/ 'I Was a Teenage Werewolf', plus their cover of the Sonics' 'Strychnine'.

These few records originated a whole aesthetic – often called Psychobilly – which was very popular in the early eighties. A better exploration of the Cramps' exhumation of forgotten, extreme trash can be found on the *Born Bad* compilations, volumes 1–5 (Born Bad Records, 1987).

The major label pick-up of both Devo and Pere Ubu in early 1978 encouraged a flood of recordings from this area, which Stiff saw fit to package as 'the Akron Sound' in mid 1978. One fine group benefited from this space:

THE BIZARROS
Bizarros (Mercury, 1979). Great Lou Reed readymades from the Rubber Belt. Also *Underground* recorded in 1979 (Sordide Sentimental, 1981).

After April 1977, there were the post-Damned groups:

Los Angeles
25.8.78: Laurie O'Donnell and two of the men from W.Im.P (World Imitation Products) pick me up in the Hollywood Hills. W.Im.P are an outpost of the mid seventies Mail Art/Neo Dada scene: the introduction has come through Genesis P. Orridge, whose friend Skot Armst worked with them on a tiny montage magazine, *Science Holiday*. W.Im.P don't quite have Armst's skewered brilliance, but they shower me with their zines, exquisite playthings in editions of 50 with titles like *Computer Buddy*, *Teslarama*, *I Hate this Trip* and, my favourite, *Alien Roundup*. They produce about one a month. I get it immediately: they don't have Linder's viciousness or pain, but their sheer playfulness is liberating. Not for the last time, I feel part of a dialogue that is being carried on over 5000 miles.

I accept W.Im.P's deadpan aesthetic as one way of dealing with the extreme peculiarity of Los Angeles. This is my first visit to the US, let alone the West

Azteca handbill, August 1978 (artist unknown)

Coast, and I know that I'm on another planet, especially when, at Griffith Park Observatory, the blood-red moon bathes an endless strip of freeways with an apocalyptic, killing glow. Laurie has spent the day in driving me round a succession of thrift stores, where we load up on Martin Denny albums and tab-collared shirts – impossible to find in the UK. We hit Sunset to the strains of the Sonics' 'Boss Hoss': abrasive kitsch seems like a good place to start making sense of this parallel world.

Our destination is the Azteca, a Chicano club not used to punk, situated deep in the Valley about forty minutes' drive from Hollywood. When we arrive, there already is a group of people on the pavement – an extreme rarity in Los Angeles, and in itself tantamount to provocation. Inside, the switch from the deserted streets is startling: clusters of men and women in the US equivalent of punk dress – fifties clothes from the thrift store profusion matched with the regulation black – rotate urgently, swimming in the Azteca's gold and glitter. All the local faces are there. It's all very similar to what I've just (thankfully) left behind in London; as I pass around a pillar, the distance between Los Angeles and London is completely wiped out as Mick Jones comes into vision, sitting at a table.

We say hello, with a certain restraint. In the winter of 1976, when I was hanging around Portobello and Ladbroke Grove, MJ and I fell in with each other; we'd meet in Mick's caff and discuss matters punk, artistic and political – J. G. Ballard's *High Rise* and Tom Wicker's book on the Attica jail riot. This all evaporated as soon as our roles became defined: MJ as rock star and me as rock journalist. I'd already found out that the two cannot be friends unless there is a great degree of mutual tolerance – not a great 1978 attribute. Anyway by now I can no longer lie and say how fabulous the Clash are: 'Clash City Rockers' was a poor 45 and all the laddish behaviour they encourage in their entourage has turned me right off. We regard each other, therefore, with mutual suspicion: I don't know what I'm doing here and I don't know what he's doing here. The winter of 1976 might as well be a lifetime ago, so much has happened.

The first band walk out on the long, low stage and plug in. The Middle Class, with three young brothers from Santa Ana, with similar long noses, pissed off expressions, and tousled black hair. They're dressed down in sixties jackets, jeans, nondescript shirts. They play punk sped up to what, in 1978, sounds like the limits of intelligibility: words, melodies and instrumentation telescoped into a queasy blare. '1!2!3!4!' they yell regularly, as if their very own creed; 'Out! A! Vogue!' they bark before the blur restarts. Their sheer velocity makes tangible the desperate urge to communicate – something, anything, before . . . what? – that is a hallmark of these times. There is also a stuttering self-critique, a harbinger of the moment when Punk will finally fall in on itself: 'Growing tired of the s-s-s-situations/that you created/in your own mind.'

27.8.78: Claude Bessy's apartment right on the beach at Venice. I look at the sea and spin out: there are only a few islands between here and Japan. A few fanatics perform complicated yoga postures at this world's edge. Lunch with Claude, his wife Philomena, and a young woman called Debbie Dub, who has badgered me transatlantic to write something for her fanzine, called *Starting Fires*: my response is an ill-tempered, apocalyptic blast that says more about my mental state than any objective reality. Punk talk. Debbie is very enthusiastic about the UK, raving about the new hype, Tom Robinson. I am not, so we are at cross purposes. It's not her fault, but things go from bad to worse. Over lunch, Debbie punctuates her polite-ical discussion with several pauses where, toying with a boiled potato, she loads her knife with amphetamine sulphate and sniffs lustily. 'Do you want some?' she asks brightly. I suddenly realise how tired I am.

25.8.78: By the time the next band – Negative Trend: more blokeish, lumpy, key song 'Mercenaries' – have finished, the club is much livelier and my headache has settled in well. Laurie makes several introductions on my behalf; I reciprocate by taking her over to MJ who – settled into the rock star mode he will never shake – is polite but noncommittal. This total congruity of familiarity and strangeness deepens as the evening continues: the next band on, the Dils, are at first sight complete Clash clones – Russian iconography, angry stance, barked slogan lyrics. Their two singles – 'I Hate the Rich' and 'Class War' – are at once exciting and unsettling, but live their individuality is subject to the same old breakneck thrash.

Two brothers share the frontline: although both have the same white trash face – lean, bad skin – singer/guitarist Chip Kinman is blond and passionate as bassist Tony is saturnine. They cover a lot of space, filling the stage with jacknife jerks and souped up fury. Less desperate than the Middle Class, the Dils are more established, if such a thing is possible in this tiny enclave of about 150 people in Los Angeles' millions. Their lyrics are exhortatory instructions to the community they have been elected to represent. The crowd start to pogo enthusiastically, just like they do in the UK – which does not surprise me after seeing a replicant punk on Melrose the previous day, with a suntan for god's sake. MJ and I allow each other a little smirk: we have seen this before, haven't we?

Except that we haven't. The wild card in this situation is the presence of two Rent-A-Cops, hired by the Azteca's owners to prevent nihilist damage to their glittering décor. They're big and beefy – very much the standard US shape – and look askance at the skinny punks, almost all to a person drugged or starved in an approximation of that wasted, as-though-rationing-had-never-gone-away English look. By the look of disgust on their faces, they no doubt think we're all gay: well some of us are. As the crowd hots up during the Dils' set, the cops look itchy: what to the punks is fun – pogoing and slamming – is to them something approaching a riot situation. They wear helmets, truncheons, and some dangerous looking object that resembles a machine gun. In fact, as Laurie explains, it's a Mace gun, which does not make me feel a whole lot better.

John Ingham's group, the Weirdos, take the stage last. They're like a mixture of the New York Dolls and the Sex Pistols with a unique Angeleno spin: their striking lead singer, John Denney, walks the tightrope between ludicrousness and mania with great aplomb. He's to be seen wandering around Hollywood late at night, a monkish figure in his destroyed Op Art costume of contrasting stripes. The crowd go berserk at their local heroes and, three numbers in, the Rent-A-Cops lose it. They take the stage and start blustering – 'OK, that's it: no more' – which infuriates the punks, who begin to chant 'White riot! White riot!'. I think this is a little ill mannered in a Chicano club and glance at the person who wrote that song, who, like myself and the W.Im.P crowd, is beginning to melt into the middle distance, having decided that discretion is the better part of valour. They can have their riot without us.

As so often happens, however, voyeurism beats fear, and we hover near the exit. Within an instant, the tension escalates and things look very ugly. For a few minutes, there is a stand-off, with both sides locked into their respective postures: the punks play-acting for real, the Rent-A-Cops taking as reality the authority they have been paid to assume for the night. They dominate the stage with their brandished Mace guns, gross physical manifestations of the (state) authoritarianism that the punks think they wish to provoke. Behind them, the Weirdos look very frail in their smart collaged costume, like children forced to stop their games by bullying adults. When the moment passes and they're allowed to resume, it's hard for them to recapture the suspension of belief – or statement of faith – that this event is convened to achieve.

The Weirdos wind up quickly and we're herded into the night by the Rent-A-Cops with a minimum of grace; they're disappointed at not being able to vent their adrenalin. The rumour that has been passed around inside is shown to be true, as the black and white cruisers of the LA Metro Squad circle the punks like sharks around a raft. The very existence of more than five people on the sidewalk seems to constitute an illegal gathering, if not in law then in practice. The cops get out and start harassing the crowd – for drinking in public, among other misdemeanours – and again, there is this possibility of instant, dangerous escalation. Despite its low-density and the late sixties freedom rhetoric pouring out of its airwaves, Los Angeles is very tightly

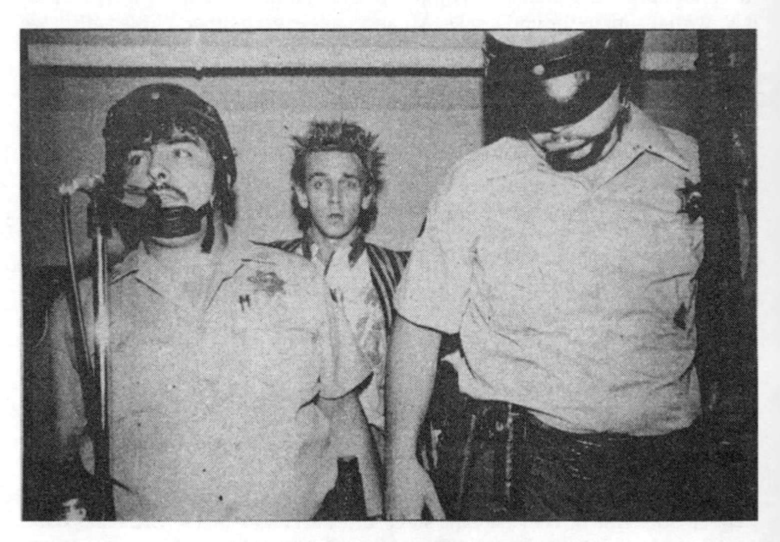

The Weirdos at the Azteca, August 1978 (© Melanie Nissen)

parcelled up, with less free space than on London's packed tube stations. For all their manifest lack of power, the local punks have succeeded in making this very clear.

'We're told, then we're sold/Affection's conspiracies
Life is so meaningful/With pop sensibilities
Teenage self-pity/The feelings are all wrong
The ideals don't apply/My life's not a love song.'
Middle Class: 'Love is Just a Tool', 1978

3.9.78: I'm in San Francisco to stay with Vale, the editor of *Search and Destroy* – the best magazine in the world at this point. I pick up some interviews with the Screamers (irritatingly smartass, by degrees charming) and the Dils. We sit in a White Castle and discuss tactics over cheeseburgers. The group and their manager, Peter Urban, have a lot to say about politics – basically orthodox Marxism with some boho workerism thrown in – and talk coherently and cogently. Until it comes to the music industry: when asked the basic questions that any British group would brush away like an errant fly, the Dils flounder. What will you do when you get a record deal? How far are you prepared to compromise? What will you do when you appear on TV? I'm bemused until I grasp a profound difference: what most Brits take for granted – ie: immediate media and music industry interest – is so far away from the experience and expectations of these guys that they haven't even considered the possibilities.

Here on the West Coast, the hippies – or their mediated versions – won with no contest. The whole Los Angeles ethic – which dominates the US music industry – is still stuck in 1970: all you seem to hear on the FM dial is a locked groove of Cream, Led Zeppelin, Creedence, the Beatles. This stasis is comfortable, and suits the vast majority; despite the transcendent trappings, it

V. Vale and Jon Savage, North Beach, September 1978 (© Ruby Ray)

can be policed – like the event at the Azteca, by a numbingly simple display of pure power. The LA punks rail against this in a succession of more extreme postures – current records include the Deadbeats' 'Kill The Hippies' and the Rotters' 'Sit On My Face, Stevie Nix' – that if anything, reemphasise their powerlessness. There is absolutely no chance that the American music and media industry will let them in. If they do not exist commercially, can they exist at all?

'Friends warehouse pain/Attack their own kind
A thousand kids bury their parents/There's laughing outside
We're locked out of the public eye/Some smooth chords
On the car radio/No hard chords
We set the trash on fire.'
X: 'The Unheard Music', 1980

THE GERMS

Fronted by Iggy disciple Darby Crash. Def first 45: 'Forming'/ 'Sex Boy (live)' (What, 1977); def first LP produced by Joan Jett: *Germs (GI)* (Slash, 1979) contains such gems as 'Communist Eyes'/ 'Lexicon Devil'/ 'Manimal'/ 'American Leather'/ 'Media Blitz'.
What We Do Is Secret (Slash, 1981) collects non LP 45s like 'Lexicon Devil' and 'No God'. Crash (born Jan Paul Behm, also known as Bobby Pyn) OD'd from heroin in December 1980. The complete works of the Germs are now collected on *The Complete Anthology* (Slash/Rhino, 2001).

For a great document of the LA Punks' run at the wall of US culture, try *Germs Live at the Whiskey June 1977* (Mohawk/BOMP, 1981: now as *Germicide: Live at the Whiskey 77* BOMP CD). Includes much pushing and shoving as well as a mutilation of 'Sugar Sugar'.

THE DILS

Teenage Red Rockers. Two great 45s: 'I Hate the Rich'/ 'You're Not Blank' (What, 1977) and 'Class War' (Dangerhouse, 1977). 'I Hate the Rich' is included, along with other What? Records by the Controllers and the Germs, on the *What? Stuff* CD (BOMP). After which, there was nothing until 'Made in Canada' (Rogelletti, EP, 1980) ('It's Not Worth It'/ 'Sound of the Rain'). The latter appears on the first of their two archetypal albums as Rank and File: *Sundown* (Slash, 1982); *Long Gone Dead* (Slash, 1984).

THE WEIRDOS

LA's finest. Essential 45s: 'Destroy All Music'/ 'A Life of Crime'/ 'Why Do You Exist' (BOMP, 1977): 'Sold my records and my stereo/ Ripped up my tickets to see ELO!' 'We Got the Neutron Bomb' (Dangerhouse, 1978). 'Drop it!' 'Who? What? When? Why?' (BOMP, EP, 1979, still available on US vinyl) features classics like: 'Happy People'/ 'Hitman'/ 'Idle Life'. Some of this material is collected on *Weird World: 1977–1981* (Frontier CD, 1991).

Plus another great bootleg (I don't do this on purpose, it's just that most of this music was buried): 'It Means Nothing' (Punk Vault, 1990) presents some of the philosophical quiddities confronting teenage nihilists all over the world: 'If it means nothing to you/ It ought to mean nothing to me.'

HE ZEROS

Chicano Punks. Two great 45s: 'Wimp' (BOMP, 1977) and 'Beat Your Heart)ut'/ 'Wild Weekend' (BOMP, 1978). 'Weekend' is 'Friday on My Mind' recast or an accelerated age: over in one minute thirty-one. Available on CD as *Don't ʾush Me Around* (BOMP CD, early singles and demos).

ɪLACK RANDY & METROSQUAD

Trouble at the Cup' (Dangerhouse, 1977). Rent-boy agitprop: *Pass the Dust, I ˀhink I'm Bowie* (Dangerhouse, 1979).

ˀHE SCREAMERS

Recorded numerous demos of synth hysteria, including 'Mater Dolores'/ 122 Hours of Fear'/ '(You Don't Love Me, You Love) Magazines'/ '(If I Can't ɨave What I Want, Then I Don't Want) Anything' and their standard: 'Peer ʾressure'. None were ever released.

ᴛHE RANDOMS

Urbanist anthem: 'A-B-C-D' (Dangerhouse, 1977).

ᴀLLEYCATS

Nothing Means Nothing Anymore' (Dangerhouse, 1978).

ᴛHE BAGS

'Survive'/ 'Babylonian Gorgon' (Dangerhouse, 1978).

MIDDLE CLASS

Two terrific EPs: 'Out of Vogue' (Joke Records, 1978) contains four songs, that, barely over a minute each, are the start of Hardcore. These are 'Insurgence'/ 'You Belong'/ 'Out of Vogue'/ 'Situations'. The last two appear on *Earcom 3* (Fast, 1979). 'Scavenged Luxury' (Torture Garden, 1980) is slower but no less intense. Picks: 'Home Is Where', 'Blueprint for Joy'.

THE DEADBEATS

'Kill the Hippies' (Dangerhouse, 1978).

THE ROTTERS

'Sit On My Face Stevie Nix' (Rotten, 1978).

THE DICKIES

Cartoon Punk. Just one moment: 'You Drive Me Ape' (A&M, UK, 1978).

THE URINALS

Three essential 45s: 'Surfin' with the Shah' (Happy Squid, 1979); 'I'm a Bug' (Happy Squid, 1979); 'Sex' (Happy Squid, 1980). These are available on the 31 tracker *Negative Capability . . . Check it Out!* (Amphetamine Reptile US CD, 1996); also featured are versions of 'You're Gonna Miss Me' and 'The Jetsons Theme', with the culminating 'You Piss Me Off'.

X

LA's most likely to. First 45: 'Adult Books'/ 'We're Desperate' (Dangerhouse, 1978). Then the first of many fine albums throughout the eighties, *Los Angeles* (Slash, 1980, now CD), includes 'Johnny Hit and Pauline'/ 'Nausea'/

'Sex and Dying in High Society' and their tribute to LA's 'Unheard Music from this period.

Compilations of Los Angeles bands include:

Yes L.A. (Dangerhouse, 1979; one-sided) is a skimpy answer record to 'No New York'. It includes cuts by the Bags ('We Don't Need the English' – quite right!), Black Randy and X.

Tooth and Nail (Upsetter Records, 1979) is a fantastic compilation of fifteen cuts including the Flesh Eaters ('Pony Dress'), UXA ('UXA'), Negative Trend ('Mercenaries') and Middle Class ('Love Is Just a Tool').

Apart from the *What? Stuff* BOMP compilation, the only general reissue of this lost rock moment is the 21 track *We're Desperate: the L.A. Scene* (1976–79) (Rhino CD, 1993), which features all the biggies – the Dils, the Germs, the Weirdos, the Zeros, X, etc. Highly recommended. In 1996, a company called Year One released a 24 song collection of live performances from the Masque in 1978, featuring the Weirdos, the Bags, the Germs and the Skulls. In 1991, arty LA metal group Jane's Addiction paid their own tribute to the era with live versions of 'Lexicon Devil', 'Nausea' and 'LA Woman' (*LA Medley*, WB UK, 1991). For more information about Los Angeles during this period, read Barney Hoskyns's *Waiting for the Sun* (St Martin's, US, 1996) and the collected reprints of *Search and Destroy* – journal of the SF and LA punk scenes – published by Re/Search Publications, 20 Romolo #B, San Francisco, California 94133 USA.

San Francisco

CRIME

Two essential 45s are 'Hot Wire My Heart' (Crime, 1977) – covered by Sonic Youth on their 1988 *Sister* LP – and 'Murder by Guitar'/ 'Frustration' (Crime, 1977).

THE NUNS

Late, lumpy 45: 'Savage'/ 'Decadent Jew'/ 'Suicide Child' (415 Records, 1978).

THE AVENGERS

Essential 45: 'Car Crash'/ 'We Are the One'/ 'I Believe in Me' (Dangerhouse, 1977). This and their second EP, producted by Steve Jones, 'The American in Me' (Orig: White Noise, 1979) are collected on *Avengers* (CD Presents, 1983). I'm afraid the recording of 'End of the World' from 14 January 1978 is from a scarce bootleg 45. A collection of live and demo material from 1977/8 (plus two re-recordings from 1998) was released as *Died for Your Sins* (Lookout! CD). The original single and Steve Jones EP are still hard to find.

TUXEDO MOON

Arty, but one early electro-pop 45: 'JoeBoy'/ 'Pinheads on the Move' (Tidal Wave, 1978).

SLEEPERS

The sound of the unconscious. 'The Sleepers' (Win, EP, 1978) includes 'No Time' and 'Flying'; after which 'Mirror'/ 'Theory' (Search & Destroy/ Trans

Target flyer, May 1978 (© Target Productions)

Time Records, 1980). One late but great LP: *Painless Nights* (Adolescent, 1981). All three records are now available on *The Less an Object* (Tim Kerr Records CD, 1996, plus 3 unreleased tracks) – highly recommended.

DEAD KENNEDYS

The definitive Punk name. 'California über Alles' (Alternative Tentacles, 1979) was the start of a long career in serious troublemaking.

California

THE TWINKEYZ

From Davis, one classic single from 1977: 'Aliens In Our Midst', peerless garage/psych with a rare gay twist. Follow up 'E.S.P.' (not the Buzzcocks' song) wasn't bad either. Both are collected, with sundry live cuts and demos on *Aliens in Our Midst* (Anopheles, 1998).

New York

Most of the action is away from CBGBs at this point: note these second-generation Punks:

THE DEAD BOYS

Young Loud and Snotty (Sire, 1977: re Sire, UK, 1977) includes their great moment, 'Sonic Reducer'. Also *We Have Cum for Your Children* (Sire, 1978).

A superior example of the buried power-pop style is The Fleshtones 'American Beat' (Red Star, 1979).

For the Downtown crossover, look no further than *No New York* (Antilles, 1978), which features an Eno production of the following at the height of their powers: Contortions ('Dish It Out'/ 'Flip Your Face' plus their cover of James Brown's 'I Can't Stand Myself'); Teenage Jesus and the Jerks ('Burning Rubber'/ 'The Closet'/ 'Red Alert'); Mars ('Helen Forsdale'/ 'Tunnel'); D.N.A. ('Egomaniac's Kiss'/ 'Not Moving'/ 'Size'). This wild LP threw down a formal gauntlet not taken up until the mid eighties by Sonic Youth et al.

Two noteworthy compilations are Lydia Lunch, *Hysterie 1975–1986* (Widowspeak, 1986), which collates early Teenage Jesus and the Jerks, Eight Eyed Spy, and her great Beirut Slump 45, 'Try Me'; and Mars, *Seventy Eight* (Widowspeak, 1986), which contains not only 'Helen Forsdale' but the '3E' EP.

The Diaspora

These records mark the full UK take-up of the challenge posed by Buzzcocks' 'Spiral Scratch'. Unlike the US, where major label deals were rarely an option and putting your own records out was a matter of necessity, UK Independent label releases were often the result of choice becoming ideology.

As the sleeve to *Streets* states: '1977 was the year that the music came out of the concert halls and onto the streets; when independent labels sprang out of the woodwork to feed new tastes; when rock music once again became about energy and fun; when the majors' boardrooms lost control. Suddenly we could do anything.'

Streets (Beggar's Banquet, 1977) collated independent label material from around the country: the Drones (OHMS), Slaughter, John Cooper Clarke and the Nosebleeds (Rabid) from Manchester; the Members, the Art Attacks, and the Lurkers from London. Too often, the utopian 'anything' turned out like sped-up bad rock but a filthy good time was had by all.

DESPERATE BICYCLES

Two essential 45s: 'Smokescreen'/ 'Handlebars' (Refill, 1977); 'The Medium Was Tedium'/ 'Don't Back the Front' (Refill, 1977). 'Xerox Music's here at last'; 'It was easy, it was cheap, go and do it.'

THROBBING GRISTLE

The start of Industrial Culture. All these early records are essential:

Second Annual Report (Industrial, 1977; re Fetish 1978).

'United'/ 'Zyklon B Zombie' (Industrial, 1978). One of the first electro pop singles.

D.O.A. – the Third and Final Report (Industrial, 1978) spans pure electro – 'I.B.M.'/ 'AB/7A' – and holocaust noise: 'Blood on the Floor'/ 'Hit by Rock'. 'Deaththreats' gives you an idea of TG's popularity during this period.

'We Hate You (Little Girls)'/ 'Five Knuckle Shuffle' (Sordide Sentimental, France, 1979).

All of Throbbing Gristle's albums were collected by Fetish: *Five Albums* (Fetish, 1981), which includes their most fully realized studio album, *20 Jazz Funk Greats* (Industrial, 1979), the hypnotic, live *Heathen Earth* (Industrial, 1980) and the record of their final concert in San Francisco, *Mission of Dead Souls*. All are now available individually through Mute/Grey Area. Also reissued by

Mute/Grey Area: the 1980 compilation, *Greatest Hits: Entertainment Through Pain* (Rough Trade, US), which contains singles like 'United' and 'Adrenalin', with great sleeve notes by Claude Bessy. There are many other Throbbing Gristle CDs available, like *Kreeme Horn* (Dossier CD, Germany): studio recordings from 1975. TG recorded all their concerts: a good, humanly feasible collection is collected on the *Throbbing Gristle Live Vols* 1–4 CD box set (Mute/Grey Area) – arranged in chronological order from 1976 to 1980. For a fuller discography and a good history of the group, read Simon Ford's *Wreckers of Civilisation: The Story of COUM Transmissions and Throbbing Gristle* (published by Black Dog, 1999).

THE NORMAL

(i.e. Daniel Miller) 'T.V.O.D.'/ 'Warm Leatherette' (Mute Records, 1978) is a fantastic early electro-pop single. Pure Ballard, and the start of England's most successful independent labels, as these techno dystopias (well, dystopia was how utopia was couched in this period) prefigure the worldwide success of Erasure and Depeche Mode in the late eighties.

Daniel Miller, interviewed in February 1991: 'Two things happened with Punk. It meant that a lot of people with no ability but a lot of ideas could make a lot of records. It also meant that a lot of failed musos made New Wave records. It gave people an opportunity to do things that were unattainable dreams before and all of a sudden became an attainable reality – like putting out your own record, forming a group, and you didn't have to know how to play. The spirit is still there, the Indie spirit. The cheapness of modern technology has made music very accessible again: particularly with dance music.'

Some examples of this in action:

CABARET VOLTAIRE

Bedroom synth noir band from Sheffield benefits from the space opened by Punk. Essential first 45: 'Extended Play' (Rough Trade, 1978) includes 'Do the Mussolini (Headkick)'/ 'Talkover'/ 'The Set up' and their version of the Velvets' 'Here She Comes Now'. The first two albums are essential: *The Mix Up* (Rough Trade, 1979) and *Voice of America* (Rough Trade, 1980) – the latter features the classic 'Partially Submerged'. These are now issued on Mute/Grey Area, as is *74–76*, a collection of those hard-to-find early cassettes. After which, many recordings throughout the eighties: early material (including the first 45) is collected on: *The Living Legends* (Mute, 1990). Also recommended: *Listen up* (Mute, CD) includes other non-LP cuts 'Baader Meinhof' and 'Sex in Secret' from 'The Factory Sample'. In 1991, founder CV member Richard Kirk made a great Techno record as Sweet Exorcist: C. C. C. D. (Warp); he followed it up with a welter of records as Sandoz and Alphaphone, of which *Dark Continent* (1996) is highly recommended.

THIS HEAT

This Heat (Piano Records, 1979; now Recommended) contains ferocious looping, driving instrumentals like 'Testcard', and a wonderful musical setting of Stevie Smith's 'Not Waving but Drowning'. This was released on CD in the early nineties, as was their still powerful second album, *Deceit*. Also available *Made Available* (These), a record of the Peel sessions that made their name. *This Heat* was produced by David Cunningham, whose

FLYING LIZARDS

Had a big hit in 1979 with their minimalist version of 'Money' (Virgin, 1979) #5. Their first 45 was 'Summertime Blues' (Virgin, 1978). Look for their fine second album, *The Fourth Wall* (Virgin, 1981), featuring the Patti Paladin vocal singles, 'Move On Up' and 'Hands 2 Take' ('At least in self-abuse, there's a certain dignity'). A Flying Lizards compilation, *Money and Other Love Songs*, is now available (Virgin, 2000).

NIGEL SIMPKINS

'X.Enc' (Waldo's Swing Records, 1978). Pure drum loops unreleasable a year earlier.

'O' LEVEL/TELEVISION PERSONALITIES

Snapshot ditties from the Punk subculture: 'We Love Malcolm' (King's Road, EP, 1978) includes their ode to McLaren – 'We love Malcolm because nobody else does' – as well as: 'Stairway to Boredom'/ 'Everybody's on Revolver'. 'Where's Bill Grundy Now?' (King's Road, EP, 1978; re Rough Trade, 1978) includes such gems as: 'Part Time Punks'/ 'Where's Bill Grundy Now?'/ 'Posing at the Roundhouse'.

SCRITTI POLITTI

'Skank Bloc Bologna' (St Pancras, EP, 1978) contains 'Is and Ought the Western World' and the minatory '26.6.78'. The sleeve lists the means of production – sleeves, pressing, and so on – while the music is a patient mixture of dub and found sound bonded by Green's high voice.

THE POP GROUP

Teenage Rimbauds from Bristol. Essential Nietzschean 45: 'She Is Beyond Good and Evil'/ '3.38' (Radar, 1979). Chaos seeps into the *Y* album (Radar, 1979, now Y/Radarscope CD, 1996) which, despite fine songs like 'Thief of Fire'/ 'We Are Time'/ 'Words Disobey Me', prefigures their messy dissolution. Some are better heard on *We Are Time* (Y Records, 1980) – 1978 demos and live tapes.

THE UNDERTONES

Londonderry. Late, incandescent pop/Punk flash. Classic first 45 'Teenage Kicks' (Good Vibrations, EP, 1978; re Sire, 1978) #31. The first LP includes 'Teenage Kicks'/ 'True Confessions'/ 'The Undertones' (Sire, 1979, now Essential CD, 2000) #13. Picks: 'Male Model'/ 'Jump Boys'/ 'Get over You'/ 'Jimmy Jimmy'/ 'Listen in'. The missing link between the 13th Floor Elevators, the Stooges, and Irish traditional music. Subsequent albums of value include *Hypnotised* (Sire, 1980) and *The Sin of Pride* (Ardeck/EMI, 1983). Both are now available on Essential CD. In the mid eighties, Feargal Sharkey worked with Vince Clarke – as the Assembly – before a briefly successful pop career; John O'Neill kept the loud fast and hard flag flying with That Petrol Emotion, whose second album, *Babble* (Polydor, 1986; reissued with extra tracks, 2001) is worth hearing if you can find it.

Feargal Sharkey, 1990: 'We were extremely angry young men, and it was a way of getting it out. We lived in Northern Ireland and the option was to go and join the IRA. It was an option that lots of friends of ours took. I didn't want to join up, out of simple fear. The Undertones was a way of getting out of that situation. People used to ask early on why we didn't write songs about the troubles: we were doing our best to escape from it.' In contrast:

STIFF LITTLE FINGERS

Belfast social realism. 'Alternative Ulster'/ '78 Revolutions a Minute' (Rigid Digits/Rough Trade, 1978). *Inflammable Material* (Rough Trade, 1979; now EMI, CD) #14, was the first big 'new Indie' success. Storming material like 'White Noise'/ 'Wasted Life'/ 'Suspect Device' is undercut by social realism's tabloid discourse.

Three labels chart Punk's diaspora throughout the North of England from 1978 on. Fast in Edinburgh was run by Bob Last. This was the start of New Pop.

THE MEKONS

'Never Been in a Riot' (Fast, 1978). Here the access principle was taken to the limit. Not everybody who couldn't play had something to say, but the serious pop/Punk of 'Where Were You' (Fast, 1978) begins a string of many fine records in the eighties and nineties (on CNT, Sin and Blast First).

THE HUMAN LEAGUE

Early synth pop from Sheffield. 'Being Boiled'/ 'Circus of Death' (Fast, 1978). Also terrific, 'The Dignity of Labour Pts 1-4' (Fast, 1979) – driving synth instrumentals. Many other records as the Human League and BEF, including 1981's global breakthrough, 'Dare'.

GANG OF FOUR

Leeds post-Situ funk. Essential early 45s: 'Damaged Goods'/ 'Love Like Anthrax'/ 'Armalite Rifle' (FAST, 1978, first copies with stickers); 'At Home He's a Tourist'/ 'It's Her Factory' (EMI, 1979) #58. Both are collected on: *A Brief History of the Twentieth Century* (EMI, 1990) with eighteen other cuts from the group's six-year career (including 'I Love a Man in Uniform') with a sleeve note by Greil Marcus. The fine first album, *Entertainment*, is available on EMI CD; in 1998 Rhino US released a 2xCD compilation, *100 Flowers Bloom*, of material from 1978–84 and their early nineties reformation.

Other Fast Products included 45s by the Scars and 2:3, three issues of the *Earcom* samplers (including Joy Division and the Middle Class) plus two xerox magazines: *The Quality of Life* and *Sexex*. The early singles are on: *Fast Product: the First Year Plan* (EMI, 1979), recompiled (with extra material from Fire Engines and the Human League) on the 1993 EMI CD, *Rigour, Discipline and Disgust*.

The Zoo label was based in Liverpool and run by Dave Balfe and the KLF's Bill Drummond. They released:

BIG IN JAPAN

Liverpool shriekerama includes Jayne Casey, Holly, Bill Drummond, Budgie, Ian Broudie. 'From Y to Z and Never Again' (Zoo, 1978), EP with 'Cindy and the Barbie Dolls'/ 'Suicide a Go Go'.

TEARDROP EXPLODES

Great first 45: 'Sleeping Gas'/ 'Camera Camera'/ 'Kirby Workers Dream Fades' (Zoo, 1978). 'Bouncing Babies' (Zoo, 1979), after which many others, including 1980's *Kilimanjaro* (available on Polygram CD) and 1981's big hit, 'Reward'. Singer Julian Cope still records.

ECHO AND THE BUNNYMEN

The new psychedelia. 'The Pictures on My Wall'/ 'Read It in Books' (Zoo, 1979). Def first major label 45 and album: *Rescue* (Korova/WEA, 1980) #62. The 12" includes the killer 'Simple Stuff'. *Crocodile* (Korova/WEA, 1980) #16 includes such subcultural classics as 'Villiers Terrace' and 'All That Jazz'. After which many hits, collected on: *Songs to Learn and Sing*. (WEA, 1985 – replaced by *Ballyhoo*, WEA CD). In the late nineties, the Bunnymen reformed for a couple of poor albums; guitarist Will Sergeant shines, however, on the ambient/experimental albums *Themes for GRIND* (Ninety-Two Happy Customers LP 1982, CD 1998) and, as Glide, *Space Age Freak Out* (Ochre, 1997).

Compilations of this material include:
To the Shores of Lake Placid (Zoo, 1982) with rare cuts by Big In Japan ('Society for Cutting Up Men'), Teardrop and Echo. *The Zoo Uncaged* (Document, CD, 1990) contains almost every Zoo A and B side from 1978 to 1982.

Pete Fulwell and Roger Eagle's Inevitable Records begin in 1980 with Peter Wylie as Wah! Heat!: 'Better Scream' (Inevitable, 1980). Future releases include Dead or Alive, Holly.

Factory was a Manchester label run by Rob Gretton, Tony Wilson, and Alan Erasmus. Two of the label's first three releases are posters by Peter Saville – one start of the eighties' design obsession. Otherwise:

JOY DIVISION

The post-Punk move to inner space. 'Ideal for Living' (Enigma, EP, 1978; re Anonymous, 12", 1978) marks the name change from Warsaw and contains 'Warsaw'/ 'Leaders of Men'/ 'No Love Lost'/ 'Failures'.

The story really starts with 'The Factory Sample' EP – with three other acts: John Dowie, Durutti Column and Cabaret Voltaire – 'Digital' and 'Glass' (Factory, 1978). Other 45s: two cuts on 'Earcom 2' (FAST, EP, 1979); 'Autosuggestion' and 'From Safety to Where?'; 'Dead Souls'/ 'Atmosphere' (Sordide Sentimental, 1980).

These are collected, plus the other Factory 45s, on *Substance* (Factory, 1988), while *Still* (Factory, 1981) wraps up early outtakes like 'The Sound of Music', 'Exercise One' and 'The Only Mistake'.

Sometime in 1979–80, the eleven songs Joy Division recorded in May 1978 as *Warsaw* were released on a bootleg. Most are better heard on *Unknown*

Pleasures (Factory 1979), a definitive, ambient Rock album which set the post-Punk mood. Picks: the whole damn thing, but especially 'She's Lost Control'/ 'Day of the Lords'/ 'Insight'/ 'Interzone'/ 'I Remember Nothing'/ 'New Dawn Fades': 'A change of speed, a change of style/ A change of scene, with no regrets/ A chance to watch, admire the distance/ Still occupying – though you forget/ Different colours, different shades/ Over each mistakes were made/ I took the blame/ Directionless, so plain to see/ A loaded gun won't set you free/ So you say.'

All these albums, plus 1980's extraordinary *Closer*, have been reissued on London CD. In 1997, the boxed set *Heart and Soul* (London 4xCD) collected all the group's released studio recordings with a CD of demos and radio shots (including versions of 'Ceremony' and 'In a Lonely Place') and a live CD from 1979 and 1980. The booklet contains an essay by Paul Morley. In 2000, their John Peel recordings were released on CD (*Complete Radio Sessions*, Strange Fruit), with extra material from their infamous 1979 performance on the youth TV programme, *Something Else*.

JOHN LYDON

By some extraordinary sleight of hand, John Lydon managed to pull all this together with his new group Public Image Limited, usually shortened to PIL. These essential records dominated the first post-Punk eighteen months:

'Public Image' (Virgin, 1978) #9

'Death Disco' (Virgin, 1979) #20

'Memories' (Virgin, 1979) #60

Public Image (Virgin, 1978; now CD) #20. Picks: 'Theme'/ 'Religion I & II'/ 'Annalisa'/ 'Low Life'/ 'Attack'

Metal Box (Virgin, 1979) #18. A limited edition of 50,000 was replaced by *Second Edition* (Virgin, 1980; now re in tin, 1990) #46. Picks: all twelve tracks right through to Keith Levene's archetypal instrumental, 'Radio 4'.

John Lydon continues to record with various PILs. Some kind of high spot was reached with 1981's terrific 'Flowers of Romance' 45 and LP (Virgin, 1981; now on CD with the non-LP 'Home Is Where the Heart Is') #11, but after this suffocating intensity, a retreat.

Two more great singles: 'This Is Not a Love Song' (VS, 1983) #5 and (as Time Zone, with Afrika Bambaataa) 'World Destruction' (Tommy Boy/ Celluloid/ Virgin, 1984); then disasters with 1983–4 LPs like *Live in Tokyo* and *This is What You Want . . . This is What You Get*. Despite fine albums like *Album* (Virgin, CD, 1986), Lydon's career has not fully recovered.

In late 1990, he had a Top Thirty hit with the eco 'Don't Ask Me', and a handy compilation was released of 45s plus the best tracks from the 1987–8 albums, *Happy* and *9*: *P.I.L. the Greatest Hits So Far* (Virgin, CD, 1990). In 1998, the whole PIL output was compiled on *Plastic Box* (Virgin, 4xCD), from the first single to a 1992 Radio 1 session.

By the early nineties, Lydon had settled into his continued role as a fascinating, often vituperative media personality, but was still marked – as he is today – by an extreme bitterness towards Malcolm McLaren. Thankfully, this obsessive drive to regain control of his past resulted in the entertaining and recommended autobiography, *Rotten: No Irish, No Blacks, No Dogs* (1994). Great photos, well-edited rants and sharp glimpses into the five Sex Pistols' often extreme lack of personal accord make up for the occasionally poor organization of the material. Not the full story, but an essential part.

Lydon's first solo album, *Psycho's Path* (Virgin) was released in 1997. In 2000, Lydon was actively involved – along with Paul Cook, Steve Jones and Glen Matlock – in the promotion of the authorized film. His current media activities can be traced on the following websites: the official website, with news and links (www.johnlydon.com); his VH1 show (www.rottentv.co); his weekly Rotten Radio show (www.eyada.com) – recent guests have included Chrissie Hynde, Wayne Kramer, the Chieftains' Paddy Moloney, Motorhead's Lemmy, Greil Marcus and the Rev. Billy from the Church of Stop Shopping.

By the early nineties, the Sex Pistols had already become a pop myth, up there in the Pantheon along with Elvis Presley, the Beatles, and Jimi Hendrix. The remaining four – largely through the non-mythic 'Filthy Lucre' tour – have escaped the worst aspects of this human divinity, but the one dead member remains a teenage fuck-up archetype as powerful as James Dean or Jim Morrison. Note the claustrophobic second half of Alex Cox's *Sid and Nancy* (1986) – featuring Courtney Love in a bit part – or this 1991 *Guardian* report from Budapest: 'In Vorosmarty Square, there is a statue which attracts the eye with its strong form and determined stance. What also attracts the eye to it is the defiant slogan, SID VICIOUS!, painted in broad swipes on top of the original inscription and accompanied by a carelessly drawn letter A. The statue is one of several in the city which have become the focus for a new generation of disaffected youths.'

The Sex Pistols' (and punk's) influence on eighties and nineties rock was considerable, ranging from major rock bands like U2 and Guns'n'Roses through to Rap as a genre: self-assertion, politics, empowerment and shock value translated into blackamerican music after 1982. The punk principle of autonomy was taken up by many local scenes: for one account, read Clark Humphrey's history of Seattle music from the sixties to the nineties, *Loser* (Feral House, 1995). For another view, consider the impact of punk on the Welsh-language music scene from 1986 onwards: a long historical march which has resulted in the late nineties international acceptance of groups like Catatonia, Gorky's Zygotic Mynci and Super Furry Animals – whose Welsh-language 'Mwng' (Placid Casual, 2000) justifies the whole idea by itself.

With the extraordinary success of Nirvana in autumn 1991, American Punk finally came of age: shut out by the media in the late seventies, it went deep underground through various permutations (Hardcore, Straight Edge, then Grunge (in Kurt Cobain's equation: punk + Beatles + Black Sabbath)) – a phase captured in the pages of keep-the-faith 'zine *Maximum Rock'n'Roll*. Just as the title of the breakthrough *Nevermind* echoed *Never Mind the Bollocks*, so Nirvana – with their feral rage and keening hurt – were seen as more than a rock group: harbingers of family break-up, teen abjection and economic meltdown. Kurt Cobain's suicide in April 1994 was in part – if we are to accept his final note – an ultimate enactment of the Punk Loser script. Since his death, rock has

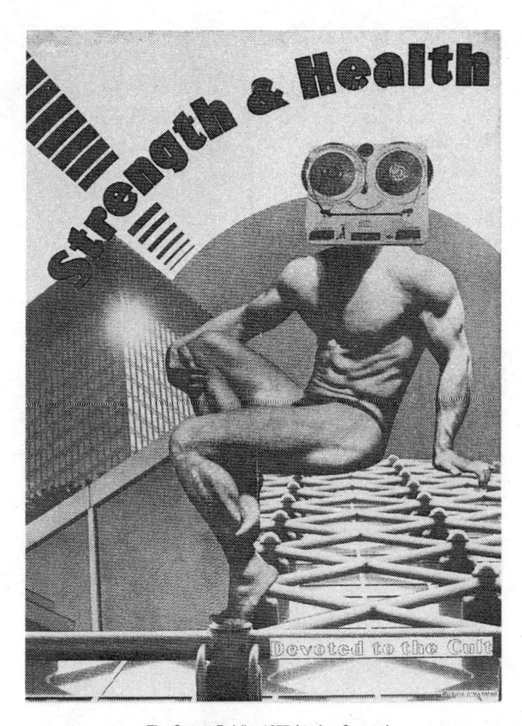

The Secret Public, 1977 (© Jon Savage)

largely avoided progressive politics, social confrontation and personal truth-telling.

With Nirvana and associated nineties' punk-poppers like Green Day, the direct punk influence (music + ideology) on the pop mainstream came to an end. Punk continues as a genre – much like the perennial rock'n'roll revivals that continued through the seventies – but is best seen as a diffuse, pervasive presence. You could point, for instance, to the Punk in Eminem (peroxided bad attitude); Madonna (female autonomy + explorative sexuality); Oasis (that Steve Jones wall of sound, when they rock); Public Enemy (social critique + practical autonomy); Rage Against the Machine (agitpop); Manic Street Preachers (early thrash + pro-situ sloganeering); Elastica (that Wire stop/start thing); Blink 182 and Limp Bizkit (shock tactics = lad grossness); even the Spice Girls (Girl Power). But that's like pointing out the Beatles' continued influence on pop. Punk and the Sex Pistols are now *in* history – until the next bunch of screamers comes along to source this quarter-century old package of concentrated emotion.

With thanks to Alan Holmes of Ectogram and Cob Records, Bangor, for his help with this updated discography.

Acknowledgements

Many thanks to all the following, who agreed to be interviewed: Roger Armstrong, Simon Barker, Berlin, Adèle Bertei, Claude Bessy, Anne Beverley, Richard Boon, Peter Buck, Sue Carrington, Ted Carroll, Jayne Casey, Leee Black Childers, Al Clark, Edwyn Collins, Crass (G., Steve Ignorant, Penny Rimbaud, Peter Wright), Andy Czezowski, Howard Devoto, Danny Fields, Malcolm Garrett, Johnny Gems, Andy Gill, Vic Godard, Gerry Goldstein, Dave Goodman, Rob Gretton, Bob Gruen, the late Martin Hannett, Mary Harron, Shanne Hasler, John Holmstrom, Peter Hook, Chrissie Hynde, Tony James, Rory Johnston, Alan Jones, Nick Kent, Richard Kirk, Ed Kuepper, Don Letts, Graham Lewis, Linder, Max, Al McDowell, Angus MacKinnon, Legs McNeil, Trevor Miles, Daniel Miller, Dennis Morris, Morrissey, Pauline Murray, Warwick Nightingale, Thom Oatman, Mark Perry, Marco Pirroni, Theodore Ramos, Bernard Rhodes, Sophie Richmond, Roadent (SteveConnolly), Paul Robinson, Gareth Sager, Robin Scott, Captain Sensible (Ray Burns), Steve Severin, Feargal Sharkey, Pete Shelley, Siouxsie, T. V. Smith, Brian Southall, Neil Spencer, Seymour Stein, Nils Stevenson, Ray Stevenson, Joe Strummer, Poly Styrene, Jane Suck, Syl Sylvain, Julien Temple, Geoff Travis, Vale, Keith Wainwright, Steve Walsh, Steven Wells, Ben Westwood, Debbie Wilson, Tony Wilson, Simon Withers, Jah Wobble (John Wardle).

Thanks also to the following for interviews and/or help beyond the call of duty: Viv Albertine, Adam Ant, Roberta Bayley, Margi Clarke, Caroline Coon,

Stuart Edwards, Bill Forsyth and Bill Allerton of Plastic Passion, Barbara Harwood, Stewart Home, Jonh Ingham, Derek Jarman, Jordan, Mandy Merck, Genesis P. Orridge, Peter Rogers, Paul Sieveking, Kate Simon, Joe Stevens, John Tiberi, John Varnom, Nick Wapshott, Helen Wallington-Lloyd.

Without the following all this material would never have made into book form: Ian Birch, Adair Brouwer, David Chipp, Charlotte Greig, Nigel Hart, Sandy Hemingway, Sue Holding, Tessa Hughes-Freeland, Carlo McCormick, Thom Oatman, Patti Palladin, Tony Peake, Howard Schuman, Tracey Scoffield, Lisa Gail Smith, Neil Tennant, Pete Townshend, Graham Willett, Wendy Wolf, John Wozencroft. Thanks in particular to Simon Frith and Greil Marcus who read the manuscript and made vital suggestions, and to Marc Issue who did the bulk of the tape transcriptions.

Above all, thanks to all the Sex Pistols and the people who instigated the events which are the subject of this book: Paul Cook, Steve Jones, Jordan, John Lydon, Glen Matlock, Jamie Reid (the inspiration), Sophie Richmond, and to Malcolm McLaren who gave me access to his archives.

Finally, all my thanks to my grandmother and my parents, who lived through this with me twice. I hope it was worth it.

Index